D1565940

The Old Testament
explained and applied

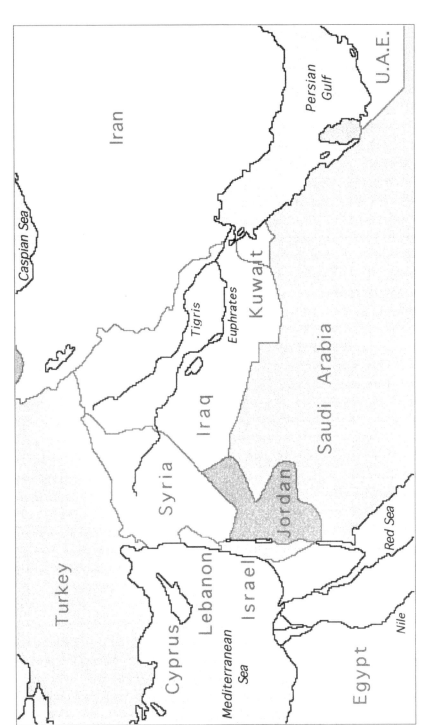

Modern map of Bible lands

The Old Testament
explained and applied

Gareth Crossley

 EVANGELICAL PRESS

EVANGELICAL PRESS
Faverdale North, Darlington, DL3 0PH, England

e-mail: sales@evangelicalpress.org

Evangelical Press USA
P. O. Box 825, Webster, New York 14580, USA

e-mail: usa.sales@evangelicalpress.org

web: http://www.evangelicalpress.org

First published 2002
Reprinted 2006

British Library Cataloguing in Publication Data available

ISBN-13 978-0-85234-523-8   ISBN 0-85234-523-2

Dedicated to
the brothers and sisters
known as
West Park Church, Wolverhampton,
beloved members of
Christ and his church

Contents

Maps, illustrations and charts

Preface

This project started out as ministry at the midweek meetings of West Park Church, Wolverhampton. Designed to give an overview of the books of the Old Testament, the object was to cover one book in the space of fifty minutes — an impossible undertaking!

Jim Gough, my colleague in eldership, and John Cooke, one of the deacons, urged that the notes should be sent to the publishers for the benefit of the church of Jesus Christ in other places. The publishers responded favourably but with recommendations that would involve a substantial enlargement and considerably more work. The prospect was daunting.

Over the past five years my wife Joan Mary and I have spent days off, holidays and extended study leave, thoroughly engrossed in this project. There can be no greater subject for study and meditation, no greater privilege than to be freed to give time, energy and effort to this end.

We owe a great debt of gratitude to the Saviour for such a great salvation, to the Father for such a great preparation and to the Holy Spirit for such a great record in Holy Scripture.

Our thanks too to the brothers and sisters in Christ who compose West Park Church, Wolverhampton, for their loving support and encouragement over many years.

Gareth Crossley

Introduction

Many Christians find the reading of the Old Testament a trial. The self-discipline imposed by a commitment to read through the whole Bible in three years, or in some cases in twelve months, may indicate the reluctance with which some believers approach the Old Testament Scriptures. Like the man who continually beat his head against the wall because he felt so good when he stopped, the enforced reading of the Old Testament may produce only a similar benefit — the sense of achievement at completion. The task has been accomplished, but the benefit derived along the way may be little different from having read the full works of William Shakespeare.

There may be a number of reasons for this reticence in turning to the Old Testament with enthusiasm. It may reside in the fact that the Old Testament is often read like irrelevant history. Does the average Christian see his or her own history there in its pages? What are the possible applications for today of the particulars of the law in Deuteronomy, or the details of the sacrifices in Leviticus, or the histories of the kings, or the philosophies of Ecclesiastes?

A second reason for the reticence may be that so many of those who preach from the Old Testament seem to 'spiritualize' every text and often betray more of a vivid imagination than clear principles of biblical interpretation. Lacking such imaginative skills, the average Christian avoids the thirty-nine books except for the occasional dip into a well-worn passage in the Psalms, or Isaiah, or a favourite story in Genesis.

A third explanation may rest in the fact that few Christians see the thread, or understand the flow, of the Old Testament. They are not gripped by the unfolding historical drama, not thrilled by the evidences of the providence and purpose of God, nor enthralled by the developing picture of the promised Messiah, the Christ.

When, for example, Genesis is read, the understanding is affected by previous information obtained from other places such as Exodus, the prophets, the kings, or the New Testament record. This often occurs in nothing more than a haphazard way. Every reading of the Old Testament is inevitably coloured by the other Old Testament Scriptures which have been read. It is also influenced by the New Testament insights and blessings which have been received. But what are the connections? What are the associations which God intends? Are the Old Testament Scriptures a mass of random events, indiscriminate biographies and arbitrary sayings, with the occasional Messianic promise or prophecy thrown in for good measure? Is there a unifying theme, a plan, a purpose, to which everything is subservient and by which everything is measured for inclusion or exclusion? How should the Old Testament be approached? The Lord's challenge to the lawyer, as recorded in Luke, is the challenge to all Christians: 'What is your reading of it?' (Luke 10:26).

The importance of the Old Testament for present-day Christians cannot be overstated. From the earliest days of the Christian era these thirty-nine books have held a vital place. The new Christian converts on the Day of Pentecost, once baptized, committed themselves with great enthusiasm to the apostles' doctrine, fellowship with other believers, the breaking of bread and united prayer (Acts 2:42). The teaching of the apostles was composed of a number of elements: relating the teaching they received directly from the Lord Jesus Christ, bearing witness to the things concerning the Lord which they had seen and heard for themselves, and interpreting and applying the Old Testament Scriptures with specific reference to the Lord Jesus Christ. The apostles were at great pains, whether among unbelieving Jews or believing Christians, to relate everything that Jesus said and did to the thirty-nine books of the Old Testament (Acts 2:22-36; 4:9-12,24-28; 13:29-41). The Scriptures, as composed at that time, were the firm foundation for understanding and explaining the ministry, life, suffering, death, resurrection, ascension and glorification of the Lord Jesus Christ. This was the doctrine, or teaching, of the apostles.

From the beginning the apostles' doctrine was a vital ingredient of Christian worship. There is abundant evidence throughout the Acts of the Apostles that this teaching played an important part in church life (e.g. Acts 2:42; 6:2,4). The Word of God was to be read and carefully and faithfully explained to the church (1 Tim. 4:13; 2 Tim. 2:15).

Knowledge and understanding of the Scriptures was not, however, to be restricted to that which was gained through meetings for worship and teaching. The private study of God's Word was invaluable. How else could believers maintain a Berean mentality and check out what the preacher said? (Acts 17:11). Without the personal study of the Scriptures believers would be vulnerable, all too easily 'tossed to and fro and carried about with every wind of doctrine' (Eph. 4:14).

Fundamental, therefore, to the Christian church in its worship, witness and work was the correct understanding and application of the Old Testament Scriptures. Rightly understood, by that illumination which comes only from heaven, the Holy Scriptures 'are able to make ... wise for salvation through faith which is in Christ Jesus' (2 Tim. 3:15; cf. 2 Cor. 3:14-18). Once saved, once converted, the Christian can be educated and 'equipped for every good work', through the contents of those Old Testament Scriptures 'given by inspiration of God, and ... profitable for doctrine, for reproof, for correction, for instruction in righteousness' (2 Tim. 3:16-17).

Sadly, however, that central feature, the relating of the person and work of the Lord Jesus Christ to the Old Testament Scriptures, seems largely to have been eliminated from modern-day Christianity. With many distractions, the Bible has been sidelined and marginalized. In many quarters enthusiasm for the New Testament is waning, and appreciation of the Old Testament has almost gone.

This book is written with a clear goal in mind — to encourage the people of God in their private reading and study of the Old Testament Scriptures. Without help, reading this first and largest portion of the Bible may appear a daunting prospect.

How is the Old Testament to be read? Should it be treated like a workshop manual and dipped into only when there is a problem to solve or a question to answer? Is it best to start at the beginning and read it through like a novel? Is it important for Christians to read and understand the message of the Old Testament? Why are there thirty-nine different books in this section of the Bible and what is their relationship to each other and to the New Testament? What are the key thoughts in each book and is there a progression? These questions and others like them will be addressed as this overview of the Old Testament unfolds.

The approach

This is an overview of the thirty-nine books of the Old Testament. It is not intended to be an exhaustive study. Aids to more detailed Bible study will be suggested along the way. The objective for this book is to present a glimpse of the contents of each Old Testament book so that the overall plan and purpose of God might be clearly perceived.

The Old and New Testaments are treated as the inspired Word of God and therefore to be regarded as without error and without lack as originally given; therefore a chapter is included on the nature of inspiration. (It is usual in all definitions of inspiration to distinguish between the original Scriptures in Hebrew and Greek and any subsequent translations into Latin, English, etc. Translations are not believed to be inspired in the same sense as the original writings.) This chapter may be omitted by those eager to delve into the Scriptures themselves, or left until some later occasion.

Beneficial study of God's Word requires clear perspective — seeing each book in relation to its neighbours.

The Hebrew Old Testament is divided into three major sections:

Law (Torah)	Prophets		Writings
	Former Prophets	*Latter Prophets*	*(a) Poetical books*
Genesis	Joshua	Isaiah	Psalms
Exodus	Judges	Jeremiah	Proverbs
Leviticus	Samuel	Ezekiel	Job
Numbers	Kings	Hosea	
Deuteronomy		Joel	*(b) Five Rolls (Megilloth)*
		Amos	Song of Songs
		Obadiah	Ruth
		Jonah	Lamentations
		Micah	Ecclesiastes
		Nahum	Esther
		Habakkuk	
		Zephaniah	*(c) Historical Books*
		Haggai	Daniel
		Zechariah	Ezra / Nehemiah
		Malachi	Chronicles

The English Old Testament is arranged differently under four headings:

Law	History	Poetry	Prophecy	
			Major	*Minor*
Genesis	Joshua	Job	Isaiah	Hosea
Exodus	Judges	Psalms	Jeremiah	Joel
Leviticus	Ruth	Proverbs	Lamentations	Amos
Numbers	I Samuel	Ecclesiastes	Ezekiel	Obadiah
Deuteronomy	2 Samuel	Song of Solomon	Daniel	Jonah
	I Kings			Micah
	2 Kings			Nahum
	I Chronicles			Habakkuk
	2 Chronicles			Zephaniah

Law	History	Poetry	Prophecy	
			Major	*Minor*
	Ezra			Haggai
	Nehemiah			Zechariah
	Esther			Malachi

The overall theme of God's revelation needs to be kept in mind. The controlling thought for the whole of the Old Testament is preparation for the coming of the Messiah, the Son of God. For those of a more academic bent there is a chapter presenting the reasoned argument for this central theme. For others this chapter may be passed over without loss of benefit.

Throughout this overview there are many biblical references cited. Consulting these references at the first reading will interrupt the flow and cause discontinuity of perspective. It will also take hours. Copious references are provided for the benefit of the preacher, the student, or anyone unconvinced about any particular point being made.

Each chapter will follow an outline like this:

Introduction
Author
Historical setting
Outline
Christ and his church
Application
Conclusion

So as to ensure the historical integrity of each book, the Christological content and the present-day applications will be kept separate.

The inspiration of Scripture

For nineteen centuries Christians recognized the vital importance of the Scriptures. Over recent years that conviction and confidence has been seriously eroded. The question might well be asked: 'If the foundations are destroyed, what can the righteous do?' (Ps. 11:3). Take away the Scriptures as the authoritative and utterly reliable Word from God, and chaos will soon ensue. So many believers seem to be 'tossed to and fro and carried about with every wind of doctrine' (Eph. 4:14). In teaching and in practice — in the home, in the church, and in society — human ideas and the counsel of the ungodly are prevalent (Col. 2:8; Ps. 1:1). A return to confidence in the Scriptures as the Word of God is urgently needed.

Because of the confusion which is permeating the Christian church, it is important to crystallize the view of the Bible which is taken throughout this present book. Quoting 2 Timothy 3:16-17, which states that 'All Scripture is given by inspiration of God, and is profitable for doctrine, for reproof, for correction, for instruction in righteousness, that the man of God may be complete, thoroughly equipped for every good work,' seems insufficient for some of God's people today. It is necessary, therefore, to be more specific about the actual stance taken on Scripture throughout these pages.

The understanding of inspiration basic to this book is that the written Scriptures are the Word which God spoke and still speaks to his church. This is the final and sufficient source and authority for Christian faith and Christian living. Here in Scripture the Lord has provided 'all things that pertain to life and godliness' (2 Peter 1:3). To know God's Word is to know God's revealed will. And we can trust that Word. It is infallible (without error, entirely dependable) because an infallible God has spoken an infallible Word. He is Sovereign Lord over all things. 'Whatever the LORD pleases he does, in heaven and in earth' (Ps. 135:6). There is nothing incongruous, therefore, about God's producing a book which, while arising out of the experience of his children, is also, through his sovereign ordering, his precise Word to them.[1] If God is not sovereign in his revelation of himself to human beings, then he is not sovereign in anything.

It is nonsense to believe in an all-powerful God if he is incapable of communicating accurately and infallibly to his human creatures.

The relationship between the Word of God and the words of men in the writing of the Bible may be expressed like this: 'The Holy Spirit moved men to write. He allowed them to use their own style, culture, gifts and character, to use the results of their own study and research, to write of their own experiences and to express what was in their mind. At the same time, the Holy Spirit did not allow sin to influence their writings; he overruled in the expression of thought and in the choice of words. Thus they recorded accurately all that God wanted them to say and exactly how he wanted them to say it, in their own character, style and language.'[2]

God inspired the Bible word for word (this is known as 'verbal inspiration'). The Bible throughout exhibits a God who speaks. He uses words. He communicates predominantly, though not exclusively, through words. Throughout the Scriptures there is clear evidence that these things were spoken by the Lord, were spoken in words. The living God spoke them.[3] 'What Scripture says, God says. The Bible is inspired in the sense of being word-for-word God-given... The Bible, therefore, does not need to be supplemented and interpreted by tradition, or revised and corrected by reason. Instead, it demands to sit in judgement on the dictates of both; for the words of men must be tried by the Word of God.'[4]

The men who recorded Scripture knew full well what they were doing. They were not in a trance. They were not 'taken over' by a spirit personality. They were fully conscious, fully rational. They did not, however, always understand the *meaning* and *significance* of what they said or wrote. The prophets were 'curious', in the best sense of that word, to comprehend God's purposes and timing, and went to considerable effort to discover answers (1 Peter 1:10-12).

God inspired the whole Bible, from Genesis to Revelation. All sixty-six books are infallible and inerrant. They are entirely without error as originally given. As Francis Schaeffer declares, '... the Bible is without error not only when it speaks of values, the meaning system, and religious things, but it is also without error when it speaks of history and the cosmos.'[5]

One Author: many authors!

There are at least thirty different authors of the books of the Bible, the first writer living more than fifteen hundred years before the last. God used

Amos the farm labourer as well as Ezekiel the priest. God used uneducated working-class men, like the apostles Peter and John (Acts 4:13), together with middle-class intellectuals like the apostle Paul (Acts 22:3; Gal. 1:14) and Dr Luke, author of the third Gospel and the Acts of the Apostles. God used diverse men and welded their work together into one great and glorious composition — the Scriptures, the Word of God. These human agents appear to have been 'of every kind of temperament, of every degree of endowment, of every time of life, of every grade of attainment, of every condition in the social scale'.[6] The personality of each writer shines through the pages of his writings. The letters of Peter are distinct from those of John. The epistle of James contrasts with those of Paul.

God loves variety. This is obvious in *natural revelation,* in creation, where there is such an assortment of colours, sizes, shapes, sounds, textures, tastes and smells. It is also evident in *special revelation,* in the Scriptures, where God's 'chosen vessels' are of such differing background, experience and ability. Not only are the human authors different, but the kinds of written composition are equally varied. There are historic records, biographies, extracts from civic documents, moral laws, civil and ceremonial rules and regulations, laws of hygiene, sermons, theological discourses, official decrees, personal letters, visions, dreams, poems and songs. The Bible is anything but monotonous and dull.

Authors of the biblical books retained their own temperaments, their unique experiences, their personal strengths and their personal weaknesses. Their biblical writings were infallible. The men themselves were not. In their personal lives they were capable of making mistakes — sometimes serious mistakes, as when Peter at Antioch behaved inconsistently to New Covenant principles (Gal. 2:11-21). One author, David, was responsible for sins in relation to Bathsheba and Uriah when lust led to adultery and murder (2 Sam. 11). In spite of their sins and imperfections God chose them and God used them. He made sure that what they recorded as Scripture was accurate: firstly, the impulse to write was given from God; secondly, their understanding was enlightened by the Holy Spirit so that their writings were preserved from all material error; thirdly, they were divinely guided in the selection of their materials so that nothing was omitted or added against the will of God; and, fourthly, they received special divine help in order to complete their work accurately.[7]

One further point about the inspiration of Scripture needs to be made. As God used imperfect human instruments to communicate his Word, so he also chose to record the uninspired words of sinful men. While the words of sinful men found in Scripture were not inspired, the *record* of those words was inspired by God. An example of this distinction is seen in the book of Job. The Scriptures accurately record the words that Job's three friends used when they came to comfort him in his great distress. Many of those words are clearly contrary to some of the teaching of the Bible — they were not inspired words, but the *record* of them was inspired.[8] When the whole incident reached its climax, the Lord reprimanded Eliphaz: 'My wrath is aroused against you and your two friends, for you have not spoken of me what is right, as my servant Job has' (Job 42:7). This strikes a note of real caution in evaluating the arguments which form the bulk of the book of Job. The account is thoroughly inspired and consequently totally infallible — the arguments are neither. Assessment and analysis of the advice found there must be made by comparing it with other scriptures where truth from God is clearly stated.

Without a clear grasp and a decided conviction concerning the nature of biblical inspiration, there can be no confident and beneficial study of its contents. 'Grant that the Bible *is* (in its original manuscripts) inerrant and infallible, and you reach the place where study of its contents is both practicable and profitable.'[9]

The Old Testament Scriptures

'Your word is truth,' says the Lord Jesus Christ in prayer to his heavenly Father (John 17:17). 'What Christ has said concerning the authority of the Bible must itself always be regarded as having the utmost authority.'[10] The Lord Jesus clearly indicates that the Spirit of God was the author of the Old Testament Scriptures (e.g. Matt. 19:3-5; 22:41-44; cf. Ps. 110:1). He refers to twenty Old Testament characters. He quotes from nineteen different books. From *Genesis* he refers to the creation of man, the institution of marriage, the history of Noah, Abraham and Lot, and to the overthrow of Sodom and Gomorrah; from *Exodus*, to the appearing of God to Moses in the bush, to the manna, the Ten Commandments and the tribute money. He refers to the ceremonial law for the purification of lepers and to the great moral law, 'You shall love your neighbour as yourself,' both contained in *Leviticus*, to the bronze serpent, and the law regarding vows, in *Numbers*. At our Lord's temptations we have three quotations from *Deuteronomy*. He refers to David's flight to Abiathar the priest at Nob, to the glory of Solomon and the visit of the Queen of Sheba, to Elijah's stay with the widow of Zarephath, to the healing of Naaman, and to the killing of Zechariah — from various *historical books*. The ground of Christ's constant appeal is: 'Have you not read?' or 'It is written...' His constant assertion is: 'The Scripture cannot be broken'; 'The Scriptures testify of me,' and 'The Scripture must be fulfilled.'[11]

The writers of the New Testament consistently shared this view of the Old Testament Scriptures. There is an undisputed acceptance of their full inspiration and absolute authority. It is not sufficient that the Lord should inspire the Scriptures; he must also lead the church to recognize those Scriptures. Accuracy in the formation of the canon, the finished collection of Scripture, is as vital as its original inspiration. Christians must be confident that that which is placed in their hands is the full, unabridged and entire Word of God. 'It was not enough that God inspired the *writing* of each book of the Bible. He also gave to His people, in a collective sense, the spiritual perception to *recognize* in each of those books the genuine marks of divine inspiration and authority. With the Holy Spirit's guidance, they knew what spurious writings to reject, as well as what genuine writings to accept. Thus, over the centuries as the Old Testament books were being written, the Old Testament canon (list or group of inspired books) kept growing until it reached its completed form.'[12]

Fifty-six times the New Testament writers refer to God as the Author of the Old Testament. And even where the human writer is known, the divine authorship is often stated instead.[13] In Hebrews 1:5-13, for example, quotations are taken from 2 Samuel 7:14; Psalm 2:7; 104:4; 45:6-7; 102:25-27 and 110:1. The human writers are ignored and five times the apostle introduces a quotation with the phrase: 'He [i.e. God] says...' The four Gospel historians refer to Old Testament writings and declare them to be words which were 'spoken by the Lord through the prophet' (Matt. 1:22-23), or words of Scripture which must be fulfilled (John 19:24; cf. vv. 36,37). The early church praised God for his prophetic words recorded in the book of Psalms (Acts 4:24-26; cf. Ps. 2:1-2). Then, some years later, the apostle Paul refers to God's Word in Psalm 2:7, Isaiah 55:3 and Psalm 16:10 (Acts 13:33-35).

The attitude of the Lord Jesus Christ to the Old Testament Scriptures and the attitude of the New Testament writers to the Old Testament Scriptures lead us to understand that everything from Genesis 1:1 through to Malachi 4:6 should be received, 'not as the word of men, but as it is in truth, the word of God' (1 Thess. 2:13).

In spite of the multifarious human authors, there is only one divine Author. The prophets of the Old Testament knew they were speaking under the influence of the living God (e.g. Isa. 28:16; Jer. 7:20; Ezek. 3:11; Amos 3:11). The consistent view of the New Testament writers is that God was speaking in and through those prophets. They were convinced that what was recorded in the Old Testament Scriptures was and is the actual Word of God (2 Tim. 3:16-17; Heb. 1:1-2; 2 Peter 1:20-21).

The New Testament Scriptures

In arguing for the inspiration of the Old Testament Scriptures, that they are God-breathed and hence without error, the authority of the Lord Jesus Christ, his apostles and the other writers of the New Testament has been presented as conclusive proof. This, however, begs the question of the inspiration and reliability of the New Testament Scriptures. What is the ground upon which Christians may place their entire confidence in the twenty-seven books and letters of the New Testament?

The New Testament has two overlapping and interwoven parts. The first is an infallible (error-free as originally given) record of the life, ministry, suffering, death and resurrection of the Lord Jesus Christ, the Son of God. The second is an infallible record of the teaching of God through the apostles of the Lord Jesus Christ.

Confidence that the New Testament provides an infallible record concerning the person and work of the Saviour and the teaching of God through the apostles is based upon a number of considerations.

The Spirit of truth

Before his departure back to the Father, the Lord Jesus Christ promised the assistance and supernatural help of the Holy Spirit: 'These things I have spoken to you while being present with you. But the Helper, the Holy Spirit, whom the Father will send in my name, he will teach you all things, and bring to your remembrance all things that I said to you' (John 14:25-26). The Lord did not need to choose special men with outstanding memories. Nor did the apostles need to worry about forgetting vital information entrusted to them by the Lord. The Son of God promised the Spirit of God, especially under his name as 'the Spirit of truth'.

The work of the Spirit of God was not, however, restricted to the ability to recall information already received. Jesus had not communicated everything during his earthly lifetime (John 16:12). The Holy Spirit would eventually supply additional information: 'When he, the Spirit of truth, has come, he will guide you into all truth; for he will not speak on his own authority, but whatever he hears he will speak; and *he will tell you things to come*. He will glorify me, for he will take of what is mine and declare it to you' (John 16:13-14, emphasis added).

The last book of the New Testament is one of many testimonies to this promise. In 'the Revelation of Jesus Christ, which God gave him [i.e. Christ] to show his servants — things which must shortly take place' (Rev. 1:1), the Saviour communicates with the apostle John. Later we learn that the risen Christ used the services of the Holy Spirit as his agent. At the end of each of the letters to the seven churches in Asia Minor are the words: 'He who has an ear, let him hear what the Spirit says to the churches' (Rev. 2:7,11,17,29; 3:6,13,22).

Three facts are implied by the Lord's promise of the Holy Spirit to assist the apostles:

1. That which depended upon their memory was kept free from error.

2. That which was recorded of their own observations was kept free from error.

3. God also gave them 'truths imparted ... directly by the Spirit of God, which they could never have arrived at by the unaided exercise of their own minds'. [14]

The internal testimony

The Lord Jesus promised the Holy Spirit to his twelve apostles. Consequently the record of the life and teaching of the Lord Jesus Christ as found in Matthew and John (both apostles of Christ) is accepted as bearing the marks of that promise. But what about the writings of Luke and Mark? They were not apostles. There is no record to show that they were included in the promise concerning the Spirit.

It is evident that Luke was a respected member of the early Christian church. He accompanied the apostle Paul on many of his travels. Paul refers to Luke as 'the beloved physician' present with him as he writes the letter to the Colossians (Col. 4:14). Paul also mentions the presence of Luke when he writes his second letter to Timothy: 'Only Luke is with me' (2 Tim. 4:11). A further reference is found in Paul's letter to his good friend Philemon. At the conclusion Paul writes, 'Epaphras, my fellow prisoner in Christ Jesus, greets you, as do Mark, Aristarchus, Demas, Luke, my fellow labourers' (Phil. 23-24).

Dr Luke accompanied Paul on his missionary journeys. He met other apostles and was ideally suited to draw together a mass of information and detail. As he states at the beginning of his record of the life and teaching of the Lord Jesus Christ, 'Inasmuch as many have taken in hand to set in order a narrative of those things which are most surely believed among us, just as those who from the beginning were eyewitnesses and ministers of the word delivered them to us, it seemed good to me also, having had perfect [i.e. a complete or full] understanding of all things from the very first, to write to you an orderly account, most excellent Theophilus, that you may know the certainty of those things in which you were instructed' (Luke 1:1-4).

Luke gathered together all the available information, both oral (by word of mouth) and written. He examined the material carefully and verified it with the eyewitnesses, apostles and disciples, and then set it down in a coherent fashion. Nevertheless his claim alone does not demonstrate the confidence of the apostles in this record of the life and teaching of the Lord Jesus Christ. True, he was a respected member of the church, a gifted and able man. He had spent many hours, weeks, months, even years, with apostles of Christ. He had researched his subject carefully and painstakingly. But what did the apostles think of the finished result? The apostle Paul supplies an answer, almost inadvertently. He evidently accepted Luke's record as 'Scripture', as can be seen from his first letter to Timothy: 'For the Scripture says, "You shall not muzzle an ox while it treads out the grain," and, "The labourer is worthy of his wages" ' (1 Tim. 5:18).

The first quotation is taken from Deuteronomy 25:4 and the second from Luke 10:7. There could be no clearer association of the writings of Luke and the Old Testament Scriptures. The Bible is bearing its own testimony to the writings of Luke. The Gospel according to Luke and the Acts of the Apostles are therefore authenticated as Scripture breathed out by God. The promise of the assistance of the Holy Spirit was not given to Luke. He did not bring teaching of Christ back to memory, nor did he experience revelations of things to come. He merely recorded accurately the remembrance and revelations of the apostles and eyewitnesses. He is an accurate historian authenticated by an apostle.

The apostles' scribes

The second New Testament historian who is not an apostle is Mark, the nephew of Barnabas, sometimes called 'John Mark' (Acts 12:12,25; 15:37). While there is no internal verification of Mark's record as inspired Scripture, it has been generally agreed in the church through the ages that the apostle Peter provided the eyewitness material. Church Fathers Papias and Tertullian, both of whom lived in the middle of the second century

A.D., claimed that Mark wrote his Gospel in partnership with the apostle Peter. Papias says, 'Mark, having become Peter's interpreter, wrote accurately all that he remembered...' Tertullian was even more clear in his statement: 'That which Mark had published may be affirmed to be Peter's whose interpreter Mark was.'[15] A careful study of 'the Gospel According to Mark' will substantially support this conclusion.

Both Peter and Paul used others, on occasions, to write their letters for them (1 Peter 5:12; Rom. 16:22).

The apostles' authentication

It is important to see the unique position of these apostles. They were a personally chosen and a uniquely authenticated group of men (John 15:16). Speaking of our 'great salvation', the writer to the Hebrews continues, 'which at the first began to be spoken by the Lord, and *was confirmed to us* by those who heard him, *God also bearing witness both with signs and wonders, with various miracles, and gifts of the Holy Spirit, according to his own will*' (Heb. 2:3-4, emphasis added). Here it is clearly stated that God authenticated the Lord Jesus Christ *and* his apostles by the demonstration of supernatural miracles.

Peter spoke of this endorsement of Christ when he preached to a large Jewish congregation on the Day of Pentecost: 'Men of Israel, hear these words: Jesus of Nazareth, a man attested by God to you by miracles, wonders, and signs which God did through him in your midst, as you yourselves also know...' (Acts 2:22).

Paul speaks of the authorization of the apostles when he wrote to the Corinthian church: 'Truly the signs of an apostle were accomplished among you with all perseverance, in signs and wonders and mighty deeds' (2 Cor. 12:12).

The Lord Jesus is attested to be the Christ of God and the Son of God through the miraculous signs he performed (John 5:36; Matt. 11:3-5; John 3:2). Miraculous signs were also given to attest the twelve disciples and Paul as apostles of Christ and consequently they were authorized to act as the Saviour's unique representatives (Acts 5:12; Heb. 2:3-4; 2 Cor. 12:12).

The apostles' awareness

Together with this authentication from the Holy Spirit, the apostles had also a personal awareness, a personal consciousness of authority in the church of Christ:

We are of God. He who knows God hears us; he who is not of God does not hear us. By this we know the spirit of truth and the spirit of error (1 John 4:6).

These things we also speak, not in words which man's wisdom teaches but which the Holy Spirit teaches (1 Cor. 2:13).

For I received from the Lord that which I also delivered to you (1 Cor. 11:23).

If anyone thinks himself to be a prophet or spiritual, let him acknowledge that the things which I write to you are the commandments of the Lord (1 Cor. 14:37).

Therefore he who rejects this does not reject man, but God, who has also given us his Holy Spirit (1 Thess. 4:8).

Consequently it is a failure to understand and believe the Scriptures' own testimony that results in the suggestion, by some, that the teaching of Paul is not as important as the teaching of the Lord Jesus Christ. In reality Paul often refers to Christ as the source of his teaching (1 Cor. 11:23; 14:37). He is conscious of receiving authority from Christ to function as an apostle (Gal. 1:1; 1 Tim. 2:7). The apostles were the servants of Christ. They would not knowingly transmit incorrect information or communicate inaccurate commandments to the church. Paul says he and his colleagues should be considered 'as servants of Christ and stewards of the mysteries of God'. He then adds, 'Moreover it is required in stewards that one be found faithful' (1 Cor. 4:1-2). The teaching which is found in the New Testament Scriptures is *all* the teaching of the Lord Jesus Christ.

Along with this individual consciousness of authority, the apostles also possessed a sense of collective authority. This is a very important aspect of the New Testament. In spite of their great differences in personality, background and experiences, the apostles had a great respect for each other as apostles. Some twenty or thirty years after Pentecost, the apostle Peter places his words, along with those of the other apostles, on the same level with, and bearing the same authority as, the Scriptures of the Old Testament: 'Beloved, I now write to you this second epistle (in both of which I stir up your pure minds by way of reminder), that you may be mindful of the words which were spoken before by the holy prophets, and the commandment of us the apostles of the Lord and Saviour' (2 Peter 3:1-2).

The New Testament was already almost entirely formed during the lifetime of the apostles. They understood their writings to be on a par with Old Testament Scripture. Hence Peter writes of the letters of Paul that there are 'some things hard to understand, which those who are untaught and unstable twist to their own destruction, as they do also the rest of the Scriptures' (2 Peter 3:16). Considering the public rebuke which Peter received from Paul at Antioch (Gal. 2:11-14), the reference to Paul as 'our beloved brother Paul' (2 Peter 3:15), and the acknowledgement of his writings as Scripture, is all the more powerful a testimony!

Conclusion

In a brief and broad sweep the inspiration, and therefore the reliability, of the Scriptures of the Old and New Testaments, has been examined. The living God has given the necessary confirmation that the writings of the prophets and the writings of the apostles are to be regarded as breathed out by God. Holy men of God not only spoke as they were moved by the Holy Spirit (2 Peter 1:20-21), they also wrote the Old Testament, and they wrote the New Testament, as moved by the same Spirit. Thus the solid 'foundation of the apostles and prophets' is laid, 'Jesus Christ himself being the chief cornerstone' (Eph. 2:20).

The Holy Spirit was the overseer who personally ensured that the thirty-nine books of the Old Testament are the truth which God wants to reveal to his church, and nothing but the truth. The Holy Spirit ensured that the Jewish nation first, and then the Christian church later, recognized these books which had been given by inspiration of God. The same Spirit of truth guarded the recording, the communication and the selection of the New Testament Scriptures. But the work of the Holy Spirit in relation to the Scriptures is by no means over. As the Spirit of God alone inspired the Scriptures, safeguarded the transmission of the Scriptures and gave the perception to recognize those Scriptures, so he alone interprets the Scriptures. The reading of the Bible in and of itself does not bring illumination and understanding. In the days of the apostle Paul there were Jews reading the Old Testament without understanding. They lacked enlightenment from the Spirit because they had not turned in faith to Christ (2 Cor. 3:14-18). Even those who have turned to Christ need constantly to reiterate the prayer of the psalmist: 'Open my eyes, that I may see wondrous things from your law' (Ps. 119:18).

Here is the reliable Word from God which needs faithful translation from the original languages to communicate its truth; prayerful meditation to understand its truth; careful interpretation, comparing scripture with scripture, to apply its truth; and living devotion to obey its truth.

The central theme of Old Testament Scripture

E. A. Martens maintains that the 'Old Testament supplies the fibre for the Christian faith. But unless the message of the Old Testament is clearly articulated, its relevance to the New Testament and to Christians today will remain fuzzy.' Clarity about the Christian faith will depend on a grasp of the Old Testament, he asserts, and then sets out in search of 'a single central message' which he believes will be 'the key to the content of the Old Testament'.[1] But does such a key exist to reveal an orderly and progressive development of the subjects, themes and teachings of the Old Testament?

The divine covenant

William Dumbrell, along with others, finds his centre point for Old Testament revelation in the concept of the *berît* (the covenant) which occurs almost three hundred times in the Old Testament and is first introduced by the Lord in relation to Noah: 'And behold, I myself am bringing the flood of waters on the earth, to destroy from under heaven all flesh in which is the breath of life; and everything that is on the earth shall die. But I will establish my covenant with you; and you shall go into the ark — you, your sons, your wife, and your sons' wives with you' (Gen. 6:17-18).

The Hebrew word *berît* is normally translated as 'covenant' in most English versions, but Dumbrell points out that this is misleading: 'Basically, the notion conveyed by the English word is that of agreement, with the nuance of legal agreement whereby rights and privileges, commitments and obligations are set up between two parties, an agreement which may have involved extended or protracted negotiations. Admittedly, the English word can also bear the note of an undertaking or a pledge advanced by one party and thus can mean substantially a unilateral vow or a promise. Most naturally, however, the English word embodies the idea of an agreement which has involved mutual consent. This latter meaning would not fit at Genesis 6:18, for there the divine announcement appears to point to a one-sided arrangement.'[2]

While this understanding of *berît* points to the unilateral character of the covenant, with the initiative being entirely with God, nevertheless responses are required. These responses result either in receiving the blessings attached to the covenant, or suffering the curses which the rejection of the covenant entails. The Lord takes on an obligation to care for Noah and his family. As the Old Testament revelation progresses and further clarification is given, the Lord becomes more specific. To Moses God says, 'I am the LORD. I appeared to Abraham, to Isaac, and to Jacob, as God Almighty, but by my name, LORD, I was not known to them. I have also established my covenant with them, to give them the land of Canaan, the land of their pilgrimage, in which they were strangers. And I have also heard the groaning of the children of Israel whom the Egyptians keep in bondage, and I have remembered my covenant. Therefore say to the children of Israel: "I am the LORD; I will bring you out from under the burdens of the Egyptians, I will rescue you from their bondage, and I will redeem you with an outstretched arm and with great judgements. I will take you as my people, and I will be your God. Then you shall know that I am the LORD your God who brings you out from under the burdens of the Egyptians. And I will bring you into the land which I swore to give to Abraham, Isaac, and Jacob; and I will give it to you as a heritage: I am the LORD"' (Exod. 6:2-8).

Such passages lead to the conclusion that the 'essence of a covenant … is the bonded *relationship* between two parties' (emphasis added).[3] The people of God during the Old Testament period are the 'covenant community'. The Lord declares his responsibilities towards his people, and marks out their responsibilities towards him. But the concept of a covenant community does not end with the Old Testament. The New Testament church of Jesus Christ is just as strongly a community under covenant. Indeed, in outlining the blessings of 'a new heaven and a new earth' where there is 'no more death, nor sorrow, nor crying; and there shall be no more pain', the highlight is that 'The tabernacle of God is with men, and he will dwell with them, and they shall be his people, and God himself will be with them and be their God' (Rev. 21:1,4,3).

The divine promise

Closely aligned with the concept of the divine covenant is the notion of the divine promise. Walter Kaiser argues for the central theme of Old Testament revelation as 'the divine blessing-promise'.[4] Asserting that the New Testament writers eventually refer to this focal point as 'the promise', he maintains that the Old Testament 'knew it under a constellation of such words as promise, oath, blessing, rest, and seed'. He continues: 'It was also known under such formulas as the tripartite saying: "I will be your God, you shall be My people, and I will dwell in the midst of you" or the redemptive self-assertion formula scattered in part or in full form 125 times throughout the OT: "I am the Lord your God who brought you up out of the Land of Egypt." It could also be seen as a divine plan in history which promised to bring a universal blessing through the agency of an unmerited, divine choice of a human offspring: "In thee shall all families of the earth be blessed" (Genesis 12:3).'[5]

The blessing-promises of Genesis 12:1-3 which relate specifically to Abraham are: firstly, that he will become a great nation (v. 2); secondly, that he will be blessed (v. 2); and, thirdly, that his name will become great (v. 2). The elements of the blessing-promise that reach beyond Abraham are: firstly, that he will be a blessing (v. 2); secondly, that the Lord will bless those who favour Abraham and curse any who do not (v. 3); and, thirdly, that all peoples of the earth will be blessed through him (v. 3). Later, when Abraham arrives in Canaan, the Lord amplifies the earlier promise by saying, 'To your descendants I will give this land' (Gen. 12:7). This was implicit in the earlier words, 'I will make you a great nation' (Gen. 12:2). It serves to refine that earlier statement by more narrowly defining the 'great nation' as Abraham's offspring and it amplifies the statement by designating the land of Canaan as the country in which his posterity would become a nation.[6] Later the Lord reinforces his promise to Abraham that he will have numerous descendants from his own body (Gen. 15:4-5).

Thirteen years after the birth of Ishmael to Abraham and Hagar, the Lord appears to Abraham and again expands the divine blessing-promise. Now Abraham's numerous descendants are to include royalty (Gen. 17:6). Another new note is struck: the divine-human relationship is highlighted; to Abraham the Lord promises, 'I will establish my covenant between me and you and your descendants after you in their generations, for an everlasting covenant, to be God to you and your descendants after you' (Gen. 17:7). It is now evident that the Lord meant every word literally when he spoke about 'an everlasting covenant' and 'an everlasting possession' (Gen.

17:7,8). 'The promise covenant, made with Abraham and his offspring, is an eternal covenant that never loses its force or integrity.'[7]

Drawing together all the strands of the blessing-promise results in a remarkable list of blessings:

- Abraham will be singularly blessed by God.
- Abraham's name will become great.
- Abraham and Sarah will have numerous descendants.
- Abraham and Sarah's descendants will include royalty.
- Abraham's descendants will receive the land of Canaan.
- Abraham and his descendants will enjoy a personal relationship with God.
- Abraham will be a source of blessing for the Gentiles.
- Abraham's blessings will have everlasting implications.

The divine purpose

In seeking a central theme for the Old Testament, rather than beginning with Genesis 6 and the divine covenant, or Genesis 12 and the divine blessing-promise, Martens leaps to the second book of the Bible and maintains that Exodus 5:22 – 6:8 is 'a pivotal text about Yahweh and his purpose'.[8] There Moses is seen confronting the Lord with a breach of promise, and while a rebuke might have been expected, Moses receives instead an amplification of the promise. God's reply to Moses begins with a simple but highly significant assertion: 'I am the LORD' (6:2). In the English translation the force of this statement is not immediately apparent. 'It is essentially the name of the deity that is at issue.'[9] In his reply God declares three times: 'I am the LORD' (vv. 2,6,8). When the word 'LORD' appears in capital letters in our English versions it is translating the Hebrew word YHWH (Yahweh). In seeking to determine the meaning of the word Martens lays aside the idea that 'at the time of the exodus, the name Yahweh was to be associated with the keeping of promises' and prefers instead to conclude from the immediate context that 'Yahweh is the name by which God represents himself as present, here and now, to act, especially to deliver. It is in this way, essentially in a new way, that Israel will experience Yahweh. Yahweh is a salvation name. This name, the most frequent name for God (YHWH occurs more than 6,800 times in the Old Testament) becomes a frequent reminder that God is the saving God.'[10]

YHWH is God's name of self-disclosure or revelation with particular reference to his redemptive undertaking.[11] Following this self-identification in Exodus 6:2, the relationship of God to the patriarchs Abraham, Isaac and Jacob, in terms of the covenant, is recalled. The covenant embracing the triple promise of offspring, land and blessing, was given to Abraham at the age of ninety-nine (Gen. 17:1-8), and repeated to Isaac (Gen. 26:3) and to Jacob (Gen. 28:13-15; 35:9-12). By the time of the Exodus one of the three blessings had already been realized, for 'The children of Israel were fruitful and increased abundantly, multiplied and grew exceedingly mighty; and the land [Egypt] was filled with them' (Exod. 1:7). Under the leadership of Moses and Joshua a second strand of the covenant is about to be fulfilled: Israel is to inherit the promised land (Exod. 6:8).

From the record in Exodus 6 the Lord's design may be understood as:

- Deliverance for his people: 'I will bring you out...' (v. 6).
- The formation of a godly community: 'I will take you as my people, and I will be your God' (v. 7).
- An ongoing relationship with his people: 'Then you shall know that I am Yahweh your God who brings you out...' (v. 7).
- The enjoyment of the good life for his people: 'I will bring you into the land...' (v. 8); cf. '... flowing with milk and honey' (3:17).

Martens continues: 'If in the name Yahweh there is disclosed a new feature of Yahweh, and if the covenant with the patriarchs was already made earlier, apart from the name, then we must look for a new feature other than covenant as linked in a particular way with the name Yahweh. Is that new feature not to be found in the statement of the fourfold design? Salvation, a new people, a new relationship, and the gift of the land — these are the components of the purpose. Yahweh is the name that is associated at this crucial juncture with purpose, that which God intends or is about.'[12]

The divine purpose is summed up as: deliverance, a covenant community, relationship with God and inheriting a land.

Evaluation

So far we have considered three themes for the Old Testament — the divine covenant, the divine promise and the divine purpose. They provide a thread to link the many different strands of Old Testament revelation together and to form, with the New Testament, a unified whole. These three have many features in common, either stated or implied. They point to a seed, a race, a family, a land and a blessing of everlasting and universal proportions. In that covenant, promise or purpose, there is plenty of room for manoeuvre: for development, for clarification, for amplification and for application. In seeking a central theme for the Old Testament the concept of the divine covenant begins at Genesis 6, of divine blessing-promise at Genesis 12, or of divine purpose at Exodus 6. The weakness of these three approaches is that they neither go far enough forward nor far enough back; while ultimately they each find their fulfilment in the Saviour and his people, none of the three approaches to the Old Testament *begins* with Christ and his church. Is this not the theme which integrates the Old Testament as it so obviously does the New Testament? This approach, that the true theme is Christ and his church, looks back from a vantage-point 2,400 to 6,000 years after the events — seeing so many of the fulfilments, the extent of which could not have been envisaged in those early days. But lest it be thought that prophecy, types and revelations can be so easily coloured in a favourable light by a backward glance, the predictions concerning Christ and his church will be seen to have been in the heart of God from eternity: '… you were not redeemed with corruptible things … but with the precious blood of Christ, as of a lamb without blemish and without spot. *He indeed was foreordained before the foundation of the world,* but was made manifest in these last times for you who through him believe in God, who raised him from the dead and gave him glory, so that your faith and hope are in God' (1 Peter 1:18-21, emphasis added). 'Blessed be the God and Father of our Lord Jesus Christ, who has blessed us with every spiritual blessing in the heavenly places in Christ, *just as he chose us in him before the foundation of the world…*' (Eph. 1:3-4, emphasis added).

In asking the question, 'Where does the story of Jesus Christ begin?' we must travel back with Matthew to Abraham (Matt. 1:1-16), further back still with Luke to Adam (Luke 3:23-38) and with John to the eternity before time and creation (John 1:1-3). The Old Testament is then seen as the unfolding of a carefully prepared plan for the coming of his Son into the world which the Master Architect slowly and painstakingly reveals.

The questions remain to intrigue and to humble: 'Why the sending of that Divine Redeemer and Restorer, which had been purposed from eternity, did not immediately succeed the fall; — why four thousand years must first elapse, and in the meantime diseased humanity seek in vain to heal itself, in the absence of the divine Physician, who alone could give relief; is a question too profound for human wisdom…'[13]

With Hengstenberg we can only stand in awe and wonder. And with the apostle Paul we readily confess that God's timing is always perfect — for 'When the fulness of the time had come, God sent forth his Son, born of a woman, born under the law, to redeem those who were under the law, that we might receive the adoption as sons' (Gal. 4:4-5). The advent of Christ could not have happened one single moment earlier or one single moment later.

> Remember the former things of old,
> For I am God, and there is no other;
> I am God, and there is none like me,
> Declaring the end from the beginning,
> And from ancient times things that are not yet done,
> Saying, 'My counsel shall stand,
> And I will do all my pleasure.' ...
> Indeed I have spoken it;
> I will also bring it to pass.
> I have purposed it;
> I will also do it
>
> (Isa. 46:9-11).

Christ and his church

The central theme of Old Testament Scripture need not remain veiled and hidden under symbolic representations. The promise of God in the New Testament is that in coming to faith in Jesus Christ the veil is removed (2 Cor. 3:14). The Spirit of God grants illumination and insight: '... we all, with unveiled face, beholding as in a mirror [i.e. in the Old Testament Scriptures] the glory of the Lord, are being transformed into the same image from glory to glory, just as by the Spirit of the Lord' (2 Cor. 3:18).

Jesus Christ, the Son of God, is the grand subject, the central theme, of the Old Testament. When the Lord is challenged about his claims to unique sonship, he presents, as one of a number of proofs, the content of Old Testament Scripture: 'You search the Scriptures, for in them you think you have eternal life; and these are they which testify of me. But you are not willing to come to me that you may have life... Do not think that I shall accuse you to the Father; there is one who accuses you — Moses, in whom you trust. For if you believed Moses, you would believe me; for he wrote about me' (John 5:39-40,45-46).

After his resurrection, the Lord joined two of his disciples as they walked to the village of Emmaus. For some time these disciples were not permitted to recognize their Master. In the course of conversation they expressed their sadness and disappointment at the recent events surrounding the crucifixion and their discomfort at the claims which were circulating that Jesus was in fact alive.

The Lord rebuked them, not because they did not believe the reports of his resurrection, but because they were 'slow of heart to believe in all that the prophets have spoken! Ought not the Christ to have suffered these things and to enter into his glory?' (Luke 24:25-26). The Saviour's criticism is based upon their unbelief of the Old Testament Scriptures. He then enlightens them from those very writings: '... beginning at Moses and all the prophets, he expounded to them in all the Scriptures the things concerning himself' (Luke 24:27).

Returning immediately to the apostles and disciples in Jerusalem, these two disciples reported the encounter. As they were speaking, the Lord appeared before them. Again he confirmed his connection with the Old Testament: '"These are the words which I spoke to you while I was still with you, that all things must be fulfilled which were written in the Law of Moses and the Prophets and the Psalms concerning me." And he opened their understanding, that they might comprehend the Scriptures. Then he said to them, "Thus it is written, and thus it was necessary for the Christ to suffer and to rise from the dead the third day, and that repentance and remission of sins should be preached in his name to all nations, beginning at Jerusalem"'(Luke 24:44-47).

The apostle Paul insists upon the same solid Old Testament base for the death, burial and resurrection of Christ. Not only the events, but also the theological significance of those events is declared to be 'according to the Scriptures' (1 Cor. 15:3-4). Christ was seen by Paul in the Old Testament just as vividly as we can see him in the New Testament. Paul could see Christ in such things as the first institution of marriage (Eph. 5:31-32); the promise to Abraham's Seed (Gal. 3:16); the rock in the wilderness journey (1 Cor. 10:4); and the words of Moses in Deuteronomy 30:12-14 (Rom. 10:6-8).

How else could Paul argue so convincingly before the Jews if Christ is not the subject of the Old Testament? At Achaia, 'He vigorously refuted the Jews publicly, showing from the Scriptures that Jesus is the Christ' (Acts 18:28). Before King Agrippa Paul makes a bold claim: 'Therefore, having obtained help from God, to this day I stand, witnessing both to small and great, *saying no other things than those which the prophets and Moses said would come* — that the Christ would suffer, that he would be the first to rise from the dead, and would proclaim light to the Jewish people and to the Gentiles' (Acts 26:22-23, emphasis added).

The secret is out. That mystery is revealed which was 'kept secret since the world began but now has been made manifest, and by the prophetic Scriptures has been made known to all nations, according to the commandment of the everlasting God' (Rom. 16:25-26). This mystery 'from the beginning of the ages has been hidden in God who created all things through Jesus Christ' (Eph. 3:9). The living God has had an 'eternal purpose which he accomplished in Christ Jesus our Lord' (Eph. 3:11).

It is not that the Old Testament has a great theme to which are added occasional prophecies and predictions about the coming of the Messiah. Nor is it a random history with the occasional spiritual gem hidden here or there. Everything found in the Old Testament has relevance at some point to the incarnation, humiliation, death, resurrection, ascension, glorification, triumphant return or future kingdom of the Lord Jesus Christ, Son of the living God (cf. Luke 24:27). Without undermining the literal and historical sense of Old Testament Scripture, this principle will be applied throughout this entire book. Andrew Bonar took the same approach to the Psalms: '... our principle is, that having once found the literal sense, the exact meaning of the terms, and the primary application ... we are then to ask what the Holy Spirit intended to teach in all ages by this formula...'[14] Bonar made no apology in seeing Christ and his church throughout the Psalms. This principle of looking for Christ will be basic to this overview of the thirty-nine books of the Old Testament.

Revelation concerning Christ occurs in three major forms in the Old Testament: theophanies, types and prophecies. The Son of God appears in a theophany immediately following the fall of humanity in Adam and Eve. He speaks of the woman's seed, and he predicts a violent contest with a victorious outcome (Gen. 3:15).[15] Revelation by theophany, type and prophecy has begun. Frequent new revelations will keep the expectation of the people alive, and make it continually more and more definite. Consequently the doctrine of a coming Redeemer, even when partially misunderstood, becomes 'the soul and centre of all theocratic expectations'.[16] Each subsequent revelation in history contributes to the development, progress and enlargement of the grand and glorious purpose of God in Christ.

Theophanies

Theophanies are temporary appearances of God in human form. 'Christo-phanies' might be a more accurate term, as any manifestation of God in human form is an appearance of the Second Person of the Godhead, for 'No one has seen God at any time. The only begotten Son, who is in the bosom of the Father, he has declared him' (John 1:18).

Christophanies are 'those unsought, intermittent and temporary, visible and audible manifestations of God the Son in human form, by which God communicated something to certain conscious human beings on earth prior to the birth of Jesus Christ'.[17] Distinguishing Christophanies from dreams, visions, the pillar of cloud, the Shekinah glory and the incarnation of Christ, James Borland contends that the purpose of Christophanies 'was not only to provide immediate revelation but also to prepare ... for the in-carnation of Christ'.[18]

Each appearance of the Son of God in human form reveals something about the Godhead, or something about God's will. There is an implied reference to regular appearances, or Christophanies, for fellowship with Adam and Eve before the Fall (Gen. 3:8), but after the Fall, with the ex-ception of fellowship with Enoch (Gen. 5:22,24), the appearances have specific functions, such as the giving of a warning, a promise, instruction, or blessing. By this means God gave warnings of judgement to the serpent and to Adam and Eve (Gen. 3:14-19), to Cain (Gen. 4:9-12), to Noah (Gen. 6:9,13-14) and in response to the sin of Sodom and Gomorrah (Gen. 18:20-21). He made promises to Hagar (Gen. 16:7-13), to Abraham (Gen. 17:1-22), to both Abraham and Sarah (Gen. 18) and to Isaac (Gen. 26:2,24). He blessed Jacob at Peniel (Gen. 32:24-30; cf. 35:1,9-13). He gave instructions to Joshua outside Jericho (Josh. 5:13-15), to Gideon in Ophrah (Judg. 6:11-23) and to Manoah and his wife about their as yet un-born son Samson (Judg. 13:3-6,8-23).

Borland suggests the following purposes behind the theophanies:

• God the Son anticipated his future incarnation, intimated its possibility, prefigured its human form and even prophesied its coming reality.
• God was using a form of revelation suited to his purposes in the early history of his redemptive plan.
• God connected his work in the Old and New Testaments by appearing in human form in both.

- God was able to reveal aspects of his person in this way that no other form of revelation allowed.
- God may have sought to intimate Christ's deity and the Godhead.[19]

Types

A more difficult area of revelation is that of types. The Old Testament gives us types that foreshadow the New Testament fulfilment. A type is a form of analogy that is distinctive to the Bible. Like all analogies, a type combines identity and difference. David is a type of Christ; David and Christ were both given kingly power and rule. 'In spite of the vast differences between David's royalty and Christ's, there are points of formal identity that make the comparison meaningful.'[20]

This is the area of Christology (the study of Christ) which is most susceptible to a vivid imagination rather than the application of carefully determined principles of interpretation. We must not make an Old Testament passage mean what we would like it to mean. We must not impose our ideas upon the text. But how to safeguard against such abuse is not easy to define. The typology of Scripture does not depend upon the usage or meaning of the word 'type' in the Scriptures. It is grounded upon a whole series of references where an object, person or event in the Old Testament is seen to reflect in the natural realm a truth or feature in the New Testament in the spiritual realm. A type may be defined as 'a figure, episode, or symbolic factor resembling some future reality in such a way as to foreshadow or prefigure it'. An antitype is the future reality of the symbol. Just as little children are taught with the help of pictures and models, so the Lord graciously teaches his people with the assistance of visual aids. But these pictures and emblems are not restricted to those young in the faith. Their significance may be best discovered by those who have a thorough acquaintance with the Scriptures.

Andrew Jukes suggests that the neglect of the study of the types in Scripture may be explained in part in 'that they require more spiritual intelligence than many Christians can bring to them. To apprehend them requires a certain measure of spiritual capacity and habitual exercise in the things of God, which all do not possess, for want of abiding fellowship with Jesus... The types are, indeed, pictures, but to understand the picture it is necessary we should know something of the reality... The real secret of our difficulty is that we know so little, and, what is worse, we do not know our ignorance.'[21] As it is 'by reason of use' that mature Christians 'have their senses exercised to discern both good and evil' (Heb. 5:14), so it is by that same using of truth already possessed that spiritual advancement is made and spiritual growth takes place.

By the use of types the Lord gives detailed insight into the person and work of his Son that no mere words could ever convey: 'Though sacrifices and ceremonies can be no ground or foundation to build up — that is, though we can prove nought with them — yet, when we have once found out Christ and His mysteries, then we may borrow figures, that is to say, allegories, similitudes, and examples, *to open Christ, and the secrets of God hid in Christ* ... and can declare them more lively and sensibly with them than with all the words of the world. For similitudes have more virtue and power with them than bare words, and lead a man's understanding further into the pith and marrow and spiritual understanding of the thing, than all the words that can be imagined.'[22]

The institution of marriage is shown to be a type of Christ and his church (Gen. 2:24; Eph. 5:31-32). The flood is seen as the type of Christian baptism (Gen. 7:1,4,10; 1 Peter 3:21). Melchizedek is a type of Christ in his priesthood (Gen. 14:18-20; Ps. 110:4; Heb. 6:20 – 7:28). The whole structure of the tabernacle, with its ministry and services, is designated 'a copy and shadow of ... heavenly things' (Heb. 8:5; cf. Exod. 25:1 – 28:43; Lev. 23:3-43). It gives symbolic expression to the great truths and principles of the spiritual life: truths respecting sin and salvation, the purification of the heart, and the dedication of the person and the life to God; truths and principles common to both Old and New Testament times but which could only find their proper development and full realization in the New Testament revelation of Christ and his church.

As well as the clear identifications of types of Christ in the New Testament, such as the Passover (1 Cor. 5:7), the water-giving rock (1 Cor. 10:4) and the whole sacrificial system (Heb. 10:1-10), there are others by implication, such as the manna in the wilderness (John 6:31-33), the ladder in Jacob's dream (John 1:51) and the temple (John 2:19). These are not the results of coincidence. They are the outworking of a brilliantly conceived and carefully executed divine plan, for resemblance or coincidence alone is not sufficient: '... to constitute one thing the type of another, something more is wanted than mere resemblance. The former must not only resemble the latter, but must have been *designed* to resemble the latter. The type as well as the antitype must have been pre-ordained; and they must have been pre-ordained as constituent parts of the same general scheme of Divine Providence.'[23]

Old Testament religious buildings, ceremonies and priesthood, chosen articles and objects — whether actual, or seen in dreams or visions — are types of Christ and his unique work of salvation. But are only Old Testament *symbols* to be seen as types of Christ? Could it not be that *historic events* recorded in the Old Testament are also designed and overruled to provide glorious types of Christ and his unique saving work? Is not this the principle by which the Lord Jesus points to the serpent raised up in the wilderness? (John 3:14-15). It is not simply in the coincidence of elevation into the vertical position that the connection is made. There are features about that period in Israel's history which shed a profound light upon the Crucified One: the people had sinned (Num. 21:5; cf. v. 7); the Lord sent punishment (Num. 21:6); the people repented and sought forgiveness (v. 7); and the Lord provided the means of healing which required faith and obedience (v. 8). Now it is to be noted that the means which the Lord adopted was horrific. The serpent is the symbol of everything that is evil, from the first book of the Bible even to the last. It was the serpent in the Garden of Eden that Satan used as his agent in tempting Adam and Eve to sin. In the book of Revelation the devil is referred to as 'that serpent of old' (Rev. 12:9). The associations could not be more unpalatable. Nevertheless, the Lord's self-identification with the serpent in the wilderness cannot be passed over lightly. He identified himself with the solution to the problem of sin. That solution was itself related to the curse of God (the poisonous serpents). Christ is seen therefore as identified, at great personal cost, with the sin (2 Cor. 5:21), with the curse (Gal. 3:13) and with the cure (John 3:14-16; cf. Num. 21:9). 'There is life for a look at the Crucified One!'

Christians may derive great benefit from these divinely inspired Scriptures of the Old Testament: 'For whatever things were written before were written for our learning, that we through the patience and comfort of the Scriptures might have hope' (Rom. 15:4). Speaking of God's dealings with the Israelites during the wilderness journey, Paul affirms: 'Now all these things happened to them *as examples*, and they were written for our admonition, on whom the ends of the ages have come' (1 Cor. 10:11, emphasis added).

In Israel's history we can trace the providential workings of God. We can follow also a pattern, or type of things spiritual, concerning Christ and his church — things to come. Who can read the history of Joseph without reflecting upon the circumstances surrounding the life, suffering, death and resurrection of the Lord Jesus Christ? Born among brethren and persecuted in infancy, he finds sanctuary in Egypt, is sold by someone close to him, falsely accused, treated as an outcast, envied and persecuted, yet remains upright and blameless through trials and imprisonment; he is raised up to the right hand of power and glory and given a wife; the hostility of his fellow Israelites leads to blessing for the Gentiles; we see him distributing life-giving resources, receiving his brethren again through repentance and providing a home of plenty, safety and peace for all persons under his charge.

Joseph displays a deep spiritual discernment regarding the providence of God. Speaking to his brothers he says, '… you meant evil against me; but God meant it for good, in order to bring it about as it is this day, to save many people alive' (Gen. 50:20). Joseph skilfully distinguishes between the wicked purposes in the minds of his brothers and the gracious purpose in the mind of God. The seriousness and evil of their deeds is not reduced in the slightest degree. The selling of Joseph was a despicable crime. Yet, at one and the same time, he was sold by the will of God. The Lord did not permit Joseph's death; the Lord did permit Joseph's enslavement. The Lord 'used' the expression of human hostility for his own greater purposes: 'Joseph was sold by the wicked consent of his brethren, and by the secret providence of God.' [24]

Years later a similar crime would be perpetrated, but this time upon the only begotten Son of God. He was betrayed by his 'brethren' and sold, not to slavery, but to death. Following Christ's resurrection and the outpouring of the Holy Spirit at Pentecost, the apostle Peter views the Saviour's death from two vastly different perspectives: 'Jesus of Nazareth … being delivered by the carefully planned intention and foreknowledge of God, you have taken by lawless hands, have crucified, and put to death…' (Acts 2:22-23).

As with Joseph's words, so with the apostle Peter's: no lessening of guilt is permitted. The Lord of glory was falsely accused, disgracefully tried, unlawfully sentenced and viciously executed by corrupt men.

Having traced the Old Testament revelation of Christ by means of Christophanies and types, we still need to explore one further area, that of prophecies. In the numerous Messianic predictions of the Old Testament we find the clearest, most detailed anticipation of Christ and his church.

Prophecies

'The chief object of prophecy,' declares E. W. Hengstenberg, 'was to prepare the way for Christ, that, when He should come, He might be identified by a comparison of the prediction with its fulfilment.'[25] 'For the testimony of Jesus is the spirit of prophecy' (Rev. 19:10). Yet it is readily admitted that the earliest prophecies were remarkably vague. Like a skilful artist, God begins with light sketches which to the onlooker may appear quite indistinct and unrecognizable. Little by little, colour and detail are added — nothing is rushed — until it is quite obvious what the finished product will be like. The lack of clarity and the shortage of specific detail must not be misconstrued as marks of error. Nothing is calculated to mislead. The great Artist has the finished picture in his mind's eye.

As Fairbairn, Vos and others have shown, there is a fundamental connection throughout. Fairbairn speaks of 'the inter-connected and progressive character of prophecy' and uses the analogy of an acorn and an oak tree: 'At first, the word of God is as a seed, it may be of the oak, or of any other plant, in which the whole majestic form and various parts of the future lie undisclosed, ready to reveal themselves when the times and the seasons, and other conditions which God has appointed to determine its being, shall have taken their course. And there is no break, nor leap, nor start in its course, which proceeds by a slow, and sweet, and beautiful progression, to perfect that purpose or word of God, which said at the beginning, "Let the earth bring forth grass, the herb that yields seed, and the fruit tree that yields fruit according to its kind, whose seed is in itself."'[26]

Vos insists that 'In the seed-form the minimum of indispensable knowledge was already present.'[27] From the first moment of creation God has one overriding thought in his mind — his Son and his people. Even as God creates Eve from the side of Adam and presents her back to him, so we glimpse the creation of a people through the Son to be returned to him, bound to him by love in the closest of ties, for all eternity. The centre and soul of the Old Testament is the same as that of the New Testament. It is Christ and his church.

In the Old Testament it is evident that a divinely determined principle of selectivity is in operation. In the formula, 'Thus says the Lord...', there is a single principle, a single understanding of all prophetic revelation which left the prophets and the people in no doubt concerning the divine disclosure: '... no prophecy of Scripture is of any private origin [see RAV footnote], for prophecy never came by the will of man, but holy men of God spoke as they were moved by the Holy Spirit' (2 Peter 1:20-21).

If the key, then, for an orderly and progressive arrangement of the subjects, themes and teachings of the Old Testament is Christ and his church, then a related question arises: 'Were the Old Testament authors consciously aware of this theme?' Did the prophets understand what they uttered? The same New Testament apostle provides the answer. Writing to new covenant believers in the Dispersion he says, 'Of this salvation the prophets have inquired and searched diligently, who prophesied of the grace that would come to you, searching what, or what manner of time, the Spirit of Christ who was in them was indicating when he testified before-hand of the sufferings of Christ and the glories that would follow. To them it was revealed that not to themselves but to us they were ministering the things which now have been reported to you through those who have preached the gospel to you by the Holy Spirit sent from heaven — things which angels desire to look into' (1 Peter 1:10-12).

It would seem that not only the prophets wanted to understand God's purposes in Christ; the angels in heaven were also intrigued by what God was doing and revealing to the Old Testament church. They were evidently not party to the secret (Rom. 16:25-26; Eph. 3:9). Yet while the prophets studied the revelation at the time to understand its meaning and its appli-cation, they were not ignorant of the general drift or scheme which united their words with the past and pointed on towards the future.

By theophany, type and prophecy the way is prepared for the coming of the Son of God to earth. Israel's history is itself part of the prophetic preparation. With Patrick Fairbairn we affirm: 'Christ … is the end of the *history* as well as of the *law* of the Old Testament' (emphasis added).[28]

The author of Hebrews welds together the revelation of God in the Old Testament and the revelation of God in Christ when he says, 'God, who at various times and in different ways spoke in time past to the fathers by the prophets, has in these last days spoken to us by his Son' (Heb. 1:1-2).

The history of Israel is the history of the Old Testament church prepar-ing for the coming of the Redeemer. It also provides analogies and insights into the New Testament church in its conflicts and ultimate victory in Christ. Since the days of Eve, the church (i.e. the Old Testament church) has been 'with child' — crying 'out in labour and in pain to give birth' (Rev. 12:2). Satan has been constantly active seeking to destroy 'her child [i.e. Christ] as soon as it was born' (v. 4). Once the child-king is born, he is 'caught up to God and to his throne' (v. 5). Unable to molest the child further, Satan turns his attention back to the woman (now the New Testament church) who 'fled into the wilderness, where she has a place prepared by God, that they should feed her there' (v. 6). There is a living union between the Old Testament church and the New Testament church. The unity of the people of God in all ages is not simply the participation in a common salvation. It is an integral unity which means that the blessings of the inheritance promised to the remnant in the Old Testament are blessings shared by the church in the New. We share the same faith, the same hope, as the believing Jews of the Old Testament. United under our common Head, we shall together inherit the promised blessings: 'And all these, having obtained a good testimony through faith, did not receive the promise, God having provided something better for us, that they should not be made perfect apart from us' (Heb. 11:39-40).

It is not only our Lord and Saviour who has this solid bond with the past, and especially with the history recorded in the thirty-nine books of the Old Testament; we too have an unbroken (and unbreakable) link with Old Testament history. It is not only Christ who is to be seen there, it is his church also. Christians have an inseparable bond with the history of the Old Testament: 'Israel's theology — and ours — is rooted in history.'[29] Furthermore, the history of Israel is *our* history: 'For you are all sons of God through faith in Christ Jesus. For as many of you as were baptized into Christ have put on Christ. There is neither Jew nor Greek, there is neither slave nor free, there is neither male nor female; for you are all one in Christ Jesus. And if you are Christ's, then you are Abraham's seed, and heirs according to the promise' (Gal. 3:26-29).

Conclusion

The search for the central theme of the Old Testament has been undertaken by examining the concepts of the divine covenant, the divine promise and the divine purpose. All these approaches have a great deal in common, but fail to identify with sufficient clarity the theme of the Old Testament. The Scriptures have been explored to see if Christ and his church are the theme which to a large extent lies hidden in the Old and in a glorious way is revealed in the New. An examination of theophanies (or rather, Christophanies), typology and prophecy has confirmed that Christ and his church is indeed the unifying thread. The Bible's story is about Christ. History is 'his story'. The Old Testament Scriptures outline the remarkable steps which the Father took to prepare for the coming of his Son. Those who believe the Old Testament Scriptures receive Jesus Christ as that long-awaited Son and deliverer (John 5:39-40,45-47). These sacred writings 'are able to make ... wise for salvation through faith which is in Christ Jesus' (2 Tim. 3:15). They act as 'our tutor to bring us to Christ, that we might be justified by faith' (Gal. 3:24).

The Old Testament is the logical introduction, the firm foundation and the ultimate authority for the life of Christ recorded in the New Testament. The whole Bible is God's message about his Son, our Saviour. God's chief purpose in writing this book was to reveal Christ. The Old Testament is the preparation for Christ. The New Testament is the manifestation of Christ. The Scriptures reveal Christ from Genesis to Revelation. The entire Bible finds meaning in him. Jesus Christ is the origin, the substance and the object of all divine revelation: 'In a word, the blessed Redeemer, whom the Gospel reveals, is Himself the beginning and the end of the scheme of God's dispensations; in Him is found alike the centre of Heaven's plan, and the one foundation of human confidence and hope. So that *before* His coming into the world, all things of necessity pointed toward Him; types and prophecies bore testimony to the things that concerned His work and kingdom; the children of blessing were blessed in anticipation of His promised redemption; and *with* His coming, the grand reality itself came, and the higher purposes of Heaven entered on their fulfilment.'[30]

As William Hendriksen asserts, no Old Testament book is 'interpreted fully until it is viewed in the light of New Testament revelation'.[31] The fulfilment is always greater than the promise, and the reality than the expectation. To the prophets of the Old Testament the vision of the Coming One, the promised Seed, was indeed glorious, but greater far is that reality by which we now know the one who loved us and gave himself for us. The mystery of Christ as the Lamb of God who takes away the sin of the world could only be known *in part* by the church of the Old Testament.

In the Scriptures there is a whole Christ presented: Christ in his offices — as Prophet, Priest and King; Christ in his character — as holy, harmless, undefiled; Christ in his person — as God and man; Christ in his relation to God and humanity; Christ in his body the church; Christ as giving to God all that God requires from his people; Christ as bringing to his people all that they require from God; Christ seen in his suffering; Christ viewed in glory; Christ as the first and the last; the all in all to his people.

'The different books are but God's chapters in which He arranges and illustrates some one or more of these or other aspects of His Beloved.'[32]

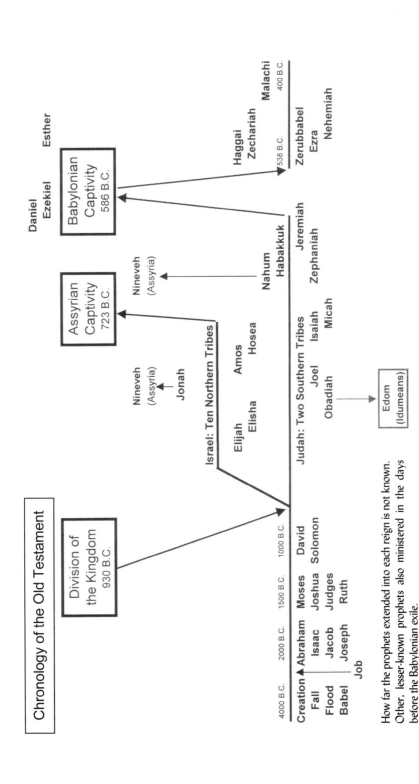

Chronology of the Old Testament

4000 B.C.	2000 B.C.	1500 B.C.	1000 B.C.

Creation   Abraham   Moses   David
Fall   Isaac   Joshua   Solomon
Flood   Jacob   Judges
Babel   Joseph   Ruth
            Job

Division of the Kingdom
930 B.C.

Israel: Ten Northern Tribes

Elijah   Amos
Elisha   Hosea

Nineveh (Assyria)
Jonah

Assyrian Captivity
723 B.C.

Nineveh (Assyria)

Nahum
Habakkuk

Judah: Two Southern Tribes

Joel   Isaiah
Obadiah Micah

Edom (Idumeans)

Jeremiah
Zephaniah

Daniel
Ezekiel   Esther

Babylonian Captivity
586 B.C.

Haggai
Zechariah

538 B.C.   Zerubbabel
            Ezra
            Nehemiah

Malachi
400 B.C.

How far the prophets extended into each reign is not known. Other, lesser-known prophets also ministered in the days before the Babylonian exile.

Genesis

('origins')

Author: Moses
(commonly accepted)

Key thought: 'Beginning'

Theme:
Human failure and God's glorious purpose

'In the beginning, God created the
heavens and the earth.'

Genesis 1:1

Summary

2. Isaac

i.	Isaac's birth	21:3
ii.	Isaac's marriage to Rebekah	24:1-67
iii.	The birth of twin sons Jacob and Esau	25:20-26
iv.	Isaac's later years	26:1-35

3. Jacob

i.	Jacob's deceit to secure the birthright	27:1-46
ii.	Jacob's vision of the heavenly ladder	28:10-22
iii.	Life with Laban, Leah and Rachel	29:1 – 31:55
iv.	Wrestling with God and man	32:1-32
v.	His brother Esau's family	36:1-43
vi.	Jacob's journey to Egypt	46:1 – 47:31
vii.	Jacob blesses Joseph's sons	48:1-22
viii.	Jacob's last words to his twelve sons	49:1-33

4. Joseph

i.	Joseph's birth	30:1,22-24
ii.	Conflict with his brothers	37:1-36
iii.	A slave in Egypt	39:1-23
iv.	Dreams in the prison	40:1-23
v.	Joseph's rise to power	41:1-57
vi.	Joseph's brothers travel to Egypt	42:1 – 45:28
vii.	Joseph buries his father	50:1-21
viii.	Joseph's death	50:22-26

Genesis

The first five books of the Old Testament, Genesis, Exodus, Leviticus, Numbers and Deuteronomy, are known among the Jews as the Torah (meaning 'law'). Among non-Jews they are known as the Pentateuch (from the Septuagint, the Greek translation of the Old Testament, meaning 'five books') or simply 'the Law'.

Genesis is the first book of the Pentateuch, the first book of the Old Testament, the first book of the Bible. It holds a strategic and vital place in God's revelation. Here is the record of how Israel was selected from among the nations of the world to become the chosen people. The choice was not made on account of any merit or excellence on their part; it is, therefore, 'the story of God's free grace in establishing Israel for Himself as His people'.[1] Opening with the account of creation, the book concludes with the death of Joseph and with the Israelites established and prospering in the land of Egypt.

Genesis is in many respects the most important book in the Bible. As its name implies, it is the book of 'beginnings', or the book of 'origins'. Without it, the origin of life, the birth of sin and the first promise of a radical solution would have remained a mystery and left the rest of the Scriptures seriously impoverished. Almost all the truths of God's revelation, the great doctrines which are afterwards fully developed in the books of Scripture, are here in seed form.

Author

Of the five books traditionally ascribed to Moses, only Exodus is directly credited to him in Scripture (Mark 12:26). The other four, Genesis, Leviticus, Numbers and Deuteronomy, are not referred to individually by name. The Lord Jesus Christ and the New Testament writers do, however, make a number of collective references to the writings of Moses (Luke 16:29,31; 24:27,44; John 1:45; 5:45-47; 2 Cor. 3:15).

Of ultimate concern is not the human author but the assurance that this book is part of the Scriptures breathed out by God (2 Tim. 3:16). That the ultimate authorship is divine all biblical writers are agreed. The Lord Jesus clearly accepted Genesis as written by God, as we see in his debate with the Pharisees on the issue of divorce: 'The Pharisees also came to him, testing him, and saying to him, "Is it lawful for a man to divorce his wife for just any reason?" And he answered and said to them, "Have you not read that he who made them at the beginning 'made them male and female', and said, 'For this reason a man shall leave his father and mother and be joined to his wife, and the two shall become one flesh'? So then, they are no longer two but one flesh. Therefore what God has joined together, let not man separate"' (Matt. 19:3-5).

The reliability of the early history which Moses records is often challenged on the ground that the events in the opening chapter occurred 2,500 years, and those in the closing chapter took place at least 300 years, before the time of Moses. There is, however, no biblically based reason to assume that written records had not been produced earlier. Moses may have in fact made use of existing manuscripts, records, as well as oral traditions, in his compilation. He certainly had the qualifications for the task — for he 'was learned in all the wisdom of the Egyptians, and was mighty in words and deeds' (Acts 7:22). More importantly, Moses was singularly favoured by God:

> If there is a prophet among you,
> I, the LORD, make myself known to him in a vision,
> And I speak to him in a dream.
> Not so with my servant Moses;
> He is faithful in all my house.
> I speak with him face to face,
> Even plainly, and not in dark sayings;
> And he sees the form of the LORD
>
> (Num. 12:6-8)

The contents of Genesis were revealed by God. As the Lord Jesus Christ promised the assistance of the Holy Spirit to aid the memories of his apostles (John 14:26), so God could easily ensure the accuracy of what was transmitted down the years until a written form was adopted. And as the Lord Jesus Christ promised his apostles further revelations by his Spirit of 'things to come' (John 16:13), so God could effortlessly reveal 'things to come' to Abraham, Isaac, Jacob and Moses. Geerhardus Vos speaks for all

Bible-believing Christians when he insists that 'revelation' implies an infallible communication: 'If God be personal and conscious, then the inference
is inevitable that in every mode of self-disclosure He will make a faultless
expression of His nature and purpose. He will communicate His thought to
the world with the stamp of divinity on it.'[2]

Historical setting

The book of Genesis covers a period in excess of 2,200 years, from the
days of creation (4000+ B.C.) to the death of Joseph (1804 B.C.).

Outline

The first eleven chapters are governed by four momentous events: Creation, the Fall, the Flood and the Tower of Babel. The second half of the
book, the remaining thirty-nine chapters, is taken up with the biographies
of four major personalities: Abraham, Isaac, Jacob and Joseph.

Part I: Four momentous events (1:1 – 11:32)

1. Creation

Genesis opens with the declaration: 'In the beginning God created the
heavens and the earth' (1:1; cf.[3] Ps. 19:1-6; 24:1; 33:6-9). Here is the only
correct and satisfactory information concerning prehistoric times. Acceptance of the doctrine of creation is, however, dependent upon the disposition of the heart. It is 'by faith we understand that the worlds were framed
by the word of God' (Heb. 11:1). The teaching of Scripture is clear and
unequivocal: 'that God created the universe on six successive days, limited
by morning and evening, six real, ordinary days like our days of twenty-
four hours.'[4]

   In the first two chapters information is supplied which forms the backcloth for all subsequent events. Human beings are shown to be the high
point of God's creative work. They, of all creation, bear the image of God

(1:26-27). Of all created beings it is only human beings who are capable of a deep relationship with God. This is our outstanding privilege. Created to enjoy fellowship with God, to rule over the rest of creation as his vice-gerents, to produce children and to enjoy the fruit of the earth — the conditions of life for the first human beings were idyllic. Only one restriction had been placed upon them: 'From every tree of the garden you may freely eat; but from the tree of the knowledge of good and evil you shall not eat, for in the day that you eat the fruit of it you shall surely die' (2:16-17).

2. The Fall

In spite of the serious warning which God issues, the first human beings, Adam and Eve, disobey through unbelief, and their relationship with the Creator is never to be the same again — until the Restorer comes and permanently corrects the problem at source. The changes which take place as a result of this second momentous event, the Fall, cannot be overstated. In Genesis the 'wiles of the devil' (Eph. 6:11) are exposed. Here there is a clear indication of how the Evil One operates. Studying Genesis should mean that 'we are not ignorant of his devices' (2 Cor. 2:11). He calls into question the Word of God: 'Has God indeed said...?' (3:1). He casts doubt on its trustworthiness, denies its truth: 'You will not surely die. For God knows that in the day you eat it your eyes will be opened, and you will be like God, knowing good and evil' (3:4-5).

When Adam and Eve respond to the insidious insinuations of Satan and rebel against God, the results are catastrophic. God keeps his word. The death penalty is enforced. From that moment the human body is subject to decay. And not only Adam and Eve and their posterity are to suffer: 'For the creation was subjected to futility, not willingly...' (Rom. 8:20).

Exclusion from the Garden of Eden is only the beginning. Humanity now has a sinful bias, and that sinful nature, which was not there at creation, is soon exhibited in hatred and violence. Adam and Eve are to witness the appalling results of their transgression when their older son murders his younger brother. The issue is really between Cain and the Lord, not between Cain and his brother. But because 'The LORD respected Abel and his offering' (4:4), Cain takes out his anger upon his brother (1 John 3:12). The first murder graphically illustrates the corrupting power of sin that now flows through humanity — from the Fall.

Following Abel's death a third son is born to Adam and Eve. The line is traced through Seth showing the early ancestors of the promised Seed (3:15; see chart below).

The line of descent from Adam to Noah

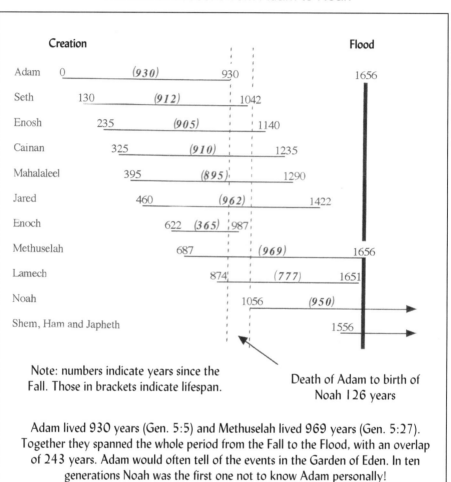

Note: numbers indicate years since the Fall. Those in brackets indicate lifespan.

Death of Adam to birth of Noah 126 years

Adam lived 930 years (Gen. 5:5) and Methuselah lived 969 years (Gen. 5:27). Together they spanned the whole period from the Fall to the Flood, with an overlap of 243 years. Adam would often tell of the events in the Garden of Eden. In ten generations Noah was the first one not to know Adam personally!

The descendants of Cain prove to be as ungodly as their father. In Lamech the ungodliness of the Cainite line appears in his defiance and arrogance in abusing the words of the Lord (4:24). The wickedness of humanity continues its downward spiral, reaching such depths that 'The LORD was sorry that he had made man on the earth, and he was grieved in his heart' (6:6). The third momentous event is on the horizon — judgement!

3. The Flood

The Flood destroys every living thing except those who are saved in Noah's ark — for 'Noah found grace in the eyes of the LORD' (6:8). 'By faith Noah, being divinely warned of things not yet seen, moved with godly fear, prepared an ark for the saving of his household, by which he condemned the world and became heir of the righteousness which is according to faith' (Heb. 11:7)

The dimensions of the ark are supplied by the Lord. It would have been quite unlike the representation given in most illustrations. Longer than a football pitch, it was three hundred cubits long, fifty cubits wide, and thirty cubits high (approximately 459 x 75 x 44 feet, or 140 x 23 x 13.5 metres, giving a volume of 1.5 million cubic feet, or 43,500 cubic metres). Built with three floors, the ark had room for 432 double-decker buses or 125,000 sheep! This would have been enough room for pairs of all living land-dwelling animals and also some prehistoric kinds. Designed as it was to float rather than to sail, marine experts say that these are the best proportions possible in order to ride storm waves with maximum stability.[5]

The dimensions of Noah's ark

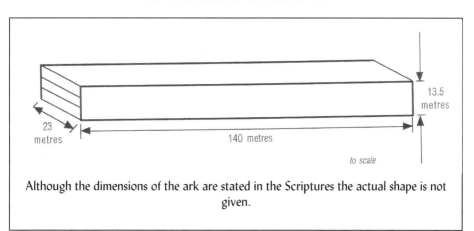

23 metres

140 metres

13.5 metres

to scale

Although the dimensions of the ark are stated in the Scriptures the actual shape is not given.

The mercy of God is shown in that Noah was 'a preacher of righteousness' (2 Peter 2:5), and declared the judgement of God well before the event.

Following the Flood there is the establishment of the covenant with Noah and creation (9:9-11). Some time later an incident, brought about as a result of Noah's intoxication and Ham's lack of discretion, is to have far-reaching implications for the sons of Noah and their descendants. The ancestral line of the promised Seed — that is Christ — is to pass through Shem (Luke 3:36). The words of Noah to this son have a prophetic character. The opening phrase indicates that true religion will be preserved in the descendants of Shem: 'Blessed be the LORD, the God of Shem...' (9:26-27). This is the second Messianic prophecy (the first is recorded in 3:15). The families of the earth will be blessed only through their association and relationship with the descendants of Shem. In connection with the descendants of Shem the descendants of Japheth will be received among the true worshippers of God (9:27).[6]

4. The Tower of Babel

The Tower of Babel is built on 'a plain in the land of Shinar' (11:2), probably located in ancient Babylonia in southern Mesopotamia. It symbolizes godless arrogance. In an attempt to make a monument of unsurpassed proportions, 'a tower' is planned 'whose top is in the heavens', so that the architects can 'make a name' for themselves (11:4).

Apparently quite aware that God had said, 'Be fruitful and multiply, and fill the earth' (9:1), these people react and, filled with self-importance, commence to build a construction which would bind them together so that they should not 'be scattered abroad over the face of the whole earth' (11:4).

The Lord prevents the proceedings by the simple expedient of confusing 'their language, that they may not understand one another's speech' (11:7). The basic languages of the world come into being. Unable to communicate, the builders disperse. The project is discontinued. The people separate into their various language groups.

These four major occurrences, creation, the Fall, the Flood and the Tower of Babel, form the backcloth for all subsequent history. Human rebellion, foolishness, spiritual blindness and religious incompetence find their first expression and explanation here in Genesis. These are the dominant issues in the first eleven chapters of this book.

The line of descent from Shem to Abraham

Flood

Shem	-98	(600)			502	
Arphachshad	2	(438)		440		
Shalah	37	(433)		470		
Eber	67	(464)			531	
Peleg	101	(239)	340			
Reu	131	(239)	370			
Serug	163	(230)	393			
Nahor	193	(148)	341			
Terah	222	(205)	427			
Abraham	292	(175)	467			
Isaac	392	(180)	572			

Note: numbers indicate years since the
Flood. Those in brackets indicate lifespan.

Death of Shem

Part II: Four chosen leaders (12:1 - 50:26)

Against the backcloth of human rebellion and sin, Genesis presents the beginnings of divine activity. Plans, promises, covenants and the provision of a wonderful solution for the human predicament are initiated. The family line of Shem serves to introduce Terah's eldest son, Abram (11:10-26).

The second part of Genesis records the biographies of Abraham, Isaac, Jacob and Joseph. God's dealings with these men are highly significant. From the time reached at the conclusion of the book of Genesis, and thereafter, the Lord will be known as 'the God of Abraham, the God of Isaac, and the God of Jacob' (Exod. 3:6; cf. Matt. 22:31-32).

1. Abraham

The story of Abraham in this book is by no means a full biography. Only the main features of his life are noted. The selection of material is based upon the central theme — the early preparation for the coming of the promised Seed (3:15), who is to be the Son of God, Jesus the Christ.

Abraham is chosen from an idolatrous background. His father Terah 'served other gods' (Josh. 24:2).

The Lord's call to Abraham to move out to an unnamed destination demanded considerable trust and confidence. Abraham was to travel almost 1,000 miles from Ur to Haran, and then on to Canaan. He is the first one to be called a 'Hebrew' (`*Ibrîy* meaning 'one from beyond' — 14:13).

The journeys of Abraham

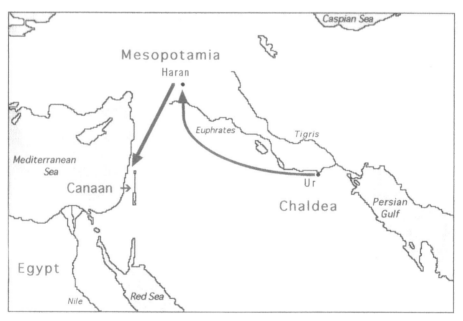

Whether Abraham became a believer in Ur or in Haran is not stated. It is clear, however, that he was a believer before he left Haran (Heb. 11:8).

Abraham's initial call includes promises of personal blessing, numerous offspring, a great name and his being made a blessing to 'all the families of the earth' (12:2-3). On arrival in Canaan the Lord adds the blessing of the land (12:7). A few years later, after the division between the shepherds of

Lot and the shepherds of Abraham, the Lord indicates the extent of the land promised to Abraham and reinforces his promise of numerous offspring (13:14-17). The promise of descendants and the gift of land is repeated and confirmed by a dramatic covenant (15:1-21). The involvement of Hagar to bear the offspring seems to have been entirely Sarah's idea and may have been motivated by a misguided attempt to fulfil the promise of God regarding a son for Abraham (16:1-16). Thirteen years later the Lord appears to Abraham and reinforces his promises of offspring, adding that the covenant and the promise of the land of Canaan as a possession are 'everlasting', that God 'will be God' (suggesting a close personal relationship) to Abraham and his descendants, that Sarah will be the mother of the promised son and that Abraham and Sarah's natural descendants will include royalty (17:1-21). In Genesis 18 the promise of a son and a multitude of descendants is repeated to Abraham and Sarah. Some years later, after the successful test of obedience in the offering of his son Isaac, the promises of blessing are given once again to Abraham: 'descendants as the stars of the heaven and as the sand which is on the seashore,' together with victory over their enemies and blessing for all nations of the earth (22:17-18).

These great promises to Abraham are in one sense only a qualifying of the original promise to Adam and Eve (3:15). They merely mark out 'a particular channel, through which divine grace should flow in raising up a spiritual seed, to resist and baffle and drive out the tempter'.[7]

2. Isaac

The prophetic disclosures successively made to Isaac and Jacob (26:3-4; 28:13-15) are little more than renewals of the original promise to Abraham. Ernest Hengstenberg concludes: 'The undeniable meaning of these promises made to the patriarchs is, that through their posterity salvation should be conferred upon all the nations of the earth. The nature of this blessing, however, is not accurately defined.'[8]

The son of Abraham and Sarah receives the name Isaac (meaning 'laughter') since his father and mother laughed on hearing that Sarah was to give birth to a son when they were both well advanced in years (17:17; 18:10-15). Incredulous laughter turns to the laughter of joy (21:6). Isaac is the long-awaited son of promise. His half-brother Ishmael seems to have resented his arrival in the family (21:9). Probably when Isaac is in his teens, he is taken by his father to the land of Moriah to be sacrificed. The Lord intervenes (22:1-2,11-12).

Abraham takes great care in providing a suitable wife for Isaac, and while theirs is an arranged marriage, Isaac clearly loves his wife Rebekah (24:67). Isaac and Rebekah have twin sons, Jacob and Esau. In mid-life famine drives Isaac to Gerar. Here he repeats his father's earlier deception by insisting that his wife is his sister (26:7-11; cf. 12:19; 20:2). Following the fraud perpetrated by Jacob by which he obtains the blessing of the first-born, Isaac sends his son away to Padan Aram. Twenty years later he sees his son return prosperous and with a large family. Isaac lives 180 years.

3. Jacob

Jacob (meaning 'supplanter' or 'deceiver') receives his name following the unusual nature of his birth (25:26). He is a meek and quiet-tempered man who appreciates the peaceful life of a shepherd. Esau, his brother is, by contrast, a fiery personality and loves hunting. Esau shows his disdain for his birthright as the first-born by selling it flippantly to Jacob for a bowl of stew. He thereby reveals his total lack of spiritual interest and disregard for the promises of God.

Spurred on by his mother, Jacob fraudulently obtains his father's blessing. When Esau discovers the deception he is livid and vows to kill Jacob (27:41). Jacob goes in fear of his life. On the pretext of seeking a wife, Jacob is dispatched to Padan Aram to the home of his uncle Laban. Through their deception, mother and son are separated, for Rebekah dies years before Jacob returns.

Before setting out for Padan Aram Jacob receives 'the blessing of Abraham' from his father Isaac (28:3-4). On the journey the Lord appears to him in a dream, reinforces the divine promise and assures Jacob of divine protection (28:10-15). Once in Padan Aram the deceiver is himself deceived. Jacob labours seven years for the hand of Rachel only to be tricked by Laban into marrying her older sister Leah. Not content with one wife, Jacob labours a further seven years for Rachel, whom he loves. Jacob is constantly cheated in his wages and it is only through the providence of God that he prospers. After twenty years Laban's sons become more and more critical of Jacob. Laban too is increasingly ill-disposed towards him. Under divine instruction Jacob takes his family and livestock and returns home to the land of promise (31:3).

The turning-point of Jacob's life comes at Peniel, where he is humbled by the Angel (Hosea 12:3-5). He turns from his old ways of craftiness and deceit and begins to rely solely upon the Lord in prayer.

Jacob's home life is frequently traumatic: the tensions between his two wives, the distress of Rachel at her childlessness, the incident surrounding his daughter Dinah, the corruption of Reuben, the violence of Simeon and Levi and the loss of his favourite son Joseph, presumed dead for so many years. But the Lord is with him. Jacob's latter days are calm, happy and prosperous in the land of Egypt with his extended family.

Jacob functions as a prophet when, on his deathbed, he blesses his twelve sons (49:1-28). Bypassing Reuben, Simeon and Levi, he addresses his fourth son as the heir of the promise (vv. 9-12). To Judah is given the blessing of the first-born. His will be the family from which the promised Seed, the Shiloh, will be born.[9] Following the blessing Jacob gives instruction for his burial back in the promised land. On his death his son Joseph makes the necessary arrangements (50:2-13).

4. Joseph

The fourth person whose history is recorded in some detail in the book of Genesis is Joseph. Whereas the line of promise was to pass from Abraham through Isaac, Jacob and Judah, it is not to Judah that detailed attention is given. It is one of his younger brothers whom the Lord uses to illustrate forcefully how he keeps his promises. God keeps his covenant with Abraham, Isaac and Jacob in the life of Joseph, whose experiences in Egypt are recalled by the psalmist:

[God] called for a famine in the land;
He destroyed all the provision of bread.
He sent a man before them —
Joseph — who was sold as a slave.
They hurt his feet with fetters,
He was laid in irons.
Until the time that his word came to pass,
The word of the LORD tested him.
The king sent and released him,
The ruler of the people let him go free.
He made him lord of his house,
And ruler of all his possessions,

To bind his princes at his pleasure,
And teach his elders wisdom.
Israel also came into Egypt,
And Jacob sojourned in the land of Ham

(Ps. 105:16-23).

To Jacob, the famine is an added affliction following the loss of his beloved son. Nevertheless God uses the one to provide for the other. In later life godly Joseph will trace the providential hand of God and say to his brothers, 'You meant evil against me; but God meant it for good, in order to bring it about as it is this day, to save many people alive' (50:20).

God's dealings with these four great men — Abraham, Isaac, Jacob and Joseph — are concisely traced by Stephen before the Jewish council in Jerusalem (Acts 7:1-16).

From the historical outline, we turn to the spiritual message of the book of Genesis.

Christ and his church

Genesis is packed full of Christological significance.

As Creator God reveals himself in the mysterious plurality of his being: 'Let *us* make man in *our* image' (1:26, emphasis added). Clarity is given in the New Testament, where it is revealed that God the Father and 'the Son of his love' were co-Creators (Col. 1:13,16-17; Heb. 1:2-3; John 1:1-3).

From the Fall, the Creator is Lord over two kingdoms: the kingdom of nature and the kingdom of grace. In the first he is Elohim — the Creator, Preserver and Ruler. In the second he is also Jehovah — the Saviour, Guardian and Friend. All his arrangement and organization of the universe have the ultimate goal to prepare, establish and confirm the kingdom of grace in humanity. 'As mercy presupposes misery, so grace presupposes sin.'[10] Christ has been given all authority over the kingdom of nature to ensure the well-being of his kingdom of grace (Eph. 1:22; Matt. 28:18).

Theophanies

The Angel of the LORD appears in the pages of Scripture in such a way that his deity cannot be denied. Here is the Son of God appearing momentarily in human form before his incarnation.[11] Appearing to Abraham's second 'wife' Hagar, he is called 'the angel of the LORD' four times (16:7,9,10,11). Moses the historian identifies him as 'the LORD [YHWH] who spoke to her' (16:13). Hagar speaks of him as 'God' (16:13). Moses records the testimony of Jacob: 'Then the Angel of God spoke to me in a dream, saying… "I am the God of Bethel"' (31:11,13). Years later, when Jacob blesses Joseph, he speaks of the 'God, before whom my fathers Abraham and Isaac walked, the God who has fed me all my life long to this day' as 'the Angel who has redeemed me from all evil' (48:15,16). This is further confirmed by the prophet Hosea, who declares of Jacob:

> He took his brother by the heel in the womb,
> And in his strength he struggled with God.
> Yes, he struggled with the Angel and prevailed
>
> (Hosea 12:3-4).

Types

Adam 'is a type[12] of him who was to come' (Rom. 5:14), that is, Christ. The first Adam is to be followed by the Last Adam. The apostle Paul quotes Genesis 2:7: 'The first man Adam became a living being,' and adds, 'The last Adam became a life-giving spirit' (1 Cor. 15:45). Adam is treated by God as the representative head of the whole human race. The punishment which the Lord laid upon Adam was laid upon all humanity (Rom. 5:12). What Adam did brought guilt upon all human beings, since all human beings are united to him by birth (all who are born are 'in Adam'). The Lord Jesus Christ, as the second Adam, is treated in the same manner. He is the representative head of *his* people. What he did brought blessing upon all human beings united to him (all who are twice-born, as evidenced by repentance and faith, are 'in Christ').

Adam and Eve in their relationship are a type of Christ and his church (2:20-24; Eph. 5:28-32). In the forming of Eve from Adam's side, and in the exclusive love of Adam for Eve as part of his own flesh, Christ is seen in his exclusive and jealous love for his church (2 Cor. 11:2). The New Testament reveals the Lord Jesus as the Bridegroom who has come to claim his people as his bride (John 3:29-30; cf. Rev. 19:6-9).

The sabbath rest after the six days of creative work is a type of the blessings enjoyed by believers in Christ (2:2-3; cf. Heb. 4:1-10). The promised rest symbolized in creation was not fulfilled in Canaan (Josh.

23:1); otherwise David 'would not afterwards have spoken of another day' (Heb. 4:8; cf. Ps. 95:7-11). The remaining 'rest' (Heb. 4:9 — the Greek word *sabbatismos* means a 'sabbatism', or a 'sabbath rest') is not realized until the believer rests by faith in Christ (Heb. 4:10; Matt. 11:28; Eph. 2:8-9).

The temptations of Eve bear a strong connection with the Lord's temptations. Satan appealed to 'the lust of the flesh, the lust of the eyes, and the pride of life' (1 John 2:16). This is evident in Eve's thoughts, 'that the [forbidden] tree was good for food, that it was pleasant to the eyes, and a tree desirable to make one wise' (3:6). The same parallels are discernible in the temptations of Christ — 'the lust of the flesh' (cf. Luke 4:2-3), 'the lust of the eyes' (cf. Luke 4:5-7) 'and the pride of life' (cf. Luke 4:9-11). While the devil still uses the same three-pronged attack on the Lord's people, it is obvious that the temptations of our Lord were tailored specifically for him. Twice Satan confronted the Lord with the challenge: 'If you are the Son of God...'

The delivery of Noah and his family in the ark is seen as a type of the believer's union with Christ in baptism (6:14 – 8:19; cf. 1 Peter 3:20-21). The Lord determined to punish humanity for its great wickedness (6:5-7). He set a day for the Flood and then proceeded to warn the people through the preaching of Noah (2 Peter 2:5). The people took no notice of the warning (cf. Luke 17:26-27). The ark symbolizes Christ as the only means of salvation from the judgement of God (cf. Acts 4:12). It is later prophesied that 'A man will be as a hiding place from the wind, and a cover from the tempest' (Isa. 32:2). The ark had only one door (cf. John 10:7). The ark was entered by faith (Heb. 11:7). The ark took the full force of the storm (cf. Ps. 69:1-2; 42:7).

The building of *the Tower of Babel*, 'whose top' was intended to be 'in the heavens', was foiled by the Lord. Only one bridge between heaven and earth is possible. Jacob is privileged to dream about the ladder which is a type of Christ (11:1-9; 28:12-17; cf. John 1:51). 'The stairway-tower of Jacob's dream was God's answer to the tower of Babel. The top of it did reach to heaven, for God was the builder, not man. God alone establishes communication between heaven and earth.'[13] On the Day of Pentecost there was an anticipation of the ultimate restoration of one common language throughout the regenerated earth (Acts 2:6-11).

In *Melchizedek* there is a type of Christ in his unique role as King and Priest of God Most High (14:18-20; Ps. 110:1-4; Heb. 7:1-3). He is 'king of righteousness' and 'king of peace'. He holds the unique office of royal priest and is superior to Abraham and, therefore, by implication, to the

Aaronic or Levitical priesthood (Heb. 7:4-10). It is later predicted that Messiah, under the title of 'the Branch', will build the temple of the Lord and be 'a priest on his throne, and the counsel of peace shall be between them both' (Zech. 6:12-13). In other words, there will be perfect harmony between his kingly rule and his priestly office. Christ as the Royal Priest will promote the peace of his people.

In *Ishmael and Isaac* the hostility of unregenerate Israelites towards spiritual children of God is symbolized (21:9-10; cf. Gal. 4:21-31). This is reminiscent of the hostility felt by Cain towards Abel (4:8; cf. 1 John 3:11-15).

While there are many more links which may be located between the book of Genesis and Christ and his church, one further reference will suffice for this overview — *Joseph* as a type of Christ. Many lessons may be drawn from the character and experiences of Joseph.

George Lawson notes that '... there is very remarkable similarity between the character of Joseph and that of Christ, as well as between the events of their lives — only an allowance must be made for the incomparable excellency of our great Redeemer above all the sons of men. As the shadow is to the body, so were all the types and figures of our Lord Jesus Christ to Him, whom they represented.'[14]

Resemblances of a more or less typical character cannot fail to be observed between Joseph and Christ, and between his varied life and Christ's, 'by the most literal and unimaginative commentator.'[15] We see him rejected and despised by his brethren; sold; becoming a servant; severely tempted yet without yielding to sin; falsely accused; offering no defence; cast into prison; suffering at the hands of Gentiles; innocent yet suffering; winning the respect of his jailer; numbered with transgressors; a blessing to one and judgement on the other; delivered from prison by the hand of God; the revealer of secrets; warning of impending danger and the steps to take to prepare for it; exalted to the right hand of the king; given a wife by the king; thirty years old when he begins his life's work; making bread available for a starving world.

Joseph's words to his brothers sum up his experience and also the experiences of the Israelites in Egypt in later years: 'But as for you, you meant evil against me; but God meant it for good, in order to bring it about as it is this day, to save many people alive' (50:20). These words also sum up our Lord's experiences at the hands of the high priest and the Sanhedrin: 'Him, being delivered by the carefully planned intention and foreknowledge of God, you have taken by lawless hands, have crucified, and put to death...' (Acts 2:23).

Prophecies

1. The promised Seed

The first prophecy comes immediately after the Fall. Even as the living God is pronouncing judgement upon Adam and Eve for their wilful disobedience, he includes a wonderful promise (3:15). This first prophecy concerning the promised 'seed' is indistinct. The only factor that is clear is the certainty of victory for the seed of the woman. It is not explicitly stated whether the fulfilment will come through some peculiarly gifted race, or by a single individual from among the descendants of the woman. This prophecy concerning a seed, a descendant or descendants, is the reason why genealogies and ancestral lines are given such prominence in Genesis. The line of descent of the following men is distinctly recorded in order to see God's promise fulfilled: Adam (5:1); Noah (6:9); the sons of Noah (10:1); Shem (11:10); Terah, the father of Abraham (11:27); Ishmael (25:12); Isaac (25:19); Esau (36:1,9); Jacob (37:2). These serve to prove that God has not forgotten his initial promise.

The Hebrew word translated 'seed' *(zera`)* is ambiguous. It may refer to one individual, or it may refer to a group. Genesis does not resolve the question. It simply shows that the chosen line is Abraham, Isaac and Jacob. Even in the New Testament the ambiguity is perpetuated. The plural and singular are traceable:

1. The seed are *all the true children of God*. At first it seems that the seed of Abraham (in the New Testament the Greek word for seed is *sperma*) refers to the physical descendants of Abraham (Luke 1:55; John 8:33,37; Acts 7:5-6; Rom. 11:1; 2 Cor. 11:22; Heb. 11:18). The apostle Paul, however, broadens the promise to immense proportions by arguing that 'the seed of Abraham' includes only those Hebrews who share his faith and also all Gentiles who share that faith (Rom. 4:13-16; 9:6-8; Gal. 3:7,26-29). The early recipients of the promise could not have imagined the remarkable way in which the Lord would fulfil his word!

2. At the same time the New Testament argues that the promised 'seed' refers to *Christ*. Peter implies this as he preaches in the temple at Jerusalem shortly after the Pentecost experience (Acts 3:25-26). Paul argues strongly that the word 'seed' in Genesis is not a grammatical plural and so refers to Christ (Gal. 3:16); yet at the same

time, within a few verses, he interprets 'the seed of Abraham' as composed of all believers (Gal. 3:29). It is evident that the collective function of *zera`* (seed) 'allows the writer to refer to the group or to a representative individual of that group'.[16] The ambiguity of the original promise is further reinforced by Paul when he makes evident allusion to Genesis 3:15 in saying to the Christians at Rome, '... the God of peace will crush Satan under your feet shortly' (Rom. 16:20).[17]

2. The promised land

The land is an important motif throughout the Scriptures. Adam and Eve were driven from their homeland as a result of their rebellion and sin (3:23-24). Years later the land of Canaan was given to Abraham and his descendants for their possession (12:7; 13:15). But Abraham only received title to a small plot of that land during his lifetime. He purchased the cave of Machpelah from Ephron the Hittite, son of Zohar (23:3-18). 'And after this Abraham buried Sarah his wife in the cave of the field of Machpelah, before Mamre (that is, Hebron) in the land of Canaan. So the field and the cave that is in it were legally transferred to Abraham by the sons of Heth as property for a burial place...' (23:19-20).

The New Testament leaves us in no doubt that Abraham had his eyes set on a distant and spiritual fulfilment of the promise which was going to be no less real, and no less material: 'By faith he [Abraham] sojourned in the land of promise as in a foreign country, dwelling in tents with Isaac and Jacob, the heirs with him of the same promise; for he waited for the city which has foundations, whose builder and maker is God... These all died in faith, not having received the promises, but having seen them afar off, they were assured of them, embraced them, and confessed that they were strangers and pilgrims on the earth. For those who say such things declare plainly that they seek a homeland. And truly if they had called to mind that country from which they had come out, they would have had opportunity to return. But now they desire a better, that is, a heavenly country. Therefore God is not ashamed to be called their God, for he has prepared a city for them' (Heb. 11:9-10,13-16).

3. The promised blessing

The promises made to Abraham were also made to Christ before his incarnation (Gal. 3:16). 'I will establish my covenant between me and you and your descendants after you in their generations, for an everlasting covenant, to be God to you and your descendants after you' (17:7).

The promised blessing is a deep personal relationship with the living God. It is a full restoration of the intimate bond and friendship that existed between the Lord and Adam and Eve in the earliest days. In Genesis the glorious characteristics of salvation in Christ are set before us in symbolic form. From the very beginning it is God who takes the initiative to deal with the problem of sin. God himself clothes Adam and Eve after their sin (3:21). The clothing is made of skin. The death of an animal is required. God provides a covering. Years later Isaiah will say:

> … we are all like an unclean thing,
> And all our righteousnesses are like filthy rags;
> We all fade as a leaf,
> And our iniquities, like the wind,
> Have taken us away
>
> (Isa. 64:6).

Isaiah will also say:

> I will greatly rejoice in the LORD,
> My soul shall be joyful in my God;
> For he has clothed me with the garments of salvation.
> He has covered me with the robe of righteousness
>
> (Isa. 61:10).

Only in this way could humanity's shame be covered and sinners be made fit to stand in the presence of God. God is operating on the basis of his abiding principle: 'Without shedding of blood there is no remission' (Heb. 9:22). Was the animal that died a lamb? Genesis does not say, but it would be entirely in harmony with the flow of Scripture if this were the case.

The first open statement regarding a lamb appears in the fourth chapter in relation to Cain and Abel and their offerings in worship. Judged from the standpoint of the record of revelation up to that point in history, it would seem quite arbitrary for the Lord to receive Abel's offering of a lamb and reject Cain's offering of vegetables. The unfolding significance of a lamb as sacrifice is indisputable (Exod. 12:3,5-13; John 1:29; Rev. 5:6), but was Abel blessed merely on the basis of a coincidence? He was a shepherd. He brought a lamb and was consequently accepted. Cain, a horticulturist, brought vegetables and was rejected. This might be seen to suggest that God deals with people in a somewhat arbitrary fashion. The truth is, however, far from the case, as the New Testament later makes clear. In the letter to the Hebrews it is said, 'By faith Abel offered to God a more excellent sacrifice than Cain, through which he obtained witness that he was righteous...' (Heb. 11:4). In Scripture 'faith' is never a matter of chance. It is never a 'leap in the dark', as some have erroneously taught. It is always the right response to God's Word — spoken or written. If Abel brought the right offering 'by faith', then the Lord must have previously revealed the kind of offering which would be acceptable. Abel is then seen as believing the Word of God and being obedient in coming to God in God's own way. Cain, with the hard heart of unbelief, wanted to come to God on his own terms. He wanted to use his own means in finding acceptance. These two then become symbolic, on the one hand, of the true believer coming to God by the means he has provided, and, on the other, of the unbeliever trying to find acceptance on his own basis.

This interpretation finds further confirmation in the fact that the Lord provided *coverings of skin* for Adam and Eve in replacement of their coverings of vegetation (3:21; cf. 3:7). Even though there is no *recorded* institution of a sacrificial system, Noah offered animal sacrifices (8:20), and Abraham built altars (12:7,8; 13:18).

Further confirmation that God had revealed his will with regard to sacrifice is shown when Abraham's son Isaac accompanies his father to the land of Moriah to offer a burnt offering to the Lord, and he asks the question: 'Where is the lamb for a burnt offering?' (22:7). From Abraham come the prophetic words, 'God will provide for himself the lamb for a burnt offering' (22:8). On that particular occasion a ram is provided, not a lamb. The words of Abraham are to find a glorious fulfilment nearly two thousand years later when the Lamb of God offered himself in that same geographic area. What God requested from Abraham, but did not allow him to fulfil, God did when he gave up his Son, his only Son Jesus, whom he loves (cf. 22:2).

A further prophecy of Christ is given by Jacob on his deathbed. Giving prophetic blessing to the twelve tribes through his twelve sons, Jacob says of his fourth son:

The sceptre shall not depart from Judah,
Nor a law-giver from between his feet,
Until Shiloh comes;
And to him shall be the obedience of the people

(49:10).

The Hebrew word *Shîylôh* (Shiloh) means 'pacifier,' 'peacemaker' or 'man of rest'.[18] From the tribe of Judah a great peacemaker will arise. Years later Isaiah predicts:

For unto us a child is born,
Unto us a Son is given;
And the government will be upon his shoulder.
And his name will be called
Wonderful, Counsellor, Mighty God,
Everlasting Father, Prince of Peace.
Of the increase of his government and peace
There will be no end,
Upon the throne of David and over his kingdom,
To order it and establish it with judgement and justice
From that time forward, even for ever

(Isa. 9:6-7).

God kept his word given through Jacob. The tribe's capacity for rule and sovereignty was not lost. The tribe of Judah did not lose its identity, as did the other tribes of Israel. Though perilously close to annihilation in the dark days of the Babylonian exile (Esth. 3:13), God ensured their survival (Esth. 4:13-14). It was not until about forty years after the death and resurrection of Christ that the Jewish nation was entirely destroyed (A.D. 70). By then the promise had been fulfilled. Shiloh had come, to whom 'the obedience of the people' is to be. The promised Son had come down from heaven, suffered, bled and died, and in his last resurrection appearance revealed to his aged apostle the fulfilment of the prophecy.

In Revelation, John records seeing a vision of the heavenly order (Rev. 4-5). He hears a question ring out: 'Who is worthy to open the scroll and to loose its seals?' In other words, 'Who can bring about the will and purpose of God on earth? Who can bring the world to its God-appointed end?' There is a painful silence which causes John to weep until one of the elders says to him, 'Do not weep. Behold, the Lion of the tribe of Judah, the Root of David, has prevailed to open the scroll and to loose its seven seals' (Rev. 5:5).

When John looks up he does not see a lion; he sees a lamb — with the marks of death upon it (Rev. 5:6). The Lion of Jacob's prophecy (Gen. 49:9-10) is none other than 'the Lamb of God who takes away the sin of the world!' (John 1:29). Two great types of Christ are united — the Lion is the Lamb!

Application

1. Sovereign free choice

Each book of the Bible has a 'prominent and dominant theme'.[19] Historically considered, the book of Genesis is the book of beginnings, but viewed doctrinally, it is seen to be the book that deals with election — God's free and sovereign choice. In Genesis God chooses Shem from the three sons of Noah as the one from whose line, ultimately, the Saviour will come; God chooses Abraham from an idolatrous people, and makes him the father of the chosen nation; God passes by Ishmael in favour of Isaac (Rom. 9:7); he calls Jacob and not Esau (Rom. 9:10–13); he appoints Joseph from all the twelve sons of Jacob/Israel to be the honoured instrument in providing for the family during famine, raising him to the second place of rule and authority in all Egypt; and finally he passes by the elder of Joseph's sons and grants the blessing of the first-born to Ephraim (48:13-20). Time and again the principle of God's sovereign choice is illustrated in the book of Genesis. Clear teaching regarding the sovereignty of God cannot be avoided by any who read the first book of the Bible.

2. Only by grace

The story of Genesis is the story of God's free grace (love and favour towards the undeserving). Having passed the death sentence upon Adam and Eve for their rebellion and sin, the Lord keeps his word. 'Sin entered the world, and death through sin, and thus death spread to all men, because all sinned' (Rom. 5:12). Yet, even as he pronounces judgement against them, the Lord gives a gracious promise. God will put enmity between the seed of the serpent and the seed of the woman. God will ensure the victory for the seed of the woman. When corruption is so widespread that God regrets having created human beings and determines, as a just punishment, to destroy every living thing, one man, Noah, finds grace in his eyes (6:8). In the face of total destruction grace prevails and one family is saved. When human pride, arrogance and godlessness reach new heights, God punishes the people by scattering them over the earth. But by sovereign grace God chooses and calls Abraham. The corruption and evil of Sodom and Gomorrah result in the Lord's raining down 'brimstone and fire ... from the LORD out of the heavens', overthrowing 'those cities, all the plain, all the inhabitants of the cities, and what grew on the ground' (19:24-25). Yet grace prevails in the rescue of Lot. Grace overrules nature in the gift of a son to Abraham and Sarah (Rom. 4:19-21). With Martens we conclude, 'The gospel of God's intervention is unmistakable.'[20]

3. Justification by faith

In Genesis the truth of justification by faith is first made known: 'And he [Abraham] believed in the LORD, and he accounted it to him for righteousness' (15:6). God's dealings with Abraham were not on account of Abraham's obedience, or service, or love, but on account of his faith. Abraham's own body might be dead and Sarah long past the age of childbearing, yet Abraham was fully convinced that God had power to keep his word. As God accounted righteousness to Abraham, then Abraham evidently had none of his own. Abraham, the sinner, was declared righteous. Believing God, he had righteousness reckoned to his account.

Christians enjoy the same blessing, but with one important difference: Abraham trusted God and looked forward to the promised son; we trust God and look back and see the glorious fulfilment in the promised Son. While Abraham had believed in the Lord for many years (Heb. 11:8), it is here revealed that the faith which was 'counted for righteousness' was the faith which believed what God had said concerning the promised Seed. Abraham believed the promise of God which pointed to Christ.[21] Justification by faith is first indicated in the Scriptures in connection with the Saviour, in order that no one should separate justification from him.[22] There is no justification apart from Christ (Acts 13:38-39).

When Paul demonstrates that justification by faith alone is no novel idea, but one that has been always the case before God since the Fall, he uses the stalwarts of the faith, Abraham and David. Of Abraham he says,

'For what does the Scripture say? "Abraham believed God, and it was accounted to him for righteousness." Now to him who works, the wages are not counted as grace but as debt. But to him who does not work but believes on him who justifies the ungodly, his faith is accounted for righteousness...' (Rom. 4:3-5).

While the people of the Old Covenant period had a far less distinct picture of the Messiah than those believers who are under the New Covenant, the essence of their faith was just the same — that is, 'trust in God's grace and power to bring deliverance from sin'.[23]

4. Prevailing prayer

The importance and value of prayer are indicated in Genesis. Abraham prayed for the righteous in Sodom and Lot was spared (18:22-32; 19:15-16). Abraham prayed to God and the life of Abimelech was spared (20:7,17). Abraham's servant prayed for guidance in the choice of a bride for Isaac and God answered his prayer (24:12-15). 'Isaac pleaded with the LORD for his wife, because she was barren; and the LORD granted his plea, and Rebekah his wife conceived' (25:21). Jacob wrestled with God and prevailed (32:28).

'Jacob's victory was not, of course, a conquest. He had not mastered the Angel of God. Lame and helpless, he could only cling to the One who had laid hold of him. His victory was a victory of faith. He did not let go because he *could* not. God's blessing was all his hope and desire. Faith wins when it knows that all is lost, and clings to God alone. "Israel," the name God gave to Jacob, reflects this ambiguity. Normally it would be taken to mean "God Prevails". But the Lord turns the meaning around as He gives the name to Jacob: Jacob has prevailed with God. In that name Jacob's desperate faith is acknowledged by the Lord.'[24]

While God is undoubtedly the Sovereign Lord, 'who works all things according to the counsel of his will' (Eph. 1:11), and 'does whatever he pleases' (Ps. 115:3), he nevertheless honours the prayers of his people. 'The effective, fervent prayer of a righteous man avails much' (James 5:16).

Conclusion

Genesis is packed full of good things from the Lord. Four momentous events overshadow the first section of the book; four great men dominate the pages of the latter. In and through it all God is at work. Human sin is repugnant to the holy God. Punishment is well deserved by every person, young or old. Yet God's grace triumphs, for 'Where sin abounded, grace abounded much more' (Rom. 5:20). Faced with human inability, weakness and sinfulness, the Lord achieves his purposes. He has made his plans; nothing will thwart him.

Genesis is a treasury of spiritual gems. Here all the major doctrines are to be found 'in germ form' and attest to its divine authorship. The truths which are embodied here are expanded and developed throughout the rest of the Bible. Here is evidence that this book 'is given by inspiration of God' (2 Tim. 3:16). Here is demonstrated the truth that 'Prophecy never came by the will of man, but holy men of God spoke as they were moved by the Holy Spirit' (2 Peter 1:21). Who but the one who knows the end from the beginning could have provided such a reliable introduction?

> For I am God, and there is no other;
> I am God, and there is none like me,
> Declaring the end from the beginning,
> And from ancient times things that are not yet done,
> Saying, 'My counsel shall stand,
> And I will do all my pleasure'
>
> (Isa. 46:9-10).

Through the ups and downs, the rebellions and sin, judgements and punishment, God has been working. A chosen people, the Israelites, has been established in the land of Egypt. But that is not to be their homeland. God has promised them the land of Canaan. As he prophesied to Abraham, 'Know certainly that your descendants will be strangers in a land that is not theirs, and will serve its people and be afflicted by them four hundred years. And also the nation whom they serve I will judge; afterwards they shall come out with great possessions' (15:13-14).

Three hundred years and more are to pass before there dawns the next great epoch in God's unfolding purposes — moving ever on towards the coming of Christ for his church.

Exodus

('departure')

Author: Moses
(see Mark 12:26)

Key thought: 'Redeemed by blood'

Theme:
Delivery from slavery and laws for life

'You in your mercy have led forth
The people whom you have redeemed...'
Exodus 15:13

Summary

Exodus

At the close of the book of Genesis, God's people were enjoying life in Egypt. Their days of famine were over and they were benefiting from the comfort and security of a new land. The Egyptians had accepted and respected them on account of all that Joseph had done for their nation. The book of Exodus opens three and a half centuries later with a brief reference to the members of Jacob's family who had joined Joseph in Egypt. In the intervening years the experiences of the Israelites have changed dramatically. From respect, friendship and appreciation, the attitude of the Egyptians towards the Israelites has turned to dislike, distrust and persecution. The turning-point is noted in the words: 'Now there arose a new king over Egypt, who did not know Joseph' (1:8).

The Israelites went into Egypt as an extended family of seventy people (Gen. 46:27); they came out as a nation of almost two million men, women and children.[1] Once favoured friends, they had now become feared foes. They entered as honoured relatives of the Prime Minister of all Egypt; they left as the fugitive slaves of a despotic and oppressive government.

Author

Our Lord places the authorship of Exodus beyond all dispute. Replying to a trick question of the Sadducees concerning the resurrection, he says, 'Concerning the dead, that they rise, have you not read in the book of Moses, in the burning bush passage, how God spoke to him, saying, "I am the God of Abraham, the God of Isaac, and the God of Jacob"? He is not the God of the dead, but the God of the living. You are therefore greatly mistaken' (Mark 12:26-27; cf. Luke 20:37-38).

Historical setting

The overriding theme of the book of Exodus is *deliverance*. The events recorded cover a period of Israel's history from slavery in Egypt to emancipation and consolidation on Mount Sinai (approximately 1524–1443 B.C.). The book opens in darkness and gloom, yet ends in glory. 'It commences by telling how *God came down in grace* to deliver an enslaved people, and ends by declaring how *God came down in glory* to dwell in the midst of a redeemed people.'[2] This portion of Israel's history is intimately tied up with the life of its central figure, Moses. Whereas Joseph was the man raised up by God as the deliverer of his people on their *entry* into Egypt, Moses was the man raised up by God four centuries later as the deliverer of his people on their *exit* from Egypt.

At the time of his death, 'Moses was one hundred and twenty years old… His eyes were not dim nor his natural vigour abated' (Deut. 34:7). His life falls naturally into three distinct periods of forty years' duration: with Pharaoh's daughter in the royal court of Egypt (2:2-15); with Jethro in the land of Midian (2:16 – 4:19); and with the children of Israel in Egypt and in the wilderness (Exod. 4:20 – Deut. 34:5). Robert Lee summarizes the life of Moses like this: firstly, forty years thinking he was somebody; secondly, forty years learning he was a nobody; and, thirdly, forty years discovering what God can do with a nobody.[3]

Outline

After a brief introduction setting the scene, the book of Exodus records the history of Israel in four sections, the first two occurring in Egypt and the last two in the wilderness: slavery, confrontation, liberation and law and order. The first eighty years in the life of Moses fit within the first section of slavery in Egypt. The last forty years cover the three remaining more detailed sections — first in Egypt, then on the journey in the wilderness, and finally at Mount Sinai.

Part I: Slavery (1:8 - 4:17)

After a brief introduction indicating the growth in the Israelite population in Egypt, Moses the historian introduces the conditions of acute persecution. Fearing the rising numbers and the force of arms which this could represent, Pharaoh and the Egyptian authorities take steps to try to influence the birth-rate of the Hebrews. Initiating a process of hard labour, they subject the Israelites to demanding tasks. The Egyptians 'made their lives bitter with hard bondage — in mortar, in brick, and in all manner of service in the field' (1:14). When it is evident that this procedure is not having the desired effect, Pharaoh turns to more drastic measures. The Hebrew midwives, Shiphrah and Puah, are commanded to kill all male children at birth. Fearing God more than they fear the king, they let the boys live. In answer to criticism they claim that the Israelite mothers spend less time in labour and give birth *before* the midwives arrive.

Into this dreadful situation a boy is born to a Levite couple, Amram and Jochebed (6:20). The mother conceals the child in the house for three months. Changing the hiding place to a waterproof basket in the bulrushes leads to discovery by Pharaoh's daughter. By a remarkable providence the life of Moses is spared. The child is adopted; his own mother rears him; he eventually takes his place as a royal prince under the guardianship of Pharaoh's daughter. In consequence, 'Moses was learned in all the wisdom of the Egyptians, and was mighty in words and deeds' (Acts 7:22). The education and upbringing Moses receives in the Egyptian court provide him with rich intellectual resources which are to stand him in good stead for the task to which the Lord calls him later. Nevertheless Moses evidently considered himself to be lacking in communication skills (4:10).

When he is forty years old, Moses visits his Israelite brethren and thus the events are set in motion which are to culminate in his flight from Egypt into the land of Midian (Acts 7:23-29). He sees an Egyptian guard beating an Israelite. The only way Moses can restrain the aggressor is to kill him. The only witness to the incident is the man on whose behalf he intervenes! The following day Moses sees two Hebrews fighting. It is not sufficient that they are a people beaten by the Egyptians; they are also beating each other! When Moses tries to stop the fight he discovers that his killing of the Egyptian is well known. The Hebrew he had rescued on the previous occasion had evidently informed on him. What is more, the news is not kept within the Israelite community. Pharaoh is informed, and Moses is sought on a charge of murder. He flees from Egypt to the land of Midian, settles with the priest Jethro, whose daughter he marries, and has two sons.

Moses spends the next forty years as a shepherd in Midian. It is likely that those years of quiet reflection gave him a spiritual depth which it might have been difficult to acquire in all the worldly activity of a pagan palace.[4]

At the age of eighty Moses is called to the service of God. The third period of forty years in his life begins. The cry of the Israelites in their bondage in Egypt has been heard: '… and God remembered his covenant with Abraham, with Isaac, and with Jacob. And God looked upon the children of Israel, and God acknowledged them' (2:24-25).

Through the miraculous burning bush God makes Moses aware of his 'life's work'. At eighty Moses is to deliver the Israelites from their bondage and slavery in Egypt (Acts 7:30-34). God always has a man or woman prepared for his work, but they are not always willing to serve him. Moses is reluctant to begin his difficult assignment. He presents many excuses. He is a reluctant leader. Yet what the Lord later says to Jeremiah might equally have been said to Moses:

Before I formed you in the womb I knew you;
Before you were born I sanctified you;
And I ordained you a prophet

(Jer. 1:5).

God's providential dealings with Moses have prepared him for his ministry. Moses is to prove a faithful servant in the household of God (Heb. 3:5).

Moses has to convince the Israelites, as well as Pharaoh and the Egyptian authorities, that his assignment is from the Lord. In order to do this God gives him power to perform three miracles — turning his rod into a snake, making his hand leprous and turning water taken from the river into blood. Claiming a lack of eloquence, Moses is given his older brother Aaron to be his assistant and his official mouthpiece.

Part II: Confrontation (4:18 - 12:30)

Returning to Egypt, Moses and Aaron convince the Israelite leadership of their divine commission. The two brothers then visit Pharaoh with the request that they might take the Israelites into the wilderness to hold a service of worship. They are under no obligation to explain the ulterior motive behind their request. Pharaoh's response is to increase the workload for the Israelites, who then in turn react against Moses. Moses remonstrates with the Lord, who graciously reinforces his promise to deliver the children of

Israel from the Egyptian bondage: 'I am the LORD. I appeared to Abraham, to Isaac, and to Jacob… I have also established my covenant with them, to give them the land of Canaan… And I have also heard the groaning of the children of Israel … and I have remembered my covenant… I will take you as my people, and I will be your God… And I will bring you into the land which I swore to give to Abraham, Isaac, and Jacob; and I will give it to you as a heritage: I am the LORD' (6:2-8).

With this statement the relationship of God to the patriarchs, described in Genesis, is reaffirmed. The triple promise of seed, land and blessing was established in a covenant given to Abraham at the age of ninety-nine (Gen. 17:1-8), reiterated to Isaac (Gen. 26:3), and to Jacob (Gen. 28:14; 35:9-12). By the time of the Exodus, the first facet of the promise, that of seed (offspring, or descendants), has been realized. The families of Israel have been exceptionally fruitful (1:7). Fulfilment of the remaining parts of the promise, land and blessing, is now to be undertaken.

The ten plagues of Egypt

Over a period of about nine months ten terrible plagues come upon the Egyptians. Throughout them all the Israelites are protected.

1. The Nile is turned into blood — Pharaoh's heart grows hard (7:20,22).
2. Frogs cover the land — Pharaoh begs, promises freedom, hardens his heart again (8:6,8,15).
3. Lice on humans and animals — Pharaoh's heart grows hard (8:17,19).
4. Thick swarms of flies — Pharaoh bargains, hardens his heart again (8:24,28,32).
5. The livestock of the Egyptians die — Pharaoh's heart becomes hard (9:6,7).
6. Boils on humans and animals — the LORD hardens Pharaoh's heart (9:10,12).
7. Thunder, hail and fire — Pharaoh apologizes, promises, hardens his heart (9:23,27,28,34).
8. Locusts over all the land — Pharaoh begs, but the LORD hardens his heart (10:13,16-17,20).
9. Three days of thick darkness — Pharaoh bargains, but the LORD hardens his heart (10:22,24,27).

10. Death of all Egypt's first-born — Pharaoh commands the Israelites to leave Egypt (12:29,31).

The most serious of the ten plagues of Egypt is kept till last. The wrath of
God comes upon the Egyptians and the eldest son in every home dies on
an appointed night (4:22-23). At the same time God calls for faith and
obedience from his people Israel. The only way they are able to escape the
coming judgement is to believe and obey the word of the Lord.

The Hebrews are instructed to take an unblemished lamb, offer it as a
sacrifice, paint its blood on the doorposts and lintels of their homes, and
cook and eat the flesh that very night. 'And when I see the blood, I will pass
over you; and the plague shall not be on you to destroy you when I strike
the land of Egypt' (12:13).

Part III: Liberation (12:31 - 18:27)

The last devastating plague, the death of the first-born throughout all
Egypt, results in the command of Pharaoh that the Israelites should leave
immediately. The great migration of just under two million people begins
(see map, page 86). The Israelites are miraculously led by a pillar of cloud
by day and a pillar of fire by night.

When the Egyptians recover from the shock surrounding the departure
of the Hebrew slaves, the army is dispatched and pursues them as far as
the Red Sea. With the great sea before them, the wilderness to their left and
to their right, and the Egyptians on the skyline behind them, the people react with great fear and bitterly criticize Moses. Moses responds by telling
them, 'Do not be afraid. Stand still, and see the salvation of the LORD,
which he will accomplish for you today. For the Egyptians whom you see
today, you shall see again no more for ever. The LORD will fight for you,
and you shall hold your peace' (14:13-14).

They are warned against panic. God delivers them in a remarkable and
most unexpected manner — the sea divides and the children of Israel pass
through the midst of the sea on dry ground, and the waters are a wall to
them on either side.

The Lord hinders the Egyptian army as they try to follow over the bed
of the Red Sea. Their chariot wheels come off, 'so that they drove them
with difficulty' (14:25). Returning the sea to its normal flow kills all the soldiers. Israel is free. Moses leads the people in a song of thanksgiving and
praise to the Lord.

The two-month journey to Sinai continues in the Wilderness of Shur.

Israel's journey from Egypt to Mount Sinai

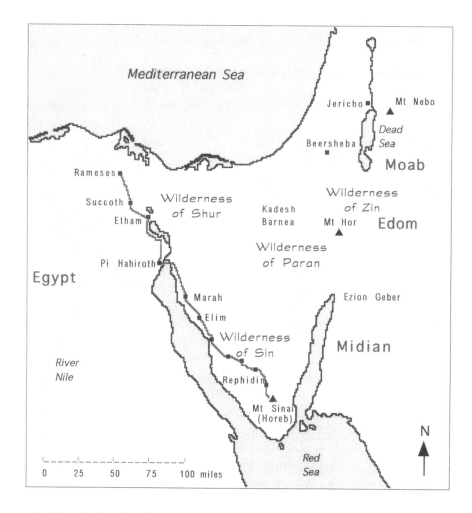

At Marah the Israelites complain that the water is bitter and unfit to drink. The Lord shows Moses how to make it sweet. At Elim they enjoy a pleasant oasis. In the Wilderness of Sin they begin to grumble again, regretting having left the meat and bread of Egypt. The Lord provides quails and manna in abundance. At Rephidim the people once more contend with Moses about the lack of water. A desperately needed supply miraculously flows from the rock struck by Moses. The Amalekites attack but are defeated. Success is attributed to the arms of Moses being held up by

Aaron and Hur (to show the importance of prayer and reliance upon the Lord).

The arrival of his wife, his two sons and his father-in-law Jethro from Midian leads to some sound advice that eases the workload for Moses. A large number of assistants are appointed to make judgement in simple cases, thus leaving Moses free to tackle only the more serious problems which arise among the people.

Part IV: Law and order (19:1 - 40:38)

In the third month after leaving Egypt, the Israelites arrive at Mount Sinai. Over a period of ten months events are to occur here which will have profound influence upon the whole of God's dealings with his people. All subsequent divine revelation throughout the Scriptures will connect in some measure with this encounter. On Mount Sinai God gives Moses the particulars of his law and instructions about the detailed design and construction of the tabernacle.

The law of Moses

In the history of the world nothing has happened, with the exception of the incarnation and the cross, which is so significant, so solemn, so profound, as the giving of the law by God himself at Sinai.[5] The ethos in which the law was given is striking. There was the warning of instant death to any person or animal that touched the mountain or its base. This was accompanied by 'thunderings and lightnings, and a thick cloud on the mountain; and the sound of the trumpet was very loud, so that all the people who were in the camp trembled' (19:16). It was essential for humanity to learn the nature of God's holiness and the character of human sinfulness. The Lord uses various means to instil a right appreciation of the moral gulf that exists between the Creator and his human creatures.

The law makes sin recognizable for what it is. By this the Israelites could see their corruption and sense their misery. God's commandments are addressed to the heart. The commandments require not only outward actions, but also inward affections; they require not only the outward act of obedience, but also the inward affection of love. The law of God forbids not only the act of sin, but the desire and inclination: 'Man's law binds the hands only, God's law binds the heart.'[6]

The covenant established with Moses (19:5) is a continuation of the one established first with Noah and then later with Abraham. In the covenant with Moses, the Lord keeps his promise made 400 years earlier (Gen. 15:13). Through Moses God provides additional instructions to show the Israelites how they are to conduct themselves as the people of God — as God's 'special treasure … above all people … a kingdom of priests and a holy nation' (19:5-6). Here the Lord sets out the principles and rules by which he will govern his people. Israel is to be governed, not by a democracy, the rule of the majority; nor by an aristocracy, the rule of the few; but by a theocracy, the rule of God. Consequently the Old Covenant law is an intermingling of moral, civil and ceremonial laws.

The Ten Commandments summarize the duties of the Israelites as the people of God (20:1-17).

In the wisdom and grace of God, that which most glorifies the Lord also tends most to the good of his people. The Lord gives laws which, when obeyed, would be most beneficial for the Israelites.

The LORD came from Sinai…
From his right hand came a fiery law for them.
Yes, he loves the people

(Deut. 33:2-3).

Love *from* God provided the law; love *for* God seeks to fulfil the law (Ps. 119:97; 9-10; cf. John 14:15).

The tabernacle

Central to the worship life of the Israelites was to be 'the tabernacle of the tent of meeting' (39:32). At the heart of the tabernacle was the altar of sacrifice. A tribe was selected and ordained to function as priests. Men had served in this capacity before the establishment of the priesthood under Aaron (19:22,24). Abel, Noah, Abraham and Jacob functioned in a priestly capacity when they built altars and offered sacrifices to the Lord (Gen. 4:4; 8:20; 22:13; 31:54). These 'occasional priests' were now to be replaced by a hereditary priesthood to carry out all the services associated with the tabernacle and the worship of God.

Plan of the tabernacle in the wilderness

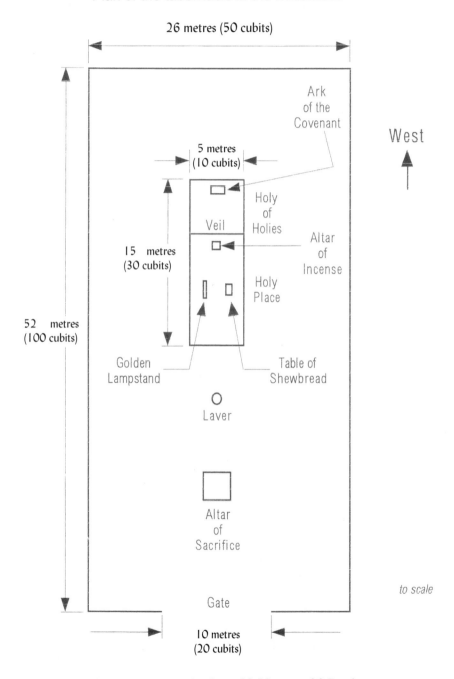

26 metres (50 cubits)

Ark
of the
Covenant

West

5 metres
(10 cubits)

Holy
of
Holies

Veil

Altar
of
Incense

15 metres
(30 cubits)

Holy
Place

52 metres
(100 cubits)

Golden
Lampstand

Table of
Shewbread

Laver

Altar
of
Sacrifice

to scale

Gate

10 metres
(20 cubits)

Measurement conversion: 1 cubit = 52.52 cm. or 20.7 inches

God's design for the tabernacle, entrusted to Moses on Mount Sinai, was to be followed to the letter (25:9). The people contributed materials, skills and labour. The outer courtyard was a fenced rectangle with one wide door for entry (27:9,13,16).[7] In the courtyard stood the altar for animal sacrifices, constructed of acacia wood overlaid with bronze. Between the tabernacle proper and the altar stood the laver of bronze, a large bowl filled with water for the priests to wash their hands and their feet before entering the enclosed tabernacle (30:17-21).

In the tabernacle proper there were two rooms, 'the holy place and the Most Holy' (26:33), separated by a thick veil. In the first room, the holy place, 'the sanctuary' (Heb. 9:2), stood three items: the lampstand, the table of shewbread and the altar of incense. The solid gold lampstand, with its seven branches (25:31-40; 26:35), burned day and night and gave light to the holy place. The table of shewbread was made of acacia wood overlaid with gold (25:23-30). Newly baked bread was placed on the table on the Sabbath and replaced every seven days. The twelve loaves, representing the tribes of Israel, were a thank-offering placed, or 'shown', before the face of the Lord continually. The altar of incense was also made of acacia wood overlaid with gold (30:1-10). The name 'altar' links it with the altar of sacrifice. The atonement was symbolized in the altar of sacrifice reconciling the Israelite with God. The altar of incense represented the reconciled Israelites in their prayer and worship ascending to the Lord.[8]

The second room, the Most Holy, the Holy of Holies, or 'the Holiest of All' (Heb. 9:3), housed the ark of the covenant, also called the ark of the Testimony (26:34). The ark contained 'the golden pot that had the manna, Aaron's rod that budded, and the tablets of the covenant' (Heb. 9:4).[9] This inner room was entered only once a year by the high priest on the Day of Atonement to sprinkle the sacrificial blood upon the mercy seat (Lev. 16;14-15; Heb. 9:7).

The ark of the covenant, made of acacia wood, was overlaid with pure gold, inside and out. The lid of the ark was the mercy seat made of pure gold with two golden cherubim on either end facing the mercy seat (25:10-22): '... draw a straight line from the centre of the Gate to the Mercy-Seat. You go through the Altar, through the Laver, through the Door; you pass the Table of Shewbread on your right hand, and the golden Lampstand on your left; through the Altar of Incense, through the Veil, to the Ark, covered by the Mercy-Seat, in the Holy of Holies. This is the true Pilgrim's Progress from the camp outside to the immediate presence of God.'[10]

On completion of all the work, the tabernacle was consecrated by the Lord: 'Then the cloud covered the tabernacle of meeting, and the glory of the LORD filled the tabernacle. And Moses was not able to enter the tabernacle of meeting, because the cloud rested above it, and the glory of the LORD filled the tabernacle' (40:34-35).

Christ and his church

In 1 Corinthians 10 the apostle Paul refers back to the events covered by the book of Exodus. He speaks of the Israelites being under the cloud, passing through the sea, drinking from the rock. Some of those Israelites became idolaters; others committed sexual immorality; still others, he says, tempted Christ and were destroyed by serpents, and numerous individuals murmured and complained against God. Paul sums up all these references in this way: 'Now all these things happened to them as examples, and they were written for our admonition, on whom the ends of the ages have come. Therefore let him who thinks he stands take heed lest he fall' (1 Cor. 10:11-12).

So much in this book of Exodus has a spiritual message and application for Christians: 'For whatever things were written before were written for our learning, that we through the patience and comfort of the Scriptures might have hope' (Rom. 15:4). Exodus is packed full of Christological significance.

- *Israel's bondage* in Egypt (1:11-14) is a symbol of the sinner's slavery to sin (Rom. 6:17-18).
- The *Passover Lamb* (12:5,7,13) is a type[11] of Christ and his precious blood (John 1:29; 1 Peter 1:19; 1 Cor. 5:7; Rev. 5:6). Not one of its bones shall be broken (12:46; cf. Num. 9:12; Ps. 34:20; John 19:36).
- The *pillar of cloud and fire* (14:19; cf. 13:21-22) is a type of Christ's presence with his people (John 14:18; Matt. 28:20).
- The *song of Moses* (15:1-19) is a type of songs of spiritual victory (Rev. 15:3-4).
- The *mixed multitude* (12:38) symbolizes the regenerate and unregenerate in the visible church (Matt. 13:24-30,36-43).
- The *waters of Marah and Elim* (15:23-27) are a type of bittersweet experiences in the Christian life (1 Peter 1:6).

- The *manna* (16:4) is a type of Christ, the bread of life (John 6:31-35).
- *Water from the rock* (17:6) is a type of Christ, who provides living water (1 Cor. 10:4; John 4:10; 7:37-39).

The tabernacle

The earthly tabernacle was built to God's exact specifications (25:9). It was designed to represent spiritual realities (Heb. 8:5). The person and work of the Lord Jesus Christ are prefigured in the construction, materials and furnishings of the tabernacle in the wilderness.[12] The tabernacle in the wilderness represents our Saviour's incarnation on earth: 'And the Word became flesh and dwelt among us, and we beheld his glory, the glory as of the only begotten of the Father, full of grace and truth' (John 1:14 — the Greek word translated 'dwelt' is from a root word meaning 'tabernacled').

All the beauty of the earthly tabernacle was internal. Viewed externally it was a long, dark-coloured, unattractive tent of badger skin. Inside it was beautiful in the extreme, glistening with gold and exquisitely coloured tapestries. Here is the 'ordinary', plain, external appearance and extraordinary internal beauty of Christ (Isa. 53:2; 52:14; Heb. 7:26; 4:15; 1 John 3:5). Not only is there an absence of all sin in Christ; there is also a positive holiness and righteousness. He is Jehovah Tsidkenu, 'the LORD our Righteousness' (Jer. 23:6); for he is altogether righteous. He is righteous in name, righteous in deed, righteous in mind, righteous in heart; he is righteous altogether — through and through, inside and out.

The *altar of sacrifice* speaks of the atoning work of the Saviour and the fellowship with God which we enjoy through him (Heb. 13:10; 1 John 1:7).

The *ark* containing the unbroken law of God speaks of Christ, who alone kept it utterly and completely in spirit and in letter (Ps. 40:8; cf. Heb. 10:5-7).

The *mercy seat* over the ark was covered with gold to symbolize God's royal throne. To those who come to God through Jesus Christ, that royal throne of judgement is none other than the mercy seat. We are 'justified freely by his grace through the redemption that is in Christ Jesus, whom God set forth to be a propitiation by his blood' (Rom. 3:24-25). The Greek word translated 'propitiation' is from *hilasterion* meaning 'mercy seat' (cf. Heb. 9:5).

'In the court stood the altar of burnt offering and the laver, pointing forward to Christ through whose blood we are justified and through whose

Spirit we are sanctified. In the holy place were to be found the table of shewbread, the seven-branched candlestick, and the altar of incense, respectively foreshadowing Christ as our Bread of Life, our source of Light, and our Intercessor. Finally, there was the Holy of Holies with its ark of the covenant, containing the law. But between the Glorious Presence and God's holy law which man had transgressed was the blood-sprinkled cover, the "mercy seat", an appropriate symbol and type of Christ, our Atonement. The holy of holies was the image of heaven itself; the ark, a symbol of God's throne. The entire tabernacle, being the abode of Jehovah, was a beautiful and most appropriate prophecy of Christ, in whom all the fulness of the Godhead dwells bodily.'[13]

The priesthood

On Mount Sinai God gave Moses the details of the Old Covenant law. He also directed Moses about the particular construction of the tabernacle and its furnishings. The third area of instruction given on the holy mount concerned the establishment of a priesthood.

The priestly line of Aaron foreshadows the work of the Lord Jesus Christ as the great High Priest for his people. Aaron and his sons are mentioned twenty-four times in this book of the Scriptures. Neither Aaron nor Christ is self-appointed (28:1; cf. Heb. 5:4-6). The Lord Jesus Christ is now in heaven for 'We have a great high priest who has passed through the heavens' (Heb. 4:14). His service is not yet completed; he is needed to function as our High Priest. His service as High Priest will continue until the whole church is complete and delivered safely to the Father (Heb. 7:25).[14]

Clothing for the high priest

In the book of Exodus detailed attention is given to the making of clothing and ornaments for the high priest to wear. A number of Bible scholars, past and present, have seen significance and meaning in these articles, drawing comparison with the person and work of the Saviour.[15] A word of caution must, however, be expressed. While the parallels may well be intended by the Lord, there is no clear New Testament warrant for being dogmatic on all details.

The *high priest's garments* (28:1-43; 39:1-31 — see page 98) may be seen to set forth the varied excellencies and glories of our High Priest, Jesus Christ.

God uses types as pictures to teach his people what would otherwise be virtually incomprehensible. Not only do the furnishings of the tabernacle add to the vision of Christ's glory, but the clothing of the high priest speaks much of Christ. God designed each part of the clothing and ornaments 'for glory and for beauty' (28:2). But this was not in order that Aaron might appear admirable, magnificent, or stunning — though he did. It was designed to represent the glories of the Lord Jesus Christ. Of that there can be no doubt. Every brilliant colour shone; the richest jewels dazzled. 'The rainbow's varied hues, the sun's meridian light, seemed to concentrate in a human form. Earth brought her best. Art framed them with a Spirit-given skill… This workmanship would never have seen birth, except to show His all-surpassing worth.'[16]

The *tunic* was made of finely woven linen. It covered the whole body from the neck to the feet, and the arms down to the wrists. It was worn next to the skin. The spotless pure cotton was of the finest possible quality. This symbolizes the personal perfection and purity of our Saviour, from head to toe.

The *robe* was slightly smaller than the tunic and worn over it. It did not cover the arms and reached only just below the knees. This robe was entirely blue. Blue is the colour of the sky. By this colour the heavenly origins of the Lord are displayed.

The *ephod* was a tunic shorter than the robe, like a tabard, or two aprons, one covering the front, the other covering the back, with broad shoulder straps for support (28:7). It was a mixture of dazzling colour — 'gold and blue and purple and scarlet thread, and fine linen thread, artistically woven' (28:6). The most skilful artisans worked these materials. This embroidery may be intended to signify the fact that all rare and beautiful graces are beautifully combined in the person of Jesus Christ.

The *belt* (band) for the ephod, made of the same material and design, was fastened around the waist, holding the ephod, the robe and the tunic (28:8). This belt signifies service. It speaks of the Lord Jesus Christ in all his matchless perfections demonstrating his peerless character, serving and ministering for his church and to his church (Matt. 20:28; cf. John 13:4).

The *breastplate,* made of the same material and design, was worn over the ephod, above the belt (28:15). Composed of two pieces of cloth the same size, it was fastened together at the bottom and formed a kind of pocket in which were placed the Urim and Thummim. It measured a hand-span across and a hand-span down. On the front of this richly embroidered breastplate, twelve precious stones were set, each one representing one of the tribes of Israel. This signifies how much the church is loved. We who are the Lord's have been loved 'with an everlasting love' and with loving-kindness God has drawn us to himself (Jer. 31:3). We are always upon the heart of our High Priest, our Lord and Saviour. Christ Jesus the great High Priest knows his own, loves his own, prays for his own, guards his own, cherishes his own, delights in his own.

The *turban* of fine white linen is surrounded with a belt of blue. (Does this suggest that all our Saviour's thoughts are centred in heaven?) On this a golden plate is fixed, engraved with the words: 'Holiness to the LORD' (28:36). So everything that Jesus Christ is, that Jesus thinks, that Jesus has done, and is doing, *and* all his people in him, are 'Holiness to the LORD'.

Application

The opening books of the Bible contain much more than an inspired history of events that happened thousands of years ago. They are filled with illustrations and pictures of the great doctrines of our faith which are explained and amplified in the New Testament.

1. Redemption

Each book of the Bible has a 'prominent and dominant theme'. As we noted in the previous chapter, historically considered, the book of Genesis is the book of beginnings, but viewed doctrinally it is seen to be the book which deals with election — God's free and sovereign choice. Historically, the book of Exodus deals with the deliverance of Israel from Egypt, but viewed doctrinally it is concerned with *redemption*. Just as the first book teaches *that* God elects, or chooses, for salvation, so the second book teaches *how* God saves: by redemption — that is, by costly deliverance. Exodus is therefore a powerful illustration, or type, of that redemption from sin which comes through the incarnation, suffering and sacrificial death of the Lord Jesus Christ. [17]

Taking the theme of redemption, A. W. Pink bases his outline on one verse:

You in your mercy have led forth
the people whom you have redeemed;

you have guided them in your strength
to your holy habitation

(15:13)

From this Pink draws out a fivefold division for the book of Exodus:

The structure of the book of Exodus	
1. The need for redemption — a people enslaved	Exod. 1-6.
2. The might of the Redeemer — displayed in the plagues of Egypt	Exod. 7 – 11
3. The character of redemption — purchased by blood, emancipated by power	Exod. 12-18
4. The duty of the redeemed — obedience to the Lord	Exod. 19-24
5. The provisions made for the failures of the redeemed — tabernacle and services	Exod. 25-40

2. Faith and obedience

These two, faith and obedience, belong together: '… faith without works is dead' (James 2:20). The obedience of the Hebrew slaves made their deliverance possible (12:7,13). God told them what they had to do and they acted upon it. Obedience to the gospel is essential to salvation (Heb. 5:9; cf. 1 Peter 4:17). Paul, the great champion of justification by faith alone, speaks of 'obedience to the faith' (Rom. 1:5; 16:26). Biblical writers use the word 'faith' in two different ways. It is used objectively as in 'the faith which was once for all delivered to the saints' (Jude 3). In this usage it is the body of truth, the doctrines given by God. The translation of Romans 1:5 in the Revised Authorised Version would then be correct, namely 'obedience to the faith' — in other words, obedience to the fundamental doctrines of Christianity which a regenerate person exhibits. Alternatively 'faith' may be understood subjectively as the impulse of a regenerate soul: 'By grace you have been saved through faith, and that not of yourselves; it is the gift of God' (Eph. 2:8). Consequently Romans 1:5 would then be understood as 'the obedience of faith', meaning the obedience to the Word of God which true faith produces. Either way it amounts to much the same thing. Scripture testifies clearly that God-given faith obeys the doctrines of God's Word. There is no real conflict between Paul and James. Paul is as convinced as James that real faith produces obedience (James 2:26).

Scale model of the tabernacle of God

Reproduced by permission from Kiene, *The Tabernacle of God in the Wilderness of Sinai*, p.174.

The high priest
Reproduced by permission from Kiene, *The Tabernacle of God in the Wilderness,*
p.165.

3. Prevailing prayer

When the Amalekite soldiers came to intercept the Israelite travellers, Moses knew that this emergency situation called for prayer. Moses' arms upheld (17:12) are symbolic of mutual support in prevailing prayer (Acts 2:42; 4:23-31; Eph. 6:18-19; James 5:16-18).

4. The law

The law of Sinai was a burden placed upon the Israelites. It was impossible, even for the most devout and zealous, to keep it. The law made the Israelites conscious of their inability and sinfulness and caused them to seek mercy from God through the appointed sacrificial system. They waited 'for the consolation of Israel' and longed for the coming of the promised deliverer (Luke 2:25; Gal. 3:24). The Old Covenant could not bring salvation, but those who trusted in the mercy of God were forgiven in anticipation of the death of Christ. The law of Moses was holy (Rom. 7:12) and spiritual (Rom. 7:14), but 'weak through the flesh' (Rom. 8:3). Sinners have no ability to obey the whole of the law of God, which is why God gave the promise of a new covenant at the same time as he gave the Old Covenant law: 'The LORD your God will circumcise your heart and the heart of your descendants, to love the LORD your God with all your heart and with all your soul, that you may live' (Deut. 30:6). This promise was to be amplified by the prophets: for example, 'I will give you a new heart and put a new spirit within you... I will put my Spirit within you and cause you to walk in my statutes, and you will keep my judgements and do them' (Ezek. 36:26-27). Everything in the command was to be fulfilled in the promise.

In the New Covenant the Lord keeps his promises given through Moses and the prophets. Nearly fifteen hundred years after Sinai, at the Jerusalem Council in the early years of the Christian church, the relation of believers to the law of Moses comes under discussion. The apostle Peter resists the imposition of the law of Moses upon Gentile converts in words that are highly instructive: 'Now therefore, why do you test God by putting a yoke on the neck of the disciples which neither our fathers nor we were able to bear? But we believe that through the grace of the Lord Jesus Christ we shall be saved in the same manner as they' (Acts 15:10-11). Peter claims that such a requirement would offend God. He calls it a weight that no Jew could bear. He emphasizes that, whether Jew or Gentile, the way of salvation is now the same: we are saved by grace alone, through faith alone, in Christ alone! 'But some of the sect of the Pharisees who believed rose up, saying, "It is necessary to circumcise them, and to command them to keep the law of Moses" ' (Acts 15:5). To these Pharisees it seems to have been less important that Jews become Christians than that all nations should become Jews. Peter insists that requiring Gentiles to obey the law of Moses is to 'test' or 'tempt' God. Peter's argument is plain: circumcision and the observance of the law of Moses cannot be necessary for Gentile converts because God has acknowledged them (Acts 15:7-9). The Lord demonstrated his acceptance of Gentiles, uncircumcised and without the law of Moses, when his Holy Spirit descended upon Cornelius, his family and his friends (Acts 10:44-48). To require Gentiles to obey the law of Moses would not only tempt God, it would put an impossible yoke upon Gentile believers. A yoke is an emblem of slavery (1 Tim. 6:1). From Sinai onwards the law was a yoke. The history of Israel from Sinai to Christ was a record of heartache and struggle under the weight. They often broke the yoke and burst the bonds in rebellion and transgression (Jer. 5:5). Even for the godly the law of Moses was a stern disciplinarian to prepare them to receive Christ that they might be justified by faith in him alone (Gal. 3:24). If this yoke could not be borne by those Jews at the council nor by their fathers[18] (Acts 15:10), then it follows that the law of Moses should no longer be required of anyone, Jew or Gentile, since converted Jews now 'believe that through the grace of the Lord Jesus Christ' they will be saved in the same manner as Gentiles (Acts 15:11).

So the apostle Peter settles the debate by asserting in effect that salvation is by grace alone through faith alone in Christ alone. The reasoning of Acts 15 would seem to answer the issue for all time. Sadly that is not the case. Since the days of the New Testament the relationship of the law of Moses to Christians, whether Jew or Gentile, has been the focus of widely differing opinions often resulting in a considerable lack of Christian charity.

The difficulty centres in the meaning and definition of 'the law of Moses'. What is 'the yoke' of Acts 15:10 which is not to be imposed upon Gentile believers? Some maintain that the yoke 'is not the moral law, and the just restraints of religion; but the ceremonial laws and customs of the Jews'.[19] Others insist that the yoke is not 'circumcision, but the Mosaic law in general, and that viewed chiefly as a condition of salvation... The law, indeed, itself was a heavy burden, but it was insupportable when regarded as a condition of salvation.'[20] But it is difficult, if not impossible, to see how either of these interpretations can be derived from the words of Peter.

Calvin, with characteristic clarity and forcefulness argues: '... it is easy to gather from the actual situation that he [Peter] is not speaking about ceremonies alone … not only holy men, but also a great many hypocrites acquitted themselves correctly and punctiliously in the outward observation of the rites. Yes, and what is more, it would not be such a difficult thing to satisfy the moral law, if it were satisfied with bodily obedience only, and did not demand spiritual righteousness. For it is given to many to control their hands and feet, but it is really extremely hard to manage all the affections, so that perfect self-restraint and purity reign in the soul as well as in the body. Accordingly it is ridiculous for people to limit Peter's word to ceremonies… When he says that they were unable to bear the yoke of the Law, it is established that it is impossible to keep the Law.'[21]

Many of the Puritans viewed the Ten Commandments as the moral law of God.[22] They then reasoned that this moral law is still in force for believers. The law, they asserted, is only abolished in regard to justification and in reference to its curse. In other respects 'Believers are to make great use of the moral law.'[23]

It is argued by some Christians that the yoke, the law of Moses, was completely superseded by the incarnation, suffering, death, resurrection and ascension of the Lord Jesus Christ, followed by the sending of the Holy Spirit to establish the New Covenant: 'For the law was given through Moses, but grace and truth came through Jesus Christ' (John 1:17). The Christian, in distinction from the believing Jew under the Old Covenant, is freed from all responsibilities to obey Moses. The Christian loves and obeys Jesus Christ (Rom. 7:1-6; John 14:15). Freed from the heavy and burdensome law of Moses, the New Covenant believer is constrained by the love of Christ (2 Cor. 5:14). He or she is never antinomian (without moral law) but is always 'under law towards Christ' (1 Cor. 9:21, see context).[24]

No man who lived under the Old Covenant ever fulfilled the law of Moses and in that sense really bore its yoke. That is why the Old Covenant had its Day of Atonement and its many arrangements with offerings and sacrifices to remove sins. All these sacrifices were types of the sacrifice of Christ, and through faith the Old Covenant believer was linked to the Promised One, that is, Christ himself. For the intolerable yoke of the law, the Saviour substituted his gospel yoke, a wonderful yoke which itself bears every believer.[25] Jesus invites: 'Come to me, all you who labour and are heavy laden, and I will give you rest. Take my yoke upon you and learn from me, for I am gentle and lowly in heart, and you will find rest for your souls' (Matt. 11:28-29).

Paul shows the connection between circumcision and the Old Covenant law when he warns the Christians of Galatia, 'Stand fast therefore in the liberty by which Christ has made us free, and do not be entangled again with a yoke of bondage' (Gal. 5:1; cf. vv. 2-3). In accord with the apostle Peter at the Jerusalem Council, Paul insists that the only remedy that is effective for salvation is 'faith working through love' (Gal. 5:6).

The Lord Jesus criticized the scribes and Pharisees, 'for they bind heavy burdens, hard to bear, and lay them on men's shoulders' (Matt. 23:4). The one and only means of salvation ordained by God is ' "the grace of the Lord Jesus", and not … observance of the law. Even in the Old Covenant the saving means was the Old Testament gospel and promise of the Messiah, and not the law.'[26] Nothing, be it the law of the rabbis, or the law of Moses, or anything else, must be added 'to the sole-sufficing grace of the only Saviour'.[27]

Conclusion

The great theme of the book of Exodus is redemption accomplished. Responding to the cries of the Israelites in slavery under the Egyptians, God comes down to rescue his people. They are liberated, led through the wilderness, and taught the fundamentals of God-honouring behaviour — in society, home and personal life. Here the foundational truths of salvation are established, not so much in the form of explicit and systematic doctrine, but rather through types, symbols and Israel's history. In the book of Exodus the glorious types of our Saviour and Redeemer, the Lord Jesus Christ, shine forth. We meet him on every page, in every event. The New Testament guards us against excess and error by leading us to see, with the eye of faith, the Christ who is 'in all the Scriptures' (Luke 24:27). We see Christ as the spotless Lamb, the water-giving Rock, the manna from heaven, the cloud and fire of the constant presence of the living God. We see him at Sinai — in the tabernacle, the altar, the shewbread, the lampstand, the veil, the ark, the mercy seat — in the priesthood, its garments and breastplate.

In Exodus we see our deliverance from the slavery of sin (Rom. 6:6), and our hazardous journey to the promised land (1 Peter 1:4-6), following after the Lord Jesus Christ (Heb. 12:1-2).

Through the law of God at Sinai the people were taught the need for the tabernacle and all that it represents. The law serves to highlight human inability, guilt and sin. The tabernacle, with its furnishings, priesthood and ceremonies, is a type, a preparation for the one sacrifice and the one High Priest, who having 'by himself purged our sins' (Heb. 1:3), has entered the heavenly sanctuary bearing his own precious blood on behalf of his people. He is 'able to save to the uttermost' because he lives for ever to make intercession for us (Heb. 7:25).

The book of Exodus points distinctly and unwaveringly to Jesus Christ, the Son of God!

Leviticus

('referring to the Levites')

Author: Moses
(commonly accepted)

Key thought: 'God is holy'

Theme:
Worshipping and serving the Lord

'You shall be holy, for I the
LORD your God am holy.'
Leviticus 19:2

Summary

Leviticus

'Pursue … holiness, without which no one will see the Lord'
(Heb. 12:14).

Leviticus (meaning, 'pertaining to the Levites') is the third of the first five books of the Bible known as the Pentateuch. As we have seen, viewed historically, the first book, Genesis, is the book of beginnings; viewed doctrinally it is the book of election — God sovereignly choosing as he wills. The second book, Exodus, viewed historically, deals with the deliverance of Israel from Egypt, whereas doctrinally it deals with redemption. As the first book of the Bible teaches that God elects, or chooses, those who shall be saved, so the second instructs as to how God saves — that is, through the payment of a ransom. The third book, Leviticus, teaches the holy requirements of God in worship and life, and the gracious provisions he has made to meet those requirements. Viewed historically, the book of Leviticus is an account of the institution of an elaborate sacrificial system and the inauguration of a meticulous priesthood. From the doctrinal perspective it is profound teaching concerning the work of the Lord Jesus Christ as sacrifice and High Priest.[1]

Author

'Now the LORD called to Moses, and spoke to him...' (1:1). There are two clear implications from this statement: firstly, that which follows is from Moses; and, secondly, it was not the product of his mind and thinking, but the revelation of Almighty God to him. While these words strictly refer only to the section of the book which immediately follows (1:1 – 3:17), nevertheless, the same or a similar expression is used no less than fifty-six times in the twenty-seven chapters. It seems not unreasonable therefore to conclude that they cover the entire book. The contents of Leviticus are God's Word communicated to, and through, his servant Moses. The Lord Jesus speaks of Moses as the recipient of God's Word contained in Leviticus when, having healed a leper, he says, 'See that you tell no one; but go your way, show yourself to the priest, and offer the gift that Moses commanded, as a testimony to them' (Matt. 8:4). Such a command is found only in Leviticus (14:2-10).

The Bible does not inform us whether or not Moses wrote down every word himself, or whether the Spirit of God directed and inspired other people, in the days of Moses or afterwards, to commit these laws to writing (cf. Ezra 6:18). The important point, as always, is knowing with confidence that they form part of the inspired Scriptures given by God.

That God is the ultimate author of Leviticus is confirmed, if such confirmation is needed, by the Lord Jesus Christ. For instance, in justifying his disciples for plucking ears of corn on the Sabbath day, he refers to the example of David, who ate the shewbread, 'which was not lawful for him to eat, nor for those who were with him, but only for the priests' (Matt. 12:4). The law of which our Lord speaks is found only in Leviticus (24:9). Such a reference is only relevant on the assumption that he regarded the prohibition of the shewbread as having the same inspired authority as the obligation of the Sabbath. In other words, it is clear that Jesus regards both the Levitical law and the Sabbath law as from God.

A second confirmation is also related to the Sabbath, this time when Jesus refers to Moses as having renewed the institution of circumcision originally given to Abraham (John 7:22-23). As before, divine authority is seen to be behind the command. But this renewal of circumcision is not found in the Pentateuch except in Leviticus (12:3). From these examples it is clear that the Lord Jesus Christ 'believed, and intended to be understood as teaching, that the law of Leviticus was, in a true sense, of Mosaic origin, and of inspired, and therefore infallible, authority'. [2] Andrew Bonar says there is no book in the whole of the Scriptures 'that contains more of the very words of God than Leviticus. It is God that is the direct speaker in almost every page... This consideration cannot fail to send us to the study of it with singular interest and attention.'[3]

Historical setting

The laws of Leviticus were given in the wilderness. The book covers a period in Israel's history of less than two months at the beginning of the second year after the exodus from Egypt: from the first day of the first month to the twentieth day of the second month (Exod. 40:17; Num. 10:11 — 1443 B.C.). The book is closely connected with Exodus and Numbers but, unlike those books, Leviticus contains only a small amount of historical narrative (8-10; 24:10-23).

There is a natural flow from Exodus to Leviticus. This is highlighted in the closing words of the former and the opening words of the latter: 'Then the cloud covered the tabernacle of meeting, and the glory of the LORD filled the tabernacle...' 'Now the LORD called to Moses, and spoke to him from the tabernacle of meeting, saying...' (Exod. 40:34; Lev. 1:1).

At Sinai the Israelites are organized into a theocracy — the Lord is to govern his people personally. Basic laws are given covering moral, civil and ceremonial duties (Exod. 20-24). The covenant between God and Israel is confirmed. The tabernacle is constructed. Before the Lord continues to lead the Israelites to the promised land, he provides detailed instruction as to how worship is to be conducted in the tabernacle. An elaborate sacrificial system is instituted together with a series of annual festivals. These remind of the past and point to the future.

Outline

There is a clear and simple structure: ceremonies and laws are set out in a straightforward manner. The emphasis throughout the book is placed upon the holiness of God: 'You shall be holy, for I the LORD your God am holy' (19:2; cf. 11:45). The underlying purpose is to provide guidelines to the priests and people for the appropriate worship of God. At the root of the concept of holiness is 'separation'. The Israelites are to understand that they are separated by God, to God, for God. Their view of worship is to extend beyond the confines of the tabernacle and embrace every aspect of their lives. Their behaviour is to reflect the distinction and dignity of their relationship with the living God (20:26). It is this personal relationship which is the key and motivation for their obedience and faithfulness: 'I am the LORD your God. You shall therefore...' (11:44; cf. 18:2-5; 19:2-4).

Part I: The law of sacrifice (1:1 - 7:38)

The sacrificial system formed the core of Israel's public worship. It is surprising that there is no explanation regarding the meaning of the ceremonies. It seems to be taken for granted that the original participants understood the significance and only needed to be reminded of the correct procedures. The meaning of sacrifice as a whole and of individual sacrifices in particular can be determined by the symbolism employed and how they were used in worship.[4] Two emphases are apparent: sin must be pardoned and removed, and lost fellowship with God must be restored and preserved. The New Testament, especially the letter to the Hebrews, enables Christians to understand the meaning and relevance of the sacrifices both in their original context and for today.

God is holy and he will not permit sin and uncleanness in his presence. In order to establish a relationship between God and sinners, a sacrifice has to be made substituting a pure life for a sinful one. Throughout the Old Testament period, animals (without moral discernment and therefore free from moral responsibility and from guilt) were used as the substituted sacrifice to atone for sin. Atonement — 'at-one-ment' — means the reconciling through substitution of those who have been estranged. God is righteously angry with sinful humans; sinful humans are hostile towards the holy God. The atonement, or reconciling sacrifice, brings harmony through the removal of sin and guilt. The life of the animal is accepted in the place of the life of the sinner (Heb. 9:22). The punishment of death for sin is exacted on the substitute. The sacrificed animal does not in fact remove sin but symbolizes the one who successfully accomplishes this great purpose (Heb. 10:4,10).

A progression may be traced in the offerings of Leviticus: atonement, consecration, fellowship and preservation. The *burnt offering* (1:1-17) is the sacrifice for atonement. This is the major sacrifice since it initiates a right relationship between God and sinners. The sacrificial animal or bird has to be without blemish. The connection of the sinner with the sacrifice is visualized when 'he shall put his hand on the head of the burnt offering, and it will be accepted on his behalf to make atonement for him' (1:4). The whole of the creature, with the exception of the skin (7:8), is sacrificed to God by fire.

A right relationship is first established by God through the burnt offering, the atonement. The justified sinner, now declared righteous through the atoning sacrifice, gratefully responds in bringing the *cereal offering* (2:1-16; 6:14-23), signifying the consecration of the whole life to the service of God. Once reconciled to God, the pardoned sinner responds with wholehearted commitment.

The best grain is carefully and thoroughly sieved. Oil is poured upon it. Incense is then added to a small amount of this mixture and burned, usually with the burnt offering. The remaining oil and flour is then given to the priests as food.

A right relationship having been established between God and the sinner, and the forgiven sinner having responded with wholehearted devotion, the benefits of this fellowship are now to be experienced. So the third offering, the *peace offering* (3:1-17; 7:11-34), signifies the enjoyment of the reconciled relationship. Unlike the burnt offering, where the whole of the animal was consumed in the fire upon the altar, in this sacrifice only the fat surrounding the internal organs and also the kidneys are burnt (3:3-5). The rest, the flesh, is cooked and eaten by the priests and people (7:15,31-34). Fellowship with God means fellowship also with God's people.

The fourth and fifth sacrifices provide for those who have already been reconciled to God through the atoning sacrifice. These offerings symbolize the maintenance of the already established relationship. The *sin offering* (4:1-35; 6:24-30) serves to maintain the relationship where sin has been committed unintentionally. This offering is the basis of restoration. In a similar way the *guilt offering* (5:1-19; 7:1-10) also serves to maintain an existing relationship. The difference is seen in the emphasis placed upon the notion of 'trespass'. This relates to an invasion of the rights of others, divine or human. Idolatry, for example, is a trespass against God, an invasion of his rights, in that it robs him of the worship, offerings and tithes that are rightfully his. The same Hebrew word for 'trespass' is also used in connection with adultery (Num. 5:12, cf. AV). Marital unfaithfulness involves the invasion of the rights of the spouse. Every trespass is a sin, but not every sin is a trespass. In this fifth sacrifice relating to the invasion of the rights of others there must not only be the removal of the sin but also compensation for the damage caused.[5]

Part II: The consecration of priests (8:1 – 10:20)

Along with the sacrificial system, the priesthood is a prime concern of Leviticus, as its name implies ('pertaining to the Levites, i.e. the priests'). Priests functioned as mediators. They represented God to the people and the people to God.

Moses prepares and anoints Aaron and his sons for the priesthood on the basis of previous instructions (Exod. 29:1-36; 40:12-15). These are elaborate and detailed in order to instil into the minds of priests and people the entire holiness and spotless purity of the Lord of glory. No one is to rush carelessly into the presence of the Almighty. No one may approach him without being thoroughly washed, without wearing spotlessly clean clothing, without the provision of an appropriate sacrifice — that is, one that God has authorized. The priestly garments and the ceremony of anointing with oil linked these men with the tabernacle as separated exclusively to the service of God.

Aaron and his sons commence their duties. The strictness of the Lord in relation to the functioning of the priests is brought home dramatically when two of Aaron's sons, Nabad and Abihu, offer 'profane fire before the LORD, which he had not commanded them' (10:1). They are immediately slain and the Lord utters a solemn warning:

> By those who come near me
> I must be regarded as holy;
> And before all the people
> I must be glorified
>
> (10:3).

Priests are appointed by God to protect his honour and glory and promote his holiness among the people. This is to be achieved through their personal example, meticulous service and regular instruction (10:11).

Part III: Clean and unclean (11:1 - 15:33)

The laws of purity emphasize in their own way the holiness of God. Holiness in God's people concerns the body as well as the soul. It is evident that the hygiene laws inculcated a sense of responsibility to live in a wholesome manner before the Lord. They also served to protect the Israelites from many of the diseases common to other nations of the time (Exod. 15:26).[6]

What criteria are used to distinguish between clean and unclean animals, between clean fish and unclean crustaceans, is not readily apparent. Many theories have been presented. It is quite possible that the Lord made an arbitrary distinction on purpose! Though there was nothing morally different between one animal and another, the fact that God made a distinction meant that the Israelites must regard them as such. Consequently they would be faced with the issue of clean or unclean *every day of their lives*. In preparing meals the dominant thought would not be, 'Is this healthy?' or 'Is this nutritious?' but rather, 'Is this kosher? Is this permitted, or is this forbidden, *in the sight of the living God*?'

Following the list of clean and unclean species, the Lord gives directions for purification after childbirth, procedures in cases of leprosy in people, clothing and buildings, and cleansing after bodily secretions of various kinds. Holiness in the people of God involves pure food, pure bodies, pure homes and pure habits.

Part IV: The Day of Atonement (16:1-34)

Central to the worship of God was the sacrificial system. At the heart of the sacrificial system was the annual Day of Atonement *(Yom Kippur)*. Only on this day could the high priest enter into the Holy of Holies, the most holy place of the tabernacle. This was a day of solemn reflection, a day of humbling before the Lord. The people were to reflect deeply upon the seriousness of sin. This was the only day of the year where fasting was compulsory. All other annual festivals and feast days had an atmosphere of celebration, of rejoicing. While the sense of God's holiness would be impressed upon the people, there was nevertheless the triumphant note that the Lord had provided the means for forgiveness: 'For the life of the flesh is in the blood, and I have given it to you upon the altar to make atonement for your souls; for it is the blood that makes atonement for the soul' (17:11).

This Day of Atonement was the high point of all sacrifices. It was intentionally comprehensive. Here was provision for any and every sin not covered by the specific offerings detailed in the first seven chapters.

Part V: The law of holiness (17:1 - 25:55)

The people of God are to ensure holiness in life. They are to separate themselves from the practices of the surrounding nations. The key to this section is found in the eighteenth chapter: 'According to the doings of the land of Egypt, where you dwelt, you shall not do; and according to the doings of the land of Canaan, where I am bringing you, you shall not do; nor shall you walk in their ordinances. You shall observe my judgements and keep my ordinances; to walk in them; I am the LORD your God' (18:3-4).

The Israelites were to maintain a distinctive lifestyle. This was to be achieved by obedience to the laws that God gave through his servant Moses. They were not only to abstain from food forbidden by God (11:1-47), they also had to prepare and consume permitted food in a way that was pleasing to God. They were to avoid even the appearance of following the idolatrous practices of the surrounding heathens. To kill an animal in the open field might have given the impression that they were pouring the blood on the ground and thereby sacrificing to 'field-devils' (17:3-7).[7] Consequently all animals permitted for food were to be slaughtered at the door of the tabernacle. Their blood was to be sprinkled on the altar of burnt offering and the fat parts burnt 'for a sweet aroma to the LORD' (17:6). Only then, after the priest had taken his appropriate portion, were the people to eat the flesh. (The diet of the Israelites contained very little meat. It was eaten mainly on feast days,[8] so the restrictions here were not really a burden upon the people.)

The Israelites were not to consume blood, otherwise they would be excommunicated — driven from the community of Israel. Eating carrion (dead and rotting flesh) carried with it a day-long penalty with appropriate washings. These laws were not intended simply to supplement the food laws of chapter 11. They raised the eating of food into an act of worship. This had two implications: it kept the Israelites from participating in idolatrous sacrificial meals; and it reminded them that their daily food was provided for them by the Lord.

The Israelites were also to be distinct in their sexual relationships. Incest — that is, physical intimacy with those who constitute close family, either by blood or marriage — was forbidden. Homosexuality was designated 'an abomination'; bestiality was classed as a 'perversion' (18:22,23). The penalty for these corruptions was excommunication — permanent banishment (18:29).

This section includes a list of various moral and ceremonial laws followed by specified punishments (19:1 – 20:27).

The holiness required of priests receives special attention (22:1-16). They were the appointed leaders and needed to set a good and godly example to the people. The laws concerning defilement through contact with a dead body and restrictions regarding marriage were stricter for them than for the Israelite population as a whole.

Festivals and special days

The seventh day of each week was to be kept as 'a *Sabbath* of solemn rest' (23:3; cf. Exod. 20:8-11). The day was to be kept free from work in accordance with God's example at creation (Exod. 31:12-17). The Sabbath principle was also to be applied to the land once the Israelites were settled (25:2-7; Exod. 23:10-11).

On the evening of the fourteenth day of the first month (Hebrew —
Abib, corresponding to our March/April) the *Feast of the Passover* was to
be commemorated with the eating of a lamb (23:5; cf. Exod. 12:1-28). This
reminded the Israelites of God's deliverance of their ancestors from Egyptian slavery, passing over their homes and destroying the first-born in Egypt
(Exod. 12:27).

On that evening no leaven was to be consumed — in fact none was to
be found in their homes. The *Feast of Unleavened Bread* was to be observed for seven days (23:6-8; cf. Exod. 12:15-20, 13:3-10; Num.
28:17-25). This served to remind the Israelites of the haste and distress with
which their ancestors departed from Egypt (Exod. 12:39).

During the Feast of Unleavened Bread, on the day after the Sabbath,
the *Feast of First-fruits* (a sheaf of first-fruits was used as a wave offering,
23:15) was to be celebrated (23:9-14). This was the day when they were to
bring the first-fruits of the early (barley) harvest. In this way the Israelites
would offer the first cut of harvest to the Lord as an expression of gratitude
and thanksgiving for his daily provision of their food.

Seven weeks later the Israelites were to celebrate the *Feast of Weeks*,
also known as Pentecost (23:15-22). Falling on the fiftieth day (seven
weeks, or the seventh of the seventh days) calculated from the Feast of
First-fruits, this was the first-fruits of the late (wheat) harvest, the main harvest (Num. 28:26).

Each year on the first day of the seventh month the *Feast of Trumpets*
was observed (23:23-25; Num. 29:1-6) to announce the dawn of the sab-
batical month. Nine days later the *Day of Atonement* was to be enacted
(23:26-32), to make atonement for the priests and people (16:1-34). When
the sacrificial blood was shed the work of the priest was not over. The
blood had to be taken beyond the veil into the Holy of Holies, there to be
sprinkled upon the mercy seat over the ark of the covenant (16:14). Every
fifty years a jubilee year was observed from the Day of Atonement. This
was calculated on the sabbath principle (23:3) and applied to the sabbath
of sabbath years (seven times seven). All land taken in payment of debt
had to be returned to its rightful owner. All servants had to be released so
that they could return to their own plots of land (25:8-17).

Five days after the Day of Atonement, the *Feast of Tabernacles* was to
be observed (23:33-43). The festivities included the construction of shelters,
or booths, in which the people slept for seven nights. During seven days
seventy bullocks were sacrificed: thirteen on the first day, twelve on the
second, eleven on the third, and so on (Num. 29:12-38). This feast is also
called 'the Feast of Ingathering' (Exod. 23:16) and marked the end of the

year's harvest of barley, wheat and grapes (Deut. 16:13). The law of Moses was to be read *every* seventh year during the time of this feast (Deut. 31:9-13). The Feast of Tabernacles reminded the Israelites in a graphic manner that their ancestors had been homeless wanderers in the desert, and the Lord had protected them and provided for them.

Attendance at three of the festivals (held initially in the tabernacle, the tent of meeting, and later in the temple) was compulsory to all male adults — the Feast of Unleavened Bread (including Passover and First-fruits), the Feast of Pentecost and the Feast of Tabernacles (Deut. 16:16).

Part VI: Promises, warning and appendix (26:1 – 27:34)

The whole of the law is summed up in the first two verses — idolatry is forbidden and the pure worship of the Lord is required (26:1-2). Following the death of two of Aaron's sons, the priests would have been in no doubt about the seriousness of obedience.

Christ and his church

The importance of the book of Leviticus is evident from the use made of it by the Lord Jesus and the writers of the New Testament.[9] Whereas some books of the Bible, such as Isaiah and Psalms, abound in prophecies concerning the Lord Jesus Christ and his church, the book of Leviticus bursts with typology. It is essentially and intentionally a book of types.[10] Here are vivid pictures illustrating wonderful truths about the Saviour and his people.

The Epistle to the Hebrews is the New Testament counterpart to Leviticus, containing the explanation of so many of the types found there. The manner in which that letter was composed suggests that it was not a new idea to understand the ceremonies of the Old Covenant as illustrations of something more glorious to come.

1. The sacrifices as types of Christ and his church

Here in Leviticus we find demonstrated the horror and consequences of sin and the nature of the sinner before a holy God. But here is also grace, amazing grace, and a vivid picture of the Saviour of sinners. Leviticus reveals, in vivid picture language, the glorious person and work of our Saviour. The use of types or symbols is part of God's design before the full revelation in his Son. The blood of bulls and goats cannot make atonement for sin (Heb. 10:4). Yet the blood of sacrificial animals does convey significance. It serves as a sign, 'a symbol that points beyond itself to the reality of Christ's atoning sacrifice'.[11] The blood of animals with which the earthly tabernacle was purified prefigured 'better sacrifices than these' — that is, the Lord Jesus Christ our Saviour, who 'has appeared to put away sin by the sacrifice of himself' (Heb. 9:23,26). The Levitical law at its best is only 'a shadow of the good things to come' (Heb. 10:1).

The *burnt offering* is the sacrifice for atonement offered to God by fire. This is the sacrifice of substitution establishing a right relationship with God (2 Cor. 5:21). The fire symbolizes the wrath of God, for 'Our God is a consuming fire' (Heb. 12:29). The Saviour experienced hell while still alive on the cross. His devastating agony is expressed in his cry: 'My God, my God, why have you forsaken me?' (Matt. 27:46). 'For Christ also suffered once for sins, the just for the unjust, that he might bring us to God' (1 Peter 3:18). It is the living God 'who has reconciled us to himself through Jesus Christ' (2 Cor. 5:18). He demonstrated 'his righteousness, that he might be just and the justifier of the one who has faith in Jesus' (Rom. 3:26).

The *cereal offering* signifies the consecration of the whole life to the service of God. When Christ came into the world he said, 'A body you have prepared for me... Behold, I have come ... to do your will, O God' (Heb. 10:5,7). The Son of God says, 'Here am I and the children whom God has given me' (Heb. 2:13). Accepted believers respond in Christ; we 'walk in love, as Christ also has loved us and given himself for us, an offering and a sacrifice to God for a sweet-smelling aroma' (Eph. 5:2). We present our 'bodies a living sacrifice, holy, acceptable to God' which is our 'reasonable service' (Rom. 12:1). Our bodies are 'holy' because of the consecration of the Holy Spirit (represented by the 'oil' of the cereal offering) and 'acceptable to God' because God 'has made us accepted in the Beloved' (Eph. 1:6).

The *peace offering* signifies the enjoyment of the reconciled relationship. The Lord Jesus exhibited a deep fellowship with God the Father throughout the whole of his earthly life. He yielded to God what he most desires, 'truth in the inward parts' (Ps. 51:6). He 'poured out his soul unto death' (Isa. 53:12). He 'humbled himself and became obedient to death, even the death of the cross' (Phil. 2:8). Christ is our peace offering, 'having made peace through the blood of his cross' (Col. 1:20). Consequently the 'Prince of Peace' (Isa. 9:6) bequeaths peace to all his followers (John 14:27).

'Therefore, having been justified by faith, we have peace with God through our Lord Jesus Christ' (Rom. 5:1).

The fourth and fifth sacrifices provide for those who have already been reconciled to God through the atoning sacrifice. These offerings symbolize the maintenance of an already established relationship. The *sin offering* and the *guilt offering* maintain the reconciled relationship. The purpose of the atonement is to free sinners from the 'law of sin and death' (Rom. 8:2). We are urged not to present our 'members as instruments of unrighteousness to sin', but to yield them 'as instruments of righteousness to God' (Rom. 6:13). But who is able? Thank God there is, even so, the assurance that '... if anyone sins, we have an advocate with the Father, Jesus Christ the righteous. And he himself is the propitiation[12] for our sins' (1 John 2:1-2).

The whole sacrificial system of the Old Covenant is abolished. Every detail of every offering pointed to some aspect of the perfect sacrifice of Christ. In the humble, obedient life of Christ, culminating in a holy sinless death, the sacrifices instituted in Leviticus are rendered obsolete. When Christ came into the world he said, 'Behold, I have come to do your will, O God,' from which the writer to the Hebrews concludes: 'He takes away the first that he may establish the second. By that will we have been sanctified through the offering of the body of Jesus Christ once' (Heb. 10:9-10).

> Not all the blood of beasts,
> On Jewish altars slain,
> Could give the guilty conscience peace,
> Or wash away the stain.
>
> But Christ, the heavenly Lamb,
> Takes all our sins away;
> A sacrifice of nobler name
> And richer blood than they.
>
> My faith would lay her hand
> On that dear head of thine,
> While like a penitent I stand,
> And there confess my sin.
>
> (Isaac Watts)

'What we have in type in Leviticus we have in reality in the Cross of Christ.' [13]

2. The priesthood as types of Christ and his church

The contrast between the earthly and the heavenly priesthood is brought out in detail in Hebrews:

Earthly priests	Christ, the Heavenly Priest
are sinners, they offer sacrifice for their own sins first (Heb. 9:7)	is 'holy, harmless, undefiled, separate from sinners' and has no sin for which to atone (Heb. 7:26; cf. I John 3:5)
die and need to be replaced (Heb. 7:23)	lives for ever (Heb. 7:24-25)
entered the Holy of Holies once a year (Heb. 9:7)	entered heaven's Holy of Holies and stayed there, having 'sat down at the right hand of the Majesty on high' (Heb. 7:27; 1:3)
carried the blood of goats and calves (Heb. 9:12-13)	presented his own precious blood (Heb. 9:12)
brought the sacrifices for sins (Heb. 5:1)	is the sacrifice for sins; High Priest and sacrifice are one, it is he 'who through the eternal Spirit offered himself without spot to God' (Heb. 9:14; cf. John 10:17-18)
repeated the sacrifices daily (Heb. 10:11)	'offered one sacrifice for sins for ever' (Heb. 10:12)
offered sacrifices that could not take away sin (Heb. 10:4)	offered the perfect sacrifice for sin (Heb. 9:26; I John 1:7; I Peter 1:19)

'His one surrender of Himself as the atoning Lamb, for ever quenched all wrath, for ever took away all curse, for ever satisfied all claims, for ever saved the family of faith, for ever opened heaven, for ever vanquished hell. To add to infinite perfection is impossible. Woe be to them who think such offering incomplete!'[14]

The Levitical priesthood and sacrifices are gone, but the spiritual truth they represent stays for ever. There is no entry into the kingdom of God, no enjoyment of everlasting bliss and happiness, without the services of a high priest and mediator bearing a sacrifice for sin: 'But Christ came as high priest of the good things to come, with the greater and more perfect tabernacle not made with hands, that is, not of this creation. Not with the blood of goats and calves, but with his own blood he entered the Most Holy Place once for all, having obtained eternal redemption' (Heb. 9:11-12).

The Lord Jesus Christ 'loved us and washed us from our sins in his own blood' (Rev. 1:5). We are 'a holy priesthood, to offer up spiritual sacrifices acceptable to God through Jesus Christ' (1 Peter 2:5). The Christian church does not *have* a priesthood; it *is* a priesthood. As priests believers have direct access to God, speak to God on behalf of others and speak to others on behalf of God (1 Peter 2:9-10).

3. The festivals as types of Christ and his church

As with the various sacrifices of Leviticus, so too with the different festivals — all are types of Christ and his church. Festival, new moon or sabbaths, are 'a shadow of things to come, but the substance is of Christ' (Col. 2:17). Our task now is to discern the spiritual significance of the annual festivals.

The *Feast of Passover* finds its glorious fulfilment in the sacrifice of the true Paschal Lamb, the Lord Jesus Christ (1 Cor. 5:7; John 1:29,36; 19:36; 1 Peter 1:18-19). Uniting the Feast of Passover and the *Feast of Unleavened Bread,* and replacing them, is the New Covenant symbolic meal of bread and wine — representing the body and blood of the Saviour (Matt. 26:17-18,26-28; John 6:33-35,48-58). His is the pure life — 'holy, harmless, undefiled' (Heb. 7:26). We, his followers, are to 'keep the feast, not with old leaven, nor with the leaven of malice and wickedness, but with the unleavened bread of sincerity and truth' (1 Cor. 5:7-8).

Linked with the Feast of the Passover and the Feast of Unleavened Bread is the *Feast of First-fruits.* It was on this day of the year that the Lord Jesus arose from the dead, becoming 'the first-fruits of those who have fallen asleep' (1 Cor. 15:20). His resurrection is the sign and seal of the resurrection of all who believe in him (1 Cor. 15:23; cf. John 6:39-40; 1 Thess. 4:14,16-17).

Exactly seven weeks later the *Feast of Pentecost* is observed.

Jewish tradition links the celebration of Pentecost with the giving of the law to Moses. Arnot draws a Christian parallel from this tradition: 'At the feast of the Passover, the lamb was slain; at the feast of Pentecost, the law was given. Coincident with the slaying of the lamb was the death of Christ; coincident with the giving of the law was the descent of the Spirit... On the first Pentecost the law was written on tables of stone; on the last Pentecost came the Spirit, whose office it is to write that law on the living tables of the heart.'[15] While being an attractive idea this theory has one major flaw: there is no evidence to be found in either the Old or the New Testament for linking Pentecost to the giving of the law.

A more satisfactory approach is to look at the connection between the Feast of Pentecost and the coming of the Holy Spirit. It was on the Day of Pentecost that the Holy Spirit first descended to bring the promised blessing of the New Covenant to the nations of the earth (Acts 2:1-4). The Lord Jesus had to die in order to produce the harvest (John 12:24). Following his death, resurrection and glorification, the Holy Spirit was sent from heaven (John 7:39). The great harvest of the nations was to begin (Matt. 28:18-20; Acts 1:8; Luke 10:2; John 4:35-38; cf. Acts 2:41; 4:4; 5:14). Ingathering will be achieved through the worldwide proclamation of the gospel, the Word of God (Acts 2:6-11; 1 Peter 1:23,25; Rev. 7:9).

The seventh month of the religious calendar of the Israelites (September/October) was to form a high point of the year. It began with the *Feast of Trumpets* on the first day, followed by the *Day of Atonement* on the tenth day. From the fifteenth day the *Feast of Tabernacles* was observed for seven days. These festivals combine to make a powerful symbol of the finished work of Christ which culminates in his return to establish his everlasting kingdom on earth. The sound of trumpets is associated with the return of the Lord Jesus Christ (Matt. 24:31; 1 Cor. 15:52; 1 Thess. 4:16).

Christ is the atoning sacrifice (Heb. 9:26). On the Day of Atonement the high priest carried a censer of burning coals into the Holy of Holies. Once inside he sprinkled incense upon the coals so that 'the cloud of incense may cover the mercy seat' (Lev. 16:12-13). 'Thus Jesus fills the heavens with fragrance. His precious intercession sheds precious odours round. He pleads that all His work on earth is done. He spreads His wounded hands. He shows His wounded side. He proves that every term of the vast covenant of grace is kept, that sin is punished, and His people free… "Who shall lay anything to the charge of God's elect?"' [16]

The constant theme of the Levitical sacrifices is atonement through substitution — sin is removed by being carried by another (2 Cor. 5:21). The scapegoat released into the wilderness emphasizes the point: 'Aaron shall lay both his hands on the head of the live goat, confess over it all the iniquities of the children of Israel, and all their transgressions, concerning all their sins, putting them on the head of the goat, and shall send it away into the wilderness by the hand of a suitable man. The goat shall bear on itself all their iniquities…' (16:21-22).

The seventy bullocks sacrificed at the Feast of Tabernacles are thought to represent the seventy nations of the earth.[17] The one bullock additional to the seventy and sacrificed on the eighth day would then be understood to represent Israel. The final church will be composed 'of all nations, tribes, peoples, and tongues' (Rev. 7:9). This feast points to the end of the journey, the prosperous and peaceful life of the new world (2 Peter 3:13; Rev. 21:1-4), following the return of the Lord Jesus.

The Old Testament saints looked upon a hidden Saviour. The prophets struggled to understand the meaning and the timing 'of the sufferings of Christ and the glories that would follow' (1 Peter 1:11). We 'look upon an unveiled Saviour; and, going back to the Old, we can see far better than the Jews could, the features and form of Jesus the Beloved, under that veil'.[18]

The feasts of the Israelites (Lev. 23)

'… let no one judge you in food or in drink, or regarding a festival or a new moon or sabbaths, which are a shadow of things to come, but the substance is of Christ' (Col. 2:16-17).

	Feast	Day/Month	Meaning for Israel	Meaning for Christians	Biblical References
v.3	Sabbath	every seventh day	God's rest after creation	Salvation rest in Christ	Heb. 4:8-10; Matt. 11:28-30
v.5	Passover	14th of the first	Deliverance from Egypt (death of lamb)	Deliverance from sin (death of Christ)	I Cor. 5:7; I Peter 1:19; John 1:29; 19:31,36
vv.6-7	Unleavened Bread	15th of the first (7 days)	Haste of departure from Egypt	Sinless life of Christ	Heb. 7:26; I Cor. 5:7-8
vv.10-11	First-fruits	16th of the first	First crop early (barley) harvest	Resurrection (Christ the first-fruits from the dead)	Matt. 28:1,6; I Cor. 15:20; I Cor. 15:23
vv.15-16	Weeks (Pentecost)	50th day from First-fruits	First crop main (wheat) harvest	The Spirit comes: power for world evangelization	Acts 2:1-4; 1:8 Matt. 28:18-20
v.24	Trumpets	1st of the seventh	Sabbatical month	Announcing the imminent return of Christ	I Cor. 15:52; Matt. 24:31; I Thess. 4:16

	Feast	Day/Month	Meaning for Israel	Meaning for Christians	Biblical References
v.27	Day of Atonement	10th of the seventh	Humbling — reconciliation through sacrifice	Humbling — reconciliation through Christ's sacrifice	1 John 1:6-9; Rom. 5:11 2 Cor. 5:19
v.34	Tabernacles (Booths)	15th of the seventh (7 days)	End of all harvests	New heavens and a new earth	2 Peter 3:13; Rev. 21:1-4

Note: The Jewish day was calculated from evening to evening, that is, sunset to sunset (cf. Gen. 1:5,8,13).

Application

1. Holiness

The stress which this book places upon sacrifices is calculated to impress upon the reader two great truths: the holiness of the Lord and the sinfulness of humanity. No one can approach the living God except on the grounds of atonement. The seriousness of sin is evident in the number and nature of the sacrifices. It is also apparent in the punishments that the Lord specifies for wrongdoing.

There are those who are uncomfortable with the severity of some of the laws in Leviticus, and what seem to them to be the arbitrary and even trivial character of other requirements. They judge that these appear to them to be irreconcilable, on the one hand, with the mercy, and on the other hand, with the dignity and majesty of God. [19]

The severity of the penalties which were attached to the Levitical laws are consistent with the impeccable holy character of God. Liberal-minded critics may call these punishments harsh, but they underestimate the seriousness of sin, and how repugnant and insulting sin really is to the all-holy and all-glorious God (cf. Hab. 1:13). Even what we dare to call 'small' sins are singularly offensive to one who is morally perfect and unspeakably pure! No one can deny that Leviticus impresses the Israelite, and every serious reader, with God's absolute intolerance of sin and impurity (cf. 1 Cor. 6:9-10; Gal. 5:19-21; Rom. 1:18-32).

But here in Leviticus the very book which emphasizes the message from heaven that 'Without shedding of blood there is no remission' (Heb. 9:22) also shows with equal clarity and force that *with shedding of blood there is full remission of sins* for every believing penitent. 'For I will forgive their iniquity, and their sin I will remember no more' (Jer. 31:34) is clearly the promised implication within the sacrificial system. Even under the Old Covenant, believers may rejoice and praise God for the reality of pardon: 'As far as the east is from the west, so far has he removed our transgressions from us' (Ps. 103:12).

2. Worship

'God is a Spirit, and those who worship him must worship in spirit and truth' (John 4:24). Leadership in worship and teaching is still a serious responsibility. Those who teach the people of God 'shall receive a stricter judgement' (James 3:1). 'Let all things be done decently and in order' (1 Cor. 14:40).

It is interesting to note that, for a book so full of Christology, there is no reference in Leviticus to the Holy Spirit. Yet that is not surprising. The Holy Spirit's main task is not to draw attention to himself but to glorify Christ (John 16:13-14).

3. Separation

The apostle Peter quotes Leviticus when he urges Christians to live as obedient and transformed children of God: '… as he who called you is holy, you also be holy in all your conduct, because it is written, "Be holy, for I am holy"' (1 Peter 1:15-16; cf. Lev. 11:44,45; 19:2).

God makes the distinction between clean and unclean foods to symbolize the necessity of separation from ungodliness and corruption (20:22-26). The detailed regulations emphasize the importance of inward and outward purity. They instil the conviction that believers are to be separate from all that is ungodly and impure — a thought that permeates the whole of the Old and New Testaments (2 Cor. 6:14-18).[20]

Under the New Covenant the distinction between foods as clean or unclean has been abrogated (Acts 10:9-16). We receive our food with thanksgiving to God, 'for it is sanctified by the word of God and prayer' (1 Tim. 4:4-5). In matters of food and drink there is, nevertheless, an abiding principle which governs the manner and the amount of that which we consume: 'Whether you eat or drink, or whatever you do, do all to the glory of God' (1 Cor. 10:31). All areas of daily life are important to the Lord: whether in food or drink, in clothing or behaviour; whether single or married; whether in family, in church, or in the world; whether domestic, agricultural, trade or business, 'Let us cleanse ourselves from all filthiness of the flesh and spirit, perfecting holiness in the fear of God' (2 Cor. 7:1).

Conclusion

'Leviticus begins after redemption is known, and speaks of things connected with the access of a chosen people to God... Christ in His work is the sum and substance of these types, it is Christ as discerned by one who already knows the certainty of redemption: it is Christ as seen by one, who, possessing peace with God and deliverance, is able to look with joy at all that Christ has so fully been for him. Christ as the priest, the offerer, the offering; Christ as meeting all that a saved sinner needs to approach to God; Christ for the believer, and all that Christ is to the believer, as keeping up his communion with God; this is what we have distinctly set forth in the varied types of Leviticus. Exodus gives us the blood of the lamb, saving Israel in the land of Egypt. Leviticus gives us the priest and the offerings, meeting Israel's need in *their access to Jehovah*.' [21]

Leviticus teaches laws to establish Israel's physical, moral and spiritual well-being. The law of Leviticus was intended to prepare Israel for its world mission. Through Israel, the unapproachable holiness of God was to be communicated to the nations. He is still exactly what he was when he spoke to Moses on Mount Sinai or called to him out of the tent of meeting. The God of the New Testament is no different from the God of the Old. He is just as holy as he was then, just as intolerant of sin, just as merciful to the penitent sinner who trusts in the appointed blood of atonement as he was then. The message of Leviticus is loud and clear: 'Without shedding of blood there is no remission' (Heb. 9:22), and at the same time, by God's gracious provision, with the shedding of blood there is full remission.

The works of the LORD are great,
Studied by all who have pleasure in them.
His work is honourable and glorious,
And his righteousness endures for ever.
He has made his wonderful works to be remembered;
The LORD is gracious and full of compassion

(Ps. 111:2-4).

Numbers

(from 'numbering' Israel)

Author: Moses
(commonly accepted)

Key thought: 'Trials in the wilderness'

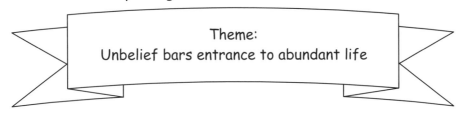

Theme:
Unbelief bars entrance to abundant life

'Do not harden your hearts, as in the
rebellion,
And as the day of trial in the
wilderness...'

Psalm 95:8

Summary

Numbers

The title 'Numbers' is likely to provoke a reaction of anticipated boredom. Derived from the Septuagint, the name conjures up thoughts of endless lists and registers. While the book does contain records of families, names and duties to perform, it also holds considerable interest for the Christian who begins with the conviction that 'All Scripture is given by inspiration of God, *and is profitable...*' (2 Tim. 3:16, emphasis added). There is much Christological interest contained in its pages, such as the smitten rock, the bronze serpent and the cities of refuge. There are also many spiritual lessons of great relevance to the Christian life. It would be better known by its Hebrew name *bemidhbar,* which means simply, 'In the wilderness', for this is the setting: from 'the Wilderness of Sinai' (1:1) to 'the Wilderness of Paran' (10:12) and on to 'the plains of Moab' (22:1).

The book of Numbers records a pathetic story. It carries various details about the wanderings of the Israelites in the wilderness. Here is the account of their frequent lapses into idolatry and immorality, together with God's judgement upon them for their sins. It covers the forty years in which the vast majority of the adults who left Egypt died in the wilderness through unbelief and disobedience (Heb. 3:17-19).

Author

The journeys of the children of Israel were recorded by Moses (33:2). There are no other references that indicate Moses as the author of this book, though he is frequently mentioned as receiving communication directly from God (1:1; 2:1; 3:5,11,14,40,44; 4:1,17,21, etc., — more than eighty references in all). While attributing the authorship to Moses we note that it is extremely unlikely that Moses wrote about his own humility! (12:3). This was probably added by Joshua or a later editor.[1]

Historical setting

The book of Exodus closed with the establishment of the children of Israel as a theocratic nation. A year after the departure from Egypt, the tent of meeting was completed, '... and the glory of the LORD filled the tabernacle' (Exod. 40:34). Two weeks later the Israelites celebrated, for the second time, the Passover instituted in Egypt as an annual memorial (Exod. 12:14,24; Num. 9:2-3,5). Leviticus links Exodus and Numbers in stipulating, in great detail, the manner and mode of worship and service for the Lord. The laws of Leviticus regulate the lifestyle of the Israelites in preparation for their entry into the land of Canaan. The bulk of the information in Leviticus was given over a seven-week period spanning the completion of the tabernacle to its dismantling for transportation (Exod. 40:17; Num. 10:11 — see table below).

Second year out of Egypt			
Occasion	Day	Month	Reference
Tabernacle erected	1	1	Exod. 40:2,17
Passover celebrated	14	1	Num. 9:2-3,5
Census ordered	1	2	Num. 1:1-2
Tabernacle dismantled	20	2	Num. 10:11

The book of Numbers in its commencement overlaps part of the period covered by Leviticus, though with a different purpose in mind. Here the preparation for leaving the Wilderness of Sinai is recorded, followed by the journey to Kadesh Barnea. After the failure of the Israelites to occupy Canaan, they are consigned to thirty-eight more years of wandering in the wilderness. When the punishment has been exacted by God upon the unbelieving adult males and they have died in the wilderness, the events which took place on the plains of Moab on the threshold of the promised land form the concluding section of the book. Numbers covers the years 1443–1404 B.C.

Outline

The flow of history and the unfolding of revelation are seen clearly in the Pentateuch. Genesis is the book of beginnings and teaches God's sovereignty in choosing whom he wills. Exodus deals with the deliverance of

Israel from Egypt and teaches how God redeems and delivers his people from the bondage of sin. Leviticus elucidates the holy requirements of God in worship and fellowship and the gracious provisions he has made to meet these requirements. Numbers follows, not just in a chronological order, but also in a thematic and theological sequence. This is the record of Israel's walk and warfare in the wilderness. Through this historic record Christians are taught spiritual lessons as to how believers pass through this life, with its sin and trials, with their repeated failures always without excuse, yet nevertheless experiencing God's faithfulness and long-suffering.[2]

God had given a promise to Abraham: 'I will establish my covenant between me and you and your descendants after you in their generations, for an everlasting covenant, to be God to you and your descendants after you. Also I give to you and your descendants after you the land in which you are a stranger, all the land of Canaan, as an everlasting possession; and I will be their God' (Gen. 17:7-8).

From Egypt the Israelites are being led by the Lord to the land promised to their fathers — to Abraham (Gen. 12:7; 13:15,17; 15:7; 17:7-8), to Isaac (Gen. 26:3-4), to Jacob (Gen. 28:13; 35:12; 48:3-4) and to their descendants (Exod. 12:25).

Part I: Preparation for leaving Sinai (1:1 - 10:10)

This first section covers a period of nineteen days from the 1st to the 20th of the second month of the second year after the departure from Egypt. The Lord requires a census to be taken exactly one month after the erection of the tabernacle. The first and the second census of Israel which the Lord ordered are both for the purpose of recording the number of men of twenty years and over, capable of military service (1:3; 26:2). This suggests an estimated total population of roughly two million.[3] For the Lord to miraculously feed such a vast company in the wilderness for forty years was no minor achievement.

The opening chapters provide information about the composition and numerical strength of the various tribes. Distinct places are assigned to each tribe while they are in the camp and also as they are on the move. Always the tabernacle is to be central. Encamped, three tribes are located on each of the four sides of the tent of meeting. On the move, six tribes, those to the east and south, move out first. The tabernacle follows. The six remaining tribes, those dwelling to the west and north, bring up the rear.

As well as marching instructions, God provides rules to govern the spiritual welfare of his people. To assist Aaron and the priests in the duties and responsibilities of the tabernacle, the tribe of Levi is separated instead of the first-born of every family of all twelve tribes (3:5-13).

The Lord is never merely concerned with the spiritual realm. He is equally concerned with the physical and moral welfare of his people. Contact with certain diseases would expose the people to obvious dangers, so strict laws of quarantine are laid down (5:1-4). Provision is also made for establishing innocence or guilt in the case of suspected infidelity (5:11-31). Because family life is so very important to God, he gives laws to protect and promote the stability of the family.

On a brighter note, when any of the Israelites have real cause for thanksgiving, then they can take 'the vow of a Nazirite' (6:1-21). This vow involves abstinence from eating or drinking anything produced from grapes, such as wine, vinegar, grape juice, fresh grapes or raisins. Vines are a symbol of the settled life. To refrain from the produce of the vine emphasizes the pilgrim nature of a godly life. They are not to cut their hair nor go near a dead body. Letting the hair grow is probably to give public indication of the vow. During this period such people are to be regarded as 'separated' or 'consecrated' to the Lord (6:8-9).

In relation to the second celebration of the Passover a question arises about what to do if someone is ceremonially unclean, for example, by touching a corpse. Moses turns to the Lord and receives instruction for the people (9:1-14). The Passover is a festival to remember what great actions God has performed in the past. God also provides guidance for the present. In the daytime the pillar of cloud represents God's guiding presence. At night the symbol is a pillar of fire (9:15-23; cf. Exod. 13:21-22). When the cloud moves then, and only then, the people are to move.

Two silver trumpets are made so that they can be blown when it is necessary to gather the people together (10:1-10). Different sounds on the trumpets indicate different messages for the people. At this point the Lord also provides Hobab, evidently a highly skilled Midianite guide (10:29-32). So together with the cloud of his presence, God provides a human guide.

Part II: Sinai to the plains of Moab (10:11 – 21:35)

The children of Israel have been in the wilderness for fourteen months when instructions are given to move north in the direction of the promised land. The camp at Mount Sinai, which has been their home for almost a year, is dismantled and once more the huge company is on the move. After walking for three days the people begin to display a spirit of unrest. The adults in this huge company are prone to murmuring and disobedience (cf. Exod. 15:24; 16:20; 17:3). They forget their former hardships and the extraordinary kindness the Lord has shown towards them. They look back to their life in Egypt and long for those former days. They talk about the food they used to eat when they were in that land — the fish, cucumbers, melons, leeks, onions and garlic. They remember the delicious savouries — but forget the disastrous slavery. The Lord reacts this time to their grumbling, and the fire of his judgement strikes the outskirts of the camp (11:1). He further responds to their criticism by giving them plenty of meat and predicts that they will react by gorging themselves on quails for a whole month until they are literally sick of the meat (11:19-20).[4] The Lord's anger is expressed towards those who 'yielded to craving' and he strikes them with a great plague (11:33-34).

The journey which should have taken eleven days (Deut. 1:2) takes over a month. Eventually they arrive at Kadesh Barnea. Approaching Canaan from the south, Moses sends spies from the Wilderness of Paran into the promised land to reconnoitre the area (13:2; see map, page 136). The spies spend almost six weeks walking through the land of Canaan and then return to their own people at Kadesh. The reports these men bring back test the faith and confidence of the Israelites. From a human perspective the odds are overwhelmingly against them. Ten spies give a bad report and discourage the Israelites. Two spies, Caleb and Joshua, though realistic about the strength of the enemy, nevertheless encourage the people to invade the land: 'The majority declared the land to be fair and beautiful, but impossible of possession, because of the giants and the walled cities. The men of the minority also saw the giants, and the walled cities, but they saw God. The majority had lost the clear vision of God, and therefore were filled with fear by the Anakim and the walled cities. With the loss of clear vision there was the loss of perfect confidence.'[5]

Moses and Aaron join Joshua and Caleb in trying to persuade the people to trust the Lord and enter Canaan. Joshua publicly voices his confidence in God: 'If the LORD delights in us, then he will bring us into this land and give it to us, "a land which flows with milk and honey"' (14:8; cf. Exod. 3:8).

Israel's journey from Mount Sinai to the plains of Moab

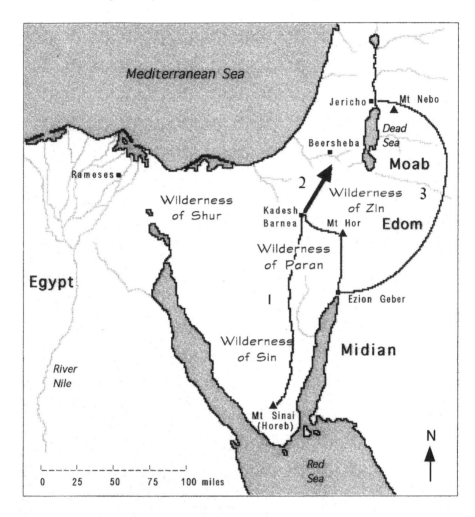

1	———	likely route from Mt Sinai to Kadesh Barnea
2	——▶	entry of the spies to reconnoitre the promised land
3	———	journey from Kadesh Barnea to the plains of Moab

Six weeks journeying to Sinai (Exod. 19:1).
Almost a year camped at Sinai (Num. 10:11).
Over a month journeying from Mt Sinai to Kadesh Barnea).

The people respond by accepting the report of the ten spies. This is the great turning-point in the history of Israel. The people will not go up and take the land of Canaan. Here is the tragic failure of the mass of the people at Kadesh Barnea. They are lost — in sight of home. What a catastrophe! Unbelief debars them from the promised land. The reluctance of the vast majority to listen to the voice of the Lord, to be confident in his promises and to obey his command, in spite of the obstacles, results in serious punishment: 'The carcasses of you who have murmured against me shall fall in this wilderness... Except for Caleb ... and Joshua... But your little ones, whom you said would be victims, I will bring in, and they shall know the land which you have despised... And your sons shall be shepherds in the wilderness forty years, and bear the brunt of your infidelity, until your carcasses are consumed in the wilderness. According to the number of the days in which you spied out the land, forty days, for each day you shall bear your guilt one year, namely forty years, and you shall know my rejection' (14:29-34).

And so the Israelites are destined to spend a further thirty-eight years in aimless wandering in the wilderness between the Mediterranean Sea and the two large forks of the Red Sea. Their history during this period is one of unbelief and fear, of quarrels and division, of rebellion and strife.

Forty years in the wilderness

Little is recorded about the events during those long years in the wilderness. When the thirty-eight years of judgement and punishment are ended, the people return again to Kadesh Barnea (20:1). 600,000 fighting men died during those years. Some were killed in the futile attack on the Amalekites, as Moses prophesied (14:40-45); others died under the direct judgement of God (e.g. 16:31-32,35), or as a result of the plague (16:49), or by suffering snake bites (21:6), while the remainder died of natural causes.

In spite of the discontent and complaining of the Israelites the Lord provides for them, often miraculously: 'If we are faithless, he remains faithful; he cannot deny himself' (2 Tim. 2:13).

At Kadesh an event occurs which is to have serious implications for Moses and Aaron. The Lord is once more to supply water for the vast company as he had done at Rephidim (20:7-12; cf. Exod. 17:1-7). The people, desperate for water, criticize Moses and Aaron. The two brothers respond by seeking God in prayer. When they turn to the Lord for help at 'the door of the tabernacle of meeting … they fell on their faces. And the glory of the LORD appeared to them. Then the LORD spoke to Moses, saying, "Take the rod; you and your brother Aaron gather the assembly together. Speak to the rock before their eyes, and it will yield its water; thus you shall bring water for them out of the rock, and give drink to the congregation and their animals." … And Moses and Aaron gathered the congregation together before the rock; and he said to them, "Hear now, you rebels! Must we bring water for you out of this rock?" Then Moses lifted his hand and struck the rock twice with his rod; and water came out abundantly, and the congregation and their animals drank' (Num. 20:6-11).

Moses does not obey the Word of the Lord. Instead of speaking to the rock with the rod of God in his hand, as God directed him, he speaks to the congregation with caustic words demonstrating considerable impatience. While the words do not actually express doubt and unbelief, they are highly inappropriate. Years later the psalmist explains what happened:

[The people] angered [God] also at the waters of strife,
So that it went ill with Moses on account of them;
Because they rebelled against his Spirit,
So that he spoke rashly with his lips

(Ps. 106:32-33).

Contrary to the instructions of the Lord, Moses strikes the rock twice with the rod, as though it somehow depended upon human exertion and not upon the power of God alone, or as if the promise of God would not have been fulfilled without all the smiting on his part. In the ill will expressed in his words the weakness of faith is displayed. This normally faithful servant of God, worn out with the numerous temptations, allows himself to be overcome, so that he stumbles and does not honour the Lord before the people. Moses discredits the Lord in his harsh words and rash action. The sin is all the more grievous in that Moses is leader of the people and he acts unworthily of his office. God punishes him by withdrawing his office from him before he has finished the work entrusted to him. He is not to lead the congregation over Jordan. He will not set foot in the promised land (27:12-14).

In some ways the behaviour of Moses is understandable. Forty years earlier the Lord had promised to bring water from a rock. On that occasion Moses was commanded to 'strike the rock, and water will come out of it, that the people may drink' (Exod. 17:6). This servant of God noted for his scrupulous care in communicating the details of God's law forgets himself for a moment, with serious consequences.

The Israelites move and journey south-east to Mount Hor. Aaron is succeeded in the office of high priest by his son Eleazar just before he dies on Mount Hor. Following thirty days of mourning for their departed leader, the children of Israel resume their travels. They travel south to Ezion Geber on the tip of the Red Sea before passing west then north to go around the land of Edom (see map, page 136). The journey from Mount Hor takes them in the opposite direction to the land of Canaan, and 'The soul of the people became very discouraged on the way' (21:4). Rebellion erupts again in the ranks. Once more the people sin against the Lord. They are critical of the food that the Lord supplies for them. They have come to loathe what they now describe as 'this worthless bread' (21:5). Responding to their murmuring and complaining, God sends swift punishment — a plague of poisonous snakes. The camp of the Israelites is overrun and many of the people are bitten and die. In desperation the people acknowledge their sin and plead with Moses to pray for them. Moses accedes to their request and in answer to his prayers the Lord provides a means of healing that requires faith and obedience. A bronze serpent is to be made and erected in the centre of the camp with instructions that anyone bitten by a snake should look at the bronze serpent and healing will then be assured (21:4-9).

The children of Israel continue their journey. Rapidly moving from one camp to another, they progress towards the promised land. As they approach the land of the Amorites they seek permission to pass through the territory without conflict. They are happy to give an undertaking of non-interference but Sihon King of the Amorites will not hear of it. He fights against Israel and is defeated. Og, the King of Bashan, also seeks to resist Israel's passage through his land. He too suffers defeat.

Part III: Events on the plains of Moab (22:1 - 36:13)

The children of Israel arrive on the threshold of the promised land — 'in the plains of Moab on the side of the Jordan across from Jericho' (22:1). Balak, the King of Moab, becomes increasingly disturbed. He does not want Israelites as his neighbours. He is well aware of the defeat of Sihon, King of the Amorites, and Og, King of Bashan. Balak's strategy is significantly different from that of Sihon and Og. He sends for Balaam, a non-Israelite prophet, to curse the Israelites as they draw close to his realm. The

Lord overrules and Balaam, rather than cursing, blesses Israel instead (22:1 – 24:25).

Although the Lord continually performs marvellous deeds for his people they still fall to the temptations of the flesh and indulge in idolatry and immorality (25:1-18). What the enemy cannot achieve through force of arms, the devil can accomplish through subtle insinuation and corruption.

Forty years after the exodus from Egypt a new census is taken of the children of Israel (26:1-51; cf. 1:1-46). Excluding the tribe of Levi, there are now 601,730 males twenty years of age and older. Only two of the original men out of 603,550 of the first census (1:46) are still alive — Caleb and Joshua (26:64-65). These are the only two adult males of those who left Egypt who are to be allowed to enter into the promised land. The Lord keeps his word — of judgement as well as of promise.

A new leader is appointed for the second generation of wilderness Israelites (27:16-23). Joshua is to succeed Moses as their commander-in-chief. He will lead the nation into Canaan. From this point to the end of the book of Numbers the outlook is positive. The second generation faces a new test of faith: will they willingly and wholeheartedly follow Joshua into Canaan?

The Lord listens to the concerns of the daughters of Zelophehad and a new law is enacted to safeguard the transference of inheritance to a daughter where there is no son (27:1-11). In several areas, for example those of ceremonies and vows, the law is finalized in preparation for settling in Canaan.

The book of Numbers concludes on the threshold of the promised land: 'These are the commandments and the judgements which the LORD commanded the children of Israel by the hand of Moses in the plains of Moab by the Jordan, across from Jericho' (Num. 36:13).

Christ and his church

As in the wilderness days covered in Exodus, the tabernacle, the pillar of cloud, the pillar of fire, the manna and the water from the rock are all found here in Numbers. These signify the providence of God: the tabernacle and pillar represent God's presence; the manna and the water from the rock represent God's provision. All these have special importance in relation to Christ (see pages 91-2). He is the great presence of God with his people. He is the great provision of God for his people.

Here in Numbers there is a repeat of the command of God to bring *water from a rock* (20:7-11; cf. Exod. 17:5-6). On the first occasion Moses had to 'strike' the rock (Exod. 17:6). On the second occasion he has to 'speak' to the rock (20:8). The Hebrew for the first-mentioned rock [*tsuwr*] signifies low-lying bedrock, whereas the Hebrew for the second rock [*celà*] is a high and exalted rock. The rods which Moses is instructed to take with him are different. The first time, at the beginning of the wilderness journey, God told him, 'Take in your hand your rod with which you struck the river' (Exod. 17:5). This rod was to strike the rock. The second time, forty years later, not long before the entry into the promised land, God told Moses to take a different rod. 'So Moses took the rod *from before the LORD as he commanded him*' (20:8-9, emphasis added; cf. 17:10). This rod is not the rod of Moses but the rod of Aaron the priest ('before the LORD' in 20:9 means the same as 'before the Testimony' in 17:10). To strengthen the concept of the priestly rod, this time Moses is to take Aaron with him (20:8). On the first occasion Aaron is not mentioned!

The striking of the rock the second time is even more serious when its significance is understood. Paul says of the Israelites, '... they drank of that spiritual Rock that followed them, and that Rock was Christ' (1 Cor. 10:4). Christ is symbolized on both occasions: in the first striking of a low-lying (humble) rock as a Saviour 'smitten by God, and afflicted ... for our transgressions' (Isa. 53:4-5). By his death he supplies living water, spiritual life, to his needy people (John 4:10; 7:37-39; 19:34). The second rock denotes him as the exalted Saviour, the High Priest in heaven. He is not to be smitten twice.[6] 'We have such a high priest, who is seated at the right hand of the throne of the Majesty in the heavens' (Heb. 8:1). He continually supplies the living water of spiritual life (Rev. 22:1,17).

On account of his disobedience Moses is not permitted to enter the land of Canaan. In terms of spiritual analogy, it would not have been appropriate for him to enter the promised land. He represents the law (John 1:17). The law is not able to bring a sinner to heaven; only Christ is able to do that (Rom. 8:1-4; 3:20-24; Gal. 2:19-21). Moses is replaced by Joshua (the Hebrew equivalent of the name 'Jesus'), the captain who leads God's people home (Heb. 12:1-2).

Another outstanding type of Christ found in the book of Numbers is the *bronze serpent* (21:6-9). It is the only occasion when the Lord God presents a type of his Son that is disturbing and offensive. Thoughts of a type of Christ here would be immediately dismissed if it were not for the fact that the Lord Jesus likens himself to the serpent raised up in the wilderness (John 3:14-15). The analogy is not simply that the Saviour would be nailed to a cross, as the snake was fastened to a pole, and erected for all to see. There is a far deeper meaning to this analogy. There are features about this period in Israel's history which shed a profound light upon the Crucified One. The people sin (21:5; cf. v.7). The Lord sends punishment (21:6). The people repent and seek forgiveness (21:7). The Lord provides the means of healing which requires faith and obedience (21:8).

The measures which the Lord adopts for healing of the snakebites are highly disturbing. The serpent is the symbol of everything that is evil from the first book of the Bible even to the last. It is the serpent in the Garden of Eden that Satan uses as his agent in tempting Adam and Eve to sin. In the book of Revelation the devil is referred to as 'that serpent of old' (Rev. 12:9). The associations could not be more unpalatable. Nevertheless, the Lord's self-identification with the serpent in the wilderness cannot be passed over lightly. He identifies himself with the solution to the problem of sin. That solution is itself related to the curse of God (the poisonous serpents). Christ is seen therefore as identified, at great personal cost, with the sin (2 Cor. 5:21), with the curse (Gal. 3:13), and with the cure (John 3:14-16; cf. Num. 21:9).

Where was the power of healing? It is clear that the power to heal did not reside in the serpent of bronze. There was no answer to that question until the day a young Jew was executed just outside the capital city of Judah.

A type of Christ is suggested in the *water of purification* (19:9-22). This was God's gracious provision for symbolic cleansing (cf. Ezek. 36:25; Titus 3:5; John 13:8). The water contained the ashes of a red heifer offered as a burnt offering for sin. The water symbolizes cleansing; the ashes of the heifer represent the atoning sacrifice. Together these two point to 'the blood of Jesus Christ' which 'cleanses us from all sin' and 'from all unrighteousness' (1 John 1:7,9).

The *cities of refuge* (35:9-34) remind Christians that the Saviour is our hiding place. Six cities were scattered throughout Israel — three on the west side of the River Jordan and three on its east side. They were to be easily accessible so that the one who had committed manslaughter could take sanctuary from the avenger of blood. In the same way the Saviour is always within reach. In him we hide. To him we have 'fled for refuge' (Heb. 6:18), echoing the words of David who cried out, 'Deliver me, O LORD, from my enemies; in you I take shelter' (Ps. 143:9). The apostle Paul says he has renounced all his natural advantages as a Hebrew, counting 'all things loss for the excellence of the knowledge of Christ Jesus' so that he might be 'found in him' not having his 'own righteousness, which is from the law, but that which is through faith in Christ, the righteousness which is from God by faith' (Phil. 3:8-9).

Prophecies of Christ

When Balak the King of Moab called in the non-Israelite prophet Balaam, he expected him to curse Israel and enable the Moabites to win a decisive victory. In the event Balaam did not curse them but uttered four prophetic blessings upon Israel. The final prophecy includes these words:

I see him, but not now;
I behold him, but not near;
A Star shall come out of Jacob;
A sceptre shall rise out of Israel,
And batter the brow of Moab,
And destroy all the sons of tumult.

And Edom shall be a possession;
Seir also, his enemies, shall be a possession,
While Israel does valiantly.
Out of Jacob one shall have dominion,
And destroy the remains of the city

(24:17-19).

Some time in the future a powerful ruler will rise from the Israelites and win a remarkable victory over their enemies. The rising star represents the appearance of a glorious ruler or king, and this is confirmed by saying, 'A sceptre shall rise out of Israel,' for the sceptre is a symbol of dominion (Gen. 49:10). 'By this Ruler, the Jews from the earliest times have understood the Messiah, either exclusively, or else principally, with a secondary reference to David.'[7] 'The fulfilment of this prophecy commenced with the subjugation of the Edomites by David (2 Samuel 8:14; 1 Kings 11:15-16; 1 Chronicles 18:12-13), but it will not be completed till "the end of the days," when all the enemies of God and His Church will be made the footstool of Christ (Psalm 110:1 sqq.).'[8]

One of the reasons given by Hengstenberg for rejecting this prophecy as a prediction of Christ is that 'No evidence can be drawn from the New Testament.'[9] This would appear to be an unusual oversight for such a scholar. At least two significant verses are to be found: 'We also have the prophetic word made more sure, which you do well to heed as to a light that shines in a dark place, until the day dawns and the morning star rises in your hearts...' (2 Peter 1:19). 'I, Jesus, have sent my angel to testify to you these things in the churches. I am the Root and the Offspring of David, the Bright and Morning Star' (Rev. 22:16).

This prophecy of Balaam may also be connected with the leading of the wise men by means of a star (Matt. 2:2,9). Christ is 'the Bright and Morning Star'. He is the Ruling Star out of Jacob.

Application

Numbers is a bewildering book in many ways. Its style and arrangement are baffling: 'Lists of tribes are followed by accounts of historical events, regulations about sacrifice are given alongside details of intricate legal controversies. It is all very important as history, for we want to know the route of God's people as they made their way to the promised land, but what are the main lessons of this book for a Christian today?'[10]

That this book is designed to be of benefit for Christians is beyond dispute (cf. 1 Cor. 10:1-13). 'For whatever things were written before were written for our learning, that we through the patience and comfort of the Scriptures might have hope' (Rom. 15:4).

1. Prepared for service

The 'numbering' which takes place is, in reality, a registration for service. It shows that every believer is a soldier and that every soldier has something to do (2 Tim. 2:3-4; Eph. 6:13-17). It further demonstrates that there is strength in organization (2:1-34). God wants his work done, in the same way as he requires his worship to be conducted — 'decently and in order' (1 Cor. 14:40). Every believer has his special task to perform in the kingdom of God (Rom. 12:4-8; 1 Cor. 12:4-31; Eph. 4:16). Special tasks require special talents: spiritual gifts and graces are more necessary than mental or physical qualifications.

2. Gifts for the work of God

The seventh chapter enumerates at great length the offerings of the tribal princes. They each brought exactly the same gifts. Rather than mentioning them as a whole, the narrative spells out each man's contribution individually. The repetition makes the point: 'God delights to honour the gifts of His children.'[11] The New Testament reinforces the same truth. The Lord Jesus takes special note of the poor widow placing her two mites in the treasury. He draws the attention of his disciples to her sacrificial giving (Mark 12:42-44). When a woman pours expensive perfume over his feet, the Lord Jesus defends her action and declares it to be the extravagance of faith and love (Luke 7:37-38,47).

The tithe (ten per cent of real income) became the standard for the Israelites in their giving (Gen. 14:20; 28:20-22; Neh. 10:38-39; Mal. 3:8-10; Prov. 3:9-10). But the tithe was not the sum total of their giving. There were many other free-will contributions that the people made to the work of God.

If the principles of giving outlined in the New Testament were observed by the church there would be no shortage of funds for ministry, evangelism or church-planting at home or abroad: 'He who sows sparingly will also reap sparingly, and he who sows bountifully will also reap bountifully. So let each one give as he purposes in his heart, not grudgingly or of necessity; for God loves a cheerful giver' (2 Cor. 9:6-7).

Tithing is a guideline, and only a guideline, for New Covenant believers. For some believers the giving of ten per cent of income will involve real self-sacrifice. For others in the Western world it is too easy and leaves far too much room for self-indulgence. To the Israelites the Lord said, 'You shall remember the LORD your God, for it is he who gives you power to get wealth' (Deut. 8:18). And to Christians, Paul sends the message: 'Command those who are rich in this present age not to be haughty, nor to trust in uncertain riches but in the living God, who gives us richly all things to enjoy, and to do good, to be rich in good works, ready to give, willing to share, storing up for themselves a good foundation for the time to come, that they may lay hold on eternal life' (1 Tim. 6:17-19).

3. Grumbling

The first twenty-five chapters in the book of Numbers illustrate a disgruntled people. The Israelites were constantly moaning — about the journey, the desert, the food, the giants, their leaders. The book of Numbers might well be named 'the book of murmurings', for it contains several major incidents of despondency and gloom. Seven distinct episodes of grumbling and complaining are noted from chapters 11-21. The children of Israel complained:

- about the journey (?) (11:1-3);
- about the food (11:4-6);
- about the giants (13:33 – 14:3);
- about their leaders (16:3);
- about divine judgement (16:41);
- about the desert (20:2-5);
- about the manna (21:5; cf. 11:6).

From the many references to grumbling, murmuring and complaining which appear in Scripture, it might well be concluded that this is one of the major failings in the spiritual life: 'Do all things without murmuring and disputing, that you may become blameless and harmless, children of God without fault in the midst of a crooked and perverse generation, among whom you shine as lights in the world, holding fast the word of life...' (Phil. 2:14-16).

4. Unbelief

This fourth book of the Pentateuch contains warnings regarding the dangers and serious consequences of sin and unbelief. The wilderness was the testing-ground of faith: 'And you shall remember that the LORD your God led you all the way these forty years in the wilderness, to humble you and test you, to know what was in your heart, whether you would keep his commandments or not' (Deut. 8:2).

Failure to trust God and enter into the promised land resulted in thirty-eight more years of wandering in the wilderness. Under the sentence of death through their unbelief, the large proportion was doomed to die for their sins there in the wastelands. They were not to enter the promised land. 'Beware, brethren, lest there be in any of you an evil heart of unbelief in departing from the living God... For who, having heard, rebelled? Indeed, was it not all who came out of Egypt, led by Moses? Now with whom was he angry forty years? Was it not with those who sinned, whose corpses fell in the wilderness? And to whom did he swear that they would not enter his rest, but to those who did not obey? So we see that they could not enter in because of unbelief. Therefore, since a promise remains of entering his rest, let us fear lest any of you seem to have come short of it. For indeed the gospel was preached to us as well as to them; but the word which they heard did not profit them, not being mixed with faith in those who heard it' (Heb. 3:12,16-19; 4:1-2).

Illness and death are sometimes *directly* related to individual sin. Such is the connection in the case of the paralysed man at the pool of Bethesda (John 5:1-15).[12] The same is true in the deaths of Ananias and Sapphira (Acts 5:1-11). Their instant deaths were the result of the immediate judgement of God. The link between sin and suffering, and sin and death, is such that Paul warns the Corinthians about insincerity at the Lord's Supper: 'For he who eats and drinks in an unworthy manner eats and drinks judgement to himself, not discerning the Lord's body. *For this reason many are weak and sick among you, and many sleep'* (1 Cor. 11:29-30, emphasis added).

All suffering, illness and death is related to sin (Rom. 5:12; 6:23), but not all suffering, illness and death is directly related to specific sins committed by that individual. There is the classic case of Job, who suffered though he was righteous before God. There is the instance of the man born blind, where neither his parents nor himself were directly responsible for his affliction (John 9:2-3).

5. Pressing forward

As we read this story of the Hebrew people and their travels, our thoughts turn to our own walk with God. The Bible pictures the Christian life as a journey: 'For here we have no continuing city, but we seek the one to come' (Heb. 13:14). We are to live 'as sojourners and pilgrims' (1 Peter 2:11). Having entered the narrow gate or door (which is Christ, John 10:9), we are to walk the 'difficult ... way which leads to life' (Matt. 7:13-14). When the apostle Paul pleads with the Christians at Ephesus 'to lead a life worthy of the calling with which [they] were called', his actual words are, '*walk* worthily...' (Eph. 4:1). And again to the Corinthians he writes, 'For though we *walk* in the flesh, we do not war according to the flesh' (2 Cor. 10:3). 'For we *walk* by faith, not by sight' (2 Cor. 5:7). The Word of God recognizes that, as we walk, it is easy to take a wrong turn and lose a sense of direction. This is what the book of Numbers is all about. In the period of history covered by this fourth book of the Bible, the children of Israel made a number of serious mistakes. These events and occurrences were recorded for our learning and instruction.

It is an insult to God to look back with longing to the old sinful, pre-conversion days. Within a relatively short time in the wilderness, the Israelites were looking back to their life in Egypt and hankering for those former days. They talked about the food they used to eat when they were in that land — the fish, cucumbers, melons, leeks, onions and garlic. They did not appreciate the blessings which they were experiencing — freedom from slavery, fellowship with God, miraculous provision of food and guidance, and the constant prospect of the promised land before them — 'a land which flows with milk and honey' (14:8).

The Lord Jesus warned the Jews of his day to 'remember Lot's wife', who looked back (Luke 17:32; cf. Gen. 19:17,26). He also said, 'No one, having put his hand to the plough, and looking back, is fit for the kingdom of God' (Luke 9:62).

The Lord not only teaches the danger of looking back with longing; he also encourages believers to be constantly pressing forward: '... forgetting those things which are behind and reaching forward to those things which are ahead, I press towards the goal for the prize of the upward call of God in Christ Jesus' (Phil. 3:13-14). When faced with seemingly insurmountable obstacles, such as giants and impregnable cities (Num. 13:28), the outcome will depend upon whether we see 'the difficulties in the light of God, or God in the shadow of the difficulties'.[13] The Lord wants realism in his people, but above all else he requires a strong confidence in his purposes and power (2 Kings 6:16). Let us run with patience ... 'looking unto Jesus' (Heb. 12:2).

Conclusion

The Lord leads his people from the bondage of Egypt out into the great unknown with the promised land as the ultimate goal. The first phase of the wilderness journey requires trust and confidence in the Lord's leading and the Lord's providing. The second phase displays the failure of the vast majority of the Israelites through their unbelief and disobedience. The result is thirty-eight more years spent in the wilderness. The third and final phase shows a new generation following Joshua and Caleb and taking up positions for entry into the promised land.

God is concerned about the practical details of our everyday life. He cares about his people's well-being. He provides for their needs. He sustains them daily. He guides them repeatedly. He fights their battles. He frustrates their enemies. He is constantly close at hand. The thing that God cannot abide is sin. The thing that none can hide is sin. For, 'Be sure your sin will find you out' (32:23).

Deuteronomy

('second law')

Author: Moses
(commonly accepted)

Key thought: 'Obedience'

Theme:
Preparation for entry into the promised land

'For … by this word you shall prolong
your days in the land which you cross
over the Jordan to possess.'
                    Deuteronomy 32:47

Summary

Deuteronomy

The name 'Deuteronomy' derives from the Septuagint translation of the Old Testament. It means 'second law' and came about because of a mistranslation of the phrase, 'a copy of this law' (17:18). 'Second law' suggests a new law in addition to the first one. This is not the case here. This book contains the original law given almost forty years earlier, repeated and amplified in preparation for the new generation of Israelites to enter into Canaan. It also includes a renewal of covenant obligations as Israel reaffirms a commitment to walk in obedience to the Lord. Under the Lord's direction, Moses also appoints his successor, the man who will lead Israel into the promised land.

In Exodus, Leviticus and Numbers, the Lord speaks directly to Moses, or through Moses to Israel. In Deuteronomy Moses himself addresses Israel. The gist of his message is this: the Lord is a *unique* God, the God of heaven and earth, spiritual in his being; Israel is a *unique* people especially loved by the Lord. The relationship between God and Israel is *unique:* he is their Father; they are his children and must love him and serve him. Israel owes the Lord a great debt of gratitude.[1]

The book contains a number of discourses, or sermons, given by Moses, with a final chapter recording his death.

Author

No man was more qualified to receive revelations and instructions from God than 'a prophet like Moses, whom the LORD knew face to face' (34:10). When it comes to any passage in the Pentateuch where the authorship of Moses is questioned there seems little to be gained from long and involved arguments in defence. Where the Bible speaks of Moses as the author, there the Christian reader will be content: 'Whatever in Scripture — be it Old or New Testament — is directly or by clear implication ascribed to Moses should be assigned to his authorship.'[2] That the occasional insertion was made by later editors, adding a comment here or there to update or clarify geographical (3:13b-14) or historical (10:6-9) detail, does not undermine this position.[3] What is of paramount importance is that the real and ultimate Author of the whole of the Pentateuch is not in doubt — he is God the Holy Spirit (2 Peter 1:20-21; 2 Tim. 3:16). The record can therefore be trusted.

Deuteronomy makes it clear that its contents are substantially the work of Moses. For example: 'So Moses wrote this law and delivered it to the priests, the sons of Levi, who bore the ark of the covenant of the LORD, and to all the elders of Israel. And Moses commanded them, saying... So it was, when Moses had completed writing the words of this law in a book, when they were finished, that Moses commanded the Levites, who bore the ark of the covenant of the LORD, saying: "Take this Book of the Law, and put it beside the ark of the covenant of the LORD your God, that it may be there as a witness..." ' (31:9-10,24-26).

The Sadducees in New Testament times attributed the authorship of Deuteronomy to Moses (Mark 12:19; cf. Deut. 25:5–6). There was no word to the contrary from the Lord Jesus Christ.

It has been suggested that the book of Deuteronomy may have been 'a special favourite' of the Lord Jesus Christ in his childhood, youth and manhood.[4] To support this view it is pointed out that the Saviour quoted *only* from this book in his conflict with Satan in the great temptations. He was in the wilderness preparing for his ministry of preaching, teaching and healing, spending almost six weeks fasting, and being tempted by Satan (Matt. 4:1-11; Luke 4:1-13; cf. Deut. 8:3; 6:16; 6:13). A more likely explanation for his quotations exclusively from Deuteronomy is that the Lord was indicating the profound link between his period of trial in the wilderness (forty days and forty nights) and the wanderings of the Israelites in the wilderness for forty years.[5] Jesus is the Captain of our salvation (Heb. 2:10 AV); he is the New Covenant Joshua, about to commence his ministry. He will do all that is necessary to gather his people together ready to lead them into the heavenly Canaan, the ultimate promised land.

Historical setting

The forty years of wandering in the wilderness have almost ended (1:3). Israel is camped in the plains of Moab on the east of the Jordan, across from Jericho. The adult generation of Israelites which left Egypt has died in the wilderness: 'For who, having heard, rebelled? Indeed, was it not all who came out of Egypt, led by Moses? Now with whom was [God] angry forty years? Was it not with those who sinned, whose corpses fell in the wilderness? And to whom did he swear that they would not enter his rest, but to those who did not obey? So we see that they could not enter in because of unbelief' (Heb. 3:16-19).

This was the punishment exacted by the Lord upon all those males over twenty years of age who refused to enter the promised land when the first opportunity arose. Caleb and Joshua, the two faithful spies who honoured God and trusted him, were rewarded by being given the distinction to lead Israel into Canaan.

This fifth book of the Pentateuch is a collection of the final addresses given by Moses to the Israelites in the plains of Moab: 'These are the words which Moses spoke to all Israel on this side of the Jordan in the wilderness' (1:1). Deuteronomy begins where Numbers ended (cf. Num. 36:13), and covers a period of about a month immediately prior to the successful crossing of the Jordan to take possession of Canaan. It is important that the law should be repeated and expounded to the new generation before they make their entry into their own land. Moses prepares the people for two highly significant and imminent events: his death, and the battles to gain the promised land.

The larger part of the contents of Deuteronomy was probably committed to writing soon after the addresses were given by Moses and shortly before his death (1404 B.C.). At 120 years of age, 'His eyes were not dim nor his natural vigour abated' (34:7).

Outline

Part I: God's acts (1:1 – 4:43)

Moses summarizes the Lord's guidance from Horeb (Mount Sinai) to Kadesh Barnea. He once more reminds the people of the rebellion and unbelief of their parents who refused to enter into Canaan. This resulted in another thirty-eight years being spent in the wilderness. When the forty years of wandering in the wilderness came to an end, the Lord directed the Israelites back to Kadesh Barnea in preparation for taking the land of Canaan. From Kadesh Barnea they moved in a roundabout way to the plains of Moab, on the east of the River Jordan opposite Jericho. En route the Lord gave them victory over the attacking forces of King Sihon and King Og. God also foiled the plans of Balak, King of the Amorites. The land east of Jordan was made secure so that the Israelites could proceed in crossing the river and taking Canaan.

Moses reminds the people of what the Lord has done in bringing them out of Egypt. He recounts the mighty deeds of God. God is about to fulfil another of his promises by giving them their own land (1:8). The threefold blessing which God gave Abraham concerned the promise of land, the promise of numerous descendants and the promise of outstanding blessing (Gen. 12:1-3,7). During the years spent in Egypt, the years covered by the book of Exodus, the family of Abraham increased rapidly through his grandson Jacob. The promise of numerous descendants was moving towards realization. In Deuteronomy the Israelites are on the threshold of receiving the second part of the promise — their own land. The final aspect of the threefold promise is that in Abraham 'all the families of the earth shall be blessed'. That promise will await the coming of the Messiah with his worldwide blessing of salvation.

Moses urges the people to faithfulness and calls for their obedience to the Lord and his law (4:1-40). He then establishes three cities of refuge in the land to the east of Jordan, for those who commit manslaughter (that is, unintentional killing, as distinct from murder).

Part II: God's laws (4:44 - 26:19)

This main section deals with a series of laws and exhortations about various aspects of life. Moses begins by expounding the Decalogue (the Ten Commandments) given by the Lord on Mount Sinai. He then reminds the congregation of their covenantal obligations to worship and serve the true God and instructs the Israelites to preserve these laws and communicate them to succeeding generations: 'Hear, O Israel: The LORD our God, the LORD is one! You shall love the LORD your God with all your heart, with all your soul, and with all your might. And these words which I command you today shall be in your heart: you shall teach them diligently to your children, and shall talk of them when you sit in your house, when you walk by the way, when you lie down, and when you rise up' (Deut. 6:4-7).

These laws have not only to be taught; they have also to be obeyed. If the people do not obey, they will soon be drawn into idolatry instead of the pure worship of the living God. In order to remove the temptation to idolatry the Israelites are commanded to exterminate the Canaanites. They are to be the instruments of God's righteous judgement against wicked and idolatrous nations (9:4-5).

Possessing and maintaining possession of the promised land is made dependent upon the loving obedience of the Israelites as the people of God (8:1; 11:8-9; 16:20). The people are reminded of the sins of past generations and warned about self-righteousness. They will owe their conquest and possession of Canaan, not to their own righteousness, but solely to the compassion and covenant faithfulness of the Lord.

Love and obedience will be rewarded with blessing (7:12-24; 11:1-25). Disobedience will bring a curse (11:28).

In expounding the main laws originally given at Sinai, Moses adds others that have direct relevance to living in a settled community in Canaan. Worship will be in a central location appointed by God (12:1-28). Idolatry is a great evil (12:29-32) and must be dealt with decisively. Three cases are cited. The first is that of a false prophet who leads the people into idolatry. He is to be put to death (13:1-5). The second is that of a close member of the family who entices others to idolatry. The guilty party has to be stoned to death (13:6-11). The third case refers to a whole city that has been led into idolatry. Upon hearing an accusation, a full investigation has to be carried out. If the case is proven then all the inhabitants of that city are to be put to the sword (13:12-18).

In anticipation of the death of Moses attention is given to providing orderly government for Israel by the establishment of judges, courts of appeal, priests, Levites, kings and prophets (16:18 – 18:22). Israel is a theocracy — a nation governed by God. The Lord does the choosing. Twenty-five times the verb 'choose' occurs in this section, emphasizing the Lord's sovereign choice. God chose Israel. He chose the priests and the Levites (18:5). He will choose the place where he will be worshipped (12:26). He will choose a king (17:15).

In seeking to discern God's choice of a king the people are to note that the qualifications for kingship are quite strict:

1. He must be an Israelite.

2. He must not increase the number of horses because this may lead the Israelites back to Egypt (good horses were bred by the Egyptians — 1 Kings 10:28).

3. He must not have many wives because they may turn his heart from the true God.

4. He must not amass silver and gold because these may make him self-sufficient, self-indulgent and arrogant.

5. He must have his own copy of the law and read it, meditate upon it, and obey it (17:14-20).

When Israel comes into her own land there will be need for further revelations from the Lord. The Lord will establish the prophetic office for this purpose. Detailed guidelines are laid down to distinguish the true from the false prophet. The nine abominations of the Canaanites, for which they are to be dispossessed, are spelt out (18:9-14). These practices must never be found among the people of God. The true prophet must be: firstly, an Israelite; secondly, like Moses, a mediator between God and the people; thirdly, one who speaks only the words of God; and, fourthly, one whose prophecies come true (18:15-22).

Once the land has been occupied, three cities of refuge are to be set up so that anyone guilty of manslaughter — that is, accidental, unpremeditated killing — might run there and be safe (19:1-7; cf. 4:41-43; Exod. 21:12-14; Num. 35:9-34). Changing a neighbour's land boundaries is forbidden (19:14), and laws of witness are laid down (19:15-21). Even the principles governing warfare are spelt out (20:1-20). Only when the offer of peace has been rejected by the enemy should an attack be mounted (20:10-15).

The laws of Deuteronomy indicate that spirituality is not to be divorced from the rest of life. Love for God is to be expressed in every area of life: civil, domestic and personal. Numerous practical issues are covered, including the treatment of women captured in war, the inheritance rights of the first-born, punishment for a disobedient son, the burial of criminals who have been hanged on a tree, respect for a neighbour's animals and property, various laws governing sexual behaviour, grounds for exclusion from the congregation, maintenance of cleanliness in the camp, treatment of runaway slaves, divorce and remarriage, freedom from military service for one year following marriage, articles taken as security against a loan, warnings against injustice, restrictions on corporal punishment, levirate marriage,[6] and fighting and fraud (21:10 – 25:16). Instruction is also given that the Amalekites are to be destroyed because of their unprovoked attack upon Israel (25:17-19).

This section ends with rules about services of thanksgiving to God for his mercy and providence. Offerings of first-fruits and tithes are to be brought to the priest (26:1-15).

Part III: God's covenant (27:1 - 30:20)

On entry into the promised land the Israelites are to assemble in two companies, one upon Mount Gerizim and the other upon Mount Ebal. Six tribes on Mount Gerizim are to speak blessings upon those who are obedient and believing (27:12; 28:1-14). Six tribes on Mount Ebal are to declare the curses that will fall upon those who are disobedient and unbelieving (27:13-26; 28:15-68). These blessings and curses are listed in detail to enforce the vital importance of obedience and faith.

The covenant renewed by Israel is not simply a commitment to the legal requirements of a contract (29:1-29).[7] It is the pledge and promise of a living relationship expressed in the loving, faithful commitment of both God and his people (6:5; 7:9,12-13; 11:1). 'God's covenant with His people is a proclamation of His sovereignty and an instrument for binding His elect to Himself in a commitment of absolute allegiance.'[8] Nevertheless the people are still responsible *to choose* to obey God.

The reiteration of the covenant is followed by an overview of covenantal promise (30:1-10). 'The blessings God has promised will all be fulfilled; Israel will enter the land and drive out their enemies; God will set His name in their midst at the place of His choosing. But Israel will continue to rebel and the curses of the covenant will also be realized. The people will be driven from the land into exile. Then, after the blessings and the curses, God will gather His scattered people and circumcise their hearts to love the Lord with all their heart and soul, that they may live.'[9]

Part IV: God's servants (31:1 - 34:12)

The closing chapters of this magnificent book direct our attention to two servants of God: Moses and Joshua. Moses is nearing the end of his days and he knows full well that his days of service are fast drawing to a close: 'Then Moses went and spoke these words to all Israel, and he said to them: "I am one hundred and twenty years old today. I can no longer go out and come in. Also the LORD has said to me, 'You shall not cross over this Jordan'"' (Deut. 31:1-3).

The expression, 'I can no longer go out and come in,' is not an indication of infirmity and lack of mobility for, at his death, it is testified of Moses: 'His eyes were not dim nor his natural vigour abated' (34:7). It means that he could no longer work for the nation (cf. Num. 27:16-17).

The law is to be read every seven years (31:10-11). A copy of the completed law is to be placed beside the ark of the covenant (31:26).

The Song of Moses is a magnificent psalm that contrasts the faithfulness of God with the unfaithfulness of his people. Did Moses and Joshua sing this as a duet in the presence of the congregation? (32:44).

Ascribe greatness to our God.
He is the Rock, his work is perfect;
For all his ways are justice.
A God of truth and without injustice;
Righteous and upright is he...

(32:3-4, part of the first stanza).

The four stanzas in Moses' song outline the entire history of Israel from start to finish: Israel's creation and gracious treatment (32:1-14); her ingratitude and apostasy (32:15-19); God's judgement (32:20-35); and Israel's salvation through the fire of judgement (32:36-43).[10]

Joshua is appointed as successor to Moses (31:3,23). He is to take up the mantle from Moses. He will take the Israelites into the promised land: 'Now Joshua the son of Nun was full of the spirit of wisdom, for Moses had laid his hands on him; so the children of Israel heeded him, and did as the LORD had commanded Moses. But since then there has not arisen in Israel a prophet like Moses, whom the LORD knew face to face, in all the signs and wonders which the LORD sent him to do in the land of Egypt, before Pharaoh, before all his servants, and in all his land, and by all that mighty power and all the great terror which Moses performed in the sight of all Israel' (Deut. 34:9-12).

There is no resistance in Moses the man of God, no resentment towards the Lord for his judgements. Moses dies, as he has lived, 'a spiritual giant'. He dies 'the death of the righteous' for, unlike Balaam, he has lived the life of the righteous (see Num. 23:10).

The attitude of Moses is reflected in the death of Mr Valiant for Truth in John Bunyan's *Pilgrim's Progress*. Just as he is about to cross the river he testifies to his friends: 'I am going to my Father's, and tho' with great difficulty I am got hither, yet now I do not repent me of all the trouble I have been at to arrive where I am. *My Sword* I give to him that shall succeed me in my Pilgrimage, and my *Courage* and *Skill* to him that can get it. My *marks* and *scars* I carry with me, to be a witness for me, that I have fought His battles, who now will be my Rewarder.'[11]

Christ and his church

Every book of the Pentateuch makes its distinct and lasting contribution to the unfolding of revelation and preparation for the coming of the Lord Jesus Christ. The book of Deuteronomy provides unique material in laying the foundation for the work of the Son of God who became Jesus the Christ.

Prophecies of Christ

1. The great Prophet

'The LORD your God will raise up for you a Prophet like me from your midst, from your brethren. Him you shall hear, according to all you desired of the LORD your God in Horeb in the day of the assembly, saying, "Let me not hear again the voice of the LORD my God, nor let me see this great fire any more, lest I die." And the LORD said to me: "What they have spoken is good. I will raise up for them a Prophet like you from among their brethren, and will put my words in his mouth, and he shall speak to them all that I command him. And it shall be that whoever will not hear my words, which he speaks in my name, I will require it of him" ' (18:15-19).

When the book of Deuteronomy ends by declaring that 'There has not arisen in Israel a prophet like Moses, whom the LORD knew face to face' (34:10), the way is paved for Israel to keep looking for the coming of 'the Prophet'. This explains the question of the priests and Levites, many years later, when they addressed John the Baptist and, among other things, asked, 'Are you the Prophet?' (John 1:21). It also explains the reaction of the crowd when the Lord Jesus fed the five thousand: 'Then those men, when they had seen the sign that Jesus did, said, "This is truly the Prophet who is to come into the world" ' (John 6:14). We might have expected the Lord to have been delighted that they were beginning to see him as the promised Prophet. But he was not pleased. They had missed the point. What is the most significant part of being a prophet? Is it not *the words* that he speaks from God? (18:18-19). These men were rightly linking the miracles of Jesus with the credentials of Messiah and associating Messiah with 'the Prophet', but they were not listening to his words. Miracles and wonders do not in themselves prove the authenticity of a prophet. That depends supremely upon *the content* of his teaching (13:1-4).

The priority for the Lord Jesus was *teaching*, not *miracles*. Just before the feeding of the five thousand, when he was followed by a great crowd, it is recorded that '… he received them and spoke to them about the kingdom of God, and healed those who had need of healing' (Luke 9:11). Jesus is the Prophet. He speaks the authentic word from God. His words are life and death.

The promised Prophet is the promised Messiah

That the promised Prophet was linked in the thinking of the Jews to the promised Messiah is clear from the manner in which the apostle Peter and Stephen the martyr take this connection for granted (Acts 3:18,22; 7:37). Both take it as the general view held by all Jews. Neither of them considers it necessary to elaborate this point when affirming Jesus as the promised Messiah *and* the promised Prophet. It is also likely that Philip had this passage in Deuteronomy in mind when he found Nathanael and told him, 'We have found him of whom *Moses in the law … wrote* — Jesus of Nazareth, the son of Joseph' (John 1:45, emphasis added).

Even the woman of Samaria, with her religious education that restricted her to receiving only the five books of Moses as the Word of God, was able to declare, 'I know that Messiah is coming… When he comes, he will tell us all things' (John 4:25). The connection with the concluding words of Deuteronomy 18:18 seems evident: '… and will put my words in his mouth, and he shall speak to them all that I command him.'

On the Mount of Transfiguration the words of the Father from the cloud revealed the Messiah: 'This is my beloved Son in whom I am well pleased. Hear him!' (Matt. 17:5). As the first sentence is a paraphrase of the prophecy in Isaiah 42:1, so the last instruction points to the great Prophet under consideration. To listen to Christ is to listen to 'the Prophet'. His words are life and death. It is crucial that he is heard. 'Hear him!' says the Father.

When Jesus invited all who were thirsty to come to him and receive a constant 'flow of living water', many of his hearers saw the link between the miraculous supply of water in the wilderness (Exod. 17:1-6; Num. 20:7-12) and the promise of a prophet (Deut. 18:15-19): 'Therefore many from the crowd, when they heard this saying, said, "Truly, this is the Prophet"' (John 7:40).

2. The great curse

How significant that the altar of sacrifice for burnt offering and for peace offering was to be built upon Mount Ebal, the mountain of cursing (27:4-7,13-26). It points to the Lord Jesus Christ becoming accursed and replacing the curse upon his people by blessing. Deuteronomy is even more specific in relation to Christ's sacrificial work. This is the first time we hear of death by hanging on a tree: 'If a man has committed a sin worthy of death, and he is put to death, and you hang him on a tree, his body shall not remain overnight on the tree, but you shall surely bury him that day, so that you do not defile the land which the LORD your God is giving you as an inheritance; for he who is hanged is accursed of God' (21:22-23). The apostle Paul reveals the implications: 'For as many as are of the works of the law are under the curse; for it is written, "Cursed is everyone who does not continue in all things which are written in the book of the law, to do them." But that no one is justified by the law in the sight of God is evident, for "The just shall live by faith." Yet the law is not of faith, but "The man who does them shall live by them." Christ has redeemed us from the curse of the law, having become a curse for us (for it is written, "Cursed is everyone who hangs on a tree"), that the blessing of Abraham might come upon the Gentiles in Christ Jesus, that we might receive the promise of the Spirit through faith' (Gal. 3:10-14).

This is the gospel: 'Christ has redeemed us from the curse of the law, having become a curse for us' (Gal. 3:13). The law of Deuteronomy is preparation for the profound significance of the crucifixion. Believers are freed from the curse by the Saviour who became accursed. In the New Testament, five times the cross is spoken of as 'a tree' (Acts 5:30; 10:39; 13:29; Gal. 3:13; 1 Peter 2:24). The apostles Peter and Paul obviously see the immense importance of the linkage between the cross of Christ and the curse of Deuteronomy 21:22-23. Yet this still leaves the question: 'Why did God choose to single out this death — death by hanging on a tree — as the one to be particularly and specifically accursed? Why not death by stoning? Why not death by fire? Why not death by drowning? Why death upon a tree? Why did the Lord isolate this mode of death as the special one to be accursed? Clearly it was to prepare for the cross, with the humiliation and shame experienced by the Saviour. But is there more to be discovered here?

Why should 'tree' be used in place of 'cross'? Why should the sinner who had committed a sin worthy of death be hanged upon a tree? What association would Moses have been able to form? He could certainly think about the significance of a tree. The prophets 'enquired and searched diligently' to understand words given to them by God (1 Peter 1:10-11). He was the historian of Genesis. He had recorded the first 'sin to death' (Rom. 6:16). That first sin of all sin was associated with a tree. Moses had noted that two special trees were planted in the Garden of Eden: 'And out of the ground the LORD God made every tree grow that is pleasant to the sight and good for food. The tree of life was also in the midst of the garden, and the tree of the knowledge of good and evil' (Gen. 2:9).

'The tree of the knowledge of good and evil' was to Adam and Eve the tree of death.[12] Contact with that tree brought the sentence of death. From that moment they had to be kept from the tree of life: 'Then the LORD God said, "Behold, the man has become like one of us, to know good and evil. And now, lest he put out his hand and take also from the tree of life, and eat, and live for ever" — therefore the LORD God sent him out of the garden of Eden to till the ground from which he was taken. So he drove out the man; and he placed cherubim at the east of the garden of Eden, and a flaming sword which turned every way, to guard the way to the tree of life' (Gen. 3:22-24).

The Lord Jesus Christ is *the tree of life* who dies upon *the tree of death.* He is cut down, cast into Marah, the waters of the bitterness of God's wrath (Exod. 15:25). On the way to Golgotha, having been unjustly sentenced to death, the Lord Jesus Christ carried his cross to the place of execution. Along the way he passed a group of women who were weeping for him. The Lord told them not to weep for him, but rather to weep for themselves because they were going to face dreadful days ahead. He went on to say, 'For if they do these things in the green wood, what will be done in the dry?' (Luke 23:31). The Greek word translated here as 'wood' is the same one that is translated as 'tree' in Galatians 3:13, where we read that 'Cursed is everyone who hangs on a tree', and in 1 Peter 2:24, where the apostle says that Christ 'himself bore our sins in his own body on the tree'.

In his words to the women Jesus is drawing a contrast between 'green' wood and 'dry' wood. Dry wood burns and is consumed easily. Green wood is wet and does not burn easily. If the Gentile Romans will crucify the Lord Jesus, dealing so with a green and yielding tree, what will they do to the Jews, who are a hard and unyielding dry tree? John Calvin delves deeper: Jesus 'takes an everyday simile to show that they cannot avoid the divine fire lighting on them and at once devouring them in its flame. We know how dry wood is usually thrown first on the fire, but if the wet and green wood is already alight, there will be far less delay for the dry.'[13] The divine judgement is falling upon the Lord Jesus Christ. He is to be crucified 'by the carefully planned intention and foreknowledge of God' (Acts 2:23) — he who is the green wood; the young tree; ever yielding to the Father, ever obedient to the Law; without sin; without fault; without flaw. 'Jesus suffered the agonies of hell especially on Calvary, but when that suffering was finished he sat down at the right hand of the Father, full of glory, honour and power. But for the impenitents the suffering will never end: Jerusalem's fall will be only a foretaste of their everlasting damnation.' [14]

Application

1. Moses and Christ

Moses is one of the greatest of all the Old Testament characters: he had a profound and lasting impact upon the whole nation of Israel. He was the nation's leader, lawgiver, prophet and historian. No Israelite ever questioned what he wrote. Appeal was made to his law as the final arbitrator in all disputes. Born of Hebrew stock, educated in the Egyptian court, having forty years' communion with the Lord in the solitude of the district of Midian, no one was more suited as the mouthpiece of the living God.

Though not permitted to lead Israel into the promised land, a greater honour awaited him many years later. On the Mount of Transfiguration he was privileged to stand once more on the earth, this time in the company of the prophet Elijah and the apostles Peter, James and John. The greater honour still was to be standing there in the presence of the Lord Jesus Christ and discuss the Saviour's death (*exodos*, lit. departure — Luke 9:31). They were talking about the crucifixion!

The writer to the Hebrews indicates some of the comparisons and contrasts between Moses and the Lord Jesus (Heb. 3:1-6) and also gives this testimony of him: 'Moses indeed was faithful in all his house as a servant, for a testimony of those things which would be spoken afterwards' (Heb. 3:5).

The contrast between that which Moses and Christ each represent is brought out in the words of the apostle John: 'For the law was given through Moses, but grace and truth came through Jesus Christ' (John 1:17). With this distinction in mind it is interesting to consider the latter days of Moses, especially with regard to his being a symbol, or type, of the law of God.

Moses, as the representative of the law, could not lead the children of Israel into the promised land.[15] 'For what the law could not do in that it was weak through the flesh, God did by sending his own Son in the likeness of sinful flesh...' (Rom. 8:3-4; cf. 3:21-22). A new leader was necessary. In the providence of God the man appointed was Joshua (the Hebrew form of the Greek name 'Jesus'). He was to take up the mantle from Moses. At 120 years of age '[Moses'] eyes were not dim nor his natural vigour abated' (34:7), for the law of God never loses its strength. Moses was buried in an unknown grave (34:6). In like manner believers 'have become dead to the law through the body of Christ' (Rom. 7:4; cf. vv.1-3). 'For Christ is the end of the law for righteousness to everyone who believes' (Rom. 10:4).

2. Instructing the young

The necessity of godly parenting, by example and by education, is delightfully expressed: 'Hear, O Israel: The LORD our God, the LORD is one! You shall love the LORD your God with all your heart, with all your soul, and with all your might. And these words which I command you today shall be in your heart: you shall teach them diligently to your children, and shall talk of them when you sit in your house, when you walk by the way, when you lie down, and when you rise up' (6:4-7).

The apostle Paul reinforces the duty of parents to train their children in the ways of the Lord (Eph. 6:4). 'Children are a heritage from the LORD' (Ps. 127:3). With such a blessing comes also serious and sober responsibility. The Lord 'seeks godly offspring' (Mal. 2:15). The Christian home is to be a loving centre of education — training children up in the things of God. They are to be taught and guided in how to live life with God and live life for God.

3. Things to remember

The key word in Deuteronomy is 'remember' (occurring fourteen times). In order to promote obedience, God calls upon the people to recollect the events and experiences of the past. This word invites the children of Israel to look over their shoulder. They are told that they must not forget that God has done great things for them. Years later David will compose many psalms which remind the Israelites of God's mercy and goodness in many wonderful and tangible ways. For example:

> One generation shall praise your works to another,
> And shall declare your mighty acts.
> I will meditate on the glorious splendour of your majesty,
> And on your wondrous works.
> Men shall speak of the might of your awesome acts,
> And I will declare your greatness.
> They shall utter the memory of your great goodness,
> And shall sing of your righteousness
>
> (Ps. 145:4-7).

In the wilderness Moses called the people to remember:

- the giving of the law on Mount Sinai (also called Horeb — 4:9-10);
- the covenant of the LORD (4:23);
- their slavery in Egypt (5:15);
- their great deliverance (7:18);
- the providence of God in the wilderness (8:2-6);
- their rebellion and sin (9:7);
- the punishments inflicted by God (24:9);
- their history (32:7).

Christians are also to remember. With spiritual insight believers can remember that once we were slaves of sin and the Lord our God brought us 'out from there by a mighty hand and by an outstretched arm' (5:15; cf. Rom. 6:17-18). We are to remember the injunctions of Scripture: 'Beloved, I now write to you this second epistle (in both of which I stir up your pure minds by way of reminder), that you may be mindful of the words which were spoken before by the holy prophets, and of the commandment of us the apostles of the Lord and Saviour...' (2 Peter 3:1-2).

4. Obedience

Together with 'remember', there are other key words such as 'hear' (over thirty times) and 'do' (about 100 times). Obedience from the Israelites does not earn the favour of God, but is required because they already enjoy his favour. They are not expected to purchase their redemption by obedience, but to obey because they are already redeemed. Time and again they are told that God loves them and has chosen them. Because he loves them and has chosen them he took them out of bondage in Egypt. He has made them his special people; therefore they should respond by loving him in return, by being holy, and by keeping his laws. This same order, grace then good works, is also emphasized in the New Testament: 'For by grace you have been saved through faith, and that not of yourselves; it is the gift of God, not of works, lest anyone should boast. For we are his workmanship, created in Christ Jesus for good works...' (Eph. 2:8-10; cf. Titus 2:13-14).

Possessing the land of promise and keeping it were dependent upon the obedience of the children of Israel to the commandments of God. The obedience which the Lord requires is not servile obedience. It is to be obedience motivated and promoted by love. The word 'love', as express-ing the relationship between God and his people, occurs only once in Exodus, when God declares that he shows 'mercy to thousands, to those who love [him] and keep [his] commandments' (Exod. 20:6). It is applied to the relationship between people in Leviticus: 'You shall love your neigh-bour as yourself' (Lev. 19:18; cf. v. 34). The word 'love' is a lonely stranger in the first four books. Everything is changed in the book of Deuteronomy. 'Its supreme and overwhelming message is that of love. To understand this will enable us to state the permanent values, and to deduce the living message... God's love of man is the motive of His government; and ... man's love of God is the motive of his obedience.'[16]

Conclusion

The book of Deuteronomy is not merely a repetition of things commanded and done as already recorded in Exodus, Leviticus and Numbers. It is rather '... a description, explanation, and enforcement of the most essential contents of the covenant revelation and covenant laws, with emphatic prominence given to the spiritual principle of the law and its fulfilment, and with a further development of the ecclesiastical, judicial, political, and civil organization, which was intended as a permanent foundation for the life and well-being of the people in the land of Canaan.'[17]

In some respects Deuteronomy portrays what an ideal Israel should be. It presents an Israel with 'one God, one people, one land, one sanctuary, and one law'.[18] The church of Jesus Christ as revealed in the New

Testament embodies this same sense of unity. In his high priestly prayer the Lord Jesus prayed that his people might be one (John 17:21). And the apostle Paul reiterates this singular concord in the church: 'There is one body and one Spirit, just as you were called in one hope of your calling; one Lord, one faith, one baptism; one God and Father of all, who is above all, and through all, and in you all' (Eph. 4:4-6).

Joshua

('Jehovah is salvation')

Author: Joshua
(predominantly)

Key thought: 'Trusting brings victory'

Theme:
Success and failure in the life of faith

'Be strong and of good courage; do
not be afraid, nor be dismayed, for the
LORD your God is with you
wherever you go.'

Joshua 1:9

Summary

Joshua

The book of Joshua records one of the most interesting and important periods in Israel's history. It deals with the establishment of the children of Israel as a nation in their own land. Genesis provides the prophecy, and the other four books of Moses provide the preparation. The first section of our Bibles, the Pentateuch (the first five books), is followed by the twelve historical books (Joshua to Esther).

The book of Joshua represents a distinct turning-point. It marks the end of Israel's trials and wanderings in the wilderness, and at the same time sets out the beginning of their new life as a settled community in their own land. What the Lord began in the great exodus from Egypt he now completes in the settlement of Israel in the promised land.

Author

In its present form the book cannot have been written by Joshua, for it includes records of events which did not take place until after his death. Among these are the conquest of Debir (Kirjath Sepher) by Othniel (15:15-17) and of Leshem by the Danites (19:47). The accounts of the death of Joshua and of Eleazar show that the book is later than Joshua's time.[1] (Jewish tradition maintains that Eleazar added the account of Joshua's death, and that Phinehas added the account of Eleazar's death.) Another pointer that the final composition may have been made by a later editor or compiler is the frequent expression 'to this day' (4:9; 5:9; 6:25; 7:26; 8:28; 13:13; 15:63). Within the book itself there is no evidence upon which to reject Joshua's authorship of the major part. Alternatively a historian could have used substantial written or spoken material from Joshua (see 18:8-9; 24:26), adding other information to amplify or clarify (e.g. 10:13). Confidence in this portion of God's Word, as in any other, does not depend upon its human author. The divine origin is not in question.

The book of Joshua may therefore be trusted as a reliable and trustworthy record.

Joshua's original name was Hoshea (Num. 13:8; Deut. 32:44), which literally means 'salvation'. During the wilderness journey Moses renamed him Jehoshua (Joshua is a contracted form), meaning 'Jehovah is salvation' (Num. 13:16).

Joshua was born in the land of Egypt and, with the sole exception of Caleb, he was the only adult Israelite in the great Exodus who survived the forty years of wandering in the wilderness and entered Canaan. He is first mentioned in Exodus 17:9, where Moses instructs him: 'Choose us some men and go out, fight with Amalek.' At this point there is no indication of Joshua's parentage, early history, or his piety, yet from this brief statement we can form some idea of the man. It is evident that Joshua had already attracted the attention of Moses, had gained his confidence as a man of courage and competence and was suited to be a captain over others. There was an immediate response from Joshua, for the next verse reads, 'So Joshua did as Moses said to him, and fought with Amalek' (Exod. 17:10). Success was on Joshua's side, for 'Joshua defeated Amalek and his people with the edge of the sword' (Exod. 17:13). This first mention of Joshua seems to set the tone and content of his future work for the Lord as captain of the people of God successfully winning victories over God's enemies. Later the Lord gave him illumination, wisdom and authority to lead the whole congregation (Num. 27:18-23). He was a great ruler, and because of his wisdom and godliness, he commanded the respect of all his subjects (Deut. 34:9). He maintained order and discipline, putting the worship of God central in the nation's government and life. He encouraged the people to greater godliness. He was also a great military leader, using his God-given talents of wisdom, confidence and courage to outwit his enemies.

Historical setting

550 years earlier the Lord had led Abraham away from his home in Ur of the Chaldeans to the land of Canaan (Gen. 11:31; 12:1). Once in Canaan, the Lord gave Abraham a solemn promise: 'To your descendants I will give this land' (Gen. 12:7). There was, however, to be a time lapse. The Lord revealed to Abraham the extent of the intervening years: 'Know certainly that your descendants will be strangers in a land that is not theirs, and will serve its people and be afflicted by them four hundred years. And also the

nation whom they serve I will judge; afterwards they shall come out with great possessions' (Gen. 15:13-14).

Twenty-four years after leaving Haran, the Lord amplified and confirmed his earlier promise: 'I will establish my covenant between me and you and your descendants after you in their generations, for an everlasting covenant, to be God to you and your descendants after you. Also I give to you and your descendants after you the land in which you are a stranger, all the land of Canaan, as an everlasting possession; and I will be their God' (Gen. 17:7-8).

The book of Genesis ends with the settlement of the Israelites in Egypt. Exodus takes up the history with a brief mention of the intervening 400 years. From being treated as honoured guests in the land of Egypt, the Israelites become persecuted slaves. Exodus records how the Lord delivers his people and leads them from Egypt, through the Red Sea and the wilderness to arrive, after six weeks or so, at Mount Sinai in Horeb, where they receive the Ten Commandments. Leviticus takes up the story of the eleven-month stay at Mount Sinai, with the construction of the tabernacle, the establishment of an elaborate sacrificial system and the inauguration of detailed annual festivals. Numbers records the dismantling of the tabernacle at Sinai, the journey to Kadesh Barnea, the failed entry into the promised land, thirty-eight further years of wandering in the wilderness, and finally the trek around Edom and Moab to arrive on the plains of Moab. Deuteronomy continues the history of the Israelites with the preparation of the new generation for entry into the promised land, concluding with the appointment of Joshua as the new national leader and the death of Moses.

The book of Joshua spans a period of about twenty-four years from the death of Moses on Mount Nebo, east of the River Jordan, to the settlement of Israel in her tribal districts (1404–1380 B.C.). It is a story of a military campaign led by Joshua, Moses' successor, in which Israel gains possession of Canaan. The land promised to Abraham's descendants extended from the 'river of Egypt to the great river, the River Euphrates' (Gen. 15:18). The land promised to the Israelites in the days of Moses and Joshua extended from the 'Red Sea to the Sea of the Philistines, and from the desert to the River [Euphrates]' (Exod. 23:31; Josh. 1:4). This places Israel between Egypt, the one world-power on her south-western border, and Babylon, the power on her eastern side.

Joshua is an aggressive book; consequently it has been suggested that Joshua bears the same relationship to the five books of Moses that the Acts of the Apostles holds to the four Gospels.[2] The invasion of Canaan and the wars with the Canaanites indicate God's horror and hatred of sin. The

Canaanites were so immersed in sin, and so given over to sin and vices of the most awful nature, that God's wrath burned against them. The behaviour of the Canaanites was bad in the time of Abraham. At that time God predicted that it would grow worse; when it reached an all-time low God would move in judgement against them. To Abraham God said, 'But in the fourth generation they shall return here, for the iniquity of the Amorites [note: all the Canaanites are represented by their strongest family] is not yet complete' (Gen. 15:16). The invasions under Joshua show that the iniquity and wickedness of the Canaanites had by now reached the point where divine tolerance would bear with it no longer. During the four intervening centuries, between Abraham and Joshua, these wicked nations had forfeited their right to live. They were now to be replaced by the Israelites.[3]

is it only the Canaanites who are to be singled out for this kind of judgement? History shows that the righteous government of God extends over all nations. Each is punished when its wickedness has come to the full — not necessarily punished to the same extent, nor in the same way, but punished as God sees fit. The Canaanites were not only idolaters; they were guilty of practices that were even regarded among other heathens as abhorrent and debasing. Furthermore this generation of Israelites was probably the godliest in all their long history as a nation (24:31). They burned with a holy zeal — not only against their pagan enemies, but also against their dishonest and wayward brethren (as in the case of Achan — 7:10-26). Later generations of Israelites were themselves to be severely punished when they turned away from the Lord and began to practise abominations:

'Shall I not punish them for these things?' says the LORD.
'And shall I not avenge myself on such a nation as this?'

(Jer. 5:9).

Righteousness exalts a nation,
But sin is a reproach to any people

(Prov. 14:34).

It is to be noted that not all Israel's enemies were defeated. Some of the cities within the boundaries were not taken until the days of David and Solomon. This may be partially explained by the failure of the Israelites fully to obey God's commands. At the same time it is recorded that God designed a delay: 'I will not drive them out from before you in one year, lest the land become desolate and the beast of the field become too numerous for you. Little by little I will drive them out from before you, until you have increased, and you inherit the land' (Exod. 23:29-30). Perhaps the delay was intended to span more than the seven years of warfare under Joshua.

Outline

The book of Joshua is the record of the conquest of Canaan. Under the leadership of Joshua, Israel makes a carefully planned and well-executed invasion of the land. Joshua's skills in military strategy are displayed when, having been instructed by God to enter Canaan via Jericho, he proceeds to drive a wedge through central Canaan, separating the territory to the north from that to the south. He then moves in on the nearest enemies to the south. Having conquered them, he turns his attention to the enemies further afield in the north. There are many enemies in the land of Canaan. As well as the Canaanites, there are the Hittites, Amorites, Perizzites, Hivites, Jebusites, Geshurites, Gazites, Ashdodites, Ashkelonites, Gittites, Ekronites, Avites, Gebalites and others (Exod. 3:8; Josh. 13:2-6).

Part I: Entry into the promised land (1:1 - 5:12)

The book opens with the Lord's directions to Joshua, who had already been designated as the successor of Moses. God directs Joshua to lead the children of Israel into the promised land. The Lord promises Joshua that he will have success. In fact, the Lord says, 'No man shall be able to stand before you all the days of your life; as I was with Moses, so I will be with you. I will not leave you nor forsake you' (1:5). Responding to the command, Joshua immediately begins to make the necessary preparations. Although the Lord has given him a solemn promise that he will be invincible, Joshua still sees the necessity of thoughtful planning and precise strategy on his part. He gives instructions to the people to make ready for the crossing of the Jordan; he reminds the tribes of Reuben, Gad and half Manasseh of their promise to assist the other tribes in the conquest of Canaan (see map on page 184), and he sends two spies into Jericho to reconnoitre the city.

Jericho is situated two hours' journey to the west of the Jordan. The two spies enter the city and take lodgings at the home of Rahab the prostitute.

Staying overnight in such a house would not draw attention to the men or create suspicion. The house was also located on the city wall. This would facilitate an easier escape if their identity and mission became known, as in the event it did. Rahab shows herself as a true friend to the people of God. She informs the spies that the inhabitants are afraid of Israel because their God, Jehovah, 'is God in heaven above and on earth beneath' (2:11). She demonstrates her true faith in the Lord God by concealing the spies at great personal risk (Heb. 11:31).[4] The two Israelites promise to safeguard Rahab and her household when the attack is launched on the city provided she hangs a scarlet cord from her window. They then escape to the mountains and hide for three days until their pursuers return to Jericho. When it is safe they make their way back to the Jordan and to the camp of Israelites.

The following day, having received the report from the spies, Joshua moves the whole company to the banks of the Jordan. Three days are spent in final preparation and prayer. The Israelites move out with the priests bearing the ark of the covenant in front of them (3:14). Whereas Moses divided the waters of the Red Sea with his rod, Joshua divides the waters of the Jordan river with the ark of the covenant, the appointed symbol of the presence of Almighty God since the covenant established on Mount Sinai. When the feet of the priests touch the waters of the Jordan, a pathway is made through the river. Although the river is in full flood, the Lord, by a remarkable miracle, makes a wide passage for the Israelites. The priests stand on firm, dry ground in the middle of the riverbed until all the people have passed over. Twelve stones from the dry riverbed are set up in the middle of the Jordan, and another twelve are erected as a permanent monument on the western bank. As soon as the priests come up out of the riverbed the waters return to their natural flow.

Aware that the Lord's promise of preservation and victory depends upon obedience to the law of God (1:7-9), Joshua ensures that the generation born in the wilderness receives the covenant sign of circumcision. Although all those who came out of Egypt had been circumcised, the practice had not been carried out during the years in the wilderness (5:5). This may have been due to the judgement of God upon the grumbling unbelieving adult generation that left Egypt: '... their children bore the reproach ... by being denied the "token" or "sign of the covenant" (Genesis 17:11).'[5] Now in the promised land the new generation is under the blessing of God and it is appropriate for the rite to be administered once more.

After a few days' rest the Israelites keep the Feast of Passover. In their first Passover celebration in the land of Canaan they sample the produce of their new land. The miraculous supply of manna ceases for ever on the following day.

Part II: Conquest of the promised land (5:13 – 12:24)

The Angel of the LORD appears to Joshua to encourage him to proceed with the conquest of Canaan. Joshua is instructed as to how the Israelites are to proceed. Jericho is a strong and secure fortress city. It is to be taken with the aid of an outstanding miracle. With the ark of the covenant at the head, the army of Israel is to march in silence around the city walls once a day for six days. On the seventh day they are to march around the walls seven times. On the final circuit the priests are to blow the trumpet and the people are to shout. The walls of the city will fall down and the soldiers are to move in to kill the enemy and destroy the city. Joshua obeys the Lord and the city is taken. Only Rahab and her household are spared, for the Israelites honour the promise made by the two spies (2:14; 6:25).

Later, in moving out from Jericho against the town of Ai, the Israelites are to learn that they will only succeed if they are faithful and obedient to the Lord. They cannot win victories in their own strength. Although the inhabitants of Ai are few, the Israelite forces sent against them are defeated. The Lord informs Joshua that his instructions are not being respected. This leads to the public exposure and execution of Achan and his family. A new attack is mounted against Ai and the Israelites win a decisive victory (8:1-23).

After the capture of Ai Israel has established a firm foothold in central Canaan. Joshua is therefore able to proceed with the building of an altar on Mount Ebal in accordance with the instructions received from Moses (8:30-35; Deut. 27:5-8).

News of the victories of the Israelites in taking the cities of Jericho and Ai soon spreads to the surrounding Canaanites. Their kings form an alliance against the Israelites. One tribe, the Hivites, does not join this coalition. They choose rather to adopt a more subtle approach. Travelling from their major city, Gibeon, six miles south-west of Ai and five miles north-west of Jerusalem, a few of their number come to the Israelites pretending to be ambassadors who have travelled many miles in order to form a treaty with Israel. Without enquiring from the Lord, Joshua agrees to a pact. When the deception is uncovered the Gibeonites have to be spared because of the oath that Joshua has made, but are consigned to a life of servitude under the Israelites.

Military strategy in taking the city of Ai

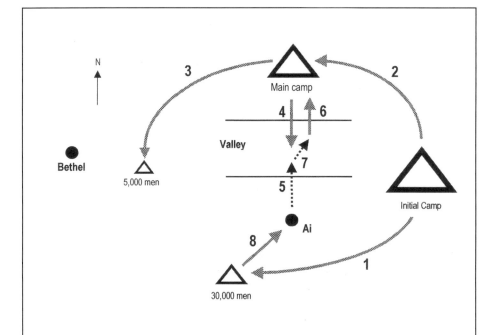

Key based on Joshua 8:1-23

1. 30,000 men are sent by night to lie in ambush near to the city (vv. 2-4,9).
2. Early the following morning, Joshua leads the main forces to the north (vv. 10-11).
3. A small contingent is sent to guard the approach from Bethel to Ai (v. 12).
4. The Israelites advance into the valley (v. 13).
5. The King of Ai sees the advance and leads his forces out to meet it (v. 14).
6. With the arrival of the enemy, the Israelites turn back as though retreating (v. 15).
7. The King of Ai and his forces pursue the Israelites (v. 16).
8. The signal is given and the men in ambush take the city and set fire to it (vv. 18-19). The men of Ai see the smoke. They turn back towards their city only to be trapped in a pincer movement by the Israelites (v. 22).

News of the treaty between the Gibeonites and the Israelites comes to the attention of Adoni-Zedek, the Amorite king of Jerusalem. He gathers another four Amorite kings to form an army to punish the Gibeonites, and to check the advance of the Israelites. In the event Israel triumphs. The Lord fights for them, casting down large hailstones which kill many of the enemy (10:11) and answering Joshua's prayer:

'Sun, stand still over Gibeon;
And Moon, in the Valley of Aijalon.'
So the sun stood still,
And the moon stopped,
Till the people had revenge
Upon their enemies…

And there has been no day like that, before it or after it, that the LORD heeded the voice of a man; for the LORD fought for Israel (10:12-14).

The five Amorite kings are defeated and executed. Having conquered the armies, Joshua then proceeds to secure their cities (see map, page 182). Moving further south, the Israelites win victory after victory until they control the southern region as far as Kadesh Barnea (10:41-42).

The Canaanite tribes to the north hear of Israel's successes and organize a joint army, comprising thousands of fighting men, to resist Israel. Mounting a surprise attack, the Israelites, though seriously outnumbered, are nevertheless victorious: '… the Lord delivered them into the hand of Israel, who defeated them' (11:8). Joshua succeeds in subduing the northern territory. Canaan belongs to Israel. Seven years of heavy fighting have come to an end. Joshua and his army have conquered thirty-one kings (12:24).

Part III: Division of the promised land (13:1 - 22:34)

The Israelites are allotted portions of land as their inheritance. The Lord had given specific and detailed instruction as to ownership, sale and redemption of the land (Lev. 25:23-28). An intermingling of justice and mercy is embodied in these laws. Any inclination towards capitalism is curbed, and no allowance is made for state ownership. No one could take advantage for long over another who had fallen on hard times.

The conquest of the promised land

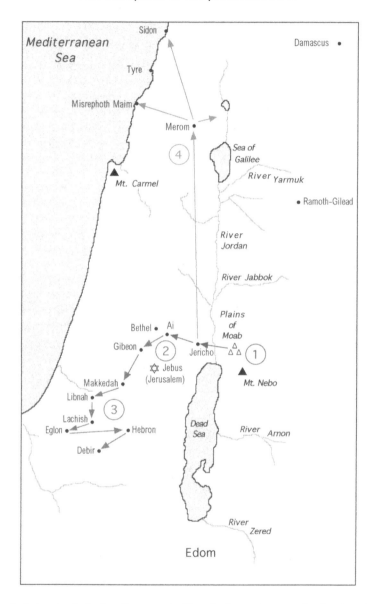

1. Joshua leads the Israelites over the River Jordan and on to take the city of Jericho.
2. After an abortive attempt to take Ai, the city falls to the Israelites.
3. The Israelites move against the southern tribes of the Canaanites.
4. Having subdued the southern tribes, the Israelites move against the northern tribes and with miraculous help win decisive victories.

Although some of the towns and villages within the boundaries of Canaan are still to be conquered, the Lord issues instructions for the distribution of the land to the individual tribes of Israel (13:1-7; cf. Judg. 1:27-36).

The tribes of Reuben and Gad had very large flocks and herds and the land on the east of the Jordan was rich in excellent pastureland. Their leaders had asked Moses and Eleazar the priest for permission to take that area as their inheritance (Num. 32:1-5). Although the land on the east of the Jordan formed part of the original territory promised to Abraham (Gen. 15:18) — a promise later reiterated to Moses (Exod. 23:31) — the Reubenites and Gadites were being motivated by materialistic considerations similar to those which influenced Lot and failed to take other important factors into account (Gen. 13:10-13); the eastern territory requested by half the tribe of Manasseh, the tribe of Gad and the tribe of Reuben was to be constantly troubled by Moabites to the south, Canaanites and Syrians to the north and Ammonites, Midianites and Amalekites from the eastern deserts.

Moses had agreed to the request from the three tribes on condition that their fighting men accompany the remaining tribes until they had all inherited their lands.

The names of the twelve tribes to whom land is apportioned differ slightly from the names of Jacob's twelve sons. There are two reasons for this discrepancy. Firstly, the tribe of Levi does not inherit a tract of land in the same way as the other tribes. Soon after the Exodus the Levites became a tribe of priests; as their inheritance they receive forty-eight cities and the surrounding land, dotted amongst the land apportioned to the other tribes (21:41). Six of these cities are designated as cities of refuge for the protection of those who commit manslaughter (20:1-9; cf. Num. 35:9-15, see map, page 184). Secondly, the tribe of Joseph does not appear. Instead that tribe receives a double portion through the tribes of Joseph's two sons Manasseh and Ephraim. Consequently the number of tribal territories still remains as twelve.

Once the distribution of the land to the west of the Jordan has been accomplished, the fighting men from the two and a half tribes whose inheritance is on the east of Jordan (Reuben, Gad and half of Manasseh) return home. They erect an impressive altar by the eastern banks of the River Jordan. The tribes of Reuben and Gad call the altar 'Ed' (meaning 'witness'): 'For it is a witness between us that the LORD is God' (22:34). Several years then pass without comment.

Division of the promised land

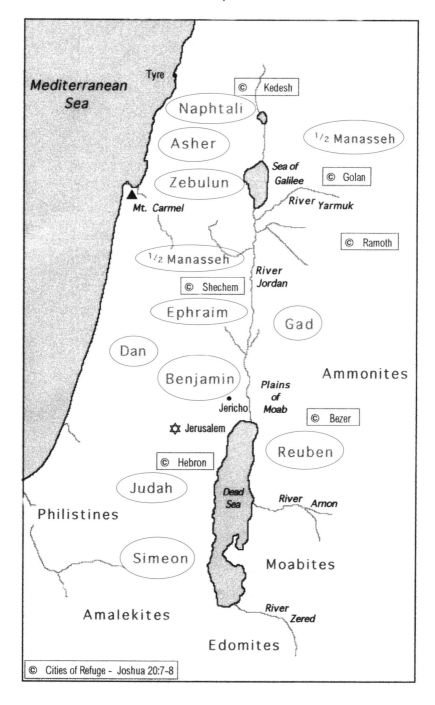

Mediterranean Sea

Tyre

© Kedesh

Naphtali

½ Manasseh

Asher

Zebulun

Sea of Galilee

© Golan

Mt. Carmel

River Yarmuk

© Ramoth

½ Manasseh

River Jordan

© Shechem

Ephraim

Gad

Dan

Benjamin

Ammonites

Plains of Moab

Jericho

© Bezer

☆ Jerusalem

Reuben

© Hebron

Judah

Dead Sea

River Arnon

Philistines

Simeon

Moabites

Amalekites

River Zered

Edomites

© Cities of Refuge - Joshua 20:7-8

Part IV: The last days of Joshua (23:1 - 24:33)

Joshua's final addresses to the leaders and to the people form a natural conclusion to the book as a whole. He gathers the leaders of the tribes together and reminds them of God's purposes and blessings.

Joshua reiterates the history of Israel from the days when the Lord brought Terah and Abraham from idolatry beyond the River Euphrates. He then urges the Israelites once more to be obedient and faithful to the Lord: 'Now therefore, fear the LORD, serve him in sincerity and in truth, and put away the gods which your fathers served on the other side of the River and in Egypt. Serve the LORD!' (24:14).

He calls upon the Israelites to remember their covenant obligations. The living God has established his covenant with them. He has kept his promises and blessed them. He will also keep his threats and punish them if they transgress the covenant of the Lord their God and turn away to other gods (23:15-16). They must not fail in their responsibilities. Their enjoyment of the promised land depends upon their faithfulness to the Lord.

Implicitly undergirding Joshua's address is the threefold covenant promise given to Abraham of a vast number of descendants, of possessing their own land and of enjoying singular blessing in relationship with the living God. Failure to keep the covenant will result in suffering and death, the loss of their land, and the great displeasure of God.

Joshua and the people renew their covenant to serve the Lord.

Joshua dies at the age of 110 after having driven out most of the Canaanites from the new land of Israel.

Christ and his church

Theophany

After the celebration of the Passover and before the invasion of Jericho, Joshua is confronted with an intriguing figure who introduces himself as 'Commander of the army of the LORD' (5:14). Joshua is 'by Jericho', in all probability trying to work out his strategy. It is surprising that Joshua responds to this 'man' by falling to the ground and worshipping him. Such behaviour from one who is so evidently God-fearing and walking in the law of the Lord can only mean that Joshua understands this 'man' to be the Angel of the LORD who is to be treated as God himself! There is 'no hesitation on his part in yielding to Him the Divine honour due to the Most High'.[6] Joshua would have known of the Angel's visit to Abraham and to Hagar, and of the Angel's wrestling with Jacob at Peniel. Now he sees the Angel of the LORD for himself. Having fallen to the ground, Joshua seeks instruction from this exalted being. He is told to take his sandals from his feet (5:15; cf. Exod. 3:5), for he is in the presence of Deity. The Lord then instructs Joshua as to how he is to take the impregnable city of Jericho (6:1-5). Jehovah is to fight for him.

At Jericho, and in several later battles, the Son of God fought with a sword; now, since the days of the New Covenant, he fights with the sharp two-edged sword of the Spirit, which is the Word of God (Rev. 19:15; cf. Heb. 4:12; Rev. 1:16; 2:12,16).

Types

There are no direct prophecies concerning the Lord Jesus Christ in the book of Joshua. There is however, in the person of *Joshua*, an allusion to a type of Christ. The name Joshua means 'Jehovah is salvation'. It is the Hebrew equivalent of the Greek name *Iesous*, meaning 'Jesus'. In his role as captain over the people of God, leading them safely into the promised land, Joshua is a type of the one who, as 'captain of their salvation', will bring 'many sons to glory' (Heb. 2:10, AV; cf. 2 Cor. 2:14; Heb. 4:8-10). The inheritance that Jesus gives is not just the tract of land between the Mediterranean Sea and the desert, the Red Sea and the River Euphrates, but the 'new heavens and a new earth in which righteousness dwells' (2 Peter 3:13; Rev. 21:1-4).

Crossing Jordan is a type of the believer's dying with Christ (1 Cor. 10:2; Rom. 6:3-4).

The *scarlet cord* (2:18) which the spies required as a sign also seems to be significant. There may be an allusion to the precious blood of Christ by which we are safe and saved (Heb. 10:19; cf. Exod. 12:13).

Canaan — A type of heaven or of the Christian life?

Canaan has been regarded as a type of heaven to which the church is journeying through this wilderness. However, there is difficulty in making too strong an association between the promised land of Canaan and heaven. Heaven will not be a place of fighting, but of eternal rest and blessedness. In a sense it is legitimate to view Canaan as the end of the trials in the wilderness. But a slightly different perspective provides a more satisfactory application. When viewed in the light of all the battles that are recorded in the book of Joshua then *entry into Canaan* may be better seen as personal conversion — entering into Christ. The battles which occur in Canaan are then seen as typical of spiritual battles in the Christian life. The *conquest of Canaan* typifies victories over spiritual enemies (2 Cor. 10:3-5; Eph. 6:12). The *partial subjugation of the Canaanites* typifies the existence of besetting sins which remain unconquered (Heb. 12:1).

In Genesis we hear the promises of God that there will be a country, and a people chosen to inherit that country. In Exodus we see our unconverted self, in bondage to sin and Satan. In Leviticus we hear God speaking, making known his holy requirements. In Numbers we find ourselves in a great howling wilderness, which is what the world appears to those who have been awakened by the Spirit of God. In Deuteronomy the strictness and spirituality of the law is revealed. This shatters self-righteousness and reveals that someone other than Moses must become the captain of our salvation if ever we are to arrive in the promised rest. That rest prefigures Christ: 'For if Joshua had given them rest, then he would not afterwards have spoken of another day. There remains therefore a rest for the people of God. For he who has entered his rest has himself also ceased from his works as God did from his. Let us therefore be diligent to enter that rest, lest anyone should fall after the same example of disobedience' (Heb. 4:8-11).

Entry into Canaan was a time of new beginnings. There was *a new generation*, for all the adults who left Egypt died in the wilderness (Num. 14:29-32). There was *a new leader*. Joshua replaced Moses, for grace achieves what the law could never accomplish. There was *a new sphere of life*: the wilderness was replaced by the land of Canaan. Here is a spiritual picture of those who have passed through a period of conviction for sin, who have felt the terrors of the law, and have now been brought to put their trust in Jesus Christ.[7] At conversion we enter into rest in Christ.

After conversion there is the blessing of victory, of resting, with the heavenly 'Joshua', who is the Lord Jesus Christ, the captain of our salvation (Heb. 2:10, AV). There is also a note of battle: 'The flesh lusts against the Spirit, and the Spirit against the flesh; and these are contrary to one another, so that you do not do the things that you wish' (Gal. 5:17). Paul brings these two elements, victory and fighting, fighting and victory, into stark relief in Romans 7 and 8: 'For the good that I will to do, I do not do; but the evil I will not to do, that I practise. Now if I do what I will not to do, it is no longer I who do it, but sin that dwells in me. I find then a law, that evil is present with me, the person who wills to do good. For I delight in the law of God according to the inward man. But I see another law in my members, warring against the law of my mind, and bringing me into captivity to the law of sin which is in my members. O wretched man that I am! Who will deliver me from this body of death? I thank God — through Jesus Christ our Lord! So then, with the mind I myself serve the law of God, but with the flesh the law of sin. There is therefore now no condemnation to those who are in Christ Jesus, who do not walk according to the flesh, but according to the Spirit...' (Rom. 7:19-25; 8:1).

The military campaign under Joshua 'typifies the warfare of the spirit. The Canaanites represent our lusts, besetting sins and spiritual enemies, and in the record we discover the *secret of an all-conquering life*':[8] 'One man of you shall chase a thousand, for the LORD your God is he who fights for you, as he has promised you. Therefore take diligent heed to yourselves, that you love the LORD your God' (23:10-11).

The Canaanites were only partially subdued, not totally eradicated! We must 'lay aside every weight, and the sin which so easily ensnares us, and … run with endurance the race that is set before us, looking unto Jesus, the author and finisher of our faith' (Heb. 12:1-2).

Application

1. Revelation

One notable fact concerning this book is its introduction to a new method of teaching. Up to this time God had spoken through dreams, visions and ministering angels; from this point he communicates primarily through the Book of the Law written by Moses, and Joshua is urged to obey it: 'Be strong and of good courage, for to this people you shall divide as an inheritance the land which I swore to their fathers to give them. Only be strong and very courageous, that you may observe to do according to all the law which Moses my servant commanded you; do not turn from it to the right hand or to the left, that you may prosper wherever you go. This Book of the Law shall not depart from your mouth, but you shall meditate in it day and night, that you may observe to do according to all that is written in it. For then you will make your way prosperous, and then you will have good success. Have I not commanded you? Be strong and of good courage; do not be afraid, nor be dismayed, for the LORD your God is with you wherever you go' (1:6-9).

Here in the book of Joshua God's major means of communication is the Word which has already been transmitted, but there are periods in history, and in the unfolding of revelation, when God uses other methods of communication. With Moses he spoke face to face (Deut. 34:10). There are times when the Lord has used dreams, visions and ministering angels. At other times he has spoken through prophets (Heb. 1:1). In our day he communicates through the written Word, the Bible, and the Spirit of God opens our minds and hearts to the meaning and message of the Scriptures (John 16:13).

2. Models of faith

Israel at the battle of Jericho and Rahab the prostitute are presented in the New Testament as examples of faith (Heb. 11:30-31). Rahab is also found among the ancestors of the Lord Jesus (Matt. 1:5). Some time after the fall of Jericho she married Salmon of the tribe of Judah and gave birth to a son, Boaz, who eventually married Ruth the Moabitess. So Rahab was ultimately Ruth's mother-in-law! This illustrates how the grace of God triumphs over sin. The Saviour is the friend of sinners and not ashamed to call us his brethren (Matt. 11:19; Heb. 2:11).

Another example of faith found in the pages of the book of Joshua is that of Caleb. With Joshua he had stood against the ten spies who, through lack of faith and confidence in God, talked the Israelites out of entering the promised land (Num. 14:6-10). Though Joshua has been elevated to the highest position of responsibility in the nation, there is not the slightest indication of a bad spirit in Caleb. He could have been disgruntled that Joshua had such authority. When aged eighty-five Caleb, with humility, reminds Joshua of the promise made to him by Moses forty-five years earlier (14:6-15). Joshua honours the pledge of Moses and it is recorded: 'Hebron therefore became the inheritance of Caleb the son of Jephunneh the Kenizzite ... because he wholly followed the LORD God of Israel' (14:14; cf. Num. 32:11-12). A glorious testimony to Caleb's faith and obedience is recorded for posterity!

Caleb's ancestry is of interest, for when he accompanied Joshua and the other ten spies to reconnoitre Canaan, he represented the tribe of Judah

(Num. 13:6). He also appears as a regular member of the family of Judah in the tribal record (1 Chr. 4:15). Yet he is described as 'the son of Jephunneh the Kenizzite' (14:6,14).⁹ The family was of Canaanite extraction, yet Caleb is not himself spoken of as a Kenizzite but simply 'the son of Jephunneh the Kenizzite'. So it would seem that Jephunneh joined the Israelites, was accepted as a member of the children of Israel, and consequently brought up his sons, Caleb and Kenaz, as full members of the tribe of Judah. So Caleb's family were originally outside the covenant family of Israel and, like Rahab before and Ruth afterwards, they were incorporated because of their faith and allegiance to the true God, the God of Israel. This provides further illustration of the ease with which outsiders could be assimilated into the commonwealth of Israel and share in the covenants of promise — through faith (cf. Eph. 2:12-13).

3. Separation

The incident with the Gibeonites warns of two dangers: the possibility of deception by unbelievers, and the consequences of unholy alliances. The Israelites entered into a treaty with the Gibeonites without first seeking the counsel of the Lord (9:14-15). This is a warning to the church of God of all ages against the trickery and cunning craftiness of the world that often seeks a peaceful coexistence with the church, and even acceptance into it, whenever it is to its advantage to do so.¹⁰ Paul warns the Ephesians, and their elders, of the enemy within as well as without (Eph. 4:14; Acts 20:29-30). The Lord also taught the parable of the wheat and tares to illustrate that believers are not always capable of detecting unbelievers among them (Matt. 13:36-43).

Unholy alliances also include marriage to unbelievers. The Lord warns the Israelites of the serious problems that will arise if they disobey his command and marry peoples of other nations: 'Therefore take diligent heed to yourselves, that you love the LORD your God. Or else, if indeed you do go back, and cling to the remnant of these nations — these that remain among you — and make marriages with them, and go in to them and they to you, know for certain that the LORD your God will no longer drive out these nations from before you. But they shall be snares and traps to you, and scourges on your sides and thorns in your eyes, until you perish from this good land which the LORD your God has given you' (23:11-13).

4. Ministry support

The tribe of Levi did not receive any division of land in the same way as the other tribes of Israel. After the settlement the ten tribes together with Manasseh and Ephraim allocated cities and surrounding land to the Levites. In total they were provided with forty-eight cities and so they lived dispersed throughout the other tribes (Num. 35:1-8). The Levites also received a generous portion of the heave and wave offerings as their food, as well as the best of the oil, the wine and the first-fruits, with the tithes of the children of Israel (Num. 18:9-19,24; Deut. 18:1-3). In this way they were sustained by the gifts of the people. In this the Levites are a type of the ministers of the gospel in the Christian era. The apostle Paul points out this comparison: 'Do you not know that those who minister the holy things eat of the things of the temple, and those who serve at the altar partake of the offerings of the altar? Even so the Lord has commanded that those who preach the gospel should live from the gospel' (1 Cor. 9:13-14).

While points of comparison are legitimately drawn between the Levites of old and present-day ministers of the gospel, there are marked differences which must not be overlooked. The likeness is shown in terms of material support, not in regard to their function or task. Unlike Christian ministers, Levitical priests were not commissioned to evangelize; that was the work of the prophets. Gospel ministers are not priests, do not offer sacrifices (except sacrifices of devotion and praise which *all* Christians are to render — Rom. 12:1; 1 Peter 2:5), and are not intermediaries between God and sinners any more than any other believers (1 Peter 2:9).

Where possible ministers of the gospel are not to entangle themselves 'with the affairs of this life' (2 Tim. 2:4). The Lord provides for the support of the ministry through the gifts and kindness of the brethren: 'Let him who is taught the word share in all good things with him who teaches' (Gal. 6:6). 'Thus it is laid down as an unchanging principle that spiritual benefits demand a temporal return. Not that any price can be put upon the invaluable ministry of the Gospel, but that those whom God has set apart to preach it have a just claim for generous compensation. And that not in the way of charity or gratuity, but as *a sacred debt* — a debt which professing Christians fail to discharge at the peril of their souls. For let none be deceived: if they fail to support the Gospel, God will severely chastise them.'[11]

Such gifts in support of the ministry are 'a sweet-smelling aroma, an acceptable sacrifice, well pleasing to God' (Phil. 4:18).

Conclusion

This book has many lessons for the Christian in the twenty-first century.

Firstly, it shows that being a child of God is not easy. Let us note that there is a battle to be fought, a race to be run, a crown to be won. This will influence our evangelism. We shall not present an 'easy' faith with a weak commitment. Following Christ means a daily self-denial, a daily taking up of our cross, a being crucified to the world and the world being crucified to us (Mark 8:34; Gal. 6:14). Faith and obedience must never be parted.

Secondly, and at the other extreme, neither is the Christian life one of constant defeats. While the warfare is fierce against the world, the flesh and the devil, nevertheless there is a note of triumph. 'For whatever is born of God overcomes the world, And this is the victory that has overcome the world — our faith. Who is he who overcomes the world, but he who believes that Jesus is the Son of God?' (1 John 5:4-5). 'Who shall separate us from the love of Christ? Shall tribulation, or distress, or persecution, or famine, or nakedness, or peril, or sword? … in all these things we are more than conquerors through him who loved us' (Rom. 8:35,37).

Joshua is a book about a land and a people. The land is an inheritance promised by God, waiting to be occupied. The people are the elect nation of God, facing human obstacles in the way of taking the land. And the obstacles are the occasion for battle — a holy war — designed by God to remove the idolatrous and corrupt enemies from the land. It is for this reason that Joshua is called the 'Book of Conquest'.[12]

> Blessed be the God and Father of our Lord Jesus Christ, who according to his abundant mercy has begotten us again to a living hope through the resurrection of Jesus Christ from the dead, to an inheritance incorruptible and undefiled and that does not fade away, reserved in heaven for you, who are kept by the power of God through faith for salvation ready to be revealed in the last time. In this you greatly rejoice, though now for a little while, if need be, you have been grieved by various trials, that the genuineness of your faith … may be found to praise, honour, and glory at the revelation of Jesus Christ, whom having not seen you love (1 Peter 1:3-8).

Judges

(from 'deliverers' and 'rulers')

Author: Unknown
(probably Samuel)

Key thought: 'Rebellion and repentance'

Theme:
Causes and cure in backsliding

'In those days there was no king in
Israel; everyone did what was right
in his own eyes.'

Judges 17:6; 21:25

Summary

6. Civil war

Abimelech (Gideon's son) takes control by treachery (three years)	9:1-57
Tola saves Israel and judges (twenty-three years)	10:1-2
Jair judges Israel (twenty-two years)	10:3-5

7. From the east

Oppression by the Ammonites (eighteen years)	10:6-9
Israel's sorrow and the Lord's response	10:10-18
Jephthah delivers Israel and judges (six years)	11:1 – 12:7
Ibzan judges Israel (seven years)	12:8-10
Elon judges Israel (ten years)	12:11-12
Abdon judges Israel (eight years)	12:13-15

8. From the west

Oppression by the Philistines (forty years)	13:1
Samson begins to deliver Israel and judges (twenty years)	13:2 – 16:31

III. Examples of corruption within Israel — 17:1 – 21:25

i.	Personal and tribal idolatry	17:1 – 18:31
ii.	The evil of the men of Gibeah	19:1-30
iii.	War between Israel and the tribe of Benjamin	20:1-48
iv.	Drastic steps to preserve the tribe of Benjamin	21:1-25

Judges

The book of Judges takes up the history of the people of Israel where that of Joshua closes, with the death of Joshua, Israel's commander-in-chief (1:1; Josh. 24:29). Whereas Joshua recounts one of the high points in the spiritual state of the nation of Israel, Judges records one of the darkest periods of their history. Although Israel had conquered the whole land of Canaan in a general sense, there still remained pockets of enemy heathen nations here and there. The reasons given for the continuing existence of these enemies within the borders of Israel are: firstly, to test the obedience of the people to the laws of God (2:22; 3:4); and, secondly, in order that the new generation might learn how to fight (3:1-3). To 'be taught to know war' (3:2) here means to learn to depend upon the Lord for help in fighting against the Canaanites. So both reasons blend into one — walking with God in obedience to, and dependence upon, him and him alone. There were temptations all around them: temptations to intermarry with their heathen neighbours, temptations to establish close friendships with Gentiles, temptations through the beauty of the Canaanite women, the pomp and self-pleasing of their pagan religious rituals, the hope of learning the future by idolatrous divination and superstitious fears of the supposed gods of the localities in which they settled.[1] The Lord uses the nations who tempt the Israelites to become periodically the instruments of their punishment.

According to Robert Lee, the book of Judges is notable for several reasons. In the first place, it has two beginnings (1:1; 2:6). Secondly, it contains the first record in history of the emergence of a woman into prominence and leadership of a nation (4:4-5). Thirdly, it contains the greatest and grandest battle-song in the world (5:2-31). Finally, it contains the oldest known parable in the world (9:8-15).[2]

Author

The writer of this book is unknown. From the phrase found four times in the closing chapters — 'In those days there was no king in Israel' (17:6; 18:1; 19:1; 21:25) — it seems evident that the book was written after the establishment of the monarchy (c. 1000 B.C., not long after the death in 1051 B.C. of Samson, the last main character of the book). Probably it was written by Samuel the prophet, the last judge in Israel, during his partial retirement from the leadership of the people at the accession of Saul to the throne of Israel. According to the Jewish Talmud, 'Samuel wrote the book which bears his name and the book of Judges and Ruth.'[3]

Historical setting

The book of Judges covers a period of about 330 years from the death of Joshua (c. 1380 B.C.) to the rise of Samuel as a prophet of the Lord (c. 1050 B.C.). It portrays a series of relapses into idolatry on the part of God's people. These are followed by invasion of the promised land and periods of oppression by their enemies. The history centres around the personalities of the heroic judges who were raised up to become deliverers of Israel whenever the people sincerely repented of their sins. The dark side of their disobedience is especially emphasized in the record.

From the attention given to Israel's repeated backsliding and spiritual failure, the impression may be given that Israel was almost constantly in a bad relationship with the Lord. This is not the case. Of the years mentioned in this book, Israel enjoyed the majority of the time in faithfulness to the one true God — at least externally and formally.[4] It is also to be noticed that only certain areas had international problems at any one time. The problem may be located at one time in the north, at another time in the south, or then again in the west or east. Where the tribes are at least outwardly showing allegiance to the true God, their history passes without comment. A study of the dates would seem to show that the Israelites maintained an outward loyalty to Jehovah for the larger part of the time. This is not evident from a casual reading of the book of Judges.

The 'judges'

The book receives its title from the 'rulers' or 'judges' who led Israel during this period. The term 'judge' had a broader meaning at that time than its English counterpart has today. These 'judges' were not merely civil magistrates who administered justice and adjudicated disputes. Primarily, they were 'deliverers ... endued with the Spirit of God [3:10; 6:34; 11:29; 13:25], who were called upon to deliver and to govern the people' in times of spiritual decline and enemy oppression.[5] Though the judges were given spiritual powers, it is evident that the possession of supernatural gifts was not always accompanied by a right use of those gifts.

Gideon introduced the golden ephod and brought disaster upon his family and people (8:27). Jephthah brought heartache into his family circle when he made a rash vow (11:30-31,34-40). He also gratified his own violent spirit in taking revenge on Ephraim (12:1-6). The history of Samson, the last judge, illustrates the strength and the weakness of Israel: strength when separated to God, utter weakness when the relationship with God became severed by lust. Samson brought heartache to his godly parents through his lust and arrogance.

These judges are not to be confused with the judges set up by Moses following the advice received from Jethro, his father-in-law (Exod. 18:21-23; cf. Deut. 1:13,16–17; 16:18-20). The men appointed by Moses were to judge in the sense of making a decision between two or more alternative possibilities. Those men were like magistrates and their role was very different from that of the judges here in the book of that name. The latter are *shophetim,* commissioned by God to deliver the Israelites from the oppression of their enemies, usually by war, and then to rule the people during the era of peace that followed (2:16; 3:9).[6] God's 'eternal principle is, when His people return to Him in penitence, He returns to them in mercy'.[7]

God's salvation and God's righteousness go hand in hand:

Rain down, you heavens, from above,
And let the skies pour down righteousness;
Let the earth open, let them bring forth salvation,
And let righteousness spring up together.
I, the LORD, have created it

(Isa. 45:8).

Consequently these individuals were judges of righteousness not only *in* Israel, but *for* Israel. The divine principle in dealing with Israel is summed up in chapter 2: 'Then the LORD raised up judges who delivered them out of the hand of those who plundered them. Yet they would not listen to their judges, but they played the prostitute with other gods, and bowed down to them. They turned quickly from the way in which their fathers walked, in obeying the commandments of the LORD; they did not do so. And when the LORD raised up judges for them, the LORD was with the judge and delivered [saved] them out of the hand of their enemies all the days of the judge; for the LORD was moved to pity by their groaning because of those who oppressed them and harassed them. And it came to pass, when the judge was dead, that they reverted and behaved more corruptly than their fathers, by following other gods, to serve them and bow down to them. They did not cease from their own doings nor from their stubborn way' (2:16-19).

The number of 'judges'

There is a difference of opinion as to how many individuals are to be identified in this book as 'judges'. One commentator favours eight on the strict usage of the word 'judge'. Another says twelve by adding Ehud, Shamgar, Deborah and Gideon. Others say fourteen by including Barak with Deborah, and Abimelech the usurper. Leon Wood favours fourteen by excluding Barak who, he says, merely assisted Deborah, and Abimelech who was a usurper, and including instead Eli the priest and Samuel the prophet. Wood then divides the fourteen into eight major and six minor judges. The 'major' ones he sees as Othniel, Ehud, Deborah, Gideon, Jephthah, Samson, Eli and Samuel, while the six 'minor' ones are Shamgar, Tola, Jair, Ibzan, Elon and Abdon.[8]

It is probably wisest not to try to identify with exactness who is to be regarded as a judge, but to recognize that in the period known as the days of 'the judges' a number of men and one woman are presented as heroes of Israel. Some are said to be endued with the Holy Spirit to achieve great exploits: Othniel, Gideon, Jephthah and Samson. Some go down in history as people of great faith: Gideon, Barak, Samson and Jephthah (Heb. 11:32).

In the book of Judges itself some are mentioned as judging but not recorded as delivering (Jair, Ibzan, Elon and Abdon). Others delivered Israel but are not said to have judged (Ehud, Shamgar and Gideon). Samson is stated to have been a judge but only to have begun to deliver Israel (13:5). Those said to have both judged *and* delivered (or saved) Israel are Othniel, Deborah, Tola and Jephthah.

The majority of the judges were local or national heroes raised up to deliver the Israelites. They continued their rule after the end of the war. None of them established a hereditary rule; there was no dynasty, no family succession. Each judge delivered only part of Israel: Shamgar, the south-west district; Deborah, together with Barak, and Gideon, northern Israel; Jephthah, the eastern side of the Jordan; and Samson, the mid-west territories of Judah and Dan.

Outline

At first sight the book seems confusing and quite disorderly. It is not in chronological order. If it were to be given in correct sequence of events then it would begin with 2:6-9; followed by 1:1 – 2:5; then to 2:10-13; followed by chapters 17-21, and finally the section from 2:14 – 16:31. The Holy Spirit's concern in this book is not primarily historical but spiritual.

Part I: Introduction and interpretation (1:1 – 3:6)

The theological explanation for Israel's history during this period is bound up with the covenant that God had made with their fathers (2:20). Through unfaithfulness to God in turning to worship and serve other gods, Israel breaks its solemn historic covenant. This brings the disapproval and punishment of God upon them. They suffer under God's righteous anger until they cry out to the Lord and he sends delivery once again.

To enjoy the blessing of God the Israelites must be faithful to him. The promises of blessing from God in the covenant with Abraham (Gen. 15), and the obligations of faithfulness and obedience from Israel in the covenant with Moses (Exod. 6:2-8; 19:5-6; 20:1-17), form the central core by which the history of Israel is to be interpreted.

When the Israelites seek guidance and the help of the Lord he responds powerfully on their behalf. It is clear from the book of Judges that Israel as a nation fails to obey the Lord in some important areas. The promised land has been given to them but they have not carried out their instructions to drive out the Canaanites (1:21,27,29-33). Though the Lord has been entirely faithful in honouring his part of the covenant, they have not kept their side. Time and again the tribes of Israel fail to complete their assignment — for whatever reason, whether out of pity for the Canaanites, or from a feeling of power in subduing them and using and abusing them as forced labour, or from sympathy towards their religious beliefs and practices, or in thinking they knew better than the Lord and the divinely appointed leadership. It seems clear that they deliberately ignored God's command to destroy the Canaanites.

For their failure and disobedience the Israelites are rebuked by 'the Angel of the LORD' (2:1-5). The phrase, 'The Angel of the LORD came up from Gilgal to Bochim' (2:1) is not an indication of any journey he has made, but in order to connect this event with the last time the Angel appeared — that is, years before to Joshua at Gilgal, just before the invasion of Jericho (Josh. 5:13-15).

The people respond to the Angel's rebuke with tears of repentance. They are so overcome with sorrow and penitence that they rename the place Bochim, meaning 'weeping'.

With the death of Joshua and all the elders who served with him, the people of Israel go into serious moral and spiritual decline (2:11-23).

Part II: Waves of oppression followed by delivery (3:7 – 16:31)

All the history in the book of Judges is accurate history, but the arrangement is not based on chronology (the sequence of events); instead it is presented in a repeated sequence of sin → oppression → delivery. This recurring pattern is often called a 'cycle' and further defined as having five steps: 'sin, servitude, supplication, salvation, and silence',[9] or 'rest, rebellion, retribution, repentance and restoration'.[10] The problem with these distinctions is that every episode related in Judges does not necessarily contain evidence of each stage of the 'cycle'. It may therefore be more accurate to describe the recorded history as a 'downward spiral'.[11]

There is a general pattern discernible:

1. The children of Israel do evil in the sight of the Lord (3:7,12; 4:1; 6:1; 10:6; 13:1). What this evil consists of is summarized as breaking covenant with the Lord (2:1-2), turning from him, worshipping and serving other gods, and friendship and intermarriage with the Canaanites (2:11 – 3:7).

Israel's oppressors in the days of the judges

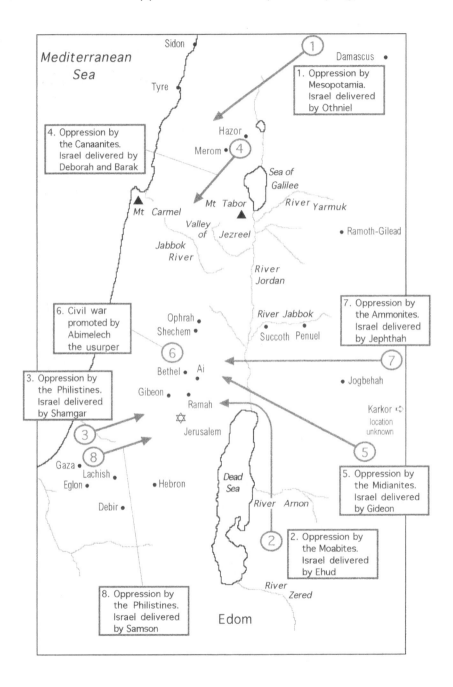

2. In response to this evil, the anger of the Lord burns hot. He withdraws his protection and power from the Israelites and sends fierce foreign oppressors against them (3:8,12; 4:2; 6:1; 10:7; 13:1).

3. Eventually, under the oppressors, the Israelites repent and cry to God for help (3:9,15; 4:3; 6:6-7; 10:10).

4. The Lord responds to their repentance by raising up judges to deliver them from their oppressors and to lead them back to a life of fellowship with him (3:9,15; 10:12). The deliverer is sometimes declared to be empowered by the Spirit of God, as in the case of Othniel (3:10), Gideon (6:34), Jephthah (11:29) and Samson (13:25; 14:6,19).

5. The enemy is subdued, the Israelites are delivered and a period of peace usually follows (3:11,30; 5:31; 8:28). Upon the death of the judge the people revert back to idolatry and immorality. The sequence begins over again.

The downward spiral

The first judge of Israel is *Othniel* (3:9-10), Caleb's nephew and son-in-law (1:13). He is a fine example of what a judge/deliverer should be — raised up by the Lord, empowered by the Holy Spirit, a highly capable and experienced soldier (Josh. 15:16-17). He leads Israel in a successful war with Mesopotamia. Upon his death the 'downward spiral' of Israel begins in earnest.

Israel 'again did evil in the sight of the LORD' (3:12).

The second deliverer, *Ehud*, though raised up by the Lord, is not said to be endued with the Spirit of the Lord, nor is there any comment to indicate whether he has a personal relationship with the Lord. Ehud is of the tribe of Benjamin (3:15). Like so many of his tribe, he is left-handed (20:15-16), a feature which enables him to take King Eglon by surprise, and stab him to death. After the deed Ehud escapes and rallies his men, who proceed to win an overwhelming victory against their oppressors.

The third deliverer is *Shamgar* (3:31). During eighty years of national rest the spiritual and moral tone of the nation deteriorates. This time the Lord uses the Canaanites, under King Jabin, to punish the Israelites from within their own land (4:2-3). These were the people whom the Lord had told the Israelites to destroy! (Deut. 20:17). Jabin reigned at Hazor, eight miles west north-west of Merom, in the land given to Naphtali. For twenty years the children of Israel in the northern region suffer painfully under the powerful army of Jabin's general, Sisera.

Responding to the cry of the people, the Lord inspires as deliverer one who is already functioning as a judge in the central region just a mile or two south of Bethel in the territory of Ephraim — Judge *Deborah* the prophetess, wife of Lapidoth. Deborah was not the first prophetess in Israel,[12] but she was the first prophet, male or female, since Moses. Deborah also has the distinction of being 'the first and only woman ever to exercise civil authority in Israel'.[13]

Forty years of peace ensue. Extended peace is once more attended by increased laxity in matters spiritual and moral: 'And the children of Israel did evil in the sight of the LORD' (6:1).

This time the Lord uses the Midianites[14] as the taskmasters to bring Israel to her knees. Repeatedly invaded, the Israelites eventually return in sorrow to the living God. The Lord responds, not by sending an immediate deliverer as previously, but by first sending a prophet. This unnamed prophet delivers a message designed to make the people aware of their sins, in order that they may understand the reason for their suffering. The prophet also acts as a herald preparing the way for the Lord's deliverer, *Gideon*, 'the mighty man of valour' of the tribe of Manasseh.

'The Angel of the LORD' visits Gideon. This manifestation was unusual for that period. Previous men, Othniel, Ehud and Barak, had been moved by the Spirit of God, but Gideon is privileged to see a Christophany.

Although Gideon has genuine faith in the living God (Heb. 11:32) it is intermingled with unbelief. In spite of the visit of the Angel of the LORD, he needs constant reassurance. His forces number 32,000 and the opposition has 135,000 (7:3; 8:10). He asks the Lord for a sign to confirm his Word (6:36-37). Not content with one miracle, he asks for another (6:39). Despite of these misgivings he has outstanding confidence in the power and purposes of God. With 300 men Gideon defeats the vast army of the Midianites.

On his return home the people of Israel offer Gideon a hereditary throne (8:22). He shows commendable modesty and humility by refusing, on the grounds that the Lord is the true King of Israel. While Moses had given directions for the appointment of a king over Israel (Deut. 17:14-20), the ideal was for Israel to function under a direct theocracy — that is, the rule of God (1 Sam. 12:12,17). Commendable as this refusal is, Gideon falls into a more subtle temptation. Requesting the gold earrings taken from the slaughtered enemy, he uses this vast quantity of gold to have an ephod (high priest's tunic) made (Exod. 28:5-14), which he houses in his home town of Ophrah. Gideon has formed wrong conclusions from a series of events: he had been visited by the Angel of the LORD; he had been commissioned to deliver Israel; his gift had been accepted as a sacrifice by fire; under God's instruction he had built an altar to the Lord and sacrificed a bullock using the wood from the idolatrous image; and he had subsequently received several revelations from the Lord. Gideon wrongly concludes from these events that he is to serve as a high priest to Israel. The Word of God does not permit him to serve in this capacity; he does not fulfil the requirements. The high priest must be a descendant of Aaron and is appointed to function in the tabernacle at Shiloh (Josh. 18:1; Judg. 18:31). Gideon sins on both counts. The people also sin in accepting Gideon's ephod as approved by God. The priesthood at Shiloh may have been abused by men of low calibre at the time, but this did not justify Gideon in making his own substitute. This sin brings serious repercussions upon Gideon's family and upon the Israelites in years to come. It opens the way for disregarding strict obedience to the revealed will of God, leading the nation to fall back into the worship of Baal upon Gideon's death (8:33). Further blots upon an otherwise upright character are Gideon's numerous wives and a concubine (8:30-31).

After Gideon's death, his son Abimelech seizes power. He is not a deliverer but an oppressor from within. He murders seventy of his half brothers to establish himself as king over Israel (9:1-6). Only one brother, Jotham, escapes death. On Mount Gerizim Jotham declares a parable of curse against the people of Shechem and against Abimelech. Abimelech the usurper rules in Shechem for three years and then dies a humiliating death: 'Thus God repaid the wickedness of Abimelech... And all the evil of the men of Shechem God returned on their own heads, and on them came the curse of Jotham the son of Jerubbaal' (9:56-57).[15]

After Abimelech two judges are briefly mentioned, *Tola* and *Jair* (10:1-5). After some years of relative calm in the nation, the spiritual and moral state of the nation once more deteriorates: 'Then the children of Israel again did evil in the sight of the LORD ... and they forsook the LORD and did not serve him' (10:6).

In his anger the Lord sends the Philistines from the south-west and the Ammonites from the east to harass and oppress the children of Israel for eighteen years. Eventually the people acknowledge their wickedness in turning from the true God to idols. They cry out to the Lord that he may have mercy upon them and deliver them. The Lord refuses to help. 'Such repulse is but intended to quicken and to deepen repentance.'[16] The people show true contrition. They destroy their idols, cease to practise idolatry and recommence with seriousness the worship of Jehovah.

Battle lines are drawn between the Ammonite army at Gilead and the Israelites at Mizpah, and *Jephthah* becomes commander-in-chief. He is successful in battle and wins a decisive victory over the Ammonites.

Following the death of Jephthah three men judge Israel: *Ibzan, Elon* and *Abdon* (12:8-15). Whether they function concurrently with other judges in different areas of Israel is not made clear. Upon the death of Abdon deterioration once more takes place: 'Again the children of Israel did evil in the sight of the LORD' (13:1). The Israelites repeatedly fail to see the connection between their faithfulness and obedience to the Lord, on the one hand, and their security and well-being as a nation, on the other.

This time the Lord uses the Philistines to the south-west of Israel to punish his people. Israel is to face forty years of affliction, its longest period throughout the whole time of the judges. During this period the Lord raises up a man who will 'begin to deliver Israel out of the hand of the Philistines' (13:5).

Unlike his great predecessors, *Samson* gathers no army, nor brings remarkable delivery for the children of Israel. With superhuman power he single-handedly performs exploits among the Philistine enemy, illustrating what all Israel could achieve if only they would rely upon the Lord and the strength of his might.

Samson's birth is announced in a most unusual manner. His parents-to-be are visited by the Angel of the LORD (13:3; cf. Gen. 18:10). Their son is to be consecrated to the Lord, for 'No razor shall come upon his head, for the child shall be a Nazirite to God from the womb; and he shall begin to deliver Israel' (13:5). The Angel implies the strongest connection between the former and the latter: success in his work will depend upon Samson's adherence to the prescribed lifestyle (Num. 6:1-8). Whereas this vow of separation was normally of temporary duration, for Samson it is to be life-long. These outward forms are intentionally to be matched by true inner dedication to the Lord. In this Samson did not always succeed. He is the epitome of 'the weak strong man'.

Samson is full of self-indulgence. In this respect he is a living symbol of the spiritual corruption of the nation as a whole (2:17; 8:27,33). Lust and love for forbidden women lead to Samson's ultimate downfall. He falls in love with Delilah, a Philistine woman. Eventually succumbing to Delilah's pleas, Samson discloses the secret of his strength. He is overpowered, blinded and made a slave in the prison workhouse. But his hair grows again and his strength returns once more.

Taken to the temple of Dagon, the god of the Philistines, Samson is paraded before a vast crowd of spectators. Making one last request for power from the Lord, Samson dies taking over 3,000 Philistines with him. He is more successful in death than in life (16:30). 'Samson, when strong and brave, strangled a lion; but he could not strangle his own love. He burst the fetters of his foes, but not the cords of his own lusts. He burned up the crops of others, and lost the fruit of his own virtue when burning with the flame enkindled by a single woman.'[17]

Part III: Examples of corruption within Israel (17:1 - 21:25)

The purpose of this section appears to be that of illustrating the extent to which the Hebrews have transgressed the Ten Commandments and the Book of the Covenant. The evils which result when 'everyone did what was right in his own eyes' (21:25) include theft (17:2), idolatry (17:5), immorality (19:2), homosexuality (19:22) and mass abduction (21:23).

Micah

An Ephraimite called Micah builds a shrine, makes an ephod to wear that he might determine the will of God, sets up idols and establishes one of his sons as his priest. A little later a Levite from Bethlehem travelling in the area is invited to lodge with Micah and offered the position of family priest. Micah foolishly concludes that the presence of the Levitical priest, in spite of the idolatrous paraphernalia, will ensure the Lord's blessing upon him (17:13).

The Benjamites

Around the same time another Levite, from Ephraim, and his concubine, while on a journey, stop at the Benjamite city of Gibeah to spend the night there. The men of Gibeah surround the house and demand that the Levite be sent out to them for their perverted purpose. God's nation of Israel has become as evil as Sodom (cf. Gen. 19:5-8). The Levite's concubine is handed over to the perverted mob. Discovering her dead the following morning, the Levite transports her body back to the mountains of Ephraim.

Once at home he dismembers her body into twelve parts and sends these to the twelve tribes.

Outraged by the incident at Gibeah, the leaders of the tribes gather together at Mizpah to determine what course of action to take against the men of Gibeah. They form a representative force that is dispatched to Gibeah. Once they arrive at the city, word is sent for the Benjamites to deliver up the perpetrators of the atrocious crime. The Benjamites refuse, choosing to side with the evil men of their community. The other tribes of Israel are forced to confront the whole tribe of Benjamin.

In the first battle Israel suffers very heavy losses: 22,000 men are killed. In the second battle Israel is defeated again, this time with a loss of 18,000 soldiers. Then at the third attempt the Benjamites are defeated and routed. Eventually only 600 men remain of the tribe of Benjamin. The question inevitably rises as to why the Israelites experience two defeats and such heavy losses when they are seeking to obey the law of God in respect to purging the land. The answer is not immediately obvious. Careful examination reveals that the Israelites do not consult the Lord in an appropriate manner. Commendable as it is that they consult God at Bethel. their sin is 'the state of mind with which they had entered upon the war, their strong self-consciousness, and great confidence in their own might and power'. [18] Their first consultation with the Lord only asks, 'Which of us shall go up first to battle against the children of Benjamin?' (20:18). The second, though accompanied by weeping before the Lord, raises the question: 'Shall I again draw near for battle against the children of my brother Benjamin?' (20:23). On both occasions the Israelites are confident in their own strength and their greater numbers. It is only when they humble themselves before the Lord and acknowledge their weakness and inadequacy, with fasting, penitence and sacrifice, that they rise successfully above the Benjamites. The final battle sees the defeat of the tribe of Benjamin to such an extent that the tribe is very nearly annihilated. Only 600 men remain of the whole tribe! Drastic steps are taken to provide the remaining Benjamites with virgin wives from other tribes.

The book of Judges documents the weakness and waywardness of the Israelites during the period between the death of Joshua and the establishment of the monarchy in Israel. Preparation is made for Israel to have a king in the repeated reference to the fact that 'In those days there was no king in Israel' (17:6; 18:1; cf. 19:1; 21:25), and summed up in the final verse of the book: 'In those days there was no king in Israel; everyone did what was right in his own eyes' (21:25). When the Israelites did what was right in their own eyes it was invariably what was evil in the sight of the Lord.

Christ and his church

The book of Judges contains three Christophanies: 'the Angel of the LORD' rebukes the Israelites (2:1-5); appoints Gideon to his work as judge and deliverer of Israel (6:11-24); and informs Manoah's wife that she will bear a son, whom she calls Samson (13:3-5,9-23). In the last of these visitations, when asked his name, the Angel replies, 'Why do you ask my name, seeing it is wonderful?' (13:18). This is not the proper name of the Angel of the LORD so much as an expression of the uniqueness of his character — 'absolutely and supremely wonderful' (cf. Isa. 9:6).[19] God alone is described in such terms. When Manoah offers food prepared for the Angel as a burnt offering, 'the Angel of the LORD ascended in the flame of the altar' (13:20). From this miracle Manoah and his wife knew that their visitor was none other than the Angel of the LORD. The deity of the Angel is confirmed beyond all doubt in the words of Manoah: 'We shall surely die, because we have seen God!' (13:22). With spiritual logic his wife reassures him that they will not die.

There are no obvious types of Christ in the book of Judges. Some commentators see Samson as a type of Christ but the arguments in favour are unconvincing.[20]

Application

1. The human heart is prone to wander away from God

There is a potential 'prodigal' in the heart of every believer. We find it hard to believe some of the things God teaches. We find it hard to obey some of the commandments he gives. We find it hard to walk in holiness and subdue self-interest and deny ourselves our sinful pleasures. We find it hard to pray as we ought, to read Scripture as we should, to attend worship as God directs. We find it hard to love our brethren as our Saviour requires. We find it hard to seek the lost, share the gospel, do good to all, to love our neighbour. In a hundred and one ways it is evident that our greatest enemy is within. It is our 'self'. My greatest enemy is me! 'The heart is deceitful above all things, and desperately wicked' (Jer. 17:9). 'For the good that I will to do, I do not do; but the evil I will not to do, that I practise' (Rom. 7:19).

> Oh to grace how great a debtor
> Daily I'm constrained to be!
> Let that grace, Lord, like a fetter,
> Bind my wandering heart to thee.
> Prone to wander, Lord, I feel it,
> Prone to leave the God I love;
> Take my heart, O take and seal it,
> Seal it from thy courts above!
>
> (Robert Robinson)

2. God pursues and restores his backslidden people

In this book of the Bible there are seven accounts of backsliding, seven periods of oppression, seven cries to God and seven deliveries:

> Thus they were defiled by their own works,
> And played the prostitute by their own deeds.
> Therefore the wrath of the LORD was kindled against his people,
> So that he abhorred his own inheritance.
> And he gave them into the hand of the Gentiles,
> And those who hated them ruled over them.
> Their enemies also oppressed them,
> And they were brought into subjection under their hand.
> Many times he delivered them;
> But they rebelled against him by their counsel,
> And were brought low for their iniquity.
> Nevertheless he regarded their affliction,
> When he heard their cry;
> And for their sake he remembered his covenant,
> And relented according to the multitude of his mercies
>
> (Ps. 106:39-45).

Those whom the Lord loves he disciplines (Heb. 12:6). Affliction is good for the soul. The psalmist declares: 'Before I was afflicted I went astray, but now I keep your word' (Ps. 119:67). In love and grace towards his wayward people, the Lord 'commands and raises the stormy wind' so that:

Their soul melts because of trouble.
They reel to and fro, and stagger like a drunken man,
And are at their wits' end

                                                                        (Ps. 107:26-27).

God's people get into difficulties in numerous ways. They reach a point of desperation. Four times in Psalm 107 we read the words: 'Then they cried out to the LORD in their trouble, and he delivered them out of their distresses' (vv. 6,13,19,28). There are repeated statements in the book of Judges that Israel 'cried out' to the Lord and he heard them and rescued them: 'When the children of Israel cried out to the LORD, the LORD raised up a deliverer for the children of Israel, who delivered them' (3:9; cf. 3:15; 4:3; 6:6-7; 10:10). The testimony of David is: 'This poor man cried out, and the LORD heard him, and saved him out of all his troubles' (Ps. 34:6).

God calls his people to faithful obedience. Nevertheless if they wander from him, or wilfully turn from him, there is a way back. They can cry out to the Lord in times of affliction and distress. 'Cast your burden on the LORD, and he shall sustain you' (Ps. 55:22). 'God … gives grace to the humble', so cast 'all your care upon him for he cares for you' (1 Peter 5:5,7).

3. Vows to the Lord

Jephthah made a rash vow. The words he used meant that he had in mind the possibility of a human being coming to meet him.[21] Making a vow is not unlawful, but Jephthah seems to have shown a distinct lack of faith. The Spirit of God had come upon him. That should have been enough to assure him of victory. Maybe he foolishly thought that by promising some great sacrifice to God, he would somehow make sure of success. Vows ought not to be made in order to obtain God's favour and blessing, but to witness to our gratitude and thankfulness.

When you make a vow to the LORD your God, you shall not delay to pay it; for the LORD your God will surely require it of you, and

it would be sin to you. But if you abstain from vowing, it shall not be
sin to you

(Deut. 23:21-22).

Do not be rash with your mouth,
And let not your heart utter anything hastily before God.
For God is in heaven, and you on earth;
Therefore let your words be few.
For a dream comes through much activity,
And a fool's voice is known by his many words.
When you make a vow to God, do not delay to pay it;
For he has no pleasure in fools.
Pay what you have vowed.
It is better not to vow than to vow and not pay.

Do not let your mouth cause your flesh to sin, nor say before the
messenger of God that it was an error. Why should God be angry at
your excuse and destroy the work of your hands?

(Eccles. 5:2-6).

It is a snare for a man to devote rashly something as holy,
And afterwards to reconsider his vows

(Prov. 20:25)

When a vow is made, the promise ought to be fulfilled (Num. 30:2). But
there are exceptional promises, such as that of Herod (Mark 6:23-27), involving the life or welfare of another human being, where breaking the vow
would involve less sin than keeping it. In such a case it is necessary to withdraw from the vow and seek pardon for having rashly made it. Jephthah
was wrong to make the vow he did. Human sacrifice was abhorrent to the
Lord (Lev. 18:21; 20:2-5). God would have seriously disapproved of such
action. In those early days human sacrifices were never heard of among
the Israelites. Such practices were only introduced to Jerusalem by the
godless kings Ahaz and Manasseh (2 Kings 16:3; 21:6). They were not
even the general practice among the heathens.

Fausset argues in defence of Jephthah on the following lines: Firstly,
Jephthah knew what he was doing right from the beginning. It was not a
hasty vow. Secondly, Jephthah knew the Pentateuch well enough to know
that human sacrifices were contrary to the law of God. Thirdly, if Jephthah
had sacrificed his daughter he could not possibly have been listed as an

example of 'faith' among the heroes of Hebrews 11 (v. 32). Fausset concludes by saying, '… all the requirements of the case are fulfilled, if we suppose he devoted his only daughter to lifelong virginity as a spiritual burnt-offering consecrated to Jehovah.'[22] This harmonizes with the sequel where Jephthah's daughter asks for permission to go away to the mountains, with her close female friends, to mourn her virginity (11:37-38). To mourn her virginity is not to mourn because she has to die a virgin, but because she has to live and remain a virgin.[23] The statement in verse 39 that 'She knew no man' would be utterly superfluous if she had been put to death. She was to commit her life to a life of celibacy in the service of the tabernacle (cf. Exod. 38:8; 1 Sam. 2:22; Luke 2:37).

From that day there was an annual remembrance of Jephthah's daughter (11:40). What the daughters of Israel gathered yearly to 'praise' was her willingness to sacrifice for ever her natural aspirations 'from motives of filial obedience, patriotic devotion, and self-renouncing piety'. [24] Literal burnt offerings could only be offered at the lawful altar and by the Levitical priests and they would never have consented to such an unlawful act. If Jephthah himself had offered her upon an altar of his own, then he would not have said '[It] shall surely be the LORD's, and I will offer it up as a burnt-offering' (11:31).[25] Young suggests: 'In fulfilment of the vow, he probably devoted her to perpetual virginity, but of this one cannot be certain.'[26] Even this would be an abuse of his responsibility as a father. On the basis of 1 Samuel 12:11 and Hebrews 11:32, Leon Wood suggests that what he did with his daughter 'was something approved of God and that he was himself in right relation to God'.[27] The true honour, however, must rest upon Jephthah's daughter. The Lord turned the foolish vow of a father into a glorious memorial to his mercy and grace 'through the lovely submissiveness and self-sacrifice of a godly daughter'. [28]

4. Strength and weakness

Sometimes the people of God are brought low so that all glory for achievements will be given to the Lord. Gideon's army was drastically reduced in size, 'lest Israel claim glory for itself against [God], saying, "My own hand has saved me" ' (7:2). The same truth is underlined in the New Testament where Paul says, 'God has chosen the foolish things of the world to put to shame the wise, and God has chosen the weak things of the world to put to shame the things which are mighty; and the base things of the world and the things which are despised God has chosen, and the things which are not, to bring to nothing the things that are, that no flesh should glory in his presence … as it is written, "He who glories, let him glory in the LORD" ' (1 Cor. 1:27-29,31).

The divine power displayed in the judges culminates in Samson, who possessed his extraordinary power by virtue of being a Nazirite consecrated to the Lord. In his natural character he was a weak man. 'In Samson we have the spectacle of a man in whom faith was mighty, but who, nevertheless, failed to subdue his own passions, and to keep his body under subjection.'[29] We may see something here of an illustration of the believer with and without close fellowship with God. When weak and yet leaning hard upon the Lord, then we are strong: 'And he said to me, "My grace is sufficient for you, for my strength is made perfect in weakness." Therefore most gladly I will rather boast in my infirmities, that the power of Christ may rest upon me. Therefore I take pleasure in infirmities, in reproaches, in needs, in persecutions, in distresses, for Christ's sake. For when I am weak, then I am strong' (2 Cor. 12:9-10).

5. The weakness of the law

The reference to Phinehas the priest (20:28) locates the appalling incidents of chapters 17-21 in the years immediately following the death of Joshua since Phinehas the son of Eleazar was already functioning as high priest in the days of Joshua (Josh. 22:13,30-32; 24:33). The good days for Israel under Joshua's leadership soon evaporated upon his death. The Israelites proved to be constantly attracted to, and influenced by, the idolatry and sexual perversion of the Canaanite fertility religions. The fact that Phinehas was the grandson of Aaron indicates too how quickly the Israelites departed from the covenant of the Lord at Sinai.

Throughout the book of Judges the weakness of the law of Sinai is all too apparent. The apostle Paul explains the reason for this failure: '… it was weak through the flesh' (Rom. 8:3). Sinful human nature cannot obey the law. The law brings the knowledge of sin (Rom. 3:20). Only drastic action by an intermediary and drastic transformation within believers can solve the problem. The Son of God provides the answer to the first and the Spirit of God provides the answer to the second: 'There is therefore now no condemnation to those who are in Christ Jesus, who do not walk according to the flesh, but according to the Spirit. For the law of the Spirit of life in Christ Jesus has made me free from the law of sin and death. For what the law could not do in that it was weak through the flesh, God did by sending his own Son in the likeness of sinful flesh, on account of sin: he condemned sin in the flesh, that the righteous requirement of the law might be fulfilled in us who do not walk according to the flesh but according to the Spirit' (Rom. 8:1-4).

Conclusion

Judges is another great book of God. Here we see what happens when people disobey, or only partially obey, the Lord. When people do what they like instead of doing what God commands, it always leads to disaster. Problems arose for the Israelites when 'everyone did what was right in his own eyes' (17:6; 21:25).

The Canaanites who were allowed to remain in the conquered land symbolize sinful tendencies and lusts remaining in the believer's heart and mind. Paul urges Christians to mortify (put to death) the sinful inclinations: 'fornication, uncleanness, passion, evil desire, and covetousness, which is idolatry' (Col. 3:5).

> If we wilfully spare a single Canaanite, or enter into a tacit agreement with the enemy, though we may perhaps not fail of heaven at last, we shall have stripes of sorrow on our journey thither: 'they shall be as thorns in your sides, and their gods shall be a snare unto you' [2:3, AV]. Our prospects will be dim, our usefulness will be impaired, our light will be turned into darkness, and our songs into dirges of lamentation; while the remorseless, tyrannous lust humbles us again and again, sinks us lower than the dust, and reduces us to exquisite and abject misery: the just penalty of refusing to take up the cross and deny self, that we might follow Christ.
>
> Merciful Lord! Deliver me and Thy whole Church from the humiliation and bitterness of being subject to the Canaanite![30]

Ruth

(after main character)

Author: Unknown
(probably Samuel)

Key thought: 'Kinsman-redeemer'

Theme:
A stranger brought into the family of God

'For wherever you go, I will go...
Your people shall be my people,
And your God, my God.'
Ruth 1:16

Summary

Ruth

The book of Ruth is a literary and spiritual gem. Alexander Schroder declares: 'No poet in the world has written a more beautiful short story.'[1] In the eighteenth century Dr Samuel Johnson read this book to his friends in a literary club in London. In his introduction he did not disclose its title or origins but simply read through its pages. The people who listened responded with high praise. They thought it a recent composition and were outspoken in their appreciation and acclaim. Dr Johnson then informed them that it was the book of Ruth which he had read to them from a book which they all despised — the Bible.[2]

The book of Ruth is a story about very ordinary people facing ordinary events. It tells of Naomi, a wife and mother bereft of husband and sons, who experiences great hardship in famine and bereavement, eventually being brought to a place of peace and security. It tells of Ruth, the foreign woman from Moab, who attaches herself to Naomi, her mother-in-law, and to Naomi's God, and receives immense blessing in later life. It tells of Boaz, Naomi's kinsman by marriage, who shows great kindness to Ruth and Naomi. By his obedience to the law of God and his respectful dealings with Ruth, Boaz becomes an honoured ancestor of the Lord Jesus Christ.

Author

The writer is unknown. Jewish tradition accredits the book to the prophet Samuel. Judging from the first verse of this book, 'Now it came to pass, in the days when the judges ruled...' (1:1), and its last verse, 'Obed begot Jesse, and Jesse begot David (4:22), it must have been written when the rule of the Judges had ceased, at the introduction of the monarchy, and after the birth of David.

Historical setting

The book of Ruth illustrates a peaceful period during the time of the judges. Whereas Judges provides us with a bleak portrayal of spiritual conditions in the nation, Ruth paints another side to the picture: a time between the fighting and the wars; a time of calm and tranquillity in the life of the nation of Israel. The times covered by this book occurred during the first one hundred years of 'the days when the judges ruled' (1:1), some time after the Moabite oppression and delivery by Ehud (Judg. 3:12-14,30). This is based on the fact that Ruth married Boaz, who was the son of Salmon and Rahab, the converted Canaanite prostitute (Matt. 1:5; Heb. 11:31) and that Israel was not at war with Moab.[3]

These were real people, with real problems, real difficulties, real experiences, who enjoyed real blessing from God. The book of Ruth presents a brief picture of rural life in Israel during the thirteenth century B.C. There are the everyday routines of life: the need to work, the joys of the family, the pains of bereavement, parting from relatives and relationships with a mother-in-law.

Outline

This book is notable because it is the only instance in the Bible where a whole book is devoted to the history of a woman (the book of Esther contains far more than the history of Esther herself).

Part I: Emigration to Moab (1: 1- 5)

Elimelech and his wife Naomi of the tribe of Judah leave their home town of Bethlehem (i.e. Ephrath, Gen. 35:19) because of a severe famine and out of desperation, having lost their ancestral land to pay debts. They journey with their two sons Mahlon and Chilion to the east, crossing over the River Jordan and going down the west coast of the Dead Sea, over the River Arnon, and into the land of Moab.[4] Elimelech dies and the two sons marry women of Moab. After having been in the land of Moab for ten years Mahlon and Chilion also die.

Part II: The sad return to Judah (1: 6-22)

Naomi, left with two Moabite daughters-in-law, and hearing that the famine is over in Judah, decides to return to her own people. She urges her two daughters-in-law to return to their parental homes, and seeks God's blessing upon each one in finding a new husband and home. Tears flow as the three women contemplate separation. Both women propose to accompany Naomi back to Bethlehem. Naomi insists that they will have no benefit from remaining with her. She cannot herself provide any more husbands for them. Naomi urges them to return to their own people. Tears flow once more and Orpah bids farewell, but Ruth will not be parted from her mother-in-law, for she has been converted to faith in the God of Israel, the only true and living God. Ruth professes her allegiance to Naomi, to Naomi's people and to Naomi's God.

Seeing the determination in her daughter-in-law, Naomi realizes that further protestations on her part will be useless. The two women continue on their journey to Bethlehem.

On their arrival in Bethlehem the local women are surprised to see Naomi returning after a ten-year absence. When they enquire, 'Is this Naomi?' she takes the opportunity to testify to her great grief: 'Do not call me Naomi [pleasant]; call me Mara [bitter], for the Almighty has dealt very bitterly with me' (1:20).

Part III: Ruth and Boaz (2:1 - 4:17)

It is harvest-time when the two women arrive in Bethlehem. Ruth obtains permission from the servant in charge to follow the reapers in order to glean what remains in the fields. The law of God provides for those who are poor and strangers: 'When you reap the harvest of your land, you shall not wholly reap the corners of your field when you reap, nor shall you gather any gleaning from your harvest. You shall leave them for the poor and for the stranger: I am the LORD your God' (Lev. 23:22).

Boaz, a relative of Naomi by marriage, comes from the city, sees Ruth gleaning, and asks his servant about her. Hearing that she is Ruth the Moabitess who returned with Naomi, Boaz is pleased to assist her. He has heard of her reputation and seeks God's blessing upon her: 'The LORD repay your work, and a full reward be given you by the LORD God of Israel, under whose wings you have come for refuge' (Ruth 2:12).

Boaz encourages Ruth to stay with his young women workers. He takes steps with the men to ensure Ruth's safety and also to provide for more grain to be dropped for her to glean. Ruth works daily in the fields of Boaz through the barley harvest and the wheat harvest, probably for a period of just under two months.

Naomi's strategy

Naomi is concerned to provide some degree of security for her daughter-in-law Ruth.[5] Widows do not seem to have been included among those who could inherit property from a man who died without leaving a male heir (Num. 27:8-11). On the basis of the provisions laid down in the law of God, Naomi seeks the restoration of her husband's land through property redemption and the continuance of her husband's name through levirate marriage.

The first part of the plan requires the buying back of the land: 'If one of your brethren becomes poor, and has sold some of his possession, and if his kinsman-redeemer comes to redeem it, then he may redeem what his brother sold. Or if the man has no one to redeem it, but he himself be-comes able to redeem it, then let him count the years since its sale, and restore the balance to the man to whom he sold it, that he may return to his possession' (Lev. 25:25-27).

The second part of the plan requires the marriage of Ruth to a near kinsman: 'If brothers dwell together, and one of them dies and has no son, the widow of the dead man shall not be married to a stranger outside the family; her husband's brother shall go in to her, take her as his wife, and perform the duty of a husband's brother to her. And it shall be that the first-born son which she bears will succeed to the name of his dead brother, that his name may not be blotted out of Israel. But if the man does not want to take his brother's wife, then let his brother's wife go up to the gate to the elders, and say, "My husband's brother refuses to raise up a name to his brother in Israel; he will not perform the duty of my husband's brother." Then the elders of his city shall call him and speak to him; and if he stands firm and says, "I do not want to take her," then his brother's wife shall come to him in the presence of the elders, remove his sandal from his foot, spit in his face, and answer and say, "So shall it be done to the man who will not build up his brother's house." And his name shall be called in Is-rael, "The house of him who had his sandal removed" ' (Deut. 25:5-10).

The threshing-floor

Ruth follows Naomi's advice, bathes, dresses in her finest outfit and goes to the threshing-floor to wait for Boaz to take a rest. Once he has fallen asleep Ruth lies at his feet. A startled Boaz discovers Ruth at midnight. She identifies herself and adds, 'Spread the corner of your garment over your maidservant' (3:9, alternative reading). This is not an invitation to immorality, but 'a formal proposal of marriage couched in the picturesque language of the time'.[6] Boaz, an honourable man of mature years (3:10), praises Ruth for having taken refuge with him, and promises to fulfil her wishes when he has satisfied himself that a closer relative will renounce his right and duty.

True to his word, Boaz takes the necessary steps required by the law of God to see that the land of Elimelech and the wife of Elimelech's son are redeemed by the next of kin. Finding the nearest kinsman to Elimelech, and in the presence of ten elders of the town, Boaz asks him if he will redeem the land of Elimelech. This the near kinsman is prepared to do. Then Boaz links the redemption of the land to the redemption of the family line. This second part the near kinsman will not fulfil since he fears it would jeopardize his existing inheritance (if Ruth bears a son, this kinsman and his family will lose a considerable amount of money in buying land that neither he nor his existing family can ever possess). Atkinson may well be right in his assessment: 'The kinsman was now placed in a predicament — which was exactly what Boaz had intended! Here Boaz' deep personal care for Ruth shines through. It was in order that he might marry her that Boaz had engineered this ploy, mentioning the land first, and Ruth afterwards. And his "masterstroke" came off. He skilfully used the possibilities of the law to place the nearest kinsman in an impossible position. The unnamed goel [i.e. kinsman-redeemer] now realized that he had two responsibilities and not one, and that both belonged together … he could hardly accept one without the other.'[7]

Boaz steps into the breach, redeems the land and redeems Ruth by taking her to be his wife. As kinsman-redeemer Boaz does not take possession of the land but holds it in trust for the first son born to Ruth. According to levirate law that son would take the name and the inheritance of Mahlon, Ruth's first husband.

Boaz and Ruth have a son, Obed. He is to become the grandfather of King David.

Part IV: Ancestors of King David (4:18-22)

The book of Ruth closes by showing how, in the providence of Almighty God, the family fits into the ancestral line of the great King David (cf. Matt. 1:3-6).

Christ and his church

The New Testament does not provide a reference to Boaz as a type of Christ, nor to Ruth as a type of the church. With the benefits of the completed Scriptures, the position of Boaz and Ruth in this representative character seems unavoidable. As Jensen warns, 'In a study of types, one should always be careful to make the antitype, not the type, the pre-eminent fact; and also to avoid forcing types for the mere sake of typology.'[8]

1. Ruth as a type of the Gentile church

Ruth symbolizes the Gentile portion of the church of Jesus Christ. Her story is a prophetic insight into God's love for the world beyond the Jews. It demonstrates his amazing grace in reaching out to those who are accursed. Ruth was a Moabitess. The *law* of God excluded her; the *grace* of God included her: 'An Ammonite or Moabite shall not enter the congregation of the LORD; even to the tenth generation none of his descendants shall enter the congregation of the LORD for ever, because they did not meet you with bread and water on the road when you came out of Egypt, and because they hired against you Balaam the son of Beor from Pethor of Mesopotamia, to curse you' (Deut. 23:3-4).

Ruth was a stranger away from God

'... at that time you were without Christ, being aliens from the commonwealth of Israel and strangers from the covenants of promise, having no hope and without God in the world. But now in Christ Jesus you who once were far off have been made near by the blood of Christ... Now, therefore, you are no longer strangers and foreigners, but fellow citizens with the saints and members of the household of God' (Eph. 2:12-13,19).

Ruth turns from father and mother, homeland and kindred

'If anyone comes to me and does not hate his father and mother, wife and children, brothers and sisters, yes, and his own life also, he cannot be my disciple' (Luke 14:26).

Listen, O daughter,
Consider and incline your ear;
Forget your own people also, and your father's house;
So the King will greatly desire your beauty;
Because he is your Lord, worship him

(Ps. 45:10-11).

'And everyone who has left houses or brothers or sisters or father or mother or wife or children or lands, for my name's sake, shall receive a hundredfold, and inherit everlasting life' (Matt. 19:29).

It has been said that there is nothing in human literature more beautiful than Ruth's address to her mother-in-law:

Entreat me not to leave you,
Or to turn back from following after you;
For wherever you go, I will go;
And wherever you lodge, I will lodge;
Your people shall be my people,
And your God, my God.
Where you die, I will die,
And there will I be buried.
The LORD do so to me, and more also,
If anything but death parts you and me

(Ruth 1:16-17).

Ruth was poor and needy

'For when we were still without strength, in due time Christ died for the ungodly... God demonstrates his own love towards us, in that while we were still sinners, Christ died for us' (Rom. 5:6,8).

Ruth was redeemed by union in marriage

'I am jealous for you with godly jealousy. For I have betrothed you to one husband, that I may present you as a chaste virgin to Christ' (2 Cor. 11:2).

'Christ ... loved the church and gave himself for it, that he might sanctify and cleanse it with the washing of water by the word, that he might present it to himself a glorious church, not having spot or wrinkle or any such thing, but that it should be holy and without blemish' (Eph. 5:25-27).

To 'redeem' means to pay the price (to pay a ransom) necessary to buy the freedom of a captive or slave. Christians 'were bought at a price' (1 Cor. 6:20), at a very high price (1 Peter 1:19).

When united with Christ loneliness ceases, believers become fruitful and a blessing to others (John 15:4).

2. Boaz as a type of Christ

Boaz as the kinsman-redeemer is a type of Christ *the* Redeemer.

The kinsman-redeemer must be a blood relative

'But when the fulness of the time had come, God sent forth his son, born of a woman, born under the law, to redeem those who were under the law, that we might receive the adoption as sons' (Gal. 4:4-5).

'Inasmuch then as the children have partaken of flesh and blood, he himself likewise shared in the same ... in all things he had to be made like his brethren, that he might be a merciful and faithful high priest in things pertaining to God, to make propitiation for the sins of the people...' (Heb. 2:14,17).

The kinsman-redeemer must be able to pay the price

The expression 'a man of great wealth' (2:1) sometimes means a 'valiant' man: it is used of Gideon and Jephthah, each of whom is described as a 'mighty man of valour' (Judg. 6:12; 11:1). Sometimes it means a man of 'substance', as in Moses' prayer for Levi: 'Bless his substance, LORD' (Deut. 33:11). Sometimes it means 'riches', a word used several times by Isaiah (Isa. 8:4; 61:6). It also carries the sense of moral worth —

it is the word used by Boaz to commend Ruth when he says, 'All the people of my town know that you are a *virtuous* woman' (Ruth 3:11). 'In Boaz, therefore, we are introduced to a man of integrity, a man of influence, a man of means.'[9] Yet a greater one than Boaz has come: 'For you know the grace of our Lord Jesus Christ, that though he was rich, yet for your sakes he became poor, that you through his poverty might become rich' (2 Cor. 8:9). 'You were not redeemed with corruptible things, like silver or gold … but with the precious blood of Christ, as of a lamb without blemish and without spot' (1 Peter 1:18-19).

The kinsman-redeemer must look with kindness upon the poor and needy (2:5)

The Lord Jesus is like the Good Samaritan who 'came where he [the bruised and bleeding man] was. And when he saw him, he had compassion on him, and went to him and bandaged his wounds, pouring in oil and wine' (Luke 10:33-34). The four Gospels record a Saviour 'who went about doing good and healing all who were oppressed by the devil, for God was with him' (Acts 10:38). And 'When in penitence we come and lie at His pierced feet, and beseeching Him to spread over us the crimson mantle of His love, how immediate is His response.'[10]

The kinsman-redeemer must redeem people and property (4:5)

The kinsman-redeemer is 'one who redeems or recovers possession or ownership by payment of a price or by rendering service'. In like manner Christ redeems his people by giving his life for us (Titus 2:14), shedding his blood to pay the price for our release (Rev. 5:9). He also redeems creation (Rom. 8:19-23). The Hebrew word for 'kinsman-redeemer' appears over twenty times in the book of Ruth. In the RAV it is translated as 'kinsman', 'kinsmen', 'redeem', 'duty' or 'right of redemption'.

The kinsman-redeemer must be willing to redeem (3:11; 4:9-10)

'Therefore my Father loves me, because I lay down my life that I may take it again. No one takes it from me, but I lay it down of myself. I have power to lay it down, and I have power to take it again. This command I have received from my Father' (John 10:17-18). '… who loved me and gave himself for me' (Gal. 2:20).

Application

1. Providence

The ordinary outworking of providence is the underlying thread of this book. Ruth's meeting with her kinsman-redeemer is described as being by chance: 'And she happened to come to the part of the field belonging to Boaz' (2:3). The verse means the exact opposite of what it seems to say.[11] The clear implication is the involvement of the Lord in guiding and leading Ruth to meet her kinsman-redeemer.

> Trust in the LORD with all your heart,
> And lean not on your own understanding;
> In all your ways acknowledge him,
> And he shall direct your paths
>
> (Prov. 3:5-6).

God's name occurs twenty-three times in this brief book and thus it instructs its readers concerning God's ongoing work in the life of ordinary people.[12] There are no miracles, no heavenly revelations, no prophetic disclosures, and yet there is the strong underlying sense of God's purpose and God's providence, or 'providing', being unfolded. From 'the illustration we are given of purity ... faithfulness and loyalty, duty and love, the writer is wanting his readers to discern the hand of a God who cares, sustains and provides'.[13] 'And we know that all things work together for good to those who love God, to those who are the called according to his purpose' (Rom. 8:28).

2. True conversion

Ruth the Moabitess is a unique illustration of God's grace extending beyond Israel. Here is the grace of God in all its splendour and glory. God so orders providence that Ruth comes from the outside. She is not seeking the true and living God. For in the natural state and condition, 'There is no one who seeks after God' (Rom. 3:11). She has not sought God. She has been sought by God. She has a Good Shepherd in heaven who leads her to the truth in his own inimitable fashion.

Ruth turns 'to God from idols to serve the living and true God' (1 Thess. 1:9). The declaration, 'Your people shall be my people, and your God, my God' (1:16), demonstrates her rejection of her past allegiances and commitments (Ps. 45:10). The Saviour says, 'Everyone who has left houses or brothers or sisters or father or mother or wife or children or lands, for my name's sake, shall receive a hundredfold, and inherit everlasting life' (Matt. 19:29).

3. Love for God's people

Ruth's conversion from paganism to faith in the living and true God is evidenced by her love for the people of God. To Naomi she expresses her faith: '… your people shall be my people, and your God, my God' (1:16).

In the New Testament the apostle John develops the connection between love for God and love for those who are God's: 'Everyone who loves him who begot also loves him who is begotten of him' (1 John 5:1). He also shows that this love for God's people is evidence of conversion: 'We know that we have passed from death to life, because we love the brethren. He who does not love his brother abides in death' (1 John 3:14).

4. Signs of backsliding

Why did Naomi and her husband Elimelech leave Judah? Those who remained and lived through the famine seemed to have fared far better (1:6). Was it right to leave the land of promise? And why choose the land of Moab? The Moabites worshipped Chemosh and apparently offered human sacrifices (2 Kings 3:27). There was also widespread practice of Canaanite fertility rites. This was no place for a God-fearing man and his family. Moving to Moab may have been calculated to save life, but the tragedy for this family was that all three males died in this foreign land.

There is no indication of Naomi's role in the move. She may have instigated the move, agreed with her husband's suggestion, or gone along out of respect for, and submission to, her husband. Nor is there any indication as to whether or not she was in agreement with her two sons marrying women of Moab contrary to the commandment of God (Deut. 23:3).[14] There is, however, other clear evidence that she is in a poor spiritual state though she is not totally without some degree of faith in the true God.

The first obvious indication is in *the advice she gives to her two daughters-in-law*. After she has encouraged them both to go home to their parents, Orpah leaves and Ruth cleaves to her. Naomi then gives her the most staggering advice: 'Look, your sister-in-law has gone back to her people and to her gods; return after your sister-in-law' (Ruth 1:15). While it might be argued that Naomi is showing marked unselfishness in releasing her daughters-in-law, nevertheless she is tacitly recommending Ruth to return 'to her gods'. The words of Naomi imply that Ruth has been converted to faith in the God of Israel, the only true God. She has turned to the LORD. What Naomi is recommending is apostasy — turning back to her Moabite gods!

The second pointer to a poor spiritual state is in *Naomi's response to the providence of God*. To Orpah and Ruth, Naomi says, 'It grieves me very much for your sakes that *the hand of the LORD has gone out against me!*' (1:13, emphasis added). And later this spirit of resentment is present when she meets the women of Bethlehem: 'Do not call me Naomi [pleasant]; call me Mara [bitter], for the Almighty has dealt very bitterly with me. I went out full, and the LORD has brought me home again empty. Why do you call me Naomi, since the LORD has testified against me, and the Almighty has afflicted me?' (Ruth 1:20-21).

How different the response of godly Job at the news of the death of his whole family:

Then Job arose and tore his robe and shaved his head, and he fell to the ground and worshipped. And he said:

'Naked I came from my mother's womb,
And naked shall I return there.
The LORD gave, and the LORD has taken away;
Blessed be the name of the LORD.'

In all this Job did not sin nor charge God with wrong (Job 1:20-22).

The third feature which indicates something not quite right with Naomi is *the strategy she uses* to enlist the help of Boaz. Naomi acknowledges the Lord without really actively trusting in his providence. She has a belief in God, yet also there is an element of disobedience. There is an awareness of his law, but she forgets that the means used to achieve the ends are just as important to God as the ends themselves. The advice she gives to Ruth could have seriously compromised Ruth and Boaz, who were both virtuous people. It is not sound advice to creep into a man's 'bedroom' and lie at his feet even when that man has a fine moral and spiritual reputation. Their presence together through the night could well have been misconstrued. From a moral standpoint this action promoted by Naomi and carried out by Ruth appears most unacceptable. Nevertheless those familiar with the history of the time suggest that it would not have been judged so shocking by the customs of the people of Israel at that time.[15] But if that is so, why is Ruth so careful to leave the threshing floor before anyone could recognize her, and Boaz so insistent that her presence there that night should not be disclosed? (3:14).

We need to be alert to any signs of 'departing from the living God' (Heb. 3:12), such as finding excuses to miss worship, reluctance to be with the people of God, pulling out of church responsibilities, prayerlessness and not finding time to read and meditate upon the Word of God. Backsliding begins in the heart: leaving our first love (Rev. 2:4); losing the joy of the Lord (Ps. 51:12); or no longer delighting in the law of God (Ps. 1:2; Rom. 7:22).

5. Women in the Bible

No impartial reader could ever conclude that the Bible has a low view of women. In studying the book of Judges we noted that it contains the first record in history of the emergence of a woman into prominence and the leadership of a nation (Judg. 4:4). Deborah is presented as a highly capable person and a 'judge' in Israel in her own right.

Male chauvinism — the smug irrational belief in the superiority of men over women — is rebuked and corrected by the teaching, illustrations and examples found in the Word of God. There are occasional illustrations of chauvinism, as with Lot offering his daughters to the perverted crowd, or the Levite his concubine (Gen. 19:8; Judg. 19:24). While such incidents are horrifying and inexplicable, there is no word of approval. That such things are recorded in Holy Scripture does not mean that the Lord sanctions these practices any more than he approved of the later vile behaviour of Lot's daughters, or Tamar's deceitful sin with her father-in-law (Gen. 19:31-36; 38:14-18). The Lord clearly assumes that his people will read the Scriptures with care and great thoughtfulness and so arrive at moral and spiritual conclusions that will be honouring to God.

Also rebuked and corrected is radical feminism, with its aggressive attack upon God as being against women. To maintain their cause men and women of radical feminist persuasion have to overlook or twist the clear implications in the pages of this great book. They have to ignore, or to interpret in a distorted manner, the beautiful illustrations of godly women found here. The Bible portrays their character, their deeds, and the respect which they gained among their fellow Israelites — both male and female.

Two of these outstanding godly women are Ruth and Esther. These two, each with a book bearing her name, shine out as examples of godliness, loyalty, devotion, obedience and service. They bring honour to God and provide a worthy example for all who follow after them — whether male or female. Ruth is the Gentile, Esther the Jew. Ruth, a Gentile, marries a Hebrew man. Esther, a Jewess, marries a Gentile king.

Conclusion

The book of Ruth recounts the story of three ordinary people whose lives are interwoven by providence. First, we see Naomi the Israelitess, bereaved of husband and two sons, advising and helping Ruth and ultimately rejoicing in the birth of a grandson. Secondly, there is Ruth the Gentile, choosing to be faithful to the true God whatever the cost and personal inconvenience, seeking to be obedient to God and accepting Naomi's counsel and receiving blessing in union with Boaz. Finally, we are introduced to Boaz, the upright godly Israelite, without guile or deceit, full of respect for the laws of God, and full of benevolent love and friendliness towards a poor stranger.

Here is a beautiful picture of the behaviour of a woman of God, and the behaviour of a man of God. This book encourages the virtues of love and faithfulness in family relationships. It teaches purity and integrity in all relationships.

A stranger comes into the central line of the covenant people through marriage to a godly Israelite. Through these two an aged Israelitess, having passed through much hardship and suffering (famine and triple bereavement), eventually comes to a place of peace and contentment.

This book also presents the ancestry of David, but more especially the ancestry of David's Lord (Matt. 1:5-6). Here is a family tree that beautifully illustrates the amazing love of God and his unique redemptive work. Perez (4:18; Matt. 1:3), Boaz's great-great-great-great-grandfather, was one of the twins conceived as a result of an immoral union between Judah and his Canaanite daughter-in-law Tamar (Gen. 38). Rahab, the former prostitute, was adopted into the congregation of Israel (Josh. 6:25) and married Salmon, Boaz's father. Ruth, the converted Moabitess, was taken by Boaz as his wife.

The blood of Ruth ran in the veins of the Lord Jesus Christ. The blood of the Lord Jesus Christ is the real redemption for Ruth.

Harmony: Samuel, Kings, Chronicles, Ezra and Nehemiah

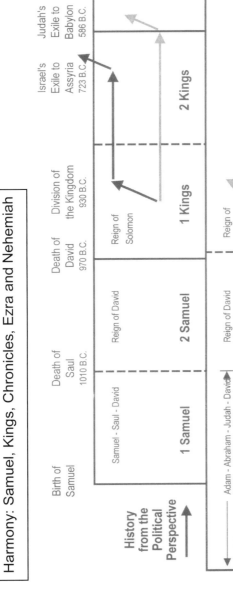
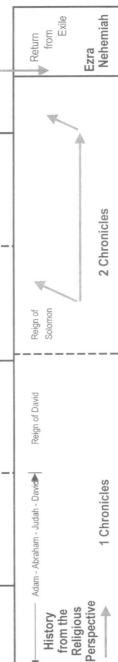

| Birth of Samuel | Death of Saul 1010 B.C. | Death of David 970 B.C. | Division of the Kingdom 930 B.C. | Israel's Exile to Assyria 723 B.C. | Judah's Exile to Babylon 586 B.C. | Decree of Cyrus 538 B.C. |

History from the Political Perspective

Samuel - Saul - David

Reign of David

Reign of Solomon

1 Samuel

2 Samuel

1 Kings

2 Kings

History from the Religious Perspective

Adam - Abraham - Judah - David

Reign of David

Reign of Solomon

1 Chronicles

2 Chronicles

Return from Exile

Ezra Nehemiah

Northern Kingdom of Israel (Ten Tribes)

Southern Kingdom of Judah (Two Tribes)

I Samuel

('heard by God')

Author: Samuel

Key thought: 'Heard by God'

Theme: The place and power
of prayer in all experiences of life

'For this child I prayed, and the
LORD has granted me my petition
which I asked of him.'

I Samuel 1:27

Summary

1 Samuel

In the original Hebrew Bible 1 and 2 Samuel formed one book, as also did 1 and 2 Kings and 1 and 2 Chronicles. These three books were first divided by scholars working on the Septuagint, when they translated the Old Testament into the Greek language. The reason for the division in each case seems to have been that written Greek requires at least one third more space than Hebrew. The translators were consequently forced to divide each of Samuel, Kings and Chronicles into two, either because there was a limit to the length of scroll available, or in order to make the scrolls easier to handle.

Although this kind of biblical literature is generally classified among the 'historical books', the Jews listed them under 'the former prophets'. The books from Joshua through to 2 Kings became known as 'the former prophets', whereas later prophetic writings were gathered together under the heading of 'the latter prophets'. This shows that the Jews believed that God was speaking just as clearly through the historical events as through the overtly prophetic books.

Author

Samuel, the prophet and judge, wrote the bulk of 1 and 2 Samuel, with Nathan and Gad completing it: 'Now the acts of King David, first and last, indeed they are written in the book of Samuel the seer, in the book of Nathan the prophet, and in the book of Gad the seer, with all his reign and his might, and the events that happened to him, to Israel, and to all the kingdoms of the lands' (1 Chr. 29:29-30).

The Jews regarded Samuel as a national leader, second only to Moses. The Lord also links Samuel with Moses as an intercessor when he addresses Jeremiah the prophet: 'Then the LORD said to me, "Though Moses and Samuel stood before me, yet my mind could not be favourable

towards this people. Cast them out of my sight, and let them go forth"'
(Jer. 15:1).

The connection between Samuel and Moses is not accidental. Samuel
was a prophet whose office, like that of all God's other prophets, can be
traced back to the promise of God through Moses: 'I will raise up for them
a Prophet like you from among their brethren, and will put my words in his
mouth, and he shall speak to them all that I command him. And it shall be
that whoever will not hear my words, which he speaks in my name, I will
require it of him' (Deut. 18:18-19).

Samuel's role was to summon Israel back to the Old Covenant. The Israelites were a favoured people: the Lord loved them and had taken them
as his own (12:22). Their responsibility was to respond to his great kindness by loving and obeying him (12:24-25). Samuel was personally committed to love God and to obey his law (12:3-5).

At the same time, the call of Samuel to be the prophet and judge of Israel formed a turning-point in the history of the Old Testament kingdom of
God. As the prophet of Jehovah, Samuel was to lead the people of Israel
out of the times of the judges into those of the kings, 'and lay the foundation for a prosperous development of the monarchy'.[1]

Historical setting

The First Book of Samuel covers the history of Israel from the time of
Judge Eli the priest (c. 1060 B.C.) to the death of Saul (1010 B.C.). The
book covers a period of transition. The rule of the judges draws to a close;
the establishment of the monarchy is introduced. Two great institutions are
now to be prominently brought forward and established, both marking a
distinct advance in the history of Israel. These two institutions, the office of
prophet and the office of king, are connected with the history of Samuel.
This explains why the two books bear his name and why they do not close
with the death of David, as might have been expected in a biography, or in
a history of his reign.

The book centres around three main characters: Samuel, the last of the
judges; Saul, the first of the kings; and David, Israel's greatest king. The
history is not presented in a strictly chronological order. There are large
gaps in the history of all three men. Long periods and important facts are
omitted as the record is made. Sometimes the author refers back, providing
the additional details later. As Alfred Edersheim explains, 'All these

peculiarities are not accidental, but designed, and in accordance with the general plan of the work.' As in other parts of Scripture, the record is governed by a purpose to provide 'a *history of the kingdom of God* during a new period in its development, and in a fresh stage of its onward movement towards the end'.[2] The goal constantly in mind is the establishment of the kingdom of God in Christ; the priesthood of Eli, the prophetic order of Samuel and the kingly rule of David all point to this. This is always the Scriptures' chief end and goal. The reader is constantly urged to look for the Christ who is Prophet, Priest and King. The value of biblical history in the Old Testament is in what it teaches about the Saviour, and how it prepares for his coming.

Outline

Part I: Samuel the prophet (1:1 – 7:17)

The book of Judges ends with this disturbing comment upon the times: 'In those days there was no king in Israel; everyone did what was right in his own eyes' (Judg. 21:25; cf. 17:6; 18:1). The opening chapters of 1 Samuel give an account of life in Israel under the last two judges, Eli and Samuel. While the official capacity of Eli was that of a priest, and Samuel's was that of a prophet, they both functioned in positions of national leadership well beyond their religious duties. Eli 'judged Israel forty years' (4:18). Samuel 'judged Israel all the days of his life' (7:15).

Samuel is a child given by God in response to the persistent prayers of a barren wife. Consequently his mother Hannah dedicates him to the Lord and after a few years she hands her young son into the care and training of Eli the priest. Samuel may legitimately perform priestly functions since he is a Levite by birth (1 Chr. 6:34-38).

Hophni and Phinehas, two sons of Eli, behave wickedly. Because their father Eli rebukes them but does not restrain them, he comes under censure from the Lord. Samuel is called to the prophetic office while still a boy. His first duty is to confront Eli with the judgement of God. The Lord is with Samuel and within a short time he is recognized throughout the land as one 'established as a prophet of the LORD' (3:20). A new period in the history of the kingdom of God has begun.

The Philistines are still occupying parts of Israel (cf. Judg. 13:1). Growing stronger by the year, this enemy poses a serious threat to the children of

Israel. In the first battle the Israelites want the ark of the covenant among them as though its presence alone will somehow assure them of victory. The Philistines win the battle and capture the ark. Hophni and Phinehas, the two sons of Eli, and 30,000 Israelite foot soldiers are killed. When news is relayed to Eli that his sons are dead, and the ark captured, he falls backwards from his seat and breaks his neck in the fall.

After Eli's grim death responsibility as judge in Israel falls to Samuel. He is the last of the judges, but not a military judge — not ruling like Samson by physical strength, but by high spiritual qualities and prayer; not so much wrestling against flesh and blood as against principalities and powers, and the rulers of the darkness of this world, and spiritual wickedness in high places. In this respect his function as judge blends with his work as prophet. In a real sense he is the first of the prophets, for before him the prophetic office was more a casual illumination; under him it becomes a more steady and systematic light.[3] It is also probable that Samuel founded the school of the prophets mentioned in this book (10:5).

The presence of the ark of the covenant brings disaster upon thousands of Philistines. Eventually it is returned to Israel. Samuel uses the occasion as an opportunity to call the people to repentance and prayer. The people respond, confess their sins and enjoy victory over the Philistines for the remaining years of Samuel's leadership (7:13).

Part II: Saul, the first king (8:1 – 15:35)

In his old age Samuel appoints his two sons as successors to the office of judge, but they prove godless and dishonest. The people cry out to Samuel for a king to judge Israel 'like all the nations' (8:5). The Lord chooses Saul as the first king of Israel. Industrious, generous, honest and modest, he is chosen by God to institute the monarchy.

Saul quickly vindicates his appointment as King of Israel, rallying the people and winning decisive battles against their enemies. However, when the Philistine army encamps at Mishmash in preparation for battle it seriously outnumbers Saul's army, whose men are afraid and deserting. After waiting seven days for the prophet Samuel, Saul wilfully oversteps his authority and, in direct contravention of the law of God, offers a burnt offering to the Lord. As soon as he has finished, the prophet Samuel arrives on the scene. What Saul has done in offering a sacrifice is so serious that he loses the perpetuity of his throne. He has demonstrated a lack of faith in God and disobedience to his Word. There will be no hereditary reign for his offspring though Saul is not himself rejected. In spite of having only 600 men Saul could have known great victory had he relied upon the Lord and been obedient to his commandments (13:13-15; cf. Gideon and his 300 — Judg. 7:7). Saul is the king after Israel's own heart (12:13): he offered sacrifices to God, but not properly; he willingly fought against the enemies of Israel, but did not seek God's blessing before setting out; he trusted God until he saw his men deserting him; he believed in the outward forms of sacrifice without having internal faith, love and obedience. These reflect the character of Israel at the time. By contrast, Samuel announces that the hereditary throne is to pass to someone 'after [God's] own heart' (13:14).

Saul's son Jonathan proves to be of a different character from what his father became. 'Whatever fitness he might have shown for "the kingdom", had he been called to it, a more unselfish, warm-hearted, genuine, or noble character is not presented to us in Scripture than that of Jonathan.'[4] Jonathan is a man of faith and courage. He is also a man of action. In his words to his armour-bearer he displays his confidence in the Lord: 'Come, let us go over to the garrison of these uncircumcised; it may be that the LORD will work for us. For nothing restrains the LORD from saving by many or by few' (1 Sam. 14:6).

Further disobedience over Agag (15:9) results in the Lord's rejecting Saul as king:

Then Samuel said:

'Has the LORD as great delight in burnt offerings and sacrifices,
As in obeying the voice of the LORD?
Behold, to obey is better than sacrifice,
And to heed than the fat of rams.
For rebellion is as the sin of witchcraft,
And stubbornness is as iniquity and idolatry.
Because you have rejected the word of the LORD,
He also has rejected you from being king'
(1 Sam. 15:22-23).

Saul's only excuse is that he 'feared the people and obeyed their voice' (15:24).

Part III: David, the greatest king (16:1 – 31:13)

With the rejection of King Saul, the Lord directs the prophet Samuel to visit Bethlehem to anoint one of Jesse's sons as heir to the throne. David is anointed with oil and the Spirit of the Lord comes upon him from that day (16:13). He is not, however, to be revealed to Israel for some time, so he returns to his duties among his brothers.

Meanwhile the Spirit of the Lord, who gives might and power and a sound mind, has departed from Saul. In the providence of God this is to be the means of introducing David to the royal court. David, a skilful musician, is brought in to soothe Saul by playing the harp when he is troubled by 'a distressing spirit from the LORD' (16:14,23). Periodically David returns home for rest and refreshment in the quiet solitude of the surroundings of Bethlehem (17:15), until he takes up Goliath's challenge. With courage inspired by a living faith, David confronts the giant: 'You come to me with a sword, with a spear, and with a javelin. But I come to you in the name of the LORD of hosts, the God of the armies of Israel, whom you have defied' (1 Sam. 17:45). David slays the giant. The Israelites are inspired, the Philistines dismayed. Israel rises up and wins a mighty victory.

From that day a bond of extraordinary strength is established between David and Saul's son Jonathan. A pure, God-honouring relationship between two godly men with mutual respect and mutual affection is forged (18:3).

King Saul appoints David as a captain in his army and such is the popularity and success of this young officer that women sing,

Saul has slain his thousands,
And David his ten thousands

(18:7).

In a fit of jealousy Saul twice attempts to kill him. Failing, Saul concludes that the Lord who has departed from him is now with David. He employs many schemes to seek to destroy David.

Taking painful leave of his great friend, David begins the life of the persecuted and hunted. He finds refuge in the Cave of Adullam. The solitude of the cave proves helpful to David in the exercise of the life of prayer and in living in utter dependence upon the Lord. Psalms 57 and 142 are composed here and indicate his confidence in the Lord.

Opportunities arise for David easily to take Saul's life, but David will not harm King Saul, 'the anointed of the LORD' (24:6; 26:9,11), and he is even conscience-stricken at having cut off the corner from Saul's cloak. David seeks to convince Saul that he is in no danger whatsoever from him. Saul declares his appreciation and confesses his folly.

With all Saul's protestations, David remains certain that the king will not rest until he has sought him out and killed him (27:1). Failing to seek the Lord and depend upon him alone, David resolves to move out of Israel to the land of the Philistines.

Some time later war is declared between the Philistines and the Israelites. Opposing camps are set up and King Saul, fearful of the prospect of war, seeks counsel from the Lord. But 'The Lord did not answer him, either by dreams or by Urim or by the prophets' (28:6). In desperation Saul disobeys the covenant law contained in the revealed Word of God and turns to a medium at En Dor (Lev. 19:31). His wickedness is compounded when he asks her to 'bring up Samuel' so that he can seek his advice and counsel.[5] Saul receives confirmation that God has rejected him and the news that he and his sons are soon to die in battle.

Assembling for battle with the Israelites, the Philistine princes take stock of their forces. Seeing David and his men at the rear of their own company, they are horrified that Israelites should be going out against Israelites. The princes show understandable distrust and command that these Hebrews should be removed from their ranks. David gives further indication of his poor spiritual state at this time for he remonstrates with the Philistine king, Achish, for not being permitted to fight against these 'enemies of my lord the king' (29:8).

Returning home to Ziklag in the land of the Philistines, David and his men discover the town on fire and all their wives and children taken captive by the Amalekites. This extreme incident brings him back to his knees: 'Then David was greatly distressed, for the people spoke of stoning him, because the soul of all the people was grieved, every man for his sons and his daughters. But David strengthened himself in the LORD his God ' (30:6).

David no doubt felt the guilt of his behaviour in leadership. To compound his deception and lies he had commanded the slaughter of men and women when attacking the Amalekites (27:8-9). It was no thanks to him that the Amalekites did not slaughter the families at Ziklag. It was the Lord who overruled to ensure the safety of the women and children. Guilt becomes conviction; conviction becomes confession, and 'David strengthened himself in the LORD his God' (30:6).

Meanwhile the Philistines make war against Israel, win a decisive victory and pursue Saul and his sons. Jonathan, Abinadab and Malchishua are killed and their father Saul is severely wounded. He falls upon his sword to avoid being humiliated by the Philistines.

Christ and his church

It is in this book that we first find the expression 'the LORD of hosts' (1:3). This is the first of the 281 occurrences of that name and title that signify the God of Israel as the Lord of all the multitudes in heaven and earth. That 'Jehovah of Hosts' is a title sometimes applied to Christ is seen by comparing Isaiah 6:1-5 with John 12:41, and Isaiah 8:13-14 with 1 Peter 2:5-8.

1. Priest

The judgement of God upon Eli and his family includes a wonderful promise: 'Then I will raise up for myself a faithful priest who shall do according to what is in my heart and in my mind. I will build him a sure house, and he shall walk before my anointed [Messiah] for ever ' (2:35).

This promise no doubt includes a reference to Samuel and then Zadok, but goes beyond them, and applies to the priesthood generally, and points for its final fulfilment to the Lord Jesus Christ.[6]

2. Prophet

'Dark days call for great men. Often God gives His choicest gifts to those who lead when times are the most difficult.'[7] Judged against the backcloth of the terrible spiritual state of Israel at this time, the prophet Samuel brought an enormous influence for good, and well deserves his place among the greatest of the Old Testament heroes. He was God's man for one of the most significant points in Israel's history. Given by God in answer to prayer, he was returned to God in adoration and praise. Raised and instructed by the high priest Eli, he was thoroughly acquainted with the ceremonies of the tabernacle. He also had easy access to the Scriptures kept there, and was well informed about the spiritual state of the nation through the regular visits of priests from all parts. Added to this were the remarkable revelations he received directly from the Lord. He was well equipped for the ministry God gave him. The testimony of Saul's servant is borne out by the whole record of Scripture: 'Look now, there is in this city a man of God, and he is an honourable man; all that he says surely comes to pass' (9:6).

Samuel lived at a time when 'The word of the Lord was rare ... there was no widespread revelation' (3:1). He was most likely the founder/leader of a group or company of prophets (10:5-10; 19:20). With travel being difficult and time-consuming, it was important to have reliable messengers of the Word of God to dispatch it throughout the land. The tradition of training men for this kind of ministry was continued by the prophets Elijah and Elisha (2 Kings 2:3-7,15-18; 6:1).

Samuel 'is the actual starting-point of the series of prophets after Moses' (cf. Acts 3:24).[8] He preached repentance to the whole of Israel (7:2-6). He was the forerunner of David, as John was of Christ.'[9] Samuel the prophet provides another strong link in the chain between the promise of a great Prophet given through Moses (Deut. 18:15) and the coming of the Lord Jesus Christ.[10] He provides a fitting type of Christ as a prophet, priest and judge. Of young Samuel it is said that he 'grew in stature, and in favour both with the LORD and men' (2:26); of the Saviour when young it is said that he 'increased in wisdom and stature, and in favour with God and men' (Luke 2:52; cf. v. 40).

3. King

In prayer Hannah prophesied:

> The adversaries of the LORD shall be broken in pieces;
> From heaven he will thunder against them.
> The LORD will judge the ends of the earth.
> He will give strength to his king,
> And exalt the horn of his anointed [Messiah].
>
> (2:10).

The style and subject matter of her prayer are later reflected in many of the psalms.

The purpose behind the First Book of Samuel is to record the establishment of the monarchy and of the part played by Samuel, the last of the judges and the first in a long line of great prophets. In Saul we see a picture of a selfish autocrat, a ruler who possesses absolute and unrestricted authority. In David, the second king of Israel, we see the man after God's own heart (13:14). Yet before David comes to rule he must undergo many trials, setbacks and disappointments: 'For whom the Lord loves he chastens, and scourges every son whom he receives' (Heb. 12:6; cf. Prov. 3:12).

David is one of the primary Old Testament types of the Lord Jesus Christ. Born at Bethlehem, working as a shepherd, reigning as the anointed King of Israel — in all these things he prefigures his glorious descendant in whom all the types and prophecies find wonderful and glorious fulfilment.[11] The early experiences of David tending sheep provided ample material for spiritual reflection. Psalm 23 is no doubt built upon those formative years. How many of the Lord's people, generation after generation, have found unique help and encouragement in that profound analogy! 'The LORD is my shepherd; I shall not want' (Ps. 23:1) finds enriched meaning in the appearing of 'the Good Shepherd' who lays down 'his life for the sheep' (John 10:11), the 'Great Shepherd' who is brought up from the dead (Heb. 13:20) and the 'Chief Shepherd' who is now in glory (1 Peter 5:4).

Application

1. Prayer and Intercession

The key to the message of the book is the meaning of Samuel's name ('Heard by God') and the frequent occurrence of the words, 'prayer' and 'prayed'. Like Moses years before, Samuel was a great intercessor (Jer. 15:1). 1 Samuel is a book full of prayer. Here are examples of prayer offered in various situations:

Hannah

While the opening verses give insight into the problems of polygamy (1:2-7), they contain the moving account of Hannah's supplication to the Lord. Well does the apostle Paul exhort the Philippians: 'Be anxious for nothing, but in everything by prayer and supplication, with thanksgiving, let your requests be made known to God...' (Phil. 4:6).

Hannah prayed. 'She was in bitterness of soul, and ... wept in anguish' — but she prayed (1:10). Her song of thanksgiving (2:1-10) is close in content to the song of the Virgin Mary (Luke 1:46-55). This no doubt indicates how familiar Mary was with the prayer of Hannah recorded in the Scriptures.

It is interesting to observe the sequence of events. Hannah prays in the vicinity of the door of the tabernacle (1:9-10). Eli sees Hannah's lips moving and assumes she has been drinking far too much wine. Hannah explains her behaviour. Eli blesses her: 'Go in peace, and the God of Israel grant your petition which you have asked of him' (1:17). The following morning she rises 'early in the morning and [worships] before the LORD' (1:19). What a challenge! Sadly it seems to be the pattern that when Christians face difficulties, afflictions and disappointments, they do not pray, they do not worship. They stay at home or take a weekend break from their church in order to cheer themselves up. The solution to problems is never found in absence from the assembly of God's people (Heb. 10:24-25).

Mizpah

The prayers of Samuel are linked with the delivery of Israel at Mizpah (7:2-13). This marks a notable turning-point in the condition of Israel in relation to her near neighbours, the Philistines. Like Joshua before him, Samuel calls a national convocation (Josh. 23:2; 24:1-2), for the confession of national sins and renewal of national obligations towards the Lord. 'He desired to unite all who were like-minded in a purpose of repentance and reformation, and to rouse them to a higher pitch of intensity by contact with a great multitude animated by the same spirit. When the assembly met, it was in a most proper spirit.'[12]

In humility and repentance the Israelites acknowledge their sins. Meanwhile the Philistines learn of the gathering together of all Israel and plan their attack. The Israelites hear of the advancement of their enemy and plead with the prophet to intercede for them. Samuel offers sacrifices and then cries out to the Lord for Israel, 'and the LORD answered him' (7:9).

'Give us a king'

The people's request for a king was sinful. Israel was a theocracy with the Lord as an invisible king. Asking for a (visible) king, like the other nations, was firstly a symptom of unbelief, and secondly a rejection of God's rule over them (8:7). It reflected an increasing trust in the outward and visible, in distinction from the inward and spiritual.

When the people pleaded for a king, Samuel turned to the Lord in prayer: 'Then all the elders of Israel gathered together and came to Samuel at Ramah, and said to him, "Look, you are old, and your sons do not walk in your ways. Now make for us a king to judge us like all the nations." But the thing displeased Samuel when they said, "Give us a king to judge us." So Samuel prayed to the LORD' (8:4-6).

Prayer for Israel

In his last public address Samuel promises unceasing prayer for the people of Israel: 'For the LORD will not forsake his people, for his great name's sake, because it has pleased the LORD to make you his people. Moreover, as for me, far be it from me that I should sin against the LORD in ceasing to pray for you; but I will teach you the good and the right way. Only fear the LORD, and serve him in truth with all your heart; for consider what great things he has done for you' (12:22-25).

The prophet Samuel was a great intercessor. His commitment to this aspect of prayer is evident when he says, 'Far be it from me that I should sin against the LORD in ceasing to pray for you.' Such commitment is a worthy example to the people of God. Intercession is a vital part of prayer (1 Tim. 2:1-2; Eph. 6:18-19; Matt. 9:38).

2. A father's responsibility

Eli the priest is represented as a devout man. Yet at the same time he seems to have lacked a sense of parental responsibility. Both his sons are described as 'corrupt [literally, sons of Belial]; they did not know the LORD' (2:12). The fact that they were not spiritual cannot be laid at Eli's door. Parents have no power, and consequently no responsibility, to convert their offspring. Eli was not punished for something totally out of his control. He was punished because he did not curb the behaviour of his sons: 'Then the LORD said to Samuel: "Behold, I will do something in Israel at which both ears of everyone who hears it will tingle. In that day I will perform against Eli all that I have spoken concerning his house, from beginning to end. For I have told him that I will judge his house for ever for the iniquity which he knows, because his sons made themselves vile, and he did not restrain them. And therefore I have sworn to the house of Eli that the iniquity of Eli's house shall not be atoned for by sacrifice or offering for ever' (3:11-14).

The failure and neglect of Eli in relation to his two sons was all the worse in that he was a priest and a judge, and his sons were also in the priestly office. Eli had not only a domestic responsibility, but also an ecclesiastical responsibility for his sons. Leadership among the people of God not only means good and faithful oversight of the saints in the church, but also good and faithful oversight of the family in the home: 'A bishop [i.e. an overseer] then must be blameless, the husband of one wife, temperate, sober-minded, of good behaviour, hospitable, able to teach; not given to wine, not violent, not greedy for money, but gentle, not quarrelsome, not covetous; one who rules his own house well, having his children in submission with all reverence (for if a man does not know how to rule his own house, how will he take care of the church of God?)' (1 Tim. 3:2-5). This domestic rule not only includes elders, for it is applied to deacons as well: 'Let deacons be the husbands of one wife, ruling their children and their own houses well' (1 Tim. 3:12).

The word translated 'rule' might accurately be translated into modern idiom as 'exercise management skills'. Such activity involves 'planning, organization, enlistment, training and deployment of personnel, administration and discipline'.[13] Clearly the modern practice of reasoning without restraint and talking without training is the error for which Eli was punished. Of course this does not mean that *only* elders and deacons should rule their homes in this manner. All fathers should do so. Nevertheless it is especially important that leaders give a right example in this matter. In our own day there is much discredit brought upon church leaders by the unruly behaviour of their children. How many ministers, elders and deacons would be caused to resign their office if the domestic test were seriously applied?

The judgement of God against Eli for failure as a father was communicated through Samuel while the latter was still a boy (3:1). The sad sequel is that Samuel also failed in this regard. Godly as he undoubtedly was, spiritually-minded as he most certainly was, prayerful as he decidedly was, nevertheless he was a poor father: 'Now it came to pass when Samuel was old that he made his sons judges over Israel. The name of his first-born was Joel, and the name of his second, Abijah; they were judges in Beersheba. But his sons did not walk in his ways; they turned aside after dishonest gain, took bribes, and perverted justice' (8:1-3).

3. Friendship

Two extremes of friendship are illustrated — one the purest and most noble, the other sinful and worldly: the first between David and Jonathan, the second between David and Achish. Behaviour is usually affected (infected?) by the company we keep (1 Cor. 15:33). Between David and Jonathan there was an unusual bond. It was a pure, God-honouring relationship between two godly men with mutual respect and mutual affection, for '… the soul of Jonathan was knit to the soul of David, and Jonathan loved him as his own soul' (18:1). The Lord's people can experience a deep and a rich relationship with members of their own gender. Freud is wrong in supposing that all relationships have elements of libido (sexual urge or desire). This is just another satanic attempt to provide grounds to besmirch the good name of the righteous:

Let the lying lips be put to silence,
Which speak insolent things proudly and contemptuously against the
    righteous
                                    (Ps. 31:18 — a psalm of David).

The wicked plots against the just,
And gnashes at him with his teeth.
The Lord laughs at him,
For he sees that his day is coming.
The wicked have drawn the sword
And have bent their bow …
To slay those who are of upright conduct.
Their sword shall enter their own heart,
And their bows shall be broken
                                    (Ps. 37:12-15 — a psalm of David).

The Lord Jesus sanctified friendship in his close companionship with the twelve apostles, the three — Peter, James and John (Matt. 17:1; 26:36-37) — and with the apostle John in particular (John 19:26-27; 20:2; 21:7,20).

Whereas the friendship between David and Jonathan indicates the heights to which friendship with the godly may rise, that between David and Achish shows the depths to which friendship with the worldly can sometimes plunge. David was wrong in seeking protection from Saul by turning to King Achish of the Philistines. He placed himself under obligation to an enemy of Israel. Trapped by his own deceit and lies, David professed allegiance to King Achish (28:1-2), who was thoroughly taken in by David's prevarications. The man who had twice insisted that Saul should not be killed (24:6; 26:9) was now in league with the army that would destroy both Saul and Jonathan too! Friendship with the world always leads to serious problems for the Lord's people (1 John 2:15-16; Rom. 12:2; 2 Cor. 6:17-18).

4. Obedience

The importance of obeying the Word of God is brought into sharp focus in the Lord's punishment of King Saul. His first disobedience occurred when he performed the function of a priest (a duty which, under the Mosaic covenant, only a Levite could fulfil). On the brink of a major battle against the Philistines, with his army unsettled and dispersing, and the priest Samuel not having arrived at the appointed time, Saul took matters into his own hands (13:9) with disastrous results. The second major disobedience occurred when the Lord ordered King Saul to carry out the total destruction of the Amalekites and all their livestock (15:2-3). In the event, Saul spared the life of Agag, the King of Amalek, and confiscated the best of the livestock as booty (15:9). Samuel confronted Saul with the Lord's judgement against him:

> Has the LORD as great delight in burnt offerings and sacrifices,
> As in obeying the voice of the LORD?
> Behold, to obey is better than sacrifice,
> And to heed than the fat of rams.
> For rebellion is as the sin of witchcraft,
> And stubbornness is as iniquity and idolatry.
> Because you have rejected the word of the LORD,
> He also has rejected you from being king
>
> (15:22-23).

The same emphasis upon obedience to the Lord is found in the New Testament. The Lord Jesus expects love to be demonstrated practically in obedience (John 14:15; 15:10,14). Also the connection between faith and obedience is so strong that the Scripture which says, 'Abraham believed God, and it was accounted to him for righteousness,' is seen by one New Testament writer as a fine example of faith, and by another as an indisputable illustration of obedience (Rom. 4:2-5; James 2:21-24).

5. Overruling providence

Among the many, two major incidents illustrate this point. The first concerns David's intended revenge upon Nabal, who would not give supplies to David's servants (25:21-22). Rebuffed by this rich farmer, David responds immediately. 'How did David now receive their report? Did he humble himself and commend his cause to God the Lord? On the contrary, we meet him now, for the first time, not master of his own spirit, but hurried along by his natural passionateness of disposition. With a flaming anger … glowing with a spirit of revenge he led his band of four hundred armed men to the little town of Carmel… Surely he had not this time either prayed or enquired of the Lord by the "Urim and Thummim". If he had carried out what his anger suggested to him … he would have given the death-blow to his own honour and to his cause. Then he would have appeared before God and all the world as an outlaw: a man over whom not only his enemies would have triumphed, but who must also be given up by his *friends* as unworthy of the crown of Israel.'[14]

In the providence of God there is someone there to save the day. Abigail intervenes and not only averts a tragedy for her husband and servants, but also prevents David from ruining his reputation.

The second illustration of the overruling providence of God is seen in David's foolish alliance with King Achish of the Philistines. Having placed himself under obligation to this enemy of Israel, David is determined to go to war on the side of the Philistines against Israel (29:1-2,8). The Lord uses the princes of the Philistines to block David's stupidity (29:3-4). Had David gone to battle against Israel it would have destroyed his credibility before his own people for ever.

6. Grace and gifts

When the people cried out for a king, their acceptance of Saul was probably based on his striking appearance and his natural skills which suited him as a military leader. However, his religious commitment and spiritual state reflected the state of the nation at the time: 'that of combining zeal for the religion of Jehovah, and outward conformity to it, with utter want of real heart submission to the Lord, and of true devotedness to Him'.[15] Saul was never born again and yet, following his anointing to the office of King of Israel, he was granted 'signs' that God was with him (10:7). One of these signs was that the Spirit of the Lord would come upon him and he would prophesy together with a group of prophets (10:6). This raises the serious question of the relationship between the grace of God and the gifts of the Holy Spirit. Here is a man, Saul, who evidently prophesied by the power of the Holy Spirit and yet he was not a child of God and was ultimately totally rejected.

The Lord Jesus Christ draws attention to this possibility that someone might exercise spiritual gifts and yet not possess spiritual grace when he declares: 'Not everyone who says to me, "Lord, Lord," shall enter the kingdom of heaven, but he who does the will of my Father in heaven. Many will say to me in that day, "Lord, Lord, have we not prophesied in your name, cast out demons in your name, and done many wonders in your name?" And then I will declare to them, "I never knew you; depart from me, you who practise lawlessness!" ' (Matt. 7:21-23).

The apostle Paul makes the same sober assessment: 'Though I speak with the tongues of men and of angels, but have not love, I have become as sounding brass or a clanging cymbal. And though I have the gift of prophecy, and understand all mysteries and all knowledge, and though I have all faith, so that I could remove mountains, but have not love, I am nothing' (1 Cor. 13:1-2).

Love for God and obedience to God are the marks of true godliness, not the exercise of gifts — natural or spiritual!

7. Religious superstition

The ark of the covenant (or 'ark of the Testimony') built according to the exact specifications given by God (Exod. 25:10-21) was the place where God met with Moses as he had promised: 'And there I will meet with you, and I will speak with you from above the mercy seat, from between the two cherubim which are on the ark of the Testimony, of all things which I will give you in commandment to the children of Israel' (Exod. 25:22).

The ark of the covenant held a prominent place in the history of Israel. The mercy seat, forming the lid of the ark and supporting the two golden cherubim, was associated with the presence of God (Ps. 80:1). When the priests carrying the ark entered the waters of the River Jordan a pathway was miraculously opened up and the huge company of Israelites walked on the dry riverbed into the land of Canaan (Josh. 3:14-17). Shortly after-wards the ark was carried for seven days around Jericho before the walls of the city fell (Josh. 6:6-20). After Israel's settlement in Canaan the ark remained for a while in the tabernacle at Gilgal and then it was relocated to Shiloh, where it remained until the days of Eli.

Entering into battle with the Philistines, Israel was defeated (4:1-2). They rightly concluded that their failure to succeed was evidence that the Lord had withdrawn his support. The method they used to try to secure God's help in the next battle was entirely wrong. Instead of humbling themselves and repenting, confessing their sins and their backsliding, they decided to transport the ark of the covenant from the tabernacle at Shiloh into the camp, in the misguided notion that God's presence was inseparably linked to the mercy seat (4:4). Disastrous results followed, including the capture of the ark of the covenant.

Symbols instituted by God never possess power. The Israelites, and other people since, often made the mistake of dissociating external symbols from internal realities. The true cause of Israel's defeat was the disapproval of God upon their spiritual backsliding. The answer was entirely spiritual. Let Israel repent and return in true contrition to the Lord and he would once more support and defend them.

Reliance upon the outward form without the internal spiritual reality became the trade mark of the Pharisees in New Testament times (Matt. 23:25-28).

The same error can be made with regard to the Christian symbols of bread and wine in the celebration of the Lord's Supper. Taking the symbols without sincere spiritual awareness can lead to a drastic outcome: 'For he who eats and drinks in an unworthy manner eats and drinks judgement to himself, not discerning the Lord's body. For this reason many are weak and sick among you, and many sleep' (1 Cor. 11:29-30).

Conclusion

Four main characters appear in the First Book of Samuel: Eli, Samuel, Saul and David.

Eli, the priest and judge, may be described as 'a man whose weakness impaired his witness'.[16] Failure at home brought dishonour and the judgement of God.

Although Samuel, the prophet, priest and judge, also failed in his home, he nevertheless was the man of prayer. Whether facing difficulties, confronted by hard decisions, needing guidance, or praising God for his mercy and kindness, Samuel prayed. His prayers were backed by action, for the prophet not only prayed, he obeyed (16:4).

Saul started out well, but soon fell into the snare of the autocrat. Such absolute power is not easily controlled. Disobedient to the Word of God, he violated his office, usurped that of another, burned with jealousy towards David and ended his life beset by periods of insanity.

Last of the foursome is David who, in spite of his many sins and failings, is nevertheless described as the man after God's own heart (13:14). Persecution, afflictions, trials and temptations shaped and fashioned this man of God as he was prepared to be the next and greatest king of Israel.

2 Samuel

(sequel to 1 Samuel)

Authors: Nathan and Gad
(probably — see 1 Chr. 29:29-30)

Key thought: 'Before the Lord'

Theme:
Trials and triumphs for the servant of God

'So let your name be magnified …
And let the house of your servant
David be established before you.'
2 Samuel 7:26

Summary

The reign of King David

2 Samuel

In the original Hebrew Bible 1 and 2 Samuel formed a single volume. There is an obvious cohesion between the two parts although each has characteristics of its own. The first is concerned with the history surrounding three notable figures: Samuel, the last of the judges; Saul, the first of the kings; and David, Israel's greatest king. This Second Book of Samuel is almost entirely devoted to a history of David as king. Both books emphasize the importance of prayer. In the second book the expression 'enquired of the Lord' appears four times (2:1; 5:19,23; 21:1). Furthermore there is a strong emphasis throughout almost the whole of this history that David constantly recognized the presence of God with him at all times.

Author

The authors of this second book were probably Nathan and Gad, two prophets who were contemporaries of David: 'Now the acts of King David, first and last, indeed they are written in the book of Samuel the seer, in the book of Nathan the prophet, and in the book of Gad the seer, with all his reign and his might, and the events that happened to him, to Israel, and to all the kingdoms of the lands' (1 Chr. 29:29-30).

Other sources were evidently used in compilation of this history, such as 'the Book of Jasher' (1:18).

Historical setting

The book begins with David's accession to the throne (1010 B.C. over Judah, 1003 B.C. over the united kingdom of Israel and Judah) and gives an account of significant events during his reign of forty years, to his death in 970 B.C. He rises to unparalleled power and influence nationally and internationally; falls to the temptation of lust; commits adultery and murder; and reaps the consequences of his sin in his family and in the nation.

Outline

The Second Book of Samuel records the life of David in his triumphs and his troubles. In no other biblical character is there such a variety of spiritual experiences as in the life of David.

Part I: The opening years (1:1 - 9:13)

King Saul is dead. News reaches David and his men, in their self-imposed exile in the Philistine town of Ziklag (1 Sam. 27:5-6). The messenger is a young Amalekite who claims to have ended Saul's life. The Amalekite clearly hopes for a reward, a demonstration of gratitude, some great honour on account of his professed action (4:10). But he reckons without the noble spirit and God-fearing heart of the young heir apparent to the throne of Israel. David is overwhelmed with grief over the death of Saul and Jonathan. Though Saul had persistently sought to kill him, and almost succeeded on more than one occasion, yet he was 'the LORD's anointed' (1:14; cf. 1 Sam. 24:6,10; 26:11,16,23). David would not lay a finger on him. Nor will he reward the man who does. The Amalekite is executed for his professed action.[1] 'As an Amalekite, he was doomed to destruction (Deuteronomy 25:17-19), and as the elect-king, David was now required to put the sentence into execution.'[2]

Amid the ruins of Ziklag David pays tribute to the enemy who had sought his life and to the friend who had stood by him in adversity. David is just thirty (5:4) and yet shows remarkable maturity. All the years of persecution and harassment, the countless sleepless nights, the anxiety, the distress, the journeyings — all these are gone from his heart and mind. There is no recrimination over Saul's character, no note of relief at Saul's death, not the slightest sense of joy that his enemy is no more — indeed the very opposite. As he pours out his praise and grief he does not distinguish between Saul and Jonathan until the penultimate verse of the song (1:26), where 'comparison to the love of woman is expressive of the deepest earnestness of devoted love'.[3]

'Israel lost the battle of Gilboa, but she was now standing on the threshold of undreamed-of triumphs. It was about the year 1010 B.C. and David had advanced to the foot of a throne.'[4] David would know full well that speedy and decisive action often wins the day. He could lead his men, rally support in Israel and claim the crown and throne. Instead he turns to the Lord for guidance and direction: 'David enquired of the LORD, saying, "Shall I go up to any of the cities of Judah?" And the LORD said to him, "Go up." David said, "Where shall I go up?" And he said, "To Hebron"' (2:1).

The Lord directs David to Hebron in Judah. Hebron was originally called Kirjath Arba (Josh. 14:15) and lies twenty miles east of Ziklag and eighteen miles south of Jerusalem. This move marks the first step in David's rise to supreme power. Until now Judah has been simply a province of Israel. Now it is to become a kingdom. At Hebron David is anointed 'king over the house of Judah' (2:4). Upon hearing of the courageous deed of the men of Jabesh Gilead in retrieving the bodies of Saul and his sons, David sends a message commending them for their action. This no doubt allays any fears that they or any other old friends of King Saul might have had with the ascendancy of David. Instead of trying to punish those who have faithfully served Saul, David is inclined to show them favour, to confer distinctions and honour upon them rather than forcing them into exile.

Five years after the defeat by the Philistines, Abner, commander-in-chief of Saul's army (and Saul's cousin, 1 Sam. 14:50), proclaims Saul's son Ishbosheth as King of Israel (2:8-9) — that is, the eleven tribes excluding Judah. It was Abner who brought young David to King Saul after he had slain Goliath (1 Sam. 17:57). In proclaiming Ishbosheth as king, Abner knows he is acting against the revealed will of God that the throne should pass from the house of Saul to David (3:9-10). This act of defiance leads to civil war between Israel and Judah.

It is while living in Hebron that David shows further evidence of serious weakness, in his love of women. To the two wives he had taken with him he adds four more (cf. Deut. 17:14-17). All six bear sons to David at Hebron. 'Though polygamy was not allowed to David ... this toleration of polygamy did not and could not prevent the evils to which, from its very nature, it gives rise. There could be no unity in David's family, none of that delightful feeling of oneness, which gives such a charm to the family home. On the contrary, occasions of estrangement and opposition would be perpetually apt to arise among the different branches of the household, and it would require all his gentleness and wisdom to keep these quarrels within moderate bounds.'[5]

In spite of the express warning of Moses that a king must not multiply wives (Deut. 17:17), David will take more wives and concubines when he eventually moves to Jerusalem (5:13). But great grief is to come to David through his family: his favourite wife will turn against him (6:20-22); his daughter Tamar will be raped by her half-brother (13:14); his son Amnon will be murdered by his half-brother (13:28-29); his favourite son Absalom will take the throne from him (15:13) and be murdered (18:14); another son Adonijah will also try to take the throne (1 Kings 1:5) and he too will be murdered by his half-brother (1 Kings 2:24-25). As Moses warned all Israel, '… be sure your sin will find you out' (Num. 32:23).

David's wives and sons

Wife	Son	Death
Michal	no children	
Ahinoam	Amnon (violated Tamar)	killed by Absalom
Abigail	Chileab (Daniel)	died in his youth
Maacah	Absalom (brother of Tamar)	killed by Joab
Haggith	Adonijah	killed by Solomon
Abital	Shephatiah	
Eglah	Ithream	
Bathsheba	**Solomon (Jedidiah)**	
	Shimea (Shammua)	
	Shobab	
	Nathan	
One of the above wives	Ibhar	
One of the above wives	Elishama (Elishua)	
One of the above wives	Eliphelet (Elpelet)	
One of the above wives	Nogah	
One of the above wives	Nepheg	
One of the above wives	Japhia	
One of the above wives	Elishama	
One of the above wives	Eliada (Beeliada)	
One of the above wives	Eliphelet	
Concubines	others (1 Chr. 3:9)	

At the death of King Ishbosheth and Abner, their commander-in-chief, the demoralized Israelites turn to David and yield to his rule. The elders recognize the purposes of God in the person of David. They give three reasons for choosing him as king: first, that he is of their kin; secondly, that he has experience as an army captain in war; and, thirdly, that the Lord promised the kingdom to him. The elders of Israel ought to have put the last first, for that is the most important reason of all. Had they been governed by spiritual considerations and thoughts of pleasing the Lord, then they would have been satisfied with the one reason — it was God's revealed will. That they were not motivated by high spiritual principles and concerns is clear in regard to two further factors: the fact that they took so long to take this action, since seven and a half years had passed since the death of Saul; and the way in which God's will was made a secondary consideration — they only began to express regard for it when no other course was possible.

After seven and a half years as King of Judah, David is anointed as king over the united kingdoms of Israel and Judah. He makes 'a covenant with them at Hebron before the LORD' (5:3). God's great promise is fulfilled, as David, of the tribe of Judah, becomes king over the united kingdom of Israel:

Judah, you are he whom your brothers shall praise;
Your hand shall be on the neck of your enemies;
Your father's children shall bow down before you.
Judah is a lion's whelp;
From the prey, my son, you have gone up.
He bows down, he lies down as a lion;
And as a lion, who shall rouse him?
The sceptre [the symbol of royalty] shall not depart from Judah,
Nor a law-giver [the king's long staff] from between his feet,
Until Shiloh [the Pacifier, the Prince of Peace] comes;
And to him shall be the obedience of the people

(Gen. 49:8-10).

The covenant which the elders and David made that day (5:3) would no doubt have set out the duties of king and subjects, and have included promises made on behalf of each party.

David chooses Jerusalem, the stronghold of Zion, for his royal residence. Jerusalem, with its cluster of hills, had a sacred history. Here Abraham met the mysterious Melchizedek, King of Salem (Jeru-Salem, i.e. 'Place of Peace') who gave him bread and wine and blessed him with the solemn words:

Blessed be Abram of God Most High,
Possessor of heaven and earth;

> And blessed be God Most High
> Who has delivered your enemies into your hand
>
> (Gen. 14:19-20).

Here on Mount Moriah, where Jerusalem was built, Abraham had taken his son to offer him as a burnt offering to the Lord (Gen. 22:1-2) and spoken those unforgettable words: 'God will provide for himself the lamb for a burnt offering' (Gen. 22:8). The ancient name of Salem was changed to Jebus at the time of Joshua's invasion. In the days of the judges the Jebusites (inhabitants of Jebus) were described as 'a city of foreigners, who are not of the children of Israel' (Judg. 19:12).

Jerusalem, otherwise virtually impenetrable, is taken by Joab, leading a band of David's courageous men up the water-shaft into the city (5:7-8; 1 Chr. 11:6).

The Philistines hear that David is now king of the united Israel and, lest he should have time to consolidate his position, they move immediately into action. They advance as far as the Valley of Rephaim. Though such danger is on his threshold, David turns to God for counsel. Under the Lord's direction David fights against the Philistines and wins a decisive victory.[6] A further battle ensues and, once more under the direction of the Lord, David succeeds in driving the Philistines out of Israel.

The ark of the Testimony

The ark of the Testimony, or the ark of the covenant, had been constructed according to the Lord's detailed instructions to Moses on Sinai (Exod. 25:10-22). Bearing the mercy seat as its lid, and housed in the Holy of Holies inside the tabernacle tent, it was the piece of furniture at the heart of divinely ordained, God-honouring worship in Old Testament times. It was carried in front of the Israelites as they left Mount Sinai (Num. 10:33) and the Levites became the only authorized handlers of it (Deut. 10:8). A copy of the completed law of Moses was eventually placed inside (Deut. 31:26). The ark led the way over the Jordan river and into the promised land (Josh. 3:6,8) and was carried around Jericho before the city wall collapsed (Josh. 6:8). The ark was captured by the Philistines (1 Sam. 4:10-11), but brought them so much distress that they returned it to Israel (1 Sam. 5:1 – 6:12). Eventually it was placed in the house of Abinadab (1 Sam. 7:1), where it remained until David planned to move it into Jerusalem.

About seventy years had passed since the ark of God had stood in the tabernacle.[7] With the uniting of the twelve tribes of Israel under the reign of David, it was fitting to pay careful attention to the centrality of worship, for the ark represented the presence of God. There was a no place more suitable for the ark than the capital city, Jerusalem, which became known as the City of David. So the king prepared a tent to house the ark of the Testimony, the ark of the covenant.

Tragic thoughtlessness surrounds the first attempt to transport the ark into Jerusalem (6:2-7). Obviously more concerned to follow the example of the Philistines (1 Sam. 6:7), rather than the express commandments of God, the Israelites move the ark on a new cart. The First Book of Chronicles provides a fuller account of the measures taken by David and the priests to make the second attempt according to the revealed Word of God: 'And the children of the Levites bore the ark of God on their shoulders, by its poles, as Moses had commanded according to the word of the LORD' (1 Chr. 15:15).

With great thanksgiving the ark is brought into the City of David. The king, full of spiritual excitement, dances 'before the LORD with all his might' (6:14). His wife Michal, daughter of King Saul, witnesses her husband's behaviour and despises him 'in her heart' (6:16).[8] The relationship between the two is never the same again.

Settled in Jerusalem and given rest by the Lord from all his enemies, David feels increasingly ill at ease that his house is more substantial than the place where the ark of God is kept. He longs to build a permanent building, a temple for the Lord. The prophet Nathan at first encourages David to go ahead, but when night comes God shows Nathan his presumption and error (7:4). Nathan is charged to deliver a message to the king: David will not build a house for God; God will build a house for David (7:11). There is a play on words here. God's house is a building; David's house is his descendants. Receiving the news King David responds with characteristic reverence and humility. He leaves the royal palace and makes his way to the humble tent which houses the sacred ark. There 'King David went in and sat before the LORD' (7:18). He has just received news that would have inflated many a man, filled him with a sense of his own importance and caused him to act arrogantly towards others. But this man, 'a man after [God's] own heart' (1 Sam. 13:14), is quite different. Humbled, filled with amazement at God's great kindness, David goes to the place of worship, there to pour out his heart in wonder, love and praise (cf. Ps. 132).

David's kingdom is strengthened and enlarged. The full conquest of the Philistines is followed by the subjugation of the Moabites and the expansion of the kingdom to the north-east as far as the River Euphrates. Syria falls, as do Ammon, Amalek and Edom. The 'LORD preserved David wherever he went' (8:14).

Remembering his promise made years before to his best friend, Prince Jonathan, David enquires to see if there is any member of his family still alive (1 Sam. 20:15,17). Discovering one remaining son of Jonathan, lame Mephibosheth, David restores to him the family land which belonged to his grandfather Saul. He then pledges that Mephibosheth will constantly sit as an honoured guest at his table.

Part II: The middle years (10:1 - 19:43)

David and his troops win a decisive victory against the Syrians, but the following spring he decides not to accompany his troops into battle. This marks a dreadful turning-point in the life of this God-fearing man. His early life, chequered as it was, is nevertheless characterized by triumphs. The remaining years will be characterized by troubles. Things begin to go horribly wrong. The spiritual downfall of David begins when he turns from the path of duty, stays in Jerusalem when his men are out fighting and passes his time in idleness. He sees a beautiful woman bathing. He 'is tempted when he is drawn away by his own desires and enticed. Then, when desire has conceived, it gives birth to sin' (James 1:14-15). And one sin leads to another. From taking another man's wife he is soon taking another man's life. He is guilty of adultery, scheming and murder. And God's wrath is kindled. David the king is rebuked by Nathan the prophet. In a most notable parable personally addressed by Nathan to David (12:1-15), the king is brought under spiritual conviction. David repents. Psalm 51 is wrung from his heart.

Although the sense of divine retribution is clearly and decisively portrayed in this book, yet there is also the record of the amazing grace of God. God is always ready to forgive even terrible sins (12:13). Sometimes, however, pardoned sin still has its consequences (12:14). David is no ordinary man. He is King of Israel. Position brings responsibility. The higher the position, the greater the responsibility. Failure brings requisite discipline. Those who lead, like those who teach, will 'receive a stricter judgement' (James 3:1). The whole subsequent history of David is a record of the consequences resulting from his sin. The child conceived in the sinful union dies. David's family life becomes chaotic. The man who is able to rule his nation wisely cannot rule his home. His son Amnon commits a dreadful sin against his half-sister Tamar, and David is simply 'very angry' (13:21). No further action is taken until, two years later, Absalom (full brother to Tamar, half-brother to Amnon) takes matters into his own hands, murders Amnon and flees the country. '*The tragedy in the life of King David was no more evident than in the sorrows his own sons heaped upon his head.* And it was in Absalom that he reaped the bitterest harvest of all.'[9]

David grieves for his son Absalom and longs for his return to Israel. Not a day passes in three years in which David does not miss his favourite son. Joab, commander-in-chief of Israel's army and close confidant of his uncle David, plans to resolve the difficulties and restore Absalom to his father. As with Nathan, Joab employs a scheme that will force David to pass judgement on an imaginary case which is similar to that of Absalom. Even though David learns that Joab is behind the ploy, he nevertheless accepts the point and commands that Absalom be brought home — but not brought before the king! This is an incomprehensible proviso to the agreement that he should be brought back. The father grieves for his son but refuses to see him. There is no greeting for Absalom, no opportunity for repentance and forgiveness, no restoration of relationship. The instruction is: '... do not let him see my face' (14:24). In this action David may well have contributed to the later rebellion of Absalom!

Two years pass with no change in the attitude of his father, so Absalom forces the issue himself. Joab speaks to the king and Absalom is brought to his father and reconciliation takes place. But five years of estrangement have taken their toll upon this son of David. Whatever pride and ambition may lie in his heart at this point, subsequent events are to demonstrate these sins in uncontrolled profusion.

In his late twenties, and with his brothers Amnon and Chileab both dead, Absalom is the heir to the throne of Israel. Because of his past behaviour he may doubt the support of his father and the nation. Furthermore there is young Solomon, the second son of Bathsheba, who is possibly being groomed to sit upon the throne. Absalom plans a manoeuvre. In contrast to his father the king, he determines on a high-profile strategy, regularly appearing in public with an impressive entourage. He also sits at the palace gate listening to those who come with grievances, telling them what justice he would dispense if he were in power. He embraces anyone who shows him significant respect. So by such cunning and craft, 'Absalom stole the hearts of the men of Israel' (15:6). After four years Absalom is confident of sufficient support to mount a revolt.

Psalm 41 may have been composed about this time: '... if we place this psalm into the time of the rebellion of Absalom, it would fit exceptionally well. The "bosom friend" could well be Ahithophel. The period of illness would have led to the omission of the carrying out of many duties in David's administrative work, which would explain how Absalom was able to claim that men were not getting just treatment under David's administration.'[10]

On the pretext of honouring a vow made some years earlier, Absalom visits Hebron, the town of his birth (3:2-3). 200 friends who are oblivious of his intentions go with him. He is also accompanied by one of David's most trusted counsellors, Ahithophel. So David's favourite son and his trusted friend join forces in a conspiracy to usurp the throne (15:31). Psalm 55 fits these events, though, as Spurgeon notes, 'It would be idle to fix a time, and find an occasion for this Psalm with any dogmatism. It reads like a song of the time of Absalom and Ahithophel... Altogether it seems to us to relate to that mournful era when the King was betrayed by his trusted counsellor.'[11]

When news of the rebellion reaches David he gathers his household and servants and makes a hasty departure from Jerusalem. The man who had for many years been a fugitive from godless Saul is now to become a fugitive from his own godless son (cf. Ps. 3).

> How long, O you sons of men,
> Will you turn my glory to shame?
> How long will you love worthlessness
> And seek falsehood?
> But know that the LORD has set apart for himself him who is godly;
> The LORD will hear when I call to him
>
> (Ps. 4:2-3)

During this time, David and his party are met by Ziba, the servant of Mephibosheth. Ziba lies about his master, saying he is a usurper. David believes Ziba and rewards him accordingly. One day David will learn the truth and discover that he has been deceived (19:24-30). His fault lies in believing Ziba without evidence; consequently Mephibosheth is judged an ungrateful traitor. It is difficult in these circumstances for David to know whom to trust. He ought to postpone judgement until conversant with all the facts. Believers are warned not to 'judge according to appearance, but [to] judge with righteous judgement' (John 7:24).

David recognizes the judgement of God on his life, as is evident in his reaction to Shimei, the son of Gera, of the house of Saul. When Abishai wants to kill Shimei for cursing David, the king replies, 'What have I to do with you, you sons of Zeruiah? So let him curse, because the LORD has said to him, "Curse David." Who then shall say, "Why have you done so?" ' (16:10). There is very little brightness in David's life since his sins against Uriah and Bathsheba.

He is brought very low by news of the death of Absalom. David retires to the privacy of his own room and weeps. 'It was a king who heard his armies had been victorious, but it was a father who grieved.'[12] 'O my son Absalom — my son, my son Absalom — if only I had died in your place! O Absalom my son, my son!' (18:33).

David's grief as a father completely overshadows his responsibilities as a king. He should have been joining with his people in the praise of God for victory, and publicly acknowledging the faithfulness of his loyal subjects. Joab, his commander-in-chief, rightly rebukes him. David accepts the criticism and goes out to greet the people.

With the death of Absalom and the defeat of his army David could well have returned immediately and with military force have regained the throne in Jerusalem. He chooses rather to wait until the elders of both Israel and Judah invite him back.

As David begins his return journey to Jerusalem the men of Judah cross the Jordan to escort him. A contingent of Benjamites, and Ziba with his sons, also accompany him. Once over the Jordan King David is greeted by Shimei, who is full of remorse for his past offence (16:5-8). David forgives him and will not permit anyone to harm him.

The next person to greet the returning king is lame Mephibosheth. Tricked by Ziba, his servant, he was unable to join David when he left Jerusalem. As an open gesture of his grief since David's departure Mephibosheth has neglected his appearance. His loyalty to David is now visibly evident.

The return is not without its problems. The men of Israel challenge the men of Judah for taking the honour of escorting King David over the Jordan, for it was Judah who was at first reticent to see David returned to power. Judah responds by claiming their tribal relationship as warrant for the honour. They argue fiercely and will not relent. The scene is set for a new division.

Part III: The final years (20:1 - 24:25)

A Benjamite leads the opposition. Sheba sounds the trumpet and calls upon all Israelites to turn away from King David. He has caught the spirit of the day and the Israelites respond in totality. Judah alone escorts King David to Jerusalem.

A dark shadow is once more cast over Israel: three years of famine afflict the land. At length David seeks an explanation from the Lord. It is revealed that the famine is punishment for a crime committed some years earlier: the breaking of a peace treaty with the Gibeonites that had been entered into in the days of Joshua (Josh. 9:3-15). King Saul had violated this covenant (21:2). Responding to their request, David hands over seven male descendants of Saul. They are executed and their bodies hung on trees or stakes. Rizpah, Saul's concubine, keeps vigil over the bodies. Her action in respect for the dead prompts David to recover the bodies of Saul, Jonathan and the seven grandsons who were hung. He ensures their burial in the tomb of Kish, Saul's father, in the town of Zelah of the land of Benjamin (21:14; cf. 1 Sam. 9:1-2). The famine ends.

At an age when most men have settled down to a less strenuous existence, David is still leading his army into battle.[13] While fighting the old enemy, the Philistines, David collapses on the battlefield (21:15), is rescued by Abishai and requested by his men not to accompany them to war again (21:17). At sixty-eight the courageous soldier and outstanding military leader, more often than not conscious of the Lord's enabling (22:30,35, 37-51), has to hang up his sword. But his work is not yet over.

> The righteous shall flourish like a palm tree,
> He shall grow like a cedar in Lebanon.
> Those who are planted in the house of the LORD
> Shall flourish in the courts of our God.
> They shall still bear fruit in old age;
> They shall be fresh and flourishing,
> To declare that the LORD is upright;
> He is my rock, and there is no unrighteousness in him
>
> (Ps. 92:12-15).

Retirement from military activity gives David the opportunity to reflect upon his long and eventful life. Under the influence of the Holy Spirit he composes a song of thanksgiving that forms an appropriate conclusion to the history of his active life (22:1-51; cf. Ps. 18). As David advances in years he appears to grow more thankful to the Lord, 'and it is delightful to see him, as it is delightful to see any old man, not turning sour, as the infirmities of age gathered upon him, but more grateful, more humble, more genial than ever'.[14]

David claims divine inspiration for the psalm recorded in chapter 22 (and by implication all his other psalms), for immediately following the psalm he declares:

The Spirit of the LORD spoke by me,
And his word was on my tongue.
The God of Israel said,
The Rock of Israel spoke to me…

(23:2-3).

These lines may be intentionally 'trinitarian' in their reference to God the Holy Spirit (i.e. The Spirit of the LORD spoke by me…'), God the Father (i.e. 'The God of Israel said…'), and God the Son (i.e. 'The Rock of Israel spoke to me…'; cf. Isa. 32:2; 1 Cor. 10:4: '… and that Rock was Christ').[15]

Testimony is recorded of 'David's heroes', the mighty men who were loyal to David, and an account given of an outstanding example of heroic devotion. In the early days of David's flight from the wrath of King Saul, three men came to David at harvest-time when he was in the Cave of Adullam (1 Sam. 22:1). David was on the mountain fortress and the Philistine post was then in Bethlehem. David longed for water and said, 'Oh, that someone would give me a drink of the water from the well of Bethlehem, which is by the gate!' (23:15). Bethlehem was his birthplace; he longed to be home. The three mighty men, disregarding their own safety, broke through the ranks of the enemy, by strategy or by sword, to obtain the desired water. Their deed was all the more remarkable in that David was a fugitive, had not been crowned king — nor humanly speaking was there any prospect of his being crowned king — was not in a position to honour these men and had issued no command. Their respect and devotion for David are unquestionable. When the water was brought to David he immediately understood the danger to which the men had exposed themselves and viewed the water as far too precious for his consumption, 'but poured it out to the LORD' (23:16).

The final chapter of 2 Samuel 'concerns an episode which though simple and plain in some of its features, is in other respects shrouded in deep mystery'.[16] David determines to number the nation of Israel to ascertain the strength of his people. His captains resist the idea and David himself later confesses that he has 'sinned greatly' (24:10). The Lord also indicates his displeasure by sending a plague that kills 70,000 men (24:15).

Years before, Moses had, under instruction from the Lord, numbered the people twice: immediately following the construction of the tabernacle in the Wilderness of Sinai (Num. 1:1-3), and on the plains of Moab just prior to entering the land of Canaan (Num. 26:1-2). It would seem that David had a precedent for taking a census of fighting men, so what was the nature of his great sin? Various explanations have been given. One is that David sinned in numbering the people without the express instruction to do so from the Lord; another that David was motivated by personal pride in wanting to know the extent of his military power. A third suggestion is that David failed to require the half-shekel which was to be paid by each person for the service of the sanctuary when the people were numbered (Exod. 30:12-13). When the Scriptures provide no explanation it is unwise to form any strong conclusions.

The Lord gives David a choice of punishments: seven years of famine, three months of defeat in battle, or three days of plague. David's response indicates that his confession is sincere and his repentance is genuine: 'Please let us fall into the hand of the LORD, for his mercies are great' (24:14). The plague hits the nation; 70, 000 men die; the angel is poised to strike the capital; David pleads with God; the Lord answers; an altar is to be erected 'to the LORD on the threshing-floor of Araunah' (24:18). 'And David built there an altar to the LORD; and offered burnt offerings and peace offerings. So the LORD heeded the prayers for the land, and the plague was withdrawn from Israel' (24:25).

Christ and his church

David as a type of Christ

'I will establish one shepherd over them, and he shall feed them — my servant David. He shall feed them and be their shepherd. And I, the LORD, will be their God, and my servant David a prince among them; I, the LORD, have spoken' (Ezek. 34:23-24). 'David my servant shall be king over them, and they shall all have one shepherd; they shall also walk in my judgements and observe my statutes, and do them … and my servant David shall be their prince for ever' (Ezek. 37:24-25; cf. Jer. 30:9). This posthumous use of the name 'David' in reference to the promised Messiah at least permits, if not implicitly commends, the examination of the life of David as a type of Christ.

David as a type of Christ

	David	Christ
One of his brethren	'Indeed we are your bone and your flesh' (2 Sam. 5:1). '... one from among your brethren you shall set as king over you' (Deut. 17:15).	'Inasmuch then as the children have partaken of flesh and blood, he himself likewise shared in the same...' (Heb. 2:14).
One by whom the Lord would deliver his people	'I have been with you ... and have cut off all your enemies from before you' (2 Sam. 7:9; cf. 22:38-41).	Blessed is the Lord God of Israel, For he has visited and redeemed his people And has raised up a horn of salvation for us (Luke 1:68-69). 'For he must reign till he has put all enemies under his feet' (1 Cor. 15:25).
Anointed	'Then Samuel took the horn of oil and anointed him in the midst of his brothers' (1 Sam. 16:13; 2 Sam. 2:4; 5:3).	'God, your God, has anointed you with the oil of gladness more than your companions' (Heb. 1:9; cf. Ps. 45:7).
Hated without cause	'Why then will you sin against innocent blood, to kill David without a cause?' (1 Sam. 19:5). Let them not rejoice over me who are wrongfully my enemies; Nor let them wink with the eye who hate me without a cause (Ps. 35:19; cf. Ps. 69:4).	'But this happened that the word might be fulfilled which is written in their law, "They hated me without a cause"' (John 15:25).

	David	Christ
Opposing kingdoms	'So Saul became David's enemy continually' (1 Sam. 18:29).	Satan is continually the enemy of Christ: '... the ruler of this world' (John 12:31); '... the prince of the power of the air, the spirit who now works in the sons of disobedience'(Eph. 2:2).
Gathers a motley band of followers	'And everyone who was in distress, everyone who was in debt, and everyone who was discontented gathered to him' (1 Sam. 22:2).	'God has chosen the foolish things ... the weak things ... and the things which are despised...' (1 Cor. 1:27-28).
Grants pardon for sinners	'"Shall not Shimei be put to death for this, because he cursed the LORD's anointed?" ... The king said to Shimei, "You shall not die"' (2 Sam. 19:21,23).	'Even the robbers who were crucified with him reviled him' (Matt.27:44) 'And Jesus said to him, "Assuredly, I say to you, today you will be with me in paradise"' (Luke 23:43).
Betrayed by a close friend	'Absalom sent for Ahithophel ... David's counsellor... And the conspiracy grew strong' (2 Sam. 15:12). Even my own familiar friend in whom I trusted, Who ate my bread, Has lifted up his heel against me (Ps. 41:9).	'Judas, one of the twelve, went before them... But Jesus said to him, "Judas, are you betraying the Son of Man with a kiss?"'(Luke 22:47-48). 'I know whom I have chosen; but that the Scripture may be fulfilled... "He who eats bread with me has lifted up his heel against me"' (John 13:18).

	David	Christ
The betrayer hangs himself	'Then [Ahithophel] put his household in order, and hanged himself, and died' (2 Sam. 17:23).	'Then [Judas] threw down the pieces of silver in the temple and departed, and went and hanged himself' (Matt. 27:5).
Gentiles share the king's rejection	'And Ittai answered the king and said, "As the LORD lives, and as my lord the king lives, surely in whatever place my lord the king shall be, whether in death or life, even there also your servant will be"' (2 Sam. 15:21).	'For to you it has been granted on behalf of Christ, not only to believe in him, but also to suffer for his sake' (Phil. 1:29). 'Yes, and all who desire to lead a godly life in Christ Jesus will suffer persecution' (2 Tim. 3:12).
Has devoted followers	The three mighty men risked their lives to bring water for David: '"Is this not the blood of the men who went in jeopardy of their lives?" Therefore he would not drink it' (2 Sam. 23:17).	'...our beloved Barnabas and Paul, men who have risked their lives for the name of our Lord Jesus Christ' (Acts 15:25-26; cf. 2 Cor. 11:23-27; Rev. 12:11).

Many parallels may be drawn (see table above). David was three times anointed — in his father's house, over Judah and, lastly, over Israel (1 Sam. 16:13; 2 Sam. 2:4; 5:3). God has anointed Jesus of Nazareth with the oil of gladness in the Father's house, over his people the church and ultimately over all things.

Though anointed king, David experienced exile for many years while Saul reigned over Israel. In like manner the Lord is rejected by the world and 'the god of this age' (2 Cor. 4:4) reigns in the hearts of the people. Like David, the Saviour gathers to himself a motley band of followers.

The pardoning of Shimei resembles the pardoning of such sinners as the thief on the cross who had mocked the Saviour and 'illustrates the sufficiency of God's mercy for the greatest sinner and the vilest rebel — even for those who have poured blasphemy and reproach on His holy name.'[17] We cannot form too high a view of the grace and goodness of God in Christ. No sin is too great for him to be able to forgive it.

David and Mephibosheth as a type of Christ and sinners

Mephibosheth	Sinners
Mephibosheth means 'a shameful thing'. He was unclean; he had not cared for his personal hygiene since David left (2 Sam. 19:24).	But we are all like an unclean thing, And all our righteousnesses are like filthy rags (Isa. 64:6)
He was lame in both feet as a result of a fall (2 Sam. 4:4).	Sinners are crippled by birth and behaviour as a result of Adam's fall (Rom. 5:12).
He was a fugitive from the wrath of a king (2 Sam. 4:4).	Sinners are under the wrath of God (Rom. 1:18; Eph. 2:3).
He lived in Lo Debar, which means 'the place of no pasture' (2 Sam. 9:4).	Like the prodigal, sinners are in a far country where there is a severe famine (Luke 15:13-14).
He was reconciled to the king (2 Sam. 19:24-30).	'And you, who once were alienated and enemies ... he has reconciled' (Col. 1:21).
He was brought to Jerusalem, which means 'the place of peace' (2 Sam. 9:13).	'Peace I leave with you, my peace I give to you... Let not your heart be troubled' (John 14:27).
By the unmerited favour of the king he would dine at the king's table for the rest of his life (2 Sam. 9:13).	'I will come in to him and dine with him, and he with me' (Rev. 3:20; cf. 19:9).

David's dealings with Mephibosheth provide a type of the Saviour's dealings with a sinner. The name Mephibosheth means 'a shameful thing' and, polluted by sin, 'We are all like an unclean thing' (Isa. 64:6), following 'the lusts of our flesh, fulfilling the desires of the flesh and of the mind' (Eph. 2:3). Mephibosheth was lame in both feet; in the same way, we too are by birth and behaviour crippled as a result of a fall. Mephibosheth was a fugitive from the wrath of a king; we 'were by nature children of wrath, just as the others' (Eph. 2:3), unable to please God (Rom. 8:8). Mephibosheth lived in Lo Debar, which means, 'the place of no pasture'; like the prodigal son, sinners are in a far country where there is severe famine (Luke 15:13-14). Mephibosheth was brought to Jerusalem, 'the place of peace'. By the unmerited favour of the king he would dine at the king's table for the rest of his life. Forgiven sinners will dine with Christ for eternity.

The defection of David's close companion Ahithophel is a type of the betrayal of Jesus by Judas. It is thought that Ahithophel was one whom the king included among his closest friends, with whom he had fellowship in spiritual matters, and of whom he spoke when he said that they 'took sweet counsel together, and walked to the house of God in the throng' (Ps. 55:14). David felt the betrayal deeply:

> Even my own familiar friend in whom I trusted,
> Who ate my bread,
> Has lifted up his heel against me
>
> (Ps. 41:9).

Ahithophel hanged himself, and so did Judas.

In the loyal Philistine Gittites, who fled Jerusalem with David, there is a type of Gentile believers who join the Saviour and share his dishonour in the world. The height of devotion to Christ is illustrated in the willingness and eagerness with which the three mighty men of David discounted thoughts of their own safety in order to fulfil the desire of their beloved leader (23:15-17).

Prophecies

1. The Seed of David

After David had brought the ark of the covenant to Jerusalem and had placed it in a temporary tabernacle he planned to build a beautiful and more permanent temple. The Lord responded to his desire by sending word through Nathan the prophet: David would not build the house of the Lord; the Lord would build the house of David (7:5,11). The Lord gave David a prophetic promise: '… your house and your kingdom shall be established for ever before you. Your throne shall be established for ever' (7:16).

There is an intriguing ambiguity in the promise that the Lord gives to David: 'When your days are fulfilled and you rest with your fathers, I will set up your seed after you, who will come from your body, and I will establish his kingdom. He shall build a house for my name, and I will establish the throne of his kingdom for ever' (7:12-13).

Solomon was not yet born. Was this promise to be fulfilled in Solomon, or in the Lord Jesus Christ, or in both? When God said, 'I will be his Father, and he shall be my son' (7:14) the ultimate fulfilment is reserved for the Lord Jesus Christ (Heb. 1:5).[18] Later generations would clearly see the thread of history: the promised Seed of Eve (Gen. 3:15) is the promised Seed of Abraham (Gen. 12:3, 7) who is the promised Seed of David (7:12-13; cf. Rom. 1:3). David is in the ancestral line of the promised Messiah (Matt. 1:6). This Messiah will build the true house of God (7:13): 'Christ … a son over his own house, whose house we are if we hold fast the confidence and the rejoicing of the hope firm to the end' (Heb. 3:6; cf. Zech. 6:12-13; 1 Cor. 6:19-20; Eph. 5:30).

The continuity between the covenant with Abraham and the covenant with David is highlighted by the prophet Jeremiah: 'Thus says the LORD: "If my covenant is not with day and night, and if I have not appointed the ordinances of heaven and earth, then I will cast away the descendants of Jacob and David my servant, so that I will not take any of his descendants to be rulers over the descendants of Abraham, Isaac, and Jacob. For I will cause their captives to return, and will have mercy on them"' (Jer. 33:25-26).

The elements of the promises made to David are strikingly similar to those in the promises made to Abraham (see tables on page 279). Like Abraham, David is promised that his name will be great and that the nation will have security in its own land. David is promised offspring: kings are to descend from him. God declares himself as the God of Israel and they are his very own people. The promises to Abraham and to David are eternal. The only element of the promise to Abraham that seems to be lacking in 2 Samuel 7 is the extension of the divine blessing to Gentiles.[19]

The hope of the prophets was based upon confidence in the promise of God, for 'If the promise ever came to an end, the messianic hope would die.'[20] If the promise ever failed the whole purposes of God would be shattered and the kingdom of Christ could never be established.

The promise made to Abraham of a seed to come has now, through David, 'attained the high stature of a triumphant and universal king of Judah'.[21] As we are now privileged to see, Messiah is 'King of Kings and Lord of Lords' (Rev. 19:16; 17:14), and 'He will reign … for ever, and of his kingdom there will be no end' (Luke 1:33; Heb. 1:8).

Promises to Abraham and to David

	Abraham	David
A great name	Genesis 12:2	2 Samuel 7:9
A land for his descendants	Genesis 12:7	2 Samuel 7:10
A great nation	Genesis 12:2	2 Samuel 7:12
A royal line	Genesis 17:6	2 Samuel 7:16
To be their God	Genesis 17:7	2 Samuel 7:14
An everlasting promise	Genesis 17:7	2 Samuel 7:13

Abraham	David
I will make you a great nation; I will bless you And make your name great; And you shall be a blessing. I will bless those who bless you, And I will curse him who curses you; And in you all the families of the earth shall be blessed (Gen. 12:2-3). 'To your descendants I will give this land' (Gen. 12:7). 'I will make you exceedingly fruitful; and I will make nations of you, and kings shall come from you. And I will establish my covenant between me and you and your descendants after you in their generations, for an everlasting covenant, to be God to you and your descendants after you. Also I give to you and your descendants after you the land in which you are a stranger, all the land of Canaan, as an everlasting possession; and I will be their God' (Gen. 17:6-8).	'And I have been with you wherever you have gone, and have cut off all your enemies from before you, and have made you a great name, like the name of the great men who are on the earth. Moreover I will appoint a place for my people Israel, and will plant them, that they may dwell in a place of their own and move no more; nor shall the sons of wickedness oppress them any more, as previously, since the time that I commanded judges to be over my people Israel, and have caused you to rest from all your enemies. Also the LORD tells you that he will make you a house. When your days are fulfilled and you rest with your fathers, I will set up your seed after you, who will come from your body, and I will establish his kingdom. He shall build a house for my name, and I will establish the throne of his kingdom for ever. I will be his Father, and he shall be my son. If he commits iniquity, I will chasten him with the rod of men and with the blows of the sons of men. But my mercy shall not depart from him, as I took it from Saul, whom I removed from before you. And your house and your kingdom shall be established for ever before you. Your throne shall be established for ever' (2 Sam. 7:9-16).

2. The Lord's Anointed

It is David who first describes a king as 'the LORD's anointed' (1 Sam.
24:6), a phrase which gives a high and exalted view of kingship
(1:14,16). Having witnessed his own phenomenal rise to the throne,
followed by his devastating fall into the sins of lust, adultery and murder,
David has seen his life closely aligned with the promised Messiah in his
own rising, but separate from the promised Messiah in his own falling.
By the end of his life David in his writings clearly separates himself from
the Promised One. The picture of the future in chapter 23 'is nothing else
than the image of the Messiah, which now has been entirely separated
from [David's] subjectivity, and which stands before him as purely
objective':[22]

> He who rules over men must be just,
> Ruling in the fear of God.
> And he shall be like the light of the morning when the sun rises,
> A morning without clouds,
> Like the tender grass springing out of the earth,
> By clear shining after rain
>
> (23:3-4).

The later prophets would build upon this prophecy of the 'just' or
'righteous' rule of Messiah. Although the prophecies were obscure and
built upon each other, we have the advantage, at this side of Calvary, of
seeing the fulfilment of the detail and tracing the thread back:

> Behold, your King is coming to you;
> He is just and having salvation,
> Lowly and riding on a donkey,
> A colt, the foal of a donkey
>
> (Zech. 9:9; cf. Jer. 23:5-6; Ps. 72:2).

In Psalm 2 the phrase 'the LORD's anointed' is portrayed in clear
focus: God's anointed (the Messiah) is the one whom God has appointed King of Zion and is God's Son to whom all should yield unre-
served submission and trust (Ps. 2:2,6,7,12).

Application

1. Human plans and divine purposes

Good ideas, even ideas which are honouring to God, should be brought before the Lord for his approval (7:1-17). If we do not regard God's will as *supreme,* we are entirely at fault. Our first question ought to be: 'What says the Lord?' or 'What would the Lord have me to do?' There is some credit to the Israelites that the question does come second or third in line of consideration. There is some merit that it is there at all. Yet if we would honour God it will be our first and foremost consideration. Life is short. All plans must be made in the conscious presence of God and with due consideration to the purposes of God: 'Come now, you who say, "Today or tomorrow we will go to such and such a city, spend a year there, buy and sell, and make a profit"; whereas you do not know what will happen tomorrow. For what is your life? It is even a vapour that appears for a little time and then vanishes away. Instead you ought to say, "If the Lord wills, we shall live and do this or that"' (James 4:13-15).

2. God's work in God's way

David always acknowledged that God was behind his accession to the throne of Israel and Judah: 'David knew that the LORD had established him as king over Israel, and that he had exalted his kingdom for his people Israel's sake' (5:12). Such awareness keeps a believer humble before God and others, and dependent upon God alone (Deut. 8:11-18).

David was often conscious of God's presence and involvement in his life. It was not a periodic intervention into his life and circumstances; David acknowledged God's constant involvement — though he did not always live as we would expect of one who was continually aware of it. When he fought against the Philistines he humbly acknowledged that his victory in war was the Lord's doing; before he fought he prayed to know the mind of God; having received word from the Lord that he should proceed, he won a great victory. When the Philistines were defeated David declared, 'The LORD has broken through my enemies before me, like water bursting a breach' (5:20).

David did, however, make some serious mistakes in this regard. In seeking to bring the ark of the covenant into Jerusalem, his intentions were good but his initial approach was bad. Rather than seeking the mind of God and consulting the Scriptures, David consulted his leaders (1 Chr. 13:1), making democracy his guiding principle (1 Chr. 13:2,4) with staggering and tragic results (6:6-7).

When the ark was first constructed on Mount Sinai it was made to God's exact specifications. The Lord not only laid down the dimensions; he also stipulated the materials from which each section should be composed. The Lord was not, however, concerned simply for accuracy in the manufacture of the ark, but also for its housing and transportation. It was in the moving of the ark that the covenantal law of God was violated: 'When the camp prepares to journey, Aaron and his sons shall come, and they shall take down the covering veil and cover the ark of the Testimony with it. Then they shall put on it a covering of badger skins, and spread over that a cloth entirely of blue; and they shall insert its poles' (Num. 4:5-6). 'And when Aaron and his sons have finished covering the sanctuary and all the furnishings of the sanctuary, when the camp is set to go, then the sons of Kohath shall come to carry them; but they shall not touch any holy thing, lest they die' (Num. 4:15). 'To the sons of Kohath he gave [no carts or oxen] because theirs was the service of the holy things, which they carried on their shoulders' (Num. 7:9).

The design of the ark provided for rings into which poles were inserted 'that the ark *may be carried by them*' (Exod. 25:14, emphasis added). The Israelites failed to do this and it cost Uzzah his life. It may seem that Uzzah was unfairly treated by the Lord since he was attempting to stop the ark falling to the ground. But the whole incident was another sad case of men disregarding God's instructions and warnings. God's revelation is never to be dismissed in preference for human invention. God's work must be done in God's way. Wilful defiance does not go unpunished. Furthermore the Israelites added insult to injury in that they followed the practice of the godless Philistines and built a new cart to transport the ark. What God permits the heathen to do in ignorance he will not allow his people to do in disobedience.

Three months after the death of Uzzah, the ark was removed from the house of Obed-Edom the Gittite (6:11-12) and brought to the city of Jerusalem. This time David followed the divine instructions on the transportation of the ark of the covenant (1 Chr. 15:2,11-15).

3. Monogamy

From the beginning God's design for marriage was that it should be an exclusive covenant relationship between one man and one woman (Gen. 2:24; cf. Matt. 19:3-6). David's polygamy (marriage to more than one wife) brought immense grief and heartache into his home. His numerous wives with their numerous children produced enormous pressures and problems.[23]

In our own day the widespread practices of temporary cohabitation and easy divorce not only damage the stability of society, but also bring difficult problems into the church. New converts often have complex relationships such as previous spouses and children from different partners. Pastoral wisdom, love and patience need to be exercised to ensure maximum stability for all who are in less than ideal circumstances.

4. Clouded judgement

The remarkable skill displayed by David in gathering, organizing and leading thousands of people was not so evident in the management of his own household. When his son Amnon raped his half-sister Tamar (David's daughter by another wife) the only response from King David, who was used by Amnon as an unwitting accomplice, was that 'He was very angry' (13:21; cf. v. 6). David's failure as a father to punish Amnon and ensure justice and honourable treatment for Tamar contributed to the actions of another son, Absalom, who eventually took matters into his own hands, murdered Amnon and fled from his father, his home and his country.

When after three years David permitted Absalom to return from exile, he refused to see his son for a further two years (14:24,28,33). Even when they were reconciled, the difficulties between father and son were far from over. Absalom caused untold distress in Israel and led a civil war against his father.

Despite all these immense problems David persisted in his love for Absalom, so that when his son fell in battle King David mourned with inconsolable grief: 'O my son Absalom — my son, my son Absalom — if only I had died in your place! O Absalom my son, my son!' (18:33). David's love for his son Absalom clouded his judgement; overcome with his personal grief he disregarded those who had risked their lives for him. Joab's rebuke was well deserved: 'Today you have disgraced all your servants who today have saved your life, the lives of your sons and daughters, the lives of your wives and the lives of your concubines, in that you love your enemies and hate your friends. For you have declared today that you regard neither princes nor servants; for today I perceive that if Absalom had lived and all of us had died today, then it would have pleased you well' (19:5-6).

Leaders among the people of God are responsible to ensure that family ties do not cloud their judgement. As well as the danger of nepotism (favouritism shown to relatives or friends in conferring offices or privileges) the leader is open to being more lenient towards members of his own family. Where elders are appointed from within the local church (a practice that is highly commended in the New Testament) there is the risk of their being influenced in their judgement by family members. It is crucial therefore that an elder must be 'one who rules his own house well' (1 Tim. 3:4), and is also aware of the dangers inherent in extended family relationships within the church.

5. Relying upon the promises of God

The Second Book of Samuel teaches patience and dependence upon God to keep his promises (2:1; 5:1-3). There were certainly many occasions in the life of David when he had only the bare promises of God to cling on to. Trusting in the Lord to preserve him from all danger and deliver him from all harm, David would not speed up the purposes of God by any actions of his own; though God had said that he would be King of Israel (1 Sam. 16:13), David took no action to bring it to pass. Indeed when a man came, saying that he had killed King Saul, David was horrified and had the man executed there and then. When Rechab and his brother Baanah thought to win David's favour by murdering Saul's remaining son Ishbosheth, they grossly misjudged the reaction of David. He was once more horrified and ordered the execution of these two murderers (4:12).

David had to wait years to see the unfolding of God's promises. God has often taught his people patience. Abraham had to wait twenty-five years for the son of promise. Moses had to wait forty years in obscurity before leading the children of Israel out of Egypt. 'In quietness and confidence shall be your strength' (Isa. 30:15).

6. Exposure of sin

This book also contains a serious warning which may be expressed in the words found in the book of Numbers: 'Be sure your sin will find you out' (Num. 32:23). This is illustrated in:

- The Amalekite who claimed to have killed King Saul, 'the LORD's anointed' (1:14-16);
- Abner, who ignored what he knew to be God's purpose when he made Saul's son Ishbosheth king (2:8-9; 3:9; cf. v. 27);
- Rechab and Baanah, who tried to win David's favour by means of murdering Ishbosheth (4:5-12);
- Amnon and the rape of Tamar (13:1-17; cf. vv. 28-29);
- David in his adultery with Bathsheba and murder of Uriah (11:1-27; 12:7-14).

Whenever, through the Scriptures, God shows the weakness, failing and sinfulness of his saints, we must take great care. We must take note of the exhortation of Paul when he urges, Consider 'yourself lest you also be tempted' (Gal. 6:1). 'He who is without sin among you, let him throw a stone … first' (John 8:7).

Conclusion

David was a man after God's own heart (1 Sam. 13:14). In a lifespan of about seventy years, he 'served his own generation by the will of God' (Acts 13:36).

David was Israel's greatest king, designated by God as the kingly type of Christ the Messiah. He is the only person in Scripture with the name David. There are fifty-eight New Testament references to him. David's career, though outstanding at times, was marred by atrocious sins. His honesty and sincere repentance in acknowledging and confessing those sins brought God's forgiveness. He knew how to cry to God:

Have mercy upon me, O God,
According to your loving-kindness;
According to the multitude of your tender mercies,
Blot out my transgressions.

Wash me thoroughly from my iniquity,
And cleanse me from my sin

(Ps. 51:1).

He knew also the joy of salvation and justification by faith alone:

Blessed is he whose transgression is forgiven,
Whose sin is covered.
Blessed is the man to whom the LORD does not impute iniquity,
And in whose spirit there is no guile.
When I kept silent, my bones grew old
Through my groaning all the day long.
For day and night your hand was heavy upon me;
My vitality was turned into the drought of summer.
I acknowledged my sin to you,
And my iniquity I have not hidden.
I said, "I will confess my transgressions to the LORD,"
And you forgave the iniquity of my sin

(Ps. 32:1-5).

David is a key figure in the unfolding purposes of God centring in Christ and his church.

I Kings

(the history of the kings of Israel and Judah)

Author: Unknown
(maybe Jeremiah)

Key thought: '... as did his father David'

Theme: Obedience blessed, disobedience punished, penitents forgiven

'I will tear the kingdom out of the hand of Solomon ... And to his son I will give one tribe, that my servant David may always have a lamp before me in Jerusalem...'

I Kings 11:31,36

Summary

The rise and fall of the kingdom of Israel

1. The establishment of the kingdom   1:1 – 2:46

    i. The death of David and the accession
        of Solomon   1:1 – 2:12
    ii. Solomon executes his enemies   2:13-46

2. The glory of the kingdom   3:1 – 10:29
    i. The marriage of Solomon   3:1-2
    ii. The prayer of Solomon   3:3-15
    iii. The wisdom of Solomon   3:16-28
    iv. The greatness of Solomon   4:1-34
    v. The building of the temple   5:1 – 7:51
    vi. The dedication of the temple   8:1-66
    vii. The Lord's second appearance to Solomon   9:1-9
    viii. The fame of Solomon   9:10-28
    ix. The visit of the Queen of Sheba   10:1-13
    x. The wealth of Solomon   10:14-29

3. The division of the kingdom   11:1 – 12:24
    i. Solomon's backsliding and death   11:1-43
    ii. The accession and stubbornness
        of Rehoboam   12:1-19
    iii. Jeroboam becomes king of the ten tribes
        (Israel)   12:20-24

4. The divided kingdoms of Israel and Judah   12:25 – 22:53

Judah (two southern tribes)		**Israel** (ten northern tribes)
	12:25 – 14:20	i. The reign of King Jeroboam (bad)
	12:25-33	a. Jeroboam's apostasy
	13:1-34	b prophecy against calf-worship
	14:1-20	c. destruction of the dynasty
		predicted
ii. The reign of King	14:21-31	
Rehoboam (bad)		
iii. The reign of King Abijam	15:1-8	
(bad)		
iv. The reign of King Asa	15:9-24	
(good)		

Judah (two southern tribes)		Israel (ten northern tribes)
	15:25-32	v. The reign of King Nadab (bad)
	15:33 – 16:7	vi. The reign of King Baasha (bad)
	16:8-14	vii. The reign of King Elah (bad)
	16:15-20	viii. The reign of King Zimri (bad)
	16:21-28	ix. The reign of King Omri (bad)
	16:29 – 22:40	x. The reign of King Ahab (bad)
	16:29-34	a. Ahab introduces false worship
	17:1	b. Elijah confronts Ahab
	17:2-24	c. Elijah miraculously sustained
	18:1-19	d. Elijah meets godly Obadiah
	18:20-46	e. Elijah on Mount Carmel
	19:1-18	f. Elijah's flight to the wilderness
	19:19-21	g. Elijah appoints Elisha
	20:1-43	h. Ahab defeats the Syrians
	21:1-29	i. Ahab and Naboth's vineyard
	22:1-28	j. Ahab and Jehoshaphat of Judah
	22:29-40	k. Ahab's death in battle
xi. The reign of King Jehoshaphat (good)	22:41-50	
	22:51-53	xii. The reign of King Ahaziah (bad)

I Kings

The First Book of Kings may described as 'The rise and fall of the nation of Israel'. The first half of the book recounts the notable events in the forty-year reign of King Solomon, son of David and Bathsheba. The second half presents a sketch of the history of the divided kingdom — split into Israel (the northern kingdom of the ten tribes) and Judah (the southern kingdom of the two tribes — that is, Judah and Benjamin).

The book is written to show the causes of the establishment and decline of the kingdom. When loyal to God alone ('You shall have no other gods before me' — Exod. 20:3), Israel flourished. But when the Israelites turned from God, his covenant and his law, established through Moses, their morals and their kingdom declined. Jehovah is the Sovereign Ruler 'sitting on his throne' (22:19). He blesses the obedient; he punishes the disobedient; he forgives the penitent.

Author

The author of the book is unknown, although Jewish tradition ascribes authorship to the prophet Jeremiah. Whoever he was, he compiled his history using a number of sources, such as 'the book of the acts of Solomon' (11:41), 'the book of the chronicles of the kings of Israel' (14:19; 15:31, etc.) and 'the book of the chronicles of the kings of Judah' (14:29; 15:7,23, etc.). These books appear to have been public records, probably written down by various prophets through the years. 'Under divine inspiration the author of Kings made his choice from these written documents.'[1] It is considered probable that the bulk of the work was completed before the exile and that 2 Kings 25 was added during the period of captivity.[2]

Historical setting

The two books of Kings, like the books of Samuel, were originally one book.[3] Together they cover a period of Israel's history from the accession of King Solomon (970 B.C.), to the final exile of the people of Judah to the land of Babylon (586 B.C.). The dividing point of the two books comes during the reign of Ahaziah, son of Ahab of Israel (not to be confused with Ahaziah, son of Jehoram of Judah — 2 Kings 8:25-26), about the year 853 B.C.

The history recorded in 1 Kings follows on from that of 2 Samuel, though with a notable omission: the place where the altar was erected. The punishment of God for the sin of King David in taking a census is ended when David builds 'an altar to the LORD' and offers 'burnt offerings and peace offerings' (2 Sam. 24:25; 1 Chr. 21:26). From the parallel history in 1 Chronicles it is evident that the command to 'erect an altar to the LORD on the threshing-floor of Araunah the Jebusite' (2 Sam. 24:18) is quite sufficient for David to conclude that this is the Lord's designated site for the temple which his son Solomon will build.[4] Consequently David says, 'This is the house of the LORD God, and this is the altar of burnt offering for Israel' (1 Chr. 22:1).

In appreciation of forgiveness and in anticipation of the temple to be built, David composes Psalm 30. The title given to this psalm in our English versions may be misleading, as Spurgeon notes: '"A Psalm and Song at the Dedication of the House of David"; or rather, "A Psalm; a Song *of* Dedication *for* the House. *By* David." A song of faith since the house of Jehovah, here intended, David never lived to see. A Psalm of praise, since a sore judgement had been stayed, and a great sin forgiven'[5] (emphasis added).

David prepared for the building of the temple. He began to assemble the skilled workers and gather the materials for its construction. He also instructed Solomon about his responsibilities before God (1 Chr. 22:2-19).

Outline

The history of the kings of Judah and Israel has been amplified by reference to the various historical and prophetic books of the Old Testament in order to present a composite account.

Part I: The establishment of the kingdom (1:1 – 2:46)

King David is old, and Adonijah, the next in line to the throne, determines that he will assume the throne. It is David's duty to appoint his successor. The Lord has revealed that Solomon is his choice (1 Chr. 28:5). For some reason David delays making a public announcement and in so doing gives opportunity for Adonijah to strengthen his own support.

Adonijah seems to be well aware that not only David but, more especially, the Lord, has promised the throne to his brother Solomon (2:15). David takes immediate steps to proclaim Solomon as the future king. Zadok the priest, Nathan the prophet, and Benaiah the military leader are instructed to ensure that Solomon is anointed and declared the King of Israel (cf. 1 Chr. 23:1). Once the news of the appointment breaks, the followers of Adonijah turn back from supporting his claim to the throne. In dread of his life Adonijah flees and grasps the horns of the altar, demonstrating that he is placing himself under divine protection. Solomon assures him that he is in no danger provided he behaves wisely and does not repeat his earlier blunders (1:52).

David calls together all the leaders of Israel to make detailed provision for the continuing worship of God, the organization of the army and the functioning of government (1 Chr. 23-27). This he achieves in the last year of his life (1 Chr. 26:31). This national assembly provides David with the opportunity to acknowledge Solomon publicly as the new king of Israel and to repeat in public some of the instructions and warnings which he had previously given to Solomon in private (1 Chr. 28:2-10; 22:7-19). David officially hands over to Solomon the plans, the materials, the gold and silver for the building of the temple, and the arrangements for the services of the priests and Levites (1 Chr. 28:11-21). In a fitting conclusion to his reign, David leads the whole congregation in the worship of God:

> Blessed are you, LORD God of Israel, our Father, for ever and ever.
> Yours, O LORD, is the greatness,
> The power and the glory,
> The victory and the majesty;
> For all that is in heaven and in earth is yours;
> Yours is the kingdom, O LORD,
> And you are exalted as head over all.
> Both riches and honour come from you,
> And you reign over all.
> In your hand is power and might;

In your hand it is to make great
And to give strength to all.
Now therefore, our God,
We thank you
And praise your glorious name

(1 Chr. 29:10-13).

After a long and chequered life, godly David dies 'at a good old age, full of days and riches and honour; and Solomon his son reigned in his place' (1 Chr. 29:28).

The reign of Solomon

Upon his accession to the throne Solomon sets about establishing his reign (2:12; 1 Chr. 29:23-25). First of all, he punishes the rebels. Adonijah comes through Bathsheba with a request which Solomon immediately interprets as a further attempt to usurp his throne. Although Abishag had been only the nurse to King David, in the eyes of the people she was regarded as his concubine. Taking the harem of a deceased or conquered king was equivalent to establishing a claim to the throne (2:22; 2 Sam. 12:8). Adonijah is executed, Abiathar the priest is exiled, Joab is executed and Shimei is brought to Jerusalem and placed under house arrest. Three years later Shimei breaks the terms of his agreement, leaves the city to recover two slaves and forfeits his life. So Solomon fulfils the dying requests of his father (2:5-6,8-9).

Part II: The glory of the kingdom (3:1 - 10:29)

Once Solomon has secured his throne he enters into an alliance with Egypt by marrying Pharaoh's daughter (3:1). She is not his first wife for he had married Naamah an Ammonitess before his accession (14:21; cf. 11:42-43). Marriage to an Egyptian was not forbidden, for it was only marriages contracted with women of the seven indigenous nations that were prohibited (Deut. 7:1-4; Exod. 34:16). Furthermore it seems evident that the Egyptian princess renounced all Egyptian gods and confessed faith in Jehovah as the one true God, since when he married Pharaoh's daughter it is said of him that 'Solomon loved the LORD, walking in the statutes of his father David' (3:3). In addition, the daughter of Pharaoh is distinguished from the foreign 'wives who turned his heart after other gods' (11:1,4).

The early years of Solomon's reign have been described as 'the Golden Age of Israel'. [6] These years were made famous by Solomon's character and deeds. There are seven pointers to Solomon's significance and renown during this early period: his humility, wisdom, administration, palace, temple, cities and wealth, and his distinguished visitor.

1. Solomon's humility

Seeking the blessing of God upon his reign, Solomon, accompanied by representatives of the whole nation, offers a thousand burnt offerings on the bronze altar before the tabernacle at Gibeon (the only item missing from the tabernacle is the ark of the covenant which David had brought to the city of Jerusalem — 2 Chr. 1:4). The Lord appears to Solomon in a dream and allows him one request. Showing distinct humility, aware of his inexperience, and conscious of the daunting task to which he has been called, Solomon requests of God 'an understanding heart to judge your people, that I may discern between good and evil. For who is able to judge this great people of yours?' (3:9). This request pleases the Lord and he not only gives him wisdom beyond all others, but promises him riches and honour as well. Solomon is also promised a long life on condition that he follows the example of his father David and walks faithfully before God. Returning to Jerusalem, Solomon visits the location of the ark of the covenant, offers sacrifices and holds a feast for all his servants.

2. Solomon's wisdom

Solomon's great wisdom is illustrated in his handling of two women who are arguing over a baby. Both gave birth around the same time: one child died; the other lived. Both mothers claim the living child. Solomon solves the dilemma by commanding that the child be cut in two, and one half given to each woman. One of the women immediately protests and pleads with the king to give the child to the other woman. The second woman agrees to the division of the child. Solomon thereby reveals the true mother, who 'yearned with compassion for her son' and would rather that he be given to another than put to death. Solomon restores the baby to his mother: 'And all Israel heard of the judgement which the king had rendered; and they feared the king, for they saw that the wisdom of God was in him to administer justice' (3:28).

The outstanding wisdom that God had given to Solomon was soon known by all the surrounding nations: 'God gave Solomon wisdom and exceedingly great understanding, and largeness of heart like the sand on the seashore. Thus Solomon's wisdom excelled the wisdom of all the men of the East and all the wisdom of Egypt. For he was wiser than all men... He spoke three thousand proverbs, and his songs were one thousand and five. Also he spoke of trees, from the cedar tree of Lebanon even to the hyssop that springs out of the wall; he spoke also of animals, of birds, of creeping things, and of fish. And men of all nations, from all the kings of the earth who had heard of his wisdom, came to hear the wisdom of Solomon' (4:29-34).

3. Solomon's administration

The vastness of Solomon's kingdom is described: 'Solomon reigned over all kingdoms from the River [Euphrates] to the land of the Philistines, as far as the border of Egypt. They brought tribute and served Solomon all the days of his life... For he had dominion over all the region on this side of the River from Tiphsah even to Gaza, namely over all the kings on this side of the River; and he had peace on every side all around him. And Judah and Israel dwelt safely' (4:21,24-25).

4. Solomon's temple

The building of the temple described in chapters 5 and 6 is the result of a king committed to the service of Almighty God. Solomon's concern was to obey God. He spared no expense in building a magnificent temple for the worship of Jehovah the living God. Solomon seems to have been raised up specially for the purpose of erecting the temple. His father David had said, '... of all my sons (for the LORD has given me many sons) he has chosen my son Solomon to sit on the throne of the kingdom of the LORD over Israel. Now he said to me, "It is your son Solomon who shall build my house and my courts; for I have chosen him to be my son, and I will be his Father. Moreover I will establish his kingdom for ever, if he is steadfast to observe my commandments and my judgements, as it is this day"' (1 Chr. 28:5-7).

At that time David had addressed his son directly: 'As for you, my son Solomon, know the God of your father, and serve him with a loyal heart and with a willing mind; for the LORD searches all hearts and understands all the intent of the thoughts. If you seek him, he will be found by you; but if you forsake him, he will cast you off for ever. Consider now, for the LORD has chosen you to build a house for the sanctuary; be strong, and do it' (1 Chr. 28:9-10).

5. Solomon's palace

The building of the temple took seven years (6:38); the building of the palace took thirteen years (7:1). This detail may indicate that there were significantly more workmen involved in the building of the temple. It may also, however, indicate something quite different — that the splendour of the king's palace was greater than that of the Lord's temple!

6. Solomon's cities and wealth

'And Solomon built Gezer, Lower Beth Horon, Baalath, and Tadmor, in the wilderness, in the land of Judah, all the storage cities that Solomon had, cities for his chariots and cities for his cavalry, and whatever Solomon desired to build in Jerusalem, in Lebanon, and in all the land of his dominion' (9:17-19).

'The weight of gold that came to Solomon yearly was six hundred and sixty-six talents of gold, besides that from the travelling merchants, from the income of traders, from all the kings of Arabia, and from the governors of the country... For the king had merchant ships at sea with the fleet of Hiram. Once every three years the merchant ships came bringing gold, silver, ivory, apes and monkeys. So King Solomon surpassed all the kings of the earth in riches and wisdom. And all the earth sought the presence of Solomon to hear his wisdom, which God had put in his heart' (10:14-15,22-24).

God gave Solomon that for which he did not ask. But that was no reason for him to be extravagant.

The extent of Solomon's kingdom

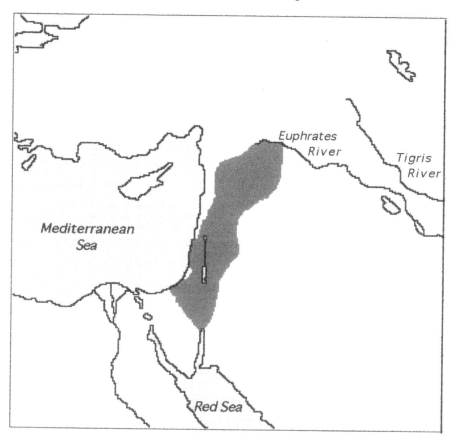

7. Solomon's distinguished visitor

The Queen of Sheba, 'the Queen of the South … came from the ends of the earth to hear the wisdom of Solomon' (Luke 11:31). She 'came to test him with hard questions' (10:1). By posing one riddle after another she intended to discover the skill and prudence of this renowned king. Nothing proved too difficult for him either to understand or to explain to her.

Part III: The division of the kingdom (11:1 – 12:24)

In the second half of Solomon's life the consequences are evident of what happens when a servant of God turns from his first love, disregards the commandments and warnings of the Word of God and yields to nearly unbridled passion. Here are some of the most sober warnings against serious backsliding. With all his wisdom Solomon is not able to control his lust. He begins well; he ends badly. Despite all the blessings God has showered upon him, Solomon nevertheless forgets the Lord his God: 'But King Solomon loved many foreign women, as well as the daughter of Pharaoh: women of the Moabites, Ammonites, Edomites, Sidonians, and Hittites — from the nations of whom the LORD had said to the children of Israel, "You shall not intermarry with them, nor they with you. For surely they will turn away your hearts after their gods." Solomon clung to these in love. And he had seven hundred wives, princesses, and three hundred concubines; and his wives turned away his heart. For it was so, when Solomon was old, that his wives turned his heart after other gods; and his heart was not loyal to the LORD his God, as was the heart of his father David… Solomon did evil in the sight of the LORD' (11:1-4,6).

Solomon could not plead ignorance, for the warnings of God had been given in the law of Moses. Concerning any king of Israel God had said, 'But he shall not multiply horses for himself, nor cause the people to return to Egypt to multiply horses, for the LORD has said to you, "You shall not return that way again." Neither shall he multiply wives for himself, lest his heart turn away; nor shall he greatly multiply silver and gold for himself' (Deut. 17:16-17). Solomon did all three. Added to these three areas of disobedience, Solomon included a fourth by marrying many *pagan* wives. He 'is an enigma, for he was both the perfecter of Israel's glory and the architect of its destruction'.[7]

The decline of Solomon's kingdom is brought about by:

* His extravagant lifestyle (10:14-29);
* His notorious lust (11:1-3);
* His turning from God (11:4-10);
* His enemies who were raised up by God (11:14-25).

So in the latter part of his life Solomon seriously falls from his spiritual walk with God. Through external and internal means the Lord brings punishment. Rebellion by some of the subject neighbour-states is accompanied by internal disruption within Israel. Solomon's servant Jeroboam rebels against the king (11:26). As the Lord had raised up adversaries outside Israel (11:14,23), so the Lord raises up this adversary inside Israel and, through the prophet Ahijah, predicts the devastating division of the kingdom of Israel (11:29-31). At the same time God confirms his earlier promise to David to maintain his line:

'And to his son I will give one tribe, that my servant David may always have a lamp before me in Jerusalem, the city which I have chosen for myself, to put my name there (11:36). Jeroboam is warned to walk in obedience to the Lord so that he may enjoy God's full blessing upon his life and reign. Hearing of the prophecy, Solomon seeks Jeroboam to take his life. Jeroboam escapes to Egypt and places himself under the protection of King Shishak.

After a reign of forty years Solomon dies and his son Rehoboam comes to the throne. At the same time, by popular request, Jeroboam is called back from Egypt. Jeroboam champions the cause of the people, making representations to King Rehoboam for a reduction of the heavy taxation. Rehoboam proves a stubborn and foolish king. Rejecting the counsel of his father's older and wiser counsellors and listening rather to the advice of his young bosom friends, he increases rather than lessens the burden upon the people. The scene is set for open revolt. When Rehoboam sends Adoram, his minister of finance, to collect the new taxes, Adoram is stoned to death by the people (12:18). King Rehoboam makes a speedy return to Jerusalem, with all Israel in uproar. Jeroboam is made king over the ten tribes of Israel. Meanwhile King Rehoboam, once in Jerusalem, assembles the armies of Judah and Benjamin, intending to attack the other ten tribes and force their submission to his rule. The Lord intervenes through Shemaiah, the man of God, and Judah and Benjamin are forbidden to go to war with Israel. The people of the two tribes obey the word of God and return to their homes.

Part IV: The divided kingdoms of Israel and Judah (12:25 - 22:53)

Solomon had reigned in Israel for forty years (11:42). God's judgement upon the twelve tribes of the nation coincides with his death. The people as a whole have turned from the true and living God. They have forgotten his law, violated his covenant and disobeyed his commands. They have turned to the heathen and pagan gods of the surrounding nations. The once strong and united kingdom of Israel and Judah is now divided into two weak and squabbling nations: the larger, ten tribes under King Jeroboam; the smaller, the two tribes of Judah and Benjamin under King Rehoboam. With the division of the kingdom in 930 B.C. the serious deterioration, decline and disintegration of the twelve tribes of Israel has begun.

The divided kingdom

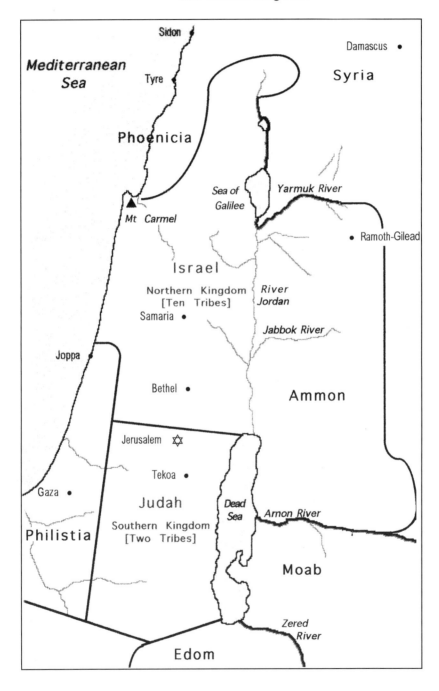

Jeroboam in Israel — 930-909 B.C.[8] (12:20-14:20)

Although the Lord had given Jeroboam wonderful promises through the prophet Ahijah (11:37-38), the new king of Israel does not trust in God and he disregards all the warnings. Seeking to consolidate his position on the throne, and in outright rebellion against the revealed will of God, Jeroboam introduces a corrupted alternative place of worship and a blasphemous form of idolatry. A golden calf is erected at Bethel and at Dan, and King Jeroboam says to the people, 'It is too much for you to go up to Jerusalem. Here are your gods, O Israel, which brought you up from the land of Egypt!' (12:28). He makes shrines on the high places and appoints a priesthood from all the tribes of Israel, contravening the law of God that priests were to come only from the tribe of Levi. Jeroboam institutes sacrifices and feast days to match those that are celebrated at Jerusalem.

The scene is set for a succession of bad kings to sit upon the throne of the northern kingdom. Had a good and godly king arisen he would of necessity have destroyed the shrines to false gods, sought reconciliation with Judah, directed the people to worship in the temple which God had appointed at Jerusalem, and yielded to the claims of the King of Judah as being in the line of God's promise to Judah, David and his descendants.

God gives a word of prophecy in the presence of King Jeroboam. Addressing the altar, a man of God says, 'O altar, altar! Thus says the LORD: "Behold, a child, Josiah by name, shall be born to the house of David; and on you he shall sacrifice the priests of the high places who burn incense on you, and men's bones shall be burned on you' (13:2).[9]

In spite of miracles King Jeroboam does not amend his ways but continues in his godless path of rebellion. His offences are so serious before the Lord as to lead to the judgement being pronounced that his family line will be exterminated (13:34).

Rehoboam in Judah: 930-913 B.C. (14:21-31; cf. 2 Chr. 11:5 – 12:16)

Following the division of the kingdom with the revolt of the ten northern tribes, Rehoboam seeks to establish himself in Judah. He builds strong cities for defence, with fortified strongholds storing large stores of food and weaponry. A further strategy is to disperse some of his many sons throughout the territory of Judah and Benjamin. He is supported and encouraged by the migration of a large number of priests and Levites expelled from Israel: 'And from all their territories the priests and the Levites who were in all Israel took their stand with him [i.e. Rehoboam]. For the Levites left their common lands and their possessions and came to Judah and Jerusalem, for Jeroboam and his sons had rejected them from serving as priests to the LORD... And after the Levites left, those from all the tribes of Israel, such as set their heart to seek the LORD God of Israel, came to Jerusalem to sacrifice to the LORD God of their fathers. So they strengthened the kingdom of Judah, and made Rehoboam the son of Solomon strong for three years, because they walked in the way of David and Solomon for three years' (2 Chr. 11:13-14,16-17).

This is a description of people committed to a life of true worship and faithful service. They move home at considerable personal sacrifice. They are loyal to the temple, the priesthood and the king, in spite of the fact that King Rehoboam is stubborn and foolish. The presence of these godly immigrants does not, however, halt the deterioration in the spiritual and moral life of the nation, for we read, 'Judah did evil in the sight of the LORD, and they provoked him to jealousy with their sins which they committed, more than all that their fathers had done' (14:22).

International superpowers after the division of the united kingdom of Israel and Judah

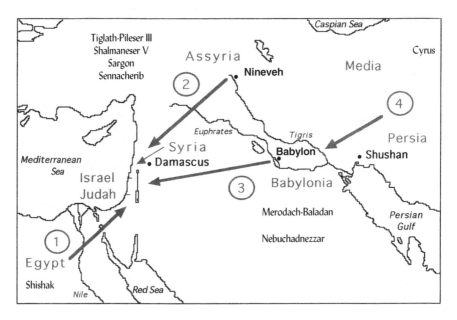

The numbers indicate the superpowers and the order in which they oppressed Israel and Judah.

Whatever his earlier sympathies concerning loyalty to the living God, once Rehoboam has established his position and strengthened his control he forsakes 'the law of the LORD, and all Israel along with him' (2 Chr. 12:1). The Lord punishes this defection through Shishak, King of Egypt. He delivers Judah from destruction but commits the people to become servants of Egypt. Shishak plunders the gold from the temple and the king's palace, and takes everything away (2 Chr. 12:9). Rehoboam is allowed to continue his reign over Judah.

Abijam[10] in Judah — 913-910 B.C. (15:1-8; cf. 2 Chr. 13:1-22)

Throughout the seventeen years of his father Rehoboam's reign there had been hostility between Israel and Judah. Abijam comes to the throne when tension is high between the two kingdoms. 1 Kings merely records the animosity, whereas 2 Chronicles provides a detailed account of a great battle fought between the two nations. Severely outnumbered by two to one when the battle lines are drawn, Abijam gives every impression of being a God-fearing king as he challenges Jeroboam from Mount Zemaraim (2 Chr. 13:4-12). As he speaks, Israelite soldiers move into position behind the army of Judah. Outflanked, the men of Judah cry out to God. The Lord responds to their prayers in spite of the fact that King Abijam is described as one who 'walked in all the sins of his father [Rehoboam], which he had done before him; his heart was not loyal to the LORD his God, as was the heart of his father David' (15:3). The Lord's kindness to Judah is evidently 'for David's sake' (15:4), and in the maintenance of his covenant purposes in relation to the tribe of Judah (Gen. 49:10; 2 Sam. 7:12-16).

Under King Abijam, Israel is subdued by Judah because the latter rely 'on the LORD God of their fathers' (2 Chr. 13:18). Judah captures a number of towns and cities from Israel. After a short reign Abijam dies and is succeeded by his son Asa.

Asa in Judah — 910-869 B.C. (15:9-24) [11]

As a result of the battle between Judah and Israel in the days of King Abijam, Judah experiences some years of rest. Asa comes to the throne and enjoys a peaceful reign for ten years. Unlike his father and his grandfather, 'Asa did what was right in the eyes of the LORD, as did his father David' (15:11). He removes pagan altars, demolishes heathen pillars, chops down wooden images and banishes perverted people from the land. He commands the people of Judah to seek the Lord and to obey his law and commandments. He also fortifies the cities of Judah with walls, towers and gates. Although he experiences considerable blessing from the Lord, he seriously backslides towards the end of his long reign. At his death he is succeeded to the throne by his godly son Jehoshaphat.

Ahab in Israel — 874-853 B.C. (16:29 – 22:40; cf. 2 Chr. 18:1-34)

For thirty-five years, from the death of Jeroboam, Israel is ruled by six godless kings. Most of them reign for very short periods and are noted only for their wickedness. Eventually there arises the most notorious of them all, Ahab. Ahab excels in wickedness, for he 'did evil in the sight of the LORD, more than all who were before him' (16:30). He shows his contempt for the Word of God and the honour of God's name by marrying Jezebel and worshipping her god, Baal. Ahab sets up an altar in a temple to Baal in the city of Samaria. In complete disregard of God's warning through Joshua, Ahab rebuilds Jericho (16:34; cf. Josh. 6:26).

The true prophets of the Lord are outlawed; the priests of the Most High are persecuted and put to the sword. The worship of the true God is banned. Baal is now the official god of Israel. The prophets and priests of Baal take over the religious life of the nation. The spiritual condition of the country is at an all-time low. From the darkness of this evil time God raises up a man; a figure stands out as a true witness for the living God. He is to be the living proof that God is quietly working onwards towards his eternal kingdom of righteousness.

Elijah the prophet in Israel[12]

It is a testimony to God's grace that he continued to send messengers to the northern kingdom of Israel. They were still his covenant people and he continued to urge them to repentance and to return to himself. This would inevitably lead to the restoration of the one nation under the one king from the tribe of Judah, with one centre of worship in the temple at Jerusalem in accordance with the law of Moses.

Elijah, the rugged prophet of the wilderness, dressed in a camel-hair tunic with a leather belt, suddenly bursts upon the scene and confronts godless King Ahab: 'As the LORD God of Israel lives, before whom I stand, there shall not be dew nor rain these years, except at my word' (17:1).

The Lord had warned the people through Moses, over 500 years earlier, when the Israelites were on the threshold of the promised land: 'Take heed to yourselves, lest your heart be deceived, and you turn aside and serve other gods and worship them, lest the LORD's anger be aroused against you, and he shut up the heavens so that there be no rain, and the land yield no produce, and you perish quickly from the good land which the LORD is giving you' (Deut. 11:16-17).

Elijah brings the message to the wicked and godless King Ahab. During the three and a half years of drought that follow, the Lord miraculously sustains the prophet. Eventually there is a confrontation on Mount Carmel and for a short while it appears as though the nation of Israel has turned back to the Lord. But their recognition of the true God is short-lived.

Elijah leaves Mount Carmel, is threatened by Queen Jezebel and makes his way south to Beersheba with his servant.[13] He leaves his servant under the jurisdiction of godly King Jehoshaphat in Judah (19:3) and journeys into the wilderness. Sustained by the Lord, he travels for over a month to arrive at 'Horeb, the mountain of God' (19:8), also called Mount Sinai. Though he thinks his ministry has largely failed and must now be over, the Lord gives him further commissions and reassures him that there are still many faithful souls to be found in Israel. Responding with renewed enthusiasm, Elijah seeks out Elisha to appoint him as his successor.

Meanwhile King Ben-Hadad of Syria, with thirty-two allies, moves against Samaria. Even though the miracle on Mount Carmel failed to influence Ahab, the Lord is determined to show mercy towards him. A prophet of God is sent to Ahab prophesying a great victory: 'Thus says the LORD: "Have you seen all this great multitude? Behold, I will deliver it into your hand today, and you shall know that I am the LORD"' (20:13). Ahab wins a double victory against Syria. These victories were 'a fruit of the seven thousand who had not bent their knee before Baal',[14] because of their faithfulness to the living God (19:18; cf. Mark 13:20; Luke 18:7). Elijah would also learn that the Lord has not yet departed from the rebellious kingdom.

Following the battles with Ben-Hadad there is peace between Israel and Syria for two years. Ahab dies of wounds received in battle the following year.

The journeys of the prophet Elijah

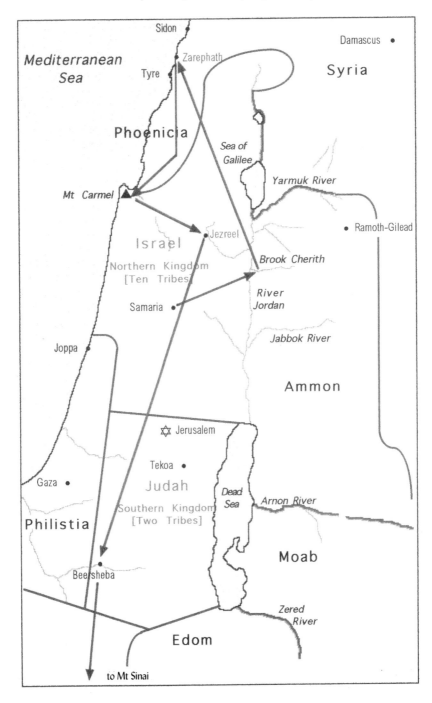

Jehoshaphat in Judah — 872-848 B.C. (22:41-50) [15]

Like his father Asa before him, Jehoshaphat is a godly king, keen to live in obedience to the Lord and to encourage the people of Judah to be faithful to the true God. He 'sought the God of his father, and walked in his commandments and not according to the acts of Israel. Therefore the LORD established the kingdom in his hand; and all Judah gave presents to Jehoshaphat, and he had riches and honour in abundance. And his heart took delight in the ways of the LORD...' (2 Chr. 17:4-6).

The blessings of God rest upon the labours of Jehoshaphat and he responds by seeking to strengthen the nation spiritually. He sends out civil leaders and Levites throughout all Judah to teach the people the law of God.

Ahaziah in Israel — 853-852 B.C. (22:51-53)

A brief reference to the reign of Ahaziah the son of Ahab draws the First Book of Kings to a close. He behaves in the same manner as his father and mother (Ahab and Jezebel) who had introduced the worship of Baal into the kingdom of Israel, and after the manner of Jeroboam who had set up the golden calves (16:30-33). The brief reign of godless King Ahaziah comes to an end when he falls 'through the lattice of his upper room in Samaria' (2 Kings 1:2). His injury, contact with Elijah the prophet and subsequent death form the opening chapter of the Second Book of Kings.

Christ and his church

The relationship of Elijah to the unfolding purposes of God for Christ and his church are discussed in the next chapter on 2 Kings.

Types

King David and King Solomon both function as types of Christ as King. While both men fall far short of that sinlessness and holiness which are so perfect and complete in the Lord Jesus Christ, nevertheless God uses these human vessels to portray something of the glory and grandeur that belong to 'the only begotten of the Father' (John 1:14) who is 'the Christ of God' (Luke 9:20).

Both men present different perspectives upon the kingly reign of the Messiah. King David stands for the Christ engaged in battle. He is the fighting monarch. In contrast, Solomon, as his name implies, is the Prince of Peace. Solomon means 'peaceful', for the name derives from the root word *'shalom'*, meaning peace, quiet, tranquillity, contentment, completeness, soundness, welfare, health. King Solomon's peaceful kingdom was the result of the victories King David had won.

1. David the king

David was three times anointed as king: first in his father's house, then over Judah and, lastly, over all Israel. God has anointed Jesus of Nazareth with the oil of gladness (Heb. 1:9; cf. Ps. 45:7). He is King of kings and Lord of lords (Rev. 17:14; 19:16). As David — though anointed king — was in exile while Saul reigned over the people, so Christ is rejected by the world, and the 'ruler of this world' (John 12:31) is reigning in the majority of human hearts.

God's promise to Israel was that he would save them from all their enemies by the hand of David. There is no indication that David was ever defeated in battle. So Christ will vanquish his (and our) enemies including the great enemy Satan. The Son of God has come to this earth 'that we, being delivered from the hand of our enemies, might serve him without fear, in holiness and righteousness before him all the days of our life' (Luke 1:74-75). Christ 'must reign till he has put all enemies under his feet' (1 Cor. 15:25). For:

> Of the increase of his government and peace
> There will be no end,
> Upon the throne of David and over his kingdom,
> To order it and establish it with judgement and justice
> From that time forward, even for ever.
> The zeal of the LORD of hosts will perform this
>
> (Isa. 9:7).

2. Solomon the king

King Solomon symbolizes the Lord Jesus Christ reigning in peace after the battle. Our Saviour is the 'Prince of Peace' (Isa. 9:6). He is 'Shiloh' the 'Pacifier', the 'Peacemaker' of the tribe of Judah (Gen. 49:10). As God promised David, 'Behold, a son shall be born to you, who shall be a man of rest; and I will give him rest from all his enemies all around. His name shall be Solomon, for I will give peace and quietness to Israel in his days' (1 Chr. 22:9).

The apostle Paul declares, '... the kingdom of God is ... righteousness *and peace* and joy in the Holy Spirit' (Rom. 14:17, emphasis added), for Christ has 'made peace through the blood of his cross' (Col. 1:20).

Solomon's kingdom is a picture of the reign of Christ in his kingdom (4:21-34; 5:4; cf. Ps. 72). There are, however, notable differences: firstly, our Lord's kingdom will stretch to every corner of the globe, for he will reign over the whole earth (Rev. 11:15); secondly, it will be composed of 'a great multitude which no one could number, of all nations, tribes, peoples, and tongues' (Rev. 7:9); and, thirdly, it will be an everlasting kingdom (Luke 1:33).

King Solomon was very rich; Christ is far richer and far more be-nevolent: 'For you know the grace of our Lord Jesus Christ, that though he was rich, yet for your sakes he became poor, that you through his poverty might become rich' (2 Cor. 8:9). 'He who did not spare his own Son, but delivered him up for us all, how shall he not with him also freely give us all things?' (Rom. 8:32). Christians have an amazing in-heritance reserved in heaven (1 Peter 1:4). Even in this present life, 'God shall supply all your need according to his riches in glory by Christ Jesus' (Phil. 4:19).

The wisdom of Solomon is a foreshadowing of the wisdom of Christ, 'in whom are hidden all the treasures of wisdom and knowledge' (Col. 2:3). The Lord Jesus said to the Jews of his day, 'The Queen of the South will rise up in the judgement with the men of this generation and condemn them, for she came from the ends of the earth to hear the wis-dom of Solomon; and indeed a greater than Solomon is here' (Luke 11:31).

The Queen of the South, the Queen of Sheba, 'came to test him [Solomon] with hard questions' (10:1). Interesting spiritual parallels made be drawn from this visit. The Queen of Sheba may be seen to symbolize a seeker coming to Christ and finding full satisfaction in him. She came a great distance in response to 'a true report' (cf. 'the gospel of

Christ'). So those 'who once were far off have been made near by the
blood of Christ' (Eph. 2:13). She came with her 'hard questions' and
'spoke with him about all that was in her heart' (10:1-2). And 'There was
nothing so difficult for the king that he could not explain it to her' (10:3).
In a greater sense 'Christ Jesus ... became for us wisdom from God'
(1 Cor. 1:30).

This is the amazing testimony that the queen gave: 'It was a true report which I heard in my own land about your words and your wisdom.
However I did not believe the words until I came and saw it with my
own eyes; and indeed the half was not told me. Your wisdom and prosperity exceed the fame of which I heard. Happy are your men and happy
are these your servants, who stand continually before you and hear your
wisdom! Blessed be the LORD your God, who delighted in you, setting you
on the throne of Israel! Because the LORD has loved Israel for ever, therefore he made you king, to do justice and righteousness' (10:6-9).

Such words are so appropriate for the Christ of God and his happy servants. Following the encounter with the Lord Jesus at the well of Sychar,
the Samaritan woman returned to proclaim him to her fellow-citizens. They
responded in words similar to those of the Queen of Sheba. After having
met Jesus they said to the woman, 'Now we believe, not because of what
you said, for we have heard for ourselves and know that this is indeed the
Christ, the Saviour of the world' (John 4:42).

Application

1. God-honouring prayer

At the dedication of the temple King Solomon led the congregation in
prayer (8:22-53). Kneeling upon a platform (or kind of pulpit) and facing
the congregation, he raised his hands towards heaven (2 Chr. 6:12-13).
The form of his prayer is that of imploring God to remember his promises
and to act in accordance with his Word (cf. Lev. 26 and Deut. 28). The
repeated theme is that of asking God to hear and forgive those who return
to him in prayer, confessing their sins. Throughout his prayer Solomon acknowledges the uniqueness, incomparable greatness and awesome splendour of God. Sadly, this is often lacking in modern-day worship. 'LORD
God of Israel, there is no God in heaven above or on earth below like you,

who keep your covenant and mercy with your servants who walk before you with all their heart' (8:23). 'Behold, heaven and the heaven of heavens cannot contain you' (8:27; cf. vv. 39,42).

Solomon had, in his father David, a special model for his prayer life. The Psalms are the divinely inspired prayer book for the church and Christians would do well to model their prayers upon those fine examples:

O LORD, our Lord,
How excellent is your name in all the earth,
You who set your glory above the heavens!

(Ps. 8:1).

LORD, you have been our dwelling-place in all generations.
Before the mountains were brought forth,
Or ever you had formed the earth and the world,
Even from everlasting to everlasting, you are God

(Ps. 90:1-2).

O God, you are my God;
Early will I seek you;
My soul thirsts for you;
My flesh longs for you
In a dry and thirsty land
Where there is no water.
So I have looked for you in the sanctuary,
To see your power and your glory.
Because your loving-kindness is better than life,
My lips shall praise you.
Thus I will bless you while I live;
I will lift up my hands in your name.
My soul shall be satisfied as with marrow and fatness,
And my mouth shall praise you with joyful lips

(Ps. 63:1-5).

I will love you, O LORD, my strength.
The LORD is my rock and my fortress and my deliverer;
My God, my strength, in whom I will trust;
My shield and the horn of my salvation, my stronghold.
I will call upon the LORD, who is worthy to be praised

(Ps. 18:1-3).

I have called upon you, for you will hear me, O God;
Incline your ear to me, and hear my speech.
Show your marvellous loving-kindness by your right hand,
O you who save those who trust in you
From those who rise up against them

(Ps. 17:6-7).

You are the God who does wonders;
You have declared your strength among the peoples.
You have with your arm redeemed your people…

(Ps. 77:14-15).

Prayers in a Christian assembly are often nothing more than coming to God with 'a shopping list'; making one request after another, without addressing God in worship, praise and blessing and without reference to his wondrous works, attributes or promises.

The model for Christian prayer was provided by the Lord Jesus Christ when he said:

In this manner, therefore, pray:

Our Father in heaven,
Hallowed be your name.
Your kingdom come.
Your will be done
on earth as it is in heaven

(Matt. 6:9-10).

Before making requests of God the priority is to show respect, honour and submission to the great God of heaven himself.

It is further to be noted that the Lord Jesus teaches to whom we are to speak in prayer: 'Our Father in heaven.' Despite the clearer revelation in the New Testament concerning the Son of God, this has not altered the person who is to be addressed in prayer. 'There has developed a trend in which prayer is almost exclusively addressed to the Lord Jesus Christ — sometimes simply to 'Jesus'. It is almost as if the Father did not exist… When, however, we turn to the New Testament we find that the consistent pattern in prayer and praise is an approach to the Father.'[16]

2. Marriage to the ungodly

Wisdom and the knowledge of God are no defence against falling into serious sin. The sad spiritual decline of Solomon was brought about by his unbridled passion. Loving many women — marrying 700 and having 300 more as concubines — resulted in his turning away from God (11:1-4,6). They influenced him to serve their gods. The Word of God through Moses warned of this danger (Deut. 17:17).

Throughout the Old Testament there is a consistent pattern showing the problems, dangers and disasters that arise when the people of God marry outside the faith. Esau brought great grief to his parents by his marriage to two Hittite women (Gen. 26:34-35). The law prohibited marriage with Canaanites (Deut. 7:1-4). Samson distressed his parents by going outside Israel and marrying a Philistine (Judg. 14:3). 'Is she a fair Philistine? Why is not the deformity of the soul more powerful to dissuade us, than the beauty of the face to allure us?'[17]

'When the interests of godliness do not govern the people of God in the choice of marital partners, irreparable confusion is the result and the interests, not only of spirituality, but also of morality, are destroyed ... marital life is to be guided, not by impulse or fancy, but by considerations which conserve and promote the interests of godliness. It is the Old Testament counterpart of the New Testament principle that Christians should marry only "in the Lord."'[18]

Under the New Covenant, as under the Old Covenant, believers are forbidden to marry those who are not God's people. Such marriages violate the fundamental principle that believers should not be unequally yoked[19] together with unbelievers: 'For what fellowship has righteousness with lawlessness? And what communion has light with darkness?' (2 Cor. 6:14).

3. Backsliding and apostasy

There are sober warnings in the Scriptures about apostasy: falling away from the faith. Of Hebrews 6:4-8, Calvin remarks: '... the apostle is not talking here about theft, or perjury, or murder, or drunkenness or adultery. He is referring to a complete falling away from the Gospel, not one in which the sinner has offended God in some one part only, but in which he has utterly renounced His grace.'[20]

Backsliding, however, means turning away from God and returning to the former way of life. It is a pardonable offence against God. As a true believer in the Lord, David was guilty of serious backsliding in his adultery with Bathsheba and the murder of Uriah (2 Sam. 11:2-17), and he repented (Ps. 51; cf. Gal. 6:1; James 5:19-20).

Did Solomon apostatize (fall away and seriously deny the faith) or just seriously backslide? The idolatry into which Solomon fell in his old age seems incomprehensible for one so wise and God-fearing as he was in earlier days. 'But great wisdom and a refined knowledge of God are not a defence against the folly of idolatry, since this has its roots in the heart, and springs from sensual desires and the lust of the flesh.'[21]

Solomon's spiritual state is more complex than that of his father, in that there is no record of repentance and a wholehearted return to the Lord. Hengstenberg makes a point which is difficult to refute when he argues: 'The first fruit of his conversion would have been to destroy the scandals which he had established.'[22] The contrary view that Solomon was eventually restored to a right relationship with God is not based upon any record of repentance (though Ecclesiastes 12:13-14 might be seen to indicate this) but upon the grace, mercy and power of God. The Lord had a special love for Solomon: 'Then David comforted Bathsheba his wife, and went in to her and lay with her. So she bore a son, and he called his name Solomon. *And the LORD loved him.* And he sent word by the hand of Nathan the prophet; so he called his name *Jedidiah* [i.e. 'Beloved of the LORD'], because of the LORD' (2 Sam. 12:24-25, emphasis added).

There is, further, the prophecy of Nathan to David: 'When your days are fulfilled and you rest with your fathers, I will set up your seed after you, who will come from your body, and I will establish his kingdom. He shall build a house for my name, and I will establish the throne of his kingdom for ever. I will be his Father, and he shall be my son. *If he commits iniquity,* I will chasten him with the rod of men and with the blows of the sons of men. *But my mercy shall not depart from him,* as I took it from Saul, whom I removed from before you. And your house and your kingdom shall be established for ever before you. Your throne shall be established for ever' (2 Sam. 7:12-16, emphasis added).

Clearly there is in this prophecy an intermingling of two promises, one relating to Solomon, the other relating to Christ. The establishment of David's kingdom and his throne 'for ever' has reference to 'the everlasting kingdom of our Lord and Saviour Jesus Christ' (2 Peter 1:11). No mere man can rule for ever and ever. Only God can do that. On the other hand, there is reference to iniquity, to wickedness, to sin, and the warning that

God would certainly punish sin; yet there is the promise that God would not take away his mercy from that one. This surely is not a reference to Christ but to Solomon. Solomon was punished 'with the rod of men and with the blows of the sons of men'. While he was still on the throne, Edom began to throw off its allegiance, under the guidance of Hadad; Rezon took Damascus and the surrounding area from Solomon, and founded a kingdom which would afterwards prove very destructive to the Israelites; a still heavier punishment came through his own family, for the greater part of his kingdom would be taken from his son. Preparation was made for the fulfilment of this threat even in Solomon's lifetime.

'Is any Christian immune from relapse into sin when for a season he relaxes his vigilance and ceases to watch and pray lest he enter into temptation? … It is because few of us have any claim to fame that our individual failures are known only to God… Those failures might be magnified a thousand times if we were exalted to positions of absolute power. Let him who is without sin cast the first stone at Solomon.'[23]

4. God's power and provision

No circumstances are too difficult for the Lord. This is vividly illustrated in this book by the fire descending upon the water-soaked altar and by other wonderful miracles experienced by the prophet Elijah. During a three-and-a-half-year famine he was first fed by ravens bringing bread and meat each morning and evening (17:6) and then sustained by a supernatural supply of oil and flour (17:16).

David confidently declared:

I have been young, and now am old;
Yet I have not seen the righteous forsaken,
Nor his descendants begging bread

(Ps. 37:25).

The apostle Paul thanks the Christians at Philippi for their kind support and generous gift and then reassures them of the provision of God: 'And my God shall supply all your need according to his riches in glory by Christ Jesus' (Phil. 4:19).

However, the Lord's ordinary providences are no less wonderful than the more spectacular display of power: 'Now to him who is able to do exceeding abundantly above all that we ask or think, according to the power that works in us, to him be glory in the church by Christ Jesus throughout all ages, world without end. Amen' (Eph. 3:20-21).

5. Fleeing persecution

Elijah has been much maligned. His experiences following the events on Mount Carmel are often used to illustrate the way in which the godly may become cowardly and depressed: 'God's heroes are never supermen. "Elijah," wrote James, "was a man just like us" (James 5:17). So from attaining heights of courage and seeming fearlessness, he suddenly plumbs the depths of fear and runs for his life. His flight, however, did not lead to freedom, but rather into a cul-de-sac of self-pity and abject depression. Indeed we find him teetering on the brink of despair. That is why he is such a help to us in facing depression.'[24] 'Alas, instead of spreading his case before God, he takes matters into his own hands; instead of waiting patiently for Him, he acts on hasty impulse, deserts the post of duty, and flees from the one who sought his destruction... His eyes were fixed on the wicked and furious queen: his mind was occupied with her power and fury, and therefore his heart was filled with terror... Elijah's mind was no longer stayed upon Jehovah, and therefore fear took possession of him ... he lost sight of the Lord.'[25]

Charles Alexander has challenged this interpretation of Elijah as a depressed coward in the strongest possible terms: 'In the case of Elijah's flight from Jezebel, no shadow of guilt is attributed to Elijah anywhere in Holy Scripture, but rather, as we shall see, his flight was divinely ordained to prepare the way prophetically for the Coming of the Saviour.'[26] No New Testament writer attributes any depression to the prophet Elijah. Alexander further points out that Elijah was the only source of information of these events, that there was neither rebuke from the Lord nor repentance from the prophet for the sin of cowardice, and that Elijah is never once criticized as though deserting the nation in its hour of need.

Flight from persecution is not only acceptable before God, but also recommended by him. Jacob fled from his brother Esau (Gen. 27:43); David fled from Saul (1 Sam. 19:10; 20:1); Joseph and Mary fled from Herod (Matt. 2:13-15); the apostle Paul fled from irate Jews (Acts 9:23-25). Are these then to be regarded as the actions of depressed cowards? The Lord Jesus Christ advised his disciples: '... when they persecute you in this city, flee to another' (Matt. 10:23).

Furthermore the Lord does not translate cowards. Moses was not permitted to enter the promised land because of one momentary lapse, yet God translated Elijah into heaven that he might not experience death.

The Hebrew of 19:3 is translated in a variety of ways. The RAV and AV read: 'And when he saw that, he arose and went for his life.' The NIV reads: 'Elijah was afraid and ran for his life.'[27] Some Hebrew manuscripts have the word for 'saw'; others have the alternative '[was] afraid'. Apart from the more complex issue of which group of manuscripts is more reliable, the straight issue to determine which word is correct here in 19:3 can be resolved by the context: 'For it is obvious that Elijah did not flee from any fear of the vain threat of Jezebel, from the fact that he did not merely withdraw into the kingdom of Judah, where he would have been safe under Jehoshaphat from all the persecutions of Jezebel, but went to Beersheba, and thence onwards into the desert, there to pour out before the Lord God his weariness of life (v. 4) … he went upon his soul … i.e. not to save his life (as I once thought, with many other commentators), for his wish to die (v. 4) is opposed to this; but to care for his soul in the manner indicated in v. 4, i.e. to commit his soul or his life to the Lord his God in the solitude of the desert, and see what He would determine concerning him.'[28]

6. Called to service

At the commandment of the Lord, Elijah called Elisha to the prophetic office (19:16). When Elijah found Elisha the latter was busy ploughing. Elisha's reaction was to leave his work. Many men, called by God to the ministry of the Word, have also responded by leaving their work. When called by the Lord Jesus Christ to accompany him, Simon Peter and Andrew his brother were fishing in the Sea of Galilee. Jesus said to them, '"Come after me, and I will make you become fishers of men." And immediately *they left their nets* and followed him' (Mark 1:17-18, emphasis added). In the same manner, when called to follow the Lord Jesus Christ and join the close company of the apostles, Matthew was busy at his work: 'And *he left all*, rose up, and followed him' (Luke 5:28, emphasis added). Today the cost is the same for some Christians in serving the Lord Jesus Christ: 'Sell all that you have and distribute to the poor, and you will have treasure in heaven; and come, follow me" (Luke 18:22).

Elisha cooked a yoke of oxen and gave them to his family and neighbours. In using the wooden yoke as fuel he forcefully demonstrated that he would not be returning to his former work. From here on he was looking to the Lord to provide for him by some other means: 'Even so the Lord has commanded that those who preach the gospel should live from the gospel' (1 Cor. 9:14), for 'The labourer is worthy of his wages' (Luke 10:7; cf. 1 Tim. 5:17-18; 1 Cor. 9:7-11; Gal. 6:6).

Conclusion

The First Book of Kings relates the history of the kingdom of Israel from the death of David to the death of Ahab. Most of the first half of the book is dominated by the reign of Solomon. The historian faithfully relates the strengths and weaknesses of this wisest of men. The second half is devoted to a description of the reigns of the early kings of the divided kingdom, 'a nation passing from affluence and influence, to poverty and paralysis'.[29] The northern kingdom is beset by a succession of bad kings. Not one good and godly king emerges. Had such a king arisen he would inevitably have taken action which would have disbanded the nation; he would have sought reconciliation with Judah and yielded to their king as being in the line of God's promise to Judah and a descendant of King David.

Through all the ups and downs of the people of Israel, there is demonstrated 'the historical reality of God's faithfulness to his promises to David'.[30]

2 Kings

(continuation of 1 Kings)

Author: Unknown
(maybe Jeremiah)

Key thought: 'According to the word of the Lord'

Theme: The word of the Lord is sure and certain to saint and sinner

'Know now that nothing shall fall to
earth of the word of the LORD
… for the LORD has done what
he spoke by his servant Elijah.'

2 Kings 10:10

Summary

Judah (two southern tribes)		Israel (ten northern tribes)
Reigning king: Jehoshaphat (good)	1:1 – 2:25	i. The reign of King Ahaziah (bad)
	1:1-18	a. Elijah calls down fire upon his enemies
	2:1-11	b. Elijah's translation into heaven
	2:12-18	c. Elisha divides the River Jordan
	2:19-22	d. Elisha heals the waters
	2:23-25	e. Elisha taunted by youths
	3:1 – 8:15	ii. The reign of King Joram (bad)
	3:1 – 4:7	a. Elisha and the miracles of water and oil
	4:8-37	b. Elisha raises the Shunammite's son
	4:38-41	c. Elisha heals the deadly stew
	4:42-44	d. Elisha feeds 100 men
	5:1-19	e. Elisha heals Naaman the leper
	5:20-27	f. Elisha's servant smitten with leprosy
	6:1-7	g. Elisha floats the iron axe-head
	6:8-12	h. Elisha discloses Syria's plans
	6:13-33	i. Elisha and the Syrians' blindness
	7:1-20	j. Prophecy: the ending of a famine
	8:1-6	k. Restoration of the Shunammite's land
	8:7-15	l. Prophecy: Hazael to be King of Syria
iii. The reign of King Jehoram (bad)	8:16-24	
iv. The reign of King Ahaziah (bad)	8:25-29	
	9:1 – 10:36	v. The reign of King Jehu
vi. The reign of Queen Athaliah (bad)	11:1-3	
vii. The reign of King Joash (good when under the influence of Jehoiada the priest)	11:4 – 12:21	
	13:1-9	viii. The reign of King Jehoahaz (bad)

2 Kings

In the original format there was only one book of Kings which 'begins with King David and ends with the King of Babylon; opens with the Temple built and closes with the Temple burnt; begins with David's first successor on the throne of his kingdom, and ends with David's last successor released from the house of his captivity'.[1] For practical reasons the original book was divided into two. Consequently what has been written concerning the author under the introduction to 1 Kings applies also to this second book.

Historical setting

Résumé

Following the death of Solomon it was not long before the twelve tribes which composed the nation of Israel experienced civil war. Jeroboam, one of Solomon's key leaders, a mighty man of valour and also highly industrious (1 Kings 11:28), rebelled against Solomon and fled to Egypt. When he heard of King Solomon's death and the coronation of his son Rehoboam, he returned to Israel and became a significant leader among the people. Jeroboam led a delegation of Israelites who visited the new king and asked for a lifting of the heavy burdens which King Solomon had imposed on the people. They assured King Rehoboam that, if he would just slacken the demands, they would willingly serve him (1 Kings 12:4). But Solomon's son, Rehoboam, was an arrogant young man. He listened more to the young men who had grown up with him than to the elders who had been in close consultation with his father Solomon (1 Kings 12:6-8). The result was that Rehoboam made even heavier demands and, consequently, stirred up a rebellion among the general populace.

The division of the kingdom

In 930 B.C. the division of the nation of Israel took place. There were now two distinct nations — Israel and Judah. Jeroboam was proclaimed King of Israel, the large northern kingdom composed of ten of the twelve tribes. Rehoboam was left with Judah, the southern kingdom composed of the two remaining tribes of Judah and Benjamin, based at Jerusalem. Israel extended from Bethel to Dan, from the Mediterranean to Syria and Ammon. The new centre for Israel became the city of Samaria.

The Second Book of Kings covers the history of the kingdoms of Israel and Judah from the reign of Ahaziah in Israel, and that of Jehoshaphat in Judah, to the time of the Assyrian and Babylonian exiles respectively. As far as the history of Israel is concerned, it is a dark picture of degenerate rulers and sinful people, ending in slavery. The only slight upturn occurs under the rule of Jehu when he enacts the punishment of God, but he cannot be described as godly. Jehu executed Joram, Ahaziah, Jezebel, seventy of Ahab's children and the worshippers of Baal (9:1 – 10:36).

The kingdom of Judah was also on the downgrade, but judgement was not visited upon her so speedily because of the influence of a number of godly kings who reigned during this period.

Outline

The history of the kings of Judah and Israel has been amplified by reference to the various historical and prophetic books of the Old Testament in order to present a composite account.

The first eight chapters are dominated by the final days of the prophet Elijah followed by the outstanding ministry of his successor, the prophet Elisha. The remaining chapters outline the decline of Israel and Judah — spiritually and morally. The majority of the kings of the divided kingdom are godless and wicked. The historian highlights the notable exceptions.

At the opening of 2 Kings, Ahaziah rules Israel and Jehoshaphat rules Judah. There is a marked contrast between these two. Of King Ahaziah of Israel it is written: 'He did evil in the sight of the LORD, and walked in the way of his father and in the way of his mother and in the way of Jeroboam the son of Nebat, who had made Israel sin; for he served Baal and worshipped him, and provoked the LORD God of Israel to anger, according to all that his father had done' (1 Kings 22:52-53). By contrast, of King

Jehoshaphat of Judah it is written: 'And he walked in all the ways of his father Asa. He did not turn aside from them, doing what was right in the eyes of the LORD' (1 Kings 22:43). So while Israel is ruled by a bad king, Judah is experiencing the benefits of the leadership of a good and godly king.

1. Ahaziah in Israel — 853-852 B.C.[2] (1:1-18)

The Moabites had been under subjection to Israel since the days of David (2 Sam. 8:2). Following the defeat of Israel by the Syrians at Ramoth Gilead (1 Kings 22:29-38), Moab takes advantage of the weakened power of Israel on the east of the River Jordan, and rebels (1:1).

The brief reign of godless King Ahaziah comes to an end when he falls 'through the lattice of his upper room in Samaria' (1:2). Since he had no son, his brother Joram (also spelt Jehoram) reigns in his place.

Meanwhile the prophet Elijah is about to be translated to heaven. Having appointed Elisha as his successor, Elijah, moved no doubt by modesty at the great honour to be conferred upon him, attempts to leave Elisha, first at Gilgal, then at Bethel and finally at Jericho. Each time Elisha is insistent on accompanying his mentor — for he knows as well as Elijah what is about to take place on the other side of the River Jordan. The Lord is to put his seal of approval upon the ministry of Elijah by translating the prophet to heaven so that he does not experience death. The Lord has also revealed the departure of Elijah to the sons of the prophets at Bethel and at Jericho (2:3,5).

Elisha the prophet in Israel[3]

Elijah performs his last miracle in dividing the waters of the River Jordan and the two prophets cross over on dry ground in full sight of fifty of the sons of the prophets. There is a strong resemblance to the crossing of the Red Sea by the Israelites years before. There Moses, the leader of the people, performed his miracle with his rod (Exod. 14:16,21); here Elijah the prophet divides the river with his prophet's cloak (2:8). Once over the river Elijah invites Elisha to make one final request. Probably basing his response upon the law of Moses regarding the first-born (Deut. 21:16-17), Elisha asks for a double portion of Elijah's spirit. If he is to take up the prophetic office where Elijah lays it down, then he will need the authority and power of the Holy Spirit. This is not in Elijah's power to grant. Leaving the matter in the Lord's hands, Elijah promises that if Elisha sees his departure, that will be the sign that God has granted his request. The chariot and horses of fire appear and transport Elijah away into heaven. Elisha witnesses the whole event. The Lord has granted his request. Returning to the River Jordan, Elisha takes Elijah's cloak, strikes the water and walks across the dry bed of the river. The sons of the prophets see the evidence that the spirit of Elijah now rests on Elisha. His call to office has been publicly confirmed.

The second and third miracles performed by Elisha are intended to establish before the people of Israel his appointment to the prophetic office. The healing of the water at Jericho has similarities to the miracle carried out by Moses when he cast a tree into the bitter waters of Marah (Exod. 15:23-25) and re-emphasizes the revelation: 'I am the LORD who heals you' (Exod. 15:26; cf. 2 Kings 2:21). Here at Jericho a blessing falls at the place of a curse (Josh. 6:26; 1 Kings 16:34). Shortly afterwards, a curse falls at Bethel, which had been the place of a blessing (Gen. 28:16-17,19); a large gang of boys, over forty of them, taunt the prophet and hurl abuse at him. They sin on at least three counts: they deride Elisha for a natural condition — premature baldness (he lived another fifty years); they show marked disrespect and contempt for an adult; and they show their hostility towards a man of God in shouting, 'Go up, you baldhead!' (2:23), which is evidently a reference to the translation of Elijah. An insult to a man of God, because he is a man of God, is an insult against God himself. The behaviour of these youths is symptomatic of the moral and spiritual disorder in the community, which is anti-God!

2. Joram in Israel — 852-841 B.C. (3:1 – 8:15)

Following the death of Ahaziah, his brother Joram accedes to the throne of Israel. He is not as evil as his parents since he tries to remove the worship of Baal from the land. He does, however, perpetuate the sin of Jeroboam in encouraging the worship of the true God through the image of the calf.

Chapters 4 to 8 record a series of miracles performed by Elisha. These confirm that he is continuing the work that Elijah had begun in seeking to turn the people of Israel from the worship of Baal to the worship of the true and living God. One of the significant contributions which Elisha makes in this connection is to continue the training and the encouragement of the sons of the prophets, who labour as itinerant preachers throughout the land. Elijah had established schools for disciples at Gilgal, Bethel and

Jericho (2:3,5; 4:38). Under Elisha's tutelage the number of students at Jericho increases to such an extent that new premises are required. It is while they are engaged in this enterprise that the head falls from the shaft of a borrowed axe and Elisha recovers it in a most unusual manner (6:6).

Since Elisha died during the reign of Jehoash of Israel (13:14) his ministry must have extended some fifty-five years or more — over the combined reigns of Joram, Jehu, Jehoahaz and Jehoash. His long ministry is not characterized by demonstrations of the power and might of Jehovah, but by 'the tender care, the sufficient provision, and the ever-present help which the Lord extends to His own servants and people'.[4] This is strikingly illustrated in many ways: the miraculous provision for a widow and her sons; the ending of the Shunammite's barrenness and the subsequent restoration of her dead son; the rendering harmless of a poisonous stew by the addition of a quantity of flour; and the miraculous increase of twenty small loaves so that there is more than sufficient to feed one hundred men.

3. Jehoram in Judah — 853-841 B.C. (8:16-24; cf. 2 Chr. 21:1-20)

Jehoram becomes king while his father Jehoshaphat is still king. They exercise a co-regency for a few years until Jehoshaphat hands over sole government to his son. Jehoram's wife is Athaliah, the daughter of Ahab and Jezebel of Israel (2 Chr. 21:6). No doubt through her evil influence, Jehoram introduces Baal-worship into Judah. Immediately following his father's death, Jehoram murders all his brothers, to whom Jehoshaphat had given great treasures and who had been strategically placed in fortified cities around Judah (2 Chr. 21:1-4). This wickedness would have resulted in the destruction of Judah had it not been for the covenant which the Lord had made with David. Jehoram will not, however, escape punishment. The Lord inspires Elijah the prophet to send a letter to Jehoram in which his sins and his subsequent punishment are clearly spelt out (2 Chr. 21:12-15). The prophecy is fulfilled and Jehoram dies of a terrible disease after a protracted illness of two years.

4. Ahaziah (Azariah)[5] in Judah — 841 B.C. (8:25-29; cf. 2 Chr. 22:1-9)

His mother Athaliah, daughter of the idolatrous Queen Jezebel and wicked King Ahab of Israel, exercises a powerful and evil influence over him, so that as King of Judah Ahaziah follows in the evil ways of Ahab of Israel.

Ahaziah joins with Joram of Israel, his mother's brother, in a war against the Syrians at Ramoth Gilead. Fighting over this city had previously cost Ahab his life (1 Kings 22:3-4,34-35).

5. Jehu in Israel — 841-814 B.C. (9:1 – 10:36)

Meanwhile Elisha the prophet continues to fulfil the ministry of his master Elijah. He sends one of the sons of the prophets to anoint Jehu as King of Israel (9:1-3; cf. 1 Kings 19:16) in the place of Joram, with a commission to avenge the death of the executed prophets and faithful servants of the Lord (1 Kings 18:4; 19:10). Jehu is to kill the male descendants of Ahab, and Jezebel is to die. With the full support of his fellow-captains, Jehu sets about planning the downfall of King Joram. He leads his troops to Jezreel and kills Joram King of Israel and his nephew Ahaziah King of Judah (9:16,24,27; 2 Chr. 22:7-9). Queen Jezebel hears of the deaths of Joram and Ahaziah, and prepares to meet Jehu. She uses make-up, not to allure Jehu by her charm but to present an imposing appearance and die as a queen.[6]

Jehu, King of Israel, continues to exterminate the family of Ahab. He uses trickery and deceit to massacre not only the descendants of Ahab but also the priests, prophets and servants of Baal. Yet in spite of this apparent zeal for the Lord and the word spoken through the prophet Elijah, Jehu seems to have been motivated more by personal ambition than by concern for the honour of the living God. 'Jehu took no heed to walk in the law of the LORD God of Israel with all his heart, for he did not depart from the sins of Jeroboam, who had made Israel sin' (10:31).

6. Queen Athaliah in Judah — 841-835 B.C. (11:1-3; cf. 2 Chr. 22:10 – 23:21)

After the death of King Ahaziah, Athaliah his mother, daughter of Ahab and Jezebel (8:18,26), seizes the throne. When Jehu of Israel murders the forty-two brothers of Ahaziah of Judah, Athaliah puts to death all the remaining members of the royal family of Judah (her grandchildren).[7] Only one son of Ahaziah, the young child Joash, escapes. As a one-year-old he is rescued by his aunt Jehosheba, daughter of Jehoram (probably by a wife other than Athaliah[8]) whose husband is the godly high priest Jehoiada

(2 Chr. 22:11). Joash and his nurse are moved into hiding in the home of the high priest in one of the buildings in the court of the temple.

7. Joash in Judah — 835-796 B.C. (11:4 – 12:21) [9]

Hidden and protected for six years, the seven-year-old Joash is revealed as the rightful King of Judah. After he is anointed king and Queen Athaliah has been put to death, Jehoiada the high priest renews the covenant between Jehovah and the king and people (cf. Exod. 24:3-8; Deut. 27:9-10). Religious reformation goes on apace, but only while the king is under the godly eye and influence of Jehoiada the high priest. Upon the priest's death Joash changes his ways — for the worse. He restores Baal-worship and the building of groves to Ashtoreth.

Hazael King of Syria marches along the coast after defeating Israel (13:3), takes the city of Gath which Rehoboam had built for the defence of Judah (2 Chr. 11:5,8) and moves against Jerusalem. Although his forces are small he conquers a much larger army because the Lord is using him to punish Judah and King Joash (2 Chr. 24:24). Having emptied the treasuries of the temple and the palace, Hazael withdraws from Jerusalem leaving King Joash seriously wounded. While Joash is recovering in bed his servants, seeking revenge for the death of a prophet named Zechariah, end his life.

8. Jehoahaz in Israel — 814-798 B.C. (13:1-9)

Upon the death of Jehu, his son Jehoahaz becomes King of Israel. Jehoahaz follows the sinful practices of Jeroboam by perpetuating the worship of the golden calf. The Lord punishes him, for throughout the whole of his reign Israel is under the domination of the Syrian king Hazael and his son Ben-Hadad, who force Jehoahaz to drastically reduce his military forces. The Syrian oppression is so severe that King Jehoahaz eventually turns in desperation to the Lord. The Lord hears his cry and sends a deliverer who frees them from the Syrian yoke.[10] After reigning for seventeen years Jehoahaz dies and is succeeded by his son Jehoash (also spelt Joash).

9. Jehoash in Israel — 798-782 B.C. (13:10-25)

During his sixteen-year reign over Israel, King Jehoash visits the prophet Elisha on his deathbed. At that meeting Jehoash is promised three victories over his enemies the Syrians. Consequently King Ben-Hadad is defeated three times and Israel regains possession of a number of cities. Jehoash is also successful in the battle with Judah. Challenged to a war he did not wish to fight, Jehoash wins a decisive victory, takes King Amaziah prisoner, sacks the city of Jerusalem, plunders the temple and the palace, and takes many prisoners back to Samaria.

10. Amaziah in Judah —796-767 B.C. (14:1-22; cf. 2 Chr. 25:1-28)

Upon the murder of his father Joash, Amaziah becomes King of Judah. His twenty-nine-year reign begins reasonably well. He seems to have been somewhat responsive to the Word of God (14:3,6), though a serious departure results in severe punishment from the Lord for, like his father Joash before him, Amaziah falls into idolatry in the closing years of his life. The Chronicler sums up Amaziah's behaviour: 'And he did what was right in the sight of the LORD, but not with a loyal heart' (2 Chr. 25:2).

11. Jeroboam II in Israel — 793-753 B.C. (14:23-29)

Jeroboam II, son of Jehoash of Israel, reigns forty-one years. The prophets Jonah, Amos and Hosea exercise their ministry during his long reign (14:25; Amos 1:1; Hosea 1:1).

The only prophecy of Jonah to Israel which has been included in Scripture is in keeping with his name. Jonah ('the Dove') brings a message of comfort and encouragement to the nation.[11] The Lord has seen the terrible distress of his people Israel and he has determined to deliver them by the hand of King Jeroboam: 'He restored the territory of Israel from the entrance of Hamath to the Sea of the Arabah, according to the word of the LORD God of Israel, which he had spoken through his servant Jonah the son of Amittai, the prophet who was from Gath Hepher. For the LORD saw that the affliction of Israel was very bitter; and whether bond or free, there was no helper for Israel. And the LORD did not say that he would blot out the name of Israel from under heaven; but he saved them by the hand of Jeroboam the son of Joash' (14:25-27).

Israel regains the territory lost through the invasions of the Syrians, restoring the ancient boundaries of the kingdom as in the days of Solomon
(cf. 1 Kings 8:65). Jeroboam not only drives out the Syrians (cf.13:4-5), but
pursues them and takes their capital city, Damascus, in fulfilment of the
prophecy of Amos (Amos 1:3,5). Jeroboam's conquest of Damascus is,
however, to prove a rash move as it destabilizes the international scene. By
weakening Syria, Israel leaves herself wide open to attack from another
enemy — the Assyrians.

Other problems arise for the Israelites during this period of international
peace and economic prosperity: the worship of the true God is corrupted
by idolatry (Hosea 4:12-14; 13:6; Amos 2:8); materialism, greed, immorality and injustice are rife throughout the land (Amos 2:6-7; 4:1; 6:6).

12. Uzziah in Judah — 792-740 B.C. (15:1-7; cf. 2 Chr. 26:1-23)

Uzziah[12] becomes King of Judah at the age of sixteen. He begins his reign
well, for '... he did what was right in the sight of the LORD, according to all
that his father Amaziah had done' (15:3). 'He sought God in the days of
Zechariah, who had understanding in the visions of God; and as long as he
sought the LORD, God made him prosper' (2 Chr. 26:5). He wins great
victories over his enemies the Philistines, the Arabians who live in Gur Baal
and against the Meunites, for 'God helped him' (2 Chr. 26:7). He strengthens the fortification of the city of Jerusalem, builds towers in strategic desert
locations, amasses a great army equipped with the finest weaponry and
becomes exceedingly powerful and famous.

These many successes, however, are to prove to be Uzziah's downfall.
He becomes proud and self-confident. Entering the temple, he violates the
declared will of God by burning incense on the altar when he is not of the
priestly tribe. Azariah the high priest and eighty of his colleagues rebuke
Uzziah, who reacts with rage. God strikes Uzziah that very moment as a
direct consequence of his serious and wilful sin; Uzziah is afflicted with leprosy to the day of his death. For the next ten years Uzziah is king in name
only for his son Jotham is the effective monarch.

Uzziah reigns for a total of fifty-two years, during which time the southern kingdom of Judah experiences a period of well-being and affluence. As
with the northern kingdom of Israel at this time, the people of Judah respond to days of prosperity by increasing self-indulgence, paganism and
godlessness, as the prophet Isaiah records (Isa. 2:1 – 3:26).

13. The reigns of five idolatrous kings in Israel — 753-732 B.C. (15:8-31)

Zechariah assumes the throne and is the fourth-generation king in Jehu's family (10:30) but his reign is terminated after only six months. *Shallum* reigns over Israel for only one month, when he is murdered by *Menahem*. After a ten-year reign, Menahem dies and is succeeded by his son *Peka-hiah* who reigns for two years. The next king, *Pekah*, follows in the godless and evil tradition of the Israelite kings.

14. Jotham in Judah — 750-732 B.C. (15:32-38; cf. 2 Chr. 27:1-9)

Jotham is the effective ruler, though his father Uzziah (Azariah) is the of-ficial king for the last ten years of his life (15:5). On Uzziah's death Jotham spends about five years as sole monarch after which he is joined by his son Ahaz. For a few years the two reign together over Judah, until Jotham's death.

King Jotham 'did what was right in the sight of the LORD, according to all that his father Uzziah had done (although he did not enter the temple of the LORD)'[13] (2 Chr. 27:2). His success is attributed to his commitment to honour and obey the living God, for he 'became mighty, because he pre-pared his ways before the LORD his God' (2 Chr. 27:6). In spite of the king's godly example, the nation as a whole still acted corruptly (2 Chr. 27:2).[14]

King Jotham must, however, bear some of the responsibility for the people's poor spiritual state since idolatry is permitted in the land (15:35). While Jotham extends the building of the Lord's temple, he does not re-move the many pagan temples scattered throughout Judah. Consequently towards the end of Jotham's reign, the Lord's displeasure is expressed against the king and nation because they are not being entirely true to the living God. Syria and Israel form an alliance against Judah: 'In those days the LORD began to send Rezin king of Syria and Pekah the son of Re-maliah against Judah' (15:37).

15. Ahaz in Judah — 735-715 B.C. (16:1-20; cf. 2 Chr. 28:1-27)

King Ahaz is unlike his father Jotham, for he has no regard for the worship and honour of the true and living God. He is an active and passionate idolater who goes further than his godless ancestors in that he sacrifices some of his own children by fire to the Baal-god Moloch in the Valley of Ben Hinnom (16:3; cf. 23:10; Jer. 7:30-31; Ezek. 16:20-21).

Upon King Ahaz's refusal to join them against Assyria, Syria and Israel attack Judah (16:5; Isa. 7:1). They intend, not only to overthrow Judah, but also to remove the descendants of David from the throne in Jerusalem (Isa. 7:6).[15]

The prophet Isaiah is commissioned by the Lord to inform King Ahaz that he must not yield to the attack from Syria and Israel. King Ahaz is urged to trust in Jehovah, for the Lord is well able to defend the king and the nation. Ahaz is invited to ask a sign from the Lord in the assurance of the Lord's protection, but he refuses on the hypocritical pretext that he would not presume to test the Lord in such a way (Isa. 7:1-12). The prophecy is nevertheless given: 'Behold, the virgin shall conceive and bear a Son, and shall call his name Immanuel [which means, God-with-us]' (Isa. 7:14).[16] But Ahaz refuses to trust in the Lord, and the kingdom of Judah suffers heavy casualties and losses under the combined forces of Syria and Israel.

Syria takes many captives back to Damascus; Israel kills 120,000 soldiers in one day, and takes 200,000 women and children captive (2 Chr. 28:5-8).[17] As the army returns to Samaria with the captives, Oded, the prophet of the Lord, confronts and rebukes them for their extreme hostility, and orders them to return the captives to their own land of Judah. The women and children are treated kindly, fed and clothed and returned home.

Judah is brought low. The cause is not military but moral, not a matter of strategy but of spirituality: 'For the LORD brought Judah low because of Ahaz King of Israel, for he had encouraged moral decline in Judah and had been continually unfaithful to the LORD. Also Tiglath-Pileser king of Assyria came to him and distressed him, and did not assist him. For Ahaz took part of the treasures from the house of the LORD, from the house of the king, and from the leaders, and he gave it to the king of Assyria; but he did not help him. Now in the time of his distress King Ahaz became increasingly unfaithful to the LORD. This is that King Ahaz. For he sacrificed to the gods of Damascus which had defeated him, saying, "Because the gods of the kings of Syria help them, I will sacrifice to them that they may help me." But they were the ruin of him and of all Israel' (2 Chr. 28:19-23).

And so, towards the close of his sixteen-year reign, the idolatrous and immoral King Ahaz adds a further insult against Jehovah when he suspends public worship by closing down the temple (2 Chr. 28:24), having first desecrated it by the introduction of a pagan altar and a corrupt sacrificial system.

16. Hoshea in Israel — 732-723 B.C. (17:1-41)

Hoshea assumes the throne of Israel after murdering King Pekah (15:30). He follows in the godless and evil tradition of so many of the kings of Israel. His reign lasts nine years and comes to an end when an attempted conspiracy with Egypt against Assyria is exposed. Shalmaneser[18] has succeeded Tiglath-Pileser as King of Assyria. He moves against Israel and in 723 B.C., following a three-year siege, the capital of Samaria is destroyed and numerous Israelites are deported to Assyria. From that time the nation of the northern kingdom, the ten tribes of Israel, ceases to exist. The judgement of God has fallen upon a godless and wicked people. Their demise comes as a direct consequence of unfaithfulness and wickedness.

The Assyrians repopulate Samaria by bringing people from the five nations of Babylon, Cuthah, Ava, Hamath and Sepharvaim. The immigrants bring their own pagan religious rituals and these are practised alongside the worship of Jehovah (17:41).

17. Hezekiah in Judah — 715-686 B.C. (18:1 – 20:21)[19]

King Hezekiah, son of wicked Ahaz, is generally regarded as one of the wisest and best of the kings of Judah (18:5-7; 2 Chr. 31:20-21). At the commencement of his reign he entirely reverses the wicked policy of his father Ahaz, and with true zeal destroys the idols and heathen temples that had been set up in the land, restoring and purifying the worship of Jehovah. Having taken extensive steps to restore God-honouring temple worship, King Hezekiah calls the nation to unite in the celebration of a great Passover (2 Chr. 30:5).

Some years later, when attacked by Sennacherib King of Assyria, Hezekiah places his entire confidence in Jehovah. With a heaven-sent miracle Judah is delivered from the enemy.

Shortly after these events Hezekiah becomes seriously ill and is dying. Isaiah the prophet visits him and says, 'Set your house in order, for you shall die, and not live' (20:1). The reaction of King Hezekiah once more indicates his godliness. He prays and weeps before the Lord. The Lord responds by giving a message through Isaiah: 'Return and tell Hezekiah the leader of my people, "Thus says the LORD, the God of David your father: 'I have heard your prayer, I have seen your tears; surely I will heal you. On the third day you shall go up to the house of the LORD. And I will add to your days fifteen years' (20:5-6).

A miraculous sign is given to King Hezekiah in confirmation of the promise of God (20:11). In response to his illness and remarkable recovery, Hezekiah composes a beautiful psalm of praise to the Lord (Isa. 38:10-20).

18. Manasseh in Judah — 697-642 B.C. (21:1-18; cf. 2 Chr. 33:1-20)

Manasseh is twelve when he becomes king and he reigns in Jerusalem for fifty-five years. He is a complete contrast to his father Hezekiah. No doubt under the influence of the corrupt priests and false prophets who unsuccessfully tried to influence his father, Manasseh succumbs and follows the pagan practices of the neighbouring nations surrounding Judah, and even exceeds their evil and corruption (21:9,11; cf. Isa. 28:7,14-15; 30:9-11). He rebuilds the pagan places of worship that his father Hezekiah had destroyed. He builds altars to the Baals, makes wooden idols and worships the gods of the Assyrians. He builds two altars to the Assyrian gods and places them in the temple of the living God. He sacrifices some of his sons as burnt offerings to the god Moloch in the Valley of the Son of Hinnom.[20] This vile practice of sacrificing children to Moloch was introduced into Judah by Manasseh's godless grandfather King Ahaz (2 Chr. 28:3). King Manasseh has a devastating influence upon the nation and brings Judah very low spiritually and morally.

'And the LORD spoke to Manasseh and his people, but they would not listen' (2 Chr. 33:10). As a result of this disobedience and refusal to listen, the Lord brings severe punishment upon Manasseh through the hands of the Assyrians. He is captured by Assyrian generals and taken with nose-hooks and chains back to Babylon.

Then a wonderful change takes place in the mind and heart of King Manasseh: 'Now when he was in affliction, he implored the LORD his God, and humbled himself greatly before the God of his fathers, and prayed to him; and he received his entreaty, heard his supplication, and brought him back to Jerusalem into his kingdom' (2 Chr. 33:12-13). Manasseh sincerely repents and turns in true faith to God. On his return to Jerusalem he begins to undo all the harm he had perpetrated. He takes away the foreign gods and the idol from the temple; he tears down all the altars that he had built in Jerusalem; he repairs the altar of the Lord and sacrifices peace offerings and thank offerings on it, and he commands the people of Judah 'to serve the LORD God of Israel' (2 Chr. 33:15-16).

19. Amon in Judah — 642-640 B.C. (21:19-26; cf. 2 Chr. 33:21-25)

Amon reigns only two years. Evidently unaffected by his father's repentance, Amon follows in the practice of idolatry.

20. Josiah in Judah — 640-609 B.C. (22:1 – 23:30)[21]

Josiah succeeds to the throne at the age of eight and by his mid-teens shows signs of true conversion (2 Chr. 34:3). At the age of twenty he begins a thorough reformation of religion throughout the whole nation. Rediscovery of the Book of the Law (22:8)[22] has a profound effect upon the king. He becomes even more concerned for himself and the people in relation to the living God.

Josiah responds with a sincere commitment to follow the Lord and obey the law of Moses. He calls upon the people to join him in making a solemn covenant with the Lord. A great Passover to the Lord is celebrated at his command. This Passover is particularly distinguished by two things: first, the inclusion of the remnant of the ten tribes of Israel together with the nation of Judah — including Benjamin (2 Chr. 35:18); and, secondly, the fact that the celebration was conducted strictly in accordance with the law of Moses (the Passover in the days of Hezekiah was held on a day other than that stipulated in God's law because there were not enough priests already consecrated for the service; neither did all the people fulfil the purification requirements — 2 Chr. 30:2-3,17-20).

The calibre and uniqueness of King Josiah are summed up as follows: 'Now before him there was no king like him, who turned to the LORD with all his heart, with all his soul, and with all his might, according to all the Law of Moses; nor after him did any arise like him' (23:25). There is an obvious allusion here to the law of Moses, where it is written: 'You shall love the LORD your God with all your heart, with all your soul, and with all your might. And these words which I command you today shall be in your heart...' (Deut. 6:5-6).

Josiah is killed in battle. For his burial in Jerusalem the prophet Jeremiah composes a funeral hymn that continued to be sung for many years afterwards (2 Chr. 35:25). A copy of that manuscript is no longer in existence.

21. Jehoahaz in Judah — 609 B.C. (23:31-34; cf. 2 Chr. 36:1-4)

Upon the death of godly Josiah the people proclaim Jehoahaz, his younger son, king. Jehoahaz reigns only three months yet earns the reputation of doing 'evil in the sight of the LORD, according to all that his fathers had done' (23:32). Jehoahaz is appropriately nicknamed 'Shallum' (meaning, 'retribution') by the prophet Jeremiah as he relays the judgement of God upon him (Jer. 22:11-17). The prophet Ezekiel compares Jehoahaz to a young lion that learned to catch prey and devour men who, when the nations hear, is captured in a pit and led to the land of Egypt (Ezek. 19:3-4).

22. Jehoiakim in Judah — 609-598 B.C. (23:35 – 24:7; cf. 2 Chr. 36:5-8)

King Jehoiakim proves no better a king than his younger brother Jehoahaz. He follows in the tradition of his ungodly ancestors. Jeremiah speaks of him as a bad king who will be 'buried with the burial of a donkey, dragged and cast out beyond the gates of Jerusalem' (Jer. 22:19), and not missed by anyone (Jer. 22:18).

In the third year of Jehoiakim's reign Nebuchadnezzar King of Babylon invades Judah and lays siege to the city of Jerusalem (Dan. 1:1-2). He fastens the king in chains in preparation for his deportation to Babylon (2 Chr. 36:6). It would seem that Jehoiakim assures Nebuchadnezzar of his willing allegiance and therefore he is released and allowed to stay on the throne of Judah paying tribute to Babylon. Some of the king's descendants and some of the nobles are taken into captivity. Among those Jewish exiles is a young man named Daniel who is destined by God to become a great prophet (Dan. 1:3-6).

King Jehoiakim is responsible for many atrocities during his reign: '… he had filled Jerusalem with innocent blood, which the LORD would not pardon' (24:4), even if great intercessors like Moses and Samuel were to stand before him (Jer. 15:1). One such victim of Jehoiakim is the prophet Urijah who prophesies against Jerusalem and Judah, is pursued into Egypt, brought back and killed in Jerusalem (Jer. 26:20-23). The evil reign of

Jehoiakim spans eleven years and terminates with his unceremonious death (Jer. 36:30).

23. Jehoiachin in Judah: 598-597 B.C. (24:8-16; cf. 2 Chr. 36:9-10)

Upon the death of his father Jehoiakim, eighteen-year-old Jehoiachin succeeds to the throne. He reigns only three months and ten days (2 Chr. 36:9) and follows in the evil practices of his godless ancestors. Jeremiah the prophet speaks words of warning to the king whom he refers to as Coniah (Jer. 22:24-30), but King Jehoiachin shows no sorrow, no repentance. Like Jehoahaz he is as a lion devouring men, until he is trapped and deported in chains to Babylon (Ezek. 19:5-7).

24. Zedekiah in Judah — 597-586 B.C. (24:17-20; cf. 2 Chr. 36:11-13)

Upon the deportation of Jehoiachin to Babylon, Nebuchadnezzar places Jehoiachin's uncle Mattaniah (whose name he changes to Zedekiah) on the throne of Judah. He is under the influence and control of the powerful nobles in the land (Jer. 38:1-6,24-26). Like them he does not listen to the Word of God through the prophet Jeremiah (Jer. 37:2; 2 Chr. 36:12).

Nebuchadnezzar marches against Judah. When Jerusalem is taken Zedekiah tries to escape. He is captured on the plains of Jericho, and blinded (25:7). Two seemingly contradictory prophecies come true: 'Zedekiah king of Judah shall not escape from the hand of the Chaldeans, but shall surely be delivered into the hand of the king of Babylon, and shall speak with him face to face, and see him eye to eye' (Jer. 32:4); and, 'I will bring him to Babylon, to the land of the Chaldeans; yet he shall not see it, though he shall die there' (Ezek. 12:13).

The Babylonians sack Jerusalem; they destroy the temple, the palace, all substantial houses and the city wall. They take all civil and religious leaders back to Babylon where they are executed (Jer. 52:24-27). The remaining people of Jerusalem are taken captive to Babylon, with the exception of poor vine-dressers and farmers who are left to tend the land (25:12) with Gedaliah as governor. In three invasions Nebuchadnezzar has taken a total of 4,600 captives (Jer. 52:30). The remaining inhabitants experience internal strife and flee to Egypt, against the word of Jeremiah the prophet (Jer. 43:5-7).

The kingdom of Judah is at an end.

Christ and his church

In many ways the spiritual encouragement of the Second Book of Kings is principally to be found in the early section recounting the lives of the two prophets Elijah and Elisha. They both play an important role in the purposes of God that centre in his Son, the Lord Jesus Christ.

1. Elijah, John and Jesus Christ

Elijah is a type of John the Baptist, the forerunner of Jesus Christ. Like Enoch (Gen. 5:24), Elijah did not experience death. He was privileged to be translated to heaven.

The return of Elijah is predicted at the close of the Old Testament period (c. 400 B.C.): 'Behold, I will send you Elijah the prophet before the coming of the great and dreadful day of the LORD' (Mal. 4:5). John the Baptist is the fulfilment of this remarkable prophecy.

John knew of his special connection with the prophet Elijah. An angel of the Lord visited his father Zacharias while he was burning incense in the temple (Luke 1:9,11). The angel informed Zacharias that he and his wife Elizabeth were to have a son in their old age, one who would be special: 'For he will be great in the sight of the Lord, and shall drink neither wine nor strong drink. He will also be filled with the Holy Spirit, even from his mother's womb. And he will turn many of the children of Israel to the Lord their God. He will also go before him in the spirit and power of Elijah, "to turn the hearts of the fathers to the children," and the disobedient to the wisdom of the just, to make ready a people prepared for the Lord' (Luke 1:15-16).

A further confirmation that John understood his connection with the prophet Elijah is indicated by the way he dressed 'in camel's hair, with a leather belt around his waist' (Matt. 3:4; cf. 2 Kings 1:8; see also Zech. 13:4, where the 'robe of coarse hair' is the 'uniform' of the true prophet, used occasionally by false prophets in order to deceive).

Years later, when challenged by priests and Levites from Jerusalem who asked who he was, John denied being Elijah and claimed to be nothing other than the forerunner of the Lord (John 1:21-23; cf. Isa. 40:3). The Lord Jesus indicates how this apparent contradiction is resolved. Speaking of John the Baptist, the Saviour says, 'Assuredly, I say to you, among those born of women there has not risen one greater than John the Baptist; but he who is least in the kingdom of heaven is greater than he… And *if you are willing to receive it, he is Elijah who is to come.* He who has ears to hear, let him hear!' (Matt. 11:11,14-15, emphasis added). John was not literally Elijah (John 1:21), but he came 'in the spirit and power of Elijah' (Luke 1:17).

Later the Lord informs his disciples, ' "Elijah truly is coming first and will restore all things. But I say to you that *Elijah has come already,* and they did not know him but did to him whatever they wished. Likewise the Son of Man is also about to suffer at their hands." *Then the disciples understood that he spoke to them of John the Baptist'* (Matt. 17:11-13, emphasis added).

2. Elijah, Moses and Jesus Christ

Elijah and Moses are linked in the final promise of the Old Testament:

Remember the Law of Moses, my servant,
Which I commanded him in Horeb for all Israel,
With the statutes and judgements.
Behold, I will send you Elijah the prophet
Before the coming of the great and dreadful day of the LORD
(Mal. 4:4-5).

In the New Testament the strongest connection is confirmed between Elijah, Moses and the Lord Jesus Christ. When the Lord Jesus took Peter, James and John to the Mount of Transfiguration, they were to witness an amazing sight. Not only did they see the remarkable splendour of deity shining from the person of the Lord Jesus Christ when the Saviour's 'face shone like the sun, and his clothes became as white as the light' (Matt. 17:2; cf. Heb. 1:3), they also heard the voice which came 'from the Excellent Glory: "This is my beloved Son, in whom I am well pleased" ' (2 Peter 1:17). Involved in the whole episode were two men from the past — Moses and Elijah, standing with the Lord Jesus. These two 'appeared in glory and spoke of his decease [Greek: *exodos*]' (Luke 9:31). 1,400 years had passed since Moses had died and been secretly buried by the Lord (Deut. 34:5-6). 850 years had passed since Elijah had been translated 'by a whirlwind into heaven' (2:11). These two great champions of the faith represent the law and the prophets respectively.

'Moses and Elijah were great men in their day; but Peter and his companions were to remember that in nature, dignity, and office, they were far below Christ. He was the true sun: they were the stars depending daily on His light. He was the root: they were the branches. He was the Master: they were the servants. Their goodness was all derived: His was original and His own. Let them honour Moses and the prophets, as holy men; but if they would be saved they must take Christ alone for their Master, and glory only in Him. "Hear ye Him." ' [23]

Jesus said, 'Do not think that I came to destroy the Law or the Prophets. I did not come to destroy but to fulfil. For assuredly, I say to you, till heaven and earth pass away, one jot or one tittle will by no means pass from the law till all is fulfilled' (Matt. 5:17-18).

3. Elijah, Elisha and Jesus Christ

Shortly after the amazing incident on Mount Carmel, Elijah journeyed far south, out of the land of Israel, through the land of Judah, into the wilderness region, arriving at his destination at Horeb, the mountain of the Lord (1 Kings 19:8). It was here on Mount Sinai in Horeb that the Lord had called Moses to be leader of the children of Israel (Exod. 3:1 – 4:17). Here too, the law was given, the priesthood instituted and the tabernacle constructed. It is to this mountain that the Lord directs the prophet Elijah. Here Elijah is given a further commission from God. His work is not yet over. One of the tasks he is to perform is to anoint Elisha the son of Shaphat of Abel Meholah as prophet in his place (1 Kings 19:16). Mount Sinai is very much associated with the law, but God's glory is not fully expressed in the law. His true glory is revealed in grace. Elijah is the forerunner of Elisha, as John the Baptist is the forerunner of Christ. Both Elijah and John the Baptist anoint their successors at the Jordan River. In the contrast of their characters and of their missions, Elijah is a type of John the Baptist and Elisha a type of our Saviour: 'The coming of Elisha was prophetic of Christ. Of all the prophets Elisha was the most remarkable type of Christ. His name means "The Salvation of God" and the name of his father Shaphat means "Justice" or "Judgement". Abel-Meholah where he dwelt signifies the place of mourning and weakness, for Christ was the Man of Sorrows, crucified through weakness — the weakness of human nature and patient submission to the holy will of the Father.'[24]

All the miracles of Elisha were miracles of mercy and link with the Lord Jesus Christ.[25] Elisha fed the hungry, cured the leper, healed the sick, raised the dead, and thereby provides a wonderful illustration of 'the Coming One' (Matt. 11:3-5). The cursing of the children at Bethel was not a miracle but a judgement. Christ came for judgement as well as for mercy (John 9:39). Even in death Elisha is a type of Christ, for when a dead man's corpse touched the bones of the prophet, the dead man revived; in the same way, there is life through the death of Christ. He has died that we might live.

Application

1. Wicked youths

The incident at Bethel is a sober reminder that 'God is not mocked' (Gal. 6:7); that children must be brought up 'in the training and admonition of the Lord' (Eph. 6:4); and that those who trouble the godly will be punished (2 Thess. 1:6). The wisest of men said, 'Even a child is known by his deeds, by whether what he does is pure and right' (Prov. 20:11). God's restraints on children operate 'largely through parental control — moral training in the home, wholesome instruction and discipline in the school, and adequate punishment of young offenders by the state'[26] (cf. Prov. 22:6,15; 13:24; 19:18).

2. Pure worship

Some time after the majority of the people of the northern kingdom of Israel had been taken into captivity to Assyria, Esarhaddon King of Assyria brought in replacements (Ezra 4:2). He brought people from the five nations of Babylon, Cuthah, Ava, Hamath and Sepharvaim (17:24), who brought their own pagan religious practices with them and amalgamated them with a corrupted form of the worship of Jehovah (17:41). These are the ancestors of the Samaritans of New Testament times who were much detested by the Jews (John 4:9).

In a remarkable way the Samaritan woman who met the Lord Jesus at the well of Sychar is a representative of her race. She had been married five times and the man she was currently living with was not her husband (John 4:18). 'She had had five husbands; and he whom she now had was not her husband, not having deigned to connect himself with her in marriage. So with the nation. It had previously been in fivefold spiritual marriage with its idols, and this marriage had been dissolved as frivolously as it had been concluded. The people sued for marriage with Jehovah; but this was denied them, because they did not belong to Israel.'[27]

The Samaritan woman, as, indeed, her whole nation, needed to turn in faith to Christ before God could be worshipped 'in spirit and truth' (John 4:24; cf. vv. 41-42). It is 'through Jesus Christ' only and exclusively that the penitent believer is able 'to offer up spiritual sacrifices acceptable to God' (1 Peter 2:5).

3. Rulers and nations

Throughout the history of Judah and Israel there is more often than not a clear correlation between the spiritual state of the king and that of the nation. Usually when a godly king governs Judah the people fear the living God. The result is that the nation prospers. When a godless, evil king rules Judah then the people tend to become more idolatrous and immoral. The result is that the nation suffers defeats in battle and domestic disasters. Occasionally there is an exception to the maxim: 'Like king, like nation.' One such exception is to be found during the reign of Jotham. King Jotham is described as a man who 'did what was right in the sight of the LORD' (2 Chr. 27:2). He 'became mighty, because he prepared his ways before the LORD his God' (2 Chr. 27:6). In spite of this godly example in the king, the nation as a whole still acted corruptly (2 Chr. 27:2; Isa. 2:5-9; 5:7-30; Micah 1:5; 2:1-2).

The spiritual message of the book as a whole is that rulers have a powerful influence for good or bad upon a nation. This should give cause for concern in our own day and our own land. While modern states are not monarchies like Israel and Judah, it is still true that 'Righteousness exalts a nation, but sin is a reproach to any people' (Prov. 14:34). It is imperative that the people of God pray for those who have the rule over them: 'Therefore I exhort first of all that supplications, prayers, intercessions, and giving of thanks be made for all men, for kings and all who are in authority, that we may lead a quiet and peaceable life in all godliness and reverence. For this is good and acceptable in the sight of God our Saviour, who desires all men to be saved and to come to the knowledge of the truth' (1 Tim. 2:1-4).

The first object of such prayer is to enable the people of God to 'lead a quiet and peaceable life in all godliness and reverence'. The second object of such prayer is to enable the work of the gospel to have free course in the land. Our prayer might be:

Oh, that you would rend the heavens!
That you would come down!
That the mountains might shake at your presence —
As fire burns brushwood,
As fire causes water to boil —
To make your name known to your adversaries,
that the nations may tremble at your presence!

(Isa. 64:1-2).

Conclusion

The reign of Solomon had a profound effect upon the nation of Israel. His rise meant prosperity and power for the nation; his fall into a terrible spiritual state opened the way for a major deterioration in the religious and moral life of the people. It can be seen how far the nation had fallen under the reign of Solomon from the fact that only a short time after his death Jeroboam could introduce the worship of golden calves without creating a public outcry.

The separate nation of Israel existed for just a little over 200 years, from 930 to 723 B.C. Its entire history is an almost unbroken chain of wickedness, with each successive king coming to the throne through the murder of his predecessor. The much smaller nation, Judah, existed longer — almost 350 years, until 586 B.C. 'The kings of Judah are judged in accordance with the promise given to David in 2 Samuel 7:12-16, whereas those of the northern kingdom, all of whom are condemned, are condemned because they have continued in the sin of Jeroboam the son of Nebat who made Israel to sin.'[28]

At the close of the Second Book of Kings the ten tribes of Israel are in exile in Assyria and the two tribes of Judah are in exile throughout Babylon. 'It lay in the plan of the divine providence to abandon them to oppression, to lead them to repentance through the school of misery.'[29] The temple, palace and city of Jerusalem lie in ruins. David's kingdom appears to have been destroyed. Disobedience to the law of God through Moses and the breaking of the covenant have resulted in God's punishment.

But the Lord will not forget his ancient promises. The nation will rise again — as from the dead!

1 Chronicles

('events of the days',
selected history from Adam to Solomon)

Author: Unknown
(possibly Ezra)

Key thought: 'God reigns over all'

Theme: The sovereignty of God: blessing
obedience, punishing disobedience

'Yours is the kingdom, O LORD,
And you are exalted as head over all.
Both riches and honour come from you,
And you reign over all.'
1 Chronicles 29:11-12

Summary

1 Chronicles

Every historian writes from a particular viewpoint. Each event is selected on a predetermined basis (cf. John 20:30-31; 21:25). Everything cannot be included. The historian of Chronicles (1 and 2 Chronicles were one book in the original version) is making his selection on the basis of a clear goal and purpose. He is tracing the history of the chosen people of Israel, and in particular the tribe of Judah from which the Messiah will rise (Gen. 49:10). The content 'is solid history, but the selective character of that content reveals a thoroughgoing theological and spiritual purpose'.[1]

Some of the historical descriptions found in 1 and 2 Chronicles are almost identical with those of the earlier books: 1 Chronicles contains material found in 2 Samuel; and 2 Chronicles contains material found in 1 and 2 Kings. Whereas in 2 Samuel the main concern is with the political aspects of David's kingdom, 1 Chronicles views David's kingdom from the religious perspective, the spiritual welfare of the nation and the continuity of the covenant promise. In a similar manner 1 and 2 Kings contain prophetic judgements and historical records of Israel and Judah, whereas 1 and 2 Chronicles contain priestly hopes and spiritual outlook on blessings and punishments of Judah only.

The books of Chronicles form, however, much more than a mere supplement to the other historical books. They are an independent work, in which the history of the chosen people is related in a new manner, and from a new vantage-point. While often the same events are recorded, they are nevertheless viewed from a different perspective. 'In Samuel and Kings we have the facts of history; here we have the Divine words and thoughts about these facts.'[2] In the former books these facts are related from a human standpoint; in Chronicles they are viewed from a divine standpoint. Chronicles provides us, therefore, with a more heavenly perspective.

Author

There is a very clear resemblance in style and language between the two books of Chronicles and those of Ezra and Nehemiah. The contents suggest a priestly authorship: emphasis on genealogies, the temple, the priesthood, obedience to the law of God, and the Davidic line from Judah. Consequently 1 and 2 Chronicles are generally credited to Ezra the priest, who was a skilled scholar and teacher of the Jewish Law (Ezra 7:6). The author functioned like a research historian drawing on a considerable range of material.[3]

The author's source material: reference books

1.	The book of the kings of Israel	I Chr. 9:1; 2 Chr. 20:34
2.	The chronicles of King David	I Chr. 27:24
3.	The book of Samuel the seer*	I Chr. 29:29
4.	The book of Nathan the prophet*	I Chr. 29:29; cf. 2 Chr. 9:29
5.	The book of Gad the seer*	I Chr. 29:29
6.	The prophecy of Ahijah the Shilonite	2 Chr. 9:29
7.	The visions of Iddo the seer	2 Chr. 9:29
8.	The book of Shemaiah the prophet	2 Chr. 12:15
9.	The book of Iddo the seer concerning genealogies	2 Chr. 12:15
10.	The annals of the prophet Iddo	2 Chr. 13:22
11.	The book of the kings of Judah and Israel (cf. no. 1 above)	2 Chr. 16:11; 25:26
12.	The book of Jehu the son of Hanani	2 Chr. 20:34
13.	The many oracles in the annals of the book of the kings	2 Chr. 24:27
14.	The writings of the prophet Isaiah the son of Amoz	2 Chr. 26:22
15.	Probably the actual letters of Sennacherib king of Assyria	2 Chr. 32:17
16.	The vision of Isaiah the prophet, the son of Amoz	2 Chr. 32:32
17.	The sayings of Hozai	2 Chr. 33:19
18.	The written instruction of David[†]	2 Chr. 35:4
19.	The written instruction of Solomon[†]	2 Chr. 35:4

*These may be references to parts of what we now know as 1 and 2 Samuel.
[†]The last two may have had joint authorship.

While a number of these books, records, genealogies and letters may refer to the same source under a different title, it is still evident that a wide range of material was available to the author.

The books of Chronicles were probably written shortly after the Babylonian captivity in 538 B.C. If this were the case it would explain why, having been written for the Jews (contraction of 'Judahs') who were returning from the Babylonian exile, it contains a more positive emphasis than either the books of Samuel or Kings. Its purpose is to encourage the returning exiles to rebuild the temple at Jerusalem, for God has not forgotten his covenant promises to his people: 'All is not lost; though the glory has departed and they are under the control of Gentile powers, God still has a future for them. The throne of David was gone but the line of David still stood.'[4]

This book teaches the strong lessons of Israel's history: apostasy, idolatry, intermarriage with Gentiles and lack of unity were the reasons for their recent ruin. The Babylonian captivity had a profound effect upon the returning Jews and their descendants: 'It is significant that after the exile, Israel never again worshipped foreign gods.'[5]

Historical setting

The two books of Chronicles cover the history of the chosen people of God over a period of thirty-five centuries, from creation to the proclamation of Cyrus, King of the Medes and Persians, encouraging the Jews to return to Jerusalem (538 B.C.).

1 Chronicles divides into two periods: the genealogies from Adam to David (1:1 – 9:44), and the reign of David over the united kingdom of Israel and Judah from 1004-971 B.C. (10:1 – 29:30).

Outline

Part I: Genealogies (1:1 - 9:44)

Of the Old Testament it is declared: 'All Scripture is given by inspiration of God, and is profitable for doctrine, for reproof, for correction, for instruction in righteousness, that the man of God may be complete, thoroughly equipped for every good work ' (2 Tim. 3:16-17).

The early genealogies might seem dry and uninspiring. The underlying purpose in presenting these ancestral lines is to show the fulfilment of the covenant promises. History is selectively reported to demonstrate that God is at work choosing and preserving a people for himself from the beginning. The line of God's covenant promise is traced from Adam through Abraham to David. The Lord is constantly selecting, constantly choosing: rejecting the unfaithful and disobedient; blessing the faithful and obedient. The one thing that counts is obedience and the character that grows out of it: 'The purpose of selection, as revealed in these genealogies, is that from the beginning the ultimate is in view ... the apparently crooked way is yet the straight way to the goal. The straight way would have followed the inheritance through the first-born, and that would often have been the straight way to failure and defeat. Whenever God made a new selection, setting aside rights and privileges ... choosing men who were not in the line of ordinary human expectation, He did so because His mind was set upon the ultimate goal.'[6]

Genealogies were very important to the Jews because of the promises associated with their tribes. The genealogies link the returning exiles with their forefathers and reassure them that they are still God's chosen people. The earliest prophecy of the Messiah simply promised a saviour from the human race (Gen. 3:15). Over time the specific race and then the particular family from which the Messiah would emerge were identified: of Abraham (Gen. 12:3); of Judah (Gen. 49:10); of David (2 Sam. 7:12-16).

The genealogies were not only important in relation to the coming of Messiah; they were also necessary for the faithful administration of the temple, its worship and all priestly functions. Carelessness in the past had brought punishment from God (1 Sam. 13:12-14). Only legitimate men of the tribe of Levi were to minister as priests of the living God.

Part II: King David's reign (10:1 - 29:30; cf. 2 Sam. 5:1 - 24:25)

Following a brief account of the death and dishonour of King Saul at the hands of the Philistines (the Lord's executioners, 10:13-14), and the courageous intervention of the men of Jabesh Gilead, the main theme is introduced: David, king over all Israel.

In 1 Chronicles King David is presented in all his strength. In consequence there are significant omissions: David's agonizing years with King Saul; his seven-year reign over Judah prior to becoming king of all Israel; his many wives; his sin with Bathsheba and treachery towards Uriah; and the rebellion of his sons Absalom and Adonijah. In this book, with the exception of the census (21:1-30),[7] the king is presented in his best light, for he personifies the hopes of the nation. He is the one to whom the Israelites look for a type of the Messiah/Deliverer.

Though David is the central character, it is God's dealings with and through David which form the true heart of the First Book of Chronicles. This is expressed in the covenant and the temple.

God's covenant

The prominent feature, indeed the pivotal point, of this book is the covenant that God made with King David: 'And it shall be, when your days are fulfilled, when you must go to be with your fathers, that I will set up your seed after you, who will be of your sons; and I will establish his kingdom. He shall build me a house, and I will establish his throne for ever. I will be his Father, and he shall be my son; and I will not take my mercy away from him, as I took it from him who was before you. And I will establish him in my house and in my kingdom for ever; and his throne shall be established for ever' (17:11-14; cf. 2 Sam. 7:12-16; 1 Kings 11:36). God promises David that a descendant will reign on the throne of Israel for ever. All covenant promises of land, blessing, honour and prosperity are tied to this Coming One. Though Solomon will fulfil something of the promises, a greater than Solomon is envisaged (cf. Matt. 12:42).

In 1 Chronicles the central nation is Judah; the central personality is David; the central issue is the covenant with David; the central objective is the temple. Nation, king, covenant and temple belong together in the unfolding purposes of God.

God's temple

This book provides information not recorded in the history of 2 Samuel: the extensive plans and preparation that David made for the temple and its services of worship. The importance of this project for David, for the Israelites, and for the cause of true religion throughout the world, gradually

emerges. The temple is to be the permanent structure to replace the tabernacle in the wilderness as the symbol of the visible presence of God among
his people. David was passionate about the cause of God; that is why he
cared about the ark of the covenant; that is why he desired to build the
temple. But God had determined that David's part in the project would
only be preparatory. While he is not permitted to build the temple (28:3),
David nevertheless prepares the site (21:18,22,28; 2 Chr. 3:1; cf. Gen.
22:2), draws up the plans, collects the building materials (22:1-5) and
structures the duties of the Levites, priests, musicians, singers, gate-keepers
and treasurers (23:1 – 26:32).

Structure of worship in the temple (25:1-31)

Three prophets

David
(Acts 2:29-30)

Nathan		Gad
(2 Chronicles 29:25)		(2 Chronicles 29:25)

Four leaders

Chenaniah
(15:22)

Asaph	Heman	Jeduthun	*total*
(25:6)	(25:6)	(25:6)	
4 sons	14 sons	6 sons	24
	each son supervised 11 singers		264

Choir: 'So the number of them, with their brethren who were instructed in the songs of the LORD, all who were skilful, was
two hundred and eighty-eight' (25:7).   288

Orchestra: '... four thousand praised the LORD with musical instruments' (23:5).

The book draws to a close with David's remarkable and beautiful public
prayer of praise to God at Solomon's coronation (29:10-25).

Christ and his church

1. 'Son of David'

The importance of David in the ancestry of the Messiah is paramount. Announcing the birth of the Lord Jesus Christ, the angel specifically referred to his stepfather as 'Joseph, son of David' (Matt. 1:20). Later, when the Lord began his ministry of preaching and healing, the sick frequently pleaded for his help calling, 'Son of David, have mercy on us!' (Matt. 9:27; cf. 20:30). As his ministry progressed the question arose among the people: 'Could this be the son of David?' (Matt. 12:23). Even a Gentile woman addressed him with the cry: 'O Lord, son of David!' (Matt. 15:22). The Messianic hopes connected with a descendant of King David reached their zenith with the adulation of the crowd at the Lord's triumphal entry into Jerusalem:

> Hosanna to the son of David!
> 'Blessed is he who comes in the name of the LORD!'
> Hosanna in the highest!
>
> (Matt. 21:9).

Not many days before his death, the Lord Jesus posed a question to a group of Pharisees: ' "What do you think about the Christ? Whose Son is he?" They said to him, "The son of David." He said to them, "How then does David in the Spirit call him 'Lord,' saying: 'The LORD said to my Lord, "Sit at my right hand, till I make your enemies your foot-stool" '? If David then calls him 'Lord', how is he his Son?" And no one was able to answer him a word...' (Matt. 22:42-46; cf. Ps. 110:1).

This is not a trick question. It is designed to provoke profound thought. The Lord Jesus is leading them from the known to the unknown, from the clear to the mysterious. Though the Messiah will descend from David, he will be greater than David. David's words in Psalm 110 indicate his insight into the person of the Messiah: Jehovah (the LORD) addresses the promised Seed as 'Lord'. In Psalm 110 God is promising the 'Lord', that is, the Messiah, 'such pre-eminence, power, authority, and majesty as would be proper only for One who, as to his person, from all eternity was, is now, and for ever will be God'[8] (Acts 2:33-36; Eph. 1:20-23; Phil. 2:5-11; Heb. 2:9; Rev. 5:1-10). The deity of the Lord Jesus Christ is not a doubtful or dubious doctrine, as present-day heretics would teach. It is clear from the New Testament that the early Christians were thoroughly convinced from the Old Testament Scriptures and from the words of Jesus. Though they never used the term 'Trinity', their teaching on the respective persons of Father, Son and Holy Spirit necessitates such a conclusion.[9] The Messiah is not only 'of the seed of David according to the flesh', but he is also 'declared to be the Son of God with power, according to the Spirit of holiness, by the resurrection from the dead' (Rom. 1:3-4).

2. King Messiah

David understood something of the profound relationship that exists between the Lord and his Messiah (Anointed). He declared God's decree concerning the position of honour ascribed to the Messiah:

> I will declare the decree:
> The LORD has said to me,
> 'You are my Son,
> Today I have begotten you'
>
> (Ps. 2:7; cf. Acts 13:33).

In the same psalm David reveals that Messiah is not only the Son of God but is also the one whom God has set as King over his 'holy hill of Zion' (Ps. 2:6). This is the Son of David, Son of God, whose throne will be established for ever (17:11-14). David and his kingdom become a type of Christ and his kingdom. The prophets provide deep insight into this connection, with its comparisons and contrasts (Isa. 9:6-7; 55:3-4; Ezek. 37:24; 34:23; Amos 9:11).

In Psalm 45 the King is declared to be 'the God whose throne is for ever and ever'. This 'is no mere mortal and his everlasting dominion is not bounded by Lebanon and Egypt's river'.[10] 'Some here see Solomon and Pharaoh's daughter only — they are short-sighted; others see both Solomon and Christ — they are cross-eyed; well-focused spiritual eyes see here Jesus only...'[11]

Application

1. Obedience

In 1 Samuel 31 it is simply recorded that King Saul met his death in battle with the Philistines. In 1 Chronicles 10:14 it is reported that the Lord killed him. The Philistines were merely executioners acting out Jehovah's justice, for King 'Saul died for his unfaithfulness which he had committed against the LORD, because he did not keep the word of the LORD' (10:13). An earlier reference to Achan also highlights the same rebellious heart (2:7). Achan knew that all the spoil had to be devoted to the Lord (Josh. 6:17-19; 7:15-25) but he did not choose to obey God's Word. These two both knew what God required and chose to disobey.

A further powerful lesson on obedience is presented in the account of the return of the ark of the covenant to Israel and its eventual trans- portation to Jerusalem. The historical record in Chronicles (13:1-14; 15:1 – 16:43) is much longer than that in Samuel (2 Sam. 6:1-23). In the present book an explanation is given as to why the Lord slew Uzzah and how David admitted Israel's serious error in not consulting the Lord 'about the proper order' (13:7,9-11; 15:2,13).

It is evident from these incidents how important obedience is in God's sight. Obedience is still a crucial aspect in the life of faith: 'Now by this we know that we know him, if we keep his commandments. He who says, "I know him," and does not keep his commandments, is a liar, and the truth is not in him. But whoever keeps his word, truly the love of God is per- fected in him. By this we know that we are in him' (1 John 2:3-5).

2. Prayer

Two fine examples of powerful prayer are presented in the early geneal- ogies. These may be easily overlooked and yet they provide a great incen- tive to resist fatalism and to plead with God. This is illustrated in the life of an individual and in a group.

Jabez is an example to all believers. He was not content to accept his name and pessimistically wait for it to be fulfilled. He sought God. He pleaded with the Lord. And God answered: 'Now Jabez was more honourable than his brothers, and his mother called his name Jabez [lit.,

"He will cause pain"], saying, "Because I bore him in pain." And Jabez called on the God of Israel saying, "Oh, that you would bless me indeed, and enlarge my territory, that your hand would be with me, and that you would keep me from evil, that I may not cause pain!" So God granted him what he requested' (4:9-10).

The second example of prayer is given in the events surrounding a large group of unnamed warriors from the tribes of Reuben, Gad and Manasseh: 'The sons of Reuben, the Gadites, and half the tribe of Manasseh had forty-four thousand seven hundred and sixty valiant men, men able to bear shield and sword, to shoot with the bow, and skilful in war, who went to war. They made war with the Hagrites, Jetur, Naphish, and Nodab. And they were helped against them, and the Hagrites were delivered into their hand, and all who were with them, for they cried out to God in the battle. He heeded their prayer, because they put their trust in him' (5:18-20).

In the Scriptures there are many instructions, illustrations and incentives in regard to prayer, whether private or public (e.g. Matt. 6:5-13; Luke 18:1-14; Acts 2:42; Eph. 6:18; Phil. 4:6-7).

'The reason so many people do not pray is because of its cost. The cost is not so much in the sweat of agonizing supplication, as in the daily fidelity to the life of prayer. It is the acid test of devotion. Nothing in the life of Faith is so difficult to maintain. There are those who resent the association of discipline and intensity with prayer...'[12]

'True praying is a strenuous spiritual exercise which demands the utmost mental discipline and concentration.'[13]

3. Service

Details are given about the Levites and their appointment 'to every kind of service of the tabernacle of the house of God' (6:48). They seem to have responded enthusiastically to their duties and responsibilities. Later some of the priests are described as 'very able men for the work of the service of the house of God' (9:13). When the historian calls them 'very able men' he is highlighting the importance that only the best is good enough for the service of God. There is here also an emphasis upon the considerable variety of gifts that were employed in God's service. Years later the apostle Paul would remind the Christians at Corinth that there is great variation in the spiritual gifts which God the Holy Spirit gives to the children of God: 'Now there are diversities of gifts, but the same Spirit. There are differences of ministries, but the same Lord. And there are diversities of activities, but it is the same God who works all in all. But the manifestation of the Spirit is given to each one for the profit of all' (1 Cor. 12:4-7).

The efficiency and effectiveness of the local church depends upon each member making his or her individual contribution for the good of the whole. It is only when 'every part does its share' that the result is the 'growth of the body for the edifying of itself in love' (Eph. 4:16).

4. No redundancy!

With the prospect of a permanent building the duties of the Levites relating to the dismantling, transportation and re-erection of the tabernacle were no longer required (23:26). They were not, however, declared redundant! David wisely designated new duties: maintaining the fabric of the temple, preparing the offerings and utensils, leading daily worship and generally assisting the priests in their religious duties (23:27-32). 'Redundancy is a word that many people in the modern world have come to dread. A person who has been made redundant has lost more than his employment and income, for he has lost his dignity. He feels like someone who has been dismissed as a superfluous human being — surplus to requirements. However, we may be thankful that in the service of God there is no such thing as a redundant person. All God's people are needed, because when one avenue of service is closed another is opened to them.'[14]

5. Leadership skills

In the mighty men surrounding David (11:10 – 12:38) there is clear evidence of David's ability to train and to inspire others. At Adullam he had attracted a motley band — men in distress, in debt and everyone who was discontented — and he had become captain over them (1 Sam. 22:2). Under his leadership these men became a disciplined, highly competent fighting unit.

Eventually David's army was composed of men who could use 'both the right hand and the left' (12:2), indicating not only their competence but also the level of training they had received. There were also men 'who could handle shield and spear' (12:8); in other words, they were experts in offensive and defensive warfare.

Of all the mighty men there was one mightier — David the king. He won their loyalty; he won their hearts (11:15-19). In this too he is a type of the Lord Jesus Christ. Christians are inspired by the Saviour's leadership.

Under the New Covenant the importance of spiritual leadership is emphasized. Besides the regular training given through the weekly exposition of the Word of God (Eph. 4:11-16), there is also the specific training of future leaders (2 Tim. 2:2). Church leaders are responsible for the training of new leaders. That training should be accompanied by a worthy example: 'Imitate me, just as I also imitate Christ' (1 Cor. 11:1; cf. Phil. 4:9). A godly example inspires others (1 Tim. 4:12).

6. Orderly worship

Though the Lord had never commanded it, or indicated that he required it, David longed to build a temple for the worship of God (17:1). Though not permitted to construct the temple, he did undertake meticulous preparation for it. David was not concerned with a beautiful building for its own sake, nor for any kudos it might bring to his kingdom or city; he was concerned for the pure worship of God. As a prophet he wrote many beautiful psalms under the inspiration of God. Most were composed for public worship. As already noted, he also made elaborate preparations for training orchestras and choirs so that a high standard of music and song would lead the people in adoration and praise to God.

The New Covenant gives great freedom to worship anywhere and at any time, but it does not give licence for shoddy, careless, ill-prepared worship under the guise of spontaneity. 'God is not the author of confusion', and he requires that worship in his church 'be done decently and in order' (1 Cor. 14:33,40). The worship of God is still of major importance to God, and to God's people. True 'worshippers will worship the Father in spirit and truth; for the Father is seeking such to worship him' (John 4:23).

The LORD loves the gates of Zion
More than all the dwellings of Jacob.
Glorious things are spoken of you,
O city of God!

(Ps. 87:2-3).

God loves his people individually ('the dwellings of Jacob'), but he delights more in the assembly of the saints at worship ('loves the gates of

Zion'). As Spurgeon comments, 'God delights in the prayers and praises of Christian families and individuals, but he has a special eye to the assemblies of the faithful, and he has a special delight in their devotions in their church capacity.'[15]

The psalmist makes reference to the new birth that makes a person a member of 'Zion' (Ps. 87:5-6).

Conclusion

Together the books of 1 and 2 Chronicles summarize not only the history, but also the theology of the Old Testament: the revelation that God gave of himself at creation, to the patriarchs, through Moses, during the monarchy, exile and restoration.[16]

The First Book of Chronicles is concerned from beginning to end to magnify God and give him his rightful place in the worship and service of Israel. King David typifies the godly person who wants his whole life to be devoted to the Lord. The apostle Paul summed up the life of David when he said, 'David ... served his own generation by the will of God' (Acts 13:36). As shepherd, king, psalmist and prophet, he lived with an eye almost continually set upon the glory and honour of God, and thus he prayed:

> Blessed are you, LORD God of Israel, our Father, for ever and ever.
> Yours, O LORD, is the greatness,
> The power and the glory,
> The victory and the majesty;
> For all that is in heaven and in earth is yours;
> Yours is the kingdom, O LORD,
> And you are exalted as head over all.
> Both riches and honour come from you,
> And you reign over all.
> In your hand is power and might;
> In your hand it is to make great
> And to give strength to all.
> Now therefore, our God,
> We thank you
> And praise your glorious name
>
> (29:10-13).

2 Chronicles

(continuation of 1 Chronicles)

Author: Unknown
(possibly Ezra)

Key thought: 'Preparing the heart to seek God'

Theme:
The slippery slope to ruin

'The LORD is with you while you
are with him. If you seek him, he will
be found by you; but if you forsake
him, he will forsake you.'
2 Chronicles 15:2

Summary

			Year (B.C.)	compare with
x.	Uzziah / Azariah (began well, ended badly)	26:1-23	792-740	2 Kings 15:1-7
xi.	Jotham (good)	27:1-9	750-732	2 Kings 15:32-38
xii.	Ahaz (bad)	28:1-27	735-715	2 Kings 16:1-20
xiii.	Hezekiah (good)	29:1 – 32:33	715-686	2 Kings 18:1 – 20:21
xiv.	Manasseh (bad but repented)	33:1-20	697-642	2 Kings 21:1-18
xv.	Amon (bad)	33:21-25	642-640	2 Kings 21:19-26
xvi.	Josiah (good)	34:1 – 35:27	640-609	2 Kings 22:1 – 23:30
xvii.	Jehoahaz (bad)	36:1-4	609	2 Kings 23:31-34
xviii.	Jehoiakim / Eliakim (bad)	36:5-8	609-598	2 Kings 23:35 – 24:7
xix.	Jehoiachin (bad)	36:9-10	598-597	2 Kings 24:8-16
xx.	Zedekiah (bad)	36:11-13	597-586	2 Kings 24:17-20

4. Babylonian captivity   **36:14-21**   586   2 Kings 25:1-21

5. The beginning of the restoration of Judah   36:22-23   538

2 Chronicles

As noted in the chapter on 1 Samuel, the division into what are now the First and Second Books of Chronicles occurred for purely practical reasons. In the original form there was only one book of Chronicles. Consequently what has been written concerning the author and his source material under the introduction to 1 Chronicles equally applies to this second book.

It is still the spiritual aspect of the nation's history that receives the emphasis: the promises of God and his constant faithfulness; the vital importance of God-centred and God-honouring worship; and the power of his Word to transform an individual or a nation.

The historian is dedicated to the encouragement of the Israelites in their Babylonian captivity. In Chronicles David and Solomon are portrayed as glorious, obedient, all-conquering figures who enjoy not only divine blessing but also the support of the nation. The Chronicler does not mention that David only saves the kingdom for Solomon at the last minute due to the intervention of his wife Bathsheba and the prophet Nathan (1 Kings 1).

God's covenant promises, as they centre in King David, Solomon and their descendants, are the overriding concern. Consequently, whereas in the book of Kings, Solomon's wisdom is expressed in terms of wisdom to rule, in 2 Chronicles it is seen primarily as wisdom for building the temple.

Historical setting

1 Chronicles closes with the death of King David. 2 Chronicles opens with the reign of his son King Solomon and traces the distinction, division and destruction of the kingdom (970 – 538 B.C.). Focusing on the history of Judah, a bleak picture is presented of a nation in decline and apostasy. Nevertheless there are striking periods of spiritual revival and religious reformation.

Much of the history recorded in 2 Chronicles is found in 1 and 2 Kings.

Outline

Part I: The reign of Solomon (1:1 - 9:31)

Solomon's reign is Israel's 'golden age' of peace and prosperity. The glory and grandeur of Solomon's kingdom span from the border of Egypt to the west and south, to the River Euphrates to the east and north (1 Kings 4:21). The area has been roughly calculated as covering 50,000 square miles[1] (about half the size of the British Isles). But in the vast kingdom of Solomon, it is the temple that predominates. Plans for the temple which dominated the latter part of 1 Chronicles find realization under the leadership of Solomon. The building is to be 'exceedingly magnificent, famous and glorious throughout all countries' (1 Chr. 22:5).

Commenced in the fourth year of Solomon's reign (3:2), 480 years after the delivery of Israel from Egypt (1 Kings 6:1), the temple was the first large single structure to be built by any ruler of Israel. Solomon realized the temple's significance as the house of God, 'since heaven and the heaven of heavens cannot contain him', and at the same time he was aware of his own inadequacy for the task (2:4-6).

The Lord appears to Solomon a second time at the dedication of the completed temple. God clearly states the basis upon which the nation will know his blessing or his punishment: 'If my people who are called by my name will humble themselves, and pray and seek my face, and turn from their wicked ways, then I will hear from heaven, and will forgive their sin and heal their land. Now my eyes will be open and my ears attentive to prayer made in this place' (7:14-15).

The worship of God is central to the nation's future; 'seeking God' is the crucial factor in its survival. This theme provides the thread throughout the remaining chapters, for even as the nation deteriorates in its spiritual and moral life there are outstanding periods of spiritual awakening and renewed faithfulness to the Lord.

God gave Solomon outstanding wisdom: he was skilled in pithy and wise sayings, a musician and poet; he was an expert botanist and zoologist; he was a prudent counsellor and king (1 Kings 4:29-34). Solomon wrote the books of Proverbs, Ecclesiastes, Song of Solomon and at least two psalms: Psalm 72 and Psalm 127.

Part II: Civil war (10:1 – 11:23)

As in 1 Chronicles, David's sins in relation to Bathsheba and Uriah are omitted (although the Chronicler does refer the reader to the books of Samuel, Nathan and Gad for a fuller account of the reign of David, 1 Chr. 29:29-30), so in 2 Chronicles there is no mention of Solomon's taking revenge on David's enemies (1 Kings 2). Nor are the sins of Solomon recounted, which in 1 Kings 11 are presented as the reason for the division of the kingdom. The emphasis here falls upon the agents of the division, Jeroboam's rebellion and the inexperience of Solomon's son Rehoboam (13:6-7).

Part III: Kings of Judah (12:1 – 36:13)

The record of the kings of the northern kingdom (Israel) is omitted from 2 Chronicles since the concern of the Chronicler is to trace the line of Judah with especial reference to the Lord's covenant promise to David (1 Chr. 17:11-14) and commitment to the true worship of God in the temple at Jerusalem. These two central concerns were abandoned by the ten tribes of the northern kingdom. There could be no restoration, no true reformation among the people called 'Israel' without repentance towards God and a return in submission to the God-ordained ruler out of Judah (Gen. 49:10), descendant of David (2 Sam. 7:12-16), and to the priesthood that God had instituted and the true temple at Jerusalem. The temple symbolizes God's presence with his people and provides a visible link for the Jews uniting their past and their future.

Although there were more bad kings ruling Judah the sum total of their years on the throne amounts to considerably less than that of the combined reigns of the good kings.

The author is tracing the spiritual line of promise and the preserving power of God. For this reason prominence is given to Judah's kings who were noted for leading significant reformations of religion: Kings Asa, Jehoshaphat, Joash (credited entirely to the godly influence exerted upon him by Jehoiada the priest), Hezekiah and Josiah. Five distinct waves of revival and reformation emphasize the connection between seeking God and the well-being of the kingdom.

1. Religious reformation under King Asa (14:1 – 16:14; cf. 1 Kings 15:9-24)

Unlike his father and his grandfather, Asa does 'what was good and right in the eyes of the LORD his God' (14:2). He removes pagan altars, demolishes heathen pillars, chops down wooden images and banishes perverted people from the land. He commands the people of Judah to seek the Lord and to obey his law and commandments.

When the Ethiopians attack with an army twice the size of Judah's, King Asa turns in total reliance upon the Lord and experiences a great and overwhelming victory. The Lord gives a promise with a condition: 'Hear me, Asa, and all Judah and Benjamin. The LORD is with you while you are with him. If you seek him, he will be found by you; but if you forsake him, he will forsake you … be strong and do not let your hands be weak, for your work shall be rewarded!' (15:2,7).

King Asa responds wholeheartedly to the prophecy: we read that he 'took courage, and removed the abominable idols from all the land of Judah and Benjamin … and he restored the altar of the LORD' (15:8). He gathers all Judah and Benjamin together with all the God-fearing people who have migrated from the tribal lands of Ephraim, Manasseh and Simeon. All these 'entered into a covenant to seek the LORD God of their fathers with all their heart and with all their soul… And the LORD gave them rest all around' (15:12,15).

Towards the end of his long reign King Asa seems to lose his earlier confidence in the Lord. Maybe the absence of war for some fifteen years or so has resulted in the king and nation becoming spiritually lethargic. Easy times rarely promote spiritual growth. When Baasha King of Israel (cf. 1 Kings 15:33 – 16:7) invades Judah, Asa makes a terrible mistake. Relying upon the 'arm of the flesh' (32:8), he does not seek the help of God. He gathers together the gold and silver from the temple and from the palace and sends them as a gift to King Ben-Hadad of Syria. With the gift is the request that Ben-Hadad would break his treaty with Israel and make a treaty with Judah, resulting in his withdrawal from Judah. The plan works but the Lord disapproves. Asa ends his days in a spiritually backslidden state and in severe physical pain.

2. Religious reformation under King Jehoshaphat (17:1 – 20:37; cf. 1 Kings 22:41-50)

Like his father Asa in his earlier days, Jehoshaphat is a godly king, keen to live in obedience to the Lord and to encourage the people of Judah to be faithful to the true God. The blessings of God rest upon his labours and Jehoshaphat responds by seeking to strengthen the nation spiritually. He sends out civil leaders and Levites throughout all Judah to teach the people the law of God from 'the Book of the Law of the LORD'[2] (17:9). This strategy has such an effect that the nations around Judah are gripped by 'the terror of Jehovah' and none of them attempts to make war with Judah. Indeed, some of the Philistines and some of the Arabians bring presents to Jehoshaphat to ensure his goodwill towards them.

As a result of a marriage alliance with Israel, followed by a state visit to King Ahab, Judah becomes involved in assisting Israel against the Syrians. The battle that follows leads to Ahab's death. The Lord disapproves of Jehoshaphat's involvement with Israel: 'Should you help the wicked and love those who hate the LORD? Therefore the wrath of the LORD is upon you. Nevertheless good things are found in you...' (19:2-3). The godly king responds to the rebuke, and the encouragement, by continuing his work of civil and spiritual reformation. The administration of justice is improved throughout the whole land of Judah.

Some years later the Ammonites, with the Moabites and the inhabitants of Mount Seir, come up against Judah. When news of this mighty invasion reaches the King of Judah, he reacts as only the godly can do: 'Jehoshaphat feared, and set himself to seek the LORD, and proclaimed a fast throughout all Judah. So Judah gathered together to ask help from the LORD; and from all the cities of Judah they came to seek the LORD' (20:3-4).

King Jehoshaphat leads the vast congregation in prayer and worship (20:6-12). The Lord responds: 'Do not be afraid nor dismayed because of this great multitude, for the battle is not yours, but God's... You will not need to fight in this battle. Position yourselves, stand still and see the salvation of the LORD, who is with you, O Judah and Jerusalem! Do not fear or be dismayed; tomorrow go out against them, for the LORD is with you' (20:15,17).

The king humbles himself before the Lord. He and the whole congregation continue to worship. The following day they experience a remarkable delivery — without wielding a single sword. The battle is indeed the Lord's!

3. Religious reformation under King Joash (24:1-27; cf. 2 Kings 11:4 – 12:21)

Wicked Queen Athaliah, daughter of Ahab and Jezebel of Israel, seizes the throne of Judah upon the death of her son King Ahaziah. She ushers in one of the bleakest episodes in the history of the Hebrews. Athaliah puts to death all the remaining members of the royal family of Judah (her grand-children). Only one son of Ahaziah, the young child Joash, escapes. As a one-year-old he is rescued by his aunt Jehoshabeath, daughter of Jehoram (probably by a wife other than Athaliah) whose husband is the godly high priest Jehoiada (22:11). Joash and his nurse are moved into hiding in the home of the high priest adjoining the court of the temple.

For some years the God-fearing people among the tribe of Judah must have thought that all their hope was lost. It must have seemed as though the Lord had failed to keep his covenant promise to David. As far as the people of Judah were concerned, there was no remaining male descendant of David (2 Sam. 7:16).

After six years with the wicked Athaliah as Queen of Judah, Jehoiada the high priest reveals the rightful heir to the throne, the seven-year-old boy Joash. The temple of Baal is pulled down, its priest killed and its images and altars destroyed. A period of prosperity follows and the worship of the true God is re-established. Joash instigates major repairs of the temple at Jerusalem.

The behaviour of Joash changes at the death of Jehoiada the high priest. He is no longer resolute in following the Lord. Without the presence of the godly priest, Joash comes under the influence of bad counsellors and restores Baal-worship and the building of groves to Ashtoreth. God sends prophets to the people, but they will not listen. Eventually the Spirit of the Lord directs Zechariah the son of Jehoiada the priest with a message for the people, but his message incenses the king and he orders the assassin-ation of Zechariah. His murder is carried out 'in the court of the house of the LORD' (24:21). This atrocity is even more obnoxious because it is per-formed between the sanctuary (the Holy Place and the Holy of Holies) and the altar of burnt sacrifice (Matt. 23:35). In effect it is done in the very pres-ence of God.[3] In commanding the death of Zechariah, Joash disregards the years of immense kindness shown to him by Zechariah's father Jehoiada.

4. Religious reformation under King Hezekiah (29:1 – 32:33; cf. 2 Kings 18:1 – 20:21)

King Hezekiah is generally regarded as one of the wisest and best of the kings of Judah: 'Hezekiah ... did what was good and right and true before the LORD his God. And in every work that he began in the service of the house of God, in the law and in the commandment, to seek his God, he did it with all his heart. So he prospered' (31:20-21). 'He trusted in the LORD God of Israel, so that after him was none like him among all the kings of Judah, nor any who were before him. For he held fast to the LORD; he did not depart from following him, but kept his commandments, which the LORD had commanded Moses. The LORD was with him; he prospered wherever he went' (2 Kings 18:5-7).

At the commencement of his reign he entirely reverses the wicked policy of his father Ahaz, and with true zeal destroys the idols and heathen temples that had been set up in the land, restoring and purifying the worship of Jehovah. Having taken extensive steps to restore God-honouring temple worship, King Hezekiah calls the nation to unite in the celebration of a great Passover (30:5). On the day set for the observance of the Passover there is an atmosphere of genuine repentance, of turning from idolatry and returning to the living God.

Some years later, when Sennacherib becomes King of Assyria (705 B.C.) and marches on Jerusalem, Hezekiah follows good military procedure by creating an aqueduct to re-route the water supply, by fortifying the city and ensuring a good supply of weapons (32:1-5). But it is his encouragement to the people which truly demonstrates his godliness: he calls the people to trust in the Lord: ' "Be strong and courageous; do not be afraid nor dismayed before the king of Assyria, nor before all the multitude that is with him; for there are more with us than with him. With him is an arm of flesh; but with us is the LORD our God, to help us and to fight our battles." And the people were strengthened by the words of Hezekiah king of Judah' (32:7-8).

Hezekiah places his entire confidence in Jehovah. When the King of Assyria blasphemes God and publishes libellous letters against the King of Judah, Hezekiah takes the letters into the temple and spreads them before the Lord and prays: 'O LORD of hosts, God of Israel, the one who dwells between the cherubim, you are God, you alone, of all the kingdoms of the earth. You have made heaven and earth. Incline your ear, O LORD, and hear; open your eyes, O LORD, and see; and hear all the words of Sennacherib, who has sent to reproach the living God. Truly, LORD, the kings of Assyria have laid waste all the nations and their lands, and have cast their gods into the fire; for they were not gods, but the work of men's hands — wood and stone. Therefore they have destroyed them. Now therefore, O LORD our God, save us from his hand, that all the kingdoms of the earth may know that you are the LORD, you alone' (Isa. 37:16-20).

The future for Jerusalem looks bleak, utterly impossible. The Lord sends Isaiah the prophet to reassure King Hezekiah that his prayers have been heard and his confidence in the living God will be rewarded (2 Kings 19:20-34).

The miraculous delivery is described: 'Then the angel of the LORD went out, and killed in the camp of the Assyrians one hundred and eighty-five thousand; and when people arose early in the morning, there were the corpses — all dead' (Isa. 37:36). The people of God can always rely upon the Lord, even when facing seemingly insurmountable opposition.

5. Religious reformation under King Josiah (34:1-35:27; cf. 2 Kings 22:1 – 23:30)

Josiah came to the throne of Judah at the age of eight years. When he was sixteen years old, the young king 'began to seek the God of his father David'. At the age of twenty he began the destruction of the pagan places of worship and the numerous images that littered the country. He travelled extensively throughout the land and personally supervised the destruction of all the paraphernalia of paganism.

At twenty-six years of age, in the eighteenth year of his reign, he began to repair the temple. It was during this work of renovation that Hilkiah the high priest found the lost Book of the Law.[4] This may have been the original copy of the law of Moses (34:14). It is likely that the reading of the law had been prohibited during the evil reigns of Manasseh and Amon.

When passages of this book were read to King Josiah, they had a remarkable effect upon him (34:19). It would seem that Josiah had never before heard these words, though many copies of the law had been made years earlier under the direction of godly King Hezekiah. It is likely that, with the passage of time and the influence of two godless kings, the people now followed only an outward form of ritual, and had little or no interest in the Word of God.

Josiah responded with great concern for himself and his people. He commanded that the Lord should be consulted. Steps were taken to understand the implications of the law of God and, although Judah was to be

punished for her many sins, King Josiah was singularly favoured by the
Lord. God said to him, '"… because your heart was tender, and you
humbled yourself before God when you heard his words against this place
and against its inhabitants, and you humbled yourself before me, and you
tore your clothes and wept before me, I also have heard you," says the
LORD. "Surely I will gather you to your fathers, and you shall be gathered
to your grave in peace; and your eyes shall not see all the calamity which I
will bring on this place and its inhabitants"' (34:27-28).

Josiah responded with a sincere commitment to follow the Lord and
obey the law given through Moses. He called the people to join him in
making a solemn covenant with the Lord (34:30-33).

Out of twenty rulers over Judah, from the division of the kingdom to the
captivity, five led spiritual reformations, two others also sought to follow the
Lord, another repented in the latter years of his reign, but the remainder
were godless and immoral.

Part IV: Babylonian captivity (36:14-21)

After godly Josiah, four godless kings follow in quick succession. Over a
period of twenty years three invasions by the Babylonians bring the nation
of Judah to her knees. Nobles (including the prophet Daniel), priests (including the prophet Ezekiel) and people are taken captive to Babylon. But
the Lord has not yet fulfilled his covenant promise to Judah and to his servant David. The promised Messiah has not yet appeared.

Part V: The beginning of the restoration of Judah
(36:22-23)

Jeremiah's prediction of a seventy-year captivity in Babylon (36:21; Jer.
29:10) is fulfilled in two ways: firstly, a political captivity in which Jerusalem
is controlled by Babylon from 605 B.C. to 536 B.C. with its inhabitants
taken into exile in three phases; and, secondly, a religious captivity from
the destruction of the temple in 586 B.C. to the completion of the new
temple in 516 B.C.[5]

Seventy years pass and Babylon is conquered by the Medes and Persians. The king of that vast empire is King Cyrus, of whom the prophet

Isaiah had spoken around two hundred years before. He will instigate the return of the Jews to Jerusalem with the object of rebuilding the temple:

> Thus says the LORD, your Redeemer...
> Who says to Jerusalem, 'You shall be inhabited,'
> To the cities of Judah, 'You shall be built' ...
> Who says of Cyrus, 'He is my shepherd,
> And he shall perform all my pleasure,
> Even saying to Jerusalem, "You shall be built,"
> And to the temple, "Your foundation shall be laid" '
>
> (Isa. 44:24,26,28).

Christ and his church

1. David's line

Satan is constantly trying to thwart the purposes of God. If he can instigate a massacre of the royal family, then the Son of God cannot fulfil the prophecies of the Old Testament. The line of promise was clear: seed of Eve (Gen. 3:15), seed of Abraham (Gen. 12:1-3) and seed of King David. The Lord made a promise to David through Nathan the prophet: 'When your days are fulfilled and you rest with your fathers, I will set up your seed after you, who will come from your body, and I will establish his kingdom. He shall build a house for my name, and I will establish the throne of his kingdom for ever' (2 Sam. 7:12-13).

Satan was constantly looking for ways to destroy the line of David so that he could discredit God and thwart the coming of his Son as the Messiah, the Promised One. Under the evil Queen Athaliah the devil almost achieved his objective. When she sought to execute all the members of the royal family of Judah (22:10) she was probably only concerned about protecting her claim to the throne. Behind her was the Evil One who was seeking the failure of the covenant promises concerning Christ and his church. She annihilated all her grandchildren. Unbeknown to her, however, and in the wonderful providence of Almighty God, one grandson, baby Joash, was rescued from slaughter.

When Syria and Israel attacked Judah they planned the removal of the royal line and the installation of a complete outsider on the throne of Judah

(Isa. 7:1,6). Had they succeeded what would have become of the promised Seed? The ruler out of Israel must be a descendant not only of Judah (Gen. 49:10), but especially of David. 'Yet the LORD would not destroy the house of David, because of the covenant that he had made with David...' (21:7).

Wars, assassinations, scheming, persecution and exile threaten the Messianic line, but it remains unbroken from Adam to Jeconiah. The throne was destroyed but the line continues. The prophecy to David that his throne would be for ever is only fulfilled in Christ. The genealogies recorded in Chronicles which demonstrate the unbroken prophetic line for the Messiah are continued in the genealogies of Luke 3:23-38 and Matthew 1:1-17.[6] Jesus of Nazareth is demonstrated to fulfil the prophetic criteria, for truly he was 'born of the seed of David according to the flesh' (Rom. 1:3). The prophecies of the Old Testament must be fulfilled. This is God's safeguard to false claims. This is God's proof that Jesus of Nazareth is 'the Christ, the Son of God' (John 20:31). The Old Testament Scriptures, together with his miracles, ministry, suffering and death, and the declarations of John the Baptist, accredit Jesus of Nazareth as the Son of God (John 5:31-47; Acts 2:22,36; 1 Cor. 15:3-4).

2. Solomon's temple

Central to the First Book of Chronicles is God's *covenant* made with David. Central to the Second Book of Chronicles is God's *temple* constructed by Solomon. The history and significance of the temple are central to the biblical teaching concerning Christ and his church.

The temple which David designed and for which he prepared materials and labourers, and which Solomon his son actually constructed, was built 'at Jerusalem on Mount Moriah' (3:1). This is the mountain range to which the Lord directed Abraham when he commanded him to sacrifice his son Isaac (Gen. 22:2). That command was never enacted. The Lord intervened. Isaac was spared. Profound connections may be seen between Abraham offering his *son,* his *only son* Isaac, *whom he loved,* and the later action of God himself offering his *Son,* his *only begotten Son,* his *beloved Son,* as the sacrifice for sin — there on that very spot! And no one intervened (Rom. 8:32).

The significance of the temple is indicated by the name which it bore in its most ancient form, Ohel Moed, which means, 'the tabernacle of congregation', the place where God met with his people (cf. Exod. 25:22, 29:43; Num. 17:4).[7]

The temple that Solomon constructed was only to have a temporary life. Solomon began construction in 966 B.C. and concluded seven years later (1 Kings 6:1,38). The building was destroyed by the invading forces of King Nebuchadnezzar of Babylon in 586 B.C., 380 years after its foundations were laid.

After seventy years of captivity the Jews were allowed to return home. Under the leadership of Zerubbabel a new temple was constructed. It was not as impressive in appearance as the first, yet through the prophet Haggai, speaking at the dedication of this second temple, God gave a wonderful promise: '"I will fill this temple with glory," says the LORD of hosts... "The glory of this latter temple shall be greater than the former," says the LORD of hosts. "And in this place I will give peace," says the LORD of hosts' (Hag. 2:7,9). Something was going to occur in this temple that would have drastic and far-reaching effects.

After many years, at the time of our Lord's life on earth, this second temple was enlarged. King Herod financed the extensive alterations that took a total of eighty-three years (19 B.C. to A.D. 64). This temple was destroyed by the invading Romans in A.D. 70. The question then remains: 'Did the Lord fulfil his promise that the glory of the second temple would exceed the glory of the first?' To those who know the living God the question is not, 'Did he fulfil his promise…?' but rather, 'How did he fulfil his promise?'

The prophet Malachi also gave a prophecy about the second temple:

'Behold, I send my messenger,
And he will prepare the way before me.
And the Lord, whom you seek,
Will suddenly come to his temple,
Even the Messenger of the covenant,
In whom you delight.
Behold, he is coming,' says the LORD of hosts

(Mal. 3:1).

John the Baptist is that messenger preparing the way for the Messenger who is Christ (Mark 1:2,4). Jesus Christ is 'the Lord, whom you seek … even the Messenger of the covenant'. This is how the glory of the second temple exceeded the first because the incarnate Son of God, the very embodiment of the true tabernacle and true temple, personally visited this temple (Matt. 12:6).

There is a further prophecy concerning the temple which was given through Zechariah:

> Thus says the LORD of hosts, saying:
> 'Behold, the man whose name is the BRANCH!
> From his place he shall branch out,
> And he shall build the temple of the LORD;
> Yes, he shall build the temple of the LORD.
> He shall bear the glory,
> And shall sit and *rule on his throne*;
> So he shall be *a priest on his throne*,
> And the counsel of peace shall be between them both'
> (Zech. 6:12-13, emphasis added).

God promises that the man spoken of here as the Branch, the Messiah (cf. Isa. 4:2; Jer. 23:5-6), will build, not *a* temple *to* the Lord, but rather *the* temple *of* the Lord. Furthermore, the Messiah would himself be the glory of the new temple and he would rule in a dual capacity as king and priest. Such a double function, bearing the two offices of king and priest, was impossible under the terms of the Old Covenant since priests were to descend from Levi and kings were to descend from Judah. Consequently the Lord had prepared a priestly order *above that* of Aaron and Levi — the order of Melchizedek, the king-priest (Gen. 14:18-20; Heb. 7:1-10).[8] Messiah comes in this order of priesthood (Ps. 110:4). Christ rules the new temple, *the temple of God*, as King and Priest. He is king over his body the church (Eph. 1:22-23), ruling, controlling, guarding. He is priest for his church having presented the one supreme sacrifice for sin (Heb. 10:10), and since he ever lives to make intercession for us (Heb. 7:24-25).

'He who was predicted as the seed of the woman, as the seed of Abraham, the Son of David, the Branch, the Servant of the Lord, the Prince of Peace, is our Lord, Jesus Christ, the Son of God, God manifest in the flesh. He, therefore, from the beginning has been held up as the hope of the world, the *Salvator hominum*. He was set forth in all his offices, as Prophet, Priest, and King. His work was described as a sacrifice as well as a redemption.'[9]

Messiah will personally build the temple the Lord, the greater temple. That temple is currently under construction. It is the spiritual temple of which Christ is the foundation (1 Cor. 3:11,16); its cornerstone (Eph. 2:20);

its centre and heart (John 2:21). Believers are living stones who come to Christ to be 'built up as a spiritual house' (1 Peter 2:5) and with him and in him to form the true temple (1 Cor. 3:16; 6:19-20). The true temple, the spiritual temple, is Christ and his church.[10]

Application

1. Seeking God

'If my people who are called by my name will humble themselves, and pray and seek my face, and turn from their wicked ways, then I will hear from heaven, and will forgive their sin and heal their land. Now my eyes will be open and my ears attentive to prayer made in this place' (7:14-15).

Striking examples are given of those who 'set their heart to seek the LORD God of Israel' (11:16).

Following the division of the kingdom there was a migration of Levites from the northern kingdom of the ten tribes. These godly people remained true to the God of Israel and at great personal cost they moved to the southern kingdom of the two tribes (11:13-14,16). They were a people committed to a life of worship and service, loyal to the priesthood and the king, in spite of the fact that King Rehoboam was stubborn and foolish.

The second illustration of seeking God occurred in connection with a battle against the ten tribes of Israel (13:13-16). God responded to the prayers of the people in spite of the fact that King Abijam is described as one who 'walked in all the sins of his father [Rehoboam], which he had done before him; his heart was not loyal to the LORD his God, as was the heart of his father David' (1 Kings 15:3).

Some years later an invasion by an overwhelming force of Ethiopians was averted when King Asa 'cried out to the LORD his God' (14:11).

His son Jehoshaphat followed him to the throne and enjoyed the blessing of God upon his reign because he 'sought the God of his father, and walked in his commandments' (17:4; cf. 20:3-4).

Years later King Uzziah (called Azariah in 2 Kings 14:21; 15:1-7) 'sought God … and as long as he sought the LORD, God made him prosper' (26:5).

King Jotham became mighty, 'because he prepared his ways before the LORD his God' (27:6).

His grandson King Hezekiah 'did what was good and right and true before the LORD his God. And in every work that he began in the service of the house of God, in the law and in the commandment, to seek his God, he did it with all his heart. So he prospered' (31:20-21).

Where the monarch and/or the people seek God in worship and prayer, God always responds. The spiritual message of 2 Chronicles is the sovereignty of God and the power of prayer.

2. Repentance

Manasseh was twelve when he followed his godly father Hezekiah to the throne. But he did not share his father's faith in God. Manasseh 'did evil in the sight of the LORD' (33:2). He followed the practices of the heathen nations. He rebuilt the pagan places of worship that his father Hezekiah had destroyed. He built altars to the Baals, made wooden idols and worshipped the gods of the Assyrians. He went so far as to build two altars to the Assyrian gods — right in the temple of God. He sacrificed some of his sons as burnt offerings to the god Moloch in the Valley of the Son of Hinnom (known in New Testament times as 'Gehenna'). This vile practice of sacrificing children to Moloch was introduced into Judah by Manasseh's godless grandfather King Ahaz (28:3). Manasseh had a devastating influence upon the nation and brought Judah very low spiritually and morally. 'And the LORD spoke to Manasseh and his people, but they would not listen' (33:10). As a result of this disobedience and refusal to listen, the Lord brought severe punishment upon Manasseh through the hands of the Assyrians.

Then a wonderful change took place in the mind and heart of King Manasseh: 'Now when he was in affliction, he implored the LORD his God, and humbled himself greatly before the God of his fathers, and prayed to him; and he received his entreaty, heard his supplication, and brought him back to Jerusalem into his kingdom' (33:12-13).

That Manasseh had sincerely repented and truly turned to God there can be no doubt. On his return to Jerusalem, he 'took away the foreign gods and the idol from the house of the LORD, and all the altars that he had built in the mount of the house of the LORD and in Jerusalem; and he cast them out of the city. He also repaired the altar of the LORD, sacrificed peace offerings and thank offerings on it, and commanded Judah to serve the LORD God of Israel' (33:15-16). 'For godly sorrow produces repentance to salvation, not to be regretted; but the sorrow of the world produces death' (2 Cor. 7:10). 'Bear fruits worthy of repentance' (Matt. 3:8).

3. Genealogies

Maintaining accurate records of the line of descent was very important in the purposes of God in preparation for the coming of the Messiah. Godly Israelites looked for the fulfilment of the promise to David and awaited, from his descendants, 'the Coming One' (Matt. 11:3). Another reason for maintaining the genealogies was that responsibilities had been uniquely designated to certain tribes: ruling to Judah; priestly functions to Levi. The God-fearing were concerned to know their ancestry and that their names were recorded because to be part of Israel meant to be part of the people of the true and living God. This theme continues to have an important place in the New Testament church (1 Peter 2:9; Eph. 2:19).

The prophets make mention of a record that the Lord keeps of those who are his people:

At that time Michael shall stand up,
The great prince who stands watch over the sons of your people;
And there shall be a time of trouble,
Such as never was since there was a nation,
Even to that time.
And at that time your people shall be delivered,
Every one who is found written in the book

(Dan. 12:1).

Then those who feared the LORD spoke to one another,
And the LORD listened and heard them;
So a book of remembrance was written before him
For those who fear the LORD
And who meditate on his name

(Mal. 3:16).

The apostle Paul writes of those 'whose names are in the book of life' (Phil. 4:3). In Revelation frequent reference is made to names that appear in 'the book of life' (Rev. 3:5; 13:8; 17:8; 20:12,15; 21:27; 22:19). Here is a clear indication that 'The Lord knows who are his' and who will enjoy eternal life with him (2 Tim. 2:19).

Conclusion

While the number of bad kings is roughly twice the number of good kings, this may lead to the wrong conclusion that life in Israel during this period was dominated by wicked rulers. In fact the sum total of years under bad rulers is no greater than the total of years under good rulers. Even though the judgement of God is upon the nation there are still notable periods of spiritual awakening and revival of true religion. When the ceremonial law is breached the Lord responds favourably to fervent prayer for cleansing and pardon. When an exceedingly wicked king truly repents there is forgiveness and restoration: '... for the LORD your God is gracious and merciful, and will not turn his face from you if you return to him' (30:9). A teenager is able to govern a nation wisely because he sought the Lord with a tender heart.

But the overriding message of the Second Book of Chronicles to the returning exiles is clear: David's line, the temple and the priesthood have not been eradicated. The line of descent is unbroken, the temple can be rebuilt and the priesthood is still in existence. God is the God of the covenant!

The Israelites will return to the land of promise: 'Thus says Cyrus king of Persia: "All the kingdoms of the earth the LORD God of heaven has given me. And he has commanded me to build him a house at Jerusalem which is in Judah. Who is there among you of all his people? May the LORD his God be with him, and let him go up!"' (36:23).

Ezra

('help')

Author: Ezra
(probably)

Key thought: 'The Word of the Lord'

Theme: The place and power
of the Word of God in the religious,
social and civil life of his people

'Ezra had prepared his heart to
seek the Law of the LORD, and
to do it, and to teach statutes and
ordinances in Israel.'

Ezra 7:10

Summary

Ezra

The nation of Israel has been sacked. With the Israelites in exile in Assyria and the Jews (a contraction of 'Judahs') banished to Babylon, the land of Israel and Judah lies desolate, farmed by a handful of poor and powerless people. The Lord's promise to Abraham lies unfulfilled: 'And the LORD said to Abram, after Lot had separated from him: "Lift your eyes now and look from the place where you are — northward, southward, eastward, and westward; for all the land which you see *I give to you and your descendants for ever*"' (Gen. 13:14-15, emphasis added).

The duration of the exile, before a return to Judah would be made possible, is contained in a prophecy of Jeremiah to which the closing words of 2 Chronicles and the opening words of Ezra refer. In a letter, which the prophet sent to the captives in Babylon, it is stated: 'For thus says the LORD: After seventy years are completed at Babylon, I will visit you and perform my good word towards you, and cause you to return to this place. For I know the thoughts that I think towards you, says the LORD, thoughts of peace and not of evil, to give you a future and a hope. Then you will call upon me and go and pray to me, and I will listen to you. And you will seek me and find me, when you search for me with all your heart. I will be found by you, says the LORD, and I will bring you back from your captivity; I will gather you from all the nations and from all the places where I have driven you, says the LORD, and I will bring you to the place from which I cause you to be carried away captive' (Jer. 29:10-14).

The Lord makes promises: the Lord keeps all his promises!

Author

The books of Chronicles, Ezra and Nehemiah form a unit. They tell one story. The language of these books is similar. There are also various references, such as the names included in the genealogies of 1 Chronicles 3 and Nehemiah 12:10,11,22, which would seem to indicate that they were brought to completion around the same time, that is, roughly two hundred years after the return of the Jews to Jerusalem under Ezra (c. 457 B.C.). They may have been compiled from a number of original sources and produced by one writer, Ezra, Nehemiah, or an unknown editor. These sources might include historic records compiled by Ezra (Ezra 8:1-9:15) and Nehemiah (Neh. 1:1 – 7:5; 12:31-43; 13:1-31) and official decrees of Persian kings (2 Chr. 36:23; Ezra 1:1-4; 6:1-12; 7:11-26), all interspersed with information culled from earlier books of the Old Testament.[1]

It is likely that Ezra and Nehemiah originally formed one book. Ezra and Nehemiah acknowledge Jehovah as the God who always fulfils his prophecies, who always keeps his promises. Ezra views the return from exile from the ceremonial standpoint, Nehemiah from the civil. Ezra is the book of the rebuilding of the altar and the temple; Nehemiah is the book of the rebuilding of the walls of the city. With the dawning of the days of Ezra and Nehemiah the nation of Israel enters a bright new era. This is the time of restoration: returning from captivity and rebuilding the shattered nation.

Historical setting

The English Old Testament is divided into three sections: History (Genesis to Esther), Poetry (Job to Song of Solomon) and Prophecy (Isaiah to Malachi). The seventeen books from Genesis to Esther present a panoramic view of the history of Israel in preparation for the coming of the Messiah. Beginning with the history of creation, followed by events leading up to the great Flood and the gracious delivery of Noah and his family, attention gradually becomes focused upon one man, Abraham, and his descendants through Isaac and then Jacob (Israel). Abraham is traced from Ur to Haran, and on to Canaan; the story unfolds. Eventually moved from Canaan by famine, the seventy-strong family of Jacob settles in Egypt and prospers. 400 years pass and their numbers have increased to such an extent that the Egyptians believe they constitute a threat to their national security. The Israelites are forced into slavery. But God has not forgotten his covenant with Abraham. He wonderfully delivers his people.

Once out of Egypt and after repeated rebellions, obstinacy and disobedience, the Israelites are led into the promised land. At last the nation is established in its own country. Eventually, after many years, Israel becomes strong and secure under godly King David. During his son's reign, however, the united kingdom of Israel reaches its peak and then begins to plummet. The kingdom is split in two by civil war. The spiritual decline of the two nations, Israel and Judah, is manifested in repeated periods of immorality, idolatry and godlessness. 250 years after David's death the peoples of the northern kingdom of the ten tribes of Israel are taken into exile in Assyria. 136 years later the two tribes of Judah and Benjamin, the southern kingdom, are taken in captivity to Babylon. God has punished his people.

The books of Kings and Chronicles record the successes and failures of the divided kingdom of God's chosen people — Israel and Judah. They register their eventual fall and captivity by foreign powers in foreign lands, as a divine punishment for their spiritual rebellion and sin. While the books of Kings are written from the political point of view, Chronicles, Ezra and Nehemiah are written from the spiritual perspective.

The book of Ezra covers a period of just over eighty years from the decree of Cyrus (538 B.C.). As the people of Judah were taken captive in three successive groups (605, 597, 586 B.C.) so, coincidentally they return in three groups. The first company returns under the leadership of Zerubbabel (2:2; 538 B.C.) and, inspired by prophets Haggai and Zechariah,[2] they eventually rebuild the temple (520–516 B.C.). Sixty years later the second wave returns from Babylon under the leadership of Ezra the priest (458 B.C.). This is the period covered by the book of Ezra. Fourteen years later Nehemiah leads the third group[3] (444 B.C.) and the book bearing his name records the essential features. The book of Esther covers momentous events that took place in Babylon from 483 to 473 B.C., that is, between the first and second return.

Outline

There is a slight overlap forming a natural continuity between the end of 2 Chronicles (36:22-23) and the opening of the book of Ezra (1:1-3). The clear theme throughout the whole book is the place and power of the Word of God in the religious, social and civil life of his people. The key phrase is 'the Word of God' expressed in a variety of words. Scripture is referred to as 'the word of the Lord' (1:1); 'the Law of Moses the man of God' (3:2); 'the commandment of the God of Israel' (6:14); 'the Book of Moses' (6:18); 'the Law of your God which is in your hand' (7:14); 'the words of the God of Israel' (9:4); and 'the commandment of our God' (10:3).

The book of Ezra falls into two distinct sections: the first six chapters deal with the first return under Zerubbabel; the remaining four chapters record the second return eighty years later under Ezra.

Part I: Zerubbabel leads the first return of exiles (1:1 – 6:22)

Cyrus King of Persia conquered Babylon in 539 B.C. The prophecy of Isaiah is in the process of fulfilment:

Thus says the LORD, your Redeemer...
Who says of Cyrus, 'He is my shepherd,
And he shall perform all my pleasure,
Even saying to Jerusalem, "You shall be built,"
And to the temple, "Your foundation shall be laid."'
Thus says the LORD to his anointed,
To Cyrus, whose right hand I have held —
To subdue nations before him
And loose the armour of kings,
To open before him the double doors,
So that the gates will not be shut:
'I will go before you
And make the crooked places straight;
I will break in pieces the gates of bronze
And cut the bars of iron.
I will give you the treasures of darkness
And hidden riches of secret places,
That you may know that I, the LORD,
Who call you by your name,
Am the God of Israel.
For Jacob my servant's sake,
And Israel my elect,
I have even called you by your name;
I have named you, though you have not known me.
I am the LORD, and there is no other;
There is no God besides me.
I will gird you, though you have not known me...'

(Isa. 44:24,28; 45:1-5).

The prophet Daniel, who was exiled to Babylon as a teenager (and never returned to Israel), 'prospered ... in the reign of Cyrus the Persian' (Dan. 6:28; cf. 10:1). Daniel probably had an influence upon King Cyrus and the proclamation which he issued in the first year of his reign in Babylon. This decree encouraged the Israelites to return and rebuild the temple in Jerusalem (1:1-4). The people of Babylon gave gifts towards the rebuilding programme (1:6). King Cyrus also restored the treasures captured from the temple (1:7). Almost 50,000 Jews (49,897 to be exact) chose to return to the land of Israel (2:64-65). Many Jews chose to remain in Babylon. Those who stayed behind did not wish to leave their secure homes or influential positions, or to face the upheaval of moving the long distance from the one country to the other. According to archaeological discoveries some of the Jews who remained succeeded reasonably well in business.[4]

When the Hebrews returned to Israel they did not begin work with the reconstruction of the city walls, but thought first of the temple, the house of God. Even then they did not commence with the foundations and walls of the temple itself. They began with the rebuilding of the altar (3:2). Appropriately the first feast they celebrated together was the Feast of Tabernacles. This would be significant for them since it had been instituted hundreds of years earlier to remind the Israelites of their long journey from Egypt, through the wilderness, and into the promised land (Lev. 23:34-43). These exiles returning from Babylon had travelled over 700 miles across another difficult wilderness. They too wanted to express their gratitude to the Lord.

After a short while the Samaritans (people brought into Israel after the Assyrian captivity to repopulate the land of Canaan — 2 Kings 17:24) offered to work with the Jews in the construction of the temple. They had been introduced to a corrupted form of worship of the one true God. Their own words highlight the problem. They say, 'Let us build with you, for we seek your God as you do; and we have sacrificed to him since the days of Esarhaddon king of Assyria, who brought us here' (4:2). To be told that the Samaritans have continued to offer sacrifices to the Lord would not have pleased a godly Jew. Sacrifices not offered in Jerusalem were regarded as equivalent to sacrifices offered to idols! (Lev. 17:1-9). Their offer of help is flatly refused. Zerubbabel and his colleagues in leadership refer to the decree of King Cyrus of Persia that only Israelites are to rebuild the temple. Consequently the leaders of the new community are legally justified in rejecting the proposal of the colonists brought in by Esarhaddon. These people are neither members of the chosen people of God, nor Israelites, nor genuine worshippers of the true God. They are non-Israelites and, indeed, they describe themselves as those whom the King of Assyria had brought into the land.[5]

In consequence of this refusal to allow them to participate in the reconstruction of the temple, the Samaritans begin to hinder the building work. They try hard to discourage and dishearten the Israelites in their task. This opposition serves to confirm the rightness of the decision of the Hebrew leadership. Had the Samaritans been sincere in their desire to help in the construction of the temple they would hardly have turned nasty and hindered the work. The main procedure they adopt to make life difficult for the Israelites is to hire 'counsellors against them to frustrate their purpose' (4:5). They write to successive kings of Persia accusing the Jews of insurrection. The opposition successfully frustrates the temple reconstruction. Following the laying of the foundation, work is hindered for fourteen years.[6]

While the historian is recounting the opposition to the rebuilding of the temple, he skips from the days of Cyrus and Darius to show how opposition continued against the rebuilding of the city for another sixty years into the reigns of Ahasuerus (Xerxes) and Artaxerxes I (4:6-23).

The fifth chapter of Ezra returns to the events that occurred during the reign of Darius the Great of Persia. It is at this point that the prophets Haggai and Zechariah encourage progress on the building project (5:1-2). The temple is completed and full worship is restored.

Part II: Ezra leads the second return of exiles (7:1 - 10:44)

Whereas about 50,000 Jews returned under the leadership of Zerubbabel, only about 2,000 returned eighty years later under the leadership of Ezra. Ezra was the great-grandson of Hilkiah (7:1), high priest in the reign of godly Josiah (640–609 B.C.). Hilkiah was the priest who found the copy of 'the Book of the Law of the LORD given by Moses' (2 Chr. 34:14). Though Ezra was by birth a priest, he was not able to function as a priest because he was in captivity in Babylon. Instead he spent a considerable amount of time studying Scripture: '… this Ezra came up from Babylon; and he was a skilled scribe in the Law of Moses, which the LORD God of Israel had given' (7:6). 'For Ezra had prepared his heart to seek the Law of the LORD, and to do it, and to teach statutes and ordinances in Israel' (7:10).

On reading 2 Chronicles, Ezra and Nehemiah it is evident that the people of Israel in general had little knowledge of the Scriptures that God had inspired. It was mainly through Ezra's ministry that the Word of God gained its rightful position for the first time in the history of Israel and Judah.

Ezra was a willing and eager Bible student. God's law was burning in his own heart and lived out in his own life before he taught it to others. This enabled him to speak with the intensity of real conviction.[7] The quality and consistency of Ezra's godly life were noted by King Artaxerxes of Persia, who gave him a letter authorizing all the people of Israel who were willing to go with him to Jerusalem (7:12-13). The letter also commanded that he should be supplied with all that was necessary for the building of the house of God (7:20). Although still under the rule of Persia, Ezra was granted power to appoint magistrates and judges to rule the people in Israel. He was also instructed to teach the people the law of God (7:25).

Only about 2,000 Jews gathered at the River Ahava, and there, with fasting and prayer, they committed their way to the Lord, no doubt remembering God's remarkable delivery of the Israelites under Queen Esther, which had occurred in the eighty-year interval between the first wave of returning exiles under Zerubbabel and this second wave. Ezra 'was ashamed' to ask for a guard of soldiers as it might reflect upon the Lord's power to deliver. Ezra attributes all his success, the kindness and benevolence of the king, the willingness of the people and safety in travelling to the good hand of his God upon him (8:22).

Arrival in Jerusalem

When Ezra arrived in Israel he found the situation to be even worse than he had expected. Since the days of Zerubbabel, the Jews in Jerusalem had once more backslidden in their devotion to the one true God. Some of the descendants of those who had returned eighty years earlier had blatantly disregarded the law of God with respect to intermarriage with non-Israelites. Ezra's response shows a characteristic depth of spiritual sensitivity: 'So when I heard this thing, I tore my garment and my robe, and plucked out some of the hair of my head and beard, and sat down appalled. Then everyone who trembled at the words of the God of Israel assembled to me, because of the transgression of those who had been carried away captive, and I sat appalled until the evening sacrifice. At the evening sacrifice I arose from my fasting; and having torn my garment and my robe, I fell on my knees and spread out my hands to the LORD my God, and said, "O my God; I am too ashamed and humiliated to lift up my face to you, my God; for our iniquities have risen higher than our heads, and our guilt has grown up to the heavens' (9:3-6).

The revival of true religion

'And now for a little while grace has been shown from the LORD our God, to leave us a remnant to escape, and to give us a nail in his holy place, that our God may enlighten our eyes and give us a measure of revival in our bondage...' (9:8).

The revival under Ezra takes the form of a revival of Bible study and obedience to the revealed will of God (cf. Neh. 8). The Word of the Lord, read and expounded by Ezra the priest, has a profound effect upon the people. Before the Babylonian exile God had spoken through Isaiah saying:

Seek the LORD while he may be found,
Call upon him while he is near.
Let the wicked forsake his way,
And the unrighteous man his thoughts;
Let him return to the LORD,
And he will have mercy on him;
And to our God,
For he will abundantly pardon

(Isa. 55:6-7).

In returning to the Lord with all their hearts the Israelites take steps to turn also from their disobedient lifestyle. The law of Moses has been transgressed in that many Israelites have intermarried with Gentile women. All the people of Judah are gathered together and a resolution is made to separate all foreign wives from their community. For three months Ezra and the appointed magistrates hear and resolve individual cases. 113 cases of mixed marriage are identified and a strict separation enacted.

Christ and his church

But for the grace of God there would have been no restoration of Israel. Not one of the tribes of Israel deserved such kind and benevolent treatment at the hands of the Lord:

If we are faithless,
    he remains faithful;
    he cannot deny himself

(2 Tim. 2:13).

The restoration of a remnant of Israel to their land was vitally important in the purposes of God. So many promises and prophecies were associated with the land of Judah — promises to Abraham, Isaac and Jacob and prophecies through Isaiah, Micah and Jeremiah — that restoration to the promised land was essential. Nevertheless there is the greater goal always in the background. The return from exile in Babylon and the re-establishment of the Jews in their own land paved the way for the coming of the promised Messiah, the Christ of God. God's Son was to be 'born of the seed of David according to the flesh' (Rom. 1:3; cf. 2 Sam. 7:12-13). Yet it was not sufficient for him to have the right ancestry. He must also be born in the right place. God had specified that place. 200 years earlier the Lord had promised through the prophet Micah:

But you, Bethlehem Ephrathah,
Though you are little among the thousands of Judah,
Yet out of you shall come forth to me
The one to be ruler in Israel,
Whose goings forth have been from of old,
From everlasting

(Micah 5:2).

The Son of God was to be born in Bethlehem, not Babylon, in the holy land of promise, not in the land of captivity. A remnant of the Jews was to return to the promised land.

Bethlehem, Nazareth and Jerusalem were some of the geographic locations woven into the promises concerning our Lord's advent. In just over 400 years after the days of Ezra, 'when the fulness of the time had come', God would send 'forth his Son, born of a woman' (Gal. 4:4). It is to the Israelites that 'pertain the adoption, the glory, the covenants, the giving of the law, the service of God, and the promises; of whom are the fathers and from whom, according to the flesh, Christ came, who is over all, the eternally blessed God' (Rom. 9:4-5).

Application

1. Right priorities

It is interesting to note the order of priority when the Hebrews returned to Israel. They did not begin with the rebuilding of the city walls. Even before they thought of building homes for themselves, the returning Jews thought first of the temple, the house of God. Nor did they commence with the foundations and walls of the temple itself. They began with the rebuilding of the altar (3:2). This is a beautiful illustration of the timeless truth that atoning work must come first and be at the heart of all of our life's concerns — in the church, in the home, and in society at large. 'Jesus Christ and him crucified' (1 Cor. 2:2) is to be the centre of concern, and the controlling principle, in all areas of life.

2. True repentance

When the Holy Spirit illuminates the Word of God wonderful results follow, one of which is genuine heartfelt repentance. So Israel responded to the teaching of Scripture, for '… a very large congregation of men, women, and children assembled to [Ezra] from Israel; for the people wept very bitterly' (10:1). There is, however, 'a sorrow of the world' and a 'godly sorrow' (2 Cor. 7:10). The first kind of grief is pain experienced through remorse or regret at the resulting consequences. This does not lead to repentance or to salvation. The second kind of grief brings a sinner to God in confession of sin and seeking forgiveness and mercy.

A further mark of 'godly sorrow [which] produces repentance to salvation, not to be regretted' is a turning away from sin, or a desperate cry to God for the grace and strength to turn away from sin (Isa. 55:7; Heb. 4:16; Gal. 5:16). Christians are motivated and empowered by the love of Christ (2 Cor. 5:14-15) to produce 'fruits worthy of repentance' (Matt. 3:8), and 'to lead a life worthy of the calling with which [they] were called' (Eph. 4:1).

3. Separation

There is a thread of separation in the book of Ezra: first, separation from Babylon (1:1-3); secondly, separation from worldly help in building the house of God (4:1-3); thirdly, separation from dependence upon human protection (8:21-23); and, fourthly, separation from sinful partnerships (10:11-12).

Drawing from the prophecies of Isaiah 52:11 and 2 Samuel 7:14, the apostle Paul pleads for spiritual separation when he urges Christians not to be 'unequally yoked together with unbelievers' (2 Cor. 6:14) with these words:

> 'Come out from among them
> And be separate,' says the Lord.
> 'Do not touch what is unclean,
> And I will receive you.'
> 'I will be a Father to you,
> And you shall be my sons and daughters,'
> Says the LORD Almighty
>
> (2 Cor. 6:17-18).

Zerubbabel and the Jewish leadership rightly refused the Samaritans' offer of help in rebuilding the temple. Though the Samaritans claimed to worship the true God (4:2), they actually practised a corrupted form of Jehovah-worship. They followed the practices of the early immigrants to Samaria who 'feared the LORD, yet served their own gods — according to the rituals of the nations from among whom they were carried away' (2 Kings 17:33). Zerubbabel knew that the worship of God had become corrupt and degraded.

A clear distinction is to be made between those who worship the true God and those who do not. It is inappropriate for non-Christians to be confused with genuine members of the church of Jesus Christ or to work on behalf of the church.

Conclusion

The book of Ezra reveals the power and grace of God in protecting his people, leading his people, teaching his people and restoring his people.

Central throughout is the importance of the revealed Word of God. Ezra himself is shown to be a man of the Word, a man of faith, a man of prayer and a man of courage. He loved the Word of God, believed in its message, taught its truths, lived by its principles and, by proclaiming it, he influenced the lives of the restored children of captivity. Such men of the Word are needed in every generation and in every nation.

The church of Jesus Christ is only spiritually strong when Christians read, study, teach and obey the Scriptures.

Nehemiah

('whom Jehovah comforts')

Author: Nehemiah
(probably)

Key thought: 'Prayer and hard work'

Theme: Building the kingdom of God
by prayer, hard work and perseverance

'Nevertheless we made our prayer
to our God, and … set a watch
… day and night…
So we laboured in the work.'
Nehemiah 4:9,21

Summary

Nehemiah

When Ezra the priest arrived in Judah he found the morale of the community in Judah very low. Disappointment had led to disillusionment, and disillusionment to religious and moral laxity. This is evident from the words of the prophet Malachi (a contemporary of Nehemiah) and those of Nehemiah. Priests, bored with their duties, offered sick and injured animals to the Lord (Mal. 1:6-14). They earned the derision and disgust of the people by showing partiality in the administration of justice (Mal. 2:7-9). God's law concerning the Sabbath was ignored: it was just another day for business and trade (Neh. 13:15-18). The non-payment of tithes forced Levites to neglect their duties in order to earn a living (Mal. 3:7-10; Neh. 13:10-13). The high incidence of divorce was a public scandal (Mal. 2:13-16). The people were spiritually totally disheartened and lost confidence in their religious leaders (Mal. 2:17; 3:13-15). There was a prevalence of witchcraft, adultery, bearing false witness and exploitation of workers and the underprivileged (Mal. 3:5). The poor, having mortgaged their fields in time of drought, or to pay taxes, found themselves and their children reduced to slavery (Neh. 5:1-5). Intermarriage with heathens was common (Mal. 2:11). As the children of those mixed marriages became more numerous there were serious implications for the future of the nation (Neh. 13:23-27).

With no sense of direction and a distinct lack of morale, there was a real danger that the Jewish community in Judah would disintegrate. Drastic measures were needed. Thoroughgoing reform of the nation's life — spiritual, social and civil — was desperately needed.

In the providence of God, two men implemented the reforms that would save the nation and provide the necessary stability for the remaining four centuries until the coming of the Messiah. These men, Ezra and Nehemiah, were to have a profound effect upon the nation. Ezra reorganized and reformed the nation's spiritual life. Nehemiah reconstituted its civil government.

Author

Since the books of Ezra and Nehemiah display similarities in style and perspective, and because they were originally one book in the Hebrew Bible, they may have been produced by one writer. Ezra, Nehemiah or an unknown editor may have drawn together a number of original sources including historic records compiled by Ezra (Ezra 7:27 – 9:15), and by Nehemiah (Neh. 1:1-7:5; 12:31-43; 13:1-31), with official decrees of Persian kings (2 Chr. 36:23; Ezra 1:1-4; 6:1-12; 7:11-26), all interspersed with information culled from earlier books of the Old Testament.[1]

Historical setting

In 550 B.C. Cyrus became King of Persia. Eleven years later he conquered Babylon. In the first year as ruler of Babylon Cyrus issued a proclamation encouraging the Jews to return to Judah and rebuild the temple of the Lord in Jerusalem. Consequently, in 538 B.C. 50,000 Jews returned to the land of Israel (Ezra 2:64-65) under the leadership of Zerubbabel (Ezra 2:2). Eventually, after considerable opposition from the Samaritans and great encouragement from the prophets Haggai and Zechariah,[2] the temple was completed and dedicated in 516 B.C. All seemed set fair for a period of stability and growth.

Little is known about the next period in Jewish history. The early enthusiasm evidently began to wane: the mass of Jews dispersed throughout the Persian Empire lost interest in the restoration programme in Israel and settled down, content to remain where they were. The future of the Jewish community in Judah became uncertain and discouraging. Babylon remained the centre of Jewish life for centuries. A number of the Israelite exiles and their descendants prospered. Some of them, like Nehemiah, rose to high positions in Persian government.

Thirteen years after the second return of exiles under the leadership of Ezra, Nehemiah hears news of the sad state of affairs in Jerusalem and is troubled. He turns from the comfort, luxury and status of Persia to join the suffering people of God in Jerusalem.

Outline

The book of Nehemiah is mostly autobiographical. Nehemiah's recorded activity takes place during the reign of King Artaxerxes I of Persia, from the twentieth year until some time after the thirty-second year of his reign (2:1; 13:6) — that is, from 445 B.C. and beyond 433 B.C. The prophet Malachi was also in Jerusalem, actively engaged in the work to which God had appointed him, during this period.[3]

This book contains a striking description of a man who works for God. As Ezra is an example of a minister of the Word, diligent to present himself 'approved to God, a worker who does not need to be ashamed, rightly dividing the word of truth' (2 Tim. 2:15), so Nehemiah is a worker for God combining hard work with the essential ingredient of regular and persistent prayer.

Part I: Nehemiah becomes Governor of Judah (1:1 - 2:10)

Nehemiah was born into the community of Jewish exiles living in Babylon. He rose to the high position of cupbearer to Artaxerxes I, the great king of the vast Persian Empire. While serving the king in Shushan the capital, Nehemiah receives news from Hanani, one of his brothers, that the city of Jerusalem is in a sad condition and the people of Judah are generally distressed and disheartened (1:1-3). Nehemiah prays. He prays persistently and earnestly.[4] He is a godly man. He is a righteous man. He is a man who fears God, obeys the law of God and is deeply concerned for the honour and glory of God. He is also a man of prayer. He prays privately; he prays among fellow believers. That is suggested by his words: 'O Lord, I pray, please let your ear be attentive to the prayer of your servant, and to the prayer of your servants who desire to fear your name' (1:11).

After four months of prayer an opportunity arises, by the providence of God, for Nehemiah to share his concern with the king. With remarkable courage Nehemiah responds to the king's enquiry and clearly presents his requests to travel to Judah to rebuild Jerusalem. King Artaxerxes, indicating something of the esteem in which Nehemiah is held, grants him everything he requires and provides him with a substantial army escort. Nehemiah knows, however, that the provision of the king is due to a higher authority. The man of God records that 'The king granted them to me according to the good hand of my God upon me' (2:8).

Part II: Rebuilding the walls of Jerusalem (2:11 – 6:19)

Once in Jerusalem Nehemiah rests for three days, no doubt recovering from the long and arduous journey. He then slips out alone by night to make a personal assessment of the damage to the city wall and its gates (2:12-16). Both Ezra and Nehemiah bring distinctive godliness to Jerusalem. They are each men of great faith, persistent prayer and ready obedience. Whereas Ezra also brings years of learning in the Scriptures, skill in exposition and application of the Word of God, Nehemiah brings keen organizational and administrative skills.[5] Moving around the city walls he would have been formulating his strategy for the rebuilding programme.

Having made his assessment and decided upon a strategy, his next task is to inform the civic leaders and enthuse them for the work. He credits the Lord's goodness as the driving force behind the whole proceedings (2:18). Once informed, men with a variety of skills come forward and receive their assignments (3:1-32). But there is no lack of opposition.

External opposition

Jerusalem comes under the jurisdiction of Sanballat and Tobiah, Gentiles living over in Samaria. They are not at all pleased with the arrival of Nehemiah. Indeed, '… they were deeply disturbed that a man had come to seek the well-being of the children of Israel' (2:10). When plans for rebuilding the city wall leak out to Sanballat and his colleagues they respond with mockery and derision (2:19). They charge the Jews with planning insurrection. They would not be slow to get that message relayed back to the Persian royal palace. Nehemiah, however, has the full approval and cooperation of King Artaxerxes so he has nothing to fear from that quarter.

Governor Sanballat's displeasure only increases as the rebuilding work commences. He 'was furious and very indignant, and mocked the Jews' (4:1). As the work proceeds Sanballat's hostility intensifies. He and Tobiah conspire with the Arabs, the Ammonites and the Ashdodites to make a secret attack against Jerusalem and generally to cause as much confusion as possible among the Israelites (4:8). Nehemiah's response is classic: 'Nevertheless we made our prayer to our God, and because of them we set a watch against them day and night' (4:9). Seeing that the Israelites are not deterred, their enemies begin to stir up fear. They instigate rumours among the Jews that their enemies are all around them, that they will all be destroyed, that they will not even see their attackers. Nehemiah counters these rumours by reminding the people of the protection of their 'great and awesome' God (4:14). He urges them to fight in God's name and in the defence of their people, their families and their homes. They continue building: 'With one hand they worked at construction, and with the other held a weapon' (4:17).

The rebuilding of the wall of the city of Jerusalem is completed in just fifty-two days (6:15). This remarkable achievement comes about because the men work hard and for long periods. Nehemiah is himself fully occupied in the rebuilding programme. He and his co-workers sleep in their work clothes and only remove them for washing (4:23).

Once the walls are rebuilt Sanballat resorts to a more subtle approach in his opposition. He and his allies send an official invitation to Nehemiah to join them for discussions. The subject for debate is the purpose behind the rebuilding of the city walls of Jerusalem. Nehemiah knows that they intend to remove him from the scene by any means they can (6:2). He therefore refuses to accept the invitation though it is made to him on five different occasions.

Part III: Organization, worship and appointments (7:1 – 12:47)

When the wall is built Nehemiah is aware that the nations around are 'very disheartened in their own eyes', since they recognize 'that this work was done by our God' (6:16). He spends a considerable period of time, maybe as long as twelve years, organizing the small nation of Judah, and the affairs of the city of Jerusalem, in preparation for his return to the Persian capital.

One of the highlights of this period is the holding of a great assembly or conference. Nehemiah and Ezra call all the Israelites together: men, women and children old enough to understand what is being said and done (8:1,3). Ezra and the trained Levites teach the people the Word of God. The Scriptures are read, translated for the benefit of those who do not know Hebrew and explained (8:8). The people worship God and celebrate the Feast of Tabernacles. There is mourning over sin (9:1-3), rejoicing in God's mercy and kindness (9:5-38) and a sense of deep spiritual exercise among the people. They seal their devotion to God with a solemn covenant (10:28-39).

A public register is set up to record the number of people living within the city walls, the number living outside and the number who are priests and Levities. Then, following the dedication of the walls of Jerusalem and the appointment of Levites to certain temple duties, Nehemiah leaves for Babylon.

Part IV: Another reformation needed (13:1-31)

After a period of absence at the Persian court Nehemiah returns to Jerusalem and finds that another reformation is needed. Eliashib the high priest has given up a large room in the forecourt of the temple (13:5,7) to Tobiah the Ammonite (cf. 2:10), probably for use as a private dwelling when he was in the city. This man was a good friend of Sanballat and neither of them had shown themselves friendly towards Israel. Nehemiah roundly condemns this worldly alliance between Eliashib and Tobiah. He throws out all Tobiah's furniture, reconsecrates the rooms and restores them to their divinely appointed use (13:8-9). Nehemiah also tackles the age-old problem of mixed marriages. The issue was not racial or cultural, but religious. Israelites must not marry Gentiles unless they become Israelites. The people of God must not marry pagans and unbelievers. The ungodly, through marriage, will lead the people of God into idolatry and sin. The example of King Solomon is cited to show how even that one who was 'beloved of his God' fell into sin through the influence of his ungodly wives (13:26). The reformation is strictly enforced with solemn warnings.

Christ and his church

By this time in the history of Israel a great many wonderful prophecies had been given concerning the promised Messiah. The full revelation of God's purposes in sending his Son into the world was almost complete; only the prophecies of Malachi remained to be disclosed. Hindering the return of exiles from Babylon was the devil's vital strategy in seeking to thwart the promises of God. Once the Jews were settled back in Israel, then the devil concentrated on instigating all manner of hindrances and obstacles to the rebuilding work. If the city walls remained in ruins then the Israelites would be vulnerable to their many enemies. The reconstruction work undertaken under the leadership of Nehemiah, both in buildings and civil government, and the spiritual reformation undertaken by Ezra form a partnership essential to the restoration of the nation of Israel.

The settlement of the Hebrews in their own land was of paramount importance to the covenant promises of God. What Nehemiah achieved with God's enabling served a vital role in the unfolding and eventual fulfilling of God's purpose for Christ and his church.

Application

1. Personal sacrifice

Nehemiah was not simply a court butler responsible for serving wine; he was evidently one of the most trusted men in the kingdom. The cupbearer to the king was responsible to taste the wine in the king's chalice just before the king drank from it, to establish that the wine was not poisoned; as was often the case such a trusted position also meant that the cupbearer acted in an advisory capacity to the king. That Nehemiah held such a privileged and respected role is evident in the king's appointment of him as Governor of Judah. Nehemiah must also have had considerable administrative skills.

The spiritual stature of Nehemiah is blatantly obvious: he is deeply distressed on hearing news of the sad situation in faraway Jerusalem; he prays hard and long for wisdom and guidance to know how he should personally respond; he willingly leaves the comfort, position and prestige of the Persian court to travel nearly 1,000 miles over rough terrain to the ruins of a once famous city — for the honour and glory of God. Nehemiah is a fine example of a man who puts God first, whose career is subservient to the needs of the kingdom of God, who willingly leaves everything when the Lord requires it.

2. Fasting and prayer

Nehemiah shows where a believer begins a significant work for God — in fasting and persistent prayer (1:4; cf. Acts 13:3; 14:23). This is also the way to deal with any major crisis or problem (Dan. 9:3-19). Fasting is an important part of a Christian's devotional life (Matt. 9:14-15; 1 Cor. 7:5). It is a secret activity intimately related to prayer (Matt. 6:16-18). As far as possible no one should know. Upon our knees we cry, 'Lord, what do you want me to do?' (Acts 9:6).

A further lesson from the prayers of Nehemiah is the way in which he addresses God, reminding him of his covenant, his character and his promises (1:5,8-10). The appeal to God is based upon all that God has revealed about himself and his purposes and will: 'Now this is the confidence that we have in him, that if we ask anything according to his will, he hears us' (1 John 5:14).

3. Strategy for the church

Nehemiah's night inspection of the city walls illustrates the place of strategy and planning in the Lord's work (2:12-16). God had put the thought in his mind, but it was his job to work out the best way of achieving the goal. All our natural talents, innate skills, learned techniques and spiritual maturity and insights are to be brought into the service of God, from whom they came. 'Every good gift and every perfect gift is from above, and comes down from the Father' (James 1:17). To present the whole of ourselves — body, mind, spirit, with all our accumulated knowledge, education and wisdom — 'a living sacrifice, holy, acceptable to God', this is our 'reasonable service' (Rom. 12:1).

Nehemiah's second step was to inspire the leadership to work hard in God's service (2:17-18). Years later in the New Testament period Joses earned the nickname 'Barnabas', meaning, 'Son of encouragement' (Acts 4:36). He had the skill of stimulating others in their work for the Lord (Acts 11:22-24).

The third part of Nehemiah's strategy was to utilize and arrange the skills and expertise of a whole variety of people (3:1-32). In this there is an illustration of the truth that all believers have a contribution to make to the well-being and progress of the church of Christ (1 Cor. 12:12-27). The task of church leaders is 'the equipping of the saints for the work of ministry, for the edifying of the body of Christ' (Eph. 4:12). This includes instructing, organizing, facilitating and inspiring members of the local church, so that the work of God is strengthened and developed.

Conclusion

Nehemiah was a remarkable man of God. With great sacrifice he devoted himself to the work of God. He exercised strategy in planning for the people of Israel. He inspired others to work for the cause of God. He used his God-given talents for the service of the Lord and the Lord's people. He was a man of deep faith, ardent prayer and willing obedience. He is a fitting example for any Christian in combining the essential ingredients of godliness, hard work and prayer for the building up of the church of God.

Nehemiah brings a fitting conclusion to Old Testament history. Everything that appears in the Bible after this book has been collated under poetry or prophecy. With the exception of Malachi, who was a contemporary of Nehemiah, all the other books precede Nehemiah in terms of chronology. Throughout three and a half millennia an amazing number of wonderful prophecies have been given to Israel: 'God … at various times and in different ways spoke in time past to the fathers by the prophets' (Heb. 1:1). The book of Nehemiah closes that Old Testament history. The Lord had determined to leave the nation with a sense of hope and expectancy. Israel, reduced to a remnant composed mainly of those of the tribe of Judah, is restored to its own land to await the Messiah. Now they are known more as Jews than Israelites.

400 years are to pass in prophetic silence until the coming of the forerunner of the Lord Jesus Christ. The silence will be broken by the messenger heralding the coming of 'the Messenger of the covenant' (Mal. 3:1). John the Baptist will break the silence by bursting upon the scene of history as 'the voice of one crying in the wilderness: "Prepare the way of the LORD"' (Isa. 40:3; cf. Mark 1:2-3).

Esther

('star')

Author: Unknown
(maybe Mordecai — see 9:20)

Key thought: 'For such a time as this'

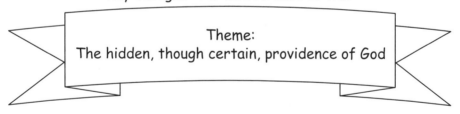

Theme:
The hidden, though certain, providence of God

'Yet who knows whether you have
come to the kingdom for such a
time as this?'

Esther 4:14

Summary

(Between chapters 1 and 2 King Ahasuerus leads five million soldiers in a historic attack on Greece. At the battle of Thermopylae the Medes and Persians suffer a severe defeat.)

Esther

Throughout history God has raised up a series of heathen kingdoms to punish his people for their rebellion and sin. Five great empires afflicted Israel during the Old Testament period and right into the era of the New. The first great empire was Assyria, with its capital at Nineveh on the River Tigris. This was ultimately overthrown by Babylon, whose capital of that name was on the River Euphrates. Then came Cyrus from Persia (present-day Iran). He conquered the Medes, establishing the kingdom of the Medes and Persians, and then he extended his vast kingdom by defeating Nebuchadnezzar of Babylon. The Greeks built the next great empire under Alexander the Great and finally, bringing us into New Testament times, the Roman Empire emerged as the world power.

The book of Esther speaks of God's faithful dealings with his people Israel during the era of the great Babylonian Empire.

Author

The author of the book of Esther is unknown, although there may be a hint that Mordecai was the historian (9:20). He was, after all, not only an eyewitness of the events that took place, but also played the principal role in them. If it was not written by Mordecai, then the author no doubt used Mordecai's records and may also have had access to the chronicles of the kings of Media and Persia (2:23; 10:2). Augustine credited Ezra with being the journalist. Yet, as we have repeatedly noted, the human author is not important to Bible-believing people. The book's divine authorship is certain.

Does the book of Esther qualify to be included in the divinely inspired Scriptures? There has not always been agreement among Jews or Christians as to whether Esther should be included in the Old Testament canon. Luther is reputed to have disliked the book and wished that it did not exist![1] There are also those of our own day who question the right of this little book to be included in the canon of Scripture. The arguments against its inclusion in Scripture are based upon its lack of spiritual content: firstly, the name of God does not appear in its pages, while a heathen king is referred to 187 times; secondly, there is no mention of prayer, no reference to the law of Moses, nor to any kind of service for God, with the possible exception of fasting; thirdly, the only reference to the supernatural is in the superstitious habit of heathens in observing lucky days (3:7); fourthly, it is never quoted in the New Testament; and, fifthly, the Feast of Purim has no connection with New Testament doctrine.

While these are strong arguments against the canonicity of the book of Esther, a simple explanation counters all the objections: the book was written for Jews living in an alien social environment. The book of Revelation was written in a similar context of persecution; hence its use of symbolism and dramatic word-pictures which only Christians would be able to interpret and understand.

In the first place, the book was written in Persia and could not be overtly God-honouring. Any use of a Persian name for God would have greatly dishonoured the Lord.

Secondly, the name of God (YHWH) does appear in acrostic form four times in the Hebrew text (1:20: 5:4,13; 7:7). The initial letters of four consecutive words in the Hebrew form the name YHWH in four different verses.

Thirdly, the absence of God's name serves the purpose of illustrating the hidden but providential care of God in spite of outward appearances (Deut. 31:18; cf. v. 8). Finally, the omission of God's name and of any direct spiritual references may be a mark of God's disapproval upon those Jews who preferred the comfort of Persia and were unwilling to emigrate and rebuild the temple and the nation in Judah.[2]

The Jews assign to this piece of ancient history a place second only to the five books of Moses. They also annually observe the Feast of Purim according to the instruction of Mordecai.

The book of Esther makes a unique contribution in highlighting the power of God to preserve his people and fulfil his covenant promises.

The crisis in Babylon recorded in the book of Esther had implications not only for the future of the Jews in Babylon itself, but throughout the whole Persian Empire, including Judah. The success of the enemies of God's people would have led to the extermination of the Jews from the face of the earth.

But God's Word will be fulfilled. His Son will come to earth 'born of a woman' (Gal. 4:4). The covenants with Abraham and David will be honoured. The prophecy of Micah will be fulfilled and Messiah will be born in Bethlehem Ephrathah (Micah 5:2). The book of Esther holds a worthy place in the Scriptures 'given by inspiration of God' (2 Tim. 3:16).

Historical setting

The greatest days of the Israelite nation were undoubtedly those enjoyed under the reign of King David. When his son Solomon became king there was an initial period of tranquillity, but although Solomon had outstanding and unmatched wisdom he was not able to curb his sinful tendencies and excesses. The king's weaknesses and sins contributed to the decline that was to result eventually in the division of the kingdom. Ten tribes formed the nation bearing the name 'Israel', while two tribes formed the nation bearing the name 'Judah'. Although the ten tribes had the name 'Israel', it was the two tribes who maintained much more of the spiritual calibre of the true Israel. Repeated sin and godlessness resulted in the Assyrians' attacking Israel and eventually taking the people of the northern kingdom into exile. The two tribes of Judah and Benjamin, based at Jerusalem, lasted longer as a nation. It was almost 350 years after the death of Solomon that these remaining members of the tribes of Israel were removed into exile: in 586 B.C. Nebuchadnezzar of Babylon took them into exile 700 miles from home. Seventy years were to pass in exile in the land of Babylon before the Lord would begin the process of restoring them to the promised land and of rebuilding the nation.

Ezra, Nehemiah and Esther fit into the latter days of the Babylonian exile. The first return from Babylonian exile took place in 538 B.C. under the leadership of Zerubbabel (Ezra 2:2) and the second took place eighty years later under the leadership of Ezra (Ezra 7:1-8). Fourteen years later still Nehemiah was to leave the Babylonian court to join Ezra in Jerusalem (Neh. 2:1,11).

The book of Esther belongs within the eighty-year period between the first and second return of exiles to Jerusalem (538–458 B.C.). This is the period between the first six chapters of the book of Ezra and the remaining four chapters. It provides the only biblical account of the events faced by the vast majority of Jews who had chosen to remain in Persia rather than to return to Israel from exile. It is possible to fix precisely the dates covered by the book of Esther by the name of the king. Ahasuerus is the Hebrew name, and Xerxes the Greek name, of King Khshayarsh of Persia (486–464 B.C.). The feast of Ahasuerus took place in the third year of his reign

4 B.C.). The feast of Ahasuerus took place in the third year of his reign
(1:3) hence the year 483 B.C. The historian Herodotus refers to this banquet as the occasion when Ahasuerus planned his war with Greece. Three
years later (480 B.C.) he was defeated by the Greeks at Salamis, and
Herodotus records that Ahasuerus sought consolation in his harem. This
corresponds to the time when young women were brought before him
and Esther was chosen and crowned queen of Persia (2:16-17). Since the
events of the rest of the book occurred in 473 B.C. (3:7-12), the time span
is a ten-year period from 483–473 B.C.[3]

Outline

Three feasts dominate the book of Esther: the feast of Ahasuerus (1:1 –
2:23), Esther's banquet (3:1 – 7:10) and the Feast of Purim (8:1 – 10:3).

1. The feast of Ahasuerus and its sequel (1:1 – 2:23)

King Ahasuerus reigned over the vast empire of the Medes and Persians
from 486 to 464 B.C. His kingdom included the land of Babylon; in fact he
'reigned from India to Ethiopia, over one hundred and twenty-seven
provinces' (1:1). He was the son of Darius, who is mentioned in the books
of Ezra and Daniel, and the grandson, on his mother's side, of King Cyrus
who issued the decree for the return of the Jews to Jerusalem to rebuild the
temple (2 Chr. 36:22-23; Ezra 1:1-4; Isa. 45:1).

In the third year of his reign Ahasuerus gives a banquet for the princes,
governors and civil servants who rule over his 127 provinces (1:3). After six
months of uninterrupted feasting with the nobility, he invites all the citizens
of his capital to join him in festivities lasting seven days (1:5). On the last
day he commands his queen, Queen Vashti, to attend the final night, but
she adamantly refuses to parade herself before her husband's male guests.
King Ahasuerus is furious and on the advice of counsellors he divorces and
dethrones Queen Vashti.

The most beautiful women in the empire are brought to the capital so
that the king might choose a new wife at his pleasure. Among these virgins
is a young Jewess named Hadassah, known by her Persian name 'Esther'.
Born a Jewish exile in the land of Persia, and having lost her parents when

very young, she had been adopted by her cousin Mordecai, an Israelite of the tribe of Benjamin.

After the customary preparation Esther is brought before the king and he chooses her to be his queen. And so, four years after divorcing Queen Vashti, Ahasuerus marries Esther and she becomes Queen of all Persia. At this time Esther does not disclose her race.

After marriage Esther continues in close communication with Mordecai, her beloved guardian and trusted mentor. During one of his daily visits to the palace grounds Mordecai overhears a plot to assassinate the king. He informs Esther, who in turn recounts the news to her husband, King Ahasuerus. The conspiracy is exposed; the would-be assassins hanged. Mordecai's action in protecting the king's life is 'written in the book of the chronicles in the presence of the king' (2:23), and then seemingly forgotten.

Some time after the marriage of King Ahasuerus and Esther, Haman the Agagite is appointed to the post of prime minister. The king commands that Haman shall be given the highest respect. In his presence the people are to bow and pay homage. But Mordecai refuses to comply (3:2). When asked for an explanation of his refusal to bow before Haman, Mordecai tells his questioners 'that he was a Jew' (3:4). Now in their long history there had been thousands upon thousands of Israelites who would not hesitate to bow down to anyone, or anything, if it was to their advantage. The mere fact of bowing to a dignitary was not a contravention of any law of God. The Israelites were in the habit of falling down to the earth before an exalted person, especially before a king (2 Sam. 14:4; 18:28; 1 Kings 1:16). Mordecai's refusal to show this honour to Haman must indicate that something else was involved here. It is likely that the Persians attached divine significance to dignitaries, especially to the king. This homage, which was probably regarded as an act of reverence and worship to a god, was, by the command of the king, to be paid to Haman as his representative. This Mordecai could not do without a denial of his faith. The man who had counselled his young charge not to reveal her people and race (2:10,20) will not now remain silent himself. In this simple statement, 'He told them that he was a Jew,' there is a declaration that he was a God-fearing Jew, a man of keen principle, a man of deep devotion to God.

Haman is incensed. The discovery that Mordecai is a Jew only serves to increase his feelings of enmity, for he is an Amalekite, a descendant of King Agag (3:1; cf. 1 Sam. 15:1-33). The age-old hostility between Amalek and Israel is reignited: Haman plans the annihilation of the whole race of Israel on one specific day. By subtle strategy and careful concealing of the truth, Haman obtains a decree from King Ahasuerus for the extermination of the

Jews throughout the whole of the empire (this would include those who had returned to Jerusalem).

Hearing the news, Mordecai sends word to Queen Esther, who is oblivious of the decree. Her cousin strongly urges her to use her influence with the king. His words form the key words to the whole book: 'Do not think in your heart that you will escape in the king's palace any more than all the other Jews. For if you remain completely silent at this time, relief and deliverance will arise for the Jews from another place, but you and your father's house will perish. Yet who knows whether you have come to the kingdom for such a time as this?' (4:13-14).

Here again there is evidence that Mordecai is a man of God in his un-spoken, though clearly implied, confidence in the providence of the God of Israel.

2. Events leading up to Esther's banquet and its sequel (3:1 – 7:10)

Esther responds. After calling upon her people in the city to join her in a full fast for seventy-two hours, Esther resolves to risk her life in approaching the king uninvited. The king grants her an audience and, before she has re-vealed her purpose, he promises to grant whatever she requests, even to the half of his kingdom. Meanwhile Haman plans the public execution of Mordecai the Jew.

That night while Haman stews in his hatred for Mordecai, King Ahasu-erus suffers insomnia. Another mark of the presence of 'the finger of God' is seen in the simple words: 'That night the king could not sleep' (6:1). Ahasuerus sends for the history books and during the reading of the recent records he stumbles across the account of Mordecai's loyalty to the king in disclosing the plot against his life. Ahasuerus enquires whether any reward or public acknowledgement has been given to Mordecai. The king is in-formed that nothing has been done for him (6:3). Immediately the king hears footsteps in the outer court. Haman has come to gain permission to execute Mordecai.

What follows then displays superb dramatic irony. The king has Morde-cai in mind, to honour him. Haman has Mordecai in mind, to hang him. Without mentioning Mordecai by name, the king asks Haman to suggest ways of honouring a man with whom the king is well pleased. The arro-gant, conceited Haman thinks the king must be referring to himself, and so piles on the honours thick and fast (6:7-9). Suddenly the truth dawns. The king is to honour Mordecai. Haman is to lead him through the streets. What humiliation for Haman!

When the king and Haman attend the second banquet, Esther pleads for her life and the life of her people (7:3-4). She reveals Haman as the would-be perpetrator of this genocide of the Jews. Full of anger and fury, the king walks out into the garden. Haman pleads for his life. The king returns to find Haman at the feet of his wife and supposes that he is about to do violence to her. Ahasuerus passes the sentence of death upon him instantly. The king gives all Haman's property to Queen Esther (8:1). She pleads for a reversal of the decree issued against the Jews, but the law of the Medes and Persians once decreed cannot be altered or rescinded. Mordecai is authorized to prepare another decree to the effect that the Jews throughout the empire may defend themselves, and retaliate against their enemies.

On the appointed day, nine months after the promulgation of the second decree, 500 enemies of the Jews are slain in Shushan the capital, and in the provinces 75,000 enemies are killed. The day following a further 300 are killed in the capital. It is estimated that the Persian Empire, from India to Ethiopia, consisted of a population of at least 100 million. The number of Jews was somewhere between two and three million, of which number at least 500,000 to 700,000 would be capable of bearing arms.[4] 'And no one could withstand them because fear of them fell upon all people' (9:2).

3. The institution of the Feast of Purim and its sequel (8:1 – 10:3)

In consequence of this remarkable turn of events, the Feast of Purim was instituted as a perpetual memorial among the Jews (9:26-27). It is called the Feast of Purim after the name Pur, the lot, because Haman had cast lots concerning the destruction of the Jews (3:7).

Christ and his church

The influence and driving force behind Haman's attempted genocide of the Jews is the devil, the great enemy of God. This portion of history recounts a classic attempt by Satan to thwart the purposes of God for Messiah's birth. The annihilation of the Israelites, especially of the tribe of Judah, would remove all possibility of God's fulfilling his promises (Gen. 49:10; 2 Sam. 7:12-16; 1 Kings 11:36). Haman acted as the agent of the devil in seeking the extermination of the Jews. Ahasuerus was king over all the Jews in Judah as well as over those in Persia and Babylon. The devil knew that the Deliverer who was to arise from the descendants of David would destroy his power. He instigated Saul's attempt at David's life in twice throwing a javelin and tracking him relentlessly across the land. He inspired Queen Athaliah in her effort to annihilate the royal line. He stirred Haman to rush from a supposed insult from one man to the proposed extermination of his whole race. The same malevolent spirit prompted Herod years later in trying to kill the Christ by the slaughter of 'all the male children who were in Bethlehem and in all its districts, from two years old and under' (Matt. 2:16).

On each occasion of satanic attack the Lord delivered his people and safeguarded his gracious plan to send his Son into the world. Scripture predicted hostility (Gen. 3:15; cf. Rom. 16:20). Satan truly inflicted pain upon the Saviour, but the Son of God triumphed over all adversity and opposition. As David predicted and the early Christian church realized, 'For truly against your holy servant Jesus, whom you anointed, both Herod and Pontius Pilate, with the Gentiles and the people of Israel, were gathered together to do whatever your hand and your purpose determined before to be done' (Acts 4:27-28; cf. vv. 25-26).

Whereas Haman illustrates the forces of evil, Esther exemplifies the powers of good. Like the Saviour, Esther put herself in danger of death for her people, but whereas she was wonderfully delivered, he was not. His death was necessary to 'save his people from their sins' (Matt. 1:21).

Another point of comparison between Esther and the Lord Jesus is seen in her interceding on behalf of her people. The Saviour intercedes for his church: 'Who is he who condemns? It is Christ who died, and furthermore is also risen, who is even at the right hand of God, who also makes intercession for us' (Rom. 8:34). 'Therefore he is also able to save to the uttermost those who come to God through him, since he ever lives to make intercession for them' (Heb. 7:25).

Application

1. Inner beauty

Esther was 'lovely and beautiful' (2:7) and no doubt her appearance was a crucial factor in Ahasuerus' choice of her for his wife. The historic record does, however, indicate that her character was a strong factor in her attractiveness. She was humble and submissive and yet not lacking in outstanding courage and determination.

The Word of God warns against concern for outward beauty: 'Charm is deceitful and beauty is vain, but a woman who fears the LORD, she shall be praised' (Prov. 31:30). 'Do not let your beauty be that outward adorning of arranging the hair, of wearing gold, or of putting on fine apparel; but let it be the hidden person of the heart, with the incorruptible ornament of a gentle and quiet spirit, which is very precious in the sight of God' (1 Peter 3:3-4).

In a day when 'the body beautiful' has become a twenty-first century idol, when obsession about physical appearance is rife throughout society, there is need for Christians to take care not to 'be conformed to this world', but rather to 'be transformed by the renewing of [their minds]' (Rom. 12:2). Dieting and weight-training may easily become a fixation and result in a serious psychological disorder. The gentle and quiet spirit commended in Scripture 'is imperishable; it is the true beauty, not one that is put on, but one that is inherent; it is not an earthly, bodily, outward thing but is inherent in the soul'.[5]

The character appropriate for godly women is also appropriate for godly men. It is 'the inner person of the heart' that matters. Is it not foretold of the Saviour: 'He has no form or comeliness; and when we see him, there is no beauty that we should desire him'? (Isa. 53:2). The beauty from within him expressed itself in 'love, joy, peace, long-suffering, kindness, goodness, faithfulness, gentleness, self-control' (Gal. 5:22-23).

2. Submission to the state

Mordecai and Esther provide an example of how the godly function under an ungodly government. In the New Testament considerable emphasis is placed upon the duty of Christians to be model citizens: 'Let every soul be subject to the governing authorities. For there is no authority except from God, and the authorities that exist are appointed by God. Therefore whoever resists the authority resists the ordinance of God' (Rom. 13:1-2; cf. 1 Peter 2:13-17).

God commands 'every God-fearing, believing Christian person to respect the properly constituted government of any nation in which he dwells, whatever its morality and whatever its standards of ethics'.[6] When a conflict occurs between obeying God and obeying the state, as it did with the apostles Peter and John (Acts 4:19), obedience to the Lord always takes priority.

There is nothing inappropriate about a godly person's being elevated to a position of responsibility and trust by an ungodly government or by a pagan king. The Jews had a fine heritage in this regard: Joseph and the Pharaoh of Egypt; Obadiah and King Ahab of Israel; Daniel and Nebuchadnezzar of Babylon; Nehemiah and Artaxerxes of Persia. In being loyal to their king, none of these men compromised their faithfulness to God. They could not prevent every evil in government, but in keeping themselves from sin they may well have influenced the course of a nation.

Nor did these men sacrifice loyalty to their own people. Of Mordecai it is testified: 'For Mordecai the Jew was second to King Ahasuerus, and was great among the Jews and well-received by the multitude of his brethren, seeking the good of his people and speaking peace to all his kindred' (10:3). Patriotism is not inconsistent with religion in its purest form. Mordecai spent his time in seeking the welfare of his people, 'but it was the welfare of his people, not of a particular class, or a few favourites... His love was without partiality; and he who could not bow to a wicked minister, was not the man to pervert judgement by respect of persons.'[7]

3. God-given opportunities

In the service of God opportunities may arise only once in a lifetime. As Mordecai said to Esther, 'Who knows whether you have come to the kingdom for such a time as this?' (4:14). There are situations that are unique to each Christian. Opportunities for honouring God and testifying to his grace in Christ Jesus may suddenly transpire. Christians should be alert and prepared for such eventualities: '... sanctify the Lord God in your hearts, and always be ready to give a defence to everyone who asks you a reason for the hope that is in you, with meekness and fear...' (1 Peter 3:15).

There may be times when, like Esther, we must be ready to take our life in our hands and risk everything for the cause of God.

4. Sovereign protection

Matthew Henry declared, 'Though the name of God be not in it, his finger is.' The book of Esther occupies its place in Scripture because of its profound message: God is always at work protecting his people, even in the darkest times. It is the supreme book of providence: 'And we know that all things work together for good to those who love God, to those who are the called according to his purpose' (Rom. 8:28).

God is involved in all that transpires on the earth. He is no absentee landlord. God sees all, hears all, knows all and controls all (Ps. 139:1-12; Eph. 1:11). The Lord Jesus Christ reigns over a kingdom of power and a kingdom of grace. His kingdom of power stretches over all the earth. His kingdom of grace extends over all the church. His reign over the one is for the benefit of the other. He rules the world for the good of his people (Eph. 1:20-23).

His purposes will ripen fast,
Unfolding every hour;
The bud may have a bitter taste,
But sweet will be the flower.

Blind unbelief is sure to err,
And scan his work in vain;
God is his own interpreter,
And he will make it plain.

(William Cowper, 1731–1800).

The book of Esther demonstrates the loving care and protection that God exercises over his people. The Lord can easily disturb a king and not permit him to sleep on one crucial night. Our God can easily turn the tables on a wicked man like Haman. 'God is wise in heart and mighty in strength. Who has hardened himself against him and prospered?' (Job 9:4).

Though the name of God does not appear throughout the entire book nevertheless his presence is abundantly evident. What a mass of 'coincidences' are contained in these pages — the singular attractiveness of Esther the Jew; the king choosing her from hundreds of candidates; Mordecai overhearing the plot against the king; a record being made of Mordecai's loyalty and faithfulness; the insomnia of the king on that particular night; the fact that he called for the chronicles to be read, that his servant read that particular piece of forgotten history and that the king asked whether Mordecai had been rewarded! All these incidents combine to form an overwhelming proof of divine control.

The doctrine of divine sovereignty is a basic feature of this book, 'but it is not a kind of fatalism. For where God's actions and purposes are not transparent, the importance of human obedience and faithfulness becomes the more apparent.'[8] Though God is sovereign he chooses to use ordinary people to overcome impossible circumstances and fulfil his gracious purposes.

Conclusion

Haman's attack upon the Jews was not a localized assault. Had he succeeded in his evil design this would have led to the annihilation of the whole Israelite race. The consequences would have been catastrophic. The covenants, the prophecies and the promises given by God would all have failed. There could have been no Messiah, no Saviour for sinners, no hope, no heaven, no glory. Haman's attack was obviously instigated, motivated and maintained by the Evil One, Satan, the devil.

Mordecai's confidence that the Jews would be preserved surely indicates his confidence in a higher power and authority than that of Haman, or indeed King Ahasuerus (4:14).

'Blessed be the God and Father of our Lord Jesus Christ, who according to his abundant mercy has begotten us again to a living hope through the resurrection of Jesus Christ from the dead, to an inheritance incorruptible and undefiled and that does not fade away, reserved in heaven for you, *who are kept by the power of God...*' (1 Peter 1:3-5, emphasis added).

Job

(after main character)

Author: Unknown
(maybe Elihu — 32:15-22)

Key thought: 'Trial'

Theme:
The mystery of suffering

'But he knows the way that I take;
When he has tested me, I shall come
forth as gold.'

Job 23:10

Summary

Job

The Hebrew Old Testament is divided into three major sections: Law *(Torah)*, Prophets *(Nebhiim)*, and Writings *(Kethubhim)*. The Protestant Old Testament is arranged quite differently under four sections: Law, History, Poetry and Prophecy.[1] In our studies so far we have covered the first seventeen books that compose the Law (Genesis to Deuteronomy) and History (Joshua to Esther). The book of Job, the eighteenth book of our Protestant Bible, begins the section on Poetry (Job to Song of Solomon). The fourth and final section comes under Prophecy, and is further sub-divided into the Major Prophets (Isaiah to Daniel) and Minor Prophets (Hosea to Malachi).

With the exception of the first two chapters and part of the last chapter, the book of Job is written in verse, in the form of poetry — that is, Hebrew poetry, not classical English poetry. Although it is largely written in a poetic style, the people and the events recorded are real. The book of Job is fact, not fiction (James 5:11; cf. Ezek. 14:14-20).

Author

The author is unknown. The fact that the name of the author is nowhere mentioned, either in the book itself or elsewhere in the Bible, means that his identity cannot be determined with any certainty. There may be a hint in chapter 32 that Elihu, who remonstrated with Job and his three friends, wrote down the record, but as we have repeatedly noted, certainty about the divine authorship is the point that really matters. The book of Job holds its rightful place in the canon of Scripture.

Historical setting

The book of Job has been the subject of a great deal of discussion. Many Bible scholars regard this as the oldest book in the Bible. Others place it as late as the Babylonian exile. In favour of the earlier date we might consider the following factors:

- The length of Job's life; he lived for another 140 years *after* the experiences described in this book (42:16), placing him in the days of the patriarchs, Abraham, Isaac and Jacob (cf. Gen. 11:10-26; 25:7);
- The fact that Job acts as high priest in his family, in the manner of Abraham, which was not allowed after the Exodus;
- The total silence of Job's 'friends' on the miracles surrounding the Exodus and the journey to the land of Canaan. These events are often used to illustrate how God delivers his friends and destroys his enemies;
- The absence of any reference to Jewish festivals and feasts, ceremonies, customs, Sabbaths or priesthood, all of which were established at Mount Sinai.

Eliphaz was a Temanite (2:11) and therefore a descendant of Esau through his eldest son (who was also called Eliphaz) and his grandson Teman (Gen. 36:10-11). These considerations would place Job some time during or immediately after the time of Jacob. While of the opinion that Job was a contemporary of the patriarchs, E. J. Young presents the arguments in favour of the opinion that the book was not actually written until the time of Solomon.[2]

Outline

Part I: Introducing Job (1:1-5)

Job lives in the land of Uz (1:1). The prophet Jeremiah refers to this country: 'Rejoice and be glad, O daughter of Edom, you who dwell in the land of Uz!' (Lam. 4:21). This may be thought to indicate that the land of Uz is identical to, or at least a part of, the land of Edom; however a more likely explanation is that the land of Uz was not the same as the country of Edom but that the Edomites (also known as Idumeans) had conquered this country that they did not originally possess. Consequently Jeremiah speaks of the 'daughter of Edom', not as dwelling in her own country properly, but as dwelling 'in the land of Uz', that is, in a foreign country, of which she had somehow obtained possession.[3]

Since Job is from the east (1:3), near the wilderness (1:19), and Edom (Idumea) lies to the south of Israel, the majority of commentators favour the location of Uz as east of Israel in the Arabian Desert, probably between Damascus and the Euphrates River, the present-day borderland of Jordan, Iraq and Saudi Arabia.

Though enjoying great prosperity Job is a truly godly man. He appears as the priest of his household and offers burnt offerings for his large family (1:5).

Part II: The heavenly court (1:6-12)

The scene changes to the heavenly court. The 'sons of God' (later used in a way that could only mean angels, 38:7) assemble and Satan challenges the sincerity of Job's piety: 'Does Job fear God for nothing?' (1:9). This insinuates that Job is good only for what he can get. This is the crux of the whole book. 'Touch all that he has', says Satan, 'and he will surely curse you to your face!' (1:11). In consequence dreadful calamities are to fall upon Job.

Part III: Disaster strikes (1:13-20)

Four messengers come to Job. Wave after wave of devastation floods over him. If the blows had not fallen so suddenly and in such quick succession he might have had time to cope with one before the next bursts upon him. But these calamities fall thick and fast. There is no time to absorb the first shock before the second, and then the third, and then the fourth hit him with merciless ferocity. All his oxen are taken; all his sheep are incinerated; all his camels are stolen and all his servants with them are put to death. Then the fourth messenger appears, informing Job that a great wind has blown down the house where all his children, seven sons and three daughters, were gathered. Not one child has escaped. Job responds to the dreadful news:

> Naked I came from my mother's womb,
> And naked shall I return there.
> The LORD gave, and the LORD has taken away;
> Blessed be the name of the LORD
>
> (1:21).

This is not the resignation of a man who yields to an inevitable fate which cannot be undone; nor is it surrender to an almighty Ruler who has the right to do as he will with his own; nor is it even the submission of a God-fearing man who surrenders to the sovereign purpose of the living God. There is far more to these words than mere resignation, surrender, or godly submission. Job declares the goodness and kindness of God. 'The bitterness of his loss is made the measure of the preciousness of the blessings God had given' him.[4] The magnitude of his loss makes him aware of the magnitude of God's kindness in giving such blessings in the first place. The more deeply he feels the taking of his children, his servants and his possessions, the greater is his appreciation of God's kindness towards him. Consequently the more profoundly he grieves, the more fervently he blesses the Lord his God. This is a staggeringly revolutionary way to think about suffering and affliction.

God's testimony to Job is recorded: 'In all this Job did not sin nor charge God with wrong' (1:22).

Part IV: The heavenly court again (2:1-6)

Back in the heavenly court Satan makes excuses for the continued piety and godliness of Job, and urges further measures against him: 'Touch his bone and his flesh, and he will surely curse you to your face!' (2:5). Permission is granted for Satan to afflict Job in his body, but not to take his life. God has confidence in his servant Job.

Part V: Disaster strikes again (2:7-10)

Job is inflicted with a dreadful disease. This may have been the disease of elephantiasis, also called black leprosy, a loathsome and dangerous form of leprosy.[5] The English word 'boils' indicates sores — painful, angry, inflamed swellings below the skin. The Hebrew word, here in the singular, suggests a burning sore, an inflamed ulcer, not localized in certain areas but covering the whole body surface. Job's disease seems to have involved ulcerations from head to toe, constantly erupting, accompanied by violent pain and constant restlessness. In elephantiasis the skin is covered with hard scabs, the legs swell, there is a loss of hair and sense of touch, a swelling of the face, and a hoarse nasal voice. It affects the whole body; the bones as well as the skin are covered with spots and tumours, at first red, but afterwards black.[6] The Scriptures record in some detail the symptoms of Job's terrible malady:

- He scrapes his body with a broken piece of pot to bring some kind of relief (2:8).
- He suffers insomnia, with constant tossing and turning through the night, longing for the dawn to come. His flesh is covered 'with worms and dust'. His skin is ulcerated and constantly breaking out afresh (7:4-5).
- The pain is so intense at times that he bites his flesh (13:14).
- His body is rotting. He is like a moth-eaten piece of clothing (13:28).
- His whole body is wrinkled and emaciated. He is like a walking skeleton (16:8).
- His face is red with crying. His eyelids are dark and shaded like death (16:16).
- He has 'one foot in the grave' (17:1).
- His bones cling to his skin and flesh (19:20).
- He has pain in his bones, and constant gnawing pains in his body (30:17).
- His skin turns black and peels away. His bones burn with fever (30:30).

All this time Job is oblivious of what is going on in the heavenly court. We have the advantage of reading the additional inspired information. Only the Lord could have communicated these details. Job's total ignorance and absolute bewilderment as to the cause of his suffering must only add far greater distress to this man of God. Job knows nothing of Satan's malicious designs in seeking to prove that his piety is pretence. Job knows nothing of the sovereign purpose of God who means to demonstrate before the world the reality and power of Job's godliness. He is on trial, but not merely for himself: the cause of true religion is represented in him, the cause of God on earth. He is unconscious of the dignity of his position. He does not know that the living God watches him with favour and approval, and confidently predicts the outcome of his trials.[7]

Part VI: Job's friends arrive (2:11-13)

Three friends, Eliphaz, Bildad and Zophar, visit Job to comfort him and sympathize with him in his distress. They are so affected and overwhelmed by the sight of Job's condition that they sit on the ground in silence for 'seven days and seven nights … for they saw that his grief was very great' (2:13).

Part VII: Job's patience is exhausted (3:1-26)

The visit of his three friends, their long silence and the increasing severity of his pain cause Job to pour out his heart. He complains. He complains about his birth. He asks why he was born. He longs for death. He asks why one suffering so much should live when life is so utterly unbearable.

Part VIII: The three friends speak (4:1 - 31:40)

The discussions between Job and his three friends go in three cycles. Eliphaz, Bildad and Zophar take turns in presenting their arguments. Immediately following each contribution there is an account of Job's reply. One friend speaks; Job replies. The second friend speaks; Job replies. The third friend speaks; Job replies. This procedure is followed through three times except that in the final round Zophar does not offer any further contribution. Instead Job makes a final response to all three friends.

The debates, at times heated, are futile philosophical speculations concerning the mystery of suffering. The arguments presented by Job's friends are basically the same: all suffering is the result of personal sin. Job's great sufferings, therefore, prove him to be a great sinner and a great hypocrite.

Round One

In the first round of discussion Eliphaz, Bildad and Zophar present their case. Eliphaz says, 'Who ever perished being innocent? Or where were the upright ever cut off?' (4:7). Bildad, more outspoken than Eliphaz, thinks that the death of Job's children is a sign of God's judgement: 'If your sons have sinned against him, he has cast them away for their transgression' (8:4). Zophar is more impetuous than the other two. He condemns what he calls 'the multitude of words' and 'empty talk' (11:2,3). In the opinion of E. J. Young, part of Zophar's speech (11:7-20) 'is of unsurpassed beauty'.[8] Zophar expresses profound and beautiful teaching that the being and ways of the living God are far beyond our comprehension and grasp. Nevertheless the abiding undercurrent is one of rebuke and censure. Zophar, along with his two companions, assumes that Job is wicked, that he is a hypocrite and consequently abandoned by God. On the basis of this wrong assumption, each of the friends concludes his speech with an appeal to Job to repent so that his prosperity will return. Such misguided treatment can only add further pain to the sufferings of Job.

In Job's replies there is good evidence to suggest that he often shares his friends' outlook as to the connection between suffering and punishment by God. He too, has a low view and limited understanding of the mystery of suffering.

Round Two

In the second round Eliphaz, Bildad and Zophar begin by criticizing Job for the empty words of his replies. They then concentrate upon the terrible sufferings and end of the wicked. Bildad begins by criticizing Job and then describes the terrors that await the wicked. He is still holding to his pagan philosophy in regard to suffering. It is during his reply to this fifth challenge and rebuke that Job confesses his unshakeable confidence in God and utters the immortal words:

Oh, that my words were written!
Oh, that they were inscribed in a book!
That they were engraved on a rock
With an iron pen and lead, for ever!
For I know that my Redeemer lives,
And he shall stand at last on the earth;

And after my skin is destroyed, this I know,
That in my flesh I shall see God,
Whom I shall see for myself,
And my eyes shall behold, and not another.
How my heart yearns within me!

(19:23-27).

Round Three

In the third round the arguments of Eliphaz and Bildad revert back to those of the first round. They maintain that suffering is the result of personal sin. Job defends himself and protests his innocence.

Eliphaz, Bildad and Zophar end their discussions with Job because they think him to be self-righteous.

Part IX: Elihu enters the discussion (32:1 - 37:24)

Elihu, the Buzite, comes nearer the truth in recognizing Job's primary concern for his own integrity. He is angry with Job 'because he justified himself rather than God' (32:2). Elihu rebukes the three brethren because they have condemned Job yet provided him with no answer to his problem. Elihu shows that suffering is sometimes God's discipline to restore the backslider:

Man is also chastened with pain on his bed,
And with strong pain in many of his bones,
So that his life abhors bread,
And his soul succulent food.
His flesh wastes away from sight,
And his bones stick out which once were not seen…
Then he is gracious to him…
He shall return to the days of his youth.
He shall pray to God, and he will delight in him…
Behold, God works all these things,
Twice, in fact, three times with a man,
To bring back his soul from the Pit,
That he may be enlightened with the light of life

(33:19-30).

Elihu declares the justice of God, the goodness of God, the righteousness of God and the majesty of God. There is a severity and harshness in
his speeches that is stronger than that of the other three friends. What he
says seems true enough in itself, but he is still missing the point.

Part X: The Lord speaks (38:1 - 41:34)

God forcefully makes the point that Job, as well as every other human
being, has great ignorance about the mysteries of the universe. If he is unable to explain the ordinary and well-known facts of natural history and
science, how can he hope to understand and interpret the mystery of the
Creator's dealings with his creation, or even his treatment of his children?
The Lord enumerates a whole range of natural phenomena about which,
even to this day, we know so little. He not only challenges Job as to his
knowledge and understanding, but also as to his power and control:

> Can you bind the cluster of the Pleiades,
> Or loose the belt of Orion?
> Can you bring out Mazzaroth [constellations of stars] in its season?
> Or can you guide the Great Bear with its cubs?
> Do you know the ordinances of the heavens?
> Can you set their dominion over the earth?
> Can you lift up your voice to the clouds,
> That an abundance of water may cover you?
>
> (38:31-34).

Up to the end of chapter 37 the book is full of reasoned arguments.
When the Lord speaks he does not use argument to explain himself or
convince Job. In fact the Lord points out the extreme ignorance and limi-
tations in power of the whole of humanity.

Part XI: Job responds to the Lord (42:1-6)

Job has been humbled by the Lord and senses his appalling ignorance.
Job has found peace, a God-given peace, even though all his questions
have not been answered. He is released from the confines of his earlier
thinking. Job and his sufferings have their place in God's all-wise, incomprehensible providence. Job does not need to understand. He needs no

explanation. God is on his throne. God will do what is best. That is to be enough for Job, and that is to be enough for every child of God. Job regrets his questioning and complaining. He repents and yields gladly to the rule of an all-glorious and all-gracious God.

Part XII: The finale: Job restored by the Lord (42:7-17)

The final scene pictures the Lord rebuking Eliphaz, Bildad and Zophar. He commands the three to take sacrifices and to go to Job so that Job may function as a priest and pray for them. Thus the Lord vindicates the integrity of Job before his friends, his family and all who read of him. Job is richly blessed and ultimately dies 'old and full of days' (42:17).

Christ and his church

1. The mystery of suffering

The connection between suffering and the punishment of an individual's sin has often been wrongly construed. Job's friends seemed incapable of drawing any other conclusion. Many years later the disciples of the Lord Jesus, seeing a man blind from birth, displayed the same kind of error in their question to the Lord: 'Rabbi, who sinned, this man or his parents, that he was born blind?' (John 9:2). On that occasion the Lord declared, 'Neither this man nor his parents sinned, but that the works of God should be revealed in him' (John 9:3).

In one sense suffering is indeed the result of sin, for 'The whole creation groans and labours with birth pangs' and 'eagerly waits for the revealing of the sons of God' (Rom. 8:22,19). Sometimes there is a direct connection between an individual's sin and the consequent suffering. Sometimes there is a direct connection between the sin of a parent and the suffering of a child. But often there is no such direct connection. Some human beings suffer more than others. Some suffer 'that the works of God should be revealed' in them (John 9:3). Some of the most godly and spiritual people suffer extraordinarily. Job was tested in this manner. He did not know the reason behind his sufferings. It was for the glory and honour of God.

To jump to a conclusion that all suffering is directly connected to personal sin inevitably increases the suffering by adding guilt, or shame, and the burden of being seriously misunderstood. Job's sufferings of bereavement, illness and disease were intensified by the rejection he experienced at the hands of his friends, grandchildren and wife (19:13-19). He pleads for their sympathy and support: 'Have pity on me, have pity on me, O you my friends, for the hand of God has struck me!' (19:21).

One man suffered more in this respect even than Job. He not only suffered the physical and mental agonies associated with crucifixion, together with the inexpressible sufferings of being 'made ... sin for us' (2 Cor. 5:21), but he also experienced utter rejection (Matt. 27:46):

> You know my reproach, my shame, and my dishonour;
> My adversaries are all before you.
> Reproach has broken my heart,
> And I am full of heaviness;
> I looked for someone to take pity, but there was none;
> And for comforters, but I found none
>
> (Ps. 69:19-20).

Isaiah prophesied of the Messiah:

> He is despised and rejected by men,
> A man of sorrows and acquainted with grief.
> And we hid, as it were, our faces from him;
> He was despised, and we did not esteem him.
> Surely he has borne our griefs
> And carried our sorrows;
> Yet we esteemed him stricken,
> Smitten by God, and afflicted
>
> (Isa. 53:3-4).

Isaiah confesses his earlier ignorance in misunderstanding the sufferings of the Saviour. He mistakenly assumed that God was punishing the sufferer for his own sins. Nothing could have been further from the truth. The Saviour provides a wonderful example of how to deal with unjust suffering: 'When he suffered, he did not threaten, but committed himself to him who judges righteously; who himself bore our sins in his own body on the tree ... by whose stripes you were healed' (1 Peter 2:23-24). His sufferings bring an end to our sufferings.

2. The glory of the resurrection

From Job is also drawn the most profound prophecy concerning the resurrection of Christ and his church:

For I know that my Redeemer lives,
And he shall stand at last on the earth;
And after my skin is destroyed, this I know,
That in my flesh I shall see God,
Whom I shall see for myself,
And my eyes shall behold, and not another.
How my heart yearns within me!

(19:25-27).

Disease had attacked Job's skin. He was covered with ulcers. The process of decay was so rapid and widespread that he expected he would be utterly consumed. If that were to be his end he would still hold fast his confidence in God. Job is certain, as Albert Barnes expresses: 'He will at length come forth, and I shall be permitted to see him, and shall have the delightful assurance that he settles this controversy in my favour, and declares that I am his friend.'[9] Whatever Job intended by these words, they nevertheless contain a glorious prophecy of the Messiah and the future resurrection.

Application

1. God rules

Nothing happens on earth until it is sanctioned in heaven. King Nebuchadnezzar of Babylon also learned the great lesson of God's sovereign rule. After behaving for some years as a brute beast, the humbled king declares:

I, Nebuchadnezzar, lifted my eyes to heaven, and my understanding returned to me; and I blessed the Most High and praised and honoured him who lives for ever:

For his dominion is an everlasting dominion,
And his kingdom is from generation to generation.

All the inhabitants of the earth are reputed as nothing;
He does according to his will in the army of heaven
And among the inhabitants of the earth.
No one can restrain his hand
Or say to him, "What have you done?

(Dan. 4:34-35).

The sovereignty of God over all creation is a cause of great reassurance and comfort to those who love him:

Who has directed the Spirit of the LORD,
Or as his counsellor has taught him?
With whom did he take counsel, and who instructed him,
And taught him in the path of justice?

(Isa. 40:13-14).

The apostle Paul reassures all Christians when he declares that God 'works all things according to the counsel of his will' (Eph. 1:11). We who believe rejoice that 'Our God is in heaven; he does whatever he pleases' (Ps. 115:3). We could not be in better or safer hands!

2. The great adversary

The Lord Jesus likened Satan to 'a strong man' (Mark 3:27) powerfully controlling his kingdom. In the book of Job, although the devil is powerful he is also depicted as subordinate to the living God. The extent of Satan's power and influence is limited by the Lord: '... there is a profound meaning in his appearing here among the sons of God before the Lord. It is designed to express his subordination and subjection to divine control. He cannot act untrammelled and at his own discretion. He is not at liberty to pursue his mischievous designs to whatever extent he may choose. There is a superior restraint to which he is obliged to bow, a superior will that sets limits to his rage... It is Satan actually exhibited in the attitude of a servant of God, and made subservient to the discipline and training of his people.'[10]

Satan's presence and power in the world are part of God's strategy to discipline and educate his chosen people. Mock combat cannot reflect the real battle. Pretend fighting has no urgency, no motivation, no life-and-death struggle. Spiritual warfare is real. The devil is a formidable foe, an extremely powerful enemy. We underestimate him at our peril. Like the apostle Paul, we should not be ignorant of Satan's devices (2 Cor. 2:11).

In the book of Job, Satan is seen as mustering a two-pronged attack: open hostility in the form of disasters and affliction, and subtle insinuation through the counsel of Job's friends. In the one he is the 'adversary the devil … like a roaring lion' (1 Peter 5:8). In the other he 'transforms himself into an angel of light' (2 Cor. 11:14).

The Lord Jesus faced the full impact of Satan's attack. At the commencement of his ministry, immediately following his anointing, he 'was led up by the Spirit into the wilderness to be tempted by the devil' (Matt. 4:1). The Saviour faced the same kind of challenges that confronted Eve in the Garden of Eden: 'the lust of the flesh, the lust of the eyes, and the pride of life' (1 John 2:16; cf. Gen. 3:6; Luke 4:3,5,9). Whereas Eve succumbed, the Saviour succeeded. Throughout his life and ministry he 'was in all points tempted as we are, yet without sin' (Heb. 4:15). He knows the power of the Evil One through personal experience. That 'serpent of old, called the Devil and Satan, who deceives the whole world' (Rev. 12:9), waited for the coming of the promised child, that he might destroy him (Rev. 12:4). At Calvary the battle was won. Satan did his worst against the Saviour but the Saviour triumphed. The first gospel promise was fulfilled: Satan inflicted pain upon Christ but Christ inflicted a death blow upon Satan (Gen. 3:15). In Christ the church will have the victory for 'The God of peace will crush Satan under [our] feet shortly' (Rom. 16:20).

'Therefore take up the whole armour of God, that you may be able to withstand in the evil day, and having done all, to stand' (Eph. 6:13). Our Father has promised that we will not be tempted beyond what we can endure (1 Cor. 10:13).

3. Discerning the will of God

Job lived in the years well before the giving of the law at Sinai. Discerning the will of God in those days of the patriarchs was fraught with difficulty. People were dependent upon oral tradition (information communicated from one generation to another), infrequent theophanies (appearances of God or 'the Angel of the LORD'), dreams (Gen. 20:3; 28:12; 31:11,24; 37:5) and visions (Gen. 15:1). God's dealings with Moses gave clarity of revelation unknown before (Num. 12:6-8). The covenant, with its law, sacrifices and priesthood, provided detailed guidelines for all who wanted faithfully to serve the living God. Now that we have the completed

Scriptures of the Old and New Testaments, the Lord no longer reveals his will by those former means.

Job's three friends claimed to know the will of God as they sought to interpret his predicament. Throughout the discussion Eliphaz backs up his argument by what he has learned from dreams and visions (4:12-16); Bildad substantiates his position by using traditions passed down from previous generations (8:8-10); while Zophar appeals to experience and reason (20:2-3).

4,000 years later, in spite of receiving the complete inspired and trustworthy Word of God, the people of God are in danger of being led astray by those who claim a superior knowledge through dreams and visions, worldly wisdom, experience or reason. The apostle Paul warned the Christian church at Colossae: 'Beware lest anyone should cheat you through philosophy and empty deceit, according to the tradition of men, according to the basic principles of the world, and not according to Christ. For in him dwells all the fulness of the Godhead bodily: and you are complete in him, who is the head of all principality and power' (Col. 2:8-10).

Our knowledge and understanding of God, and of God's dealings with his children, are not to be based on dreams and visions, worldly wisdom, experience or human reason. 'To the law and to the testimony! If they do not speak according to this word, it is because there is no light in them' (Isa. 8:20). God's Word alone shall teach us. There is no other foundation upon which to build a solid and godly life (Matt. 7:24-25). In his unsurpassed wisdom and great kindness the Lord by 'his divine power has given to us all things that pertain to life and godliness' (2 Peter 1:3). This is contained in the sixty-six books of the Bible.

4. All things work together for good

'And we know that all things work together for good to those who love God, to those who are the called according to his purpose' (Rom. 8:28). It is easy to understand how God works for our good when everything is going favourably for us. When all is well with health, family, home, work and church these things can readily be claimed as evidences of God's blessing. However, the wicked often prosper (Ps. 73:1-16) and the godly often suffer (Ps. 34:19; 2 Thess. 1:4-5). Outward circumstances are no indication of God's blessing or his censure. God disciplines those he loves (Heb. 12:5-11).

When matched against all the spiritual blessings with which we have been blessed 'in the heavenly places in Christ' (Eph. 1:3), any suffering in this present world may be viewed as 'our light affliction, which is but for a moment ... working for us a far more exceeding and eternal weight of glory' (2 Cor. 4:17).

Conclusion

The book of Job is about the physical and spiritual experience of a believer of long ago whose faith was tested to the utmost. Its main purpose is not to teach Israelite history, nor to reveal Messianic prophecy, nor to show the necessary steps for salvation, nor to disclose the mission of the church. The underlying message of Job demonstrates that '*Who God is* determines *what He does*; therefore, we must *trust Him without reservation*.'[11] God always knows what he is doing and why. Our task is to 'walk by faith, not by sight' (2 Cor. 5:7).

Sufferings are the consequences of personal sin, of the sin of others, or of the sin of the human race. The Lord uses the sufferings of his children for discipline or education. Sometimes he uses our sufferings for purposes that we may never know — to manifest his glory before unbelievers, before friends, before his enemies. The children of God 'are kept by the power of God through faith for salvation ready to be revealed in the last time'. We may be 'grieved by various trials' in order that the genuineness of our faith 'may be found to praise, honour, and glory at the revelation of Jesus Christ' (1 Peter 1:5-7).

God is not obliged to explain himself to us. This is the message of the book of Job.

Psalms

('hymns for worship')

Authors: Various

Key thought: 'Worship the Lord'

Theme: Worship: prayer and
praise to the true God

'Oh come, let us worship and bow down;
Let us kneel before the LORD our
  Maker.
For he is our God...'

Psalm 95:6-7

Summary

1. Worship	Psalms
i. Praise	34; 103; 106; 111-113; 115-117; 135; 146-150
ii. Thanksgiving	16; 18; 30; 107; 138
iii. The God of creation	8; 19; 29; 33; 65; 104; 136; 148
iv. The God of history	78; 80; 81; 83; 105; 106; 136

2. Prophecies concerning Christ (cf. Luke 24:44)		*Fulfilment*
i. The humanity of Christ	40:6	Heb. 10:5
	8:3-52	Heb. 5-9
ii. The deity of Christ	110:1-2	Matt. 22:42-45
	45:6-7	Heb. 1:8-9
iii. The sonship of Christ	2:7	Acts 13:33
		Heb. 1:5; 5:5
iv. The rejection of Christ	118:22-24	Matt. 21:42
		Acts 4:11
	41:9	Matt. 26:21-25
v. The suffering of Christ	22:1,7-8,16-18	Matt. 27:35-46
		John 20:25
	69:20-21	John 19:28-30
	31:5	Luke 23:46
vi. The sacrifice of Christ	40:6-8	Heb. 10:5-7
	34:20	John 19:33,36
vii. The resurrection of Christ	16:8-11	Acts 2:25-32
viii. The ascension of Christ	68:18	Eph. 4:8
ix. The priesthood of Christ	110:4	Heb. 5:6,10; 7:21
x. The kingdom of Christ	2:1-2	Acts 4:25-28
	2:8-9	Rev. 2:27; 19:15
	45:6-7	Heb. 1:8-9
	72:17; 22:27	
	(cf. Gen. 12:3; 2 Sam. 7:12-16)	

3. The experience of the church	
i. Repentance	6; 32; 38; 51; 102; 130; 143
ii. Conversion	32; 40
iii. Longing for God	42: 63; 143
iv. Cries for help	4; 5; 6; 13; 17; 25; 86; 88
v. Trust and confidence	3; 16; 20; 23; 27; 31; 61; 62; 91; 121
vi. Instruction	1; 5; 7; 15; 17; 50; 73; 94; 101
vii. The Word of God	1; 19; 119

(These lists and categories are not intended to be exhaustive.)

Psalms

The book of Psalms is a collection of 150 spiritual songs or poems. It is the hymn book of Israel and contains such breadth and diversity of spiritual experience that it has been a source of inspiration, guidance and comfort to the church of God since its composition. C. H. Spurgeon took twenty years to produce his classic work, *The Treasury of David.* On completion he said, 'A tinge of sadness is on my spirit as I quit "The Treasury of David", never to find on this earth a richer storehouse, though the whole palace of Revelation is open to me. Blessed have been the days spent in meditating, mourning, hoping, believing, and exulting with David. Can I hope to spend hours more joyous on this side of the golden gate? The book of Psalms instructs us in the use of wings as well as words: it sets us both mounting and singing.'[1]

Author

The psalms are a collection of works produced by various authors. The superscriptions introducing each psalm are not in the original Scriptures but have been added by scholars of the past who have ascertained the author from the psalm's content or from another part of the Scriptures. David composed at least seventy-three psalms, while twenty-five were composed by David's singers: the descendants of Korah eleven, Asaph twelve (50; 73-83), Heman one (88) and Ethan one (89). Of the remaining psalms Hezekiah composed ten; one or two were written by or for Solomon (72; maybe 127); Moses wrote one (90); and about forty are anonymous. It is likely that David also composed some of this latter group: Psalm 2 is credited to his authorship by the apostles (Acts 4:25).

   The sons of Korah were one of the oldest Levitical families, long before the time of David, and related to the still more ancient family of Kohath, the son of Levi. In the time of David, Heman the son of Joel, a member of this family, became noted for his skill in music and song. The Kohathites and Korahites had a reputation for praising 'the LORD God of Israel with voices loud and high' (2 Chr. 20:19).

It is surprising that so few psalms, two at most in this collection, are credited to Solomon, since Scripture testifies that 'He spoke three thousand proverbs, and his songs were one thousand and five' (1 Kings 4:32).

Historical setting

The psalms cover a long period of Jewish history, about 900 years, from the time of Moses (Ps. 90) to the time of the return from the Babylonian exile (Ps. 126), though the vast majority fall within the period 1000 B.C. to 500 B.C. They compose the hymn book of the Old Testament church and have long been the inspired praise-and-prayer book of the saints of both the Old and New Covenants.

Hebrew poetry

Hebrew poetry is quite distinct from English poetry, ancient or modern. It is distinguished by certain peculiarities and characteristics of its own. Its principal feature is not rhyme, but parallelism, for example:

Do not keep silent, O God!
Do not hold your peace,
And do not be still, O God!

(83:1).

Here it will be seen that the second and third lines (in the English version) express a thought that is parallel in meaning to the first line.

Three basic forms of parallelism have been identified.

1. *Synonymous parallelism*, in which the same thought is repeated in almost the same words:

Hear this, all you peoples;
Give ear, all you inhabitants of the world

(49:1).

2. *Antithetical parallelism*, in which a thought is expressed by means of contrast with its opposite:

For his anger is but for a moment,
His favour is for life

(30:5).

3. *Synthetic parallelism*, in which the second line completes, or fills out, the thought of the first:

Many are the afflictions of the righteous,
But the LORD delivers him out of them all

(34:19).

There are many more features of Hebrew poetry, but parallelism is the major characteristic.[2]

Outline

While each psalm is complete in itself, the book of Psalms in the Hebrew text has five sections: 1–41; 42–72; 73–89; 90–106 and 107–150. Many attempts have been made to explain how this fivefold division came into being and why. The only link seems to be some sort of agreement with the fivefold division of the Pentateuch.[3] Supposedly there is an attempted comparison between Genesis and Book I of the Psalms (1-41), Exodus and Book II (42-72), Leviticus and Book III (73-89), Numbers and Book IV (90-106), and between Deuteronomy and Book V (107-150). Some commentators such as Robert Lee, Jensen and the contributors to *The Companion Bible,* have tried to develop this approach further. Robert Lee, for example, has:

Book I: Man — his state of blessedness, fall and recovery;
Book II: Israel's ruin, Redeemer and redemption;
Book III: The sanctuary
Book IV: The earth
Book V: The Word of God.[4]

This seems a forced arrangement. Did the Lord really intend that such a structure and such an identity should be understood? By contrast it might be argued that the recurring themes of misery, deliverance, praise and gratitude are so randomly scattered throughout the psalms, and even on occasions in the same psalm (e.g. 95), that the conclusion of William Hendriksen seems inevitable: 'Any attempt to give a material outline of the entire Psalter, with a different descriptive phrase or title for each book, would necessarily fail. The only division that can be made is the merely formal one, into the five recognized books.'[5]

Though thoroughly interwoven, nevertheless three major themes can be identified in the book of Psalms: worship; prophecies concerning Christ; and the experience of the church.

Worship

1. The worship of God

The prime motive in worship is to acknowledge, praise, magnify and adore the living God who is Father, Son and Holy Spirit.

God is to be worshipped *for who he is* — that is, for the beauty and magnificence of his being and character:

Bless the LORD, O my soul;
And all that is within me, bless his holy name!

(103:1).

Great is the LORD, and greatly to be praised
In the city of our God,
In his holy mountain

(48:1).

Righteousness and justice are the foundation of your throne;
Mercy and truth go before your face.
Blessed are the people who know the joyful sound!

(89:14-15).

Give to the LORD, O kindreds of the peoples,
Give to the LORD glory and strength.

Give to the LORD the glory due his name;
Bring an offering, and come into his courts.
Oh, worship the LORD in the beauty of holiness!
Tremble before him, all the earth

(96:7-9).

Not unto us, O LORD, not unto us,
But to your name give glory,
Because of your mercy,
And because of your truth

(115:1).

Your mercy, O LORD, is in the heavens,
And your faithfulness reaches to the clouds.
Your righteousness is like the great mountains;
Your judgements are a great deep

(36:5-6).

God is to be worshipped *for what he has done and is doing for all his creation*:

The heavens declare the glory of God,
And the firmament shows his handiwork

(19:1).

O LORD, our Lord,
How excellent is your name in all the earth,
You who set your glory above the heavens!

(8:1).

The eyes of all look expectantly to you,
And you give them their food in due season.
You open your hand
And satisfy the desire of every living thing

(145:15-16).

God is to be worshipped *for what he has done and is doing for his people*:

> Bless the LORD, O my soul,
> And forget not all his benefits
>
> (103:2).

> I will sing to the LORD,
> Because he has dealt bountifully with me
>
> (13:6).

> I will love you, O LORD, my strength.
> The LORD is my rock and my fortress and my deliverer;
> My God, my strength, in whom I will trust
>
> (18:1-2).

> I will extol you, O LORD, for you have lifted me up
>
> (30:1).

> It is good to give thanks to the LORD,
> And to sing praises to your name, O Most High;
> To declare your loving-kindness in the morning,
> And your faithfulness every night
>
> (92:1-2).

> Oh, sing to the LORD a new song!
> For he has done marvellous things;
> His right hand and his holy arm have gained him the victory.
> The LORD has made known his salvation;
> His righteousness he has openly shown in the sight of the nations
>
> (98:1-2).

This is the benchmark of true worship. When much of modern-day worship is judged by this criteria there is a staggering and lamentable lack. Many modern songs are self-centred and fall beneath this standard. Traditional churches also exhibit a low view of worship when they rush through 'the preliminaries' (that is, singing, prayer and the reading of Scripture) in order to reach the sermon as soon as possible.

It is the duty and privilege of every human being to worship the living God. 'The wrath of God is revealed from heaven … because, although they knew God, they did not glorify him as God, nor were thankful' (Rom. 1:18,21).

The whole of creation is called upon to worship the Lord:

Praise the LORD!
Praise the LORD from the heavens;
Praise him in the heights!
Praise him, all his angels;
Praise him, all his hosts!
Praise him, sun and moon;
Praise him, all you stars of light!
Praise him, you heavens of heavens,
And you waters above the heavens!
Let them praise the name of the LORD…
Praise the LORD from the earth,
You great sea creatures and all the depths…
Beasts and all cattle;
Creeping things and flying fowl;
Kings of the earth and all peoples…
Both young men and maidens;
Old men and children.
Let them praise the name of the LORD

(148:1-5, 7,10-13).

2. Congregational blessing

Interwoven with the worship of God are encouragement, stimulus and blessing which one believer gives to another. This is so clearly stated in the New Testament: 'Let the word of Christ dwell in you richly in all wisdom, teaching and admonishing one another in psalms and hymns and spiritual songs, singing with grace in your hearts to the Lord' (Col. 3:16). 'Be filled with the Spirit, speaking to one another in psalms and hymns and spiritual songs, singing and making melody in your heart to the Lord, giving thanks always for all things to God the Father in the name of our Lord Jesus Christ' (Eph. 5:18-20).

This aspect of the benefit to others is clearly evident in the psalms also:

I will bless the LORD at all times;
His praise shall continually be in my mouth.
My soul shall make its boast in the LORD;
The humble shall hear of it and be glad.

Oh, magnify the LORD with me,
And let us exalt his name together

(34:1-4).

Rejoice in the LORD, O you righteous!
For praise from the upright is beautiful

(33:1).

Congregational singing is to be a source of encouragement and instruction to fellow-believers.

3. Personal blessing

A third element in worship is the benefit and blessing believers experience personally when they engage their minds, hearts and spirits in the enjoyment of God:

Praise the LORD!
For it is good to sing praises to our God;
For it is pleasant, and praise is beautiful

(147:1).

God is our refuge and strength,
A very present help in trouble.
Therefore we will not fear…

(46:1-2).

I will praise you, O LORD, with my whole heart;
I will tell of all your marvellous works.
I will be glad and rejoice in you;
I will sing praise to your name, O Most High

(9:1).

Some of the psalms are both a thanksgiving to God and a testimony to fellow-Christians:

I waited patiently for the LORD;
And he inclined to me,
And heard my cry.

He also brought me up out of a horrible pit,
Out of the miry clay,
And set my feet upon a rock,
And established my steps.
He has put a new song in my mouth—
Praise to our God;
Many will see it and fear,
And will trust in the LORD

(40:1-3).

Christ and his church

Prophecies concerning Christ

For two thousand years there has been difficulty in determining how much of the content of the psalms is to be understood to refer specifically to the Lord Jesus Christ. St Augustine regarded virtually all psalms as Messianic.[6] Few Christian Bible scholars have agreed. Leupold, for example, claims that Augustine 'was, indeed, carrying a New Testament approach beyond the limits that the facts warrant'.[7] Among modern commentators the pendulum has, however, swung over to the opposite extreme. Even an evangelical like Leupold is ultra-cautious and concludes that 'The Messianic element is by far not as common in the Psalter as we might have supposed.'[8]

In order to avoid the two extremes — regarding most, if not all, of the psalms as Messianic on the one hand, or regarding few if any, of them as Messianic on the other — the safe 'middle ground' will be adopted: recognizing the Messianic element of the psalms where there is New Testament authority to do so. This is far from limiting, since the New Testament writers cite from the Psalter more than from any other Old Testament book, with the possible exception of Isaiah. There are at least seventy quotations. Jensen claims there are as many as 116.[9] The actual number depends upon whether certain statements and phrases warrant the designation as a quotation.

With the remainder of the psalms, those not cited by the New Testament as referring to Messiah, we will not go far astray if, with Amyrauld, we keep 'our left eye on David, while we have our right eye full on Christ'. As Christians throughout the ages have read the psalms, they have found 'their thoughts wandering to their Lord, as the one Person in whom these breathings, these praises, these desires, these hopes, these deep feelings, found their only true and full realization'.[10]

The psalms are full of Christ and his church in prophecy and in personal experience, as expressed by Irving Jensen: 'There is a strong prophetic character of the Psalms. Many of the hymns prophesy the suffering and sorrows of God's people, Israel, and their coming deliverance, restoration, and blessing in a future glorious Kingdom. But, most of all, they prophesy of Christ in His two advents: His first advent in humiliation, and His second advent in glory. Such psalms are called Messianic psalms. Some of the Old Testament's most minute prophecies of Christ are found here. They are about His person (God and man); His character (righteous and holy); His work (death and resurrection); and His offices (priest, judge, and king).'[11]

On the day of our Lord's resurrection he appeared to two disciples on the Emmaus Road. As the three of them travelled along the road the Lord reminded them of the Old Testament predictions concerning the sufferings of the Messiah: ' "Ought not the Christ to have suffered these things and to enter into his glory?" And beginning at Moses and all the prophets, he expounded to them *in all the Scriptures* the things concerning himself' (Luke 24:26-27, emphasis added)

That evening the Lord appeared to the gathering of disciples in the upper room. Here our Lord's reference to the psalms is specifically stated: 'These are the words which I spoke to you while I was still with you, that all things must be fulfilled which were written in the Law of Moses and the Prophets *and the Psalms* concerning me' (Luke 24:44, emphasis added).

1. The humanity of Christ

In Psalm 8 the writer to the Hebrews sees the necessity for the full humanity of Messiah:

When I consider your heavens, the work of your fingers,
The moon and the stars, which you have ordained,
What is man that you are mindful of him,
And the son of man that you visit him?

For *you have made him a little lower than the angels,*
And you have crowned him with glory and honour
                              (8:3-5, emphasis added; cf. Heb. 2:5-9).

Psalm 40:6 also contains explicit reference to the humanity of Christ, as is evident from the quotation found in the letter to the Hebrews.[12] This is confirmed when the writer to the Hebrews concludes: 'By that will we have been sanctified through the offering *of the body of Jesus Christ* once for all' (Heb. 10:10, emphasis added).

2. The deity of Christ

The words 'Messiah,' 'Christ' and 'Anointed' are interchangeable since they are the Hebrew, Greek and English equivalents respectively. The one Hebrew word for Messiah occurs ten times in the book of Psalms (2:2; 18:50; 20:6; 28:8; 84:9; 89:38,51; 105:15; 132:10,17). In Psalm 105:15 the word is in the plural and refers to Israel. In Psalm 132 the immediate reference appears to be to Solomon. The other seven instances refer to David. The transition in thought from David to the Promised Messiah/King is often imperceptible: 'It is therefore here invariably applied to the king. The step in advance in the Psalms, however, is, that the Messiah gleams forth occasionally as a King far transcending David, or Solomon, or any mere man. The chief instance of this is in the 2nd Psalm, where the Lord's Anointed is described as the King, the Son of God, the heir of the heathen and of the uttermost parts of the earth, to whom homage is due, whose wrath is perdition, and whose grace is salvation. This Messiah evidently transcends the limits of humanity; and the ideal once revealed only grows in lustre till it becomes real in the Christ of the New Testament.'[13]

The Lord Jesus quotes Psalm 110 in order to demonstrate that he is greater than David and existed before David, the clear implication being that of deity:

The LORD said to my Lord, "Sit at my right hand,
Till I make your enemies your footstool."
The LORD shall send the rod of your strength out of Zion.
Rule in the midst of your enemies!
                              (110:1-2; cf. Matt. 22:42-45).

Many of the Messianic psalms contain a variety of truths concerning the promised Messiah. Consequently within a psalm that is predominantly concerned with Christ as King, there may be an explicit declaration of his deity (e.g. 'Your throne, O God, is for ever and ever... Therefore God, your God, has anointed you...' 45:6-7; cf. Heb. 1:8-9).

3. The sonship of Christ

God the Father declares that Messiah is his unique Son:

I will declare the decree:
The LORD has said to me,
'You are my Son,
Today I have begotten you'

(2:7; cf. Acts 13:33; Heb. 1:5; 5:5).

The Anointed (that is, Messiah or Christ) against whom the nations react and arise (2:2) is the King of Israel (2:6) and the Son of God (2:7) to whom the Father has given the nations (2:8) and to whom all must yield if they are to find pardon and peace with God (2:10-12).

4. The rejection of Christ

The Messiah is hated without a cause (35:19; 69:4; cf. John 15:25) and rejected:

The stone which the builders rejected
Has become the chief corner-stone.
This was the LORD's doing;
It is marvellous in our eyes
(118:22-23; cf. Matt. 21:42; Mark 12:10; Luke 20:17; Acts 4:11;
1 Peter 2:7).

The apostle Peter links the first of these two verses with later prophecies from Isaiah concerning the church:

Behold, I lay in Zion a stone for a foundation,
A tried stone, a precious corner-stone, a sure foundation;

Whoever believes will not act hastily
(Isa. 28:16; 1 Peter 2:6);

and,

He will be as a sanctuary,
But as a stone of stumbling and a rock of offence…
(Isa. 8:14; 1 Peter 2:8).

Here Peter demonstrates the two extremes of rejection and acceptance. With the apostle we testify of Christ that to us 'who believe, he is precious' (1 Peter 2:7).

5. The sufferings of Christ

Although the expression, 'that the Scriptures may be fulfilled', often appears in the New Testament (e.g. John 19:24; 13:18) no words are spoken or actions performed in order that the Scriptures may be fulfilled. The nature of prophecy is that predictions are made of that which will be said and done spontaneously at a later date. This is particularly relevant to the sufferings of Christ. When he cried out from the cross he was not consciously searching for an appropriate scripture to quote — he cried out spontaneously from his agony. Christ did not quote David; David quoted Christ, for the Spirit of Christ told David the words the Saviour would utter, 1,000 years before the event (1 Peter 1:11).

Prophecies from Psalm 22 describing the suffering of the Saviour include the following:

My God, my God, why have you forsaken me?
(v. 1; cf. Matt. 27:46; Mark 15:34).

All those who see me laugh me to scorn;
They shoot out the lip, they shake the head, saying,
'He trusted in the LORD, let him rescue him;
Let him deliver him, since he delights in him!'
(vv. 7-8; cf. Matt. 27:39-43; Mark 15:29-32).

For dogs have surrounded me;
The assembly of the wicked has enclosed me.

They pierced my hands and my feet;
I can count all my bones.
They look and stare at me.
They divide my garments among them,
And for my clothing they cast lots
                    (vv. 16-18; cf. John 20:25; Matt. 27:35; John 19:23-24).

I will declare your name to my brethren;
In the midst of the congregation I will praise you
                    (v. 22; cf. Heb. 2:11-12).

And from Psalm 31 there is a reference to the final moment upon the cross:

Into your hand I commit my spirit;
You have redeemed me, O LORD God of truth
                    (v. 5; cf. Luke 23:46).

The New Testament records the sufferings of Christ largely in terms of the external facts: the Lord Jesus is falsely accused, unjustly sentenced, brutally crucified and lovingly buried. But little is recorded in the New Testament about the Saviour's thoughts and feelings throughout his ordeal. It is in the book of Psalms that such disclosures are found. Here is insight into the Saviour's inner agony:

Reproach has broken my heart,
And I am full of heaviness;
I looked for someone to take pity, but there was none;
And for comforters, but I found none.
They also gave me gall for my food,
And for my thirst they gave me vinegar to drink
                    (69:20-21; cf. John 19:28-30).

The Lord Jesus quotes Psalm 41:9 when he refers to the treachery of Judas. The words that follow in that psalm are particularly pertinent to the Saviour:

Even my own familiar friend in whom I trusted,
  Who ate my bread,
Has lifted up his heel against me.

But you, O LORD, be merciful to me, and raise me up,
That I may repay them.
By this I know that you are well pleased with me,
Because my enemy does not triumph over me.
As for me, you uphold me in my integrity,
And set me before your face for ever

(41:9-12; cf. John 13:18).

The experience of the Lord Jesus Christ is strongly connected with the experience of David. The correlation between the Lord and Judas and the relationship of David and Ahithophel goes beyond mere coincidence. Judas and Ahithophel were both trusted friends; both were guilty of terrible betrayal (2 Sam. 15:31; John 13:21; Luke 22:47-48; Matt. 27:3); both committed suicide by hanging themselves when their treachery was disclosed (2 Sam. 17:23; Matt. 27:5). The anguish of David reflects the pain of the Saviour in being betrayed by a close and trusted friend:

For it is not an enemy who reproaches me;
Then I could bear it.
Nor is it one who hates me who has magnified himself against me;
Then I could hide from him.
But it was you, a man my equal,
My companion and my acquaintance.
We took sweet counsel together,
And walked to the house of God in the throng

(55:12-14).

6. The sacrifice of Christ

Sacrifice and offering you did not desire;
My ears you have opened;
Burnt offering and sin offering you did not require.
Then I said, 'Behold, I come;
In the scroll of the Book it is written of me.
I delight to do your will, O my God,
And your law is within my heart'

(40:6-8; cf. Heb. 10:5-10).

This quotation from the psalms links the death of Christ as a sacrifice with the whole range of sacrifices instituted by God under the Old Covenant at Sinai. The use of the various expressions, 'sacrifice', 'offering', 'burnt offering' and 'sin offering', brings the Levitical sacrifices into sharp focus and emphasizes that the Lord Jesus is the sacrifice to end all sacrifices (Heb. 10:8-10). His sacrifice was prefigured in the whole range of sacrifices ordained in the past.[14]

A connection to the sacrifice of Christ is also made through Psalm 34 where reference is made to the bones of the righteous:

> Many are the afflictions of the righteous,
> But the LORD delivers him out of them all.
> He guards all his bones;
> Not one of them is broken
>
> (vv. 19-20).

The apostle John establishes this correlation immediately upon recording the death of the Saviour (John 19:36). The link goes back beyond the psalm to the days of Moses and the insistence that the Passover lamb should not have 'one of its bones' broken (Exod. 12:46; Num. 9:12). The Passover lamb first sacrificed in Egypt was a type of 'the Lamb of God who takes away the sin of the world' (John 1:29). Satan no doubt understood the connection and implications, even if the Jews did not, when he incited the Jewish leadership to ask for the breaking of the legs of the three crucified ones (John 19:31). The Lord God once more overruled so that the perfection of the sacrifice of Christ would be utterly and absolutely maintained.

7. The resurrection of Christ

> I have set the LORD always before me;
> Because he is at my right hand I shall not be moved.
> Therefore my heart is glad, and my glory rejoices;
> My flesh also will rest in hope.
> For you will not leave my soul in Sheol,
> Nor will you allow your Holy One to see corruption
>
> (16:8-11; Acts 2:25-32).

The apostle Peter explains the grounds on which this psalm could not have referred to David but most certainly referred to the Messiah: David died and his body decayed (Acts 2:29-31).

What remarkable insight the Holy Spirit gave to David! 'So clear a light was shed over the greatness, the extent, and the range of the divine plan of salvation.' [15] This servant of God not only speaks prophetically of the experiences of Messiah; he is confident of his own resurrection too. As he says later, 'As for me, I will see your face in righteousness; I shall be satisfied when I awake in your likeness' (17:15); and, 'I will dwell in the house of the LORD for ever' (23:6).

8. The ascension of Christ

> You have ascended on high,
> You have led captivity captive;
> You have received gifts among men
>
> (68:18; cf. Eph. 4:8).

To lead 'captivity captive' indicates Messiah's complete victory; he has led all his enemies captive. The language may also express the idea that he has made captive to himself those who were captives to others, or who were in subjection to another.[16] The Saviour delivers his people from the clutches of Satan. He captures the captured. Slaves of sin are set free in order to become slaves of righteousness (Rom. 6:17-18). Being a slave of Jesus Christ (Rom. 1:1) is real freedom (John 8:31-32,34-36).

David would have been all too conscious of an apparent conflict in the prophecies between a suffering and a glorified Messiah. He was, however, among those prophets who tried extremely hard to understand the meaning and the timing 'of the sufferings of Christ and the glories that would follow' (1 Peter 1:10-11).

9. The priesthood of Christ

> The LORD has sworn
> And will not relent,
> 'You are a priest for ever
> According to the order of Melchizedek'
>
> (110:4; cf. Heb. 5:6).

Once more the psalms provide a link between the Old Covenant and the New, for David reveals that the priesthood of Messiah will be 'according to the order of Melchizedek', thus providing a foundation from which great doctrines are developed in relation to the priesthood of Christ (Heb. 7:1 – 8:6). It is in being able to trace the Spirit of God behind the events recorded in the Old Testament, and seeing their fulfilment in the Lord Jesus, that Christians are confirmed in their confidence in the living God, the God who breathed out the Scriptures (2 Tim. 3:16; cf. John 5:39). Only God could introduce Melchizedek to Abraham, inspire David with prophetic insight and enlighten the writer to the Hebrews to make the connections.

The writer of Hebrews 7 explains that the priesthood of Christ:

- Unites kingship and priesthood together in one (v. 1; cf. Zech. 6:12-13) which was not permitted under the Old Covenant law of Sinai (cf. Heb. 7:14);
- Is a permanent priesthood lasting to eternity (v. 3; cf. v.25);
- Is superior to the priesthood of Aaron (vv. 7:7-10).

10. The kingdom of Christ

Why do the nations rage,
And the people plot a vain thing?
The kings of the earth set themselves,
And the rulers take counsel together
Against the LORD and against his Anointed
(Ps. 2:1-2; cf. Acts 4:25-26).

In Acts the apostles interpret Psalm 2 as applying to the Lord Jesus Christ, to Herod, Pontius Pilate, the Gentiles and the Jews: 'For truly against your holy servant Jesus, whom you anointed, both Herod and Pontius Pilate, with the Gentiles and the people of Israel, were gathered together...' (Acts 4:27-28).

Paul connects the same psalm to the resurrection of Jesus and to the Father's giving to him 'the sure mercies of David' (Isa. 55:3; Acts 13:33-37). The kingdom of Christ is established after his resurrection: 'For he must reign till he has put all enemies under his feet. The last enemy that will be destroyed is death' (1 Cor. 15:25-26; cf. Eph. 1:20-23).

Messiah's kingdom is everlasting:

Your throne, O God, is for ever and ever;
A sceptre of righteousness is the sceptre of your kingdom.
You love righteousness and hate wickedness;
Therefore God, your God, has anointed you
With the oil of gladness more than your companions
                                        (45:6-7; cf. Heb. 1:8-9).

The everlasting reign of Christ is also implicit in Psalm 72. The language of Psalms 45 and 72 is too colourful to apply to earthly kings; the terms are too extravagant if they do not refer to Christ.

There is evident connection in the Messianic psalms with the prophecy of Nathan concerning David's kingdom (2 Sam. 7:12-16). Prophecy relating to the covenant with David never, however, loses sight of the covenant with Abraham. The words in Psalm 72:17, 'And men shall be blessed in him; all nations shall call him blessed,' have evident reference to the promise to Abraham (Gen. 12:3). The same is true of Psalm 22:27:

All the ends of the world
Shall remember and turn to the LORD,
And all the families of the nations
Shall worship before you.

In other words, then the blessing of Abraham will have come upon the Gentiles in the person of Christ.[17]

Application

The experience of the church

Every psalm has relevance, application and blessing for the Christian. Together they contain the longings of the human soul. Here poetry is adapted to be sung with the accompaniment of the harp or lyre. Such poetry is mainly 'an expression of deep *feeling*, and has its foundation in *feeling* or emotion. It is not so much the fruit of the understanding as of the heart; not so much the creation of the imagination as the utterance of deep personal emotion.'[18]

There are psalms for every occasion in life and for every spiritual condition, and they form an ideal basis for personal devotional life. There is no
experience of the believer that is not reflected here.[19] There is the
expression of distress, anguish of heart, fear, hope, joy, trust, comfort,
thankfulness, devotion to God, deep repentance for sin and delight in
God's mercy, pardon and peace. There is a distinctly spiritual purpose behind all of these songs. They are designed to raise the mind above the
things of the world, to lift the heart towards God, to inspire confidence in
God, to provide comfort in times of trial and affliction and to point forward
to a better life ahead for the people of God. Through these lyrics worshippers hear 'soul-stirring truths, uttered with ear-piercing words, but suited to
their feelings and pressed on their consciences, and riveted there by the
most mighty sanctions of life and death, present and eternal'.[20]

Through the main contributor, King David, 'the sweet psalmist of Israel'
(2 Sam. 23:1), God fashioned songs and prayers for all occasions. The
Lord raised David in the sheep pasture so that he might identify with the
lowly and simple. God took him to war so that he might be filled with
thoughts of victory and glory. He placed him in a palace so that his thinking might soar to the heights of majesty and sovereign power. He delivered
him to the solitude of the wilderness so that he might quietly contemplate
the glorious person and the mighty deeds of the living God. He kept him
there for years within a hair's breadth of death, so that David might be disciplined to trust and to depend upon the providence of God. 'His trials
were but the tuning of the instrument with which the Spirit might express
the various melodies which He designed to utter by him for the consolation
and edification of spiritual men.'[21]

David's personal testimony that he was inspired by the triune God rings
clear:

The Spirit of the LORD spoke by me,
And his word was on my tongue.
The God of Israel said,
The Rock of Israel spoke to me...

(2 Sam. 23:2-3).

The psalms of David provide the church of God with its greatest prayers
and greatest praises. There is a prayer for every condition of life. David was
an outstanding man of God who, like Elijah, was 'a man with a nature like
ours' and, also like that prophet, knew how to pray earnestly to the Lord
(James 5:17). This man David, with all his faults and failings, soared to the

spiritual heights. In him the grace of God is magnified. God is the friend of sinners. This is the 'man after [God's] own heart' (1 Sam. 13:14).

Commenting upon the Christian application of Psalm 149:6-9, C. H. Spurgeon wrote, '... under the new covenant, the enemies of the "spiritual house" are spiritual enemies (Ephesians 6:12).' He continued: 'In this Israel was not an example, but a type: we will not copy the chosen people in making literal war, but we will fulfil the emblem by carrying on spiritual war. We praise God and contend with our corruptions; we sing joyfully and war earnestly with evil of every kind. Our weapons are not carnal, but they are mighty, and wound with both back and edge. The word of God is all edge; whichever way we turn it, it strikes deadly blows at falsehood and wickedness. If we do not praise we shall grow sad in our conflict; and if we do not fight we shall become presumptuous in our song. The verse [v. 6] indicates a happy blending of the chorister and the crusader.'[22]

Conclusion

At the time it was written the twenty-third psalm was a great blessing to believing Israelites as they celebrated the Lord's goodness and mercy, but it took on an even greater significance with the coming of the Lord Jesus Christ. When believers now read, 'The LORD is my shepherd; I shall not want' (23:1), their thoughts turn to the Good Shepherd who came into the world to lay down his life for the sheep (John 10:11,15). The clearer light of the New Testament has not dimmed the quality of the psalms and the blessings to be derived from them. In fact the very opposite is the case. The content of this praise-and-prayer book of God shines all the brighter when seen from a Christ-centred perspective.

The 150 psalms make a unique contribution to the Scriptures. Here are instructions as to how God is to be worshipped and adored 'in spirit and truth' (John 4:24); here are profound insights into the person and work of the Saviour; and here are the deepest spiritual experiences of the human heart.

Proverbs

('brief sayings expressing wisdom')

Author: Solomon
(mainly)

Key thought: The fear of the Lord

Theme:
Godliness is intensely practical

'The fear of the LORD is the
beginning of knowledge,
But fools despise wisdom and
instruction.'

Proverbs 1:7

Summary

The verses in the beautiful final section (31:10-31) are arranged in Hebrew
in acrostic form.

Proverbs

As we have noted elsewhere,[1] the Protestant Old Testament is arranged in four sections:

Law	Genesis to Deuteronomy
History	Joshua to Esther
Poetry	Job to Song of Solomon
Prophecy	Major Prophets: Isaiah to Daniel
	Minor Prophets: Hosea to Malachi

Proverbs is the third book in the poetry division. Sometimes it is combined with Job and Ecclesiastes under the collective title of 'Wisdom Literature'.

The English word 'proverb' is a translation of the Hebrew word *mashal*, which comes from a root word meaning 'to be like', or 'to represent'. Most of the proverbs use comparison in order to communicate their truths, for example: 'The refining pot is for silver and the furnace for gold, but the LORD tests the hearts' (17:3). In the A.V., *mashal* is translated nineteen times by the word 'proverb' and eighteen times by the word 'parable'. *Mashal* has been defined as: 'a brief, pithy saying which expresses wisdom'.[2]

Every culture has its proverbial sayings, its witticisms. This book, however, is not simply a collection of such maxims or wise sayings from the nation of Israel. 'Underneath the superficial resemblance there is a fundamental difference between the witticisms of the nations and the proverbs of God's Word.'[3] These proverbs are included in the literature which is 'given by inspiration of God' (2 Tim. 3:16-17). This is wisdom from God. These proverbs or maxims set out what is right and what is wrong in the sight of the living God, who is all-wise and all-holy. They show the practical outworking of godliness in the spiritual, moral and social spheres. There is a universal appeal: neither Israel nor Jerusalem are referred to in Proverbs (nor incidentally in the other wisdom literature in Job and Ecclesiastes). Here the wise man is the one who lives his life according to the revealed will of God. He walks in the way of truth and righteousness. Consequently he is blessed by God and he knows real contentment and peace.

Author

The book itself contains indications of its authorship:

- 'The proverbs of Solomon the son of David, king of Israel' (1:1; cf. 10:1).
- 'The words of the wise' (22:17; 24:23; cf. Ethan, Heman, etc., in 1 Kings 4:31).
- 'These also are proverbs of Solomon which the men of Hezekiah king of Judah copied' (25:1). These proverbs were added to the collection about two hundred years after Solomon's death in 930 B.C. The 'men of Hezekiah' may have included the prophets Isaiah and Micah, who were engaged in their ministries at that time.
- 'The words of Agur the son of Jakeh, his utterance' (30:1).
- 'The words of King Lemuel, the utterance which his mother taught him' (31:1).

These references strongly suggest that Solomon was responsible for composing or compiling the majority of the proverbs and pithy sayings that this book contains. It was King Solomon, son of King David, who 'spoke three thousand proverbs, and his songs were one thousand and five' (1 Kings 4:32).[4] From this vast number of proverbs the Spirit of God led him to choose a much smaller collection for the instruction of believers in all ages and cultures. Solomon probably had this collection of proverbs in mind when he wrote elsewhere: '... because the Preacher was wise, he still taught the people knowledge; yes, he pondered and sought out *and set in order many proverbs*' (Eccles. 12:9, emphasis added).

Solomon was given an outstanding degree of wisdom. In the early days of his life, the Lord appeared to him at Gibeon and said, 'Ask! What shall I give you?' (1 Kings 3:5). Solomon responded with great respect and reverence. Aware of the tremendous responsibility of being king over Israel, he said, 'Therefore give to your servant an understanding heart to judge your people, that I may discern between good and evil. For who is able to judge this great people of yours?' (1 Kings 3:9). The Lord was pleased with this request and responded by giving him 'a wise and understanding heart', so that there has not been anyone like him before or since (1 Kings 3:12).

Solomon's wisdom extended to all branches of natural science. He 'spoke of trees ... of animals, of birds, of creeping things, and of fish' (1 Kings 4:33). He was a philosopher, musician, poet, botanist, zoologist, architect, businessman, administrator and king. But the wisdom God gave him also embraced the profound depths of true religion and personal godliness. We have no record of Solomon's knowledge in the natural sciences. Rather, it has pleased God to provide an accurate record of his knowledge of practical wisdom. This indicates the real intention of Scripture, 'not to teach philosophy, but religion; not to make men of science, but men of sound godliness'.[5]

Solomon had a keen eye for observation. He displays a profound understanding of human nature: a discernment of character and insight into motives behind actions. His teaching is intensely practical. The contents of this book make a great contribution to that body of teaching by which 'the man of God may be complete, thoroughly equipped for every good work' (2 Tim. 3:17). William Arnot aptly entitled his commentary, *Studies in Proverbs: laws from heaven for life on earth.*[6]

Solomon was the wisest of men and yet, in his latter years, he did not live out the wisdom he taught. In him we might see the fulfilment of the maxim which says, 'Do as I say, not as I do.' Solomon's son, Rehoboam, followed the example of his father in his latter years, rather than his instruction, and became a foolish and evil king.

Historical setting

Solomon died in 930 B.C., which dates the composition and compilation of his proverbs to around 970-930 B.C., but they are in no way time-bound or culture-bound. There is no mention of Israel or Jerusalem since these proverbial sayings are intended for all people of all nations. The frequent address to the reader as 'my son' (twenty-three times, e.g. 1:8,10,15), rather than to 'Israel,' may have been used in anticipation of the day when the church would extend throughout the world.

Solomon is the author of three books of the Bible. It is quite likely that these books were written at different periods of his life. It has been suggested that the Song of Solomon may have been written when he was young and in love; Proverbs may have been compiled when he was in his middle age, when it is evident that his intellectual powers were at their height; and Ecclesiastes may have been written in old age when he was disappointed and disillusioned at his own spiritual state and the weakness of his sinful nature.

Hebrew poetry

As has been pointed out in the chapter on the book of Psalms, Hebrew poetry is quite distinct from English poetry, ancient or modern. It is distinguished by certain peculiarities and characteristics of its own. Its principal feature is not rhyme, but parallelism, [7] for example:

A just weight and balance are the LORD's;
All the weights in the bag are his work

(16:11).

Here it will be seen that the second line expresses a thought that is parallel in meaning to the first line.

Three basic forms of parallelism have been identified:

1. *Synonymous parallelism*, in which the same thought is repeated in almost the same words:

Pride goes before destruction,
And a haughty spirit before a fall.

(16:18).

2. *Antithetical parallelism*, in which a thought is expressed by means of contrast with its opposite:

A soft answer turns away wrath,
But a harsh word stirs up anger.

(15:1).

3. *Synthetic parallelism*, in which the second line completes or fills out the thought of the first:

Keep your heart with all diligence,
For out of it spring the issues of life

(4:23).

Outline

The underlying theme of the whole book is contained in the seventh verse of the first chapter: 'The fear of the LORD is the beginning of knowledge, but fools despise wisdom and instruction' (1:7).

The book of Proverbs falls into three sections, with each division beginning with the phrase: 'The proverbs of Solomon' (1:1; 10:1; 25:1). Some Bible scholars have identified what they see as a significant change in the pronouns. In some cases these pronouns are in the second person, and in others the third person. On this basis they suggest that when 'you' and 'your' predominate in a section it indicates instruction *for* Solomon by his teacher. On the other hand, when 'he' and 'his' predominate that means instruction *by* Solomon. It is, however, safer to view the whole collection as part of the God-breathed Scriptures and consequently 'profitable for doctrine, for reproof, for correction, for instruction in righteousness' (2 Tim. 3:16).

The opening verses set out the purpose for which these proverbs were compiled:

To know wisdom and instruction,
To perceive the words of understanding,
To receive the instruction of wisdom,
Justice, judgement, and equity;
To give prudence to the simple [literally the 'open' — that is, the open-minded],
To the young man knowledge and discretion —
A wise man will hear and increase learning,
And a man of understanding will attain wise counsel,
To understand a proverb and an enigma,
The words of the wise and their riddles

(1:2-5).

In Ecclesiastes, Solomon also gives the reason for his collection of proverbs:

And, moreover, because the Preacher was wise, he still taught the people knowledge; yes, he pondered and sought out and set in order many proverbs. The Preacher sought to find acceptable words; and what was written was upright — words of truth. The words of the wise are like goads, and the words of scholars are like well-driven nails, given by one shepherd. And further, my son, be admonished by these. Of making many books there is no end, and much study is wearisome to the flesh. Let us hear the conclusion of the whole matter:

> Fear God and keep his commandments,
> For this is the whole duty of man.
> For God will bring every work into judgement,
> Including every secret thing,
> Whether it is good or whether it is evil
>
> (Eccles. 12:9-14).

Solomon uses poetry, parables, short stories, maxims and wise sayings to warn against the influence of bad company; against backbiting and gossip; against lying and deceit in business and trade; against taking bribes; against quarrelling, anger, controversies; against impurity of mind and body; against apathy and laziness; against pride and boasting; against greed and craving for money; against the exploitation of workers and the neglect of the poor. The style of these maxims facilitates memorization.

The concept of the family underlies many of the sayings: 'father' occurs in fifteen verses, 'mother' in eleven, 'son' in forty-four. Husband and wife are exhorted to maintain an exclusively monogamous relationship (in spite of Solomon's own confused and complex unions and the polygamy that was rife at the time). Parents share responsibility for the raising of their offspring and great respect is to be paid to mother as well as to father. Attacks on family life and relationships are roundly condemned.

Christ and his church

No prophecies, types or theophanies are found in the book of Proverbs. There are nevertheless a number of verses which provide interesting insights into the character of the Son of God.

1. The eternal generation of the Son of God

> The LORD possessed me at the beginning of his way,
> Before his works of old.

I have been established from everlasting,
From the beginning, before there was ever an earth.
When there were no depths I was brought forth,
When there were no fountains abounding with water…
Then I was beside him, as a master craftsman;
And I was daily his delight,
Rejoicing always before him,
Rejoicing in his inhabited world,
And my delight was with the sons of men

(8:22-24,30-31).

In the New Testament the Lord Jesus Christ is designated 'the only begotten Son' (John 1:18), 'the only begotten of the Father' (John 1:14), 'the only begotten Son of God' (John 3:18) and 'his only begotten Son' (John 3:16; 1 John 4:9). These words of Scripture, confirmed and supported by many more, lead to the conclusion that Jesus Christ '… is not the Son of his Father in the sense that he had a beginning. Nor is the phrase merely an exalted title, like that applied to earthly rulers. Nor is it simply a device to remind us that he became a man by supernatural means, and not by ordinary generation — though of course it does remind us of that (Luke 1:35). The First Person of the Trinity is called "Father" to show to us what is his eternal relationship with the Son. The Second Person of the Trinity is called "Son" to show us what relationship he in turn has to the First Person. "Father" and "Son" are everyday titles. But they help to convey to our poor minds something of the relationship which these two persons eternally enjoy between themselves.'[8]

The Son owes his generation to the Father, but the same cannot be said the other way round. It is also said that the Son is 'the brightness of [the Father's] glory and the express image of his person' (Heb. 1:3). It would be impossible for him to be that without the Father. But God the Father is never said to be the express image of God the Son. Yet, as it would be impossible for the Son to be what he is without the Father, so the Father could not find expression without God the Son (John 1:18; Matt. 11:27; John 14:9). This is the relationship that the First and Second Persons of the Trinity have to each other.

That the being of God is beyond our comprehension should come as no surprise. Many years ago Zophar asked his friend Job a profound question:

Can you search out the deep things of God?
Can you find out the limits of the Almighty?
They are higher than heaven — what can you do?
Deeper than Sheol — what can you know?
Their measure is longer than the earth and broader than the sea

(Job 11:7-9).

The Lord Jesus Christ is not a creature; he is God, as the Father is God. 'Both are God; both are God equally; both are God eternally, and both are God in the same sense.'[9] The Athanasian Creed is right to affirm that 'The Son is from the Father alone, neither made, nor created, but begotten.'

2. The Son's sovereignty over nature

Who has ascended into heaven, or descended?
Who has gathered the wind in his fists?
Who has bound the waters in a garment?
Who has established all the ends of the earth?
What is his name, and what is his Son's name,
If you know?

(30:4).

This wisdom of Agur the son of Jakeh (see 30:1) should be compared with the teaching of the New Testament regarding the involvement of the Son of God in creation (John 1:1-3; Col. 1:15-17; Heb. 1:1-3). The control of nature exercised by the Lord Jesus Christ is further confirmation of his unique sonship. He twice stilled a storm (Mark 4:39; 6:51) and he walked on water (John 6:18-21; cf. Ps. 107:23-30; Job 9:8,11; Mark 6:48). When he walked on the sea and stilled the storm, the disciples could form only one conclusion: they 'worshipped him, saying, "Truly you are the Son of God"' (Matt. 14:33; cf. 1 John 5:20).

3. The Son personifies wisdom

The wisdom of Solomon is a foreshadowing of the Lord Jesus Christ, 'in whom are hidden all the treasures of wisdom and knowledge' (Col. 2:3). The Lord Jesus said to the Jews of his day, 'The Queen of the South will rise up in the judgement with the men of this generation and condemn them, for she came from the ends of the earth to hear the wisdom of Solomon; and indeed a greater than Solomon is here' (Luke 11:31).

The wise man, the subject of these proverbs, is a godly man, a righteous man, a holy man. The wisdom spoken of here is found entirely and completely in Christ (Col. 2:3; cf. Prov. 8:35-36). His people have wisdom and righteousness and sanctification and redemption only as they are *in* Christ. For he 'became for us wisdom from God — and righteousness and sanctification and redemption — that, as it is written, "He who glories, let him glory in the LORD"' (1 Cor. 1:30-31).

Application

The book of Proverbs does not have a distinct structure; it is not the unfolding of history, or the development of doctrine; it is a collection of wise sayings, stated succinctly. Probably the best method of study is the topical method. This can be achieved either with the aid of a concordance, or by slow and careful reading of the text, forming categories in the process. Words to be located might include: fear (nineteen references in the RAV); anger (eight references); children (ten references); fool/fools (fifty-eight references; friend/friends (nineteen references); and tongue (nineteen references). Individual proverbs could then be grouped to give a composite view of a subject, as in the following example:

The discipline of children

He who spares his rod hates his son,
but he who loves him disciplines him promptly

(13:24).

Chasten your son while there is hope,
And do not set your heart on his destruction

(19:18).

Train up a child in the way he should go,
And when he is old he will not depart from it

(22:6).

An example of a topical study

Anger	14:17,29; 15:18; 16:32; 19:11
Benevolence	3:9-10; 11:24-26; 14:21; 19:17; 22:9
Children	13:24; 17:6; 19:18; 22:6,15; 23:13-14
Fear of God	1:7; 3:7; 9:10; 10:27; 14:26-27; 15:16,33; 16:6; 19:23; 23:17; 24:21
Fools	10:18,21,23; 12:15-16; 14:9,16; 15:2; 17:10,12,24; 20:3; 23:9; 27:22; 28:26
Friendship	17:17; 18:24; 19:4; 27:10,17
Indolence	6:6-11; 10:4-5,26; 12:27; 13:4; 15:19; 18:9; 19:15,24; 20:4,13; 24:30-34; 26:13-16
Oppression	14:31; 22:22; 28:16
Pride	6:17; 11:2; 13:10; 15:25; 16:18-19; 18:12; 21:4,24; 29:23; 30:13
Strife	3:30; 10:12; 15:18; 16:28; 17:1,14,19; 18:6,19; 20:3; 22:10; 25:8; 30:33
The tongue	4:24; 10:11-14,17-21,31-32; 12:6,17-19,22; 13:3; 14:3; 15:1-2,4-5,7,23; 16:13,23,27; 17:4; 18:6-7,21; 19:1
Wealth	10:2,15; 11:4,28; 13:7,11,22; 15:6; 16:8; 18:11; 19:4; 27:24; 28:6,22
Women	(evil) 2:16-19; 5:3-14,20; 6:24-35; 7:5-27; 9:13-18; 23:27-28
	(good) 5:18-19; 11:16; 18:22; 19:14; 31:10-31
Wisdom	1:7,20-22; 2:6-7,10-11; 3:13-18,19,21; 4:5-9; 8:1-16; 9:1-6; 12:8; 14:8; 18:4; 19:8; 24:3

New Testament references to Proverbs

A further method of study is to follow up the New Testament references to the proverbs. There are seven references (one proverb is quoted twice):

> My son, do not despise the chastening of the LORD,
> Nor be discouraged when you are rebuked by him;
> For whom the LORD loves he chastens,
> And scourges every son whom he receives
>   (Heb. 12:5-6; cf. Prov.3:11-12).

> God resists the proud,
> But gives grace to the humble
>   (James 4:6; 1 Peter 5:5; cf. Prov. 3:34).

Love will cover a multitude of sins
> (1 Peter 4:8; cf. Prov. 10:12).

If the righteous one is scarcely saved,
Where will the ungodly and the sinner appear?
> (1 Peter 4:18; cf. Prov. 11:31).

Therefore if your enemy hungers, feed him;
If he thirsts, give him a drink;
For in so doing you will heap coals of fire on his head
> (Rom. 12:20; cf. Prov. 25:21-22).

A dog returns to his own vomit
> (2 Peter 2:22; Prov. 26:11).

There are also a number of probable allusions to a proverb:

e.g.	Rom. 12:16	cf. Prov. 3:7
	Heb. 12:13	cf. Prov. 4:26
	1 Peter 2:17	cf. Prov. 24:21
	Luke 14:8-10	cf. Prov. 25:6-7
	James 4:13-14	cf. Prov. 27:1

Conclusion

The book of Proverbs contains a high view of the living God. Throughout its pages the Lord is respected and honoured. The Lord Jesus taught his disciples to begin prayer with the words: 'Our Father in heaven, *Hallowed be your name*' (Matt. 6:9, emphasis added). As the Lord is to be honoured and revered in the prayers of his people, so he must be honoured and re-vered in the principles *and* practices of his people. Whereas the psalms give an insight into the worship of Almighty God, the proverbs give under-standing of the daily life of God's people. The book of Proverbs is mainly about personal ethics, 'not as the sinner's way to God, but as the believer's walk with God on this earth'.[10] The prophets who come later show more clearly the way of salvation and call the people to a saving knowledge of God. We are saved by grace through faith, not by grace through good works. We are pardoned on account of our trusting, not on the basis of our trying. But having been saved by grace through faith, we then seek to live the life of obedience. The order is vital: faith, salvation and then good works. As the apostle Paul clearly expresses the order, 'For by grace you have been saved through faith, and that not of yourselves; it is the gift of God, not of works, lest anyone should boast. For we are his workmanship, created in Christ Jesus for good works, which God prepared beforehand that we should walk in them' (Eph. 2:8-10).

The letter of James has been described as the New Testament equivalent to the book of Proverbs. Both have a keen interest in God's people gaining wisdom from heaven to guide them into practical, godly living: 'Who is wise and understanding among you? Let him show by good conduct that his works are done in the meekness of wisdom. But if you have bitter envy and self-seeking in your hearts, do not boast and lie against the truth. This wisdom does not descend from above, but is earthly, sensual, demonic. For where envy and self-seeking exist, confusion and every evil thing will be there. But the wisdom that is from above is first pure, then peaceable, gentle, willing to yield, full of mercy and good fruits, without partiality and without hypocrisy' (James 3:13-17).

Ecclesiastes

('the preacher')

Author: Solomon
(probably)

Key thought: 'Vanity'

Theme:
Life is meaningless without God

`""Vanity of vanities,"
says the Preacher;
"Vanity of vanities, all is vanity."'
Ecclesiastes 1:2

Summary

Ecclesiastes

Ecclesiastes is a remarkably relevant book. It 'gives the appearance of being written with our time in mind', for there is 'a scepticism that sounds modern'.[1] In a world full of disillusioned people, the writer speaks as one who has tasted all that the world has to offer — the best of pleasures, the height of power, the ultimate in prestige, worldwide popularity — and still he remains unsatisfied. Nothing has any meaning. There is a futility and purposelessness about life when there is no living relationship with God. To rejoice in the gifts without delighting in the Giver leaves life empty — without meaning and without purpose. As the hymn writer testifies, 'The waters of the earth have failed; and I am thirsty still.'

In the Hebrew Bible the title of this book is *Qoheleth* or, more fully, 'The Words of Qoheleth, the son of David, king in Jerusalem'. The word *'Qoheleth'* is rare. It is found seven times in Ecclesiastes (1:1,2,12; 7:27; 12:8,9,10) and nowhere else in the Old Testament. It is not an easy word to translate; in fact it has been called an 'untranslatable title'.[2]

The English title, 'Ecclesiastes', is a simple transliteration of the Greek. The writers of the Septuagint, who translated the Hebrew Old Testament into Greek, chose the title *Ekklesiastes*, which carries the basic meaning of 'assembly' (the same root word used in the Greek New Testament for 'the church,' e.g., Matt. 16:18). *Qoheleth* is a speaker before an assembly, someone who addresses a congregation (as when Solomon assembled the people at the dedication of the temple in 1 Kings 8:1,2,5). One who addresses an assembly became associated with the function of a preacher; consequently our English version begins: 'The words of the Preacher' (1:1). The content of Ecclesiastes suggests that this translation is only an approximation, since *Qoheleth* 'appears to be philosophizing rather than preaching'.[3] Here is a speaker, a public speaker, a preacher maybe, a speaker in an assembly debating before an audience the ultimate meaning of life.

Author

There is something intriguing about the way in which the author announces himself. He comes remarkably close to calling himself Solomon, yet holds back. The name Solomon does not appear in Ecclesiastes, whereas in Proverbs and the Song of Songs Solomon is openly declared to be the author (Prov. 1:1; S. of S. 1:1). Why this silence? Why no open declaration that it is by Solomon? As much of it is autobiographical maybe he was too ashamed to put his name to it.

Tradition and some recent scholars maintain that the author *is* Solomon: 'Who else could possibly have described himself as "the son of David, king in Jerusalem"? We have before us the words of a man who, because of his privileged position, has sampled all that life has to offer. But he is now king and carries the responsibility of ruling others. He also takes upon himself the responsibility of teaching them and calls himself "the Preacher".'[4]

There is internal evidence in favour of the traditional view that Solomon is the author:

- He calls himself 'the son of David, king in Jerusalem' (1:1; cf. v. 12);
- He possesses unequalled wisdom (1:16; cf. 1 Kings 3:12; 4:29-30);
- He has indulged himself in every pleasure (2:1-3);
- He has great wealth (2:8; cf. 1 Kings 10:14-29);
- He undertook extensive building projects (2:4-6; cf. 1 Kings 5:1 – 7:51);
- He had a fine collection of proverbs (12:9; cf. 1 Kings 4:32);
- The proverbs contained in this book are like those found in the book of Proverbs.

Many Christian scholars do not agree with this traditional view. The reasons against regarding Solomon as the author are:

- The name Solomon does not occur. There is no explicit claim to be from his pen.
- All the writings of Solomon bear his name in their titles. Here the unusual designation *'Qoheleth'* appears.
- The words, 'I, *Qoheleth, was* king … in Jerusalem' (1:12), suggest that the writer has ceased to be king, whereas Solomon was King of Israel to the day of his death.

- The background of the book does not fit the time of Solomon: it was a time of misery and futility (1:2-11); the splendour of Solomon's age was gone (1:12 – 2:26); a time of death had begun for Israel (3:1-15); injustice and violence were present (4:1-3); there was heathen tyranny (5:7,9-19); death was preferred to life (7:1); 'one man ruled over other men to their hurt' (8:9).[5]

   (These comments cannot be substantiated by the texts; also there was rebellion at the end of Solomon's reign.)

The evidence is strongly in favour of Solomon as the author of the book of Ecclesiastes. 'If the Preacher is identified as Solomon, Ecclesiastes was written from a unique vantage-point. Possessing the greatest mental, material, and political resources ever combined in one man, he was qualified beyond all others to write this book.'[6]

Historical setting

The book reflects the latter part of Solomon's life immediately following a period of serious backsliding and probably close to his death (930 B.C.) when he saw himself as 'an old and foolish king' (4:13). In his early days, 'Solomon loved the LORD, walking in the statutes of his father David' (1 Kings 3:3). But in mid-life Solomon turned from God (1 Kings 11:1-10) and used his outstanding wisdom (1 Kings 3:5-12) in the search for satisfaction and happiness — without God. Consequently everything in life turned out to be futile and meaningless. 'Vanity of vanities, all is vanity' (1:2). All that he knew or experienced in the world seemed empty and pointless. Eventually he turned back to God:

> Let us hear the conclusion of the whole matter:
> Fear God and keep his commandments,
> For this is the whole duty of man
>
>   (12:13).

If Solomon was the author of the book of Ecclesiastes then 12:13-14 might be seen to indicate that, close to his death, he was restored into a right relationship with the Lord.[7]

The book of Ecclesiastes is not, like so many of the messages of the prophets, directed at one particular nation at a distinct moment in its history. This book, 'with all its lessons and illustrations, is the property of the Church and of the world in every age'.[8]

Interpretation

Before attempting an outline of this book it is necessary to discuss how it should be understood. Unlike other Bible books, any definition of the structure of Ecclesiastes will be greatly influenced by determining its purpose and why it is included in the divinely inspired Scripture. Leupold declares that 'There are few Biblical books with regard to whose purpose there is a greater lack of unanimity,'[9] and Hendriksen admits that the interpretation of this book 'is not at all an easy task'.[10] Of all the books of the Bible, Ecclesiastes requires particularly careful handling (2 Tim. 2:15).

William Hendriksen follows Martin Wyngaarden's analysis by seeing Ecclesiastes as a book containing a whole series of problems and solutions. The key, for him, is found in the last chapter: 'The words of the wise are like goads, and the words of scholars are like well-driven nails, given by one shepherd' (12:11). Goads are interpreted as the problems, and nails are viewed as the solutions. Working on this basis, Hendriksen divides Ecclesiastes into four discourses (beginning 1:1; 3:16; 6:1; 8:1), with at least one goad and one nail in each section.[11] Qoheleth repeatedly introduces problems of various kinds and then describes his struggle to arrive at solutions to these problems. Stuart Olyott identifies a similar structure (based on Jensen's outline) but calls the four sections four sermons.[12]

By contrast, Derek Kidner rejects this kind of structure and takes the approach that here we have 'a man of conviction with a faith to share'.[13] In his opinion the writer of Ecclesiastes is not expressing his own thoughts but the views of others: 'At bottom we can find the axiom of all the wise men of the Bible, that the fear of the Lord is the beginning of wisdom. But Qoheleth plans to bring us to that point last of all, when we are desperate for an answer. There are hints of it in passing, but his main approach is from the other end; the resolve to see how far a man will get with no such basis. He puts himself — and us — in the shoes of the humanist or secularist. Not the atheist, for atheism was hardly a going concern in his day, but the person who starts his thinking from man and the observable world, and knows God only from a distance.'[14]

The New Testament gives no help towards the interpretation of the book of Ecclesiastes. Although attempts have been made to link verses from this book to New Testament teaching, they have failed. Bridges admits that, with regard to the book of Ecclesiastes, 'The writers of the New Testament have not given any express reference to it.'[15]

It is difficult to know how much of what Solomon has written is from his own bitter experience. Some is obviously so, and he is looking back over his life and assessing where he went wrong:

> I set my heart to know wisdom and to know madness and folly. I perceived that this also is grasping for the wind.

> For in much wisdom is much grief,
> And he who increases knowledge increases sorrow
>
> (1:17-18).

> I said, 'I will be wise';
> But it was far from me
>
> (7:23).

Although Solomon knew much wisdom he was unable to apply it to himself. Women were his downfall and he confesses it:

> I find more bitter than death
> The woman whose heart is snares and nets,
> Whose hands are fetters.
> He who pleases God shall escape from her,
> But the sinner shall be taken by her
>
> (7:26).

When Solomon was old his wives turned his heart after other gods (1 Kings 11:4). He probably has the latter years of his own life in mind when he writes:

> Dead flies putrefy the perfumer's ointment,
> And cause it to give off a foul odour;
> So does a little folly to one respected for wisdom and honour
>
> (10:1).

There is also the possibility of the same connection when he considers his horrific backsliding and idolatry and likens himself to 'a living dog' that 'is better than a dead lion' (9:4). Does he mourn that there was no prophet like Nathan to challenge him and say, 'What are you doing?' (8:4 cf. 2 Sam. 12:7-9). Viewed in the light of an author under deep conviction by God, the book of Ecclesiastes takes on another dimension: it is deeply personal and sorrowful; it is a warning to all.

Outline

Apart from the general outline it is difficult, if not impossible, to discover an underlying structure. The style is that of the philosopher reflecting on all aspects of life: he observes; he reasons; he deduces; he concludes. Death is a prominent subject throughout the book of Ecclesiastes, featuring in eleven of the twelve chapters. Solomon contends that the pursuit of all things is futile because, whether they are attained or not, at death they will all be left behind: 'Then I hated all my labour in which I had toiled under the sun, because I must leave it to the man who will come after me. And who knows whether he will be a wise man or a fool?' (2:18-19).

Introduction (1:1-11)

The theme is introduced in the first eleven verses: everything in life is vanity. The word 'vanity' occurs thirty-seven times. It is not a good translation of the Hebrew, since 'vanity' means empty pride, arrogance, or conceit. The Hebrew word here means 'something without substance, which quickly passes away'.[16] It is better translated 'futility', 'meaninglessness', or 'pointlessness'. Linked with this word are expressions such as, 'under the sun' (twenty-nine times), 'upon the earth' (seven times) and 'under the heaven' (three times). Consequently Ecclesiastes has been called 'the book of the natural man'.[17]

The expression 'under the sun' is a key phrase throughout the pages of Ecclesiastes. Every aspect of life is considered from a purely mundane, earthly point of view. As Leupold expresses the thought, 'The presence of the little phrase "under the sun" always says in effect, "What I claim is true if one deals with purely earthly values."'[18]

Part I: The meaninglessness of everything in life
(1:12 - 6:12)

Everything in life has been tried and tested by Solomon to find fulfilment, satisfaction and happiness: science, worldly wisdom and philosophy, pleasure, drinking, building, farming, gardening, amassing possessions, accumulating wealth, pursuing music. He searched but found no answer in materialism, in fatalism (the theory that everything is predetermined and nothing can be changed), in deism (religion without revelation). Nothing answered the deepest longings of his heart and mind. He realized only the futility of life lived exclusively in these pursuits. Exclude God from the world and nothing makes sense any more.

Solomon has engaged himself in the pursuit of happiness, purpose, meaning and satisfaction. He has undertaken this quest with commitment and zeal. He looks back upon the time and energy expended and concludes it has all been pointless, a sheer waste of time. Wherever he has turned his attention, the result has eventually been the same: nothing has any point — whether power, popularity, prestige or pleasure; apart from God, nothing satisfies or answers the deepest longings of the human heart. All earthly goals and ambitions, when undertaken without reference to God, end in dissatisfaction and frustration. The world is full of oppression, envy, greed and loneliness. Human beings are ultimately no better than the animals, as the bodies of both return to dust. He asserts that it is better to eat and drink and be content daily in one's labours than to have 'laboured for the wind' (5:16). God's own work is the only work that lasts for ever (3:14). In his disillusionment Solomon recognizes that the only meaningful purpose in life is to keep oneself alive and to take care of one's soul because true wisdom and knowledge and joy come from obedience to God (2:26). It is possible to have riches and wealth and honour and yet to have no enjoyment in them: greed and avarice are never quenched because a person whose 'soul is not satisfied' has no rest even though 'he lacks nothing for himself of all he desires' (6:2,3,5). The honour, pleasure, wealth and wisdom he had so abundantly enjoyed have left him dissatisfied and disillusioned. Solomon writes from the perspective of one who has learned the meaninglessness of everything in life by bitter experience and prolonged use.

By reasoning the futility and meaninglessness of all earthly pursuits with such emphasis, '... the author first disillusions his hearers', and thus prepares the way for the second half of the book, which gives 'counsel and comfort for evil days'.[19]

Part II: How to live with meaninglessness (7:1 – 12:7)

Solomon gives practical advice on being sober-minded and being forward-looking. He recommends making the best of all life's circumstances (7:14). Negative thoughts paralyse (11:4) and there is work to be done for God even in the eventide of life (11:6). Solomon finds the answer to life in the fear of God: 'Though a sinner does evil a hundred times, and his days are prolonged, yet I surely know that it will be well with those who fear God, who fear before him' (8:12; cf. 5:7; 7:18; 12:13).

A person's effort should be in living in the fear of God, not in good works — they are of no lasting value — for no one is just; all have sinned (7:20). Death comes to all, no matter how powerful a person may be in life: 'No one has power over the spirit to retain the spirit' (8:8). The prospect of death weighs heavily upon Solomon and he recognizes that he is at the mercy of God (9:1) and will be judged by him (11:9).

The outcome is one of hope and confidence in God:

> You do not know the works of God who makes all things.
> In the morning sow your seed,
> And in the evening do not withhold your hand
>
> (11:5-6).

Conclusion (12:8-14)

Solomon remembers the days before his backsliding when he 'set in order many proverbs'; and wrote 'words of truth'; they were meaningful days. In a world of uncertainties, inequalities and injustice, the only way to find meaning and satisfaction is to respect the living God. God is morally perfect and he will bring every human being to account. Nothing will escape his attention. He notices every detail, even the hidden matters of heart and mind. The secret of life is to live in obedience to God and trust him for his goodness, wisdom and justice. Wisdom is seeing life from God's standpoint and trusting him when life makes no sense whatsoever. Solomon finds the antidote to disillusionment, cynicism and meaninglessness in fearing God and keeping his commandments:

> Let us hear the conclusion of the whole matter:
> Fear God and keep his commandments,
> For this is the whole duty of man.

For God will bring every work into judgement,
Including every secret thing,
Whether it is good or whether it is evil

(12:13-14).

Christ and his church

There are no prophecies, theophanies or types of Christ found in the book of Ecclesiastes, and yet it makes a valuable contribution to 'the holy Scriptures, which are able to make you wise for salvation through faith which is in Christ Jesus' (2 Tim. 3:15). The power of this book is in the absence rather than in the presence of Christ. This is a testimony to everything that is good and virtuous in life being tested and tried and found wanting.

In the book of Ecclesiastes there are powerful descriptions of life without meaning and without purpose — 'having no hope and without God in the world' (Eph. 2:12). Every aspect of human experience and endeavour has been tasted and tested to the full and the result is always the same — disappointment, dissatisfaction and disillusionment. The way is paved for the one who reveals the secret of life, for only Christ can provide ultimate satisfaction; only he can reveal the true meaning and purpose of our existence. The prophet Jeremiah expresses God's displeasure when people, especially his people Israel, reject him and turn in other directions to find meaning and satisfaction:

… my people have committed two evils:
They have forsaken me, the fountain of living waters,
And hewn themselves cisterns — broken cisterns that can hold no
   water

(Jer. 2:13).

Only when sinners realize that they are drinking bitter water — that is, they understand the futility and meaninglessness of all life without God — will they seek for the 'fountain of living water'. As the Lord Jesus said to the woman of Samaria, 'If you knew the gift of God, and who it is who says to you, "Give me a drink," you would have asked him, and he would have given you living water"' (John 4:10; cf. 7:37).

The Saviour has come to put meaning back into life and to fill it with richness and vitality. To his people who hear his voice, love him and follow him, he says, 'I have come that they may have life, and that they may have it more abundantly' (John 10:10).

Bruce Wilkinson and Kenneth Boa contrast 'life under the sun', as in the book of Ecclesiastes, with the believer's 'life under the Son':[20]

	Life under the sun	Life under the Son
1:3	What advantage is work under the sun?	He who has begun a good work in you will complete it until the day of Jesus Christ (Phil. 1:6).
1:9	Nothing new under the sun	Therefore, if anyone is in Christ, he is a new creation ... all things have become new (2 Cor. 5:17).
1:14	All deeds are vanity under the sun	Be steadfast, immovable ... knowing that your labour is not in vain in the Lord (1 Cor. 15:58).
2:18	The fruit of labour is hated under the sun	Being fruitful in every good work and increasing in the knowledge of God (Col. 1:10).
6:12	Man is mortal under the sun	Whoever believes in him should not perish but have everlasting life (John 3:16).
8:15	Pleasure is temporary under the sun	For it is God who works in you both to will and to do for his good pleasure (Phil. 2:13).
8:17	Man cannot discover God's work under the sun	Now I know in part, but then I shall know just as I also am known (1 Cor. 13:12).
9:3	All men die under the sun	God has given us eternal life, and this life is in his Son (1 John 5:11).
9:11	Strength and speed under the sun	God has chosen the weak things of the world to put to shame the things which are mighty (1 Cor. 1:27).
12:2	Life under the sun will cease	That you may know that you have eternal life (1 John 5:13).

Application

1. The fear of God (8:12)

Two essential aspects are contained in the fear of God: the Lord we love and the life we live.

The first involves *respect, worship and service given to God as the sovereign Lord of all life.* It encompasses the commandments of Sinai, especially that he alone is to be worshipped, no visual representations are to be made of him and his name is to be honoured in all situations and on all occasions: 'Serve the LORD with fear, and rejoice with trembling' (Ps. 2:11).

Much that passes for modern Christian worship is a thinly disguised form of self-centredness. Worship does not honour God when it centres in the thoughts, feelings, aspirations, experiences and blessings of the worshipper. While these have their place in worship, the central and overriding concern must be the adoration, exultation, praise and honouring of God. True worship renders devotion to God in prayer, in song, in reading the Scriptures and in preaching and teaching. The Father is the primary focus of worship: Christians are to worship the Father, through the Son, by the Holy Spirit. Any major shift in worship dishonours all three persons of the Godhead.

The second element in 'the fear of God' involves *holy living.* Solomon disobeyed God by marrying foreign women who influenced him into idolatry. 'Solomon did evil in the sight of the LORD, and did not fully follow the LORD, as did his father David' (1 Kings 11:6). True wisdom leads to pure and holy living (12:13) in obedience to God's revealed will: 'Behold, the fear of the Lord, that is wisdom, and to depart from evil is understanding' (Job 28:28).

The 'Spirit of the LORD' rested upon Christ:

The Spirit of wisdom and understanding,
The Spirit of counsel and might,
The Spirit of knowledge and of the fear of the LORD

(Isa. 11:2).

As Solomon said elsewhere, 'The fear of the LORD is the beginning of knowledge' (Prov. 1:7), upon which Matthew Henry commented: 'Those know enough who know how to fear God, who are careful in everything to please him and fearful of offending him in anything; this is the Alpha and Omega of knowledge.'

2. The wisdom of the world

As a young man Solomon knew the fear of the Lord, but later he turned his allegiance from God and, as he says, 'I set my heart to seek and search out by wisdom concerning all that is done under heaven' (1:13). He confesses, 'Look, I have attained greatness, and have gained more wisdom than all who were before me in Jerusalem' (1:16). But a wisdom that is devoid of the love of God and a commitment to his honour is not the wisdom that is from above: 'Who is wise and understanding among you? Let him show by good conduct that his works are done in the meekness of wisdom. But if you have bitter envy and self-seeking in your hearts, do not boast and lie against the truth. This wisdom does not descend from above, but is earthly, sensual, demonic. For where envy and self-seeking exist, confusion and every evil thing will be there. But the wisdom that is from above is first pure, then peaceable, gentle, willing to yield, full of mercy and good fruits, without partiality and without hypocrisy' (James 3:13-17).

True wisdom, that wisdom which descends from above, always leads sinners to 'fear God' (5:7; 8:12) and 'keep his commandments' (12:13). There is a wisdom in the world, but it does not lead to God or to godly living. As Paul says, 'The world through wisdom did not know God' (1 Cor. 1:21). Christians come to understand that true wisdom always centres in Jesus Christ, who is 'the wisdom of God' (1 Cor. 1:24). Hence we are to take care not to be led astray: 'Beware lest anyone should cheat you through philosophy and empty deceit, according to the tradition of men, according to the basic principles of the world, and not according to Christ' (Col. 2:8).

3. Worldliness

King Solomon had everything for which the heart could wish: 'A large, well-defined, fertile territory, peace within and around his kingdom; an enormous revenue to spend, wealth practically limitless; all the interests of new commerce and exploration. Insight and penetration above all men, sympathy with all men and things, the interest of starting classifications of science, and of forming books of maxims and songs. The respect and admiration of all his contemporaries. The power of expressing his thoughts in words…'[21] The only thing he lacked in the latter years of his reign was a good and right relationship with God! The result was that everything in his life was spoiled: 'For what will it profit a man if he gains the whole world, and loses his own soul? Or what will a man give in exchange for his soul?' (Mark 8:36-37).

Work, hobbies, sport, recreation, holidays and family may receive more attention, time and energy than is appropriate. Spiritual concerns must always take priority and regulate all else. The only way to interpret the world is to see it as a creation of God and to use and enjoy it *for his glory*.

4. Death

The backslidden Solomon was the epitome of all that humans aspire to be without God. The underlying thread of concern for the successful man of the world is leaving it all behind him. For years Solomon had not set his mind on things above, but on things on the earth (cf. Col. 3:2). He was not excited at the prospects of heaven because all that he had laboured for was here on earth; he therefore feared death because he was leaving everything behind. 'Christians can experience deep significance precisely in those areas where Qohelet felt most oppressed. Jesus has restored meaning to wisdom, labour, love, and life. After all, by facing death, Jesus conquered the biggest fear facing Qohelet, and he showed that death is not the end of all meaning, but the entrance into the very presence of God.'[22]

Conclusion

The goal of the whole book is to warn believers not to get caught up in pursuits, however good and commendable, that lead them away from God. The whole duty of human beings is the enjoyment and service of God. If we are without God, then nothing in the world has lasting benefit or value. On the other hand, if we have God, though we are poor, ill, neglected or abused in this world, we have all that really matters: 'If God is for us, who can be against us? He who did not spare his own Son, but delivered him up for us all, how shall he not with him also freely give us all things?' (Rom. 8:31-32). 'Do not love the world or the things in the world. If anyone loves the world, the love of the Father is not in him. For all that is in the world — the lust of the flesh, the lust of the eyes, and the pride of life — is not of the Father but is of the world. And the world is passing away, and the lust of it; but he who does the will of God abides for ever' (1 John 2:15-17).

Ecclesiastes is found in the Poetry section of the Protestant Old Testament. This includes the books from Job to the Song of Solomon. These five books can be seen as connected in the spiritual dimension: 'In *Job* we have the death of the self-life. In *Psalms* the resurrection-life and the idea of worship. In *Proverbs* "Laws from Heaven for life on Earth" (Dr Arnot). In *Ecclesiastes* the powerlessness of the world to satisfy the soul. In the *Song of Songs* the satisfaction of the soul in the Beloved.'[23] The disillusionment of the book of Ecclesiastes paves the way for the delights of the Song of Solomon.

The Song of Solomon

('a collection of songs')

Author: Solomon

Key thought: 'My beloved'

Theme: Love strong as death
The love expressed between Christ
and his church

'Yes, he is altogether lovely.
This is my beloved,
And this is my friend.'
    Song of Solomon 5:16

Summary

The Song of Solomon

The book 'The Song of Solomon' derives its name from the opening verse: 'The song of songs, which is Solomon's' (1:1). It is also sometimes called 'Canticles', which is derived from the Latin meaning 'a series of songs', since it is a collection of something like thirteen individual, though inter-woven, songs. On account of the introductory verse, a third title is also used, 'The Song of Songs', which indicates that of the 1,005 songs which Solomon composed, this ranks highest of them all. In the same way that the expression the 'King of kings and Lord of lords' (1 Tim. 6:15; Rev. 17:14; 19:16) means that over all kings and over all lords there is one King and Lord, the Lord Jesus Christ, who is the highest, the most powerful, and the most glorious, so the title 'The Song of Songs' indicates this composition to be the superlative song of all songs. This is not only the Song of songs out of Solomon's repertoire; it is the 'Song of songs' of all songs in the world. There is no other like it for excellence.

In the English Bible the Song of Solomon is the fifth of the poetical books: Job, Psalms, Proverbs, Ecclesiastes, Song of Solomon. The Jews have, for the most part, revered this poem as uniquely sublime despite the fact that there is no reference to God, no mention of sin, nor any religious theme whatsoever! To the Israelites, the apostle Paul says, 'were committed the oracles of God' (Rom. 3:2). It is interesting to note that one of their ancient scholars acknowledges that Solomon composed it 'by the inspiration of the Holy Spirit'. The Jews compare Proverbs to the outer court of the temple, Ecclesiastes to the holy place and the Song of Solomon to the Most Holy Place.[1] Yet though this book is held in the highest esteem it is forbidden reading to Hebrew children and young people until they reach thirty years of age.[2]

Some Christians have challenged its inclusion in the canon of Scripture because of its amorous tone, distinct lack of religious content and the disputable fact that it neither quotes from other books, nor is quoted in other books, of the Bible. The Christian church has, however, continued, with these few exceptions, in the confidence that this book belongs in the Old

Testament collection. Jonathan Edwards testified: 'The whole book of Canticles used to be pleasant to me, and I used to be much in reading it ... and found, from time to time, an increased sweetness that would carry me away in my contemplation.'³ John Gill declares, 'Its style is lovely and majestic; the manner of its composition neat and beautiful; and the matter of it full and comprehensive, being suited to all believers.'⁴ Some of the most godly people in the world have been spiritually elevated and enraptured by the contents of this inspired poem.

Author

It is fair to say that the opening words in Hebrew, 'The song of songs, which is Solomon's' (1:1), may be translated either 'which is of Solomon' or 'which is about Solomon'. This means either that it was written by him, or that it was written in his honour. In spite of this apparent ambiguity, the Jews and the Christian church have consistently held that it was composed by Solomon, the son of David and Bathsheba (2 Sam. 12:24). In other words, King Solomon, ruler of all Israel, wrote this masterpiece of poetry. His name appears within the text implying authorship (1:1). His name recurs a further six times in this composition (1:5; 3:7,9,11; 8:11,12).

'He spoke three thousand proverbs, and his songs were one thousand and five. Also he spoke of trees, from the cedar tree of Lebanon even to the hyssop that springs out of the wall; he spoke also of animals, of birds, of creeping things, and of fish. And men of all nations, from all the kings of the earth who had heard of his wisdom, came to hear the wisdom of Solomon' (1 Kings 4:32-34). According to one authority, reference is made in the Song of Solomon to fifteen species of animal and twenty-one varieties of plant.⁵

The Song of Solomon was obviously composed during a period of Solomon's life when he was in a healthy spiritual state — in other words, before his tragic decline: 'And he had seven hundred wives, princesses, and three hundred concubines; and his wives turned away his heart. For it was so, when Solomon was old, that his wives turned his heart after other gods; and his heart was not loyal to the LORD his God, as was the heart of his father David' (1 Kings 11:3-4).

The unusually large number of foreign words in the original text might indicate that King Solomon had by this time established widespread contact with surrounding nations. With this in mind, Jensen, Olyott and others suggest that it was composed somewhere around 965 B.C.,[6] which would place it at about the time of the building of the first temple in Jerusalem (966–959 B.C.).

The author speaks of many places throughout the country as though they belong to the same kingdom — Jerusalem, Kedar, En Gedi, Sharon, Bether, Lebanon, Carmel, Mount Gilead, Hermon and Tirzah. It was only during the reign of Solomon that this was the case. The comparison of the bridegroom with 'my favourite foal among Pharaoh's chariots' (1:9) is also interesting since it was Solomon who introduced horses from Egypt (1 Kings 10:28).

Interpretation and outline

In twenty of the twenty-one books of the Bible that we have studied so far it has been possible to trace an outline of the contents *before* entering into the interpretation and seeking the abiding message for the church of Jesus Christ. This twenty-second book in the inspired 'library' cannot be dealt with in the same way. To give an outline of the contents of this book depends largely upon the interpretation which is placed upon it.

If, as some suppose, there are three main characters, Solomon, the Shulamite maiden and her shepherd lover, then an overview like this will emerge: 'It is a record of the real history of a humble and virtuous woman engaged to be married to a young man of like humble circumstances, who was tempted to transfer her affections to one of the richest and most famous men that ever lived. It celebrates the victory of chaste love in humble life over all the attractions of worldly advantage, and all the allurements of courtly grandeur. It is a revelation of the chaste and virtuous love which no splendour can dazzle, and no flattery seduce.'[7] With this view we are asked to believe that Solomon cast himself in the role of the worst kind of tempter. William Hendriksen points out that this interpretation has been generally rejected because it does not fit a 'clear and consistent analysis of the book'.[8]

Another interpretation is that there are three main characters, Solomon, a Shulamite woman, and a group called the 'daughters of Jerusalem'. The scene is set like this:

King Solomon had a vineyard in the hill country of Ephraim, about fifty miles north of Jerusalem (8:11). He let it out to keepers

(8:11), consisting of a mother, two sons (1:6) and two daughters — the Shulamite (6:13), and a little sister (8:8). The Shulamite was 'the Cinderella' of the family (1:5), naturally beautiful but unnoticed. Her brothers were probably half-brothers (since she speaks of them as 'my mother's sons') (1:6). They made her work very hard tending the vineyards, so that she had little opportunity to care for her own personal appearance (1:6). She pruned the vines and set traps for the little foxes (2:15). She also kept the flocks (1:8). Being out in the open so much, she became sunburned (1:5).

One day a handsome stranger came along to the vineyard. It was Solomon disguised. He showed interest in her. She became embarrassed concerning her personal appearance (1:6). She took him for a shepherd and asked about his flocks (1:7). He answered her evasively (1:8), but also spoke loving words to her (1:8-10), and promised rich gifts for the future (1:11). He won her heart and left with the promise that some day he would return. She dreamed of him at night and sometimes thought he was near (3:1). Finally he did return in all his kingly splendour to make her his bride (3:6-7).[9]

E. J. Young gives a survey of the various interpretations that have been put forward over the years:

1. Jewish allegory, as representing God's love for his chosen people.

2. Christian allegory, representing Christ's dealings with his church. This, Professor Young admits, is the dominant view amongst Christians. (In some copies of the AV / KJV, you will find headings like this: 'The mutual love of Christ and his church', 'The graces of the church', 'Christ's love to it', 'The church professeth her faith and desire' and 'The church's love to Christ'.)

3. A drama in which 'King Solomon falls in love with a Shulamite girl and takes her to his capital Jerusalem, his love being purified from sensual to pure love'.

4. A collection of love songs.

5. A type, which means that the literal interpretation is first insisted upon. Then it is seen as bearing a typical character illustrating the love of Christ for his church.

6. An adaptation of a pagan liturgy to bring it into harmony with the religion of Israel.

7. A scene in a harem (the living quarters of wives and concubines) in which Solomon speaks to the girl from Shunem. Discussion ensues between Solomon, the girl and the women of the harem.

8. A parable — a mere song of human love, written by Solomon, possibly upon the occasion of his marriage to the daughter of Pharaoh.

Dismissing seven of these eight interpretations, E. J. Young favours the last: 'There is certainly an important element of truth in this interpretation… The Song does celebrate the dignity and purity of human love… The Song … is didactic [instructive] and moral in its purpose. It comes to us in this world of sin, where lust and passion are on every hand, where fierce temptations assail us and try to turn us aside from the God-given standard of marriage. And it reminds us, in particularly beautiful fashion, how pure and noble true love is … in the sophisticated modern world, unfaithfulness may easily be regarded as something light and trivial… So long as there is impurity in the world, we need, and need badly, the Song of Solomon.'[10]

But is it likely that this book would find a place in the collection of inspired Scripture on these grounds alone? Burrowes gives the answer: 'Impossible!' 'The universal genius and method of the sacred books exclude the idea of admitting among them songs about the ordinary love of man and woman.'[11]

There is no doubt that the message of this book clarifies the position of intimacy in God-honouring marriage; it denounces *asceticism* on the one hand and *lust* on the other.[12] All may learn here that there is a God-ordained place for the enjoyment of physical love between husband and wife and that there is no other place for physical love except in the confines of the covenant of marriage. Within that covenant relationship there is freedom for the enjoyment, the delight and the pleasure of physical intimacy. That is highlighted and confirmed by the Song of Songs.

Convinced as he is that there is no warrant for saying this book is a type of Christ, E. J. Young nevertheless admits that 'The book does turn one's eyes to Christ… The eye of faith, as it beholds this picture of exalted human love, will be reminded of the one Love that is above all earthly and human affections — even the love of the Son of God for lost humanity.'[13]

As illustrated, there are numerous interpretations, with arguments for and against, by a host of Christian scholars and commentators. We are left with the Saviour's challenge: 'What is your reading of it?' (Luke 10:26).

The song is poetry

As the first verse makes abundantly clear, this is 'the Song of Songs'. There is no claim that it is narrating historical events. The mention of Solomon, of towns and cities, of animals and plants, does not indicate any factual basis to the story. It is a love song. Stuart Olyott cautions all readers when he says, 'At no point in our study must we lose sight of the fact that we are reading an oriental love poem.'[14] It is poetry, not factual account. Much greater licence is given to the poet than to the historian. Furthermore it is Oriental. Natives of countries to the east of the Mediterranean delight in figures of speech that we in the West find most disconcerting and indecorous. At least, to those of the older generation in Western culture, some of the language appears singularly inappropriate for public reading. We are nevertheless assured, 'There is nothing here that would offend the most modest oriental.'[15] It is a poem, a love story, a parable.

In 1879 Henry Law, the Dean of Gloucester, divided this book into fifty two portions for family reading on the Lord's Day. At the outset he cautions: 'It is a Song. It is not an historic narrative, relating in plain terms the annals of the past. It is not a prophetic portrait, foreshadowing in shrouded form the semblance of the coming future. It is no scientific treatise, developing God's plan in the arrangement of nature's multitudinous wonders. It is no chain of moral precepts, directing to the beauties and bliss of holy life. It is a Song. It mounts on the wings of metaphor and figure... Thus large scope is given for lively interpretation. But to this licence strict limits are erected. No conclusion may be enforced but the obvious lessons of sound judgement and indisputable truth.'[16]

Thompson's Chain Reference Bible warns: 'It is an oriental poem, the ardent expressions of which can only be properly interpreted by a mature spiritual mind.' Robert Lee points out that this Song of Songs is sung annually by the Jews on the eighth day of the Passover Feast, which leads him to make an interesting observation: 'Only those who know the Lord Jesus as their Passover Lamb can possibly understand it.'[17]

The song viewed in the light of New Testament revelation

'What is true of every Old Testament book,' writes William Hendriksen, 'holds also with respect to the Song of Solomon: it is never interpreted fully until it is viewed in the light of New Testament revelation.'[18] In searching for the true interpretation of the Song of Solomon, like the Ethiopian minister of state on the road to Gaza, we should be asking the question: 'Of whom does the prophet say this, of himself or of some other man?' (Acts 8:34). Our conclusion will be the same in both cases. The Ethiopian was questioning Philip about Isaiah 53:7-8. Was Isaiah speaking about himself or someone else? Philip shows him that the subject of Isaiah 53 is not Isaiah the prophet but Jesus the Christ (Acts 8:35). In the same way, in this Song of Solomon, the author is not speaking about himself; he is speaking about the Lord Jesus Christ! If we expect to find Christ in this book because Christ is to be found 'in all the Scriptures' (Luke 24:27), we shall not be disappointed.

Looking at the outline of this book, it is difficult to detect a flow to its contents. Many see three sections: courtship days (1:2 – 3:5), wedding (3:6 – 5:1) and married life (5:2 – 8:14), then they try to fit Christian experience into this pattern, equating courtship days with the believer's experience of Christ before conversion, the wedding with conversion itself and married life with life lived in union with Christ. Trying to span the book in this way leads to insurmountable difficulties. Why does Christ leave us? Where is the justification for talking about pre-conversion days in terms of these first two chapters? We must search for another key.

Hendriksen points in a better direction: 'Canticles extols real, pure, unquenchable love between two human lovers: a bridegroom and a bride. This must be our starting point in the interpretation... This love between bridegroom and bride is a symbol not only of the love between Jehovah and Israel (Isa. 50:1; 54:5; 62:4; Jer. 2:2; 3:1-13; Ezek. 16; 23), but also of the love between Christ and his church. Not only is Solomon a type of Christ (II Sam. 7:12-17; Ps. 72; Matt. 12:42; Luke 11:31), but the love between husband and wife is a symbol of the close relationship which exists between our Lord and his church (Eph. 5:31-32). Moreover, the progress in our experience of this relationship is sometimes illustrated by the various elements that pertain to an Oriental wedding (Rev. 19:7; 21:9).'[19]

All these features — the love between Jehovah and Israel, the love between Christ and his church, and the elements of an Oriental wedding — dovetail beautifully if we go a little further than William Hendriksen and understand that the Song of Songs may be divided into two parts of four chapters each, with chapters 1-4 referring to Christ and the church under the Old Covenant — or Jehovah and Israel — and chapters 5-8 then referring to Christ and the church under the New Covenant. The key is to be found in the last verse of chapter 4 and the first verse of chapter 5. The Old Testament church cries out, 'Let my beloved come to his garden and eat its pleasant fruits' (4:16). The New Testament opens with the Beloved declaring, 'I have come to my garden, my sister, my spouse' (5:1). Charles Alexander asserts, 'The key to the understanding of the Song of Songs lies where few have sought for it. It is found at the centre of this great poetic drama, at the point where the Church passes from her Old Testament state into the full glory and experience of the New Covenant ushered in by the long-expected coming of the Saviour into the world.'[20]

Christ and his church

Christ's first advent: the betrothal

The long-awaited Messiah comes, but the church is asleep (5:2). He knocks at Israel's door but Israel is taken up with her present comfort. Her feet are washed (5:3). The outward washing of the law of Moses is good enough for her. Why should she defile her feet by leaving her Old Testament bed to go into the night? The Bridegroom is unwelcome. Of Christ's first coming we read, 'He came to his own, and his own did not receive him' (John 1:11). 'He is despised and rejected by men.' The Israelites hid, as it were, their faces from him, and 'did not esteem him' (Isa. 53:3).

It is claimed that the New Testament writers never quote from the Song of Solomon. This may not be so. The stirring bride, representing the spiritually awakening Israelites, testifies:

I sleep, but my heart is awake;
It is the voice of my beloved!
He knocks, saying,
'Open for me, my sister, my love,
My dove, my perfect one'

(5:2).

To the church at Laodicea the risen Christ says, 'Behold, I stand at the door and knock. If anyone hears my voice and opens the door, I will come in to him and dine with him, and he with me' (Rev. 3:20).

After the Bridegroom's departure there is an awakening in Israel. Spurned and rejected, Christ has departed, but many are now stirred to seek after him. God the Father pours down 'on the house of David and on the inhabitants of Jerusalem the Spirit of grace and supplication ... they ...

look on [him] whom they have pierced' and 'they … mourn for him …
and grieve for him' (Zech. 12:10).

> I arose to open for my beloved…
> I opened for my beloved,
> But my beloved had turned away and was gone.
> My heart went out to him when he spoke.
> I sought him, but I could not find him;
> I called him, but he gave me no answer
>
> (5:5-6).

The aroused Israelites go out into the night, the dark night of Israel, seeking
for him whom they have despised and rejected. They are met by Israel's
cruel watchmen, the scribes and Pharisees. They are beaten and put to
shame (5:7). The proud priesthood and eldership of Israel disown them,
but 'the daughters of Jerusalem', the Gentiles,[21] join the remnant of Israel to
seek him whom their souls desire (5:8). They find the bruised and persecuted bride and ask her for a description of her missing Lord. In her response (5:10-16) there is such 'an unveiling of the beauty and glory of
Christ as will fit only Deity Itself'.[22] This is the full unveiling of Christ which
is to be made in the New Testament revelation.

The Lord often uses the analogy of marriage for his relationship with his
people. In Isaiah we read:

> You shall no longer be termed Forsaken,
> Nor shall your land any more be termed Desolate;
> But you shall be called Hephzibah ['My Delight is in Her'], and your
>   land Beulah ['Married'];
> For the LORD delights in you,
> And your land shall be married…
> As the bridegroom rejoices over the bride,
> So shall your God rejoice over you
>
> (Isa. 62:4-5).

The first advent, the incarnation of Christ, is for the purpose of betrothal.
The apostle Paul tells the Corinthian Christians, 'I have betrothed you to
one husband, that I may present you as a chaste virgin to Christ' (2 Cor.
11:2).

John the Baptist testifies: 'He who has the bride is the bridegroom; but
the friend of the bridegroom, who stands and hears him, rejoices greatly

because of the bridegroom's voice. Therefore this joy of mine is fulfilled. He must increase, but I must decrease. *He who comes* from above is above all; he who is of the earth is earthly and speaks of the earth. *He who comes* from heaven is above all' (John 3:29-31, emphasis added).

Christ's second advent: the marriage feast

The Shulamite longs for the return of her Beloved:

> Make haste, my beloved,
> And be like a gazelle
> Or a young stag
> On the mountains of spices

(8:14).

'Hurry back to me,' cries the church to her Lord and years later this sentiment is repeated at the close of the final book of the Bible. The Lord promises to return and his people yearn: '"Surely I am coming quickly," Amen. Even so, come, Lord Jesus!' (Rev. 22:20). The Saviour promises to return for the marriage feast and to take his people home — never to be parted again.

Marriage among the Hebrews was quite different from marriage in modern Western culture. In the first place it was *an arranged marriage*. Secondly, instead of engagement, there was *betrothal*, or legal marriage, and then some time later the *marriage feast* took place, after which the couple began to live together as husband and wife.

This arrangement served a wonderful purpose in the incarnation of the Son of God: 'Now the birth of Jesus Christ was as follows: After his mother Mary was betrothed to Joseph, before they came together, she was found with child of the Holy Spirit. Then Joseph her husband, being a just man, and not wanting to make her a public example, was minded to put her away [that is, divorce her] secretly' (Matt. 1:18-19). This marriage arrangement safeguarded the honour and integrity of Jesus' mother Mary, ensuring that his birth was not illegitimate, and yet enabling prophecy to be fulfilled (Isa. 7:14). In Mary's own testimony responding to the announcement of the angel that she was to be a mother, 'How can this be, since I do not know a man?' (Luke 1:34), she indicates by a discreet euphemism that she was still a virgin (Matt. 1:22-23).

This marriage arrangement is also crucial to the work of the Saviour in relation to his people. The Lord Jesus 'came into the world to save sinners' (1 Tim. 1:15); the Bridegroom came for his bride (John 3:29). It is an *arranged marriage*, for Jesus said, 'All that the Father gives me will come to me' (John 6:37). The only question the bride is asked is in effect: 'Will you go with this man?' (Gen. 24:58). Responding gladly, new converts are *betrothed*. They are committed to Christ as to a husband (2 Cor. 11:2; cf. Rom. 7:4). But the *marriage feast*, followed by permanently living together, is still in the future. One day the whole believing community will join with the heavenly host in 'saying, "Alleluia! For the Lord God Omnipotent reigns! Let us be glad and rejoice and give him glory, for the marriage of the Lamb has come, and his wife has made herself ready." And to her it was granted to be arrayed in fine linen, clean and bright, for the fine linen represents the righteous acts of the saints. Then he said to me, "Write: 'Blessed are those who are called to the marriage supper of the Lamb!'" And he said to me, "These are the true sayings of God"' (Rev. 19:6-9).

There is even more which confirms and consolidates the place of the Song of Solomon at the very centre of Old Testament revelation. This book forges an unbreakable link with earlier prophecy. Solomon is intimately connected with the 'Shiloh' of Jacob's prophecy (Gen. 49:10).

Shiloh has come

Over and over again the Saviour indicates his connection with the Song of Solomon: '*I have come* to my garden, my sister, my spouse' (5:1, emphasis added). When Christ came into the world, he said, 'Behold, *I have come* — in the volume of the book it is written of me — to do your will, O God' (Heb. 10:7, emphasis added). In John's Gospel he says, 'The thief does not come except to steal, and to kill, and to destroy. *I have come* that they may have life, and that they may have it more abundantly' (John 10:10, emphasis added). And again he says, '*I have come* as a light into the world' (John 12:46, emphasis added). '*I have come* in my Father's name, and you do not receive me' (John 5:43, emphasis added). John the Baptist sends two of his disciples to the Lord Jesus with the question: 'Are you *the Coming One*, or do we look for another?' (Matt. 11:3, emphasis added).

This emphasis in the words of the Lord Jesus Christ and John the Baptist sends our minds right back to the book of Genesis and one of the most profound prophecies found within that book. In blessing his twelve sons

Jacob prophesies of his fourth son, Judah, and of the tribe that will descend from him:

> The sceptre shall not depart from Judah,
> Nor a law-giver from between his feet,
> *Until Shiloh comes;*
> And to him shall be the obedience of the people
>   (Gen. 49:10, emphasis added).

Solomon knew that the subject of his Song of Songs, 'both by intention and by inspiration, was none other than the Messiah, the Christ, the Eternal and Only Begotten Son of God, the King of kings and Lord of lords, the long-promised Redeemer of mankind'.[23] Charles Alexander argues strongly in favour of Solomon's knowing that he was writing under the inspiration of the Holy Spirit about the promised Deliverer:

> He [Solomon] was expounding the prophecy of his ancestor Jacob [Gen. 49:10]. More, he was dwelling in the 45th psalm of his father David, and was enlarging upon that glorious description of the marriage of Christ with His redeemed church, in which he [Solomon] comes face to face with one who is 'fairer than the children of men' (verse 2) — nay, who is, according to the literal meaning of the remarkable double word used in the Hebrew — One who is the 'fair-fair', the incomparable, the unique, the 'only fair' flower of all creation, into whose lips grace is poured; whom God the Father has blessed for ever, to whom it is given to go forth conquering and to conquer; who girds upon His thigh the irresistible sword of deliverance for His bride. His arrows bring down the pride of the foe; and to Him is given an eternal throne. His royal garments savour of myrrh, aloes and cassia, out of the Ivory Palaces of that gentile world from which He draws to Himself the rich reward given to Him in the love of the Father before all creation.
> Solomon lived for many years in that 45th psalm. He saw his own destiny foreshadowing the great Solomon who was to come, that Man of Peace who should make peace by the blood of His atonement, and should rise to occupy that eternal throne which was always His by right; but now doubly so, for He proved Himself and won His divine destiny by the merit of that love which gave itself to death. He would not reign alone, but would have beside Him to all eternity a Bride, a Queen. Upon Her He would place

His own beauty and with Her He would reign for ever in that Upper Garden fair, the heavenly Eden, the Paradise of God.[24]

The claim that Solomon knew he was writing about the promised Redeemer must be confirmed and consolidated if it is to be taken seriously. Is it possible to deduce this clearly and decisively from the pages of Scripture?

When Solomon entitled his composition 'The Song of Songs', that is 'the most excellent of songs', he was either presumptuous in the extreme (what about the songs of Miriam, Moses and his father David?) or aware that his subject was the greatest, most glorious subject in the whole world. It would seem that he was aware that he was writing about the promised Seed.

The proof that Solomon knew that he was writing under divine inspiration, not of himself and his own life history, but concerning the hope of Israel, concerning the promised Redeemer, the Seed of the woman who was to bruise the serpent's head (Gen. 3:15), 'lies in the deliberate use of his own name throughout the Song ... exactly seven times, and this indicates beyond doubt with what deliberation and insight he saw himself to be a type of Israel's messianic hope,' asserts Charles Alexander.[25] Solomon could not have been ignorant of Jacob's great prophecy concerning Solomon's own tribe of Judah, that the sceptre of rule would continue with the tribe until the coming of the mysterious Shiloh (Gen. 49:10). Nor could he fail to appreciate that his own name, Solomon, was derived from Shiloh, and had the meaning, 'Peace'. In the Hebrew the name Solomon is spelled *Shelomoh*. In the Song of Songs the bride of *Shelomoh* is *Shulamith*, which is derived from the same root, *Shiloh*. (*Shelomoh* and *Shulamith* differ from each other only as Cornelius differs from Cornelia).[26] *Shelomoh* means 'Prince of peace', and Shulamith means the bride of *Shelomoh*, 'the Princess of peace'. There is no other person in Scripture bearing the name Shiloh or Solomon. The sacred name Shiloh was reserved for the Saviour of the world, and given to Solomon prophetically as the son of David to point to 'great David's greater Son' (cf. Ps. 110:1; Matt. 22:41-45), the Lord of glory himself, the Prince of peace (Isa. 9:6). The prophet Micah declares Bethlehem Ephrathah to be the place of the Saviour's birth and adds, 'This man shall be peace' (Micah 5:2,5, AV). And the apostle Paul says that Christ Jesus 'himself is our peace' (Eph. 2:14), 'having made peace through the blood of his cross' (Col. 1:20).

Solomon also received another name, a name given by the Lord: 'Then David comforted Bathsheba his wife, and went in to her and lay with her. So she bore a son, and he called his name Solomon. *And the LORD loved him.* And he sent word by the hand of Nathan the prophet; so he called his name *Jedidiah,* because of the LORD' (2 Sam.12:24-25, emphasis added). Jedidiah means, 'Beloved of the LORD'. Of Christ, God the Father says, 'Behold, my servant whom I have chosen, *my beloved* in whom my soul is well pleased' (Matt. 12:18, emphasis added; cf. Isa. 42:1). And again he says, 'This is *my beloved Son,* in whom I am well pleased' (Matt. 3:17, emphasis added; cf. Matt. 17:5).

Is any further proof required that Solomon understood what he wrote, that he composed this song of all songs under the inspiration of the Holy Spirit and that he was privileged to be part of the great purpose of God — lifting back the curtain upon Christ and his church?

Application

1. Marital love

Though the Lord's primary purpose in the Song of Solomon is no doubt to communicate truth concerning Christ and his church, there is also a powerful message within the inspired story about human marital love (confined within marriage by the Word of God). In a day when sexual love is debased, exploited and publicly paraded, there is need for Christian married couples to know that sexual relationships can be pure, holy and God-honouring. 'Marriage is honourable among all, and the bed undefiled; but fornicators and adulterers God will judge' (Heb. 13:4).

Time and again over recent years in Britain and the USA, the church of Christ has been rocked by the serious fall of leading Christian preachers and teachers. While occasionally this has been due to financial greed, more often than not it is due to sinful uncontrolled sexual impulse — the vice of lust! In many cases of marital dysfunction among believers one area of ignorance constantly appears: the couple do not know, understand or apply the fundamental biblical principles of sexual relations. These principles may be clearly deduced from Paul's discussion of the subject in 1 Corinthians 7: intimacy between a husband and his wife is encouraged by God, may lead to temptations if unilaterally terminated and is to be governed by mutual respect and mutual concern.[27]

The instance of Solomon coupled with recent cases of adultery amongst prominent Christians might lead to the conclusion that men in particular are especially vulnerable in middle age. The warning of Jesus in a different context might be apposite here to the married couple: 'Watch and pray, lest you [either of you] enter into temptation' (Matt. 26:41).

2. Christ alone!

'Solomon obviously took enormous delight in the beauty of his bride, but he took even greater delight in knowing that this beautiful woman had reserved herself for him, and him alone. The images Solomon uses to describe her convey this delight. He refers to her here as "a garden enclosed", as "a spring shut up" and as "a fountain sealed" (4:12). These are terms of exclusiveness. Solomon's bride did not give herself to anyone, but only to him. A walled garden is one that only the owner and the gardener can enter. The waters of a spring that has been "shut up" and a fountain that has been "sealed" are not available to all, but only to the one who has placed them out of bounds.'[28]

The Lord Jesus Christ, the Saviour and Lord of his church, is to be loved exclusively. The church is to glorify Christ alone, love Christ alone, proclaim Christ alone and serve Christ alone. This is not, however, a response to a command so much as a response to the person and work of the Saviour. In this book Solomon paints a picture of the beloved as of singularly fine character, lovely in disposition and temperament and resplendent in all the virtues. When Christians add to this contemplation the wonderful work that Christ achieved at Calvary, then adoration, love, devotion, delight, obedience and service flow from the believer's grateful heart. The motive is not law but love. To quote Burrowes, 'Love to Jesus Christ becomes through sanctification, the strongest passion that can take possession of the human heart.'[29]

Conclusion

'We simply cannot help seeing Christ here. The theme of love causes regenerate minds to turn naturally to thinking of him. Every mention of love causes us to meditate on *his* and to bemoan the poverty of our own response. We think of our union with him and long for a closer communion. We find ourselves overwhelmed at his tenderness towards us and the sheer bliss of belonging to him for ever … many expressions of the book become the language of our own devotion. Our typical approach ceases to be an academic approach and our reading of the book becomes a precious spiritual experience.'[30]

Happy are those who hear in the bridegroom's words the love of Christ addressed to their own souls. Happy are those who can respond, who know that the words of the bride (the church) are the pure experience of their inmost feelings. M'Cheyne wrote, 'No book furnishes a better test than does the Song of the depth of a man's Christianity. If his religion be in his head only, a dry form of doctrines; or if it hath place merely in his fancy, like Pliable in *Pilgrim's Progress*, he will see nothing here to attract him. But if his religion have a hold on his heart, this will be a favourite portion of the word of God.'[31]

The Song of Songs is a prophecy in the form of an epic poem. Here is the meaning of all things — the meaning of creation, the meaning of our existence. Here too is laid bare the heart of God, the wisdom of God, the hidden purpose of God. Nothing in all creation matters to God like his Son and his church. Everything else serves this end — the glory, the honour, the blessing of Christ and his church. God, through his Son, will bind the church to himself in an eternal marriage of Creator and creature 'in an ecstasy of exquisite and eternal love'.

At the close of the New Testament we hear the Bridegroom promising to return: 'Surely I am coming quickly' (Rev. 22:20). The concluding words in the Song of Songs are those of the bride crying in longing:

Make haste, my beloved,
And be like a gazelle
Or a young stag
On the mountains of spices

(8:14).

In the penultimate verse of the completed Scripture, the bride cries: 'Amen. Even so, come, Lord Jesus!' (Rev. 22:20).

Isaiah

('Jehovah has saved')

Author: Isaiah
(of the whole book)

Key thought: 'The Holy One of Israel'

Theme:
The salvation of the nation by the living God
through judgement and grace

'For I am the LORD your God,
The Holy One of Israel, your
   Saviour.'

Isaiah 43:3

Summary

Isaiah

The book of Isaiah ranks as one of the finest books in the Old Testament Scripture. Written in the form of Hebrew poetic parallelism, in terms of sheer grandeur and majesty it is unparalleled. It is frequently quoted by our Lord and the New Testament writers. It contains outstanding insights into the character and mission of our Saviour and his wonderful relationship with his Father and with his people. Arranged into sixty-six chapters, the book parallels the sixty-six books of the Bible. The first thirty-nine chapters correspond to the books of the Old Testament and stress the holiness, justice and righteousness of God. The last twenty-seven chapters correspond to the New Testament books and display God's incomparable glory and grace.

Author

Unsurpassed for magnificence, the book of Isaiah has nevertheless been subjected, in more recent years, to repeated criticism in regard to its unity and its authorship. Until the last two centuries Jewish and Christian interpreters regarded Isaiah, the son of Amoz, the eighth-century prophet, friend and confidant of King Hezekiah, as the author of the entire book. Modern-day critical scholarship, which began in the late eighteenth century, maintains that the book is the product of at least two (1-39; 40-66) or three (1-39; 40-54; 55-66) different authors, spanning many years and from widely separated geographic locations.[1]

For those who are governed by the testimony of the New Testament, the evidence is overwhelmingly in favour of single authorship. In the New Testament Isaiah is quoted more than all the other prophets together and in such a way as to leave no doubt that the New Testament writers regarded Isaiah as the author of the entire book. Isaiah is referred to twenty-one times — *by name* — with quotations taken from twelve different chapters (seven from Isaiah 1-39, and fourteen from Isaiah 40-66). Three examples will illustrate the point:

- The apostle John makes reference to Isaiah 6:10 and 53:1 in consecutive verses, identifying both with the prophet Isaiah (John 12:38-41).
- In Acts 8:28 the Ethiopian is said to be 'reading Isaiah the prophet' as he struggles over the meaning of Isaiah 53:7-8. (Where there is a dispute over authorship, it is the second part, chapters 40-66, that is in question.)
- In Romans 9 and 10 Paul quotes extensively from Isaiah (10:22-23; 1:9; 53:1; 65:1-2) and, whether quoting from the early chapters or from the latter, in each case he attributes the authorship to Isaiah.

As E. J. Young concludes, 'To every Christian believer this testimony of the New Testament should be decisive.'[2]

The fact that the second half of Isaiah contains details of people, places, events and situations which had not yet occurred in Isaiah's day and would not occur for at least 150 years indicates, not the later addition by a second 'Isaiah', but the prophetic inspiration given by the Holy Spirit to the first (and only) Isaiah enabling him accurately to predict the future.

Isaiah actively prophesied for well over forty years until after the deliverance of Jerusalem from King Sennacherib of Assyria (701 B.C.). The name 'Isaiah' translates the shortened form of the Hebrew name *Yesha`yah*. Its full form is *Yesha`yahuw* and translates as 'Jehovah saves', 'Jehovah is salvation,' or 'Salvation is of Jehovah'.

Isaiah was the son of Amoz (1:1; 2:1), who is not to be confused with Amos the prophet. The fact that the Old Testament refers to Isaiah as 'the son of Amoz' thirteen times has led some Bible scholars to conclude that Isaiah's father was a man of some prominence. Tradition (the Jewish Talmud) maintains that Isaiah was born into nobility and mixed freely with royalty. He is said to have been a brother of King Amaziah, and so a cousin of King Uzziah. The prophet lived in Jerusalem at least until the death of Sennacherib (681 B.C.), which he records (37:38). The author of Chronicles credits Isaiah with having written a full account of the history of King Uzziah (2 Chr. 26:22). There is a tradition (in the Jewish Talmud), unsupported by any biblical evidence, that he was sawn in two during the reign of bad King Manasseh of Judah (cf. Heb. 11:37).

Little is known about Isaiah's personal history. The emphasis in Scripture is placed upon the message, not the man. Isaiah calls his wife 'the prophetess' (8:3). They had two sons, Shear-Jashub (7:3), meaning 'A remnant shall return', and Maher-Shalal-Hash-Baz (8:3), meaning 'Hastening to the spoil; hurrying to the prey' (cf. 8:4). The names of these two sons signify the twofold message of the prophet. On the one hand, there is a resounding warning; on the other, a reassuring promise. If the people will not turn away from idolatry and sin, God will punish them by raising up a foreign power to conquer them and carry them away captive. Like a wild animal pouncing on its weaker prey, so will Assyria carry Israel away. Nevertheless God will remain faithful to his ancient promises. A remnant will return to their own land.

Isaiah was evidently of keen and able intellect, one who had received a good education. He had a thorough grasp of the Scriptures and a penetrating awareness of the political circumstances of his day. The outstanding characteristic of this man is, however, his deep spirituality. He manifests an undoubted love for God and a zeal for the Lord's honour and glory. He feared God and feared no man. There is no partiality in his preaching; no toning down of judgement when addressing particular classes. He loved the people and knew that the faithful communication of the Word of God was the only way to demonstrate the reality and sincerity of that love (cf. the apostle Paul in 1 Thess. 2:4-7). Isaiah was absolutely sincere. He was bold and courageous. Jensen goes so far as to say that 'Isaiah was a many-sided genius' and that 'His ministry of prophecy was enhanced by his being gifted as a poet, a statesman, and an orator.'[3]

Isaiah was certainly a gifted communicator. He spoke to the people of Judah in plain, uncompromising language. He exhibited a broad range of vocabulary and carefully employed words to maximum effect. Occasionally he resorted to irony to expose or rebuke behaviour and attitudes (e.g. 40:19-20; 41:6-7; 44:13-20). Isaiah probably composed the last twenty-seven chapters during his later life. Whether the prophet actually preached his messages or only committed them to writing is not made clear.

Historical setting

Solomon reigned in Israel for forty years (1 Kings 11:42). On his death (930 B.C.), the kingdom of Israel was divided. Jeroboam the son of Nebat became king of the ten tribes based at Samaria and known as 'Israel', or the northern kingdom. Rehoboam, the son of King Solomon, became king of the two tribes (Judah and Benjamin) based at Jerusalem and known as 'Judah' or the southern kingdom. Generally the people had turned from God: they forgot his law, violated his covenant and disobeyed his commands. They turned to the heathen and pagan gods of the surrounding nations. God's judgement fell upon the twelve tribes.

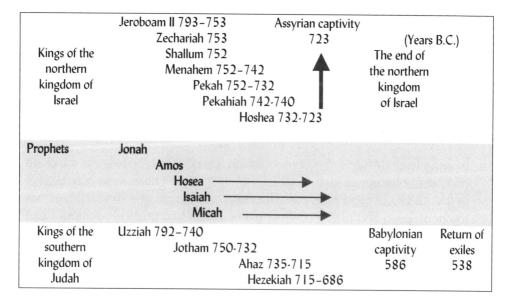

Isaiah in relation to the kings and prophets of the divided kingdom

From the time of the division of the kingdom in 930 B.C. the history of the two nations is a history of general decline and disintegration (1 Kings 12 – 2 Kings 25; 2 Chr. 10-36). Israel (the northern kingdom of the ten tribes) deteriorated more speedily, surviving as a nation for only 200 years. With the exile to Assyria in 723 B.C., the nation of Israel ceased to exist. Judah survived longer, a total of almost 350 years. Exile to Babylon in 586 B.C. destroyed the nation, but the people retained their identity as 'Jews' (the name derived in exile from 'Judeans').

Nearly 200 years after the death of King Solomon, Isaiah received his call to the prophetic office. This is 'in the year that King Uzziah [4] died' (6:1) — that is, 740 B.C. Isaiah continued to function as a prophet in Judah, the southern kingdom, during the reigns of Jotham, Ahaz and Hezekiah (1:1). The combined history of these four kings is recorded in 2 Kings 15:1 – 20:21 and 2 Chronicles 26:1 – 32:33.

Isaiah followed a long line of worthies in the prophetic office. There had been key figures such as Samuel and Nathan in the early days of the united kingdom of Israel and Judah, and men like Obadiah and Joel serving, like himself, mainly the southern kingdom of Judah. In the northern kingdom of Israel, men such as Elijah and Elisha, Amos and Jonah had earlier served as prophets.

Hosea, a prophet to Israel, preceded Isaiah in his appointment to the prophetic office by less than ten years (Hosea 1:1). Micah, serving mainly in Judah, became a prophet about ten years after Isaiah. Consequently, these three, Hosea, Isaiah and Micah, were contemporaries.

Outline

In order to understand the book of Isaiah it is necessary to keep in mind the complex political situation to which Isaiah speaks. These were critical days in the history of God's people. The Assyrian Empire was threatening from the north-east, and among the people of Judah two political solutions were being promoted. There were those who favoured a coalition with Egypt to the west, and those who preferred an alliance with Assyria. The prophet Isaiah took the middle ground and called respective kings and the people to rely entirely and exclusively upon the living God.

Part I: Prophecies against Judah and the nations (1:1 – 35:10)

Judgements on Judah in the days of Uzziah and Jotham (1:1 – 6:13)

Uzziah (Azariah) became king of the southern kingdom of Judah at the age of sixteen. He reigned for fifty-two years, although for the last ten years or so he was king in name only. His son Jotham was the effective ruler for the latter period. During Uzziah's reign Judah experienced a period of prosperity. Uzziah freed Judah from the control of the northern kingdom of Israel. He also defeated the Philistines to the west as well as the Ammonites to the east. He greatly strengthened the army and made elaborate improvements in the fortification of the city of Jerusalem (2 Chr. 26:1-15). For the people as a whole these were days of self-indulgence and godlessness. Paganism and worldliness were rife in the land (Isa. 2:1 – 3:26).

Up in the northern kingdom of Israel, Jeroboam II was king. Jeroboam's military success was even more impressive than that of King Uzziah. He extended his territory and resisted Syria to the extent that he captured the capital, Damascus (2 Kings 14:28). This, however, was to prove to be a rash move. By weakening Syria, Israel was left wide open to attack from another powerful enemy — the Assyrians.

Upon the death of Uzziah in Judah, his son Jotham continued on the throne and Isaiah was called to the prophetic office (6:1). Jotham reigned as sole monarch for about five years in Judah, after which his son Ahaz joined him and they exercised a co-regency until Jotham's death.

Jotham was a good king, a God-fearing man, for 'He did what was right in the sight of the LORD' (2 Chr. 27:2). He was a man of prayer, for 'Jotham became mighty, because he prepared his ways before the LORD his God' (2 Chr. 27:6). He was not able, however, to influence the nation in spiritual and moral concerns: 'But still the people acted corruptly' (2 Chr. 27:2). The prophets Isaiah and Micah specifically address this sinfulness of the people (2:5-9; 5:7-30; Micah 1:5; 2:1-2). Jotham was not without blame in respect to the people's sin, for while he extended the building of the temple (2 Chr. 27:3), he did not remove the many pagan temples scattered throughout Judah and '… the people still sacrificed and burned incense on the high places' (2 Kings 15:35). Consequently, 'The LORD began to send Rezin king of Syria and Pekah [the King of Israel] the son of Remaliah against Judah' (2 Kings 15:37). Syria and Israel were sent against Judah because the king and people were not being entirely true to the living God.

Prophecies concerning Judah in the days of Ahaz (7:1 – 12:6)

During the overlap of the reigns of Jotham and Ahaz, the Assyrian Empire under King Tiglath-Pileser III (745–727 B.C.) was growing stronger. Syria and the northern kingdom of Israel were becoming increasingly concerned about the threat from the north-east. Rezin, the King of Syria, and Pekah, the King of Israel, tried to persuade King Ahaz of Judah to join them against Assyria. Isaiah warned King Ahaz against participating in an anti-Assyrian coalition. When Ahaz refused to join them, Syria and Israel attacked Judah. They intended, not only to overthrow Judah, but also to remove the descendants of David from the throne in Jerusalem (7:6).

Isaiah received a commission to inform King Ahaz that he must not yield to the attack from Syria and Israel but must trust in Jehovah. The Lord would protect him and the nation. Ahaz was encouraged to ask a sign from the Lord in the assurance of his protection. In spite of the offer from Isaiah the prophet of God, King Ahaz refused to ask for a sign on the pretext that he would not dream of testing the Lord in such a manner. The sign was nevertheless given. It forms one of the amazing prophecies concerning Messiah: 'Behold, the virgin shall conceive and bear a Son, and shall call his name Immanuel [which means, God-with-us]' (7:14).

King Ahaz refused to trust in the Lord and turned to Assyria for help. Assyria, however, had plans of her own. Instead of assisting Judah, Assyria interpreted the request as a sign of weakness and so began to assert greater authority over Judah (2 Chr. 28:16-25).

The reason why Judah was being brought low like this — pressurized by the Syrians, the Israelites, the Edomites, the Philistines *and* the Assyrians — is explained in 2 Chronicles. The issue, as always in the fortunes of the ancient people of God, is not military but moral, not an issue of strategy, but a question of spirituality: 'For the LORD brought Judah low because of Ahaz king of Israel, for he had encouraged moral decline in Judah and had been continually unfaithful to the LORD. Also Tiglath-Pileser king of Assyria came to him and distressed him, and did not assist him. For Ahaz took part of the treasures from the house of the LORD, from the house of the king, and from the leaders, and he gave it to the king of Assyria; but he did not help him. Now in the time of his distress King Ahaz became increasingly unfaithful to the LORD. This is that King Ahaz. For he sacrificed to the gods of Damascus which had defeated him, saying, "Because the gods of the kings of Syria help them, I will sacrifice to them that they may help me." But they were the ruin of him and of all Israel ' (2 Chr. 28:19-23).

After the death of Tiglath-Pileser III, the Assyrian king, his successors Shalmaneser V and Sargon moved against the northern kingdom of Israel. In 722 B.C. they destroyed the capital of Samaria, deported all the Israelites and brought in immigrants from Babylon, Cuthah, Ava, Hamath and Sepharvaim to repopulate the land (2 Kings 17:24). These people were the ancestors of the Samaritans of New Testament times.

Prophecies against other nations (13:1 – 23:18)

As well as declaring God's judgement upon the unfaithful in Judah and the wicked in Israel, Isaiah also prophesies against the surrounding nations. He proclaims the fall and total destruction of Babylon at the hands of the Medes (13:17). A terrible judgement is brought upon the empire (13:1 – 14:23). Prophecies are given against Assyria (14:24-27), against Philistia (14:28-32), against Moab (15:1 – 16:14), against Syria and Israel (17:1-14), against Ethiopia (18:1-7), against Egypt (19:1 – 20:6), against Babylon (21:1-10), against Edom (21:11-12), against Arabia (21:13-17) and against Tyre (23:1-18). In the midst of these terrible prophecies against the nations there is included a prophecy against Jerusalem and her unfaithful leaders (22:1-25).

Prophecies concerning the Day of the Lord (24:1 – 27:13)

Great distress is prophesied when 'the LORD makes the earth empty and makes it waste' (24:1). This devastation will come:

Because they have transgressed the laws,
Changed the ordinance,
Broken the everlasting covenant.
Therefore the curse has devoured the earth, and those who dwell in
it are desolate

(24:5-6).

Intermingled with the prophecies of universal judgement and the description of the sins and misery of the people, there are promises of salvation, a song of confidence in God and his care over his people, his 'vineyard' (24:14-15,23; 25:6-9; 26:3-4; 27:2,12-13).

Part II: Historical interlude (36:1 – 39:8)

Hezekiah the son of Ahaz is king and rules Judah for twenty-nine years (715–686 B.C.). He is generally accounted one of the wisest and best of the kings of Judah. He has also been called 'the virtuous king', and certainly the record of many things that he did during his reign gives evidence of his God-fearing and God-honouring character: 'He trusted in the LORD God of Israel, so that after him was none like him among all the kings of Judah, nor any who were before him. For he held fast to the LORD; he did not depart from following him, but kept his commandments, which the

LORD had commanded Moses. The LORD was with him; he prospered wherever he went' (2 Kings 18:5-7).

At the very beginning of his reign he entirely reversed the wicked policy of his father Ahaz, and with true zeal destroyed the idols and heathen temples that had been set up in the land, and restored and purified the worship of Jehovah, calling all the nation to a great Passover (2 Chr. 30:5). His reign is distinguished not only by this reformation of religion, but also by many public improvements he brought about.

About ten years into his reign, King Sargon of the Assyrians died (705 B.C.) and his successor King Sennacherib faced rebellion from a number of quarters. There was unrest in Syria, and Babylon to the south-east was beginning to flex her muscles. In 701 B.C. Sennacherib turned his attention to Judah and her capital Jerusalem (36:1; 2 Kings 18:13).

When King Sennacherib and the Assyrians came up against Jerusalem, King Hezekiah placed his entire confidence in Jehovah. Tearing his clothes and covering himself with sackcloth, he went into the house of the LORD (37:1). On receiving a further communication from Sennacherib, King Hezekiah prayed: 'O LORD of hosts, God of Israel, the one who dwells between the cherubim, you are God, you alone, of all the kingdoms of the earth. You have made heaven and earth. Incline your ear, O LORD, and hear; open your eyes, O LORD, and see; and hear all the words of Sennacherib, who has sent to reproach the living God. Truly, LORD, the kings of Assyria have laid waste all the nations and their lands, and have cast their gods into the fire; for they were not gods, but the work of men's hands — wood and stone. Therefore they have destroyed them. Now therefore, O LORD our God, save us from his hand, that all the kingdoms of the earth may know that you are the LORD, you alone' (37:16-20).

The future for Jerusalem looked bleak, utterly impossible. Isaiah the prophet was sent to reassure King Hezekiah that his prayers had been heard and his confidence in the living God would be rewarded. The miraculous delivery is described: 'Then the angel of the LORD went out, and killed in the camp of the Assyrians one hundred and eighty-five thousand; and when people arose early in the morning, there were the corpses — all dead' (37:36).

Shortly after this event King Hezekiah of Judah became seriously ill. Isaiah the prophet visited the king and said to him, 'Set your house in order, for you shall die, and not live' (2 Kings 20:1). The reaction of King Hezekiah once more indicates his godliness. He prayed and wept before the Lord. The Lord responded by giving a message to Isaiah: 'Return and tell Hezekiah the leader of my people, "Thus says the LORD, the God of

David your father: 'I have heard your prayer, I have seen your tears; surely I will heal you. On the third day you shall go up to the house of the LORD. And I will add to your days fifteen years'"' (2 Kings 20:5-6). The illness and recovery of Hezekiah led him to compose a beautiful psalm (38:10-20).

When King Merodach-Baladan of Babylon sent envoys to King Hezekiah to enlist his support in a revolt against King Sennacherib of Assyria, Hezekiah unwisely showed them all his treasure (39:2). When Isaiah heard of this, he informed the king that one day all the wealth of the royal household would be carried away to Babylon.

This prophetic announcement provides the transition between the two parts of the book of Isaiah. The first part (1-39) is concerned with the Assyrian crisis, whereas the second (40-66) pays attention to the future concerns of the Jewish exiles in Babylon. Under the Spirit of the Lord Isaiah sees things that are to come. While some of the details of the second half of this book concern prophecies of actual events in the exile in Babylon and in the return to Jerusalem, Isaiah's prophecies also range far into the future. They may have an application in three periods of time and find fulfilment in the days of the return of the exiles and/or intermediate fulfilment in the days of the Messiah on earth and/or reach to the end times and find fulfilment in the new creation. The interweaving of these strands of prophecy does not make interpretation or application an easy task.

Part III: Prophecies of the nature and future of the church of God (40:1 – 66:24)

The prophecies of the last twenty-seven chapters form a composite whole. Probably composed in the latter years of Isaiah's ministry, they are intended not just for the prophet's contemporaries, but also for the future church of God.

Prophecies in the Old Testament often have more than one application and fulfilment. Four distinct periods may be identified for the application of prophecies by Isaiah:

- The days of the prophet;
- The days of the captivity in Babylon and the return;
- The days of Messiah on earth;
- The days of the new creation when the Lord will create the new heavens and a new earth.

Christ and his church

The prophet Isaiah is remembered best for his Messianic prophecies — that is, his Holy-Spirit-inspired predictions concerning the Lord Jesus Christ, the Son of God.

1. Messiah's virgin birth (7:14)

Behold, the virgin shall conceive and bear a Son, and shall call his name Immanuel [which means, 'God with us'].

Matthew, the apostle of Jesus Christ, sees the fulfilment of this prophecy in the miraculous conception and birth of the Lord Jesus Christ (Matt. 1:20-23). In that passage from Isaiah it is also predicted that Messiah will have a simple lifestyle (7:15).

2. Messiah's unique character (9:6-7)

Messiah is none other than the Son of God on the throne of David:

For unto us a child is born,
Unto us a Son is given;
And the government will be upon his shoulder.
And his name will be called
Wonderful, Counsellor, Mighty God,
Everlasting Father, Prince of Peace.
Of the increase of his government and peace
There will be no end,
Upon the throne of David and over his kingdom,
To order it and establish it with judgement and justice
From that time forward, even for ever.
The zeal of the LORD of hosts will perform this.

More than 700 years later an angel announces the arrival of the Son of God to Mary: 'And behold, you will conceive in your womb and bring forth a Son, and shall call his name JESUS. He will be great, and will be called the Son of the Highest; and the Lord God will give him the throne of his father David. And he will reign over the house of Jacob for ever, and of his kingdom there will be no end' (Luke 1:31-33).

Can there be any doubt that a connection is intended between the words of the angel here and the prophecy of Isaiah so many years earlier?

3. Messiah's outstanding qualities (11:1-12)

There shall come forth a Rod from the stem of Jesse,
And a Branch shall grow out of his roots.
The Spirit of the LORD shall rest upon him,
The Spirit of wisdom and understanding,
The Spirit of counsel and might,
The Spirit of knowledge and of the fear of the LORD...

This prophecy teaches that Messiah will be a descendant of King David's father and he will be filled with the Holy Spirit (cf. John 3:34; Matt. 3:16). He will be a faithful and righteous judge of the world (11:3-5; cf. Rev. 19:11). His reign will be characterized by peace and harmony (11:6-9). Gentile believers and Israel's faithful remnant will gather to him (11:10-12; Rom. 15:8-12).

4. Messiah's distinctive glory (6:1-3)

At his call to the prophetic office, Isaiah records:

In the year that King Uzziah died, I saw the Lord sitting on a throne, high and lifted up, and the train of his robe filled the temple. Above it stood seraphim; each one had six wings: with two he covered his face, with two he covered his feet, and with two he flew. And one cried to another and said:

'Holy, holy, holy is the LORD of hosts;
The whole earth is full of his glory!'

To remove all possible doubt and uncertainty as to whom he saw Isaiah testifies:

Woe is me, for I am undone…
For my eyes have seen the King,
The LORD [YHWH = Jehovah] of hosts

(6:5).

In vision Isaiah saw the living God. The apostle John states that Isaiah the prophet saw the glory of Messiah when he saw that vision. Having quoted from Isaiah 6 John adds, 'These things Isaiah said when he saw his glory and spoke of him' (John 12:41). That verse alone proves the deity of Jesus Christ. He is none other than Jehovah, the Son of Jehovah!

5. Messiah's gracious ministry (61:1-2)

Leaving the wilderness after the temptations of Satan, our Lord returned home to Galilee:

So he came to Nazareth, where he had been brought up. And as his custom was, he went into the synagogue on the Sabbath day, and stood up to read. And he was handed the book of the prophet Isaiah. And when he had opened the book, he found the place where it was written:

'The Spirit of the LORD is upon me,
Because he has anointed me to preach the gospel to the poor.
 He has sent me to heal the broken-hearted,
To preach deliverance to the captives
And recovery of sight to the blind,
To set at liberty those who are oppressed,
To preach the acceptable year of the LORD.'

Then he closed the book, and gave it back to the attendant and sat down. And the eyes of all who were in the synagogue were fixed on him. And he began to say to them, 'Today this scripture is fulfilled in your hearing' (Luke 4:16-21).

In declaring the fulfilment of the prophecy in Isaiah 61:1-2, the Lord is disclosing that he is the promised Messiah.

6. Messiah's excellent herald (40:3-5)

And [John the Baptist] went into all the region around the Jordan, preaching a baptism of repentance for the remission of sins, as it is written in the book of the words of Isaiah the prophet, saying:

'The voice of one crying in the wilderness:
"Prepare the way of the LORD,
Make his paths straight.
Every valley shall be filled
And every mountain and hill brought low;
And the crooked places shall be made straight
And the rough ways made smooth;
And all flesh shall see the salvation of God"'

(Luke 3:3-6).

John the Baptist understood his relationship to the Messiah in terms of the prophecy of Isaiah 40:3-5. Each of the four Gospel writers records this connection and fulfilment (Matt. 3:3; Mark 1:3; Luke 3:4-5; John 1:23). Mark also connects this prophecy with the prophecy of Malachi 3:1 (Mark 1:2-3; cf. Matt. 11:10).

7. Messiah's incomparable brilliance (9:1-2)

And leaving Nazareth, [Jesus] came and dwelt in Capernaum, which is by the sea, in the regions of Zebulun and Naphtali, that it might be fulfilled which was spoken by Isaiah the prophet, saying:

'The land of Zebulun and the land of Naphtali,
The way of the sea, beyond the Jordan,
Galilee of the Gentiles:
The people who sat in darkness saw a great light,
And upon those who sat in the region and shadow of death
Light has dawned.'

From that time Jesus began to preach and to say, 'Repent, for the kingdom of heaven is at hand' (Matt. 4:13-17).

8. Messiah's puzzling preaching (6:9-10)

When our Lord explains why he so often uses parables in his public preaching, he says:

> Therefore I speak to them in parables, because seeing they do not see, and hearing they do not hear, nor do they understand. And in them the prophecy of Isaiah is fulfilled, which says:
>
> 'Hearing you will hear and shall not understand,
> And seeing you will see and not perceive;
> For the heart of this people has grown dull.
> Their ears are hard of hearing,
> And their eyes they have closed,
> Lest they should see with their eyes and hear with their ears,
> Lest they should understand with their heart and turn,
> So that I should heal them.'
>
> But blessed are your eyes for they see, and your ears for they hear...
> (Matt. 13:13-16).

9. Messiah in the four Servant Songs (42; 49; 50; 52-53)

Messiah is a gentle servant (42:1-4)

When faced with the hostility of the Pharisees in a Galilean town, Jesus withdrew to the coast. He was followed by a great crowd from all over the region, from Galilee, Judea, Jerusalem, Idumea and beyond the Jordan, and from Tyre and Sidon (Mark 3:7-8). Jesus warned this vast company 'not to make him known' (Matt.12:16). Matthew his apostle sees this as fulfilling another prophecy of Isaiah:

> Behold, my servant whom I have chosen,
> My beloved in whom my soul is well pleased;
> I will put my Spirit upon him,
> And he will declare justice to the Gentiles.
> He will not quarrel nor cry out,
> Nor will anyone hear his voice in the streets.
> A bruised reed he will not break,

And smoking flax he will not quench,
Till he sends forth justice to victory.
And in his name Gentiles will trust

(Matt. 12:18-21; cf. Isa. 42:1-4).

Messiah is a glorious servant (49:1-6)

Identifying this Servant with our Saviour, Leupold declares that 'He is in the last analysis none less than the Messiah.'[6] There is in the opening verses a note of disappointment at the poor evidence of success. The Servant has laboured and seen little encouragement. For a short time our Lord's ministry was marked by the suffering that disappointment brings. As a man he had to hold to the prophecies that 'He shall see the travail of his soul, and be satisfied' (53:11) and to the conclusion of this prophecy, which goes on to predict that what he achieves will have worldwide significance.

And now the LORD says,
Who formed me from the womb to be his Servant,
To bring Jacob back to him,
So that Israel is gathered to him
(For I shall be glorious in the eyes of the LORD,
And my God shall be my strength),
Indeed he says,
'It is too small a thing that you should be my Servant
To raise up the tribes of Jacob,
And to restore the preserved ones of Israel;
I will also give you as a light to the Gentiles,
That you should be my salvation to the ends of the earth'

(49:5-6; cf. Luke 2:32).

Messiah is a competent servant (50:4-9)

The Lord GOD has given me
The tongue of the learned,
That I should know how to speak
A word in season to him who is weary.
He awakens me morning by morning,
He awakens my ear
To hear as the learned.
The Lord GOD has opened my ear;

And I was not rebellious,
Nor did I turn away.
I gave my back to those who struck me,
And my cheeks to those who plucked out the beard;
I did not hide my face from shame and spitting.
For the Lord GOD will help me;
Therefore I will not be disgraced;
Therefore I have set my face like a flint,
And I know that I will not be ashamed

(50:4-7).

When the Lord Jesus was arrested and brought to Caiaphas, he stood before the assembled scribes and elders to be interrogated. Exasperated by
the responses of the Son of God, 'They spat in his face and beat him; and
others struck him with the palms of their hands' (Matt. 26:67).

Messiah is a suffering servant (52:13 – 53:12)

Messiah will be exalted (52:13; cf. Phil. 2:9-10), and yet he will be disfig-
ured by suffering (52:14; cf. Mark 15:15-19; John 19:1). Relatively few will
gladly receive the gospel of Christ (53:1; cf. John 12:37-38). Messiah is to
be ordinary in appearance (53:2). He will be widely rejected and despised
(53:3; cf. John 1:10-11). He is to be the substitutionary atonement for sinners (53:5; cf. 1 Peter 3:18). He will bear our griefs and sorrows, our sins
and sickness (53:4; cf. Matt. 8:16-17). He will be our substitute (53:6,8; cf.
Rom. 5:6,8; 2 Cor. 5:21). He will exercise a voluntary silence (53:7; Mark
15:3-5; cf. Acts 8:27-35). He will willingly accept our guilt and punishment
(53:8; cf. John 10:17-18). His body will be buried in a rich man's tomb
(53:9; cf. Matt. 27:57-60). He will deliver all who believe in him (53:11;
John 3:16; Acts 16:30-31). He will die with transgressors (53:12; cf. Luke
22:37; Mark 15:27-28) and pray for transgressors (53:12; Luke 23:34;
Heb. 7:25).

10. Messiah's enemy (7:6)

As noted earlier, when Syria joined Israel (the ten tribes of the northern
kingdom) to attack Judah, they intended not only to overthrow Judah, but
also to remove the descendants of David from the throne in Jerusalem.
Had they succeeded they would have destroyed the covenant promise that

God made to David: 'When your days are fulfilled and you rest with your
fathers, I will set up your seed after you, who will come from your body,
and I will establish his kingdom. He shall build a house for my name, and I
will establish the throne of his kingdom for ever' (2 Sam. 7:12-13).

11. Messiah's feast (25:6-9)

> And in this mountain
> The LORD of hosts will make for all people
> A feast of choice pieces,
> A feast of wines on the lees,
> Of fat things full of marrow,
> Of well-refined wines on the lees.
> And he will destroy on this mountain
> The surface of the covering cast over all people,
> And the veil that is spread over all nations.
> He will swallow up death for ever,
> And the Lord GOD will wipe away tears from all faces;
> The rebuke of his people
> He will take away from all the earth;
> For the LORD has spoken.
> And it will be said in that day:
> 'Behold, this is our God;
> We have waited for him, and he will save us.
> This is the LORD;
> We have waited for him;
> We will be glad and rejoice in his salvation.'

The blessings of that new day, the Day of the Lord, are described in
terms of a feast. The guests are 'all people' (cf. Rev. 7:9-10; 19:1,6-9) for
the dividing wall between Jew and Gentile will be torn down for ever. The
covering and the veil (25:7) 'would seem to argue for a state of dense
blindness before these obstacles are eliminated'[7] (cf. 2 Cor. 4:4,6). They
have come to worship on Mount Zion, which means that the feast is a sacrificial meal (cf. Ps. 22:26-29; Matt. 8:11; 22:2-14; Luke 14:15-24). 'As
Zion here is to be taken in a figurative sense, referring to the Church of
God, so also is the banquet to be understood figuratively, as signifying the
spiritual blessings that God brings to mankind through His kingdom.'[8]

12. Messiah's universal reign (2:2-4)

> Now it shall come to pass in the latter days
> That the mountain of the LORD's house
> Shall be established on the top of the mountains,
> And shall be exalted above the hills;
> And all nations shall flow to it.
> Many people shall come and say,
> 'Come, and let us go up to the mountain of the LORD,
> To the house of the God of Jacob;
> He will teach us his ways,
> And we shall walk in his paths.'
> For out of Zion shall go forth the law,
> And the word of the LORD from Jerusalem.
> He shall judge between the nations,
> And shall rebuke many people;
> They shall beat their swords into ploughshares,
> And their spears into pruning-hooks;
> Nation shall not lift up sword against nation,
> Neither shall they learn war any more.

The prophets frequently employed the formula, 'in the latter days', to refer to the time of the Messiah, because the definite time was unknown to them. Isaiah is seeing the glorious effects of Messiah's coming into the world — a time of deliverance and salvation. In Isaiah's day the temple was situated on Mount Zion. The false gods had their mountains too: the Capitol, Olympus, Albordash, Meru and Zaphon. The promise of the Lord is that the insignificant Mount Zion will one day surpass all the others. Even Sinai, the mountain of the law, will fade into the background; for the glorious New Covenant of grace is superior to the Old Covenant of law.

The church of Christ will be exalted above all false religions, human ideologies and earthly powers. The church may look weak and insignificant but a day will dawn when she will be exalted. The Lord Jesus gave the same message through a different simile: 'The kingdom of heaven is like a mustard seed, which a man took and sowed in his field, which indeed is the least of all the seeds; but when it is grown it is greater than the herbs and becomes a tree, so that the birds of the air come and nest in its branches' (Matt. 13:31-32).

This little mountain, now eclipsed by the others, will be raised and 'established on the top of the mountains, and shall be exalted above the hills;

and all nations shall flow to it' (2:2). The picture is either of the little mountain being lifted and placed firmly upon the top of all other peaks, or of this little mountain growing larger, taller and higher than all surrounding mountains:

> A mountain of God is the mountain of Bashan;
> A mountain of many peaks is the mountain of Bashan.
> Why do you fume with envy, you mountains of many peaks?
> This is the mountain which God desires to dwell in;
> Yes, the LORD will dwell in it for ever
>
> (Ps. 68:15-16).

David compares the peaks of Mount Hermon, which lie on the northern perimeter of Bashan and tower more than 3,000 metres above sea level, with insignificant Mount Zion.[9]

In the days of Messiah, God manifested his glory on Mount Zion:

> And of Zion it will be said,
> 'This one and that one were born in her;
> And the Most High himself shall establish her.'
> The LORD will record,
> When he registers the peoples:
> 'This one was born there'
>
> (Ps. 87:5-6; cf. John 3:3-8).

Isaiah envisages the worldwide church of Jesus Christ and his universal reign:

> … all nations shall flow to it.
> Many people shall come and say,
> 'Come, and let us go up to the mountain of the LORD,
> To the house of the God of Jacob'
>
> (2:2-3).

This is the 'great multitude which no one could number, of all nations, tribes, peoples, and tongues' (Rev. 7:9). They flood to Zion because it has become the centre of true knowledge:

> The Gentiles shall come to your light,
> And kings to the brightness of your rising.
> Lift up your eyes all around, and see:

They all gather together, they come to you…
They shall ascend with acceptance on my altar,
And I will glorify the house of my glory…
Also the sons of those who afflicted you
Shall come bowing to you,
And all those who despised you shall fall prostrate at the soles of
     your feet;
And they shall call you the City of the LORD,
Zion of the Holy One of Israel

(60:3,4,7,14).

13. Messiah's remnant

The name of one of Isaiah's sons, Shear-Jashub (7:3), means, 'A remnant shall return' and highlights a recurring theme in the prophet's ministry (10:20-23; 11:11,16; 28:5; cf. Amos 5:15[10]). In every generation the Lord preserves 'a remnant according to the election of grace' (Rom. 11:5).

At the time of Isaiah's call to office, the Lord reveals his severe judgement against Israel: only one tenth of the nation will survive the exile, and even that tenth will be rigorously tried. Yet no matter how close the people come to being totally destroyed, there will still be a surviving remnant:

But yet a tenth will be in it,
And will return and be for consuming,
As a terebinth tree or as an oak,
Whose stump remains when it is cut down.
So the holy seed shall be its stump

(6:13).

A remnant who can be called holy is a spiritual remnant in whom the promises of salvation are to be realized. Although judgement must fall time after time upon the chosen people, yet no judgement will utterly wipe out the nation until the promises are fulfilled in Christ.[11] Confident of the Lord's preserving grace, the prophet declares:

Unless the LORD of hosts
Had left to us a very small remnant,

We would have become like Sodom,
We would have been made like Gomorrah

(1:9).

A confirmation that the remnant is intimately connected with the person and work of the Messiah is given by a further word from the Lord through Isaiah:

Here am I and the children whom the LORD has given me!
We are for signs and wonders in Israel
From the LORD of hosts,
Who dwells in Mount Zion

(8:18).

The writer to the Hebrews confirms the interpretation by identifying this prophecy in relation to the Lord Jesus Christ (Heb. 2:13).

Application

1. A form of religion

One of the great concerns of Isaiah, which is regularly repeated throughout his ministry, is what Paul later described as 'having a form of godliness but denying its power' (2 Tim. 3:5). False religion is a blatant disregard of the true God, but those who engage in the outward expressions of true religion without any reality in their hearts or minds show a more insidious disrespect:

He who kills a bull is as if he slays a man;
He who sacrifices a lamb, as if he breaks a dog's neck;
He who offers a grain offering, as if he offers swine's blood;
He who burns incense, as if he blesses an idol.
Just as they have chosen their own ways,
And their soul delights in their abominations,
So will I choose their delusions,
And bring their fears on them;
Because, when I called, no one answered,
When I spoke they did not hear;

But they did evil before my eyes,
And chose that in which I do not delight

(66:3-4).

When you spread out your hands,
I will hide my eyes from you;
Even though you make many prayers,
I will not hear.
Your hands are full of blood

(1:15).

The Lord Jesus was equally concerned about outward empty show. He applied Isaiah 29:13 to the Pharisees and scribes of his day:

Well did Isaiah prophesy of you hypocrites, as it is written:

'This people honours me with their lips,
But their heart is far from me.
And in vain they worship me,
Teaching as doctrines the commandments of men'

(Mark 7:6-7).

The true worship of God consists not only in the engagement of the heart and mind in worship and spiritual exercises, but also the practical outworking of service and life. Isaiah, like other great prophets of God, links the true worship of God with the practice of social justice, business integrity, active concern for the poor and oppressed and the upholding of truth and honesty in civil affairs (58:1-14; 59:14). A right relationship with God has always required a right relationship with other people. The law of God is summarized under two commands: '"You shall love the LORD your God with all your heart, with all your soul, and with all your mind." This is the first and great commandment. And the second is like it: "You shall love your neighbour as yourself." On these two commandments hang all the Law and the Prophets' (Matt. 22:37-40).

2. Worldly counsel

The people of God are constantly in danger of being influenced by worldly considerations or ungodly counsel:

'Woe to the rebellious children,' says the LORD,
'Who take counsel, but not of me,
And who devise plans, but not of my Spirit,
That they may add sin to sin…'

(30:1-2).

Living this side of Calvary and Pentecost, Christians are in the privileged position of having a completed written revelation from God. We need neither teacups nor horoscopes, neither chat shows nor advice centres to determine how to live life for God: 'To the law and to the testimony! If they do not speak according to this word, it is because there is no light in them' (8:20).

Only God can reveal his will (see 1 Cor. 2:12):

'For my thoughts are not your thoughts,
Nor are your ways my ways,' says the LORD.
'For as the heavens are higher than the earth,
So are my ways higher than your ways,
And my thoughts than your thoughts'

(55:8-9).

In the Scriptures God 'has given to us all things that pertain to life and godliness' (2 Peter 1:3), 'that the man of God may be complete' (2 Tim. 3:17; cf. v. 16). Paul warns that 'The time will come when they will not endure sound doctrine, but according to their own desires, because they have itching ears, they will heap up for themselves teachers; and they will turn their ears away from the truth, and be turned aside to fables' (2 Tim. 4:3-4). 'Blessed is the man who walks not in the counsel of the ungodly… But his delight is in the law of the LORD' (Ps. 1:1-2).

3. Affliction

A nation under the judgement of God may nevertheless have a number of citizens who are seeking faithfully to love and serve him. They suffer alongside the wicked and the temptation is to respond with Asaph of old:

Surely I have cleansed my heart in vain,
And washed my hands in innocence.

For all day long I have been plagued,
And chastened every morning

(Ps. 73:13).

In this context the prophet Isaiah is the messenger of encouragement and hope:

And though the LORD gives you
The bread of adversity and the water of affliction,
Yet your teachers will not be moved into a corner any more,
But your eyes shall see your teachers.
Your ears shall hear a word behind you, saying,
'This is the way, walk in it,'
Whenever you turn to the right hand
Or whenever you turn to the left

(30:20-21).

When you pass through the waters, I will be with you;
And through the rivers, they shall not overflow you.
When you walk through the fire, you shall not be burned,
Nor shall the flame scorch you.
For I am the LORD your God,
The Holy One of Israel, your Saviour…

(43:2-3).

Who among you fears the LORD?
Who obeys the voice of his Servant?
Who walks in darkness
And has no light?
Let him trust in the name of the LORD
And rely upon his God

(50:10).

'By "darkness" the Prophet here means not the ignorance or blindness of the human understanding, but the afflictions by which the children of God are almost always overwhelmed … he promises that they who have hitherto been discouraged and almost overwhelmed by so many distresses shall receive consolation.'[12]

Though the Lord has every reason to punish his people, two considerations hold him back: firstly, if he deals with them as harshly as they deserve, their heathen victors might conclude 'that God has left his own in the lurch, and so the honour of which he was deserving might wrongfully be attributed to other gods' (48:9-11);[13] and, secondly, though severely provoked, God will not forget his covenant:

'For a mere moment I have forsaken you,
But with great mercies I will gather you.
With a little wrath I hid my face from you for a moment;
But with everlasting kindness I will have mercy on you,'
Says the LORD, your Redeemer...
'For the mountains shall depart
And the hills be removed,
But my kindness shall not depart from you,
Nor shall my covenant of peace be removed,'
Says the LORD, who has mercy on you

(54:7-8,10).

Conclusion

The basic theme of the book of Isaiah harmonizes with the prophet's name — 'Jehovah is salvation', or 'Salvation is of Jehovah [the LORD].' While the context of the message is punishment under the righteous judgement of God, there are many remarkable revelations of grace and mercy. After the Psalms, Isaiah contains more Messianic prophecies than any other book of the Old Testament. Isaiah displays Messiah's humanity and humility, his obedience and suffering, his devotion and sacrifice, his deity and glory. He calls upon the people of God to be faithful and patient as they wait the unfolding of God's purposes. He sets before the church of God a wonderful hope for the future — 'the new heavens and the new earth' (66:22), where all who love God will worship him for ever.

Jeremiah

('Jehovah is high')

Author: Jeremiah

Key thought: Early warnings

Theme: The certainty of God's judgement
and the eternity of God's love

'Yes, I have loved you with an
    everlasting love;
Therefore with loving-kindness
    I have drawn you.'
                    Jeremiah 31:3

Summary

Jeremiah

About sixty years after the death of the prophet Isaiah the Lord raised up a young man to proclaim the imminent judgement that was about to fall upon Judah and Jerusalem. That young man, Jeremiah, is known as 'the weeping prophet', for he delivered the message of judgement with a broken heart (9:1; 13:15-17).

Author

The book of Jeremiah is the personal account of Jeremiah (1:1-2), some or all of which may have been dictated to his secretary Baruch (36:4). Jeremiah was born in 648 B.C., in Anathoth, a village a little more than two miles north-east of the city of Jerusalem. A priest by birth, Jeremiah is called to the prophetic office while still young (1:1,6). Like Moses before him (Exod. 4:10), he pleads his inexperience and inability as a speaker. The Lord reassures Jeremiah that he had been ordained to the work before his birth, and he will be given the words to speak, the authority to deliver the message and divine protection (1:7-10).

As a living symbol of the terrible judgement coming upon Judah, the prophet is commanded not to marry (16:2). His prophecies are not well received: his neighbours threaten to take his life (11:21); his own brothers spurn him (12:6); his friends turn against him (20:10); the inhabitants of Jerusalem plot against him (18:18); the priests and prophets despise him (20:1-2) and kings reject him (36:23). He is beaten, fastened in the stocks (20:2), threatened repeatedly and narrowly escapes death (26:8,11,24). He is imprisoned several times, including incarceration in a muddy dungeon (37:15; 38:6,28). At the fall of Jerusalem the Babylonians release him. He is given his freedom and chooses to remain in Jerusalem. Against the express command of God, the last inhabitants of Judah evacuate to Egypt taking Jeremiah with them (43:5-7). There the prophet dies.

The impending judgement is so severe and his love for his people so intense that it breaks his heart.

Historical setting

More is known about the life of Jeremiah than that of any other Old Testament prophet. He began his ministry in the year 627 B.C., the thirteenth year of Josiah's reign over Judah (1:2). Josiah came to the throne at the age of eight; by his mid-teens he gave evidence of true conversion, and at twenty he began a thorough religious reformation throughout the land of Judah (2 Chr. 34:1-3). So the call of Jeremiah to the prophetic office and the beginning of the extensive reformation of religion spearheaded by King Josiah both occurred within a period of twelve months.

Jeremiah ministered during the remaining eighteen years of godly King Josiah's reign and throughout the fateful reigns of four godless kings: Jehoahaz, Jehoiakim, Jehoiachin and Zedekiah.

He was a contemporary of the prophets Nahum, Zephaniah and Habakkuk in Jerusalem, and Daniel and Ezekiel in Babylon. Daniel and Ezekiel probably spent their early days under Jeremiah's ministry in Jerusalem before they were taken into exile.

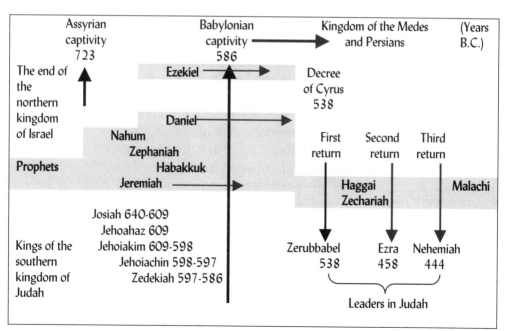

Judah and its prophets and kings before, during and after the exile

Jeremiah served God for over forty years (from 627 until 586 B.C. and beyond). He prophesied for twenty-two years while Judah was under threat from Assyria and Egypt. He prophesied for nineteen years while Judah was threatened and besieged by Babylon, being a witness to the three waves of invasion and subsequent captivities (605 B.C., 597 B.C. and 586 B.C.). He prophesied in Egypt after the destruction of Jerusalem. Thus he saw the final days of the great Assyrian Empire that had destroyed the northern kingdom of Israel and had dominated the Near East for over two hundred years. Following the death of King Ashurbanipal of Assyria (c. 626 B.C.) the Assyrian Empire went into decline. Egypt and Babylon began to assert themselves. Babylon conquered Nineveh, the capital of Assyria, in 612 B.C. and seven years later, in the inevitable confrontation, the Babylonians defeated the Egyptians at the battle of Carchemish (605 B.C.). Jeremiah exercised his ministry during these tempestuous days when the tiny nation of Judah was trying to maintain her own independence.

Outline

This book is a combination of history, biography and prophecy. It is not written in chronological order, nor is the material grouped together according to subject. It is like a collection of sermons recorded at random: 'Jeremiah's prophecies may seem to be somewhat scattered, but their arrangement enables the prophet to emphasize *repetition*. The themes of Jeremiah are *recurring* ones — the sinfulness of the nation and the approaching doom. Into his book he weaves these thoughts, and as we read on we meet them over and over again until the impression which they have made upon us is truly powerful and tremendous.'[1]

One element in the communication that God gives to the prophet Jeremiah is the use of signs and stories, in the manner of parables. A number of these messages are dramatized parables, such as, the linen sash (13:1-11), the potter and the clay (18:1-10) and the broken clay jar (19:1-13).

Through his preaching Jeremiah clearly communicates that the only way to avoid the devastating impact of God's judgement is to repent, willingly yield in allegiance to the living God and take up once more the terms and obligations of the covenant. The basic message is clear: 'the inevitable and inescapable judgement of God upon Israel for her rebellion and disobedience'.[2] These are dark days for the southern kingdom of Judah.

Jeremiah has the unenviable task of bringing rebuke, warning, pleas and words of hope to his people. By this means the Lord prepares them to some extent for the trials and difficulties that lie ahead.

Introduction: Jeremiah's call and commission (1:1-19)

Jeremiah is called to office while still young. He pleads his immaturity and lack of experience as rendering him quite unsuitable for the task. He learns that the destruction of Jerusalem is certain and that it will be carried out by a nation from the north.

Jeremiah ministers during the reign of five kings: Josiah, his three sons and a grandson.

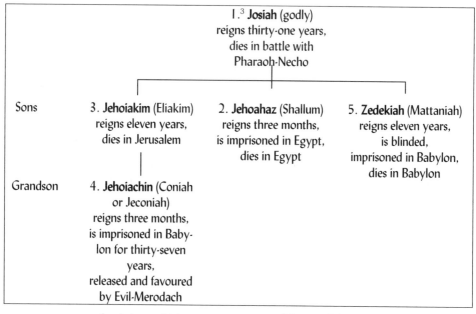

Josiah and his successors as kings of Judah

Part I: Judah in the reign of King Josiah (640–609 B.C., cf. 2 Chr. 34:1 - 35:27)[4]

Five years after Jeremiah's call to ministry, in the eighteenth year of Josiah's reign, the Book of the Law is discovered in the temple (2 Kings

22:8). The message about the breaking of the covenant and obedience to 'the words of this covenant which I commanded your fathers in the day that I brought them out of the land of Egypt' (11:3-4), sounds like a direct reference to the rediscovered written law of Moses.

The thirteen years of ministry exercised during the reign of Josiah were probably the happiest for the prophet Jeremiah, although he was no doubt constantly warning the people, during that period of religious reformation, that outward change is not sufficient for the Lord (2:22).

Jeremiah is deeply grieved when King Josiah dies in battle (609 B.C.) and probably composes a lament for his funeral (2 Chr. 35:25).

Godly Josiah is followed on the throne by three sons and a grandson, all of whom are ungodly and react with hostility and aggression to any suggestion that they should repent of their wickedness and seek the Lord. Jeremiah is uncompromising in his denunciation of these men, even though as kings they exercise the power of life and death over him.

Part II: Judah in the reign of King Jehoahaz (609 B.C., cf. 2 Kings 23:31-34)

As he announces the king's downfall, Jeremiah gives King Jehoahaz the nickname 'Shallum', meaning 'retribution' (22:11-12). The prophet speaks out against the lack of justice in the nation and the absence of equity in trade and employment. Meanwhile over in Babylon (also called the land of the Chaldeans),[5] the prophet Ezekiel compares Jehoahaz to a young lion who has learned to catch and devour men. Ezekiel also prophesies the capture, exile and imprisonment of Jehoahaz and his deportation to Egypt (Ezek. 19:3-4).

Part III: Judah in the reign of King Jehoiakim (609-598 B.C., cf. 2 Kings 23:35-37)

When Pharaoh Necho takes Jehoahaz back with him to Egypt, he places his older brother Eliakim (whom he renames Jehoiakim) on the throne to rule Judah as a vassal of Egypt.

During the reign of King Jehoiakim there is the famous battle of Carchemish where the Babylonians defeat the Egyptians and then turn against Judah. Jeremiah foretells the invasion, calls the people to repentance, warns of the dreadful outcome in rejecting the Lord and prophesies the destruction of Jerusalem and the seventy-year exile in Babylon (25:1,11). The king and people refuse to heed the warning. King Nebuchadnezzar successfully besieges Jerusalem and takes captives (among whom is Daniel) and utensils from the temple back to Babylon (Dan. 1:1-2,6).

Although the overall message committed to Jeremiah is one of terrible judgement, there is nevertheless the recurring appeal to the people to return to the living God: 'But this is what I commanded them, saying, "Obey my voice, and I will be your God, and you shall be my people. And walk in all the ways that I have commanded you, that it may be well with you." Yet they did not obey or incline their ear, but walked in the counsels and in the imagination of their evil heart, and went backward and not forward' (7:23-24).

God hates idolatry and the immorality that it produces. During the reign of Jehoiakim Jeremiah denounces the false shepherds and false prophets who mislead the people (23:1-2; 27:1,9-10); he preaches in the temple pronouncing doom on the nation unless they obey God's laws. Priests, prophets and people react with great hostility and demand Jeremiah's execution (26:1,8). The threats upon his life are only too real since when Urijah, who is also a prophet of the Lord, loses his nerve and flees to Egypt, he is followed, captured, brought back and executed (26:20-23).

During the reign of Jehoiakim the Lord instructs Jeremiah to make a permanent record of all the prophecies that God has given him. These are dictated to Baruch, who acts as Jeremiah's secretary. When Jeremiah is banned from the temple, Baruch goes and reads the prophecies to the people. When the king hears he is so angry that he cuts the scroll to pieces with a penknife, throws them into the fire and orders the arrest of Baruch and Jeremiah, 'but the LORD hid them' (36:26). A little later Jeremiah dictates a second copy to Baruch with the inclusion of additional material. Baruch, the secretary and friend of Jeremiah, has every reason to fear for his safety, but the Lord gives him a reassuring prophecy (45:1-5).

Jeremiah prophesies the ignominious death of King Jehoiakim: '... buried with the burial of a donkey, dragged and cast out beyond the gates of Jerusalem' (22:19).

Part IV: Judah in the reign of King Jehoiachin (598-597 B.C.)

Jehoiachin (Coniah or Jeconiah) reigns only three months and is taken into captivity in Babylon, just as Jeremiah predicts (22:24-30; 2 Kings 24:8-16;

Ezek. 19:9). Jehoiachin spends thirty-seven years in prison. When Evil-Merodach comes to the throne in Babylon, he releases him and treats him kindly (52:31-34). Among the aristocracy, priests, servants and army officers transported to Babylon with King Jehoiachin is young Ezekiel, who within a few years will be called to the prophetic office among the exiles.

Part V: Judah in the reign of King Zedekiah (597–586 B.C.)

When King Nebuchadnezzar of Babylon deports King Jehoiachin, he places Mattaniah (whose name he changes to Zedekiah) on the throne of Judah. Nebuchadnezzar establishes a covenant with Zedekiah (Ezek. 17:12-13), though what transpires suggests that Zedekiah has no intentions of honouring this contract. Only a short time later, he sends ambassadors to Babylon and, judging from the letter that Jeremiah the prophet sends with those same men, urging the captives to stay submissive in Babylon (29:3-28), Zedekiah has his mind on rebellion.

In the fourth year of his reign Zedekiah travels to Babylon in person (51:59), presumably to reassure the King of Babylon of his loyalty and to ascertain the situation with regard to the exiles. Five years later, no doubt with the collusion of the kings of Edom, Moab, Ammon, Tyre and Sidon (27:3), 'Zedekiah rebelled against the king of Babylon' (2 Kings 24:20). This rebellion is seen as a serious sin against God because Nebuchadnezzar 'had made him swear an oath by God' (2 Chr. 36:13; cf. Ezek. 17:13-21).

That same year (28:1; cf. 51:59) the prophet Jeremiah faces serious problems from Hananiah, a false prophet. Hananiah publicly contradicts the prophecy of Jeremiah and proclaims the delivery of Judah from the domination of Babylon and the return to Jerusalem of all the temple treasures removed by King Nebuchadnezzar. Jeremiah exposes the lies of Hananiah and privately foretells his death within the year, as a judgement from God (28:16; cf. Deut. 18:20).

Nebuchadnezzar once more marches against Judah. He lays siege to Jerusalem (52:4). The very same day the prophet Ezekiel in Babylon receives a revelation from the Lord indicating that the siege has started (Ezek. 24:1-2).

It appears that the commencement of the invasion causes King Zedekiah and his nobles to reflect upon the covenant made between the living God and his people Israel, and in particular the law on slavery: 'If you buy a Hebrew servant, he shall serve six years; and in the seventh he shall go out free and pay nothing' (Exod. 21:2). The people obey the law and set free their Hebrew slaves. But after a short time they change their minds and subjugate them once more. The Lord is angry at this further demonstration of disrespect and disobedience. Jeremiah communicates God's intense displeasure (34:13-17).

During a short respite from the siege, while the King of Babylon turns his attention to the approaching Egyptians (37:5), King Zedekiah sends men to Jeremiah to enquire of the Lord as to the outcome of the war (21:1-2). Jeremiah informs the king's ambassadors that God is fighting *against* Judah. He recommends that the people defect to Babylon (21:9), and that King Zedekiah should surrender and seek clemency. No one listens to the word from God. Jeremiah warns the people not to resist the Babylonians and some of the nobles charge him with treachery against the king, the army and the nation. He is thrown into a muddy dungeon and remains in appalling conditions until Ebed-Melech, the Ethiopian, intervenes and pleads for the king to show clemency towards the prophet. Consequently Jeremiah is brought into 'the court of the prison' (38:13).

Although Jeremiah has to communicate a message of severe judgement against Judah, he also delivers words of singular hope. The wonderful words of chapters 30 and 31 belong to this period of Judah's suffering:

Behold, I will bring back the captivity of Jacob's tents,
And have mercy on his dwelling-places...
You shall be my people,
And I will be your God

(30:18, 22).

Yes, I have loved you with an everlasting love;
Therefore with loving-kindness I have drawn you

(31:3).

Jeremiah's letter to the exiles in Babylon also contains wonderful encouragement: 'After seventy years[6] are completed at Babylon, I will visit you and perform my good word towards you, and cause you to return to this place. For I know the thoughts that I think towards you, says the LORD, thoughts of peace and not of evil, to give you a future and a hope' (29:10-11).

Only months before the fall of Jerusalem the Lord instructs Jeremiah to buy a field from his cousin Hanameel (32:6-7). The price is paid and a contract of purchase is signed before witnesses. This is a symbolic act to show that 'Houses and fields and vineyards shall be possessed again in this land' (32:15).

The city resists the Babylonian siege for eighteen months until the wall is penetrated (39:1-2). When Jerusalem is taken Zedekiah tries to escape. He is captured on the plains of Jericho, and blinded (2 Kings 25:7). Two seemingly contradictory prophecies come true: 'Zedekiah king of Judah shall not escape from the hand of the Chaldeans, but shall surely be delivered into the hand of the king of Babylon, and shall speak with him face to face, and see him eye to eye' (32:4); and 'I will bring him to Babylon, to the land of the Chaldeans; yet he shall not see it, though he shall die there' (Ezek. 12:13).

The Babylonians sack Jerusalem, destroy the temple, the palace, all substantial houses and the city wall. Jeremiah is set free and given the choice to return with the captain of the Babylonian army and live in peace in Babylon, to remain in Judah with the new governor, or to go wherever he wishes (40:4). He chooses to remain in Judah. All the civil and religious leaders are taken back to Babylon where they are executed (52:24-27). The remaining people of Jerusalem are taken captive to Babylon, with the exception of poor vine-dressers and farmers who are left to tend the land (2 Kings 25:12) with Gedaliah as governor. In three invasions Nebuchadnezzar takes a total of 4,600 captives (52:30).

The remaining inhabitants experience internal strife and, following the assassination of governor Gedaliah, flee to Egypt against the express word of the Lord (43:5-7). Jeremiah is forced to accompany them and he continues his ministry among the Jews in that land (43:8-13; 44:1-30). The people of Judah have broken their covenant with the living God. Even the devastating events of recent years have not brought them to their senses. In Egypt they forsake the Lord and turn to local idols.

Part VI: Prophecies against foreign nations
(46:1 – 51:64)

The nations which had been hostile towards Israel and Judah come under divine censure. Prophecies are directed at Egypt, the Philistines, Moab, Ammon, Edom, Damascus (i.e. Syria), Kedar (part of Arabia), Elam and Babylon. Only four of the nine nations, Egypt, Moab, Ammon and Elam, are given hope of restoration to their lands (46:26; 48:47; 49:6,39).

Christ and his church

Against the dark background of threat and punishment, there appear some of the most glorious Messianic prophecies of the entire Old Testament.[7]

1. The ark of the covenant

' "Return, O backsliding children," says the LORD... "Then it shall come to pass, when you are multiplied and increased in the land in those days," says the LORD, "that they will say no more, 'The ark of the covenant of the LORD.' It shall not come to mind, nor shall they remember it, nor shall they visit it, nor shall it be made any more. At that time Jerusalem shall be called The Throne of the LORD, and all the nations shall be gathered to it, to the name of the LORD, to Jerusalem; they shall walk no more after the stubbornness of their evil heart. In those days the house of Judah shall walk with the house of Israel, and they shall come together out of the land of the north to the land that I have given as an inheritance to your fathers" ' (3:14,16-18).

The ark symbolized the presence of God amongst his people: 'You shall make a mercy seat of pure gold... And you shall make two cherubim of gold … at the two ends of the mercy seat... You shall put the mercy seat on top of the ark, and in the ark you shall put the Testimony that I will give you. And there I will meet with you, and I will speak with you from above the mercy seat, from between the two cherubim which are on the ark of the Testimony...' (Exod. 25:17-18, 21-22).

The true 'God, who made the world and everything in it', 'the Most High' who 'does not dwell in temples made with hands' (Acts 17:24; 7:48), had chosen to become Israel's God and bind himself in a covenant relationship which stipulated privileges and obligations, blessings and curses. In order to aid people in their understanding and prepare for the coming of his Son into the world, the Lord gave types (symbolic representations) during the period of the Old Covenant, one of which is the ark of the covenant. Whoever 'would seek Him as the God of Israel, could find him only in the temple, and over the ark of the covenant'.[8]

A day is foretold in Jeremiah 3 when there will be no need, or even thought, for the ark of the covenant. 'God will supply so rich a compensation for that which is lost, that men will no longer desire it, nor, driven by this desire, make an effort to produce it again by their own hands.'[9] This is a reference to the coming Messiah.

The mercy seat which formed the lid of the ark is the symbol of the throne of God. When the people of God are urged to 'come boldly to the throne of grace, that we may obtain mercy and find grace to help in time of need' (Heb. 4:16), it is evident that 'Christ is designated as the true mercy seat, as the true ark of the covenant'.[10] In the prophecy of Jeremiah the necessity for the ark will cease when 'Jerusalem shall be called The Throne of the LORD' (3:17).

For the LORD has chosen Zion;
He has desired it for his habit-
    ation:
This is my resting place for ever;
Here I will dwell, for I have desired
    it
                          (Ps. 132:13-14).

Thus says the LORD of hosts:
'I am zealous for Zion with great
    zeal;
With great fervour I am zealous for
    her.'
Thus says the LORD:
'I will return to Zion,
And dwell in the midst of Jerusa-
    lem.
Jerusalem shall be called the City
    of Truth,
The Mountain of the LORD of
    hosts,
The Holy Mountain
                          (Zech. 8:2-3).

Zion

The first mention of Zion in the Bible is in 2 Samuel 5:7: 'David took the stronghold of Zion (that is, the City of David).' Zion, therefore, was the name of the ancient Jebusite fortress situated on the south-east hill of Jerusalem at the junction of the Kidron Valley and the Tyropoeon Valley. The name came to stand not only for the fortress, but also for the hill on which the fortress stood. After David captured 'the stronghold of Zion' by defeating the Jebusites, he called Zion 'the City of David' (1 Kings 8:1; 1 Chr. 11:5; 2 Chr. 5:2).

When Solomon built the temple on Mount Moriah (a hill distinct and separate from Mount Zion), and moved the ark of the covenant there, the word 'Zion' expanded in meaning to include also the temple and the temple area (Ps. 2:6; 48:2,1-12; 132:13). It was only a short step until Zion was used as a name for the city of Jerusalem, the land of Judah, and the people of Israel as a whole (Isa. 40:9; Jer. 31:12). The prophet Zechariah spoke of 'the sons of Zion' (Zech. 9:13). By this time the word 'Zion' had come to mean the entire nation of Israel.

The most important use of the word 'Zion' is in a religious or theological sense. Zion is used figuratively of Israel as the people of God (Isa. 60:14). The spiritual meaning of Zion (AV/KJV, Sion), is continued in the New Testament, where it is given the Christian meaning of God's spiritual kingdom, the church of God, the heavenly Jerusalem (Heb. 12:22; Rev. 14:1).[11]

These, and so many prophecies like them, came wonderfully true when 'The Word became flesh and dwelt among us, and we beheld his glory, the glory as of the only begotten of the Father, full of grace and truth' (John 1:14).

2. The righteous king

The curse on Jehoiachin/Coniah (22:28-30) meant that no physical descendant of his would succeed to the throne of David. When Matthew traces the genealogy of the Lord Jesus from David through Jehoiachin (Matt. 1:12), he is tracing the *legal* descent through his stepfather Joseph. Luke traces the *natural* descent of the Lord from David through Nathan (Luke 3:31) — and by implication through Mary — which does not include Jehoiachin. Messiah could not be born under any curse, otherwise he could not be the promised King and righteous Branch:

> 'Behold, the days are coming,' says the LORD,
> 'That I will raise to David a Branch of righteousness;
> A king shall reign and prosper,
> And execute judgement and righteousness in the earth.
> In his days Judah will be saved,
> And Israel will dwell safely;
> Now this is his name by which he will be called:
> THE LORD OUR RIGHTEOUSNESS'
>
> (23:5-6).

Since 'All our righteousnesses are like filthy rags' (Isa. 64:6), the Lord has provided his own righteousness as a gift for us who believe (Rom. 4:5-6; Ps. 24:5). 'For he made him who knew no sin to be sin for us, that we might become the righteousness of God in him' (2 Cor. 5:21). Through his substitutionary death at Calvary the Lord Jesus became righteousness for us (1 Cor. 1:30). He is most gloriously YHWH Tsidkenu, 'The LORD our Righteousness'.

3. The New Covenant

All the prophets base their accusations and challenges on the special covenant between the Lord and his people. Israel was a nation in covenant with God.

When the Lord chose Abraham and led him from his homeland and people, he entered into covenant with him to be God to him and bless him with a land, a great nation and a great privilege; for through Abraham '... all the families of the earth shall be blessed' (Gen. 12:1-3; 17:1-8). That covenant continued through Isaac and Jacob and was to form the chief hope of the Israelite nation. When the Lord delivered the Israelites from slavery in Egypt it is this covenant which he was honouring: 'So God heard their groaning, and God remembered his covenant with Abraham, with Isaac, and with Jacob. And God looked upon the children of Israel, and God acknowledged them' (Exod. 2:24-25).

On Mount Sinai the Lord distinguished the Israelites from all other nations by giving them the covenant law, the covenant tabernacle and the covenant priesthood. Moses made a record in 'the Book of the Covenant' of all that the Lord had said to him (Exod. 24:7). Forty years later, just before the death of Moses and the entry of the Israelites into the promised land, Moses and the people renewed their covenant with God (Deut. 28:1 – 30:20). The continuing history of Israel is a story of frequent disobedience and often of total disregard to their covenantal obligations to worship the Lord only and to obey his law.

Even where there was faithfulness towards God, and an earnest desire to live according to his commands, the law was a heavy and unbearable 'yoke on the neck' (Acts 15:10). There was nothing wrong with the law itself, for it 'is holy' and each 'commandment holy and just and good' (Rom. 7:12). The problem was that 'It was weak through the flesh' (Rom. 8:3). Human nature was so sinfully weak that no one could keep the law of the covenant.

Jeremiah was even more explicit than other prophets about the fact that disobedience to the covenant would bring the curses of the covenant upon the Israelites. Judah, like the northern kingdom of Israel before her, had broken that covenant (11:2-10; 31:32). The vast majority of the people had no interest in worshipping or serving the true God. Their lives were filled with corruption. Yet within these dark days of apostasy the light of a new day was prophesied. The Lord will establish a new covenant and this time he will change the hearts of his people so that they will want to keep it: ' "Behold, the days are coming," says the LORD, "when I will make a new covenant with the house of Israel and with the house of Judah — not according to the covenant that I made with their fathers in the day that I took them by the hand to bring them out of the land of Egypt, my covenant which they broke, though I was a husband to them," says the LORD. "But this is the covenant that I will make with the house of Israel: After those days, says the LORD, I will put my law in their minds, and write it on their hearts; and I will be their God, and they shall be my people. No more shall every man teach his neighbour, and every man his brother, saying, 'Know the LORD,' for they all shall know me, from the least of them to the greatest of them," says the LORD. "For I will forgive their iniquity, and their sin I will remember no more"' (Jer. 31:31-34).

The author of the letter to the Hebrews addresses the Jews who have received the Lord Jesus Christ as Messiah and Saviour. He shows how the New Covenant promises given through the prophet Jeremiah are wonderfully fulfilled in the crucified Son of God. The inadequacies of the Old Covenant and the glories of the New Covenant are spelt out: 'For if that first covenant had been faultless, then no place would have been sought for a second. Because finding fault with them, he says: "Behold, the days are coming," says the LORD, "when I will make a new covenant with the house of Israel and with the house of Judah…"' (Heb. 8:7-8, quoting Jer. 31:31-34).

The New Covenant totally replaces the Old Covenant (Heb. 8:13). At its centre is the life and death of the Lord Jesus Christ; in instituting the Lord's Supper, he said, 'This cup is the new covenant in my blood, which is shed for you' (Luke 22:20).

The New Covenant is a covenant of *grace*. 'It is of grace because it originated in the mysterious love of God for sinners who deserved only his wrath and curse. Secondly, because it promises salvation, not on the condition of works or anything meritorious on our part, but as an unmerited gift. And, thirdly, because its benefits are secured and applied not in the course of nature, or in the exercise of the natural powers of the sinner, but by the supernatural influence of the Holy Spirit, granted to him as an unmerited gift.'[12]

The Lord Jesus Christ is the 'mediator of a better covenant, which was established on better promises' (Heb. 8:6). He is the 'one mediator between God and men' (1 Tim. 2:5). The Son of God is called the 'mediator of a better covenant' and the 'surety of a better covenant' (Heb. 7:22), both phrases meaning that the Lord Jesus Christ is the personal guarantee of the terms of the new and better covenant, secured on the basis of his perfect sacrifice: 'He undertook to answer, as the Surety of the covenant, for all the sins of all those who are to be, and are made partakers of the benefits of it; that is, to undergo the punishment due unto their sins, to make an atonement for them, by offering Himself as a propitiatory sacrifice, redeeming them by the price of His blood from their state of misery and bondage under the law and the curse of it. He also undertook that those who were to be taken into this covenant should receive grace, enabling them to comply with the terms of it, fulfil its conditions, and yield the obedience therein required by God.'[13]

Under the New Covenant (31:31-34) the laws of God are written on the mind to make us *know* them, and on our hearts to make us *love* them, and we receive the indwelling Spirit to enable us to *do* them.

4. Signs and parables

As well as direct word communication, the Lord uses visual signs to teach Jeremiah. A number of these messages are dramatized parables, such as the linen sash (13:1-11), the potter and the clay (18:1-10) and the broken clay jar (19:1-13). Sometimes there is no visual presentation, but a vivid word picture conjuring up an imaginary scene, as in the case of the wine bottles (13:12-14). In each case the objective is to teach important spiritual lessons.

The Lord Jesus Christ was an expert in the use of signs and parables to communicate in a vivid and dramatic manner. So many of the miracles which he performed were not only a demonstration that he was authenticated as Messiah by God himself (Acts 2:22; Heb. 2:4; cf. Matt. 11:3-5), but they also contained an underlying spiritual message relevant to each miracle. The apostle John explains his selection of Christ's miracles on the basis that 'These are written that you may believe that Jesus is the Christ, the Son of God, and that believing you may have life' (John 20:31). His use of the word 'signs' in the preceding verse, indicates that he has chosen miracles with a profound spiritual meaning. A few examples will illustrate the point: feeding the five thousand is a miracle indicating that Jesus is the Bread of Heaven (John 6:11,35) who thoroughly satisfies the hungry soul; changing water into wine communicates the powerful truth that the purification ceremonies of the Old Covenant are inadequate and are replaced by the precious blood of the New Covenant Lamb of God, the Lord having saved the best till last (John 2:9-11; cf. Heb. 11:40); the raising of Lazarus becomes a glorious demonstration that Jesus is in himself the resurrection and the life (John 11:43-44,25); the man born blind who receives his sight at the touch of Jesus (John 9:1,6-7) represents every sinner born in sin and spiritually blind until light is commanded to shine out of his darkness (2 Cor. 4:4-6); casting the net on the other side of the boat and catching numerous fish, after the resurrection of the Lord Jesus Christ, becomes a vivid prediction of the ingathering of believing Gentiles along with believing Jews (John 21:6; cf. 10:16).

The Lord God used signs and parables to communicate in a clear and distinct manner to the prophet Jeremiah, but the Lord Jesus indicates that signs and parables, when publicly demonstrated and spoken, have another aspect to them. They restrict communication to certain people, for they have the property both to *reveal* and to *conceal* at the same time (Matt. 11:25; cf. 16:17). When asked why he spoke in parables, the Lord Jesus replied:

Therefore I speak to them in parables, because seeing they do not see, and hearing they do not hear, nor do they understand. And in them the prophecy of Isaiah is fulfilled, which says:

'Hearing you will hear and shall not understand,
And seeing you will see and not perceive...'

But blessed are your eyes for they see, and your ears for they hear...' (Matt. 13:13-14,16, quoting Isa. 6:9-10).

Application

1. The amazing love of God

At first glance Jeremiah seems an unlikely choice as a prophet of judgement. A more robust and sturdy character like Elijah might have suited the role better. Jeremiah comes over as a highly sensitive individual with a very tender heart, who grieves at having to deliver such messages:

Oh, that my head were waters,
And my eyes a fountain of tears,
That I might weep day and night
For the slain of the daughter of my people!

(9:1).

Give glory to the LORD your God
Before he causes darkness...
But if you will not hear it,
My soul will weep in secret for your pride;
My eyes will weep bitterly

And run down with tears,
Because the LORD's flock has been taken captive

(13:16-17).

Jeremiah is the prophet of the broken heart, and who better to be an ambassador for the Lord who exhibits such tenderness and sensitivity himself? Seven hundred years after Jeremiah another would express the same pain and grief over the capital: 'O Jerusalem, Jerusalem, the one who kills the prophets and stones those who are sent to her! How often I wanted to gather your children together, as a hen gathers her chicks under her wings, but you were not willing!' (Matt. 23:37).

Although Jeremiah had to deliver many words of warning, rebuke, judgement and imminent punishment, he nevertheless expresses some remarkable words of grace from God: 'For I know the thoughts that I think towards you, says the LORD, thoughts of peace and not of evil, to give you a future and a hope' (29:11). 'Yes, I have loved you with an everlasting love; therefore with loving-kindness I have drawn you' (31:3). In spite of the unfaithfulness of the people, the Lord displays amazing love and compassion.

2. Declaring the judgement of God

In spite of the evident tenderness of Jeremiah's heart and his obvious love for sinners, he faithfully delivers God's message of judgement. In uncompromising fashion he declares the wrath of God towards a wayward and rebellious people: 'Therefore thus says the Lord GOD: "Behold, my anger and my fury will be poured out on this place — on man and on beast, on the trees of the field and on the fruit of the ground. And it will burn and not be quenched." ... "For the children of Judah have done evil in my sight," says the LORD. "They have set their abominations in the house which is called by my name, to pollute it... The corpses of this people will be food for the birds of the heaven and for the beasts of the earth. And no one will frighten them away. Then I will cause to cease from the cities of Judah and from the streets of Jerusalem the voice of mirth and the voice of gladness, the voice of the bridegroom and the voice of the bride. For the land shall be desolate"' (7:20,30,33-34).

There are more references in Scripture to the anger, fury and wrath of God than there are to his love and tenderness: 'Who knows the power of your anger? For as the fear of you, so is your wrath' (Ps. 90:11).

It is the Lord Jesus Christ who speaks most about the terrors of hell and everlasting punishment. The apostles do not deal with the subjects to the same degree, and this is entirely understandable: 'For as none but God has the right, and would dare, to sentence a soul to eternal misery, for sin; and as none but God has the right, and would dare, to execute the sentence; so none but God has the right, and should presume, to delineate the nature and consequences of this sentence. This is the reason why most of the awful imagery in which the sufferings of the lost are described is found in the discourses of our Lord and Saviour.'[14]

Love for the lost demands a declaration of the judgement and justice of God. Without an awareness of the holiness and righteousness of God, without recognition of the judgement of God falling upon impenitent sinners, there will be no turning to the Saviour, no calling upon the Lord for salvation (Rom. 10:13-14). The message of the gospel is not the satisfying of human need, but the satisfaction of God's holy justice. Conviction of sin, in the awareness of the holiness and righteousness of God, is an essential prerequisite to confession and conversion (Ps. 32:3-5).

The vileness of our sin necessitated the sacrifice of the holy God-man; God's judgement on our sin exacted his agonizing suffering and death by crucifixion, bearing 'our sins in his own body on the tree' (1 Peter 2:24). Nowhere is God's wrath towards sin seen in greater clarity than at Calvary when he gave up his Son, his only Son, whom he loved (cf. Gen. 22:2).

The terrors of hell are vividly portrayed in the anguish of Calvary and that inexpressibly awful cry: 'My God, my God, why have you forsaken me?' (Matt. 27:46). Christ tasted death and hell for his people. He bore that excruciating agony so that none of his people, for whom he died, would ever experience hell for themselves. The terrors of hell for the impenitent and unbelieving will be as unending as the delights and joys of heaven for the penitent and believing. Paul reveals the judgement of God as one of the motives behind his preaching: 'Knowing, therefore, the terror of the Lord, we persuade men...' (2 Cor. 5:11).

At Athens there was a fine example of this apostle's ministry and his faithfulness in declaring the judgement of God: 'Truly, these times of ignorance God overlooked, but now he commands all men everywhere to repent, because he has appointed a day on which he will judge the world in righteousness by the man whom he has ordained. He has given assurance of this to all, by raising him from the dead' (Acts 17:30-31).

3. The condition of the human heart by nature

In sharp contrast to the revelation of the divine heart is the shocking disclosure of the human heart:

> The heart is deceitful above all things,
> And desperately wicked;
> Who can know it?
> I, the LORD, search the heart,
> I test the mind,
> Even to give every man according to his ways,
> And according to the fruit of his doings
>
> (17:9).

The Lord Jesus clarified the corruption in the human heart: '... from within, out of the heart of men, proceed evil thoughts, adulteries, fornications, murders, thefts, covetousness, wickedness, deceit, licentiousness, an evil eye, blasphemy, pride, foolishness. All these evil things come from within and defile a man' (Mark 7:21-23). The heart in its natural state not only produces these evils, but is also incapable of right judgement. While some consciousness of what is right and what is wrong is present to one degree or another in every human being, the effects of sin have been to distort and corrupt. The biblical doctrine of total depravity does not teach that every human being is as wicked as he or she could be, but that sin has infected every aspect of every human personality — in thought, mind and will. In the natural condition, therefore, no one is righteous (Ps. 14:1-3; Rom. 3:23); no one understands spiritual truth (1 Cor. 2:14); no one can please God (Rom. 8:7-8); and no one can enter the kingdom of God (John 3:5). The need for a radical change in the human condition is evident. God alone works that miracle. In Ezekiel's prophecy there is the promise of 'a new heart and ... a new spirit within' (Ezek. 36:26).

4. Plea to backsliders

In spite of the reforms brought about by good King Josiah, the nation continued in its spiritual and moral decline. The idolatry and immorality outstripped the corruptions of the northern kingdom of Israel before her exile to Assyria (3:11). Nevertheless certain words appear frequently in the prophecies of Jeremiah: 'forsaken' / 'forsake' (twenty-four times); 'backsliding' (nine times); and 'return' (forty-five times). These chapters are full of words for backsliders. Judah had forsaken the Lord; Jeremiah was commissioned to warn of impending judgement; there was still time for the people to repent and avert condemnation:

> 'Return, backsliding Israel,' says the LORD,
> 'And I will not cause my anger to fall on you;
> for I am merciful,' says the LORD,
> 'And I will not remain angry for ever.
> Only acknowledge your iniquity,
> That you have transgressed against the LORD your God...
> And you have not obeyed my voice,' says the LORD
>
> (3:12-13).

Events at the potter's house serve to illustrate the importance of returning to God quickly. A spoiled pot could be reworked and reshaped while the clay was still wet (18:4-6), but when hard and dry it can only be smashed in pieces (19:11). The opportunity for repentance is not indefinite.

A wonderful promise (reminiscent of Isaiah 55:6-7) is given to all who hear or read: 'And you will seek me and find me, when you search for me with all your heart. I will be found by you, says the LORD...' (29:13-14).

5. Standing alone

A terrible sense of isolation and aloneness must have gripped Jeremiah through those dark years. No one wanted to hear his messages from God. His family, friends, neighbours, people and rulers rejected his preaching and turned against him. Even the religious leaders despised him. Prophets and priests stood against him and sought his death. Jeremiah suffered like the greater Prophet of whom it was written: 'He is despised and rejected by men, a man of sorrows and acquainted with grief' (Isa. 53:3).

How relevant are the faithfulness and fortitude of Jeremiah for our day! With Western nations seemingly hell-bent on undermining every ethical law based upon the Scriptures, with institutional religion denying the major doctrines of the faith and actively and publicly promoting immorality and interfaith initiatives, with mysticism and existentialism dominating even evangelical churches, the sense of aloneness and pressure for conformity is almost unbearable. Religious leaders of our own day do not know 'how to blush' (8:12; cf. v. 11).

Conclusion

The phrase 'rising up early and speaking/sending' occurs six times in this book (7:13,25; 26:5; 29:19; 32:33; 35:15). The only other occurrence of this expression is found in 2 Chronicles 36:15, where Ezra probably borrowed it from Jeremiah. It has particular relevance to a book that is so full of warning, rebuke, challenge, judgement and punishment. God grants Judah many early warnings. It is a great evidence of God's mercy that he reveals judgement while there is still time to repent and avert the punishment. The prophecies of Jeremiah are sober illustrations of a greater condemnation, for 'It is appointed for men to die once, but after this the judgement' (Heb. 9:27). 'For if ... every transgression and disobedience received a just reward, how shall we escape if we neglect so great a salvation?' (Heb. 2:2) — salvation that is only to be found in the Promised One, the Messiah, Jesus the Christ.

Lamentations

('poems for a funeral')

Author: Jeremiah
(probably)

Key thought: Threatened judgement

Theme:
The misery that results from sin

'Is it nothing to you, all you who pass
   by?
Behold and see
If there is any sorrow like my sorrow...'
                      Lamentations 1:12

Summary

Lamentations

Funerals are never the happiest of occasions. Even when there is 'the sure and certain hope of the resurrection from the dead', there is still the grief and pain of those left behind. While believers do not 'sorrow as others who have no hope' (1 Thess. 4:13), they do grieve. The book of Lamentations is a collection of funeral poems. It is a sad book, probably the most distressing in the whole of the Old Testament. The 'weeping prophet', Jeremiah, composes five poems as he grieves over the capital city of Jerusalem. This once proud monument to God's glory, goodness and grace is now reduced to rubble. The people have been defeated, humiliated, slaughtered, or forced into exile. The terrible punishment, so long threatened by the living God, had burst in full fury upon the nation. For years the people had been in the habit of turning to idolatry, seeking only political solutions for their ills, and blindly and arrogantly refusing to acknowledge the Lord and return to him in repentance and obedience. Whereas other Scriptures describe the events in their historic detail (2 Kings 25:1-21; Jer. 52:7-30), the book of Lamentations expresses the feelings of utter dejection, of uncontrollable grief and of abject misery experienced by those who care about the purposes of God and the well-being of the people of God.

Author

Although there is no mention of the name of the author, either in this book or in any other part of the Scriptures, the content, style, language and circumstances all suit Jeremiah the prophet, as tradition maintains. The authorship, however, 'is not worth argument, since the text does not insist on it and its interpretation does not depend on it'.[1]

Historical setting

The continued presence of Israel in the promised land depended upon their fulfilling the terms of the covenant that God had established at Sinai (Deut. 28:63 – 29:1). In spite of repeated acts of rebellion, wilful idolatry and immorality, the Lord had faithfully urged them to repentance and restoration of relationship. Following the death of King Josiah, the people of the small southern kingdom of Judah, the last remaining Israelites in the promised land, began the final stage on the slippery slope to destruction. Now, after twenty-three years of turmoil and tragedy, four evil kings and three major invasions by Babylon, the destruction is complete. The nation is mutilated and dispersed; the city of Jerusalem lies in total ruin.

The book of Lamentations was written shortly after the third invasion of Jerusalem by the Babylonian forces of King Nebuchadnezzar (586 B.C., following earlier invasions in 605 B.C. and 597 B.C.). On this final occasion Jerusalem was sacked; the temple was destroyed, along with the king's palace, all substantial houses and the city walls (Jer. 52:12-14; 2 Kings 25:9-10). The prophecies entrusted to Jeremiah by the Lord, regarding the judgement of God on the nation, had been faithfully delivered and recorded (Jer. 36:2,27-28) and now they have been fulfilled to the letter. But there is no satisfaction in the heart of the prophet, no comfort that his predictions have proved true and that he has been vindicated as a genuine prophet of the living God. Rather he sits and weeps. He is in agony, for he grieves over his people: many have been killed; many have been taken captive; the few survivors have become emigrants, and the city lies in ruin. It is a sad sight and testifies to the arrival of the long-predicted, well-deserved, righteous judgement of God.

Jeremiah may have composed these lamentations as he sat on a hillside overlooking the ruins and desolation shortly before being taken to Egypt (Jer. 43:1-7).

Outline

Four of the five chapters in the book of Lamentations are written in acrostic form, based on the twenty-two letters of the Hebrew alphabet, each verse beginning with a letter in the order of the alphabet. Chapter 5, though it contains twenty-two verses, is nevertheless not written as an acrostic.

Chapter 3 contains sixty-six verses, three verses beginning with *Aleph*,[2] the first letter of the alphabet, three verses beginning with *Beth*, the second letter of the alphabet, and so on through the whole alphabet. This acrostic form was probably adopted as an 'aide-mémoire'.

Each chapter contains a poem: in each there is a reference to the sad, ruined state of Jerusalem, a vindication of the Lord in dealing so drastically with his people and a reference to those passing by. The first three poems each end with a prayer to the Lord. The fourth (chapter 4) has no prayer, but the fifth poem (chapter 5) is given over entirely to prayer.

First poem: The destruction of Jerusalem (1:1-22)

Lamentations describes 'the funeral of a city'.[3] It contains all the hallmarks of an *eyewitness* account of the fall of Jerusalem and the resulting desolation and despair. The city — temple, palace, houses and walls — lies in ruins. The terror so long threatened and so consistently disregarded has now fallen upon Jerusalem. Jeremiah describes the ruin of Jerusalem and the misery of the exiles. The capital is personified as a weeping widow deprived of her husband and children. Deserted, she cries out, 'See, O LORD, and consider, for I am scorned' (1:11). The nation through whom the great salvation was to come has become so idolatrous and wicked that the Lord has had to punish her severely. The devastation of Jerusalem is horrific!

Throughout the lamentations the prophet plainly declares that the present judgement is the result of rebellion and sin (1:8). He pictures Zion[4] speaking and grieving over her misery. She acknowledges that her punishment is deserved and that the Lord is entirely just in inflicting the penalty: 'The LORD is righteous, for I rebelled against his commandment' (1:18).

Although the destruction of Jerusalem is a judgement from God, nevertheless the call goes out for those who have brought about the desolation to be punished (1:21-22). While the Lord has used the neighbouring nations to punish his people, yet those nations are not free from guilt for their atrocities and wickedness.

Second poem: The righteous anger of God (2:1-22)

Although it was the Babylonians who invaded, overcame and destroyed Jerusalem, they were merely the agents. It was the Lord who was punishing his people through the Babylonian forces. The Lord, the defender of Israel, has given up his people to their awful doom:

> Standing like an enemy,
> He has bent his bow…
> He has slain…
> He has poured out his fury…
>
> (2:4).

It is the Lord who has destroyed the temple, terminated the feasts and displaced king and priest (2:6).

The reasons for the anger of God upon the nation of Israel are spelled out. The remaining people are urged: 'Pour out your heart like water before the face of the Lord' (2:19). Although the Israelites deserve everything they have received, nevertheless they are still the people of God (2:20). The prophet speaks on behalf of the people, pleading with the Lord to look with compassion upon their misery and to show mercy.

Third poem: The anguish and hope of the prophet and people (3:1-66)

The prophet identifies with the people, making their miseries and sorrows his own. He pours out his heart in anguish over the afflictions, yet in the midst of grief and agony he remains confident in the God of Israel, whose character and promises are such that the people of God can be confident; they can trust in the Lord when all the evidence before them cries out, 'Hopeless!' The believer responds:

> Great is your faithfulness!
> 'The LORD is my portion,' says my soul,
> 'Therefore I hope in him!'
>
> (3:23-24).

'In the face of death and destruction, with life seemingly coming apart at the seams, Jeremiah turns tragedy into a triumph of faith. God has never failed him in the past. God has promised to remain faithful in the future. In the light of the God he knows and loves, Jeremiah finds hope and comfort.'[5]

Even though he knows the punishment is entirely deserved and the Lord is absolutely righteous and just in his dealings with Israel, the prophet is confident in the compassion of God: 'For he does not afflict willingly, nor grieve the children of men' (3:33).

While the dominant and recurring theme is that of the wretched condition of the people of Judah, there is also a clear acknowledgement of what brought this about — unfaithfulness, disobedience and rebellion in relation to the living God. So the prophet cries out to the people:

> Let us search out and examine our ways,
> And turn back to the LORD;
> Let us lift our hearts and hands
> To God in heaven.
> We have transgressed and rebelled;
> You have not pardoned
>
> (3:40-42).

Fourth poem: The siege of Jerusalem (4:1-22)

The former glory of Israel is contrasted with her present misery. The prophet again describes the fearful judgements that have fallen upon Jerusalem. A series of images are used to describe the appalling conditions: fine gold that has become dim; precious stones as worthless as clay; nursing infants and young children starving; the well-to-do living in squalor. Under siege the people resemble the walking dead (4:8).

Jeremiah once more presents a vivid description of the fall of Jerusalem. Tragedy has struck hard; conditions are horrific: invasions, destruction, ruin and utter hopelessness.

Fifth poem: A plea for the restoration of Israel (5:1-22)

Their punishment is complete. In a poem devoted to prayer for mercy, an appeal is made for the Lord's compassion: 'Look, and behold our reproach!' (5:1). The Israelites speak and make confession and appeal to God for forgiveness and delivery. The nation has become so wicked that the Lord has left the temple, the city, the land and the people. There is no certainty of his return. The only appeal, the only hope, is that the Lord will take pity upon his people.

Christ and his church

1. Jeremiah as a type of Christ

Jeremiah, 'the weeping prophet', expresses profound grief over Jerusalem. Six hundred years later, another sees the impending doom of Jerusalem once more looming on the horizon. Of the Lord Jesus Christ it is recorded: 'Now as he drew near, he saw the city and wept over it, saying, "If you had known, even you, especially in this your day, the things that make for your peace! But now they are hidden from your eyes. For the days will come upon you when your enemies will build an embankment around you, surround you and close you in on every side, and level you, and your children within you, to the ground; and they will not leave in you one stone upon another, because you did not know the time of your visitation"' (Luke 19:41-44).

Jeremiah cried out:

> The LORD has fulfilled his fury,
> He has poured out his fierce anger.
> He kindled a fire in Zion,
> And it has devoured its foundations…
> Because of the sins of her prophets
> And the iniquities of her priests,
> Who shed in her midst
> The blood of the just
>
> (4:11,13; cf. Acts 3:14-15).

The Lord Jesus cried out: 'O Jerusalem, Jerusalem, the one who kills the prophets and stones those who are sent to her!' (Matt. 23:37)

2. The suffering Saviour

While the book of Lamentations contains no direct prophecies concerning the promised Messiah, there are a number of verses that suggestively foreshadow the Saviour's crucifixion:

Is it nothing to you, all you who pass by?
Behold and see
If there is any sorrow like my sorrow

(1:12).

All who pass by clap their hands at you;
They hiss and shake their heads...
All your enemies have opened their mouth against you;
They hiss and gnash their teeth...
(2:15-16; cf. Ps. 22:13; Matt. 27:39-44).

Even when I cry and shout,
He shuts out my prayer

(3:8; cf. Matt. 27:46).

I have become the ridicule of all my people,
And their taunting song all the day
(3:14; cf. Ps. 69:12; Matt. 26:67-68).

Remember my affliction and roaming,
The wormwood[6] and the gall
(3:19; cf. Ps. 69:21; Matt. 27:34),

Let him give his cheek to the one who strikes him,
And be full of reproach
(3:30; cf. Ps. 69:20; Isa. 50:6; Luke 22:63-64).

Application

1. Life without God

The condition of a people without God is described in terms of having 'no rest' (1:3), 'no pasture' (1:6) and 'no comforter' (1:9). In Christ these deficiencies are rectified:[7] 'Come to me, all you who labour and are heavy laden, and *I will give you rest*' (Matt. 11:28, emphasis added). 'I am the door. If anyone enters by me, he will be saved, and will go in and out *and find pasture*' (John 10:9, emphasis added, cf. Ps. 23:2). 'If you love me, keep my commandments. And I will pray the Father, and *he will give you another Helper* [AV, Comforter], that he may abide with you for ever, even the Spirit of truth...' (John 14:15-17, emphasis added).

2. The faithfulness of God

Though the present circumstances are so depressing for Jeremiah and the people of God, the note of true faith and confidence rings out:

> Through the LORD's mercies we are not consumed,
> Because his compassions fail not.
> They are new every morning;
> Great is your faithfulness
>
> (3:22-23).

Even in the bleakest circumstances the Lord's people can rely upon their God:

> Who among you fears the LORD?
> Who obeys the voice of his Servant?
> Who walks in darkness and has no light?
> Let him trust in the name of the LORD
> And rely upon his God
>
> (Isa. 50:10).

Conclusion

Jeremiah wrote two books: the first, a collection of prophecies, history and biography in the years leading up to the fall of Jerusalem, a book of warnings and challenge; the second, a set of poems looking back after the fall of Jerusalem, a book of grief and deep distress. This second book is the book of Lamentations, throughout which Jeremiah expresses the deepest agony of mind and heart, yet continually declares God's holiness, justice and sovereignty in the judgements he has sent upon Judah.

No one could charge the Lord with impatience. After hundreds of years of repeated warnings, threats and pleas, the punishment of the Lord has fallen upon Judah. Jeremiah speaks for himself and his compatriots, responding to this righteous judgement with sorrow, confession and repentance, and pleading with God for mercy. In the midst of the bleak, agonizing laments there is a ray of hope. The Lord will be faithful to his covenant promises; he will restore the nation. Great is his faithfulness (3:23). Even in the final words there is an implied hope for the future:

> Turn us back to you, O LORD, and we will be restored;
> Renew our days as of old,
> Unless you have utterly rejected us,
> And are very angry with us!
>
> (5:21-22).

The situation is critical; humanly speaking, it is hopeless. Nevertheless Jeremiah is trusting in the promises of God. The covenant promises to Abraham, Moses, David and Judah will not be broken. Like Abraham years before, of Jeremiah it may also be recorded that he, 'contrary to hope, in hope believed' (Rom. 4:18). Outward circumstances, common sense, and all the reason in the world cannot remove the believer's confidence in the Word of God: 'Let God be true but every man a liar' (Rom. 3:4).

Ezekiel

('God strengthens')

Author: Ezekiel

Key thought: The glory of the Lord

Theme:
The severity and goodness of God

'And behold, the glory of the God
of Israel came … His voice was like
the sound of many waters; and the
earth shone with his glory.'

Ezekiel 43:2

Summary

Ezekiel

The name Ezekiel means, 'God strengthens.' This prophet, taken into captivity and meeting hard opposition from fellow Israelites in exile (3:8-9), needed the courage and resolution that the Lord alone could supply. His ministry was quite extraordinary. The book bearing his name displays a man of firm resolution, thoroughly convinced of the seriousness of obeying the law of God, yet with a shepherd's tender heart. Well versed in practical theology, he had a deep love for the people of God. The prophet declares the sovereignty and glory of God on the one hand, and the personal responsibility of the sinner on the other.

The book is difficult to interpret because it is so full of imagery. The author uses visions, prophecies, parables, allegories, signs and symbolic acts to dramatize the message of God to his people in captivity and to those still in Jerusalem. Centuries later the apostle Peter was to say of the writings of his fellow-apostle Paul, '… in which are some things hard to understand, which those who are untaught and unstable twist to their own destruction, as they do also the rest of the Scriptures' (2 Peter 3:16). The book of Ezekiel is open to similar misinterpretation. The complexities must not be allowed, however, to overshadow the clear and wonderful lessons which this great prophetic book contains.

Author

Ezekiel prophesied in exile in the land of Babylon. The book is autobiographical — the first person singular is used throughout. Many of the prophecies are carefully dated and the location where they are received is described. The similarity of thought and arrangement throughout make it clear that the entire book is the work of one mind.[1] The prophet is not mentioned in the Old Testament outside his own book (1:3; 24:24).

The phrase, 'in the thirtieth year' (1:1), is most probably a reference to Ezekiel's age. If so then he was born in 622 B.C. during the reign of good

King Josiah (640–609 B.C.). A year later the Book of the Law was discovered while the temple was being renovated (2 Chr. 34:14). So Ezekiel grew up in the good days of reformation (2 Kings 22:1 – 23:25). As the son of a priest he would have had first-hand experience of Josiah's reforms in the temple and in worship. Later, as a young teenager, he would have heard the sad news of Josiah's death at the hands of Pharaoh Necho at Megiddo (2 Kings 23:29; 2 Chr. 35:20-25) and witnessed the terrible spiritual and moral decline during the years immediately following.

Ezekiel probably belonged to Jerusalem's aristocracy (1:1-3; 2 Kings 24:14) and like Jeremiah he was of the priestly line. While still in Jerusalem Ezekiel would no doubt have heard Jeremiah preaching on numerous occasions. The message of Ezekiel has distinct similarities to that of Jeremiah (see Jer. 29). It is evident throughout that in his thinking, outlook and life, Ezekiel had been affected by the prophetic message of Jeremiah: 'He never melted to tears as did Jeremiah, but his vision of the ultimate deliverance of the people by the triumph of Jehovah was even clearer.'[2]

The young Ezekiel may also have known of the prophets Habakkuk and Zephaniah, since they were prophesying in Judah during the same period. Another contemporary of Ezekiel was Daniel, who was about the same age and also grew up within the vicinity of the city of Jerusalem. Daniel was taken captive in the first invasion of Jerusalem by King Nebuchadnezzar of Babylon (605 B.C.), in his mid-teens, and began his prophetic ministry that same year (Dan. 1:1-7). Ezekiel was taken captive eight years later following Nebuchadnezzar's second invasion of Jerusalem (2 Kings 24:10-16). By this time Daniel was well known in Babylon through his involvement at the king's court.[3] Jeremiah was not taken captive but remained in Jerusalem.

Historical setting

After King Josiah's death, Pharaoh Necho of Egypt deposed Josiah's successor, King Jehoahaz, imprisoning him in Riblah (2 Kings 23:33-34), and placed his older brother Eliakim (renamed Jehoiakim) upon the throne of Judah as vassal to Egypt. When the Babylonians defeated Egypt at Carchemish (Jer. 46:2), they turned against Judah.

In the first Babylonian[4] invasion of Jerusalem (605 B.C.) King Jehoiakim of Judah was taken captive, subsequently released and allowed to remain on the throne of Judah after swearing allegiance to King

Nebuchadnezzar. King Jehoiakim's descendants, some nobles and some children were, however, taken captive into Babylon (Dan. 1:1-3; cf. 2 Chr. 36:5-6). After a short time Jehoiakim rebelled against Babylon and re-aligned himself with Egypt.

Eight years after this first invasion, the Babylonians once again attacked Jerusalem (597 B.C.), where King Jehoiakim's eighteen-year-old son, Je-hoiachin, had succeeded to the throne of Judah. After a reign of just over three months (2 Chr. 36:9-10), Jehoiachin was taken captive, along with the rest of the nobility, soldiers and craftsmen of Judah (2 Kings 24:12-16). Included among the captives was the twenty-five-year-old Ezekiel (1:1-2; 33:21). Only the poorest people still remained in Jerusalem. Eleven years later the third invasion by Babylon left Jerusalem utterly destroyed.

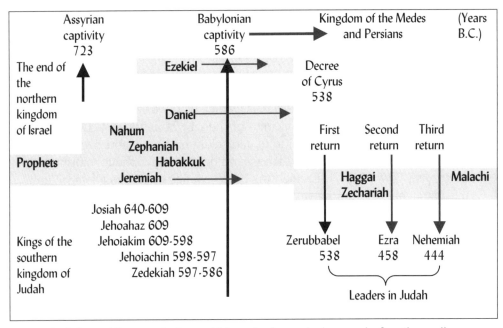

Judah and its prophets and kings before, during and after the exile

After five years in exile in the land of Babylon, Ezekiel began his minis-try in the prophetic office (1:1-2). He was called to office at the age of thirty, the same year he would have commenced service as a priest, had he remained in Jerusalem (Num. 4:3). His ministry was to span at least twenty-two years (1:2; cf. 29:17; c. 592–570 B.C.).

Some of the exiles were imprisoned or placed under house arrest; others were made slaves; the remainder were allowed to live freely in their own homes (Jer. 29:1-7; Ezra 2:59; Neh. 7:61). Ezekiel was among the privileged ones, permitted to live in his own house (8:1) in Tel Abib, one of the main Jewish ghettos near the city of Babylon (see 3:15). Ezekiel's home became a frequent meeting-place for the Jewish elders in exile (8:1; 14:1; 20:1).

Concurrently Jeremiah was ministering to the small community of Israelites back in Jerusalem, Daniel was serving in the court of King Nebuchadnezzar and Ezekiel was ministering to the Jewish exiles. Jeremiah faced problems in Jerusalem; Daniel met with fierce opposition from within the Babylonian court; and Ezekiel faced considerable resistance from the Jewish exiles and needed to have a forehead 'like adamant stone, harder than flint', because of the rebellious spirit that confronted him (3:9).

Outline

The city of Jerusalem has barely survived two major invasions, but God's judgement upon Jerusalem is not yet over. The certainty of further judgement is illustrated in Ezekiel's vision of the glory of the Lord departing first from the temple and then from the city. The surrounding Gentiles will also come under divine punishment.

Part I: The Lord commissions Ezekiel (1:1 - 3:27)

Ezekiel begins his autobiographical account by declaring that 'The heavens were opened and I saw visions of God' (1:1; cf. Isa. 6:1-5). 'A vision in Bible days was a miraculous experience of a man of God on a special occasion, whereby God revealed truth to him in some pictorial and audible form.'[5] Visions and dreams given to prophets are 'dark sayings' and not always easy to interpret:

If there is a prophet among you,
I, the LORD, make myself known to him in a vision,
And I speak to him in a dream.
Not so with my servant Moses;
He is faithful in all my house.
I speak with him face to face,
Even plainly, and not in dark sayings;
And he sees the form of the LORD

(Num. 12:6-8).

The exiles, amongst whom Ezekiel lives and works, come from the upper and skilled classes of Judean society. They are a privileged group not known for listening to warnings from prophets (2:3-8). They hope for a short period in exile and a speedy return to their wealth, rank and status in Judah. False prophets in Babylon lead the Israelite captives to believe that Jerusalem will not be destroyed and that the exiles will soon be allowed to return to their own land. The growing bond between King Zedekiah of Judah and the pharaoh in Egypt no doubt encourages the hope of entire restoration. The prophet Jeremiah hears of this and sends the Jewish exiles a letter instructing them to settle down in Babylon: 'Build houses ... plant gardens and eat their fruit... And seek the peace of the city where I have caused you to be carried away captive... For thus says the LORD: "After seventy years are completed at Babylon, I will visit you and perform my good word towards you, and cause you to return to this place"' (Jer. 29:5,7,10).

Ezekiel is called to be a watchman for Israel and to give warnings from God (3:17). He begins his ministry confirming all that Jeremiah has said and seeking to convince the exiles that they must return to the Lord *before* they can ever hope to return to Jerusalem. His task is difficult; he meets with opposition. The idolatry that Ezekiel had witnessed among the Jews in Jerusalem is also all too evident among the exiles in Babylon. The punishment of God in the first wave of captivity did not stir the first exiles to repentance. They did not believe that Jerusalem would actually be destroyed by the Babylonians. The second invasion and subsequent exile of more Israelites fail to quell the rising optimism. It is unpalatable for them to accept that the Lord has given world domination to Babylon and that the Jews should not only submit willingly to their captors but also work and pray for the peace of their enemies (Jer. 29:7). The prophets Jeremiah and Ezekiel have a united message: Jerusalem will fall and the Jews will be in exile for many years. Jeremiah predicts an exile lasting seventy years (Jer. 25:11; 29:10).[6]

Part II: Judgements against Judah before the fall of Jerusalem (4:1 - 24:27).

This section contains mainly visions, warnings and predictions concerning the guilt of the people of Judah and the coming destruction of Jerusalem. It is sin that has brought the judgement of God upon the people with the resulting captivity: 'Therefore thus says the Lord GOD: "Because you have multiplied disobedience more than the nations that are all around you, and have not walked in my statutes, nor kept my judgements, nor even done according to the judgements of the nations that are all around you," therefore thus says the Lord GOD: "Indeed I, even I, am against you and will execute judgements in your midst in the sight of the nations. And I will do among you what I have never done, and the like of which I will never do again, because of all your abominations"' (5:7-9).

In vision Ezekiel sees sins charged against the elders of the house of Israel: idols in the temple, women weeping for the fertility god Taamuz and men worshipping the sun (8:10,14,16). Following the practice of the Egyptians, they are worshipping 'crocodiles, cats, moles, beetles'. [7]

In the many visions recorded by Ezekiel those that concern the glory of God are the most significant. The departure of the glory of God from the temple and from the city is pictured: in vision the prophet sees wheels on the ark of the covenant (10:9); he watches as the glory of the Lord moves to the threshold of the temple (10:4), to the east gate (10:19) and then from the city to Mount Olivet (11:23). The departure of the glory of God from the sanctuary and the city is slow, reluctant, dignified. The 'glory of the Lord' is mentioned twelve times in the first eleven chapters. Then there is a prolonged silence. But the glory of the Lord will return (43:2,4-5; 44:4).

Ezekiel communicates not just by word of mouth, but also by the symbolic actions that he performs. The Lord says to him, 'I have made you a sign to the house of Israel' (12:6). Ezekiel willingly sacrifices his personal comfort and private interests. He is willing to do anything at God's command: 'The prophet enacted the siege of Jerusalem by using an iron pan, sketching the events on a clay tablet (4:1-8), and eating siege rations (4:9-17). He shaved his beard, divided and discarded the hair in ways that foresaw the fate of the citizens of Jerusalem (5). He packed his belongings and dug through a wall to depict the exile of the population (12:1-20). A kind of "sword dance" became an object lesson about the sword the king of Babylon was bringing against Jerusalem; the king's strategy was portrayed in a map drawn in the sand (21:8-23). Everything — from a scorched cooking pot to the death of his own wife — could serve as an object lesson about the coming fate of the nation (24).' [8]

When the contents of Ezekiel's earlier prophecies are reported back to Jerusalem King Zedekiah hears what he considers to be contradictory prophecies from Ezekiel and Jeremiah. The one states that the king will not see Babylon (12:13); the other says he will be taken captive into Babylon (Jer. 21:7). On this ground it seems that Zedekiah concludes that Jeremiah and Ezekiel are false prophets. But the Lord is to prove these two servants to be accurate in their prophecies. Both speak the inspired Word from God. Within a short time Nebuchadnezzar will come, besiege Jerusalem, take Zedekiah captive, put out his eyes, '[bind] him with bronze fetters, and [take] him to Babylon' (2 Kings 25:7).

When Nebuchadnezzar first installed Zedekiah as king of Judah he established a covenant with him (17:13). Five years later, no doubt with the collusion of the kings of Edom, Moab, Ammon, Tyre and Sidon (Jer. 27:3), 'Zedekiah rebelled against the king of Babylon' (2 Kings 24:20). This rebellion is seen as a serious sin against God because Nebuchadnezzar 'had made him swear an oath by God' (2 Chr. 36:13; cf. Ezek. 17:13-21).

Ezekiel speaks of the Israelites in Egypt in the days of the Exodus more than any other prophet. It is only here in the prophecy of Ezekiel that God records the idolatry of Israel in Egypt and tells of his deliberation to destroy them there because of it (20:1-9). The reason why he did not destroy them there and then was for his own glory: 'But I acted for my name's sake, that it should not be profaned before the Gentiles among whom they were, in whose sight I had made myself known to them, to bring them out of the land of Egypt' (20:9).

Ezekiel's dearly loved wife dies eleven years after his exile to Babylon in the sixth year of his prophetic office, the year that the final siege of Jerusalem begins (24:2,18). His wife's death is revealed to be a sign from God that Jerusalem will not be spared (24:16-24).

Part III: Judgements against the surrounding nations (25:1 - 32:32)

After declaring the severity of the judgement against Judah, the prophet is led to declare the Lord's judgements upon the seven surrounding nations. God is against these nations not just because of their sin of idolatry, but also because of their hostility towards, and persecution of, Israel. These nations openly gloated over the downfall of Jerusalem and they assisted Israel's oppressor.

The prophecies against Egypt (29:1 – 32:32) describe that country's influence over Israel spanning many years. The Egyptians had frequently brought trouble upon Israel, whether by outright hostility or pretended friendship. There are six prophecies against Egypt, each with a date calculated from the day of King Jehoiachin's exile (1:2).[9] The pharaoh addressed is Pharaoh Hophra (Jer. 44:30), the successor of Pharaoh Necho.

Unlike the nations mentioned earlier which were destroyed by Nebuchadnezzar, Egypt will continue to exist, but as 'the lowliest of kingdoms; it shall never again exalt itself above the nations' (29:15). Since that time it has not recovered its former power or influence.

Part IV: Prophecies of return and restoration (33:1 – 48:35)

Jerusalem fell in 538 B.C. After the severe judgements of God have been unleashed against Jerusalem and Judah, and the temple and the city have been destroyed, the message of the prophet changes drastically. In the aftermath of judgement there arises a clear and decisive note of hope. Up to 24:2 the prophet's message is basically: 'Jerusalem will fall.' From 34:11 onwards he looks forward and predicts, 'Jerusalem will be restored.' When Jerusalem falls the prophet's tongue is freed to speak of future hope (24:25-27). Once the misguided belief that Jerusalem would not be taken has been shattered, the people begin to give Ezekiel a hearing. There is to be a future restoration of Israel, a spiritual awakening of unique proportions. While the vast majority of adults will not see the day personally, nevertheless many of their children will have the opportunity to return to the land of Israel.

The closing chapters are packed with predictions and promises about the restoration. The means by which the glory of the nation is to be restored are spelled out:[10]

- By listening to the warning of the spiritual watchmen and repenting of sin (ch. 33).
- By removing the false shepherds and by the arrival of the Good Shepherd who will care for the flock. The time will come when the people will recognize the Lord and a true prophet will be among them (ch. 34).
- By a total reformation of religion — a new exodus, God's people returning from exile, a new covenant, a new heart and a new spirit for the restored community (ch. 36).
- By the empowering of the Holy Spirit (ch. 37).
- By the overthrow of the enemies of Israel (chs. 38-39).
- By the building of the new sanctuary (chs. 40-42).
- By the return of the glory of the Lord (chs. 43).
- By the ministry of a loyal priesthood (ch. 44).

- By life-giving waters (spiritual life) flowing from the sanctuary (ch. 47).
- By Israel's restoration to her own land (ch. 48).

Christ and his church

1. The Good Shepherd

Condemnation of the irresponsible leaders of Israel leads to the promise of God's intervention: 'For thus says the Lord God: "Indeed I myself will search for my sheep and seek them out. As a shepherd seeks out his flock on the day he is among his scattered sheep, so will I seek out my sheep and deliver them from all the places where they were scattered on a cloudy and dark day. And I will bring them out from the peoples and gather them from the countries, and will bring them to their own land... I will feed them in good pasture ... they shall lie down in a good fold and feed in rich pasture..."' (34:11-14).

With a clear allusion to the Shepherd Psalm (Ps. 23), another prophecy is given of the coming of David's Son as King and Shepherd: 'I will establish one shepherd over them, and he shall feed them — my servant David. He shall feed them and be their shepherd. And I, the LORD, will be their God, and my servant David a prince among them; I, the LORD, have spoken' (34:23-24). This is an obvious reference to Messiah, as David is dead and in his tomb (cf. Acts 2:29). The shepherd prophecies are fulfilled in the arrival of the Lord Jesus Christ as the Good Shepherd (John 10:11-16), the Chief Shepherd (1 Peter 5:4) and the Great Shepherd (Heb. 13:20). The Son of God comes to gather into one flock 'the lost sheep of the house of Israel' (Matt. 15:24) and the lost sheep from among the Gentiles. As he made clear, 'Other sheep I have which are not of this fold [that is, Judaism]; them also I must bring, and they will hear my voice; and there will be one flock [that is, Jew and Gentile] and one shepherd' (John 10:16).

2. The new temple

The destruction of Jerusalem and the temple by the invading forces of the Babylonians (586 B.C.) brought dismay to the Jews in Babylon (Ps. 137).

Thirteen years after the fall of the city, Ezekiel is given the vision of a new temple in Jerusalem (40:1; cf. 33:21). When the exiles return following the decree of Cyrus (539 B.C.) Zerubbabel, encouraged by the prophets Haggai and Zechariah, rebuilds the temple in Jerusalem (Ezra 5:2; 6:14-16). But it is not as spectacular as that prophesied by Ezekiel. Some elements of his vision seem to go beyond a reasonable literal understanding (47:1-12). Interpretation should therefore proceed with caution: 'A fair amount of mischief has been done to Ezekiel by interpreters committed to reading visions and allegories in a highly literalistic way.'[11]

Ezekiel's temple is a symbolic picture of Christ.[12] He is the true and living Temple (John 2:19-22), who draws together his people as 'living stones' to be 'built up as a spiritual house' (1 Peter 2:5), 'in whom the whole building, being joined together, grows into a holy temple in the Lord' (Eph. 2:21; cf. 1 Cor. 3:16; 6:19). On Ezekiel chapters 40-48, E. J. Young concludes, 'This elaborate representation is a picture of the Messianic age. The Lord dwells in the midst of His people... Ezekiel ... was speaking of Christ... He was, in a manner peculiar to himself, preaching Jesus Christ.'[13]

> ... the Most High does not dwell in temples made with hands, as the prophet says:
>
> 'Heaven is my throne,
> And earth is my footstool.
> What house will you build for me? says the LORD,
> Or what is the place of my rest?
> Has my hand not made all these things?'
>
> (Acts 7:48-50, quoting Isa. 66:1-2).

3. The river of life

Pouring from the temple is a stream (47:1). Everywhere this water flows it brings life where previously there had been nothing but death (47:9). 'That the description given of this stream and its effects must be understood in an ideal manner, not of any actual river, but, like all the rest of the vision, of spiritual things shadowed forth under it, is so evident as scarcely to require any proof. The source of it alone (the summit of an elevated mountain), and the manner of its increase, should put this beyond a doubt with all who would not convert the Bible into a nursery of extravagance and credulity. For a natural river like this would of necessity be in contravention of the established laws of nature, and could only exist as a perpetual miracle.'[14]

The picture of healing waters flowing from the altar in the temple holds a remarkable Christological message. The temple symbolizes Christ; the altar symbolizes Christ crucified; the healing water indicates the spiritual life that flows from the crucified Saviour (cf. John 19:34). To the woman of Samaria the Lord offered 'living water' (John 4:10), which he clearly indicated was spiritual in nature. The 'water' that he gives becomes 'a fountain of water springing up into everlasting life' (John 4:14). A little later, at the Feast of Tabernacles, the Lord Jesus cried out: '"If anyone thirsts, let him come to me and drink. He who believes in me, as the Scripture has said, out of his heart will flow rivers of living water." But this he spoke concerning the Spirit, whom those believing in him would receive; for the Holy Spirit was not yet given, because Jesus was not yet glorified' (John 7:37-39).

The river of life is flowing from the temple (47:1; Joel 3:18; Zech. 14:8-9). This is the 'river whose streams shall make glad the city of God, the holy place of the tabernacle of the Most High' (Ps. 46:4). Along its banks are trees that provide food and medicine, 'for the healing of the nations' (47:12; Rev. 22:1-2). Ezekiel's temple is to be spiritually understood. It symbolizes the Lord Jesus Christ and the spiritual life and spiritual healing which he alone supplies.

4. The New Covenant

The prophet Ezekiel makes a valuable contribution to the promises of the New Covenant. God is going to make an everlasting covenant of peace with the Israelites after they have returned to their own land (37:26-28). The context shows that there is to be a wonderful spiritual awakening; the Lord will breathe his Spirit into those who are spiritually dead (37:1-14). This will be accompanied by a remarkable transformation in the people: 'Then I will sprinkle clean water on you, and you shall be clean; I will cleanse you from all your filthiness and from all your idols. I will give you a new heart and put a new spirit within you; I will take the heart of stone out of your flesh and give you a heart of flesh. I will put my Spirit within you and cause you to walk in my statutes, and you will keep my judgements and do them' (36:25-27).

This message communicated through the prophet Ezekiel in Babylon expressed similar blessings to those communicated, around that same time, through the prophet Jeremiah in Judah: 'But this is the covenant that I will make with the house of Israel: After those days, says the LORD, I will put my law in their minds, and write it on their hearts; and I will be their God, and they shall be my people... I will forgive their iniquity, and their sin I will remember no more' (Jer. 31:33-34).[15]

The significant addition promised by God and prophesied by Ezekiel is the indwelling of the Holy Spirit in believers. This is one of the glories of the New Covenant. The indwelling of the Holy Spirit was dependent upon the completed work of the Messiah, the Lord Jesus Christ. He must be glorified (John 7:37-39), which means he must suffer and die in the place of his people, must rise again from the dead, must ascend to the Father and sit down 'at the right hand of the Majesty on high' (Heb. 1:3). After accomplishing his unique work, he is glorified by the Father and 'highly exalted' (Phil. 2:9). The New Covenant blessing of the indwelling Holy Spirit began forty-nine days after our Lord's resurrection when the Jews were celebrating the annual Feast of Weeks, also called Pentecost (Acts 2:1-4). The promise of the Lord Jesus is fulfilled: 'He dwells with you *and will be in you*' (John 14:17, emphasis added; see context vv.15-17).

The primary blessings of the New Covenant are:

- The complete removal of sin through the blood of the New Covenant / the everlasting covenant (36:25; Jer. 31:34; Luke 22:20; Heb. 13:20; cf. 10:1-4,10).
- The law of God written on a new heart — a heart of flesh which replaces the heart of stone (36:26; Jer. 31:33; cf. 2 Cor. 3:3; 5:17).
- The Holy Spirit of God indwelling all believers (Rom. 8:9; 1 Cor. 3:16; 6:19).

5. The tender twig

'Thus says the Lord GOD: "I will take also one of the highest branches of the high cedar and set it out. I will crop off from the topmost of its young twigs a tender one, and will plant it on a high and prominent mountain. On the mountain height of Israel I will plant it; and it will bring forth boughs, and bear fruit, and be a majestic cedar. Under it will dwell birds of every sort; in the shadow of its branches they will dwell. And all the trees of the field shall know that I, the LORD, have brought down the high tree and exalted the low tree, dried up the green tree and made the dry tree flourish; I, the LORD, have spoken and have done it"' (17:22-24).

In contrast to King Jehoiachin (a young twig, 17:4) and King Zedekiah (a vine, 17:7), Messiah appears as a tender twig which Jehovah plucks from the cedar of the house of David, plants upon Zion and causes to grow to a high tree exalted above all the trees of the field, under which the birds of heaven build their nests (cf. Matt. 13:31-32). This occurs after Jehoiachin, the topmost twig of the cedar, has been removed by the Chaldean eagle to Babylon, and Zedekiah, the vine which thirsted for the Nile water of the Egyptian eagle, has been rooted up and withered.[16] Messiah is the King who has the right to rule (21:26-27). There are several Messianic prophecies which refer to Christ as a branch (Isa. 4:2; 11:1; Jer. 23:5; 33:15; Zech. 3:8; 6:12) and a tender plant and a root (Isa. 53:2).

Application

1. Individual responsibility

Ezekiel's task is to convince the exiles that their predicament is the direct consequence of their sin. While the sovereignty of God is consistently portrayed throughout this book, this in no way removes personal responsibility from sinners: 'The soul who sins shall die' (18:4,20). The Lord does not delight in the death of the wicked (33:11; 18:23,32). He sincerely urges sinners to turn to him: 'Repent, and turn from all your transgressions, so that iniquity will not be your ruin' (18:30); and again, 'Turn … and live!' (33:11). In these incomparable terms the Lord declares his love for sinners.

Let the wicked forsake his way,
And the unrighteous man his thoughts;
Let him return to the LORD,
And he will have mercy on him;
And to our God,
For he will abundantly pardon

(Isa. 55:7).

In a society where governments are blamed for crime, and parents for the behaviour of their grown-up offspring, it is not fashionable to emphasize personal responsibility. Since the earliest days in the Garden of Eden the tendency of sinners has always been to incriminate others. Adam blamed Eve and God; Eve blamed the serpent. The Lord calls each one to give account of himself (18:20; Rom. 14:12).

2. A new heart

The corruption and sin of Israel have earned the Israelites the disapproval of God (36:16-20). Nothing in them, or in their behaviour, warrants even the least mercy or smallest degree of love from the Lord: ' "I do not do this for your sake, O house of Israel, but for my holy name's sake, which you have profaned among the nations wherever you went. And I will sanctify my great name, which has been profaned among the nations, which you have profaned in their midst; and the nations shall know that I am the LORD," says the Lord GOD, "when I am hallowed in you before their eyes" ' (36:22-23).

What God is about to do will be revolutionary and radical: cleansing believers from all filthiness and from all idolatry, removing the old heart (cf. Jer. 17:9-10), implanting a new heart filled with love for God and giving a new spirit of obedience (36:25-27; 11:19-20). These promises were pre-eminently fulfilled in the gospel of our Lord Jesus Christ (Titus 3:3-6; 1 John 1:9; John 14:17; 1 Cor. 6:19). When God gives a new heart and puts his Spirit within there is also a true conviction of sin (36:31; John 16:8-11; Acts 2:37-39).

3. Born of the Spirit

Twenty-five times Ezekiel refers to the Spirit of God (e.g. 2:2; 3:12,14,24).[17] The unique work of the Holy Spirit is brought to attention in the vision of the valley of dry bones (37:1-14). Here the spiritual destitution, recovery and restoration of the Israelites are envisaged. The vision denotes the collective misery of the Israelites in exile. It is not concerned with their political condition but with the absence of spiritual life. The bones are 'very dry' (37:2), indicating not so much how long those bones had been lying there but 'the depth of the misery into which Israel had fallen'.[18] The real misery of the people is their revolt against God and his Word, the dominion of sin, and the subsequent moral ruin into which they have sunk.

The Lord commands Ezekiel to prophesy both to the bones and to the breath; in other words, he is directed to preach and to pray. He is to address 'the dead bones' — that is, to preach to spiritually dead sinners (cf.

John 5:25; Eph. 2:1-5); he is also to call upon the Spirit of God to work his regenerating and renewing power (cf. Titus 3:5).

From this and other Old Testament Scriptures, the Pharisee Nicodemus, the teacher of Israel, should have understood the words of the Lord Jesus, 'You must be born again' (John 3:7; cf. Ps. 87:5-6). In that conversation the Lord Jesus is probably making reference to the breath coming to the valley of dry bones when he says, 'The wind blows where it wishes, and you hear the sound of it, but cannot tell where it comes from and where it goes. So is everyone who is born of the Spirit' (John 3:8).

On the Day of Pentecost there were phenomena that linked the coming of the Holy Spirit with the prophecy of Ezekiel: 'And suddenly there came a sound from heaven, as of a rushing mighty wind, and it filled the whole house where they were sitting... And they were all filled with the Holy Spirit...' (Acts 2:2,4).

Again the coming of the Holy Spirit in New Covenant blessing is associated with preaching to spiritually dead sinners (Acts 2:6,11,14; 4:31,33). The valley of dry bones is no longer confined to Israel. It is of universal proportions. Hence the Saviour commands, 'Go ... and make disciples of all the nations' (Matt. 28:19).

4. Church leaders

Ezekiel condemns false prophets for their self-interest (13:1-23) and leaders for their irresponsibility: 'The weak you have not strengthened, nor have you healed those who were sick, nor bound up the broken, nor brought back what was driven away, nor sought what was lost; but with force and cruelty you have ruled them. So they were scattered because there was no shepherd; and they became food for all the beasts of the field when they were scattered' (34:4-5).

In difficult circumstances, when the going was hard, there was no one prepared to 'stand in the gap' like Moses before an angry God on behalf of a guilty Israel (22:30; Ps. 106:23). Ultimately it was the Son of God who came as a man to stand in the breach between God and sinful human beings so that those who believe would not be destroyed.

In Old Testament times the responsibility of prophets was to discharge their obligations as watchmen and sound a clear note of warning to sinners (33:1-11). The duty of shepherds was the tender care of the flock: the sick, the broken, the lost (34:1-10). Leadership of the church of Jesus Christ is no less significant: the gospel must be preached to the lost; the people of

God must be lovingly pastored. The New Testament is replete with exhortations (Acts 20:28; Col. 4:17; 1 Tim. 4:16; 1 Peter 5:2-4; James 3:1). 'A
shepherd's work cannot be done effectively without a shepherd's heart.'[19]

Conclusion

Ezekiel was commissioned by God to convince the Israelites that their captivity would be prolonged, to strengthen Jeremiah's prophecy and to encourage believers in Babylon. While his opening prophecies concern
judgement, once the temple and the city of Jerusalem have fallen, the note
of doom is replaced by one of great optimism. Ezekiel sees success as the
people return to their Lord. He tells them of God's promise of restoration to
their own land.

The great and lasting impact of this prophetic book is beyond dispute.
There are at least sixty-five direct or indirect quotations of Ezekiel in the
New Testament, forty-eight of them in the book of Revelation. Hodgkin
identifies 'over eighty points of contact' between the book of Ezekiel and
the book of Revelation.[20] Ezekiel's eschatological visions of Israel's restoration clearly have a Messianic dimension. The title 'son of man' occurs
over ninety times in reference to Ezekiel. The Lord Jesus used this title as
his favourite self-designation. There are almost ninety references in the
Gospels.

When the Saviour comes to his church then the city shall from that day
be *Jehovah-Shammah* — 'The Lord is there' (Ezek. 48:35). When God left
the temple and city of Jerusalem, there was great misery (Hosea 9:12). 'His
presence in heaven makes it heaven; and his presence in the church makes
it happy.'[21]

'And he who sits on the throne will dwell among them. They shall
neither hunger any more nor thirst any more; the sun shall not strike them,
nor any heat; for the Lamb who is in the midst of the throne will shepherd
them and lead them to living fountains of waters. And God will wipe away
every tear from their eyes' (Rev. 7:15-17).

Daniel

('God is judge')

Author: Daniel

Key thought: The universal sovereignty of God

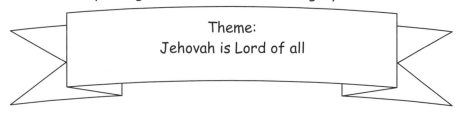

Theme:
Jehovah is Lord of all

'He does according to his will in the army
   of heaven
And among the inhabitants of the earth.
No one can stay his hand
Or say to him, "What have you done?'
                                    Daniel 4:35

Summary

Daniel

Although the name 'Daniel' means 'God is judge', his book is a message of comfort for the people of God. It asserts and confirms the sovereign control of the true God over all the kingdoms of the earth. Nothing and no one is outside his authority and command:

> For his dominion is an everlasting dominion,
> And his kingdom is from generation to generation.
> All the inhabitants of the earth are reputed as nothing;
> He does according to his will in the army of heaven
> And among the inhabitants of the earth.
> No one can restrain his hand
> Or say to him, 'What have you done?'
>
> (4:34-35).

The Babylonians, the Medes and Persians, the Greeks and the Romans will come and go, but God remains, and his kingdom endures for ever. So, while the attention of this book is upon Gentile nations and there are few direct references to Israel as the people of God, the prophecy of Daniel is a spiritual tonic to all believers of any nation or generation who are bewildered or distressed by national or international events.

The book of Daniel is not really a history either of the Israelites or of the Babylonians, nor is it an autobiography. Though the author is a Jewish exile, surrounded by fellow-countrymen in exile, there is no reference to the history of his people, no explanation for their exile and no description of their conditions, their struggles, or their sufferings in captivity. Though living upwards of sixty-seven years in the land of Babylon and having been trained and schooled in their culture, Daniel gives no account of Babylonian history or customs either. The biographical details that are included are chosen simply to illustrate the main thesis of the book: the God of Israel is the sovereign God over all the kingdoms of the world.

The factual incidents that are recorded to illustrate the theme of God's sovereignty over all life are impressive: delivery from a fiery furnace, the temporary insanity of a most powerful king, mysterious fingers writing on a wall and safety in a lion's den. These accounts have the quality of lodging deep in the memory. Furthermore, the prophecies of Daniel are amongst the most remarkable in the whole of the Bible.

Author

The entire book is obviously the work of one writer, and as Daniel is named as the one who received the revelations it follows that he is the author of the entire book.[1] The Lord commanded him to make a permanent record of the words he gave (12:4).

There is nothing of a negative nature written about Daniel. He is presented from start to finish as an outstandingly godly man: 'His life was characterized by faith, prayer, courage, consistency, and lack of compromise.'[2] He was a man 'greatly beloved' of the Lord (9:23; 10:11,19).

Daniel was taken captive in the first invasion of Jerusalem by King Nebuchadnezzar of Babylon (605 B.C.) and began his prophetic ministry the following year (1:6; 2:1,16). He may have belonged to a family of high rank in Judah, and may possibly even have been a member of the royal family (1:3). Taken to Babylon in his mid-teens, he was to remain there for the rest of his life. He was still active in his mid-eighties when Cyrus ruled Babylon (10:1; 536 B.C.), which means that he lived throughout the whole period of the Babylonian exile.

As a respected elder statesman in the land of the Medes and Persians, Daniel was probably instrumental in showing the prophecy of Isaiah (Isa. 44:24 – 45:7) to King Cyrus; with the result that Cyrus issued a decree not only allowing, but also encouraging, the Jews to return home to Judah and Jerusalem (2 Chr. 36:22-23; Ezra 1:1-4). Though he did not accompany them, Daniel witnessed the departure of the first 50,000 exiles returning home under the leadership of Zerubbabel (Ezra 2:1-2,64-65). Daniel spent his last days in Babylon with the Lord's assurance that he would die in peace and that he would enjoy the blessing of the great resurrection (12:13).

As a child in Judah Daniel would probably have known of the prophets Habakkuk and Zephaniah and no doubt he had heard the prophet Jeremiah who was exercising his ministry in Jerusalem at the time. Daniel refers to Jeremiah, and in particular to his prophecy concerning the duration of the exile in Babylon (9:2).

Along with other intelligent and fit young men, Daniel was selected for special training in the court of King Nebuchadnezzar (1:3-4). With his three Israelite colleagues, he excelled 'in all matters of wisdom and understanding' and was found to be 'ten times better than all the magicians and astrologers' throughout the whole empire (1:20). In the Babylonian royal court Daniel earned a reputation for godliness. The prophet Ezekiel, who was also taken captive to Babylon eight years after Daniel, testified to the wisdom of Daniel (Ezek. 28:3) and the righteousness of Daniel, numbering him with Noah and Job (Ezek. 14:14-20). Though an exile Daniel rose, without spiritual compromise, to the highest rank in the kingdoms of Babylon and Media and Persia. Initially elevated by King Nebuchadnezzar, he did not continue in high office during the reign of his successor King Belshazzar, but when the Medes and Persians conquered Babylon, Daniel once more came into a position of considerable importance and influence under King Darius.

Daniel was primarily a statesman. Though he had the gift of prophecy, his responsibility was to represent the Lord in a heathen royal court and to testify before the great of the land that earthly kingdoms will rise and fall but the kingdom of God stands for ever.

Historical setting

The death of King Ashurbanipal of Assyria (668–626 B.C.) marked the decline of the Assyrian Empire (the empire that 120 years earlier had destroyed Israel, the northern kingdom of the ten tribes). Three unimportant kings followed until 612 B.C. when Assyria fell to the armies of King Nabopolassar of Babylon.

The fall of Nineveh, the capital, and the conquest of Assyria left two empires to determine domination of the region: Babylon and Egypt. After seven years the conflict reached its deciding moment when Nabopolassar's son, Nebuchadnezzar, led the Babylonian army against Pharaoh Necho and the Egyptians at the great battle of Carchemish (605 B.C., Jer. 46:2-12). Nebuchadnezzar was victorious. He recovered Coele-Syria, Phoenicia and Israel, took Jerusalem (1:1-2) and was pressing forward to Egypt when news of his father's death reached him. He hurried back to Babylon accompanied only by his light troops and a group of captives from

Judah, including young Daniel (1:1-3; 2 Chr. 36:6-7). It was a long journey; Babylon, in the heart of present-day Iraq, lies almost 700 miles north-
east of Israel.

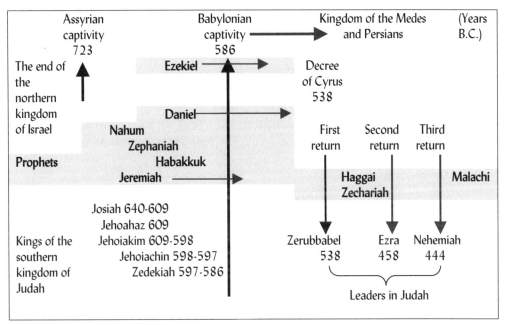

Judah and its prophets and kings before, during and after the exile

Nebuchadnezzar succeeded his father Nabopolassar, the founder of the
Babylonian Empire, to the throne. He reigned in Babylon for thirty-seven
years (cf. 2 Kings 25:27; 605–568 B.C.), during which time he led two
more invasions on Judah. At the final assault he destroyed the temple,
buildings and walls of Jerusalem, leaving it decimated (2 Kings 25:9; 2 Chr.
36:19).

The Babylonian exile was a period in which the anger of God was revealed towards his chosen people. In founding the nation of Israel Moses
had warned the people not to turn away from the Lord into idolatry and
sin. The consequences were clearly spelled out: 'Then my anger shall be
aroused against them in that day, and I will forsake them, and I will hide
my face from them, and they shall be devoured. And many evils and
troubles shall befall them, so that they will say in that day, "Have not these
evils come upon us because our God is not among us?" And I will surely
hide my face in that day because of all the evil which they have done, in
that they have turned to other gods' (Deut. 31:17-18).

Outline

The book of Daniel is often called an apocalyptic writing (from the Greek word *apokalupsis*, to take off the cover; hence 'revelation', especially of the end of the world — 2 Thess. 1:7), but it must be distinguished from the later non-biblical Jewish apocalyptic writings. There is only one other apocalypse which may be compared to it, and that is the New Testament book of Revelation.[3]

The book of Daniel was originally written in two languages: Hebrew and Aramaic. The section from the second half of 2:4 up to 7:28 was written in Aramaic and describes life in Babylon. The rest of the book was in Hebrew.

Part I: General introduction (1:1-21)

Daniel, the young Israelite exile, is selected for training in the court of King Nebuchadnezzar. 'The Hebrews were a captive people. It was natural to suppose that they would be restless, and perhaps insubordinate, in their condition, and it was a matter of policy to do all that could be done to conciliate them. Nothing would better tend to this than to select some of their own number who were of their most distinguished families; to place them at court; to provide for them from the royal bounty; to give them the advantages of the best education that the capital afforded; to make an arrangement that contemplated their future employment in the service of the state, and to furnish them every opportunity of promotion.'[4]

Evidently trained in childhood and early youth in the true faith, the religion of the Hebrews, Daniel knows the law of Moses and determines, with his three colleagues, to uphold rigorously the commandments of the Lord even in the environment of a heathen land. Given permission to abstain from certain food and drink, he is blessed by the Lord with health of body and mind. After an intensive three-year training Daniel passes the examination and is appointed to the Babylonian civil service.

Part II: Outstanding events in the life of Daniel (2: 1 - 6:28)

Following the interpretation of a dream, which none of the Chaldean wise men is able to accomplish, Daniel is elevated to a position of high rank as governor of the whole province of Babylon and chief administrator over the Chaldean wise men (2:48). King Nebuchadnezzar is impressed with Daniel's wisdom and perception. He acknowledges Daniel's God as 'God of gods' and 'Lord of kings' (2:47), but he is not converted. He is still a pagan at heart. He has not renounced his pagan gods to turn in genuine faith to the only true and living God. This is evidenced by the construction of a golden image and the command that everyone should bow down and worship it — on pain of death in the fiery furnace. Daniel's three colleagues display outstanding faith and courage in their refusal to obey the edict. Hananiah, Mishael and Azariah (Babylonian names — Shadrach, Meshach and Abed-Nego) declare their confidence in the Lord: 'Our God whom we serve is able to deliver us from the burning fiery furnace... But if not ... we do not serve your gods, nor will we worship the gold image which you have set up' (3:17-18).

The remarkable delivery of these three young Israelites from the fiery furnace once more impresses King Nebuchadnezzar, but he is still filled with pride and arrogance.

Some time later King Nebuchadnezzar has another dream. He seems to have been reluctant to turn immediately to Daniel for an interpretation. Consulting all the magicians, astrologers and soothsayers, he finds no answer. Eventually he consults Daniel. Daniel informs the king that, in consequence of his pride, he will be deprived for a while of his sanity and his throne. Living like an animal, he will eventually learn to acknowledge the true God of heaven and earth. Then his sanity and his kingdom will be restored to him. Daniel adds a tender appeal that the king might repent of his sins and show mercy to the poor in order that the threatened judgement of God might be averted (4:27).

The interpretation of the dream has no permanent effect upon Nebuchadnezzar. Twelve months later he is walking in the palace, feeling pleased with himself and proud of all his achievements, when a voice from heaven brings judgement. The dream is now to become reality, for '... a long time afterwards, when God touched his mind, he very properly recognized this punishment to have been divinely inflicted. Hence this dream was a kind of entrance and preparation for repentance.'[5] After the period appointed by God Nebuchadnezzar's sanity returns and he acknowledges the Lord: 'Now I, Nebuchadnezzar, praise and extol and honour the King of heaven, all of whose works are truth, and his ways justice' (4:37).

With the death of King Nebuchadnezzar some years later, Daniel occupies a less important position. Nothing is heard of him during the two-year reign of Nebuchadnezzar's successor, his son Evil-Merodach (562–560 B.C.), nor of his successor, Neriglisar (560–556 B.C.). It is not until the last days of King Belshazzar some twenty years later that Daniel once more rises to prominence (5:11-12).[6]

Interpreting the writing on the wall that appeared during the feast of Belshazzar, Daniel informs the king of the impending destruction of his kingdom. The rank and status subsequently promised to Daniel are not forthcoming as that night Babylon is conquered by the Medes and Persians.

Under the reign of the new king, Darius the Mede, Daniel is once more raised to a position of great influence (6:1-2). The reason for this elevation by the king of a conquering power is not stated but may not be hard to find. King Darius would benefit from having someone familiar with the affairs of state in the Babylonian Empire. Daniel was unsurpassed in qualification, with thorough knowledge of the court, the laws, customs and culture of the nation. He would know how best to secure the peace and stability of that portion of the now vast empire of the Medes and Persians. Furthermore Daniel was a foreigner and less likely to react to the domination of outsiders than would a native Chaldean.

Those who hoped to be promoted instead of Daniel react with jealousy. Using the rule of the Medes and Persians that no law once enacted by the king can be rescinded (cf. Esth. 1:19), they achieve the passing of a law that effectively alienates Daniel because of his religious principles and practices. Daniel, accused and sentenced, is ordered with great reluctance to the lion's den by King Darius. Daniel is miraculously delivered by the Lord. His accusers immediately meet their end amongst the lions.

As a result of this providence of God, Daniel is exalted to the place of highest honour in the land. From this advantageous position he is able to promote the best interests of his people, the Israelites. His influence upon King Cyrus no doubt secures the return of the exiles to their own country (6:28; 2 Chr. 36:22-23). Daniel, an octogenarian by this time, may have felt it wise not to attempt the 700-mile journey back to Jerusalem. Alternatively, he may have been convinced that he would be of more use to his own people by remaining in the court of King Cyrus.

Part III: Visions and prophecies illustrating God's control over the nations (7: 1 - 12:13)

The latter half of the book is given over to a record of the visions and prophecies which Daniel received concerning the future of the nations of the earth. The Old Testament church is to understand that the return to

Jerusalem from exile will not be an immediate prelude to a happy, peaceful and quiet life. The Holy Spirit teaches the people of God that nations are to rise and fall and Israel will often find herself tossed from pillar to post in international turmoil. Through it all and beyond it all God is building *his* unique kingdom that shall never be destroyed.

The visions Daniel receives during the first and third years of Belshazzar's reign (7:1 – 8:27) have much in common with the dream of Nebuchadnezzar (2:31-45). The use of imagery is understandable since the people of God at that time are in an alien land and this method of communication both conceals and reveals at the same time.[7]

Comparison of Nebuchadnezzar's dream and Daniel's later visions

Daniel 2	Daniel 7	Daniel 8	Interpretation of all[8]
Image	Beast	Beast	
Head of fine gold	Lion with eagle's wings		Babylon
Chest and arms silver	Like a bear	Ram with two horns	Medo-Persia
Belly and thighs bronze	Leopard with four wings and four heads	Male goat with one great horn, four horns and little horn	Greece
Legs of iron, feet of iron and clay	Terrible monster with ten horns and a little horn		Rome
A stone that becomes a great mountain	Messiah and saints receive the kingdom		Kingdom of God

Whatever may be the detailed interpretation, the overall message is unequivocal: the indisputable 'power and grotesqueness of human evil, especially on the level of the state'.[9] In both the dream and visions each kingdom feeds upon its predecessor: Medo-Persia upon Babylon, Greece upon Medo-Persia, Rome upon Greece. Represented by monstrous wild beasts, these empires are driven by human pride and arrogance; as Nebuchadnezzar boasts, 'Is not this great Babylon, that I have built for a royal dwelling by my mighty power and for the honour of my majesty?' (4:30).

There is nevertheless another kingdom of quite a different kind, represented not by beasts but by human beings: 'the Ancient of Days' and 'the Son of Man' (7:9-10,13-14):

Then the kingdom and dominion,
And the greatness of the kingdoms under the whole heaven,
Shall be given to the people, the saints of the Most High.
His kingdom is an everlasting kingdom,
And all dominions shall serve and obey him.

                                                        (7:27).

Since the early days in the Garden of Eden the battle has raged upon earth between God and Satan, good and evil. 'Sin rules the world; although it does not distort men diabolically yet it does brutally. Therefore animals are emblems of the world-powers, but the one who overthrows the world-empire and who becomes an everlasting king of an everlasting kingdom is in contrast to the secularized, bestialized human race an ideal, holy man, who in such a superhuman and yet so human way brings the history of mankind to its ideal conclusion.'[10]

Daniel prays, confessing the sins of God's people, and he receives a wonderful revelation in response (9:3-27).

The vision by the River Tigris (10:4), granted to Daniel in the third year of Cyrus, presents the future history of the great nations of the earth until the coming of Christ and then on to the final day of the resurrection.[11] The Lord has previously foretold the future condition of the Israelites after their return from Babylon and up to the advent of Christ (7:1 – 8:27), but in the eleventh chapter a more distinct prediction is given.

Daniel records his personal commitment to fasting and prayer over a period of three weeks. He then receives a vision from God. He describes the heavenly messenger (10:5-6) and outlines his own reaction, for what he experiences has a profound effect upon him: 'No strength remained in me; for my vigour was turned to frailty in me, and I retained no strength' (10:8). The scene is set for a momentous revelation, 'for the vision refers to many days yet to come' (10:14). Daniel again notes his reaction: 'My lord, because of the vision my sorrows have overwhelmed me, and I have retained no strength ... nor is any breath left in me' (10:16-17).

The angel explains his delay in attending Daniel: he was engaged in Persia in defending and safeguarding the people of God. Cambyses, son of Cyrus and King of Persia, had issued a cruel decree to prevent the Jews from rebuilding the temple in Jerusalem and he would have gone much further in his hostility towards the restoration work had it not been for the resistance imposed by the angel (10:13; Ezra 4:5).

The three kings of Persia (11:2) are Cyrus, Cambyses and Darius. The fourth, who will be 'far richer than them all' (11:2) is Khshayarsh (known

The people of Judah during the empire of the Medes and Persians

(Years B.C.)

Cyrus 539-530	Cambyses 530-522	Darius I 522-486	Xerxes 486-464	Artaxerxes I 464-423	Darius II 423-404

← Daniel prophesies →

Artaxerxes II 404-359

Artaxerxes III 359-338

Arses 338-335

Darius III 335-331

Alexander the Great establishes the Greek Empire 336-323

490
Defeated by the Greeks at Marathon

480
Defeated by the Greeks at Thermopylae

Esther delivers God's people
Esth. 1-9

432-420
Malachi prophesies

520
Haggai & Zechariah prophesy

444
Third return under Nehemiah
Neh. 1-2

458
Second return under Ezra
Ezra 7-10

516
The temple completed
Ezra 5-6

538
First return under Zerubbabel
Ezra 1-3

Rebuilding of the temple halted
Ezra 4

among the Greeks as Xerxes and among the Hebrews as Ahasuerus,[12] and the husband of Esther).[13] He was very rich (11:2; cf. Esth. 1:1-7).

The 'mighty king' (11:3) who will arise against the Persians is Alexander the Great, King of Greece. No sooner had he risen to the height of power, ruling over a vast empire, than he became ill and within a short time he died. The empire was eventually divided into four: Egypt, Syria, Greece and Asia Minor. The angel predicts, one hundred years before the birth of Alexander, that no posterity will succeed him to the throne (11:4).

The angel concentrates attention on two sections of the divided kingdom, probably because these are the near neighbours to Judah and the nations with greatest impact upon Judah and the people of God. Intrigue and wars follow between the King of the South (Egypt) and the King of the North (Syria). Secular history from that period serves to illustrate the remarkable detail and accuracy of the angel's predictions.

The people of God will be assaulted by the forces of evil (12:1) but the Lord will deliver them. These are the elect, the true people of God, whom Satan cannot destroy.

The foretelling of international events serves the purpose of consoling the people of God. God is sovereign; he knows what he will do. He reveals the future to Old Testament saints so that when it comes to pass they may be confident in him in whom they believe. The Lord Jesus Christ revealed the future to his disciples for the same reason: 'And now I have told you before it comes, that when it does come to pass, you may believe' (John 14:29; cf. 16:1,4).

The message of Daniel is emphatic, dogmatic: God will be victorious — definitely, entirely and eternally. Here is the true comfort for the people of God.

Christ and his church

Theophany

When Shadrach, Meshach and Abed-Nego are thrown into the fiery furnace a phenomenon occurs which brings an outstanding declaration from King Nebuchadnezzar: 'Then King Nebuchadnezzar was astonished; and he rose in haste and spoke, saying to his counsellors, "Did we not cast three men bound into the midst of the fire?" They answered and said to the king, "True, O king." "Look!" he answered, "I see four men loose, walking in the midst of the fire; and they are not hurt, and the form of the fourth is like the Son of God" ' (3:24-25).

The king is astonished to see the three men walking freely without the ropes or chains with which they had been bound. But it is the sight of a fourth person that is the most remarkable sight to the king. Nebuchadnezzar is not to be understood as knowingly speaking of *the* Son of God who became the human being Jesus Christ. As a pagan Nebuchadnezzar uses words describing a supernatural being, a deity figure, for his words are strictly translated, 'a son of the gods'. The meaning is, 'son of deity, that is, a Divine Person, one of the race of the gods, a supernatural being'.[14] Something about the fourth figure, maybe his countenance or his demeanour, declared him to be of heavenly origin. It cannot be concluded with any certainty that this was a Christophany, for there is no internal evidence in Scripture to lead to such a solid conclusion, yet that is a strong probability. It may be that the Lord willed that Nebuchadnezzar should utter these profound words, like Caiaphas, Pilate and others have done, without understanding their significance (John 11:49-52; 19:19-22).

Whether the angel (3:28) was *the* Angel of the LORD, or *an* angel of the Lord, the abiding message is clear: 'The vision must have been sublime; and it is a beautiful image of the children of God often walking unhurt amidst dangers, safe beneath the Divine protection.'[15] 'The angel of the LORD encamps all around those who fear him' (Ps. 34:7; cf. 91:11). This is especially fulfilled in the life of Christ, but it is extended to the whole church of Christ; God's children are under the eye and protection of these heavenly messengers (Ps. 103:20; cf. 2 Kings 6:15-17).

Similarities between the prophet Daniel's visitor by the River Tigris and the apostle John's visitor on the Isle of Patmos (Rev. 1:12-16) would suggest that this is an appearance of the Lord in human form, in other words, a Christophany. Here is another example of the Lord, the Son of God, controlling all things for the good of his church (cf. Eph. 1:22-23).

Prophecies

1. The death of Christ

Seventy weeks are determined
For your people and for your holy city,
To finish the transgression,

To make an end of sins,
To make reconciliation for iniquity,
To bring in everlasting righteousness,
To seal up vision and prophecy,
And to anoint the Most Holy.
Know therefore and understand,
That from the going forth of the command
To restore and build Jerusalem
Until Messiah the Prince,
There shall be seven weeks and sixty-two weeks…
And after the sixty-two weeks
Messiah shall be cut off, but not for himself…

(9:24-26).

Here the totality of sin is defined as 'transgression', 'sins' and 'iniquity'. These three are often combined in the Scriptures (Exod. 34:7; Ps. 51:1-2); they refer to law-breaking, guilt and wickedness respectively and 'represent in its fulness the nature of that curse which has separated man from God'.[16] This threefold designation of sin is matched by a threefold response: to 'finish' (lit., 'shut up'), to 'make an end' (lit., 'to seal') and to 'make reconciliation' (lit., to 'cover'), which contains the basic idea of removal out of sight. 'Sin, which hitherto *lay naked* and *open* before the eyes of the righteous God, is now by his mercy, *shut up,* sealed, and covered, so that it can no more be regarded as existing; a figurative designation of the forgiveness of sin, analogous to those, where it is said, "to hide the face from sin…" ' [17]

Messiah is to achieve this great work. A new clarity is given from heaven. From this time forward the spiritually enlightened people of God who understand biblical prophecy will not only await 'the Lion of the tribe of Judah, but also the sacrificial Lamb; not only a new covenant but also a mediator between God and man; not only a reconciliation with God, but also a human reconciler'.[18]

2. The return of Christ

The assertion of Daniel that God will be victorious (7:13-14) finds its fulfilment in the battle that the Saviour won against Satan at Calvary. Ironically Jesus defeated evil by his death on the cross: 'And you, being dead in your trespasses and the uncircumcision of your flesh, he has made alive together with him, having forgiven you all trespasses, having wiped out the handwriting of requirements that was against us, which was contrary to us. And he has taken it out of the way, having nailed it to the cross. Having disarmed principalities and powers, he made a public spectacle of them, triumphing over them in it' (Col. 2:13-15).

Yet though the victory is assured the war still rages, for only at the return of the Saviour in power and glory will the final curtain fall on this dramatic conflict. The day will dawn when Christ will put 'an end to all rule and all authority and power' (1 Cor. 15:24):

> I was watching in the night visions,
> And behold, one like *the Son of Man,*
> *Coming with the clouds of heaven!*
> He came to the Ancient of Days,
> And they brought him near before him.
> Then to him was given dominion and glory and a kingdom,
> That all peoples, nations, and languages should serve him.
> His dominion is an everlasting dominion,
> Which shall not pass away,
> And his kingdom the one
> Which shall not be destroyed
>
> (7:13-14, emphasis added).

The Lord Jesus Christ identified himself with this prophecy and foretold his glorious return. At his trial before the Jewish council just hours before his death, Jesus was challenged by Caiaphas the high priest: ' "I adjure you by the living God that you tell us if you are the Christ, the Son of God." Jesus said to him, "It is as you said. Nevertheless, I say to you, hereafter you will see *the Son of Man* sitting at the right hand of the Power, and *coming on the clouds of heaven*" ' (Matt. 26:63-64, emphasis added).

Application

1. The sovereign rule of God

There is only one God and he rules over everything and everyone (4:34-35; cf. 4:32). In the record which the Holy Spirit inspired Daniel to write, Gentile kings make confession of the sovereignty of God:

The king [Nebuchadnezzar] answered Daniel, and said, '"Truly your God is the God of gods, the Lord of kings, and a revealer of secrets, since you could reveal this secret' (2:47).

Now I, Nebuchadnezzar, praise and extol and honour the King of heaven, all of whose works are truth, and his ways justice. And those who walk in pride he is able to abase (4:37).

Then King Darius wrote…

I make a decree that in every dominion of my kingdom men must tremble and fear before the God of Daniel.

For he is the living God,
And steadfast for ever;
His kingdom is the one which shall not be destroyed,
And his dominion shall endure to the end

(6:25-26).

2. Prayer

Daniel was a man of prayer. The wicked scheming of jealous colleagues was based upon their confidence that Daniel would continue to pray to the Lord even though his life would depend upon his not doing so (6:5-7). They persuaded the king to pass the necessary law and then they spied on the prophet so that they could bring an accusation and have him put to death. The Lord wonderfully preserved Daniel in his subsequent incarceration in the lion's den.

In chapter 9 there is a record of the content of one of his prayers. Daniel has been thinking hard about the prophecy of Jeremiah and the number of years that Jerusalem is to be desolate. The predicted time is almost complete and yet there is not the slightest indication of a possible return to Jerusalem. Daniel knows that the exile in Babylon is a punishment for Judah's sins so, rather than enquiring about the exact meaning of Jeremiah's prophecy, he pours out his heart to the Lord in confession of the people's sins. Daniel pleads with the Lord to show mercy.

The prophet begins his prayer by addressing God and acknowledging his character, promise and behaviour: 'And I prayed to the LORD my God, and made confession, and said, "O Lord, great and awesome God, who keeps his covenant and mercy with those who love him, and with those who keep his commandments…"' (9:4).

Daniel acknowledges the Lord to be his own God; for God only hears the prayers of those who truly know him. He addresses the Lord as great and awesome and recognizes that he punishes sinful Israel on the basis of the covenant (9:4,11). The prophet appeals to the Lord on the same basis of this special covenant relationship. Even when the people of God are faithless, '… he remains faithful; he cannot deny himself' (2 Tim. 2:13).

In a similar manner Asaph makes his request:

Help us, O God of our salvation,
For the glory of your name;
And deliver us, and provide atonement for our sins,
For your name's sake!

(Ps. 79:9 emphasis added).

Though Daniel's plea is based upon God's covenant mercy, he still pours out his heart in contrition, confessing a whole multitude of sins and iniquities. So when calamity, affliction and trials fall upon us and we go to God and pray that the evil may be removed, the first thing that is required of us is that we should confess our sins and acknowledge the justice of God in the judgements that have come upon us.[19]

The Lord Jesus promised answered prayer to his disciples under similar conditions: 'And whatever you ask in my name, that I will do, that the Father may be glorified in the Son. If you ask anything in my name, I will do it. If you love me, keep my commandments' (John 14:13-15).

In his great mercy the Lord answers Daniel: 'O Daniel, man greatly beloved… Do not fear, Daniel, for from the first day that you set your heart to understand, and to humble yourself before your God, your words were heard…' (10:11-12).

3. The believer and the state

Daniel was promoted to the highest rank in the Babylonian kingdom next to the king (2:48). Like Joseph in Egypt, Daniel served without compromise. Being loyal to the king did not make him unfaithful to God. The Lord gave him favour with his tutor and his king (1:9,20; 2:48-49). Daniel for his part remained devoted to the Lord and obedient to the law and covenant of Sinai (1:8). He could not prevent every evil in government but, keeping himself from sin, he influenced the course of the nation. There is nothing inappropriate about a godly person's being elevated to a position of responsibility and trust by an ungodly government or by a pagan king.

Yet it is not without its dangers. Jealousy from others may lead to serious problems arising. In spite of great provocation at times, Daniel maintained his spiritual life in the unfriendly atmosphere of a Gentile court (6:10). When tensions arose between serving God and serving the king, Daniel did not waver for a moment. He left the consequences and outcome in God's hands. The same teaching continues under the New Covenant, for the apostle Peter exhorts Christians: 'Fear God. Honour the king' (1 Peter 2:17). Also the apostle Paul urges the church of God to pray and intercede 'for kings and all who are in authority, that we may lead a quiet and peaceable life in all godliness and reverence' (1 Tim. 2:2).

4. The final resurrection

The book of Daniel contains the clearest prophecy of the resurrection in the Old Testament Scriptures:

> And many of those who sleep in the dust of the earth shall awake,
> Some to everlasting life,
> Some to shame and everlasting contempt.
> Those who are wise shall shine
> Like the brightness of the firmament,
> And those who turn many to righteousness
> Like the stars for ever and ever
>
> (12:2-3).

Though bodies return to the dust, nevertheless they shall rise, 'implying the hope of a resurrection not founded on natural causes, but depending upon the inestimable power of God, which surpasses all our senses'.[20] Both the children of God and the wicked will be reduced to earth and dust, yet this will present no obstacle to God in raising them up again.

Conclusion

The four great prophets, Isaiah, Jeremiah, Ezekiel and Daniel, form a glorious and harmonious quartet, declaring the sovereignty of the living God. Isaiah speaks of God's sovereignty in salvation; Jeremiah of God's sovereignty in judgement; Ezekiel of God's sovereignty in glory and Daniel God's sovereignty in his kingdom.

Daniel ministered in the land of exile. Along with his people he had been torn from his home in Judah. The judgement of God rested upon the people of Israel. But it was to be of a fixed duration. Seventy years only in exile and then the Lord would restore them to their own land, the land of the covenant promise. Daniel prophesied from a Gentile royal court and declared in graphic terms the limitation of power granted to the nations. Empires may come and go, rise and fall, but God's kingdom will stand for eternity. The day will dawn when all God's people of every generation and of every nation will be raised to eternal life: 'And at that time your people shall be delivered, every one who is found written in the book' (12:1).

That book is 'the book of life' (Rev. 3:5; 13:8; 20:12,15) which is 'the Lamb's book of life' (Rev. 21:27). It is the heavenly record of those who have been loved 'from the foundation of the world' (Rev. 17:8), those who have put their wholehearted trust in God and his Christ.

Hosea

('salvation')

Author: Hosea

Key thought: 'Return'

Theme:
God's love for his wayward people

'I will heal their backsliding,
I will love them freely,
For my anger has turned away
   from him.'

Hosea 14:4

Summary

Hosea

The book of Hosea of one of the more difficult books of Old Testament Scripture. It is pre-eminently a book for the backslider. As the Lord's parable of the lost son pictures God as a loving Father yearning for the return of his wayward son (Luke 15:11-24), so Hosea pictures God as a loving Husband yearning for the return of his wayward wife. In these pages there is a vivid exposure of God's methods in restoring a backslidden people.

In the opening verses the reader is confronted with difficulties that are virtually impossible to resolve. Hosea is commanded to marry a prostitute. Many godly students of the Scriptures have concluded that this did not take place in reality but was a vision, or an analogy, or symbolism, which was set by God before the prophet Hosea. E. J. Young, the respected Old Testament scholar, while admitting that 'The prophecy reads as straightforward narrative' and at 'first sight, we receive the impression that these things are to be understood as actually having taken place', nevertheless declares that he has 'become more and more convinced that the whole episode has a symbolical significance'.[1] Calvin too objects to any suggestion that this actually took place. He argues that for the prophet to take a prostitute as a wife would have made this servant of God contemptible and a reproach.

Priests were not permitted to marry a harlot (Lev. 21:7,14) but Hosea was not a priest. Such a command of God to a church leader would not be issued under the New Covenant, for 'A bishop ... must be blameless ... Moreover he must have a good testimony among those who are outside, lest he should fall into reproach and the snare of the devil' (1 Tim. 3:2,7; cf. Titus 1:7). Nevertheless in spite of the discomfort that we feel at such a command being given in reality: '... a straightforward reading of the text leads most naturally to the conclusion that Hosea was ordered by God to marry a promiscuous woman in order to symbolize God's relationship with Israel. It is methodologically dangerous to depart from this reading based on what we consider to be moral problems with the command, and indeed this latter may be questioned. Nowhere does God command anyone but priests to avoid marriage with a prostitute.'[2]

Though attended by complex ethical problems the message itself is indisputable. Hosea's marriage to Gomer, whether history, vision, or allegory, is used by God to indicate both his loathing for Israel's unfaithfulness and his yearning love for his people.

Author

The name 'Hosea' (Hebrew, 'Hoshea') means 'salvation'. It was the family name of Joshua, the man who led the children of Israel into the promised land. During the wilderness journey Moses renamed Hoshea, later to become his successor, as Joshua, meaning 'Jehovah is salvation' (Num. 13:16). By this suffix Moses indicates the source or origin of salvation — Jehovah, the living and true God.

Hosea the son of Beeri is the author of the whole book bearing his name. He prophesies against Israel, the northern kingdom of the ten tribes. These people have turned away from the lawful worship of Jehovah. They are ripe for destruction. Hosea, however, has a message of God's tender love for a sinful and rebellious people. The people of Israel are pictured as an unfaithful wife committing spiritual adultery. God pleads with the people, through the prophet, to repent and to turn from their sinful ways. They must pass a period of humbling but they will be restored.

Hosea has been called 'the prophet of the broken heart'. [3] His commission was to plead with Israel to return to God. He probably preached for over forty years, but the people persisted in their stubborn resistance. These were days of idolatry and immorality. There was no fear of the Lord among the people. They refused to take notice of the prophet's warnings and the result was captivity. Hosea was still ministering during the Assyrian exile although there is no mention in his book of this event having taken place (cf. 2 Kings 17:5-23).

Hosea may have been a native of the northern kingdom since his style and language have a 'northern' flavour and he refers to the King of Israel as 'our king' (7:5), but this is too slight a comment to form a dogmatic conclusion.[4] If he did originate from the northern kingdom of the ten tribes, then he was the only writing prophet who came *from* Israel and wrote *to* Israel. He was certainly familiar with the evil conditions existing in Israel at that time.

Hosea addresses the northern kingdom of the ten tribes as 'Israel', 'Samaria,' 'Jacob' and 'Ephraim'. The name 'Ephraim' is used because that tribe was the largest of the ten and the leader of the rebellion against the Lord.

Hosea uses graphic illustrations to drive home his arguments:

- 'Ephraim is joined to idols' (4:17).
- 'Ephraim has mixed himself among the peoples' (7:8), for they are no longer a separated people.
- 'Ephraim is a cake unturned' (7:8) — that is, one which is still un-cooked dough on one side, but burnt on the other — expressing a divided heart.
- 'Grey hairs are here and there on him, yet he does not know it' (7:9), signifying premature old age and unconscious deterioration.
- 'Aliens have devoured his strength' (7:9), indicating that they are weakened by evil associations.
- 'Ephraim also is like a silly dove, without sense' (7:11). Israel flies here and there seeking assistance — to Egypt, to Assyria, but never to the living God.
- 'Israel is swallowed up' (8:8) — their national identity is lost.
- 'A vessel in which there is no pleasure' (8:8) — they are useless in the service of God.
- 'Her king is cut off like a twig on the water' (10:7) — one which is carried away by the current and vanishes without a trace.
- 'A cunning Canaanite! Deceitful scales are in his hand' (12:7), referring to commercial trickery in business.[5]

Hosea shows himself to be a man of deep feeling, and at times his anger against sin manifests itself in language that is somewhat harsh and severe. On the other hand, 'When the prophet sets before the nation the sublime love of the Lord the language of the book is filled with beautiful imagery.'[6]

Historical setting

Although Hosea mentions only one king of Israel, the reference to the four kings of Judah places his ministry during the reigns of the last seven kings to rule over Israel (c. 750–710 B.C.) — from King Jeroboam II, one of her most powerful kings, to King Hoshea (2 Kings 14:23-29; 15:8-31; 17:1-4).

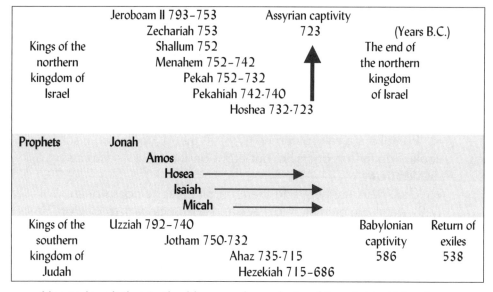

Kings of the northern kingdom of Israel	Jeroboam II 793–753 Zechariah 753 Shallum 752 Menahem 752–742 Pekah 752–732 Pekahiah 742-740 Hoshea 732-723	Assyrian captivity 723	(Years B.C.) The end of the northern kingdom of Israel
Prophets	Jonah Amos Hosea Isaiah Micah		
Kings of the southern kingdom of Judah	Uzziah 792–740 Jotham 750-732 Ahaz 735-715 Hezekiah 715–686	Babylonian captivity 586	Return of exiles 538

Hosea in relation to the kings and prophets of the divided kingdom

A contemporary of Isaiah, Micah and possibly of Amos,[7] Hosea exercised a ministry, predominantly in Israel, which extended over many years. He prophesied during the reigns of Kings Uzziah, Jotham, Ahaz and Hezekiah of Judah. This gives a period of at least forty years, and some have even suggested a ministry lasting as long as seventy-two years.[8] Hosea's ministry followed that of Amos (there may have been some overlap). The southern kingdom of Judah, under King Uzziah (Azariah), was experiencing a time of prosperity. The northern kingdom of Israel, under King Jeroboam II, was also enjoying days of economic prosperity and military success (2 Kings 14:25). But success and prosperity brought their own problems — paganism, materialism, greed, immorality and injustice.

After the death of King Jeroboam, Israel fell into rapid decline. Six kings reigned during the last thirty years of the nation's existence. Hosea does not mention these kings by name. The prophets to Israel only recognize the legitimate rulers of the kingdom of Judah as true kings of the people of God. This may indicate the Lord's disapproval of the kings of the north: 'They set up kings, but not by me; they made princes, and I did not acknowledge it' (8:4; cf. Deut. 17:15). Three of these kings reign for two years or less, and four are assassinated (2 Kings 15:8-31; 17:1-4; Hosea 7:7; 8:4; 10:3; 13:9-11).

Less than ten years after the death of Jeroboam, Assyria began to exert its military might, becoming more powerful and threatening under her king Tiglath-Pileser III. His successor King Shalmaneser V started the aggression against Israel which led to the total defeat and removal of the Israelites as captives to Assyria in 723 B.C. The threat of the Assyrian Empire provides the background to the book of Hosea.

No king of the northern kingdom of Israel could put an effective stop to her corruption. Immorality stemmed from idolatry. In turning away from the living God the Israelites turned away from the ground and foundation of true morality. If he had abolished calf-worship the King of Israel would have undermined the very existence of the northern kingdom. If the religious division between the kingdom of Israel and the kingdom of Judah had been removed then political union would have soon followed: 'Founded as it was in rebellion against the royal house of David, which God Himself had chosen, [the northern kingdom] bore within itself from the very first the spirit of rebellion and revolution, and therefore the germs of internal self-destruction.'[9]

Outline

The structure of the book of Hosea is difficult to establish. Though the first three chapters readily fall into divisions, the remaining eleven chapters are not so easily delineated. The message of the book is, however, clear and forceful. The analogy of marriage is used for God's relationship with his people. Israel's unfaithfulness is reflected in the infidelity of Hosea's wife.

Part I: Hosea's marriage symbolic of God's relationship with Israel (1:2 – 3:5)

In obedience to a divine command, Hosea takes Gomer the daughter of Diblaim as his wife. They have three children. The children of this troubled marriage are given symbolic names indicating Israel's breaking of their covenant with the Lord.

The first son is called 'Jezreel' (meaning 'God scatters'). The name Jezreel signifies the great slaughter that God would bring on the house of Jehu because of the violent acts which he had committed (2 Kings 9)

The name of Hosea's daughter, Lo-Ruhamah, means 'No mercy' (1:6). This indicates severe judgement; Israel is like a daughter whom her father casts away and disowns. God will no longer look with pity and love upon Israel. The nation has gone from bad to worse. The Lord 'will no longer have mercy on the house of Israel' (1:6). It is as though the Lord says, 'Your obstinacy is intolerable; I will not then bear with you any more.'[10]

The third child, a son, is named 'Lo-Ammi', meaning 'Not my people' (1:9). The period of weaning for Lo-Ruhamah ('No mercy') is ended. The patience of God is exhausted. Israel's wickedness is beyond healing. The final separation is to take place: 'You are not my people, and I will not be your God' (1:9).

Hosea's wife Gomer proves unfaithful and leaves her husband in search of other lovers (3:1). The sin of adultery is exacerbated by the sin of prostitution. Hosea pursues her and buys her back from harlotry (3:2). He takes her once more to his home. A period is to be spent in seclusion and true sorrow of heart until the time appointed for full restoration.

Within the account of the gross sin of Gomer, the great grief of her husband Hosea and the underlying judgement of God against Israel, there is still evidence of the triumph of grace, for the Lord says to Israel, 'I will give her … the Valley of Achor as a door of hope' (2:15). The valley was named in the days of Joshua (Josh. 7:24-26). Through the sin of Achan, disobeying the commandment of God and taking spoil from Jericho, the Israelites were defeated in their attack upon Ai (Josh. 7). Through the name 'Achor' (meaning 'trouble') this valley became a memorial, reminding the people of 'how the Lord restores His favour … after the expiation of the guilt by the punishment of the transgressor'.[11] The prophet Hosea is indicating that Israel's time of trouble and distress will become a door of hope. The Lord will deal with justice and with mercy. He will punish sin, but his grace will be supreme.

Part II: Judgements against Israel (4:1 – 11:11)

After the first three chapters, which are based on Hosea's domestic grief, the remaining chapters have no clear structure. Themes overlap, interweave, interchange, repeat and vary in emphasis as the prophecy unfolds. Hosea faithfully challenges the Israelites about their sin, warns of God's righteous judgement, appeals to them to return to their God and speaks of final hope for the nation that God loves.

Attention turns from the domestic scene to the national arena. The Lord speaks through his servant in a series of addresses. Whether these addresses were oral or written, and where each began and ended, is not stated. This section is probably a summary of Hosea's preaching over a period of forty years or more commencing in the reign of Jeroboam and concluding only a short while before the Assyrian invasion, the conquest of the capital of Samaria and the deportation of the Israelites.

The content is an interweaving of Israel's unfaithfulness with God's righteous anger and his gracious mercy. What a testimony to the character of God! 'If we are faithless, he remains faithful; he cannot deny himself' (2 Tim. 2:13).

The main topics are repeated over and over again: the calf-worship at Bethel, the idolatry and the immorality. The spiritual and moral state of Israel is as bad as it could possibly be. The evils which Jeroboam I, the son of Nebat, had introduced (1 Kings 12:25-33) have been perpetuated and strengthened over the intervening 150 years or so:

> There is no truth or mercy
> Or knowledge of God in the land.
> By swearing and lying,
> Killing and stealing and committing adultery,
> They break all restraint,
> With bloodshed after bloodshed
>
> (4:1-2).

There is far-reaching corruption among the priests, as among the people. The rulers in Israel are seeking alliances with powerful nations: 'They call to Egypt; they go to Assyria' (7:11).

The sternest warnings and the severest censure are interwoven with the tenderest appeals:

> Come, and let us return to the LORD;
> For he has torn, but he will heal us;
> He has stricken, but he will bind us up
>
> (6:1).

Part III: Israel's sin and God's anger (11:12 - 13:16)

In many ways the third section is a repeat of the second in dealing with issues of Israel's sin and God's righteous anger. The purpose is to ensure that the Israelites are thoroughly aware of their gross sinfulness. Hosea demonstrates that the impending doom falling upon them is just and inevitable because of the long history of their rebellion and sin against the Lord. It is the Lord's punishment. They have wilfully turned from the ways of Jacob their father and fallen into the godless practices of the Canaanites; and this in spite of the continual love and compassion of God towards them and in spite of the punishments which he has already inflicted in order to bring them to their senses. But neither the appeals of love nor the pains of affliction have turned the people back to God. They continue in idolatry and immorality. Nevertheless the compassion of God will not permit them to be utterly destroyed. God will redeem Israel even from death and hell.

There is a repeated rebuke to the nation for turning to Assyria and Egypt for help. 'They make a covenant with the Assyrians, and oil is carried to Egypt' (12:1; cf. 7:11). These events took place during the reign of King Hoshea (2 Kings 17:1-4).

Part IV: Israel's ultimate restoration (14:1-9)

In words reminiscent of the Song of Solomon the book of Hosea concludes with a remarkable picture of a people restored to God. Urged to godly grief (cf. 2 Cor. 7:10), Israel is called back to God. Reassurance is given that the Lord will have mercy, 'heal their backsliding' and 'love them freely' (14:4). But restoring the backslider means more than forgiveness alone. It means that the Lord will also remove the cause of the backsliding. Their hearts will be changed. There will be a new principle in operation within them:

> Ephraim shall say,
> 'What have I to do any more with idols?'
> I have heard and observed him.
> I am like a green cypress tree;
> Your fruit is found in me
>
> (14:8).

And so in just fourteen chapters the sin of Israel is exposed, the judgement of God is disclosed and the triumph of the grace of God is proposed.

Christ and his church

The beautiful theme of love and marriage as a picture of Jehovah and Israel, Christ and his church, which flows from the Song of Solomon, passes under a dark cloud here in the book of Hosea through the unfaithfulness of the spouse to her covenant. Yet even as infidelity is exposed, the love of the grieving husband reveals the agony of God in his love for sinners.

William Hendriksen draws out the symbolic significance of the book of Hosea like this:

- Just as Hosea had married Gomer, so Jehovah had become Israel's 'Husband'.
- Just as Gomer had become untrue to Hosea, so Israel had become unfaithful to Jehovah.
- Just as Gomer was enslaved by her paramours, so the Israelites would be enslaved by those very nations in which they were putting their trust.
- Just as Hosea restored Gomer, so Jehovah would restore the remnant of Israel.
- Just as Hosea, in order to restore Gomer, redeemed her with the price of silver and barley, so Christ would redeem the true Israel with the price of his own blood.[12]

The bride is chosen while still in sin (1:2; cf. Ezek. 16:4-14; cf. Eph. 2:1-10). She is thoroughly washed, purified and adorned with beautiful clothing (cf. Titus 3:3-5). The Lord takes her as his own. But the heart of the wife turns away from its primary love (cf. Rev. 2:4). She hankers after other lovers, other gods (3:1; Ezek. 16:15-34; cf. James 4:4; 1 John 2:15-16). The Lord will not forget her. He redeems her and restores her (3:2-5; Ezek. 16:60-63). God's pain will reach its zenith at Calvary (John 3:16; Rom. 5:8).

Prophecies

1. Called out of Egypt

In the prophecies of Hosea there is an allusion to a second exodus (2:14-15). God will deliver them again. The Israelites must experience bondage and slavery once more, for they have forgotten the goodness and kindness of God in bringing their fathers out of Egypt. They are an ungrateful people. God loved them in those early days, for he says, 'When Israel was a child, I loved him' (11:1). The first exodus was like the birth of the nation of Israel. God loved Israel before the nation was born. The Lord's love for Israel was such that he called the nation out of Egypt: 'And out of Egypt I called my son' (11:1).

This text had a preliminary fulfilment in Israel as a type of Christ. Its ultimate fulfilment is to be found in the Lord Jesus. Matthew applies these words to the Saviour (Matt. 2:15). Calvin reasons that 'There is no doubt, but that God in his wonderful providence intended that his Son should come forth from Egypt, that he might be a redeemer to the faithful; and thus he shows that a true, real, and perfect deliverance was at length effected, when the promised Redeemer appeared.'[13] Egypt represents the spiritual state of bondage and Christ came to identify with those in bondage, to set them free and lead them out. Christ is the Son of God in quite a different way from the people of Israel. Adoption made the children of Israel the children of God, but Christ is by nature the only begotten Son of God (John 1:18; 3:16). A further difference is also evident in that Israel was ungrateful to God and no such ingratitude ever entered the Saviour's mind. In biblical types comparison and contrast belong together. No type is perfect for there is always a great difference between the reality and its symbols.

2. Israel's rejection and restoration

Although Israel's imminent rejection and restoration is prophesied by Hosea, the state of the nation of Israel from A.D. 70 onwards is also foretold: 'Without king or prince, without sacrifice or sacred pillar, without ephod or teraphim' (3:4).

The apostle Paul appeals to Hosea (2:23; 1:10) as an indication of the call of the Gentiles:

What if God, wanting to show his wrath and to make his power known, endured with much long-suffering the vessels of wrath prepared for destruction, and that he might make known the riches of his glory on the vessels of mercy, which he had prepared beforehand for glory, even us whom he called, not of the Jews only, but also of the Gentiles? As he says also in Hosea:

'I will call them my people, who were not my people,
And her beloved, who was not beloved.'
'And it shall come to pass in the place where it was said to them,

"You are not my people," there they will be called sons of the
    living God'

(Rom. 9:22-26).

There might at first sight appear a discrepancy between the prophet's
words and the apostle's interpretation of them. In Hosea the reference is to
the tribes of Israel and not to the Gentile nations. Paul recognizes that the
rejection and restoration of Israel of which Hosea spoke have their parallel
in the exclusion of the Gentiles from God's favour, followed by their recep-
tion back into that favour.[14] The apostle Peter also takes up this theme: '...
who once were not a people but are now the people of God, who had not
obtained mercy but now have obtained mercy' (1 Peter 2:10). It may, of
course, be argued that the apostle Peter was addressing Jewish Christians
whereas the apostle Paul was seeing the wider implications in a church
composed of believing Jews and believing Gentiles. Both Peter's and
Paul's usage of this passage constitute further evidence that the apostles
interpreted Old Testament prophecy as being fulfilled in Christ and his
church.

3. Resurrection for Christ and his church

After two days he will revive us;
On the third day he will raise us up,
That we may live in his sight

(6:2).

There is here a beautiful connection between the resurrection of the Son
of God and the resurrection of his people. The Lord did not rise from the
dead for himself alone, but for his people — he is the first-fruits of those
who shall rise (1 Cor. 15:20). The prophet 'here encourages the faithful to
entertain hope of salvation, because God would raise up his only-begotten
Son, whose resurrection would be the common life of the whole Church'.[15]
    Another powerful prophecy from Hosea speaks of the great
resurrection:

I will ransom them from the power of the grave;
I will redeem them from death.
O Death, I will be your plagues!

O Grave, I will be your destruction!
Pity is hidden from my *eyes*

(13:14).

'Ransom' means rescue by the payment of a price. 'Redeem' relates to one who, as the next of kin, has the right to acquire anything as his own by paying the price. 'Both words in their most exact sense describe what Jesus did for us.'[16] The apostle Paul takes up this prophecy and reveals how it will be fulfilled. Because of the suffering of the Saviour at Calvary a day will dawn when 'The dead will be raised incorruptible, and we shall be changed' (1 Cor. 15:52). Having conquered death and the grave, the Lord will abolish death for ever (1 Cor. 15:54-55). The triumph of Christ in his death and resurrection is the seal of the believer's resurrection on the great Day of the Lord (1 Cor. 15:23,56-57).

Another New Testament reference to the prophecy of Hosea (10:8) is given by the Lord Jesus on his way to crucifixion: 'And a great multitude of the people followed him, and women who also mourned and lamented him. But Jesus, turning to them, said, "Daughters of Jerusalem, do not weep for me, but weep for yourselves and for your children. For indeed the days are coming in which they will say, 'Blessed are the barren, the wombs that never bore, and the breasts which never nursed!' Then they will begin 'to say to the mountains, "Fall on us!" and to the hills, "cover us!"' ' " ' (Luke 23:27-30).

The Saviour shows his remarkable selflessness even in the most trying circumstances. He warns the women of the impending doom. Quoting these words from Hosea, our Lord shows that there is a devastation coming upon Israel which will be like that experienced in the days of the prophet Hosea. The first fulfilment came with the invasion of the Assyrians and the deportation of the Israelites. Another calamity is being predicted by the Lord Jesus. This is the imminent invasion of the Romans and the destruction of Jerusalem (A.D. 70). But the prophecy of Hosea will have an ultimate fulfilment on the Day of Judgement. Then the godless will cry out 'to the mountains and rocks, "Fall on us and hide us from the face of him who sits on the throne and from the wrath of the Lamb!"' (Rev. 6:16-17). For when God's judgement appears, unbelievers would rather face appalling death than be faced with the fierceness of his anger.

Application

1. Chosen by grace

The marriage of Hosea and Gomer graphically teaches that God did not choose Israel on the basis of merit. Every believer of every nation and of every generation is 'a debtor to mercy alone'. The Lord God says, 'There is no saviour besides me' (13:4). 'For we ourselves were also once foolish, disobedient, deceived, serving various lusts and pleasures, living in malice and envy, hateful and hating one another. But when the kindness and the love of God our Saviour towards man appeared, not by works of right-eousness which we have done, but according to his mercy he saved us...' (Titus 3:3-4). 'But God, who is rich in mercy, because of his great love with which he loved us, even when we were dead in trespasses, made us alive together with Christ... For by grace you have been saved through faith, and that not of yourselves; it is the gift of God, not of works, lest anyone should boast. For we are his workmanship...' (Eph. 2:4-5,8-10). Believers are not chosen on the basis of any merit or desert. We are more unworthy to be the bride of Christ than Gomer was to be the bride of Hosea!

Believers are drawn 'with the cords of a man, with bands of love' (11:4, alternative reading; cf. Jer. 31:3). What a lovely description this is of the Saviour as 'a perfect man' (Eph. 4:13) drawing his people to himself by cords of Calvary love! (John 12:32).

2. Mercy, not sacrifice

After his conversion Matthew Levi, the tax collector, called together his friends for a celebration meal. Jesus was the honoured guest (Luke 5:29). The Pharisees objected to the company Jesus was keeping in eating with tax collectors and sinners. They spoke to his disciples challenging the Lord's behaviour (Matt. 9:11-13). Overhearing their criticism Jesus responded, 'Those who are well have no need of a physician, but those who are sick. But go and learn what this means: "I desire mercy and not sacri-fice." For I did not come to call the righteous, but sinners, to repentance' (Matt. 9:12-13; cf. Hosea 6:6). The Pharisees showed contempt towards tax collectors and sinners. They expelled them and made no attempt to reach or help them. Our Lord says in effect that they must learn the lesson from Hosea. By quoting from this prophet, the Lord is doing more than applying a suitable text of Scripture; he is raising before them the whole message of Hosea. Hosea's relationship with his wife expresses the covenant love and relationship of God with Israel — even wayward and faithless Israel.

Hosea addressed Israelites of his day who were openly godless and immoral:

> There is no truth or mercy
> Or knowledge of God in the land.
> By swearing and lying,
> Killing and stealing and committing adultery,
> They break all restraint,
> With bloodshed after bloodshed
>
> (4:1-2).

By bringing sacrifices to God in this kind of context, the Israelites were showing great contempt. Sacrifices are not unimportant, but they must be accompanied by a genuine effort among the people to learn from the Lord. Bringing offerings to God is of no value unless there is a real attempt to imitate God's behaviour and attitude. If the Pharisees who confronted the Lord Jesus were only to learn this great lesson then they would understand what he was doing in spending time with tax collectors and sinners.

The Lord Jesus refers again to this verse in Hosea when challenged about his disciples plucking ears of corn on the Sabbath (Matt. 12:7). Again he shows that the Pharisees had no pity. They did not love kindness. They were critical and condemning, with no compassion or tenderness towards others.

3. Leadership of God's people

The religious and political leadership of Israel come under particular criticism in the book of Hosea. The people have been led astray by their prophets (4:5), their priests (4:6; 5:1; 6:9; 10:5) and their civil rulers (5:1,10; 7:3-7; 9:15). Israel's leaders turn to other nations for political solutions rather than relying upon the living God who has constantly protected and preserved his people (5:13; 7:8-11; 8:9).

Though the Israelites possessed the law of God (8:12), they were generally ignorant of its content and application, because of the failure of their religious leaders (4:6). In our own day there have never been so many Bibles owned by the people and yet such darkness as to the contents of God's Word. The vast majority of those appointed as Christian teachers and preachers are teaching anything but the message of the Word of God. Even within the believing community there is a dearth of Bible teaching. Emphasis is often upon 'experience' and there is little evidence of that diligence in study that produces 'a worker who does not need to be ashamed, rightly dividing the word of truth' (2 Tim. 2:15). Relatively few are likely to exhaust themselves by their labour in the word and doctrine (1 Tim. 5:17).

Leadership in the church of Christ is a most serious responsibility. Each leader, as a watcher of souls, 'must give account' to God (Heb. 13:17). The great task of leadership is to equip 'the saints for the work of ministry, for the edifying of the body of Christ' (Eph. 4:12). Together with this ongoing task is the assignment to find other potential leaders and teachers (2 Tim. 2:2). Without this careful and thorough teaching from God's Word the people will be 'tossed to and fro and carried about with every wind of doctrine' (Eph. 4:14) — a situation which is all too prevalent today.

4. Restoring the backslider

Jehovah had taken Israel as his wife — cared for her, protected her, provided for her. He had treated her kindly and done so over many years. But Israel played fast and loose. She chased after other lovers, other gods. Becoming thoroughly involved with these idols, the Lord complains of Israel, 'Then she forgot me' (2:13; cf. Rev. 2:4).

There are many beautiful illustrations of the Lord's pleading with backsliders, and healing and restoring them. A century after Hosea, the prophet Jeremiah would plead: '"Return, O backsliding children," says the LORD; "for I am married to you"' (Jer. 3:14). 'Return, you backsliding children, and I will heal your backslidings' (Jer. 3:22).

In the New Testament the same tenderness is seen in the appeals that are made to those who have known the Lord and turned away from him. The parable of the lost son is arguably the finest revelation of the Lord's heart towards a returning backslider: 'Bring out the best robe and put it on him, and put a ring on his hand and sandals on his feet. And bring the fatted calf here and kill it, and let us eat and be merry; for this my son was dead and is alive again; he was lost and is found' (Luke 15:22-24). This younger son had to go away into 'a far country' and experience deprivations and want before he 'came to himself'. In similar fashion in Hosea's day the Israelites were taken to Assyria and there humbled until the time appointed for their restoration and recovery.

Restoration of backsliders is a constantly recurring theme in Scripture. There is mercy for all who will return to the Lord and pardon for all who come back to God (Isa. 55:7). In the New Testament church spiritually mature believers are called upon to care for those who fall. Paul charges the Galatians: 'If a man is overtaken in any trespass, you who are spiritual restore such a person in a spirit of gentleness, considering yourself lest you also be tempted' (Gal. 6:1).

Conclusion

The book of Hosea is full of deep feeling. There is deep passion from God towards his people. On the one hand, there is the strongest expression of his righteous anger at their sin; they have turned from the true and living God to the worship of dead idols; with paganism has also come wide-spread immorality and corruption. On the other hand, by sharp contrast, there is the tenderest passionate expression of God's yearning love over his sinful people; if they will but return to him they will receive mercy and kindness. The Lord can be like a lion, tearing the wicked and ungodly and taking them away (5:14); or he can be like gentle rain, bringing life and health to those who return to him (6:3).

The Lord has 'no pleasure in the death of the wicked, but that the wicked turn from his way and live' (Ezek. 33:11). He will not obliterate the rebellious tribes of the children of Israel. He will humble them by long and severe discipline, to bring them to a consciousness of their guilt. He will lead them to repentance so that he might have mercy upon them. He will save them from everlasting destruction.

It is with these goals in mind that the book of Hosea contains threaten-ings and punishments interwoven with gracious promises. The Lord not only presents a general hope of better days, he predicts the time of restor-ation and everlasting peace. By his almighty power and his grace the Lord will ultimately deliver his people from death and from hell.

Joel

('Jehovah is God')

Author: Joel

Key thought: 'The Day of the Lord'

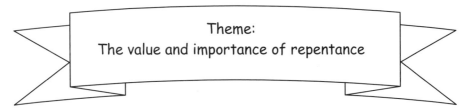

Theme:
The value and importance of repentance

'For the day of the LORD is
great and very terrible:
Who can endure it?'

Joel 2:11

Summary

Joel

A devastating infestation of locusts has hit the southern kingdom of Judah and stripped the fields bare. A drought has left the earth parched. The prophet Joel uses these events to declare a message from God: the people of Judah will be judged and punished for their sins; their only recourse is to turn in true heart repentance to the Lord; God will ultimately bring all nations to judgement and only those among the nations who have called 'on the name of the LORD shall be saved' (2:32).

It is a timeless message, forth-telling and foretelling 'the day of the LORD':

Alas for the day!
For the day of the LORD is at hand;
It shall come as destruction from the Almighty

(1:15).

Blow the trumpet in Zion,
And sound an alarm in my holy mountain!
Let all the inhabitants of the land tremble;
For the day of the LORD is coming,
For it is at hand:
A day of darkness and gloominess,
A day of clouds and thick darkness,
Like the morning clouds spread over the mountains

(2:1-2).

The LORD gives voice before his army,
For his camp is very great;
For strong is the one who executes his word.
For the day of the LORD is great and very terrible;
Who can endure it?

(2:11).

The sun shall be turned into darkness,
And the moon into blood,
Before the coming of the great and terrible day of the LORD

(2:31).

Multitudes, multitudes in the valley of decision!
For the day of the LORD is near in the valley of decision

(3:14).

The prophecy of Joel reveals that all history culminates in Christ and his church.

Author

Apart from his identifying himself as 'Joel the son of Pethuel' (1:1), no other information is given about the author of this little book. The name *yo'el* means 'Jehovah is God', and Pethuel means 'the open-heartedness, or sincerity, of God'. Twelve other men in the Old Testament bear the name 'Joel'. No satisfactory link has been made between any one of those and the prophet and author of this book. The frequent references to Zion and the house of the Lord may indicate that he lived in or near Jerusalem, but that is by no means certain. Nor can it be assumed that he was a priest as well as a prophet simply because he mentions the priesthood (1:13; 2:17). What is sure is that 'Joel was a clear, concise, and uncompromising preacher of repentance.'[1]

Historical setting

Unlike Isaiah, Hosea, Amos and others, Joel does not locate his prophecy in a distinct period in Judah's history. Opinions vary, but the contents would fit comfortably during the early days of the reign of King Joash.[2] The enemies of Judah at that time were the Phoenicians (Tyre and Sidon), the Philistines (3:4), the Egyptians and the Edomites (3:19). There is no reference to Assyria or Babylon, which suggests an earlier date than the mid-700s B.C. Nor is there any mention of a king, but rather of elders and priests (1:14; 2:16; 1:9,13; 2:17). This would accord with the early reign of

Joash since he succeeded to the throne at the tender age of seven (2 Kings
11:21) and was greatly influenced by godly Jehoiada, the high priest. Jehoiada's wife had taken him into their home and secretly raised him when
he was rescued as a one-year-old from the clutches of Queen Athaliah
(2 Chr. 22:11-12). This would mean that Joel exercised his prophetic ministry to the southern kingdom of Judah around 820 B.C., after the prophet
Obadiah; there may even have been an overlap in their ministries. At the
same time the prophet Elisha would have been engaged in his long ministry to the northern kingdom of Israel.

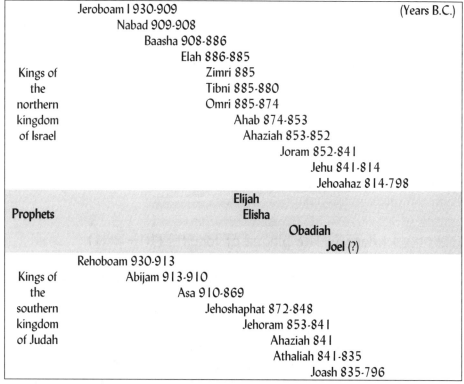

Joel in relation to the kings and prophets of the divided kingdom

The prophet Amos, who followed some fifty years later, was evidently
familiar with the prophecy of Joel and borrowed from his writings when he
himself prophesied against the northern kingdom of the ten tribes (3:16; cf.
Amos 1:2).

John Calvin was of the opinion that it is better to leave the time in
which Joel prophesied undecided since it is of no great importance.[3] The
care with which the Holy Spirit has specified the dates of other prophetic

books would seem to confirm this view; the dating of Joel adds nothing to the understanding or the interpretation of the book.

Outline

There are three periods of history in mind throughout this book: the present, the near future and a time to come. Each period is associated with the Day of the Lord. In the plague of locusts and the devastating drought the Day of the Lord has come (1:15-20); a further Day of the Lord is coming (2:1-11); whereas the great and terrible Day of the Lord is the finale, the end of this present world (2:31). The Day of the Lord is immediate, imminent and ultimate; it is now, it is close, it will be in the end; and for each of these periods described by Joel there is an associated call to repentance (1:13-14; 2:12-13; 2:32). 'He saw the near things, the sin of his people, and the locust plague; the imminent things, the coming of judgement, and the restoration following it; the far things, the day of the Spirit in which we are living, and the things beyond.'[4]

At the same time the book of Joel may be regarded as centring around three subjects: plague, penitence and promise.[5]

Part I: The plague of locusts (1:1 - 2:11)

A devastating plague of locusts has swept through the land — a phenomenon not uncommon in Israel, but the ferocity of this attack makes it unique. Drunkards have no wine, the priests have no offerings and the people have no bread. The people do not recognize that these signs indicate that the nation is under the judgement of God (Deut. 28:15,38; 1 Kings 8:37,39-40). The priests are called upon to grieve before God. They are to urge the people to fast and to gather in the temple for a national assembly in order to 'cry out to the LORD' (1:14). A trumpet is to be blown to draw the attention of the nation to the impending Day of the Lord. This invasion of locusts will be eclipsed by an even more devastating invasion of soldiers. It will be a day of darkness and gloom in which the enemy will enter the city. This vast army will sweep through the land and God will be its leader (2:11).[6]

Part II: Repentance and restoration (2:12-27)

The revelation of impending judgement is not intended to terrify the people, but to bring them back to God. The people should respond to the news by turning in heartfelt sorrow and repentance to the Lord. He will then respond to their godly grief by bringing deliverance.

> 'Now, therefore,' says the LORD,
> 'Turn to me with all your heart,
> With fasting, with weeping, and with mourning.'
> So rend your heart, and not your garments;
> Return to the LORD your God,
> For he is gracious and merciful,
> Slow to anger, and of great kindness;
> And he relents from doing harm
>
> (2:12-13).

A word in the original Hebrew is missing from this translation. It is the small word 'also' or 'even' —'Therefore also now...' (AV), 'And even now...' (Calvin) — for the judgement of God seems disastrous, catastrophic and complete, as though there could be no remedy. Yet even now, even at this disastrous stage when the situation seems hopeless, when the locusts and the drought have devastated the land, when it seems that there can be no future, that the destruction has gone too far and that nothing can reverse the process — even now God can act wondrously.

> Who knows if he will turn and relent,
> And leave a blessing behind him —
> A grain offering and a drink offering
> For the LORD your God?
>
> (2:14).

The punishment of God will not destroy them. The Lord will change the situation for good. There will be food again. There will be grain and drink offerings for the worship of the Lord.

> So I will restore to you the years that the swarming locust has eaten,
> The crawling locust,
> The consuming locust,
> And the chewing locust,

My great army which I sent among you.
You shall eat in plenty and be satisfied,
And praise the name of the LORD your God,
Who has dealt wondrously with you;
And my people shall never be put to shame

(2:25-26).

Part III: Judgement in the valley of decision
(2:28 – 3:21)

The prophet turns from consideration of the present and the immediate future to a time yet to be: 'And it shall come to pass afterwards…' (2:28). The outpouring of the Spirit (2:28) forms a parallel to the outpouring of rain (2:23); the destruction of the hostile nations (3:1-21) corresponds to the destruction of the locusts (1:4). A time will come when all God's people will receive the Holy Spirit and the gospel of God's grace will be made known to all: 'Whoever calls on the name of the LORD shall be saved' (2:32).

The people of Judah will be exiled, 'scattered among the nations', but the Lord will gather them together and restore them. 'The Prophet confirms in these words what he had before taught respecting the restoration … for it was a thing difficult to be believed: when the body of the people was so mutilated, when their name was obliterated, when all power was abolished, when the worship of God also, together with the temple, was subverted, when there was no more any form of a kingdom, or even of any civil government — who could have thought that God had any concern for a people in such a wretched condition? It is then no wonder that the Prophet speaks so much at large of the restoration … he did so, that he might more fully confirm what would have otherwise been incredible.'[7]

When the Day of the Lord comes there will be deliverance in Zion, but only for those who call upon the name of the Lord. Then, too, all the nations who have shown hostility towards God's people will be judged in the valley of decision. The curse of desolation will fall upon Egypt and Edom, whose hostility towards Judah is an example of persistent world hostility towards God's people.

Joel ends his prophecy on a glorious note of blissful promise of a time to come: 'For the LORD dwells in Zion' (3:21).

Christ and his church

Joel's prophecies reach their highest peak when declaring the outpouring of the Holy Spirit upon all flesh. Although the extent of the blessing, and the predominantly spiritual nature of that blessing, are clearly perceived and communicated by Joel, there is, however, no 'concentration of the work of salvation in one human mediator'.[8] Direct and particular prophecies about Messiah are not to be found in these pages. The connection between the outpouring of the Spirit and the mediatorial work of Christ could not have been envisaged until its full glory was revealed at Calvary and at Pentecost (John 7:39).

1. Judgement on the church

The threat of judgement is a clear indication that God will not ignore sin among his own chosen people. The fundamental truth is that, just as 'Wherever the carcass is, there the eagles will be gathered together' (Matt. 24:28), so 'Where corruption manifests itself in the Church of the Lord, there will punishment come.'[9] The apostle Peter declares, 'The time has come for judgement to begin at the house of God; and if it begins with us first, what will be the end of those who do not obey the gospel of God?' (1 Peter 4:17). Both the wise man in Proverbs and the writer to the Hebrews remind Christians that God disciplines those he loves (Prov. 3:11-12; Heb. 12:5-6) and, though it produces beneficial results, it is not a pleasant experience (Heb. 12:11).

2. New covenant blessing

Joel prophesied of a time coming when the Lord would pour out his Spirit on all flesh (2:28-32). The New Testament reveals the fulfilment of this glorious promise. On the Day of Pentecost, following the death, resurrection and ascension of the Lord Jesus Christ, strange phenomena were witnessed in Jerusalem (Acts 2:1-13). There was the sound of a rushing mighty wind, and shortly afterwards a number of people from Galilee began speaking in a variety of different languages which they had never learned. When folk in the huge crowd that gathered made fun of the preachers, and accused them of being under the influence of strong drink, the apostle Peter took the opportunity to preach:

Men of Judea and all who dwell in Jerusalem, let this be known to you, and heed my words. For these are not drunk, as you suppose, since it is only the third hour of the day. But this is what was spoken by the prophet Joel:

'And it shall come to pass in the last days, says God,
That I will pour out of my Spirit on all flesh;
Your sons and your daughters shall prophesy…
I will pour out my Spirit in those days;
And they shall prophesy'

(Acts 2:14-18).

So there is no doubt as to the fulfilment of this prophecy of Joel. The Lord has made it clear.

Nevertheless something else is needed in order to clarify the meaning of the words 'on *all flesh*'. The prophecy of Joel might be interpreted as a blessing limited to Judah alone, but the Lord is further to reveal that he means to pour out his Spirit on *every believing* man, woman and child throughout the world. Some weeks after that remarkable Pentecost the apostle Peter was sent to the home of a Roman centurion named Cornelius. Peter preached the gospel to the gathered company. Then, 'While Peter was still speaking these words, the Holy Spirit fell upon all those who heard the word. And those of the circumcision who believed were astonished, as many as came with Peter, because the gift of the Holy Spirit had been poured out on the Gentiles also. For they heard them speak with tongues and magnify God' (Acts 10:44-46). Believing Gentiles are also to be included in the fulfilment of the prophecy.

The result of the Spirit's coming in those days was the widespread exercise of the gift of prophecy. This does not mean that every individual believer would prophesy. That has never been the case, not even in New Testament days (Rom. 12:6; 1 Cor. 12:29). Under the Old Covenant the Spirit of God was particularly revealed as the Spirit 'that empowers and enables prophecy';[10] while all true believers were born of the Spirit, repented of their sins and believed in the promises of God, only a few — mainly the prophets and a few kings and priests — were filled with the Spirit of God.

Back in the early days of the Exodus, there were seventy elders appointed to assist Moses; they had the blessing of the Spirit: 'Then the LORD came down in the cloud, and spoke to [Moses], and took of the Spirit that was upon him, and placed the same upon the seventy elders; and it happened, when the Spirit rested upon them, that they prophesied, although they never did so again' (Num. 11:25).

Two of the selected men were not assembled with the rest when the Spirit came upon them. These two, Eldad and Medad, received the Spirit and prophesied while still in the camp. Joshua advised Moses to forbid them prophesying, to which Moses replied: 'Are you zealous for my sake? Oh, that all the LORD's people were prophets and that the LORD would put his Spirit upon them!' (Num. 11:29). This desire of Moses was at the same time a prophecy.[11] It became a declared prophecy in the words of Joel 2:28: 'I will pour out my Spirit on all flesh; your sons and your daughters shall prophesy...'

The complete fulfilment of Joel's prophecy could not take place until the coming of the Messiah. The promised Saviour must come into the world, suffer, die, rise from the dead and ascend to the right hand of the Father in heaven. The sending of the Spirit of God was dependent upon the completion of the whole work of Christ on earth in his humanity. This is made clear in the record of the apostle John: 'On the last day, that great day of the feast [i.e. the Feast of Tabernacles], Jesus stood and cried out, saying, "If anyone thirsts, let him come to me and drink. He who believes in me, as the Scripture has said, out of his heart will flow rivers of living water." But this he spoke concerning the Spirit, whom those believing in him would receive; for the Holy Spirit was not yet given, because Jesus was not yet glorified' (John 7:37-39).

The gift of the Holy Spirit is no longer to be confined to a few chosen men — prophets, kings priests and judges — but will extend to 'all flesh', without distinction of gender, age or social standing. The apostle Paul may have had this prophecy in mind when he wrote, 'There is neither Jew nor Greek, there is neither slave nor free, there is neither male nor female; for you are all one in Christ Jesus' (Gal. 3:28), which he links with the promise of blessing to Abraham: '... in you all the families of the earth shall be blessed' (Gen. 12:3). For, writes Paul, 'If you are Christ's, then you are Abraham's seed, and heirs according to the promise' (Gal. 3:29).

Application

1. The Day of the Lord

Five times Joel speaks of the coming of the Day of the Lord. In the Old Testament the phrase occurs over thirty times (e.g. Isa. 2:12; 13:6,9; Amos 5:18; Ezek. 30:3; Zeph. 1:7,14). The description of this day usually involves judgement and war against sinners — a necessary purge before righteousness can reign.

In the New Testament the Day of the Lord is still anticipated: 'But the day of the Lord will come as a thief in the night, in which the heavens will pass away with a great noise, and the elements will melt with fervent heat; both the earth and the works that are in it will be burned up. Therefore, since all these things will be dissolved, what manner of persons ought you to be in holy conduct and godliness, looking for and hastening the coming of the day of God...?' (2 Peter 3:10-12).[12]

2. A universal gospel

'And it shall come to pass that whoever calls on the name of the LORD shall be saved' (Joel 2:32). While in Joel the prophecy is addressed solely to Israel, and in particular to the southern kingdom of Judah, the apostle Paul argues that this promise extends way beyond the bounds of Judah and Israel: 'For there is no distinction between Jew and Greek, for the same Lord over all is rich to all who call upon him. For "whoever calls upon the name of the LORD shall be saved"' (Rom. 10:12-13). All who are saved form the true Israel of God, that is, the spiritual Israel. The nation of Israel was never composed entirely of believing people: 'For they are not all Israel who are of Israel' (Rom. 9:6). Conversely, those Gentiles who believe in the Lord are reckoned as true Israelites. The true, or spiritual, Israel is composed, therefore, of believing Jews together with believing Gentiles.

Our task is to follow the example of the prophet Joel and urge men, women and children to turn to God in true repentance of heart so that they may be saved from the judgement of the coming day of God.

3. Repentance and its fruit

The call to the nation to return to the Lord in true heart repentance is based upon the outstanding grace and mercy of the living God. In order to benefit from these wonderful characteristics the people must be genuine and sincere in heart and mind:

'Now, therefore,' says the LORD,
'Turn to me with all your heart,
With fasting, with weeping, and with mourning.'
So rend your heart, and not your garments;
Return to the LORD your God,
For he is gracious and merciful,
Slow to anger, and of great kindness;
and he relents from doing harm

(2:12-13).

The people are instructed how to show their repentance in a tangible form: they are to gather together before God as a priority over every other duty, responsibility or interest (2:15-16). The priests are to plead for the people with tears and pray on the basis of the covenant relationship: 'Spare your people, O LORD, and do not give your heritage to reproach' (2:17).

Years later the apostle Paul distinguished between 'godly sorrow' and 'the sorrow of the world' (2 Cor. 7:10). The sorrow of the world is remorse or regret over an action or a word because of the consequences which have resulted. A thief, when apprehended by the police, may be sorry he has stolen another person's property. There may even be a genuine sense of guilt because of the pain and dishonour he has brought upon his family. He may experience heartfelt shame. Such sorrow, however, though it may be real, leads to death: it has no spiritual benefit; it does not cause the thief to go to God to confess his sins and resolve before God never to steal again. Judas displayed the sorrow of the world when he went out and hung himself after betraying the Lord Jesus (Matt. 27:5). Godly sorrow is the grief of heart that brings a sinner to God in confession and with a genuine commitment to forsake sin: 'He who covers his sins will not prosper, but whoever confesses and forsakes them will have mercy' (Prov. 28:13; cf. Ps. 51:1-4; 32:3-5).

John the Baptist challenged Pharisees, Sadducees, tax collectors and soldiers who came to him for baptism to demonstrate the reality of their repentance in positive action and distinct change of behaviour (Matt. 3:7-8; Luke 3:11-14).

Conclusion

World history is moving to a climax — 'the great and terrible day of the
LORD' (2:31). This will be a time of fearful judgement upon the people and
the nations who have rebelled against God. A strong thread of disasters
runs throughout this little book of Joel — a plague of locusts, a severe
famine, raging fires, invading enemies, strange, uncanny phenomena in the
heavens and on the earth. Nevertheless throughout all the catastrophes
and calamities there is the promise of hope for those who will repent and
love and trust the Lord.

Joel visualized the unfolding of world history. As he spoke he was witnessing manifestations of sin and judgement and he proclaimed the necessity of repentance. The Day of the Lord had arrived. He also foresaw another Day of the Lord in the near future, a day of even more severe
judgement from God. He called upon the people to return to the Lord with
wholehearted repentance so that that judgement might be averted. Still
further down the ages he foresaw yet another Day of the Lord, great and
terrible. This would be the end times, the consummation, the close of this
present world. This finale would be preceded by another day when God
would pour out his Spirit upon every believer, young and old, male and
female, servant and master. To them would be entrusted the gospel message for the world: 'Whoever calls on the name of the LORD shall be saved'
(2:32).

Judgement and punishment are certain, but those who repent and turn
to the Lord will be able to rely upon his promises and to look forward to
abiding fellowship with God. This is the only way to prepare for 'the coming of the great and terrible Day of the Lord' (2:31).

Amos

('burden-bearer')

Author: Amos

Key thought: 'Punishment'

> **Theme:**
> National sin results in national punishment

'You only have I known of all the
    families of the earth;
Therefore I will punish you for all
    your iniquities.'

Amos 3:2

Summary

Amos

Righteousness and justice are the foundation of your throne;
Mercy and truth go before your face.
Blessed are the people who know the joyful sound!
They walk, O LORD, in the light of your countenance

(Ps. 89:14-15).

The Lord is a righteous King over all the earth. Because he is righteous, his rule over the earth is a righteous, or just, rule. He punishes evil in individuals and in nations. Individual sins receive individual punishment, especially in the final judgement: 'For we must all appear before the judgement seat of Christ, that each one may receive the things done in the body, according to what he has done, whether good or bad' (2 Cor. 5:10). National sins, by contrast, are dealt with distinctly in this life. Under God's government, national sins receive national punishment. 'Righteousness exalts a nation, but sin is a reproach to any people' (Prov. 14:34).

The name 'Amos' means 'burden-bearer'. This prophet's burden concerns punishment. He is the messenger delivering serious and sober words for a self-indulgent and godless age. The nations who are Israel's close neighbours are to be punished for their gross sins. But it is Israel, the people peculiarly owned and blessed by the living God, who face the greatest censure. They should know better. They 'are Israelites, to whom pertain the adoption, the glory, the covenants, the giving of the law, the service of God, and the promises; of whom are the fathers…' (Rom. 9:4-5). Because Israel has sinned so seriously in religion and morality, towards God and towards humanity, they will receive the most severe punishment: 'You only have I known of all the families of the earth; therefore I will punish you for all your iniquities' (3:2). They were idolaters, immoral, self-indulgent and complacent. Amos denounces the Israelites and warns of God's impending judgement.

Though the book of Amos is so full of judgement and rebuke, there are nevertheless wonderful displays of God's mercy and grace. In the midst of the judgements there are calls to repentance (5:4,6,14-15). A further display of outstanding grace and mercy comes at the conclusion of the whole prophecy; in spite of the awful sinfulness and failure of the Israelites God will not forget his ancient promises. He will respect his covenants. A remnant of the Israelites will be preserved. Consequently the book of Amos contains excellent examples of the goodness of God to an unworthy people and a wretched nation.

Author

The prophet Amos wrote the whole book bearing his name. He originated from Tekoa (1:1), which lay twelve miles south of Jerusalem, six miles south of Bethlehem, overlooking the Dead Sea. He therefore belonged to Judah, the southern kingdom of the divided nation. Tekoa was a rural area and may not have had any permanent housing. The shepherds and their families would have lived in a small cluster of tents. Appropriately, the name 'Tekoa' is thought to mean 'the pitching of tents'. Amos was what we might call a 'rough diamond', plain and straightforward in life and speech. He was a man of the land, 'a herdsman and a tender of sycomore fruit' (7:14). The sycomore fruit grew mainly in the plains (1 Kings 10:27). It was a wild fig eaten by only the poorest people. A 'tender' or 'dresser' (AV) means a 'nipper' or 'pincher' of sycomore figs, since the fruit ripened when pierced.

Seemingly without warning or preparation, the Lord appoints Amos to the task of prophesying against Israel, the northern kingdom. Amos testifies: 'I was no prophet, nor was I a son of a prophet' (7:14). Snatched as it were from the duties of a shepherd, he finds himself thrust into the responsibilities of a prophet. The divine call to Amos is irresistible:

A lion has roared!
Who will not fear?
The Lord GOD has spoken!
Who can but prophesy?

(3:8).

Amos is a fitting illustration of the sovereignty and wisdom of God in choosing his servants. God is as well able to call prophets and preachers from the tents of the shepherds as from the courts of the monarch. Amos was a shepherd — not a courtier like Isaiah, nor a priest like Jeremiah, but an ordinary working man. The Lord calls and equips each one for the duties to which he assigns him (Exod. 4:10-12).

Though a humble shepherd, Amos has a keen intellect, a sharp wit and a natural skill in communication. His language is strikingly graphic, drawn from experience; he describes his call to office as like the roaring of a lion in his ears (3:8); he speaks also of the Lord's heart burdened with the sinfulness of Israel as being like a cart weighed down with sheaves (2:13). The narrow escape of a remnant of Israel is compared to a shepherd recovering two legs, or a piece of an ear, from the mouth of a lion (3:12). The lack of hearing the words of the Lord is likened to a natural famine (8:11-12). His origins may be humble, but he shows all the marks of an educated mind. He is well acquainted with the Scriptures. He has a firm grasp of the political scene. He knows the pressures in society. He understands the human heart.

Historical setting

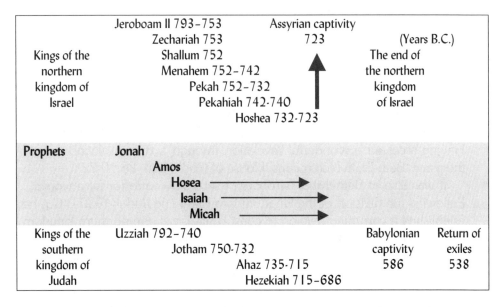

Amos in relation to the kings and prophets of the divided kingdom

The book of Amos is firmly placed in history by its opening words: ' … in the days of Uzziah king of Judah, and in the days of Jeroboam the son of

Joash, king of Israel, two years before the earthquake' (1:1). That earthquake must have been quite exceptional. There seem to be repeated allusions to this great eruption throughout the book (6:11; 8:8; 9:5; 5:8). 250 years later this earthquake is still being mentioned (Zech. 14:5).

Amos prophesied during the long and prosperous reigns of Jeroboam II of Israel (the ten tribes of the northern kingdom) and Uzziah (or Azariah) of Judah (792–740 B.C.). A brief history of King Jeroboam II is recorded in 2 Kings 14:23-29 and that of King Uzziah (Azariah) in 2 Kings 15:1-7 and 2 Chronicles 26.

It was during the reign of Jeroboam II that the territory of Israel was enlarged. A successful war against Syria restored the ancient boundaries of the kingdom. The prophecy given by the prophet Jonah came to fruition (2 Kings 14:25).[1] However, military success and economic prosperity brought their own problems in the form of materialism, greed, immorality and injustice. These were days when there was no significant world empire: neither Egypt, Syria, Assyria nor Babylon was a power of such magnitude as to pose an out-and-out threat to the region.

Although Amos lived in Judah, he was sent to prophesy against Israel (7:15). It would be like a farm labourer from Scotland standing on the steps of St Paul's Cathedral in the city of London and prophesying against England.

Location

Amos prophesied at Bethel, twelve miles north of Jerusalem. It was here, many years before, that Jacob had his remarkable encounter with God. Having received a wonderful revelation through a dream, Jacob named the place 'Beth-El,' which means 'House of God' (Gen. 28:10-22).

It was also at Bethel that Jeroboam I set up a centre for false worship. Following the division of the kingdom into Israel and Judah (930 B.C.), he established a corrupted religion to consolidate Israel, the northern kingdom of the ten tribes. He did not want any of his subjects travelling to Jerusalem in Judah to worship God. He feared that such a pilgrimage would lead to their return to the opposition at Judah, with the result that he could face execution for treason. He therefore made 'two calves of gold' and said to the people of the ten tribes, 'It is too much for you to go up to Jerusalem. Here are your gods, O Israel, which brought you up from the land of Egypt!' and proceeded to offer sacrifices to them (1 Kings 12:28,32).

Outline

Part I: Prophecies against the nations (1:3 – 2:16)

There is a certain uniformity throughout this first section as one nation after another is threatened with destruction, or with defeat and exile. In each case there is the opening phrase: 'For three transgressions and for four, I will not turn away...' This is a figurative way of demonstrating that God does not act immediately in judgement, but that he waits in order to give every nation time for repentance.[2] After this phrase an account is given of their sins, followed by the punishment to be administered by the Lord. Each foreign nation is to be punished for specific international offences. They are guilty of war crimes and the Lord will punish them.

The six nations, neighbours of Israel and Judah, are occupying land given to Israel by God. Beginning with Syria (Damascus) in the north-east, the prophet deals one by one with the enemies of Israel — Philistia (Gaza), Phoenicia (Tyre), Edom, Ammon and Moab. The first three nations are not blood-relatives of Israel, whereas the last three are.[3]

Syria is to be punished for her savage cruelty; Philistia for her slave trade; Phoenicia for her slave trade and treaty-breaking; Edom for revenge without mercy; Ammon for sadism and mad aggression; and Moab for violent and vindictive hatred. Sweeping round Israel in an ever-decreasing spiral, Amos eventually arrives on the doorstep and pronounces judgement upon Judah for idolatry and contempt for the commandments of God. It is only Judah whose sins are directly connected with her relationship to the living God. 'The arrangement of the oracles is itself clever and subversive; oracles that construct a circle of despised enemy peoples turn out to be a trap sprung on an unsuspecting Israel.'[4] What a way to draw the attention of his hearers, the Israelites! No doubt they were delighted by the announcement of God's displeasure towards the nations. But the Lord had things to say against Israel. With crushing vigour Amos delivers the first round of scathing judgements. Israel's behaviour is shameful: her practices are corrupt (2:6-8); her justice is perverted by bribery; the poor are sold into slavery for debts incurred at the hands of greedy landlords; the people are so greedy and land-grabbing that 'They would even steal the dust off the head of the poor man who has put on the traditional sack-cloth and ashes to bemoan his fate';[5] they participate in ceremonial prostitution; they violate God's law and cause unnecessary suffering (2:8; cf. Deut. 24:12-13); there is alcohol abuse among women (4:1).

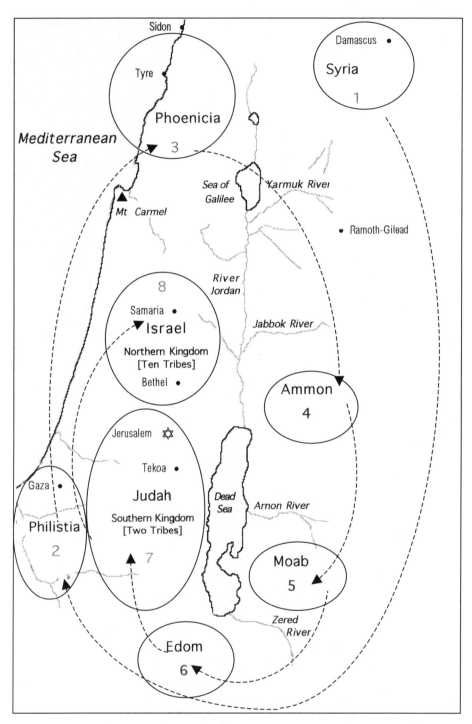

The prophecies of Amos

While it is clear that the judgement of God is consistent — judging the nations and giving to each according to its deeds — he does, however, bring a more severe judgement against Israel as his backslidden people. They have turned away from Jehovah and practise a religion which amalgamates the corrupted worship of Jehovah with the pagan practices of the heathen nations.

Part II: Judgements against Israel (3:1 - 6:14)

Although the northern kingdom of Israel is specifically addressed, its links with the southern kingdom of Judah are not overlooked: 'Hear this word that the LORD has spoken against you, O children of Israel, against the whole family which I brought up from the land of Egypt...' (3:1). Together, the southern kingdom of Judah and the northern kingdom of Israel constitute 'the whole family'.

The four chapters (3-6) divide into three discourses, or sermons, each beginning with the phrase: 'Hear this word...' (3:1; 4:1; 5:1).

In *the first address* (3:1-15) the prophet spells out the nature and ground of the Lord's quarrel with Israel.

In *the second address* (4:1-13) the prophet points out that, despite past punishments for wickedness and godlessness, the people have not turned in repentance and trust to the Lord. He is grieved at their condition and saddened that further severe punishment is necessary.

The 'earthy' language and style of Amos is illustrated in the opening words of the second sermon: 'Hear this word, you cows of Bashan...' (4:1). Bashan was a farming district noted for the health and size of its livestock. Amos addresses the rich women of Israel: 'Hear this, you fat cows...' This would not have been considered abusive or intemperate language in that day. They are 'fat' because they are gorging themselves on more than they need; they are self-indulgent, drinking too much. They greedily hold on to what they have and at the same time are taking more and more from the poor and needy (4:1; cf. Ezek. 34:18,21).

The third address (5:1 – 6:14) is divided into two by the penetrating cry: 'Woe to you who are at ease in Zion; and trust in Mount Samaria...!' (6:1). This cry is a summary of God's case against Israel. The people are selfish, self-indulgent, greedy and unjust. They practise a perverted religion formed of a mishmash of pagan ceremonies and a corrupted form of Jehovah-worship. In spite of all this, the third address includes a tender call to repentance. In the midst of severe judgement the Lord urges the people to return:

Seek me and live…
Seek the LORD and live…
Seek good and not evil, that you may live;
So the LORD God of hosts will be with you,
As you have spoken.
Hate evil, love good;
Establish justice in the gate.
It may be that the LORD God of hosts
Will be gracious to the remnant of Joseph

(5:4,6,14-15).

Part III: Five visions of judgement (7:1 – 9:10)

The third section contains five visions of judgement. The first four visions have similarities and are distinct from the fifth. In the first four the Lord shows Amos events or objects; in the fifth Amos sees the Lord himself standing by the altar. The first two visions, the locusts and the fire (possibly denoting a very severe drought), have a devastating effect upon vegetation and the life-support systems of the community. What the locusts leave, the fire will destroy. The prophet intercedes between the nation and God and the two disasters are withheld.

The third vision, unlike the first two, requires explanation, for the application is not immediately obvious. Amos is shown a plumb-line which, he is informed, represents God's requirements. The Lord is to judge the nation by his own criteria. Buildings that are seriously 'out of plumb' are unsafe and should be demolished. Israel is to be laid waste because she does not measure up to God's standards.

Historical interlude (7:10-17)

During the presentation of the five visions there is a historical interlude. Amaziah, the idolatrous priest of Bethel, reacts badly to the prophecies given by Amos. He contacts King Jeroboam II and charges Amos with conspiracy. Amaziah speaks to Amos in blunt terms:

Go, you seer!
Flee to the land of Judah.
There eat bread,
And there prophesy.
But never again prophesy at Bethel,
For it is the king's sanctuary,
And it is the royal residence

(7:12-13).

Amos responds to the charge of conspiracy by declaring his origins:

I was no prophet,
Nor was I a son of a prophet,
But I was a herdsman
And a tender of sycomore fruit.
Then the LORD took me as I followed the flock,
And the LORD said to me,
'Go, prophesy to my people Israel'

(7:14-15).

By referring in this way to his roots as a shepherd in the fields of Tekoa, Amos is seeking to indicate his lack of political connection with the government of Judah.

After this brief historical interlude the prophet returns to recounting his series of visions. The fourth vision is strongly linked with the preceding one. Here again the vision of a basket of summer fruit needs further amplification and application. The Lord explains that Israel is ripe for judgement, 'as though he said, that the vices of the people had ripened, that vengeance could no longer be deferred'.[6]

Fifth vision: the Lord by the altar (9:1-10)

The fifth and final vision is distinct from the other four. In this vision there is no event or object, but the Lord is seen standing by the altar. There is no discussion between the Lord and the prophet and no action takes place. The prophet simply listens in silence to the words of God. The Lord stands by the altar giving instruction that the temple is to be destroyed so that the whole nation will be buried under the rubble. If anyone escapes the Lord will personally pursue him and slay him, for the Lord God of hosts is ruler and judge of the whole earth. Israel has become like the heathen and does not deserve to be spared.

Yet, despite all the sinfulness and wickedness of Israel, God will not destroy her entirely. Severe judgement is inevitable but all is not lost. Though the Lord has been provoked so incessantly and to such an inordinate extent, he will, nevertheless, restore and bless the nation.

In those days of ease and plenty, with substantial military strength and good economic stability, the Israelites would have found it hard to comprehend the disaster which the prophet predicted. There is an allusion to the captivity and exile that were to come upon Israel, but Amos does not mention Assyria by name (9:8-9). Less than forty years were to pass before the final overthrow of Israel's capital at Samaria and the exile of the Israelites to the land of Assyria (723 B.C.).

Part IV: Restoration and blessing (9:11-15)

Having made allusions to the captivity, the Lord's final recorded words through the prophet Amos are words of hope and consolation. The nation which is to be destroyed because it is 'out of plumb' (7:7-9) is to be rebuilt (9:11). The people who have fallen like overripe fruit (8:1-3) shall be brought back to inhabit a fruitful land (9:13-15).

Christ and his church

Prophecy

1. Rebuilding the tabernacle of David

James, 'the Lord's brother' (Gal. 1:19), one of the 'pillars' of the church at Jerusalem (Gal. 2:9), quotes from Amos in his address to the Jerusalem Council. The council had met to discern whether Gentile believers should be circumcised and commanded to keep the laws of Moses. The apostle Peter sees no reason why the Gentiles should take on Judaism when God is saving them, giving them the Holy Spirit and making no distinction between Jew and Gentile. James supports Peter's reasoning by citing Amos:

> After this I will return
> And will rebuild the tabernacle of David which has fallen down.
> I will rebuild its ruins,
> And I will set it up,
> So that the rest of mankind may seek the LORD,
> Even all the Gentiles who are called by my name,
> Says the LORD who does all these things
>
> (Acts 15:16-17).

The prophecy as found in Amos itself is as follows:

> 'On that day I will raise up
> The tabernacle of David, which has fallen down,
> And repair its damages;
> I will raise up its ruins,
> And rebuild it as in the days of old;
> That they may possess the remnant of Edom,
> And all the Gentiles who are called by my name,'
> Says the LORD who does this thing
>
> (Amos 9:11-13).

The difference in wording may be accounted for by the fact that James is quoting from the Greek Septuagint version. There is, however, no real difference in meaning. Edom and Adam (man) are related words in Hebrew. Edom (cf. Esau — Gen. 36:1,8) means 'red', while Adam (man) means 'red earth'. James gives a remarkable interpretation to the prophecy of Amos. By substituting 'men' or 'mankind' for 'Edom', he demonstrates that it refers to the nations. The rebuilding of the 'tabernacle of David' is to be achieved when God draws to himself 'the Gentiles who are called by my name'; in other words, it will be achieved by the election of grace among the Gentiles. The rebuilding of David's fallen tent, repairing its damages and raising its ruins, does not apply to the physical nation of Israel alone; it includes the ingathering of the nations.[7] 'God had very long ago ... before-ordained the acceptance of the Gentiles, and had included them in the great plan of Israel, the building-plan of His temple upon earth! Believers of all nations were to be partakers in the sanctuary of Israel, which, after judgement, was again to be restored!

This view is laid open by James to the church at a time when the old temple was not yet destroyed, and when the preaching of the name of God to all nations had only just begun.'[8] James' interpretation of the prophecy is inspired by the Holy Spirit (otherwise it would not have appeared in the Holy Scriptures in this form). This undisputed reference to the Old Testament concludes the whole debate, pointing out that God had always intended that the elect from the Gentile nations should be saved.

Interestingly, James uses 'prophets' in the plural, for he says, 'And with this the words of the *prophets* agree...' (Acts 15:15, emphasis added). He thereby establishes, in the presence of the then leaders of the universal church, 'the key to the understanding of the prophets, taking one passage from Amos as the representative of all that class of prophecy, and spiritualizing it'.[9] Consequently, we may confidently say this is the way in which the Holy Spirit would have us interpret the Old Testament prophecies — as spiritually fulfilled in Christ and his church!

2. The remnant of Israel

Closely allied to the prophecy of the church of Christ as a community of restored believing Israelites, together with the ingathered believing Gentiles, is the biblical theme of the righteous remnant. 750 years before the birth of the Lord Jesus Christ Amos had prophesied the downfall of Israel, the northern kingdom of the ten tribes, but he had also predicted the delivery for 'the remnant of Joseph' (5:15).

Throughout history the Lord has preserved a 'remnant'. At the time of the great flood the remnant was only eight persons (Gen. 7:13). In the days of Elijah, contrary to that prophet's assessment of the situation, the Lord revealed that he had 'reserved seven thousand in Israel, all whose knees have not bowed to Baal, and every mouth that has not kissed him' (1 Kings 19:18; cf. Rom. 11:1-4). Amos graphically portrays the preservation of a remnant as a shepherd taking 'two legs or a piece of an ear' from the mouth of a lion (3:12). Isaiah prophesies the return of 'the remnant of Israel' from captivity, adding that they 'will never again depend on him who defeated them, but will depend on the LORD, the Holy One of Israel, in truth' (Isa. 10:20; cf. vv. 21-23). Micah will follow this by adding singular words of consolation and hope:

I will surely assemble all of you, O Jacob,
I will surely gather the remnant of Israel;
I will put them together like sheep of the fold.
Like a flock in the midst of their pasture;
They shall make a loud noise because of so many men.
The one who breaks open will come up before them;
They will break out,
Pass through the gate,
And go out by it;
Their king will pass before them,
With the LORD at their head

(Micah 2:12-13).

Years later the apostle Paul refers to the preservation of a small company of believers as 'a remnant according to the election of grace' (Rom. 11:5). The promises of God are sure; he will always keep a witness alive. There never will be a generation on the earth without the inclusion of some believers. Not only will there always be believers, but some of those believers will be Jews.

Application

1. Avoid idolatry and false worship

Idolatry is an abiding problem (2:8; 5:26; 8:14; cf. 1 John 5:21). Although some may try to justify the use of images as 'aids to worship', drawings, paintings, stained-glass windows and sculptures can easily assume the role of idols. Furthermore, as in the days of Amos, the worship of God can still become a formality, relying upon externals and 'going through the motions' (4:4-5; 5:21-24). God deserves worship that engages the mind, is wholehearted and involves the commitment of the will. He seeks worship that is not only sincere but also according to revealed truth. God is not only to be worshipped as he requires, but in the way that he requires — 'in spirit and truth' (John 4:24).

2. Promote social justice

'Justice' was bought by the wealthy. The poor and needy were crushed by the powerful (2:6-7; cf. James 2:5-9). The Israelites were guilty of neglecting 'the weightier matters of the law: justice and mercy and faith' (Matt. 23:23). It is our Christian duty, 'as we have opportunity', to 'do good to all, especially to those who are of the household of faith' (Gal. 6:10). Churches that neglect social responsibility and place a one-sided emphasis upon individualistic salvation clearly indicate that they have not yet caught up with Amos — or with Christ![10]

The Lord is a protector of the poor, the widow and the orphan. He defends the downtrodden (Ps. 68:5-6,10). Christians are to share his compassion and practical concern (James 1:27; Acts 2:45; 4:34-35). The godly virtuous woman 'extends her hand to the poor, yes, she reaches out her hands to the needy' (Prov. 31:20).

Social justice is required of the people of God. God speaks out against the abuse of wealth, power and privilege. The book of Amos 'stands as an eloquent witness against those who subordinate human need and dignity to the pursuit of wealth and pleasure'.[11]

3. Shun materialism

Let the wise pray:

> Give me neither poverty nor riches —
> Feed me with the food you prescribe for me;
> Lest I be full and deny you,
> And say, 'Who is the LORD?'
>
> (Prov. 30:8-9).

It is all too easy to forget the Lord in times of prosperity and to become complacent, taking credit to oneself instead of being grateful to the Lord for his provision (Deut. 8:11-18). We are servants entrusted with the Master's goods.

4. Opposition to the Word

Though Amos was a faithful messenger of the Lord. yet he experienced opposition from what we might term 'church and state'. Amaziah represented religious animosity and Jeroboam civil animosity. The Lord Jesus was crucified as a result of hostile opposition from the religious authorities of Judaism and the civil authorities of Rome.

When the apostles Peter and John were brought before the Sanhedrin, the ruling body of the Jews, they were commanded 'not to speak at all nor teach in the name of Jesus' (Acts 4:18). While God requires his people to 'be subject to the governing authorities' (Rom. 13:1) there is a limit to that submission. Submission to governing authorities is no longer appropriate when it involves a compromise of Christian principle or violation of God's Word. Hence the apostles boldly replied to the Sanhedrin: 'Whether it is right in the sight of God to listen to you more than to God, you judge. For we cannot but speak the things which we have seen and heard' (Acts 4:19-20).

The church of Jesus Christ has often been persecuted by devotees of false religion and pseudo- Christianity. They have had no hesitation in misrepresenting the true people of God before the civil authorities as troublemakers stirring up strife.

Conclusion

All nations come under the government of God. He sets the standards. Though he is amazingly patient (2 Peter 3:9), he will nevertheless punish the nations for their inhumanity and corruption. 'If cruelty makes Him angry, it is because His heart is set upon kindness. If oppression stirs up His wrath, it is because His purpose for man is that he should live in peace. If the sorrows inflicted upon man by man call down His judgement, it is because the one great desire of His heart for humanity is that of its well-being and happiness. His government always moves toward the establishment of the best and highest conditions. God is angry with everything that mars; strife, cruelty, war, oppression, because these are against the aim of His government.'[12]

God judges and God punishes the nations. But he is far more severe on those who should know better: 'For everyone to whom much is given, from him much will be required; and to whom much has been committed, of him they will ask the more' (Luke 12:48). This is a principle that applies to nations as well as to individuals. Israel, with all its privileges, is judged with greater strictness. Amos, like most prophets, exposes the sins of the people, warns of the coming judgement, emphasizes the righteousness of God and, in a most remarkable manner, reveals the outstanding mercy of God in a future deliverance.

Obadiah

('servant of God')

Author: Obadiah

Key thought: 'As you have done, it shall be done to you'

Theme: A solemn warning
to the enemies of the people of God

'As you have done, it shall be
done to you;
Your reprisal shall return upon
your own head.'
Obadiah 15

Summary

Obadiah

The book of Obadiah is the shortest book in the Old Testament. Consisting of just twenty-one verses, it deals with the bitter hostility shown by Edom, the descendants of Jacob's twin brother Esau, towards the Israelites, the chosen people of God.

'The first impression made upon the mind by the reading of this very brief prophecy is that it has very little in the nature of a message to this age. We may lay it down however, as a principle always to be observed and acted upon, that those passages or books of Scripture which seem to have least in them, need the most careful attention, and invariably yield the most remarkable results.'[1]

Author

The introductory verses of the prophetic books often contain the name of the prophet's father, information about the time in which the prophet lived, or reference to his home town (cf. Isa. 1:1; Amos 1:1; Micah 1:1). The introductory verses of Obadiah provide no such information. Even the name has been questioned as authentic in so far as 'Obadiah' means 'worshipper of God', or 'servant of God', and may be a pseudonym.[2]

There are thirteen men in the Old Testament who bear the name Obadiah. There have been many attempts to identify Obadiah the prophet with one or other of them. Some scholars, both Jewish and early Christian, identified the prophet with Obadiah the governor of King Ahab's palace (1 Kings 18:3; c. 860 B.C.). That Obadiah held a position of national importance, was a secret worshipper of Jehovah and kept a hundred prophets of the Lord alive and hidden from the persecutions of Queen Jezebel. The prophet Elijah confronted him and, in spite of Obadiah's timidity, he was persuaded to relay a message to King Ahab and set up a large-scale national meeting on Mount Carmel.

In the absence of clear testimony from anywhere in the Scriptures, it is unwise to struggle to identify Obadiah the prophet with any other person of the same name.

Historical setting

Without definite information at the opening of the book, the internal contents of the book itself are the only evidence by which to determine the historical setting. The prophecy of Obadiah is a response to an act of extreme aggression shown by Edom against Israel. This leads to a number of possibilities. Two occasions stand out as the most likely: either following the Babylonian captivity (586 B.C.) or 250 years earlier during, or soon after, the reign of Jehoram, King of Judah (853–841 B.C.). Both fit the contents of the book of Obadiah and there is no means of resolving the issue from Scripture with any degree of certainty.

1. Following the Babylonian captivity (after 586 B.C.)

Most scholars place the prophecy of Obadiah in the sixth century B.C., either close to the exile of Judah by Nebuchadnezzar or later in that century.[3] This means that verses 11-16 are seen as referring to the fall of Jerusalem and the taking away of the people of Judah into the land of Babylon: 'And the LORD God of their fathers sent warnings to them by his messengers, rising up early and sending them, because he had compassion on his people and on his dwelling-place. But they mocked the messengers of God, despised his words, and scoffed at his prophets, until the wrath of the LORD arose against his people, till there was no remedy. Therefore he brought against them the king of the Chaldeans, who killed their young men with the sword in the house of their sanctuary, and had no compassion on young man or virgin, on the aged or the weak; he gave them all into his hand. And all the articles from the house of God, great and small, the treasures of the house of the LORD, and the treasures of the king and of his leaders, all these he took to Babylon. Then they burned the house of God, broke down the wall of Jerusalem, burned all its palaces with fire, and destroyed all its precious possessions. And those who escaped from the sword he carried away to Babylon, where they became servants to him and his sons until the reign of the kingdom of Persia, to fulfil the word of the LORD by the mouth of Jeremiah, until the land had enjoyed her Sabbaths. As long as she lay desolate she kept Sabbath, to fulfil seventy years' (2 Chr. 36:15-21).

From Psalm 137 it is evident that the Edomites encouraged Nebuchadnezzar to annihilate their old enemy:

> By the rivers of Babylon,
> There we sat down, yea, we wept
> When we remembered Zion…
> Remember, O LORD, against the sons of Edom
> The day of Jerusalem,
> Who said, 'Raze it, raze it,
> To its very foundation!'
>
> (Ps. 137:1,7).

This atrocity is also remembered in the book of Lamentations:

> Rejoice and be glad, O daughter of Edom,
> You who dwell in the land of Uz!
> The cup shall also pass over to you
> And you shall become drunk and make yourself naked.
> The punishment of your iniquity is accomplished,
> O daughter of Zion;
> He will no longer send you into captivity.
> He will punish your iniquity,
> O daughter of Edom;
> He will uncover your sins
>
> (Lam. 4:21-22).

2. During, or soon after, the reign of King Jehoram of Judah (853–841 B.C.)

E. J. Young argues that it is not necessary to interpret verses 11-14 as referring to the destruction of Jerusalem.[4] These words may also refer to the events that occurred during the reign of Jehoram (2 Kings 8:16-24; 2 Chr. 21:1-20) when the Philistines and Arabians invaded Judah: 'Moreover the LORD stirred up against Jehoram the spirit of the Philistines and the Arabians who were near the Ethiopians. And they came up into Judah and invaded it, and carried away all the possessions that were found in the king's house, and also his sons and his wives, so that there was not a son left to him except Jehoahaz [i.e. Ahaziah, 22:1], the youngest of his sons' (2 Chr. 21:16-17).

Delitzsch is convinced that even the second part of the prophecy of Obadiah may be explained in the light of the circumstances and consequences of this catastrophe in Jerusalem.[5]

Further indications of the severe hostility from Edom towards Israel at that time are found in the books of Amos and Joel. The ministry of the prophet Amos is located during the reigns of King Uzziah of Judah and King Jeroboam II of Israel (Amos 1:1), which places it somewhere in the period 793–753 B.C. Amos refers to the hostility of Edom towards Israel and the severity of that ill-feeling would dovetail with Obadiah's prophecy:

Thus says the LORD:
'For three transgressions of Gaza, and for four,
I will not turn away its punishment,
Because they took captive the whole captivity
To deliver them up to Edom'

(Amos 1:6, emphasis added).

Egypt shall be a desolation,
And Edom a desolate wilderness,
Because of violence against the people of Judah,
For they have shed innocent blood in their land.
But Judah shall abide for ever,
And Jerusalem from generation to generation.
For I will acquit them of blood-guilt, whom I had not acquitted;
For the LORD dwells in Zion

(Joel 3:19-21).

The Holy Spirit has not seen fit to provide information that will place the prophecy of Obadiah in a distinct point in Israel's history. This in no way reduces the value of this little book. The hostility displayed by the Edomites towards the Israelites spanned over 800 years. 'It must suffice us that we know this prophecy to have been ever received in the canon of the church.'[6] It is God's Word; it is God's judgement on a people hostile and vicious in their attitude and behaviour towards the chosen people of God.

The strong relationship between the prophecy of Obadiah and the words of Jeremiah 49:7-22 suggest that Jeremiah probably depended upon the prophecy of Obadiah, or vice versa.

The history of the people of Edom

As the prophecy of Obadiah is confined to the judgement of God upon Edom it will be helpful to trace the history of this race as a background to considering the contents of this little book.

Trouble began between Edom and Israel before their two tribal leaders were born. Edom was the tribe descending from Esau; Israel was the tribe descending from Jacob. Esau and Jacob struggled in conflict even in their mother's womb:

> Now Isaac pleaded with the LORD for his wife, because she was barren; and the LORD granted his plea, and Rebekah his wife conceived. But the children struggled together within her; and she said, 'If all is well, why am I this way?' So she went to enquire of the LORD. And the LORD said to her:

> > 'Two nations are in your womb,
> > Two peoples shall be separated from your body;
> > One people shall be stronger than the other,
> > And the older shall serve the younger.'

> So when her days were fulfilled for her to give birth, indeed there were twins in her womb. And the first came out red. He was like a hairy garment all over; so they called his name Esau [meaning, 'Hairy']. Afterwards his brother came out, and his hand took hold of Esau's heel; so his name was called Jacob [meaning, 'Supplanter'] (Gen. 25:21-26).

In adulthood Esau was to show that he had not the slightest interest in the promises and purposes of God. Arriving home hungry from a hunting trip, he indicated how little he esteemed his birthright (which included the inheritance of the land):

> Now Jacob cooked a stew; and Esau came in from the field, and he was weary. And Esau said to Jacob, 'Please feed me with that same red stew, for I am weary.' Therefore his name was called Edom [meaning, 'Red', cf. v. 25].

> But Jacob said, 'Sell me your birthright as of this day.'

> And Esau said, 'Look, I am about to die; so what profit shall this birthright be to me?'

Then Jacob said, 'Swear to me as of this day.' So he swore to him, and sold his birthright to Jacob. And Jacob gave Esau bread and stew of lentils; then he ate and drank, arose and went his way. Thus Esau despised his birthright' (Gen. 25:29-34).

Later their father Isaac blessed Jacob, the younger of the twins, as he was leaving for Padan Aram:

May God Almighty bless you,
And make you fruitful and multiply you,
That you may be an assembly of peoples;
And give you the blessing of Abraham,
To you and your descendants with you,
That you may inherit the land
In which you are a stranger,
Which God gave to Abraham

(Gen. 28:3-4).

Over twenty years later, after the return of Jacob from his uncle Laban's home in Padan Aram, Jacob settled in Canaan (Gen. 37:1). Esau moved south beyond the Dead Sea to the land inhabited by the Horites: 'Then Esau took his wives, his sons, his daughters, and all the persons of his household, his cattle and all his animals, and all his goods which he had gained in the land of Canaan, and went to a country away from the presence of his brother Jacob. For their possessions were too great for them to dwell together, and the land where they were strangers could not support them because of their livestock. So Esau dwelt in Mount Seir. Esau is Edom. And this is the genealogy of Esau the father of the Edomites in Mount Seir…' (Gen. 36:6-9: cf. 14:6).

The land of Edom

The territory which Esau and his family took possession of is a tract of land which stretches south from the Dead Sea to the Red Sea (to the port of Ezion Geber on what we now know as the Gulf of Aqabah), and east to the desert. Today this land is part of Jordan, with Saudi Arabia on its eastern border.

Two major north-south routes passed through the region. One was known as 'the King's Highway' and it is to this that Moses refers when seeking safe passage through the land for the Israelites (Num. 20:17). This route passed through a sparse crop-growing area where there was more water but there were also deep east-west canyons to negotiate. The other route, further east, on the edge of the crop-growing belt, had no such steep canyons to cross. These were the two main trade routes on the east of the River Jordan, linking Europe, Asia and Africa. Taxes imposed on caravan traders passing along these roads provided the basis for Edom's economy.[7]

The land of Edom is dominated by a range of mountains known as Mount Seir. Here Esau settled after despising his birthright (which included the inheritance of the land), and parting from his brother Jacob.

Some years later Jacob and his whole family moved from Canaan to Egypt because of the famine.

Edom refuses a safe passage for Israel

Four hundred years pass and Jacob's family grows from seventy members to over a million and a half. They are delivered from persecution in Egypt, led through the wilderness and eventually arrive in Kadesh Barnea, to the south of the promised land and to the west of the land of Edom.

When the Lord tells Moses it is time to enter Canaan, Moses seeks permission to pass through the territory of Edom: 'Moses sent messengers from Kadesh to the king of Edom. "Thus says your brother Israel: 'You know all the hardship that has befallen us, how our fathers went down to Egypt, and we dwelt in Egypt a long time, and the Egyptians afflicted us and our fathers. When we cried out to the LORD, he heard our voice and sent the Angel and brought us up out of Egypt; now here we are in Kadesh, a city on the edge of your border. Please let us pass through your country. We will not pass through fields or vineyards, nor will we drink water from wells; we will go along the King's Highway; we will not turn aside to the right hand or to the left until we have passed through your territory'"' (Num. 20:14-17).

The Edomites refuse to let the Israelites pass through their land and threaten to come against them in war if they set foot in their country. Moses gives a further undertaking that if allowed to pass they will take nothing from the land, and they will pay for any water they drink. But the King of Edom responds by mustering his forces on the border, 'so Israel turned away from him' (Num. 20:21; cf. Judg. 11:17-18).

Some weeks later, when the non-Israelite prophet Balaam is called in by Balak, the King of Moab, to curse Israel, rather than curse he utters four prophetic blessings. The final prophecy includes these words:

> I see him, but not now;
> I behold him, but not near;
> A Star shall come out of Jacob;
> A sceptre shall rise out of Israel,
> And batter the brow of Moab,
> And destroy all the sons of tumult.
> *And Edom shall be a possession;*
> *Seir also, his enemies, shall be a possession,*
> While Israel does valiantly.
> Out of Jacob one shall have dominion,
> and destroy the remains of the city
>
> (Num. 24:17-19, emphasis added).

So, through the mouth of Balaam, the Lord predicts the conquest of Edom by Israel.

A little later, there on the plains of Moab, the Lord commands Israel, 'You shall not abhor an Edomite, for he is your brother' (Deut. 23:7).

Four hundred years later (c. 1000 B.C.) the kings of the united kingdom of Israel and Judah — Saul, David and Solomon — fight against the Edomites and eventually subdue them for a time (1 Sam. 14:47; 2 Sam. 8:13-14; 1 Kings 9:26; 11:14-22). Around 860 B.C., some seventy years or so after the death of Solomon and the division of the kingdom, Edom allies with Moab and Ammon in an invasion of Judah during the reign of Jehoshaphat (2 Chr. 20:1,22-23). A few years later Edom revolts against King Jehoram of Judah and lives in freedom for about forty years (2 Kings 8:20-22; 2 Chr. 21:8-10). King Amaziah of Judah then conquers Edom and inflicts heavy casualties — even after the battle has been won (2 Kings 14:7; 2 Chr. 25:11-12). Sixty years later (c. 725 B.C.) Edom has regained strength and is able to attack Judah and take captives (2 Chr. 28:17).

In 586 B.C., when King Nebuchadnezzar of Babylon attacks and destroys Jerusalem, Edom encourages the annihilation of her old enemy (Ps. 137:1,7). Ezekiel prophesies: 'Thus says the Lord GOD: "Because of what Edom did against the house of Judah by taking vengeance, and has greatly offended by avenging itself on them," therefore thus says the Lord GOD: "I will also stretch out my hand against Edom, cut off man and beast from it, and make it desolate from Teman; Dedan shall fall by the sword. I will lay my vengeance on Edom by the hand of my people Israel, that they may do in Edom according to my anger and according to my fury; and they shall know my vengeance," says the Lord GOD' (Ezek. 25:12-14).

There were 1,300 years of unabated hostility and aggression on the part of Edom towards Israel. The prophecy of Obadiah is the revealing of God's judgement upon the nation which descended from Esau, because of its persistent and unabating hostility and violence against the nation which descended from Jacob.

Outline

Part I: The declaration of God's judgement against Edom (vv. 1-9)

Israel has no greater enemy than the Edomites. The latter are confident in their rocky and supposedly impregnable position, but the Lord will bring them down. Their security will prove to be false. Their hidden treasure will be discovered; their mighty men will be deprived of all strength (Jer. 49:7,14-16).

Part II: The reason for God's judgement against Edom (vv. 10-14)

The Lord rebukes the Edomites for their heartless treatment of their brethren, the Israelites, and points out the error of their ways:

> For your violence against your brother Jacob,
> Shame shall cover you,
> And you shall be cut off for ever

(v. 10).

Part III: The outcome of God's judgement against Edom (vv. 15-16)

In the Day of the Lord Edom, like other nations, will be punished for her sins.

Obadiah's predictions about Edom were fulfilled in every detail. During the Babylonian supremacy Edom was involved in a conspiracy against Nebuchadnezzar (Jer. 27:1-3,8-10; etc.). Five years after the destruction of Jerusalem the people were driven from their rocky homes when Nebuchadnezzar, passing down the valley of Arabah which formed the military road to Egypt, crushed the Edomites.[8] When the Jews were restored to Jerusalem, Cyrus King of Persia conquered Edom and slaughtered thousands of her people. The Edomites lost their existence as a nation in the middle of the second century B.C., when they were crushed by the Maccabees, and their name perished at the capture of Jerusalem by the Romans: 'As you have done, it shall be done to you; your reprisal shall return upon your own head' (v. 15). They will receive the just recompense for their evil committed against Israel.

Part IV: Restoration for Israel and triumph over Edom (vv. 17-21)

In spite of the calamity which has come upon Israel, she will rise again and will return once more to Jerusalem, for:

> On Mount Zion there shall be deliverance,
> And there shall be holiness;
> The house of Jacob shall possess their possessions
>
>   (v. 17).

In other words, the people of Judah will be 'delivered, sanctified, and enriched'.[9]

The Lord intended the Israelites to be holy because they were loved: 'For you are a holy people to the LORD your God; the LORD your God has chosen you to be a people for himself, a special treasure above all the peoples on the face of the earth. The LORD did not set his love on you nor choose you because you were more in number than any other people, for you were the least of all peoples; but because the LORD loves you...' (Deut. 7:6-8).

The Israelites have suffered a severe defeat in Jerusalem. Captives were taken. The Edomites will not just suffer a similar defeat; they will be eliminated, for '... no survivor shall remain of the house of Esau' (v. 18). 'She is the only neighbour of the Israelites who was not given any promise of mercy from God.'[10] This is not because God is unmerciful, but because Edom had persistently refused that mercy.

Israel will not only possess her own land, but also the mountain land of Edom and the lowland of Philistia. Jewish exiles will return home to their enlarged fatherland. For, 'When the children of Israel should return from exile, God would restore to them their ancient country, that they might possess whatever had been promised to their father Abraham.'[11] Deliverance will come to Mount Zion and the kingdom will belong to Jehovah: 'And the kingdom shall be the LORD's' (v. 21).

Christ and his church

The New Testament does not make a single reference to this short prophecy. Nevertheless there are some interesting insights and parallels to be found in its pages.

1. Hostility against Christ

The Lord Jesus Christ is the descendant and the ultimate representative of Judah — he is 'the Lion of the tribe of Judah, the Root of David' (Rev. 5:5). In his days on earth, this descendant of Jacob was confronted by a descendant and representative of Esau. When Jesus was born at Bethlehem there was one man, an Idumean, an Edomite, a descendant of Esau, who was particularly interested in him. This was none other than Herod the Great, to whom the wise men from the east came saying, 'Where is he who has been born King of the Jews? For we have seen his star in the East and have come to worship him' (Matt. 2:2).

Herod the Great was himself 'the King of the Jews', for in 37 B.C. Emperor Augustus of Rome had increased his territory until it included the five districts of Judea, Samaria and Galilee on the west of the River Jordan, and Peraea and Idumaea on the east (what are now known as Israel,

Jordan, Syria and Lebanon). Idumea is the Greek form of the name 'Edom' (cf. Ezek. 35:15; 36:5, AV). Herod the Great was an Idumean — in other words an Edomite, a descendant of Esau. The hostility continued. Herod tried to annihilate the true King of the Jews when he ordered the slaughter of 'all the male children who were in Bethlehem and in all its districts, from two years old and under, according to the time which he had determined from the wise men' (Matt. 2:16).

Herod the Great died in 4 B.C. On his death his kingdom was divided between his three sons, Archelaus, Herod Antipas and Philip. It was Herod Antipas who was challenged by John the Baptist and subsequently executed him. It was to Herod Antipas that the Lord Jesus sent a message: 'Go and tell that fox, "Behold, I cast out demons and perform cures today and tomorrow, and the third day I shall be perfected. Nevertheless I must journey today, tomorrow, and the day following; for it cannot be that a prophet should perish outside of Jerusalem"' (Luke 13:32-33).

A year or two later, following the arrest of the Lord Jesus, Pilate sent him to Herod Antipas: 'Now when Herod saw Jesus, he was exceedingly glad; for he had desired for a long time to see him, because he had heard many things about him, and he hoped to see some miracle done by him. Then he questioned him with many words, but he answered him nothing' (Luke 23:8). The atrocities of Edom continued in the personage of Herod Antipas.

2. Hostility against the church of Christ

Some commentators see in the prophecy of Obadiah only the hostility of a nation towards the Jews and the Lord's preservation of his ancient people. The Thompson Chain Reference Bible declares this as the one spiritual lesson: 'God's special providential care over the Jews, and the certainty of punishment upon those who persecute them.' Robert Lee also writes that Obadiah contains a warning 'against hating and harming the Jews, whose cause God Himself will undertake, and whose enemies He will destroy'.[12]

The message is, however, more profound. Israel, containing as it did, the church of God under the Old Covenant, is pictured as a woman 'being with child' crying out 'in labour and in pain to give birth' (Rev. 12:2). The child in the womb of Israel is the Messiah. Any hostility expressed towards Israel during the Old Testament period was a satanic attempt to thwart the coming of Messiah. The hostility and violence of Edom towards Israel was an expression of the constant hatred between the godless and the godly.

Esau's hatred of Jacob was another expression of Cain's hatred of Abel. 'And why did he murder him? Because his works were evil and his brother's righteous. Do not marvel, my brethren, if the world hates you... Whoever hates his brother is a murderer, and you know that no murderer has eternal life abiding in him' (1 John 3:12-13,15).

During the days of Obadiah Israel looked desolate and forsaken, whereas Edom looked prosperous, secure, arrogant, rich and powerful. The Lord promised restoration to Israel and destruction to Edom. The message of Malachi is even more graphic:

'I have loved you,' says the LORD.
Yet you say, 'In what way have you loved us?'
'Was not Esau Jacob's brother?'
Says the LORD.
'Yet Jacob I have loved;
But Esau I have hated,
And laid waste his mountains and his heritage
For the jackals of the wilderness.'
Even though Edom has said,
'We have been impoverished,
But we will return and build the desolate places,'
Thus says the LORD of hosts:
'They may build, but I will throw down;
They shall be called the Territory of Wickedness,
And the people against whom the LORD will have indignation for ever.
Your eyes shall see,
And you shall say, "The LORD is magnified beyond the border of
    Israel"'

(Mal. 1:2-5).

Application

1. Jehovah is Lord of the whole world

The underlying message of the book of Obadiah is that the God of Israel is not the God of a single nation; he is the Lord of all nations, all peoples and

all places. He is 'Lord of all the earth' (Josh. 3:11). Nations rise up against
the Lord to their own destruction:

> Why do the nations rage,
> And the people plot a vain thing?
> The kings of the earth set themselves,
> And the rulers take counsel together,
> Against the LORD and against his Anointed, saying,
> 'Let us break their bonds in pieces
> And cast away their cords from us.'
> He who sits in the heavens shall laugh;
> The LORD shall hold them in derision.
> Then he shall speak to them in his wrath,
> And distress them in his deep displeasure
>
> (Ps. 2:1-5).

2. Jehovah keeps his covenant with Abraham

Under the Old Covenant Edom's destiny, along with that of all other
nations, depended upon her behaviour and attitude towards Israel as
Abraham's legitimate heir: 'I will bless those who bless you, and I will curse
him who curses you...' (Gen. 12:3).

The promise of blessing passed to Isaac and then to his son Jacob / Israel (Gen. 26:3-4; 28:13-15). Throughout the history of the Israelites God
continually remembered his covenant with Abraham, Isaac and Jacob
(Exod. 2:24-25; Deut. 9:5; 2 Kings 13:23).

3. God administers just reprisals

'As you have done, it shall be done to you; your reprisal shall return upon
your own head' (v. 15). In the New Testament we read: 'Do not be deceived, God is not mocked; for whatever a man sows, that he will also
reap' (Gal. 6:7). 'Judge not, that you be not judged. For with what judgement you judge, you will be judged; and with the same measure you use, it
will be measured back to you' (Matt. 7:1-2).

4. Salvation for Edomites

Edom was full of pride. Like their forefather Esau, they had no interest in the promises and purposes of God. They were an independent, arrogant people, so independent that they thought they could do without God:

> The pride of your heart has deceived you,
> You who dwell in the clefts of the rock,
> Whose habitation is high;
> You who say in your heart,
> 'Who will bring me down to the ground?'
>
> (v. 3).

'Pride of heart is that attitude of life which declares its ability to do without God.'[13]

Esau is described in the New Testament as an immoral and profane person, 'who for one morsel of food sold his birthright' (Heb. 12:16). A profane person is someone who shows contempt for God, who never worships, never prays, never listens to spiritual truth, never gives thought to eternity or eternal realities, and despises those who do. The Edomites looked upon the sufferings of the people of God, not just with indifference, but also with pleasure. This was the supreme manifestation of the evil in the heart of Esau. It was caused by the fact that he hated everything which Jacob represented — faith in God, trust in his promises, reliance upon his mercy, concern for the spiritual dimension of life; for, with all his failings, Jacob was still a God-fearing man, one who loved God.

In spite of all Edom's hostility, there is hope for them in Jacob's redemption, restoration and realization of the divine purpose. The nation is destroyed, yet there is salvation for Esau's descendants if they will only yield to the younger brother Jacob in his glorious representative the Lord Jesus Christ. Thus the prophecy of Balaam will come true in the highest and best sense — that is the spiritual sense:

> Edom shall be a possession [be owned by another];
> Seir also, his enemies, shall be a possession,
> While Israel does valiantly.
> Out of Jacob one shall have dominion,
> And destroy the remains of the city
>
> (Num. 24:18-19).

Does the fulfilment commence with the inclusion of Edomites in seeking out the Lord Jesus Christ? 'Jesus withdrew with his disciples to the sea. And a great multitude from Galilee followed him, and from Judea and Jerusalem *and Idumea* and beyond the Jordan; and those from Tyre and Sidon, a great multitude, when they heard how many things he was doing, came to him' (Mark 3:7-8, emphasis added).

Conclusion

'We now then perceive the design of the Prophet: as adversity might have weakened the Israelites, and even utterly broken them down, the Prophet here applies comfort and props up their dejected minds, for the Lord would shortly look on them and take due vengeance on their enemies.'[14]

Obadiah's prophecy is not merely concerned to pronounce judgement against Edom. 'Obadiah takes the general attitude of Edom towards the people of Jehovah as the groundwork of his prophecy, regards the judgement upon Edom as one feature in the universal judgement upon all nations (cf. vv.15-16), proclaims in the destruction of the power of Edom the overthrow of the power of all nations hostile to God.'[15] If the kingdoms of the world shall be the Lord's as Obadiah prophesies, then the kingdoms of the world must become the kingdoms of our Lord and of his Christ. In the book of Revelation there is recorded the ultimate fulfilment of the prophecy of Obadiah: 'Then the seventh angel sounded: and there were loud voices in heaven, saying, "The kingdoms of this world have become the kingdoms of our Lord and of his Christ, and he shall reign for ever and ever!"' (Rev. 11:15).

Jonah

('the dove')

Author: Jonah
(probably)

Key thought: 'A gracious and merciful God'

Theme: He is not the God of the Jews only;
he is the God of the Gentiles also!

'I know that you are a gracious and
merciful God, slow to anger and
abundant in loving-kindness, one who
relents from doing harm.'

Jonah 4:2

Summary

Jonah

No Old Testament character is better known than Jonah. No adventure so grips the imagination as the story of the man who was swallowed by a great fish and then, after three days, regurgitated alive on the seashore. Yet how many, knowing the story so well, understand its true import and significance?

'Jonah was a historical figure with a particular mission for God in a definite historical setting and fulfilling a vital role in the real, historical experience of God's people.'[1] True as this is, the real value of the book of Jonah goes even further. The ordeal of Jonah, brought about as it was through his own disobedience and folly, has a significance that far surpasses any localized concern for either Nineveh, Assyria, or Israel. In the purposes of God, the history of Jonah stands as a vital link in the unfolding of God's plan of salvation as found in the Old Testament Scriptures. Jonah's experiences, here recorded, are distinctly Messianic. They concern God's Son, Jesus 'the Christ, the Saviour of the world' (John 4:42).

Author

Jonah the son of Amittai was a native of Gath Hepher (2 Kings 14:25) in Zebulun. This place has been identified with the present village of El Meshed, just two and a half miles north of Nazareth. The supposed tomb of the prophet Jonah is located there. Jonah may therefore have been a Galilean. This would then suggest that the Pharisees either forgot or blatantly lied when, in their hostility towards the Lord Jesus, they said to Nicodemus, 'Search and look, for no prophet has arisen out of Galilee' (John 7:52).[2]

Many regard this little book as a myth, a story, a legend, an allegory, rather than an account of a historical event. Those who are confident in the inspiration of all Scripture (2 Tim. 3:16) find confirmation within the pages of the Bible that Jonah was a real prophet (2 Kings 14:25). That the book of Jonah is a historical account of what actually took place has been held down the years, by Jews and Christians alike, until quite recently, when sceptical scientists, who could not accept the possibility of a man being returned alive after being swallowed by a great fish, influenced the reinterpretation of the biblical material. Those who know neither 'the Scriptures nor the power of God' (Matt. 22:29) readily discount the miraculous as fictitious.

Jonah's forthright record of his own faults suggests that the book is a testimony of real experiences. A further pointer to the reality and truthfulness of this account is suggested by the fact that the Jews recognized this book as part of the Scriptures, even 'though it militated against their national prejudices in exhibiting God's mercy to another nation'.[3] With a remarkable openness, Jonah reveals his flaws and his wrong thinking. His humility is evident in his willingness to record his own serious shortcomings.

The strongest proofs that the incidents recorded in the book of Jonah actually happened as described are found in the New Testament. The Lord Jesus Christ refers to Jonah and his experience in the great fish as a real-life event. He also speaks of the repentance of the Ninevites as an actual occurrence (Matt. 12:40-41; Luke 11:30). That is sufficient to satisfy all Bible-believing Christians.

Historical setting

Jonah succeeded into the prophetic office in the line of Elijah and Elisha. Some ancient Jewish authorities supposed Jonah to be the son of the widow of Zarephath, whom Elijah raised from the dead, but there is no biblical warrant for this.[4] It is possible that Jonah was trained in the school of the prophets located at Bethel and Jericho (2 Kings 2:1-18). He prophesied during the reign of Jeroboam II of Israel (793–753 B.C.), which places his ministry just before that of the prophet Amos. So the chronology of the prophets would be Joel, Jonah, Amos, Hosea, Isaiah and Micah.

The only prophecy of Jonah to Israel which has been preserved is in keeping with his name: Jonah, 'the dove', brings a message of comfort and encouragement to his people. The Lord has seen the terrible distress of his people Israel and he has determined to deliver them by the hand of King Jeroboam. The historian of 2 Kings records of King Jeroboam II of Israel: 'He restored the territory of Israel from the entrance of Hamath to the Sea of the Arabah, according to the word of the LORD God of Israel, which he had spoken through his servant Jonah the son of Amittai, the prophet who was from Gath Hepher. For the LORD saw that the affliction of Israel was very bitter; and whether bond or free, there was no helper for Israel. And the LORD did not say that he would blot out the name of Israel from under heaven; but he saved them by the hand of Jeroboam the son of Joash' (2 Kings 14:25-27). Israel regained the territory lost through the invasion of the Syrians.

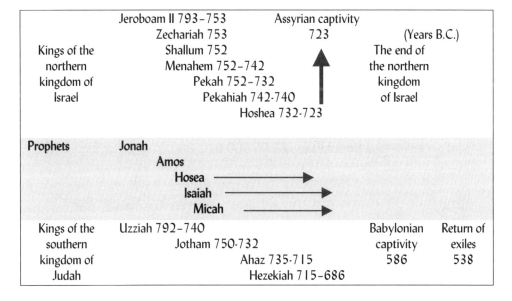

Jonah in relation to the kings and prophets of the divided kingdom

The book of Jonah is not, however, directly related to conditions in Israel. Jonah is commissioned to preach to Gentiles, and in particular to Israel's enemies, the Assyrians, dwelling in the capital of the empire, in the city of Nineveh.

Outline

The book falls into two major divisions with two chapters in each. There is a clear structure and the two sections are paralleled, as can be seen from the brief profile at the beginning of this chapter.

Part I: Jonah's commission and disobedience (1:1 – 2:10)

1. Jonah's commission (1:1-2)

The opening word, 'Now', seems to indicate that this is the continuation of his ministry, not its beginning. In other words, Jonah is already an experienced prophet when the commission comes for him to go to Nineveh.

Nineveh is described as 'an exceedingly great city'. Jonah speaks of it later as being 'a three-day journey' (3:3). Does this indicate that it would take three days to walk around the outskirts, or that it would take about three days to walk across from one side to the other? If the former then the circumference would have been about sixty miles, surrounding an area of 286 square miles. If the latter, then the area would have been over three times larger. Jonah may have been thinking about the administrative district of Nineveh rather than the city itself. In any case the area would have included considerable grassland (since there was 'much livestock' — 4:11), and an estimated population of 600,000 to 1,000,000 (including 120,000 babies and toddlers — 4:11).

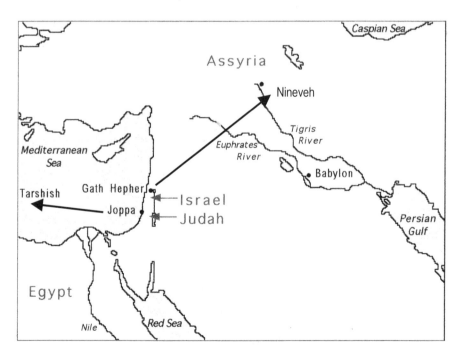

Jonah's commission and response

2. Jonah's disobedience (1:3)

Why did Jonah disobey the Lord? There is no evidence that he was a cow-ard; indeed he showed commendable courage at times (1:9-12). Perhaps he was unsympathetic to foreign missions. Maybe he was concerned for his personal honour as a prophet of Israel. It cannot have been the journey which put him off, since the voyage to Tarshish (if rightly identified as lo-cated on the coast of Spain) was a far more hazardous undertaking than the overland trek to Nineveh, which was only 550 miles overland. Tarshish, if in Spain, is located some 2,500 miles by sea in the opposite direction!

None of these speculations concerning Jonah's disobedience is accu-rate, for it seems quite evident that Jonah was motivated by patriotism. Assyria was Israel's great enemy, 'a vicious and cruel imperial power that constantly threatened his homeland'.[5] The prophet may even have known, by revelation from God, that the Assyrians were to be the means by which the Lord would later punish the Israelites (cf. Hosea 9:3). Jonah wanted to leave the Assyrians to die in their sins. He did not want them to experience the favour of the Lord. To obey the commission to preach to them might lead to their repentance. This in turn would bring forgiveness from God; resulting in their preservation rather than destruction. The key to the whole matter of Jonah's disobedience is his overwhelming awareness of the re-markable mercy of God. As Jonah later admits, 'I know that you are a gra-cious and merciful God, slow to anger and abundant in loving-kindness, one who relents from doing harm' (4:2).

Jonah, then, is God's prophet to Israel (2 Kings 14:25) and concerned for his own people. His patriotism is so intense that he is prepared to aban-don his ministry and incur God's anger, rather than risk the well-being of his countrymen. Perhaps he even fears that the Lord will transfer his love from Israel to Assyria.[6] So Jonah deliberately disobeys God; he goes south to the nearest port at Joppa, finds a ship destined for Tarshish, and pays the fare. Jonah tries to escape the command of God to preach in Nineveh by flight to Tarshish. He is angry at the thought that God might show mercy to Israel's great enemy. Boarding ship, he sails away from Joppa in a vain attempt to flee 'from the presence of the LORD'.

3. Jonah's suffering (1:4-17)

A violent storm breaks out and threatens the safety of the ship. The crew lightens the vessel by casting the cargo overboard. Meanwhile Jonah is asleep well below deck. When the captain angrily wakes him and the lot is cast to discover the cause of the disaster, Jonah confesses his sin and recommends that he should be cast overboard, since he is the cause of the dreadful storm. The sailors respond by exerting a more concerted effort to row the vessel to land, but to no avail. Accepting his punishment, Jonah is cast into the sea. But the Lord has not abandoned him; a fish is prepared to keep Jonah alive.

4. Jonah's prayer (2:1-9)

From within the great fish Jonah utters a psalm of praise. Prayer for delivery, rather than praise for delivery, might have seemed more fitting in this predicament! But Jonah functions according to the principle of faith; he understands the fact that he is alive in the great fish as 'a pledge of ultimate deliverance'.[7] In prayer he praises God for delivering him from drowning. Jonah has been swallowed alive by a great fish. The fish is not an agent of judgement but a vehicle of salvation to Jonah. There is a distinct note of confidence as to the final outcome: Jonah sings of deliverance, as though aware that his miraculous preservation in the innards of the great fish indicates that the Lord will deliver him up once more, even as from the dead.

There are many points of comparison between Jonah's psalm and the psalms of David and his contemporaries. In Jonah's prayer there are many allusions to those sacred hymns, not in the sense that he quotes from them verbatim, but more in that he is thoroughly acquainted with them and 'talks their language'. The following table lists a number of comparisons to illustrate the point.

Jonah		Psalms	
2.2	I cried out to the LORD because of my affliction And he answered me.	34:6	This poor man cried out, and the LORD heard him, And saved him out of all his troubles.
2:2	Out of the belly of Sheol I cried, And you heard my voice.	139:8	If I make my bed in hell [i.e. Sheol], behold, you are there.
		16:9-10	Therefore my heart is glad, and my glory rejoices; My flesh also will rest in hope, For you will not leave my soul in Sheol...

Jonah		Psalms	
2:3	All your billows and your waves passed over me.	42:7	All your waves and billows have gone over me.
2:4	Yet I will look again towards your holy temple.	18:6	In my distress I called upon the LORD, And cried out to my God; He heard my voice from his temple, And my cry came before him…
2:5	The waters encompassed me, even to my soul; The deep closed around me; Weeds were wrapped around my head.	69:1-2	Save me, O God! For the waters have come up to my neck. I sink in deep mire, Where there is no standing; I have come into deep waters, Where the floods overflow me.
		69:14-15	Deliver me out of the mire, And let me not sink… Let not the floodwater overflow me, Nor let the deep swallow me up; And let not the pit shut its mouth on me.
2:6	I went down to the moorings of the mountains; The earth with its bars closed behind me for ever; Yet you have brought up my life from the pit, O LORD, my God.	88:3-7	For my soul is full of troubles, And my life draws near to the grave. I am counted with those who go down to the pit… Adrift among the dead, Like the slain who lie in the grave… You have laid me in the lowest pit, In darkness, in the depths… And you have afflicted me with all your waves.
		40:2	He also brought me up out of a horrible pit…
2:8	Those who regard worthless idols Forsake their own Mercy	31:7	I will be glad and rejoice in your mercy, For you have considered my trouble; You have known my soul in adversities.

Jonah		Psalms	
2:9	But I will sacrifice to you With the voice of thanksgiving; I will pay what I have vowed. Salvation is of the LORD.	26:7	That I may proclaim with the voice of thanksgiving, And tell of all your wondrous works.
		50:14-15	Offer to God thanksgiving, And pay your vows to the Most High. Call upon me in the day of trouble: I will deliver you, and you shall glorify me.
		50:23	Whoever offers praise glorifies me; And to him who orders his conduct aright I will show the salvation of God.
		116:17-18	I will offer to you the sacrifice of thanksgiving, And will call upon the name of the LORD. I will pay my vows to the LORD ...

5. Jonah's rescue (2:10)

Whether other men have been restored after being swallowed by a great
fish is of little concern here. Even if others have lived through such an ordeal, this is vastly different. Jonah not only survives the ordeal, but he is
fully conscious and coherent, both mentally and emotionally, being able to
compose a psalm and worship God before being regurgitated by the great
fish. For many modernists this is a major obstacle to accepting a literal interpretation of this account.[8] They are heedless of the fact that Jonah's experience is in the realm of the miraculous: 'The LORD had prepared a great
fish to swallow Jonah' (1:17). An even more remarkable miracle is yet to
come in the dramatic conversion of so many of the pagan Ninevites to
serve the living and true God.

In response to Jonah's prayer, the Lord causes the fish to disgorge the
prophet on to dry ground.

Part II: Jonah's recommissioning and obedience (3:1 – 4:11)

1. Jonah's recommissioning (3:1-2)

The story begins over again. The second half of the book draws a close parallel with the first half. The outcome this time is, however, quite different. Instead of rebelling and turning from the task, Jonah responds in obedience. It will later transpire that Jonah has not really had a change of heart. He is still harbouring resentment against the Lord for his display of compassion towards the Assyrians.

2. Jonah's obedience (3:3-4)

Nineveh is the capital of the Assyrian Empire built by Nimrod (Gen. 10:11). Jonah preaches God's message of judgement and impending disaster. Our Lord says, 'Jonah became a sign to the Ninevites' (Luke 11:30). Jonah's message is not the sign; it is his person that becomes the sign. Jonah presents himself to the Ninevites as one who has miraculously escaped from death, urging them to anticipate the danger which threatened them.[9] When they hear of God's dealings with Jonah in response to his disobedience, the Ninevites are more likely to take God's message seriously.

'Yet forty days, and Nineveh shall be overthrown' (3:4) — in just under six weeks the city will experience the righteous judgement of the living God.

3. Jonah's success (3:5-10)

This message of doom and gloom has a remarkable effect: there is a widespread spiritual awakening throughout the city. The people believe God and turn to him in true repentance. When the news reaches the King of Nineveh he also repents and calls upon all citizens to repent likewise: 'Cry mightily to God; yes, let every one turn from his evil way and from the violence that is in his hands' (3:8). The reference to violence is pertinent since the Assyrians were noted for their extreme brutality. The cruelty they inflicted on their enemies went even beyond the savagery of the day.

The Lord sees that the repentance of the Ninevites is real. The people not only cover themselves with sackcloth and cry out mightily to the Lord, they also turn 'from their evil way' (3:10).

In consequence of that repentance it would seem that the judgement of God against Nineveh was suspended for a further two hundred years. Around 650 B.C. the prophet Nahum foretold the city's destruction (Nahum 1:1-10). It was destroyed in 612 B.C.

4. Jonah's prayer (4:1-3)

Jonah knows the character of God. The key to the whole book is found in this section: 'Ah, LORD, was not this what I said when I was still in my country? Therefore I fled previously to Tarshish; for I know that you are a gracious and merciful God, slow to anger and abundant in loving-kindness, one who relents from doing harm' (4:2).

In spite of the confidence in God that Jonah expresses in his psalm, he shows himself here to be antagonistic towards the mercy of the Lord. As a prophet he should have been the epitome of godliness and spirituality, but Jonah does everything in his power to disobey the Lord. Even when he reluctantly and begrudgingly discharges the duties of his office, he still resents the subsequent conversion of the Gentiles. He would rather die than witness this spectacle of amazing grace (4:3).

5. Jonah's rebuke (4:4-11)

Jonah cannot bring himself to feel compassionate towards Israel's enemy. He still holds to the hope that the Assyrians will be destroyed. Jonah's experience in the belly of the great fish does not seem to have permanently softened his heart towards the purposes of God. He resents the Lord's gracious and merciful attitude. So God teaches Jonah another vital lesson through the growth and withering of a plant!

The message of God's outstanding unmerited mercy and his compassion on the very young is the concluding word, for the Lord says to Jonah, 'And should I not pity Nineveh, that great city, in which are more than one hundred and twenty thousand persons who cannot discern between their right hand and their left...?' (4:11).

Christ and his church

Jonah: a type of Christ

The Lord Jesus Christ provides the true meaning and significance of Jonah's experiences. Jonah was a sign, says Jesus, to the Ninevites of his generation: 'And while the crowds were thickly gathered together, he began to say, "This is an evil generation. It seeks a sign, and no sign will be given to it except the sign of Jonah the prophet. For as Jonah became a sign to the Ninevites, so also the Son of Man will be to this generation"' (Luke 11:29-30). Jonah appears to the Ninevites as one brought back from the grave. In the same way, though on a far superior level, Jesus will be a sign to his generation. Indeed the death and resurrection of the Son of God will be the fulfilment of the type of Jonah. Unlike Jonah, the Saviour will be swallowed and disgorged, not by a fish but by death itself (Acts 2:23-24).

The storm of God's righteous anger was raging. As soon as Jonah was cast into the sea, 'The sea ceased from its raging' (1:15). Cast into the deep, the Saviour quenched for ever the wrath of God towards his people:

Save me, O God!
For the waters have come up to my neck.
I sink in deep mire,
Where there is no standing;
I have come into deep waters,
Where the floods overflow me

(Ps. 69:1-2).

All your waves and billows have gone over me

(Ps. 42:7).

Now from the sixth hour until the ninth hour there was darkness over all the land. And about the ninth hour Jesus cried out with a loud voice, saying 'Eli, Eli, lama sabachthani?' that is, 'My God, my God, why have you forsaken me?' (Matt. 27:45-46).

From God's dealings with Jonah it is evident yet again that the death and resurrection of the Lord Jesus Christ were in the plan and purpose of God hundreds of years before these events took place. For although Jonah

was disobedient to the command of God and consequently brought punishment upon himself, nevertheless the means which the Lord used to correct Jonah resulted in profound symbolism. Jonah's experience in the belly
of the great fish is a prophetic picture, a foreshadowing and acted prophecy
of what was to happen to the incarnate Son of God.[10] Jonah's incarceration
and release are a type of the death, burial and resurrection of Christ. 'For
as Jonah was three days and three nights in the belly of the great fish,' says
the Lord Jesus, 'so will the Son of Man be three days and three nights in
the heart of the earth' (Matt. 12:40).[11]

Speaking of his imminent death, the Lord Jesus told visiting Greeks,
'Unless an ear of wheat falls into the ground and dies, it remains alone; but
if it dies, it produces much fruit...' He continued: '"And I, if I am lifted up
from the earth, will draw all peoples to myself." This he said, signifying by
what death he would die' (John 12:24,32-33). The Saviour's death and
resurrection are crucial to the ingathering of the Gentiles. This is the important and significant link which the history of Jonah provides in the unfolding of the divine plan of salvation in the Old Testament. Through the
death of Christ the promise to Abraham is fulfilled that '... all the families of
the earth shall be blessed' (Gen. 12:3). Jonah's release from the tomb-like
belly of the fish, his preaching to the Gentile Ninevites and their subsequent
repentance constitute a wonderful type of our Lord's rising from the dead
followed by the powerful preaching of the resurrection by the apostles, with
the result that many Gentiles discovered that 'The gospel ... is the power of
God to salvation for everyone who believes' (Rom. 1:16).

Our Lord is one who is 'greater than Jonah' (Matt. 12:41), but there are
comparisons to be drawn. In Jonah's willingness to be cast into the raging
sea there is a picture of the one who willingly sacrificed his life for the safety
and salvation of others. Jesus said, 'I lay down my life that I may take it
again. No one takes it from me, but I lay it down of myself' (John
10:17-18). There is also a marked contrast: Jonah reluctantly preached to
save a city; Jesus willingly died to save the world (1 John 2:2; 4:14).

Jonah: a type of the church

Jonah the Israelite was cast into the sea because of his disobedience to
God. In the same way the Israelites in their disobedience will suffer the
judgement of God and be cast out from their own land. Assyria may devour Israel, but the Lord will preserve alive a remnant, even as he preserved Jonah in the belly of the great fish. As God dealt with Jonah when

he was without hope, so the word is revealed to the Israelites that if, even in their last extremity, they will turn to the Lord, he will have mercy upon them and abundantly pardon (Isa. 55:7). As Jonah was delivered so that he could fulfil his mission to Nineveh, so the remnant of Israel will return to fulfil the Lord's commission to make him known to the whole Gentile world. 'The mission of Jonah was a fact of symbolical and typical import-ance, which was intended not only to enlighten Israel as to the position of the Gentile world in relation to the kingdom of God, but also to typify the future adoption of such of the heathen, as should observe the word of God, into the fellowship of the salvation prepared in Israel for all nations.'[12]

When the promised Messiah came to Israel they refused to receive his message. The contrast is therefore brought out between the Gentiles in Jonah's day and the Jews in the day of our Lord: 'The men of Nineveh will rise in the judgement with this generation and condemn it, because they repented at the preaching of Jonah; and indeed a greater than Jonah is here' (Matt. 12:41).

Application

1. Providence

Note the four 'prepared' things in this book: 'Now the LORD had prepared a great fish to swallow Jonah' (1:17); 'And the LORD God prepared a plant and made it come up over Jonah' (4:6); 'God prepared a worm' (4:7); and 'God prepared a vehement east wind' (4:8). There is an undoubted recog-nition of the sovereignty of God over nature, the natural elements and all circumstances. Christians are used to the thought of the Lord stilling the storm (Mark 4:39), but are often reluctant to acknowledge that he raises the storm in the first place (Ps. 107:25).

The great fish 'vomited Jonah onto dry land' (2:10). When God works a miracle he does not do it by halves. Jonah was not required to swim to shore, nor to clamber up muddy banks. Like Moses and the children of Israel crossing the sea when escaping from Egypt, or Joshua and the Israel-ites entering into Canaan via the River Jordan, he found himself on dry land (see Exod. 14:22; Josh. 3:17).

2. Recommissioning

Jonah's experience is a warning to the servants of God against disobedience. It is also a wonderful display of divine grace in restoring one who has sinned. What a blessing not to be cast off because of faithlessness and disobedience! The apostle Peter was publicly restored after his terrible denial of the Lord (John 21:15-17). The Lord is prepared to use unworthy instruments as his messengers.

3. Prayer in time of trouble

'Is anyone among you suffering? Let him pray' (James 5:13; cf. Phil. 4:6-7; 1 Peter 5:7).

> Out of the depths I have cried to you, O LORD:
> Lord, hear my voice!
> Let your ears be attentive
> To the voice of my supplications.
>
> (Ps. 130:1-2).

> I waited patiently for the LORD;
> And he inclined to me,
> And heard my cry.
> He also brought me up out of a horrible pit,
> Out of the miry clay,
> And set my feet upon a rock,
> And established my steps
>
> (Ps. 40:1-2).

There is virtue in memorizing the Scriptures; Jonah knew the psalms. He would have been comforted and strengthened by the conviction of David, who prayed:

> Where can I go from your Spirit?
> Or where can I flee from your presence?
> If I ascend into heaven, you are there;
> If I make my bed in hell, behold, you are there.
> If I take the wings of the morning,
> And dwell in the uttermost parts of the sea,

Even there your hand shall lead me,
And your right hand shall hold me

(Ps. 139:7-10).

4. World mission

There is a right concern for our own people. The apostle Paul, in spite of being commissioned as 'an apostle to the Gentiles' (Rom. 11:13), shows a deep concern and compassion towards his own people (Rom. 9:1-5). But a regard for our own nation or race must not cloud us to our responsibilities towards the rest of the world. The book of Jonah challenges the Israelites over their failure to have a world vision. Their history ought to have served as an impetus to evangelize all nations. The Lord's promise to Abraham was that '… in you all the families of the earth shall be blessed' (Gen. 12:3). The nation of Israel was the Lord's servant with the commission to bring the knowledge of the Lord to the world.

The Lord's concern for the non-Israelite world is vividly portrayed in this book in the contrast between Jonah and God. Jonah cares for a plant; God cares for people. Jonah is interested in himself; God is interested in others. Jonah did nothing for the plant. God created and provides for human beings. God has every right to be compassionate to them; it is in his nature (4:2; Exod. 33:19; 34:6). 'But the LORD said, "You have had pity on the plant for which you have not laboured, nor made it grow, which came up in a night and perished in a night. And should I not pity Nineveh…?"' (4:9-10). 'I will have mercy on whom I will have mercy, and I will have compassion on whom I will have compassion' (Rom. 9:15). Jonah in his hatred invokes the mercy of God as a reason for refusing to preach to Gentiles. Paul in his compassion cites the mercy of God as a reason for continuing to preach to Gentiles (2 Cor. 4:1-6)

Even in New Testament days, Jewish Christians hesitated in preaching the gospel to the Gentiles. The risen Christ promised his disciples: 'You shall receive power when the Holy Spirit has come upon you; and you shall be witnesses to me in Jerusalem, and in all Judea and Samaria, and to the end of the earth.' It would seem that those disciples were not too keen to obey the worldwide commission. The persecution of the early Christian church may have been necessary in order to get the Christians moving and 'scattered throughout the regions of Judea and Samaria' (Acts 8:1). The results were certainly beneficial in terms of the spread of the gospel (Acts 8:4). A little later the apostle Peter had to be encouraged by a dream and a vision to go to the home of the Gentile Cornelius (Acts 10:9-23).

Later, Peter writes to the Christian Jews who were pilgrims of the Dispersion: 'You are a chosen generation, a royal priesthood, a holy nation, his own special people, *that you may proclaim* the praises of him who called you out of darkness into his marvellous light' (1 Peter 2:9, emphasis added). The salvation of God is not to be confined to one nation.

Conclusion

The book of Jonah holds a strategic and vital place in the purposes of God. It is an essential component in God's salvation history. God was determined to reveal all the major truths and doctrines concerning his Son before his incarnation as Jesus Christ. The experiences of Jonah when he was swallowed by the great fish speak of the Saviour's death, burial and resurrection from the dead.

This little book also prefigures the conversion blessings which will come to the whole world through an Israelite Servant of God, the Lord Jesus Christ.

Finally, the book of Jonah teaches God's people their continuing responsibility to make the gospel known to all. The church of Jesus Christ will ultimately be composed of 'a great multitude … of all nations, tribes, peoples, and tongues' (Rev. 7:9). The conversion of the Ninevites illustrates the abiding truth that 'Whoever calls on the name of the LORD shall be saved' (Joel 2:32; Acts 2:21; Rom. 10:13). 'How then shall they call on him in whom they have not believed? And how shall they believe in him of whom they have not heard? … So then faith comes by hearing, and hearing by the word of God' (Rom. 10:14,17). Our Lord has commissioned his church: 'Go into all the world and preach the gospel to every creature' (Mark 16:15).

Through Jonah this lesson is forcefully taught: God is the God of Israel, God is the God of Nineveh, God is the God of the whole world. As Paul reasons, 'Is he the God of the Jews only? Is he not also the God of the Gentiles? Yes, of the Gentiles also…' (Rom. 3:29).

God's message of salvation is intended for the whole world: Jonah needed to hear and understand this fact; Israel needed to hear and understand it; Christians today need to hear and understand it.

Micah

('Who is like Jehovah?')

Author: Micah

Key thought: The pardoning God

Theme:
God hates sin and delights to pardon

'Who is a God like you,
Pardoning iniquity…?
He does not retain his anger for ever,
Because he delights in mercy.'

Micah 7:18

Summary

Micah

Micah was a man from the country districts of the plain of Judah. He had a passionate concern for the oppressed and afflicted agricultural workers of his day. He challenged the nation about the corruption that was so evident on every hand: Judah was constantly violating her covenant with the Lord, though she continued the rituals of religion (6:6-7). Property was taken by violence (2:2); debts were collected by force (2:8); prophets and priests were corrupt (3:11); justice was perverted by the nation's leaders (3:1-3,9); witchcraft and paganism were rife throughout the land (5:12-14); false weights and deceit were frequently used in trade (6:10-12); and family relationships had broken down, with devastating consequences (7:5-6).

Micah, with a heart full of concern for the people, warned of the judgement of God upon the nation and her leaders. Spiritual corruption and social injustice were signs indicative of a people who had turned from the living God, their God, the God of the ancient covenants.

Though the sins of the people were many, yet the living God is outstanding in mercy and pardon. God would punish but God would also pardon. Micah proclaimed the grace of God as a great motive to repentance (7:18-20).

Author

The name Micah is an abbreviated form of Micaiah and means, 'Who is like Jehovah?' (cf. 7:18) — that is, 'one dedicated to Jehovah the incomparable God'.[1] The name of the prophet was suited to his character. God was everything to him. He had a high view of the holiness, righteousness and compassion of God. To judge by his writings, he was a man of powerful personality, of calm, sane judgement, tender-hearted yet faithful, and for all this he gave God the credit and the glory (3:8).[2]

Micah was a native of Moresheth Gath (1:1,14) a village about twenty-four miles south-west of the city of Jerusalem. The village was located on the edge of rolling hills as they met the coastal plains of Judah. By giving his place of birth this prophet is distinguished from another prophet called Micah, or Micaiah, the son of Imlah, who ministered over a century earlier, in the days of King Ahab of Israel (1 Kings 22:8-28).

Micah would not have been able to engage in this exacting and demanding ministry unless he had been conscious of his divine appointment to office:

> But truly I am full of power by the Spirit of the LORD,
> And of justice and might,
> To declare to Jacob his transgression
> And to Israel his sin

(3:8).

Historical setting

The prophet Micah exercised his ministry during the reigns of three kings of Judah: Jotham (750–732 B.C.), Ahaz (735–715 B.C.) and Hezekiah (715–686 B.C.). Consequently Micah functioned for at least seventeen years — commencing before 732 B.C. and continuing until after 715 B.C. He lived after the prophets Jonah and Amos and was a contemporary of Hosea and Isaiah, who had begun their ministries a few years earlier.[3]

The historical and political background of the book of Micah is the same as that of the earlier sections of the prophecy of Isaiah, although Micah has not the same familiarity with the political life of the capital. This may be readily explained in that Micah came from the countryside whereas Isaiah was from the city.

Micah began his prophetic ministry about ten years before the Assyrian invasion and subsequent captivity of the northern kingdom of Israel. While the main thrust of his ministry concerned the southern kingdom of Judah, he also included severe warnings against the northern kingdom (1:1 — 'Samaria' was the capital city of the northern kingom). Throughout his ministry the growing Assyrian Empire posed a real threat to Judah. In common with all the prophets, Micah shows that national security is not achieved by political means but by spiritual repentance and dependence upon God.

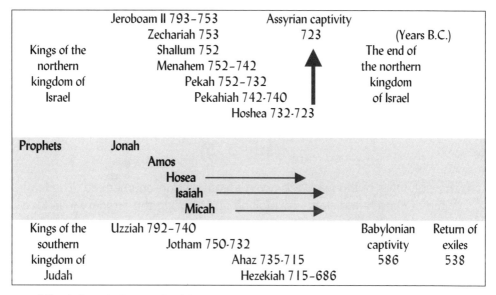

Kings of the northern kingdom of Israel	Jeroboam II 793–753 Zechariah 753 Shallum 752 Menahem 752–742 Pekah 752–732 Pekahiah 742-740 Hoshea 732-723	Assyrian captivity 723	(Years B.C.) The end of the northern kingdom of Israel
Prophets	Jonah Amos Hosea Isaiah Micah		
Kings of the southern kingdom of Judah	Uzziah 792–740 Jotham 750-732 Ahaz 735-715 Hezekiah 715–686	Babylonian captivity 586	Return of exiles 538

Micah in relation to the kings and prophets of the divided kingdom

Outline

The book of Micah does not follow a precise structure. though it falls roughly into three sections, each beginning with the word 'Hear' (1:2; 3:1; 6:1).

Part I: Judgement threatened against Israel and Judah (1:1 - 2:13)

God's anger is expressed towards Israel (Samaria) and Judah (Jerusalem) on account of the evil behaviour of their leaders and people. Micah predicts the fate of the northern kingdom of Israel (1:6-7). Judah too will not escape the judgement of God, for his anger is kindled because of their evil practices: covetousness, violence, oppression, viciousness and breaking-up of families (2:1-2,8-9). The punishment will come and the people will be brought low (2:3-5).

The section ends with wonderful words of comfort and encouragement:

I will surely assemble all of you, O Jacob,
I will surely gather the remnant of Israel;

I will put them together like sheep of the fold,
Like a flock in the midst of their pasture;
They shall make a loud noise because of so many men

(Micah 2:12).

Part II: Judgement pronounced; future events announced (3:1 - 5:15)

The sinfulness of the people is again identified and enumerated. The leadership of church and state is exploiting and abusing the ordinary folk. Censure upon the nation culminates in the prediction of the destruction of the city of Jerusalem and her temple (3:12). Well over a hundred years later elders in Jerusalem quoted this verse from Micah in defence of the ministry of the prophet Jeremiah (Jer. 26:16-19), with the result that the latter's life was spared. This reference in Jeremiah also locates the prophecy of Micah 3:12 in 'the days of Hezekiah king of Judah' and reveals the good effect which resulted from the preaching of Micah: 'Did Hezekiah king of Judah and all Judah ever put him [Micah] to death? Did he [Hezekiah] not fear the LORD and seek the LORD's favour? And the Lord relented concerning the doom which he had pronounced against them' (Jer. 26:19).

The destruction of Jerusalem was averted under the preaching of Micah. Many repented and a great reformation took place in Judah (2 Chr. 29:31 – 31:21). 'Micah's efforts probably played a large part in the revival of true religion.'[4]

Micah's prophecy was fulfilled 130 years later, in 586 B.C., when the Babylonians invaded Judah and totally destroyed the temple and Jerusalem (2 Chr. 36:15-21).

The awe-inspiring prophecy concerning the destruction of Jerusalem (3:12) is more than matched by the wonderful prophecy concerning her ultimate restoration (4:1-8). The words of 4:1-3 are virtually identical to Isaiah 2:2-4. Isaiah may have 'borrowed' from Micah; Micah may have 'borrowed' from Isaiah; both prophets may have drawn on an earlier prophecy; or the Holy Spirit may have given the same message to both independently. The prophets of the eighth century B.C. held on to glorious promises of a future salvation.

The birth of a new king and his kingdom is announced (5:2-15). The Messianic King will be unique: he will be truly human, for he shall come forth out of Bethlehem, and he will be truly divine, for his goings forth have been from of old, from days of eternity.[5]

Part III: Punishment and mercy (6:1 - 7:20)

The Lord's complaint against Judah is that he has done so much for them, but they have responded with ingratitude and rebellion. A representative speaks on behalf of the people, enquiring how to approach God (6:6-7). The answer is given that humble obedience is what is required (6:8).

The prophet responds to the threatened punishment from God: in the name of the believing remnant he confesses deep sin and widespread corruption (7:1-6). He painfully acknowledges the necessity of a severe visitation from God; all confidence is placed upon God's grace and mercy:

> Therefore I will look to the LORD;
> I will wait for the God of my salvation;
> My God will hear me
>
> (7:7).

The Lord will hear and the Lord will restore the prosperity of his people. Judah's enemies are warned not to gloat at her misfortune. The nation will rise again and the former glory will be restored. The nations will witness the raising up of God's people and be dumbfounded and humbled.

The grand climax of the whole book is reached as the pardoning grace of God is expressed in words of profound beauty and power: 'Who is a God like you, pardoning iniquity...?' (7:18-20).

Christ and his church

Prophecy

1. Messiah's birthplace

> But you, Bethlehem Ephrathah,
> Though you are little among the thousands of Judah,
> Yet out of you shall come forth to me
> The one to be ruler in Israel,

Whose goings forth have been from of old,
From everlasting

(5:2).

This prophecy was ascribed to the promised Messiah; even the godless Jewish leadership in the days of the incarnation were able to identify the birthplace of the Messiah. When Herod the Great asked the chief priests and scribes where the Christ was to be born they referred to Micah 5:2 and identified Bethlehem (Matt. 2:4-6).

God moves in mysterious ways (cf. Isa. 55:8). The chosen parents (mother and step-father) of Christ lived in Nazareth, but in the providence of God they travelled to Bethlehem for the official census, with the result that Jesus was born there in fulfilment of the prophecy (Luke 2:1-7). The fact that his earthly parents originated from Nazareth, and that Jesus was brought up in Nazareth, led to initial uncertainties that he was the Christ. When Philip announced to Nathanael that they had found Messiah and that he was 'Jesus of Nazareth, the son of Joseph' (John 1:45), Nathanael responded with the question: 'Can anything good come out of Nazareth?' The question was not motivated by prejudice but by prophecy. There were no Messianic prophecies associated with Nazareth. Philip wisely answered, 'Come and see ' (John 1:46).

2. Messiah's glorious kingdom

Now it shall come to pass in the latter days
That the mountain of the LORD's house
Shall be established on the top of the mountains,
And shall be exalted above the hills;
And peoples shall flow to it.
Many nations shall come and say,
'Come, and let us go up to the mountain of the LORD,
To the house of the God of Jacob;
He will teach us his ways,
And we shall walk in his paths.'
For out of Zion the law shall go forth,
And the word of the LORD from Jerusalem.
He shall judge between many peoples,

And rebuke strong nations afar off;
They shall beat their swords into ploughshares,
And their spears into pruning-hooks;
Nation shall not lift up sword against nation,
Neither shall they learn war any more

(4:1-3).

Although Micah addressed his messages of 'judgement and hope toward Israel and Judah of his day, he used words that transcended the immediate historical crisis and, by doing so, took his readers into the more distant future'.[6] The prophet pictures a time when the peoples of the world will flock to worship God. There will be universal peace without the least threat of war.

Micah, like Isaiah, prophesies the captivity in Babylon, but he goes beyond Isaiah in predicting the return (4:10) and rebuilding of the temple (4:2). The fulfilment of Micah 4:1-3 will pass through a number of stages: first, the return of the exiles and the rebuilding of the temple; secondly, the first advent of Messiah, with his suffering, death and resurrection leading to his entry into the heavenly sanctuary (Heb. 9:11-12,24); and, thirdly, the second advent of Messiah, when he appears in glory and establishes the 'new heavens and a new earth in which righteousness dwells' (2 Peter 3:13; cf. Rev. 21:1-4,10,22-27).

A great spiritual awakening is predicted among the nations (the Gentiles). They will turn to the God of Israel and seek to share in the blessings of believing Israelites. The Israelites were the chosen people of God under the Old Covenant, 'to whom pertain the adoption, the glory, the covenants, the giving of the law, the service of God, and the promises; of whom are the fathers and from whom, according to the flesh, Christ came, who is over all, the eternally blessed God' (Rom. 9:4-5). Gentile believers are indebted to them (Rom. 15:27). The great promise to Abraham contained blessing for 'all the families of the earth' (Gen. 12:3). The completed church of Jesus Christ will be composed of saved Israelites and saved Gentiles: 'a great multitude which no one could number, of all nations, tribes, peoples, and tongues … crying out … "Salvation belongs to our God who sits on the throne, and to the Lamb!"' (Rev. 7:9-10).

Application

1. The definition of true religion

Through the prophet Micah the Lord corrects an unhealthy emphasis on external religion:

> With what shall I come before the LORD,
> And bow myself before the High God?
> Shall I come before him with burnt offerings,
> With calves a year old?
> Will the LORD be pleased with thousands of rams
> Or ten thousand rivers of oil?
> Shall I give my first-born for my transgression,
> The fruit of my body for the sin of my soul?
> He has shown you, O man, what is good;
> And what does the LORD require of you
> But to do justly,
> To love mercy,
> And to walk humbly with your God?
>
> (6:6-8).

Whenever the prophets draw a contrast between external observations and internal heart religion they are not intending to denigrate the place of external observations but rather to emphasize the importance of heart religion (see 1 Sam. 15:22-23). Although sacrifices were instituted by God through the law, they were never to be understood as actually removing sin: 'For it is impossible for the blood of bulls and goats to take away sins' (Heb. 10:4). The design of God in those offerings was twofold: to lead the people by those rituals to repentance and faith, and to cause the people to look beyond those sacrifices to the only true sacrifice by which all sins are taken away.[7]

2. False teachers, false prophets

Severe criticism is levelled at the prophets who make the people of God go astray (3:5). Though guilty of taking bribes, of adjusting their teaching according to financial rewards and of declaring peace where there is no peace, yet they have a form of religion: 'They lean on the LORD' (3:11). The false prophets, and the rest of the establishment of Judah, fail to appreciate how far their behaviour has diverged from what the LORD requires. 'They profess to know God, but in works they deny him, being abominable, disobedient, and disqualified for every good work' (Titus 1:16). They continue to profess faith in God, and claim the blessings of the covenant as theirs by right.[8]

How is it possible to distinguish Micah as a true teacher rather than a false teacher? It is not satisfactory to quote 3:8 and declare that Micah knew he was 'full of power by the Spirit of the Lord, and of justice and might, to declare to Jacob his transgression and to Israel his sin'. Anyone could have said that. While it was true in Micah's case, it could just as easily have been claimed by false teachers. The test of teachers or prophets is not whether they claim spiritual enlightenment, but whether they are speaking in accordance with the revealed Word of God. In this way Isaiah laid a solid foundation for distinguishing the true from the false: 'To the law and to the testimony! If they do not speak according to this word, it is because there is no light in them' (Isa. 8:20).

Even the Lord Jesus Christ established his credentials upon the Word of God (John 5:39,45-47; Luke 24:25-27,44). The four Gospels are full of references to the Old Testament to verify the declaration that Jesus of Nazareth is the Christ, the Son of God. The apostle John urged his readers, 'Beloved, do not believe every spirit, but test the spirits, whether they are of God; because many false prophets have gone out into the world' (1 John 4:1). He went on to base the test upon revealed truth, especially in relation to the person and work of the Saviour. In a similar manner Jude warned of 'certain men' who 'have crept in unnoticed, who long ago were marked out for this condemnation, ungodly men, who turn the grace of our God into licentiousness and deny the only Lord God and our Lord Jesus Christ' (Jude 4; cf. 2 Peter 2:1-3). The remedy urged by Jude by which to expose and refute false teachers is 'to contend earnestly for the faith which was once for all delivered to the saints' (Jude 3; cf. Titus 1:9). Revealed truth in Scripture is the yardstick by which to test the teacher. All teachers are to remember the sober warning of James: 'My brethren, let not many of you become teachers, knowing that we shall receive a stricter judgement' (James 3:1). It is one thing to believe error; it is far worse to teach it.

3. A divisive gospel

When the Lord Jesus Christ sent out his twelve apostles to preach and heal in the towns and villages of Judah and Galilee he loosely quoted the prophet Micah (7:6): 'Do not think that I came to bring peace on earth. I did not come to bring peace but a sword. For I have come to "set a man against his father, a daughter against her mother, and a daughter-in-law against her mother-in-law". And "a man's foes will be those of his own household." He who loves father or mother more than me is not worthy of me. And he who loves son or daughter more than me is not worthy of me' (Matt. 10:34-37).

There will always be contrasting responses to the gospel: some hearers will accept Christ; others will reject him. The gospel of peace does not always bring peace. Often, at least initially, the gospel brings division in a family when one member is converted; the other members react in horror and derision. Although Jesus is the 'Prince of Peace' (Isa. 9:6), responses to him vary from great love and devotion to hatred and antagonism. The greatest war-zone for a new convert is frequently his own home.

4. Removal of sins

> Who is a God like you,
> Pardoning iniquity
> And passing over the transgression of the remnant of his heritage?
> He does not retain his anger for ever,
> Because he delights in mercy.
> He will again have compassion on us,
> And will subdue our iniquities.
> You will cast all our sins
> Into the depths of the sea
>
> (7:18-19).

The disposal of the sins of 'the remnant of his heritage', the elect, the chosen people of God, is graphically portrayed. As one preacher cryptically commented, 'God has cast our sins into the deepest ocean and put up a sign: "No fishing".' The free forgiveness of sins is a greater blessing than any human being could ever have imagined.

Conclusion

This small book presents a summary of Micah's ministry in the land of Judah. It sets out the basis of God's complaint against his people, announces the certain punishment that is coming on account of their sins and reveals a glorious salvation yet to come. The centre and soul of this great salvation will be the person of the God/Messiah. By means of the book of Micah another great step forward is taken in the preparation for the coming of Christ, the Son of the living God. His birthplace is specified; his natures are identified. In time God will reveal how his Messiah King will be the very means by which he 'will cast all our sins into the depths of the sea' and demonstrate beyond all controversy that the incomparable Jehovah is so outstanding in pardoning sin: 'In this the love of God was manifested towards us, that God has sent his only begotten Son into the world, that we might live through him. In this is love, not that we loved God, but that he loved us and sent his Son to be the propitiation for our sins' (1 John 4:9-10).

Nahum

('comfort')

Author: Nahum

Key thought: 'awful doom'

Theme:
The destruction of God's enemies

'The LORD will take vengeance
    on his adversaries,
And he reserves wrath for his
    enemies...'

Nahum 1:2

Summary

Nahum

Emphasis upon the love of God may lead to an unbalanced view of the awesome nature and majesty of Almighty God. Worship, even among converted, Bible-believing people, has deteriorated in many churches and fellowships. Concentration upon the kindness and compassion of God, to the detriment of thought and attention focused upon the might and majesty of God, has brought a low view of worship and a loss of the awesomeness of God's being. In many Christian circles there is an almost exclusive emphasis upon the person and work of God the Son and the presence and power of God the Holy Spirit, with a resultant neglect of God the Father. We need only enquire how many hymns and spiritual songs sung in our assemblies, and how many prayers prayed in our meetings, directly address God the Father. A sense of the holiness, glory, majesty and might of Almighty God needs to be recaptured in public and in private worship if we are to 'worship in spirit and truth' (John 4:24).

The book of Nahum brings such a corrective. The message of this prophet is bold and striking. The opening chapter declares who and what God is. No believer can read these words without bowing in recognition of the Lord's awesome majesty. While the destruction of Israel's great enemy gives consolation to God's people in Judah, it also demonstrates that, even for the people of God, 'It is a fearful thing to fall into the hands of the living God' (Heb. 10:31). 'Our God is a consuming fire' (Heb. 12:29), therefore we should worship and serve him 'acceptably with reverence and godly fear' (Heb. 12:28).

Author

The name 'Nahum' means 'comfort' or 'consolation'. It is a shortened form of Nehemiah, which means 'Comfort of Yahweh', or 'Comfort of Jehovah'.[1] The prophet is identified as a native of Elkosh (1:1), but there is no way of determining the location of this town or village. Various answers have been proposed through the years. One suggestion is that it was on the Tigris River north of Nineveh, and that Nahum may have been a descendant of an exiled northern Israelite family; another that it was in northern Galilee at a site now called El-Kauzeh; a third that it was in Capernaum (Caper-Nahum meaning 'place of Nahum the prophet'); and a fourth that it was in Judah, between Jerusalem and Gaza.[2] As the Lord has not seen fit to give clear indications in the Scriptures enabling us to locate Elkosh with any degree of certainty, the only possible conclusion must be that such information is irrelevant to the messenger and his message.

The book of Nahum is unique in that it is described as a 'book' (1:1). This suggests that the prophecies recorded here may not have been preached. The other writing prophets simply made a record of their public proclamations (cf. Jer. 36:2,28). From Nahum we may have 'something which was originally written as a pamphlet for circulation and discussion among the people'.[3]

Historical setting

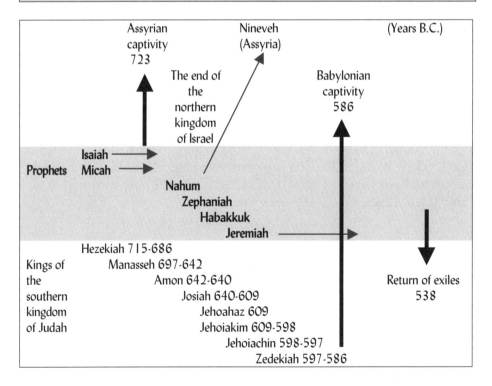

Nahum prophesied after the destruction of 'No Amon' (3:8), the strong fortress of the Egyptians on the River Nile, better known by its Greek name, 'Thebes', and before the fall of Assyria when Nineveh was demolished. This places Nahum's ministry somewhere between 663 and 612 B.C. To be more exact is not possible.

The book of Nahum stands as a sequel to the prophecy of Jonah. Both address Nineveh, the capital of Assyria, but whereas Jonah preached a call to repentance, over a hundred years later Nahum announces the destruction of the nation for its terrible apostasy.

The city of Nineveh was built around 2000 B.C. by Nimrod (Gen. 10:11). It is first implied to be the capital of Assyria in the days of King Hezekiah (2 Kings 19:36). A library in the city established by King Ashurbanipal provided a great source of knowledge of Assyrian and Babylonian affairs.[4]

Somewhere in the period 793–753 B.C. the prophet Jonah reluctantly obeyed the commission of the Lord and journeyed to Nineveh. There he preached the message given to him by God with the result that the majority of those Gentile people repented and turned to God. This was the outcome that Jonah had feared because he knew God to be 'a gracious and merciful God, slow to anger and abundant in loving-kindness, one who relents from doing harm' (Jonah 4:2). Jonah did not want the Assyrians to be given any opportunity to repent. They were a dreadful people and the enemies of Israel. In his opinion they deserved to die under the judgement of God. With the repentance of the people, however, the threatened overthrow of Nineveh within forty days (Jonah 3:4) was rescinded.

It would appear that, within a short time following that apparent spiritual awakening with numerous conversions, the people of Nineveh once more reverted to their gross idolatry and vile immorality. They were a vicious people noted for their extreme barbarity and cruelty. Their empire grew, threatening the surrounding nations.

In 726 B.C. the Assyrians invaded the northern kingdom of Israel and, following a three-year siege under the leadership of King Shalmaneser (2 Kings 18:9-10), Samaria (the capital of Israel) was taken and the majority of the people were forcibly removed into exile. The Assyrians brought in immigrants from five surrounding nations to repopulate the region of northern Israel (2 Kings 17:24). The Samaritan nation had been born.

Eight years after conquering the northern kingdom of Israel, the Assyrians, led by their new king, Sennacherib, came up against Judah (2 Kings 18:13). Sennacherib's extreme arrogance towards the Lord God illustrated how far the nation of Assyria had fallen away from God in the short time since Jonah. Under attack from the Assyrians, King Hezekiah prayed to God (2 Kings 19:15-19) and the prophet Isaiah sent a reply back from God (2 Kings 19:20-34). Overnight the Lord killed 185,000 soldiers. Sennacherib returned to Nineveh and within a short while he was murdered by two of his sons.

The Assyrians continued to plunder other nations. In 663 B.C. they attacked and destroyed the Egyptian fortress city of Thebes, that is, No Amon (3:8), which was built on both sides of the River Nile and considered to be impregnable. Both Jeremiah and Ezekiel had prophesied its destruction (Jer. 46:25; Ezek. 30:14).

Nineveh became the strongest fortress city in the world. The thirty-metre high wall surrounding the city was wide enough for three chariots to travel side by side. Huge towers were built strategically along the ramparts. A moat fifty metres wide and twenty metres deep surrounded the whole city.[5]

More than a century after the prophet Jonah, another prophet came addressing Nineveh (Assyria). Nahum's prophecy that the apparently impenetrable city of Nineveh would be invaded and destroyed must have been greeted with open incredulity. Assyria in Nahum's day was still like 'the lion' who 'tore in pieces enough for his cubs, killed for his lionesses, filled his caves with prey, and his dens with flesh' (2:12). This prophet foretold the utter destruction of Nineveh and the Assyrians because of their great turning from the Lord. They had experienced God's pardoning mercy in years past, but had so quickly deserted him. They were an apostate nation.

Nineveh was eventually destroyed in 612 B.C. under the combined forces of the Medes and Babylonians.

Outline

Israel had been destroyed by the Assyrians. Judah had been repeatedly threatened by them. Nahum communicates a message of judgement upon the enemy. Though Assyria had been blessed by God in the days of Jonah (c. 780 B.C.) and used by God in the punishment of Israel (2 Kings 17:6 — 723 B.C.), nevertheless her sins will not be overlooked. The Ninevites are an apostate people. They have known God; they have been blessed by God; they have now rejected God, and they will be punished by God.

Part I: The might and majesty of the Lord (1:1-15)

The book opens with an introductory psalm in which God is praised for his majestic power, the punishment of the Lord's enemies is announced and God's goodness is declared to all who trust in him. Under the image of a fierce storm, Nahum presents the overwhelming majesty of Almighty God (1:2-8). The grandeur, holiness, patience, power and justice of God are displayed as he comes into conflict with the cruel and defiant Assyrian Empire:

> Who can stand before his indignation?
> And who can endure the fierceness of his anger?
> His fury is poured out like fire,
> And the rocks are thrown down by him
>
> (1:6).

Yet even here, in the declaration of the most severe threatenings, there is a distinct note of grace:

> The LORD is good,
> A stronghold in the day of trouble;
> And he knows those who trust in him
>
> (1:7).

Condemned to extinction (1:8-9), the Assyrians will be overtaken at a time when they consider themselves beyond the reach of anyone. Destruction will come while they are 'tangled like thorns' (1:10). 'When thorns are entangled, we dare not, with the ends of our fingers, to touch their extreme parts; for wherever we put our hands, thorns meet and prick us. Hence the Prophet says, they who are as *entangled thorns;* that is, "However thorny ye may be, however full of poison, full of fury, full of wickedness, full of frauds, full of cruelty, ye may be, still the Lord can with one fire consume you, and consume you without any difficulty."'[6]

The 'wicked counsellor' from among them (1:11) seems to be a direct reference to the Rabshakeh, the leader of the Assyrian army, whose defiant and blasphemous words were so offensive to King Hezekiah and the people of Jerusalem, and even more offensive to the King of kings in heaven (2 Kings 18:28-37). For this effrontery the name of the Assyrians will be blotted out (1:14).

While great wrath is expressed towards Assyria, there is a note of future deliverance for Judah, the remaining Israelites in the southern region (1:15). The first chapter closes with a warning to the people of Judah to keep the terms of their covenant with the Lord: 'O Judah, keep your appointed feasts, perform your vows' (1:15). Coming after what God has said to the Assyrians in such stark and graphic terms, this warning is all the more sober and impressive. The people of Judah must turn from their wicked ways or they are in danger of a similar end to that of the Ninevites.

Part II: The destruction of Nineveh (2:1-13)

Assyria will be conquered; Judah will be restored (2:1-2). Preparation is underway for the destruction of Nineveh. The empire that has been built on violence and cruelty will perish in the same manner. Nineveh's downfall and destruction are expressed in the most vivid terms. The Lord comes as a mighty, invincible warrior against Assyria. Nahum gives a dramatic description of the siege of Nineveh. 'The prophet sees, and makes his hearers see, all the horrid sights of the tragic scene.'[7]

Part III: The Victor and the vanquished (3:1-19)

The Assyrians more than deserve the punishment that will be inflicted upon them (3:1-4). They will not escape God's justice. There is nothing they can do to avert the vengeance of the Lord. Just as Assyria invaded and conquered the seemingly impregnable fortress at No Amon, so she herself will be invaded and conquered. All that God can do with a people who have so openly and blasphemously insulted him over so many years is to destroy them (cf. Zeph. 2:13-15).

The prophecy ends with a rhetorical question (3:19). Only one other book in the Old Testament ends like this — the book of Jonah! Drawing attention to the powerful contrast is clearly intended.

Christ and his church

This prophecy of Nahum, which focuses on the judgement of Assyria, was a message of comfort and a word of hope to the Judeans of the seventh

century before Christ who first read it. Assyria had conquered and destroyed their Israelite brethren in the northern kingdom and was continually
threatening them. The people of Judah lived under this constant threat of
harassment, persecution and invasion. To hear that God was to punish
their persistent enemies severely would be a source of encouragement.

In this book we find no types or theophanies, and no prophecies that
are directly related to the Lord Jesus Christ and his church. Consequently
many Christians see little or no value or relevance in the book of Nahum
for today. This is, however, far from being the case.

The key to the book of Nahum is found in the opening psalm (1:2-15).
Here the Lord is revealed as the great Warrior who delivers his people and
punishes his enemies:

> God is jealous, and the LORD avenges;
> The LORD avenges and is furious.
> The LORD will take vengeance on his adversaries,
> And he reserves wrath for his enemies;
> The LORD is slow to anger and great in power,
> And will not at all acquit the wicked
>
> (1:2-3).

> The LORD is good,
> A stronghold in the day of trouble;
> And he knows those who trust in him.
> But with an overflowing flood
> He will make an utter end of its place,
> And darkness will pursue his enemies
>
> (1:7-8).

> O Judah, keep your appointed feasts,
> Perform your vows.
> For the wicked one shall no more pass through you;
> He is utterly cut off
>
> (1:15).

It is here that there is the strongest connection with the coming Christ, for a
similar note is struck in prophecy about the Messianic King:

> Gird your sword upon your thigh, O Mighty One,
> With your glory and your majesty.

And in your majesty ride prosperously because of truth, humility,
    and righteousness;
And your right hand shall teach you awesome things.
Your arrows are sharp in the heart of the King's enemies;
The peoples fall under you

                                 (Ps. 45:3-5).

He will bring justice to the poor of the people;
He will save the children of the needy,
And will break in pieces the oppressor...
For he will deliver the needy when he cries,
The poor also, and him who has no helper.
He will spare the poor and needy,
And will save the souls of the needy.
He will redeem their life from oppression and violence;
And precious shall be their blood in his sight

                          (Ps. 72:4,12-14).

The warrior God of the Old Testament anticipates the warrior Christ of the New Testament. There is, however, a striking difference. In the Old Testament God conducted his warfare against the physical enemies of Israel (the Assyrians, Canaanites, Philistines, etc.). In the New Testament the warfare is shown to be conducted in the spiritual domain, against Satan and his forces: 'And you, being dead in your trespasses and the uncircumcision of your flesh, he has made alive together with him, having forgiven you all trespasses, having wiped out the handwriting of requirements that was against us, which was contrary to us. And he has taken it out of the way, having nailed it to the cross. *Having disarmed principalities and powers,* he made a public spectacle of them, triumphing over them in it' (Col. 2:13-15, emphasis added). 'For he must reign till he has put all enemies under his feet' (1 Cor. 15:25).

The Warrior Christ will battle on behalf of his people, subduing all their enemies, until the finale on the great and terrible Day of the Lord: 'Then I saw heaven opened, and behold, a white horse. And he who sat on him was called Faithful and True, and in righteousness he judges and makes war. His eyes were like a flame of fire, and on his head were many crowns. He had a name written that no one knew except himself. He was clothed with a robe dipped in blood, and his name is called the Word of God. And the armies in heaven, clothed in fine linen, white and clean, followed him on white horses. Now out of his mouth goes a sharp sword, that with it he should strike the nations. And he himself will rule them with a rod of iron. He himself treads the winepress of the fierceness and wrath of Almighty God. And he has on his robe and on his thigh a name written: King of Kings and Lord of Lords' (Rev. 19:11-16).

Consequently, although Nineveh no longer exists, the abiding significance of the book of Nahum is found in the warring Christ of the New Testament.[8]

Application

1. Worship

The opening verses of the book of Nahum declare the glory, magnificence and power of Almighty God. The introduction, 'God is jealous, and the LORD avenges' (1:2), links back to the law at Sinai and the Ten Commandments, which begin with three commandments as to how the Lord is to be worshipped and served (Exod. 20:1-7). After declaring that he alone is to be worshipped and served, and that no image or visual symbol is ever to be used to represent him, the Lord gives his reasons: 'For I, the LORD your God, am a jealous God, visiting the iniquity of the fathers on the children to the third and fourth generations of those who hate me, but showing mercy to thousands, to those who love me and keep my commandments' (Exod. 20:5-6).

Right from the outset the Bible presents a revelation of the true God which is intended to inspire worship and praise. The Lord God is the sovereign Creator. 'To consider the vastness of the universe and to realize that it has come from the sovereign God and is kept in being by His power is to be moved to awe and wonder. This is the reaction which characterizes biblical religion, and which stands in marked contrast with the glib familiarity and flippancy so common in today's religious scene.'[9]

Add to the knowledge of his creative power and genius his controlling wisdom, his all-seeing, all-hearing, all-knowing awareness, his righteousness, his holiness, his mercy and his grace, and the mind is nearly overwhelmed by awe and wonder. No wonder the psalmist cries out:

Oh come, let us sing to the LORD!
Let us shout joyfully to the Rock of our salvation.

Let us come before his presence with thanksgiving;
Let us shout joyfully to him with psalms.
For the LORD is the great God,
And the great King above all gods.
In his hand are the deep places of the earth;
The heights of the hills are his also.
The sea is his, for he made it;
And his hands formed the dry land.
Oh come, let us worship and bow down;
Let us kneel before the LORD our Maker.
For he is our God,
And we are the people of his pasture,
And the sheep of his hand

(Ps. 95:1-7).

2. Prophecy fulfilled

The wicked Assyrians fell under the righteous judgement of Almighty God in 612 B.C. Nineveh, once the strongest city on earth, was destroyed. The prophecies of Nahum came to a literal fulfilment. The King of Assyria was celebrating his successes and had given a vast quantity of wine to his soldiers, who proceeded to get extremely drunk (1:10).[10] The Tigris River overflowed its banks and the flood destroyed part of the city wall (1:8; 2:6). Army deserters informed the Babylonians of the situation in the capital. The combined forces of the Medes and Babylonians grasped the opportunity and entered through the breach in the wall, plundering the city and setting fire to it (1:6,10). Considerable amounts of gold and silver not destroyed by the flames were carried away (2:9). The city of Nineveh was destroyed and 'hidden' (3:11; cf. Zeph. 2:13-15) for 2,050 years; the site was not discovered until A.D. 1842.[11]

There may have been as long as fifty years between the prophecy of Nahum and its fulfilment, which illustrates the long-suffering of God. There is a very strong parallel in the New Testament in relation to the end of this present world: 'The Lord is not slack concerning his promise, as some count slackness, but is long-suffering towards us, not willing that any should perish but that all should come to repentance. But the day of the Lord will come as a thief in the night, in which the heavens will pass away with a great noise, and the elements will melt with fervent heat; both the earth and the works that are in it will be burned up. Therefore, since all these things will be dissolved, what manner of persons ought you to be in holy conduct and godliness, looking for and hastening the coming of the day of God...' (2 Peter 3:9-12).

3. Warnings Ignored

Interspersed within this book of judgement against Assyria is a message of reassurance and warning for Judah. There is a distinct note of comfort for the people of God (1:7), a promise of delivery from oppression (12-13) and of the restoration of the nation (2:2). But the people of Judah have to face their responsibilities and walk in obedience to the Lord (1:15) or they too will know the indignation and anger of God (1:6).

Judah failed to learn the lesson and continued to break their covenant with the Lord. Seven years after the fall of Assyria, King Nebuchadnezzar and the Babylonians came against their nation (2 Kings 24:1; 605 B.C.). After repeated threats, rebellions and invasions, Judah was finally destroyed in 586 B.C., and the majority of the remaining inhabitants of the southern kingdom were taken captive. The Babylonian exile began (2 Kings 25:11,21).

Devastating as the judgement of God was against Assyria, and then against Judah, there is a far greater devastation coming upon the whole world. The first death is bad; the second death is far worse (Rev. 2:11; 20:6, 21:8). This could be called 'a living death', because it is another way of describing that everlasting hell which is the abode of unrepentant sinners, all those who are not the children of God.

The warning of this great day of God's judgement (Rom. 2:5; Matt. 12:36; 2 Peter 2:9; 3:7) has profound implications for the child of God. Peter draws attention to this implication when he asks, 'What manner of persons ought you to be in holy conduct and godliness?' Knowing that God's prophecy of the Day of Judgement will be fulfilled should have a significant impact on our lives and produce every endeavour towards holiness (cf. Titus 2:11-14).

Conclusion

Nahum stands with Obadiah and Habakkuk in proclaiming God's judgement upon the enemies of Judah. Nahum addresses Assyria; Obadiah addresses Edom, and Habakkuk addresses Babylon. Though the people of Judah were often sinful, idolatrous and immoral, the Lord always restored them after punishment. But there was to be no restoration for Assyria. Nahum clearly reveals the principles by which the Lord judges the nations while at the same time showing mercy to Judah. 'Blessed is the nation whose God is the LORD. And the people whom he has chosen as his own inheritance' (Ps. 33:12).

It is not only the grace of God, but also the righteous anger of God, which reveals the glory of God. God's righteous anger towards sin in all its forms and expressions is only an inevitable consequence of his holy love. God cannot truly love that which is pure, holy, good and true without hating those things that are opposed to purity, holiness, goodness and truth.

> For the LORD is righteous,
> He loves righteousness;
> His countenance beholds the upright
>
> (Ps. 11:7)

> God is a just judge,
> And God is angry with the wicked every day
>
> (Ps. 7:11).

There can be no genuine and true love of that which is holy and good, without there also being a corresponding hatred of that which is unholy and evil. 'Who can stand before his indignation? And who can endure the fierceness of his anger?' (1:6).

In grace the Lord God has provided an answer to his wrath for those who believe in the Saviour: 'He who believes in the Son has everlasting life; and he who does not believe the Son shall not see life, but the wrath of God abides on him' (John 3:36).

Habakkuk

('to embrace')

Author: Habakkuk

Key thought: 'Living by faith'

Theme: The mysteries of providence

'Behold the proud,
His soul is not upright in him;
But the just shall live by his faith.'
Habakkuk 2:4

Summary

Habakkuk

Why does God tolerate sinners? Why does he permit the wicked to triumph in their evil designs? Is he not the Almighty? Does he not have the authority, the right and the power to resolve bad situations?

God's people suffer and God appears unmoved. They are persecuted under evil regimes; they are molested, abused and ill-treated — and God seems distant. Does God care?

The invasion of the northern kingdom of Israel and the subsequent deportation of the majority of its citizens to Assyria (723 B.C.) had not softened the hearts of their brothers in the southern kingdom of Judah. Though the people of Judah had known, in the following 130 years, some 'times of refreshing … from the presence of the Lord' (Acts 3:19), they had fallen back yet again into serious sin. Once more leaders in church and state, in religion and politics, were corrupt. The faithful remnant was exploited and abused. When the spiritually awakened and enlightened cried out to God in their distress he appeared not to hear, not to heed.

Habakkuk, like so many before him and so many since, was utterly confused by the behaviour he witnessed around him and by the wickedness so prevalent throughout Judah. He had no doubt that the Lord of heaven and earth was almighty, just and holy, but why did he not intervene? 'Here was a man greatly troubled by what was happening. He was anxious to reconcile what he saw with what he believed.'[1]

Author

Habakkuk was a prophet (1:1; 3:1) and also evidently a member of the Levitical orchestra in the temple (3:19;[2] cf. 1 Chr. 25:1); hence he must have been a resident in Jerusalem. He does not provide any biographical material and he is not mentioned elsewhere in the Old Testament; consequently nothing more is known about him.

True to his name (Habakkuk means 'to embrace' or 'to cling'),[3] the prophet 'clings' to the Lord and pours out his difficulties in prayer.

Historical setting

Unlike many of the prophets, Habakkuk does not locate his ministry in the reign of a king, or kings, of Judah, although the words of 1:5-6 would lead to the conclusion that he ministered in the years leading up to the invasions of Judah by Nebuchadnezzar of Babylon (which took place in 605 B.C., 597 B.C. and 586 B.C.). Judging from the terrible spiritual and moral conditions in Judah (1:2-4), the beneficial effects of Josiah's reign (640–609 B.C.) and reformation (2 Chr. 34:1 – 35:27) are no longer to be seen. This would place Habakkuk's ministry in the first four years of the reign of Jehoiakim (609–598 B.C.) — that is, between the death of Josiah and the first invasion by Babylon, somewhere, therefore, between 609 and 605 B.C.

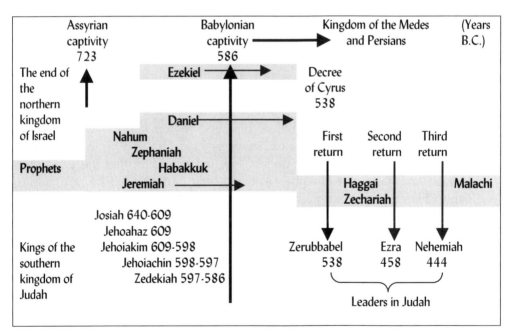

Judah and its prophets and kings before, during and after the exile

Jehoiakim was a godless king totally unlike his father King Josiah. He committed great acts of wickedness and led the people down the slippery slope to ruin (2 Kings 23:34 – 24:5). The account of the last years of Judah before the final Babylonian exile makes disturbing reading: 'Moreover all the leaders of the priests and the people transgressed more and more, according to all the abominations of the nations, and defiled the house of the LORD which he had consecrated in Jerusalem. And the LORD God of their fathers sent warnings to them by his messengers, rising up early and sending them, because he had compassion on his people and on his dwelling-place. But they mocked the messengers of God, despised his words, and scoffed at his prophets, until the wrath of the LORD arose against his people, till there was no remedy' (2 Chr. 36:14-16).

Habakkuk was one of those messengers sent by God. He was probably a contemporary of the prophets Nahum, Jeremiah and Zephaniah.

Outline

The whole book bears a poetic style 'approaching nearer to the Psalms in structure than any other of the prophetical writings'.[4]

Part I: Habakkuk's first conversation with the Lord (1:1-11)

Habakkuk sees the people of Israel in a thoroughly backslidden state. They have once more turned to idolatry and to the gross immorality with which it is so strongly associated. The authorities in the land are powerless and corrupt. These appalling conditions are weighing heavily upon the prophet's mind and heart. He has prayed frequently about the situation and called upon God, but there is no answer, no response from heaven: 'O LORD, how long shall I cry, and you will not hear?' (1:2). He is bewildered by the mystery of unpunished evil in the nations and cries out: 'Why do you show me iniquity, and cause me to see trouble?' (1:3). He cannot understand why the Lord allows such moral and spiritual wickedness.

Confident of the Lord's power, Habakkuk pours out his complaint. Judah is beset by oppression and violence on every side, the law is powerless and the righteous are constantly being victimized. The nation has once more fallen headlong into corruption and idolatry.

The Lord replies to the prophet's question, indicating that his silence does not mean that he is ignorant or indifferent to the situation. He is about to take action. He will raise up the Chaldeans (Babylonians) as an instrument of punishment (1:6), although they will not realize that the Lord is behind their successes; indeed they will credit their victories to their god (1:11). The Chaldeans will sweep through the nations in overwhelming victory, subduing all peoples before them.

Part II: Habakkuk's second conversation with the Lord (1:12 - 2:20)

The Lord's reply to Habakkuk's first question solves one difficulty but raises another: how can a holy God tolerate evil; indeed how can he use an evil nation to destroy people who are less wicked?

> Are you not from everlasting,
> O LORD my God, my Holy One? ...
> You are of purer eyes than to behold evil,
> And cannot look on wickedness.
> Why do you look on those who deal treacherously,
> And hold your tongue when the wicked devours
> One more righteous than he?
>
> (1:12-13).

The prophet climbs the watchtower to survey the land and wait to see what the Lord will do (2:1). The Lord instructs him to make a permanent record of the prophecy (2:2) so that it will be a testimony when it comes to pass. He encourages Habakkuk to be patient. The time for judgement is set. Those who love God must live with constant trust and confidence in the Lord: '... the just shall live by his faith' (2:4).

The Lord reveals that he is well aware of the wickedness of the Babylonians. The evils of this new world power are identified and swift judgement is pronounced against their dishonesty (2:6), covetousness (2:9), the use of violent means in building a town (2:12), moral corruption (2:15) and idolatry (2:18-19). The Lord promises that one day a new world order will ensue, and life will be significantly different:

> For the earth will be filled
> With the knowledge of the glory of the LORD,
> As the waters cover the sea
>
> (2:14).

Whereas idols carved out of stone and overlaid with gold and silver are lifeless and powerless, the Creator God is sovereign and will be seen to be supreme (cf. Jer. 10:1-16[5]): 'But the LORD is in his holy temple. Let all the earth keep silence before him' (2:20).

The moral character of God is such that no wickedness will go unpunished. The underlying message is that everyone will eventually stand before the Judge of all the earth.

Part III: A psalm of worship (3:1-19)

Habakkuk does not attempt to excuse or defend the people of Judah. He humbles himself before God and praises him for his holiness, justice and righteousness. He describes the appearance of God as a great Warrior overpowering and controlling all the forces of nature and the power of the nations.

The Lord is in control; the Lord knows what he is doing. Judgement will fall upon the wicked and impenitent. He works to his own timetable and according to his own counsel and purpose. The prophet prays a psalm of praise declaring the glory and majesty of the Lord, appreciated in the past and anticipated in the future. Whether this truth is demonstrated by past history or revealed by future prophecy, the Lord is in control. Habakkuk pleads with the Lord that in his anger he will remember mercy (3:2). He recalls the Lord's majesty at Sinai and in leading Israel into the promised land of Canaan. As he draws to mind the past demonstration of the might and majesty of God in delivering his people, the prophet trembles and hopes he will be safe when the destruction occurs. He utters his devotion to the living God and his glad reliance upon the Lord's purposes and providence:

Though the fig tree may not blossom,
Nor fruit be on the vines;
Though the labour of the olive may fail,
And the fields yield no food;
Though the flock be cut off from the fold,
And there be no herd in the stalls —
Yet I will rejoice in the LORD,
I will joy in the God of my salvation

(3:17-18).

Christ and his church

Opinions differ as to whether Habakkuk is describing a theophany which he himself witnessed, or whether he is reminding believers of God's appearance in the past when he says:

> God came from Teman,
> The Holy One from Mount Paran.
> His glory covered the heavens,
> And the earth was full of his praise.
> His brightness was like the light;
> He had rays flashing from his hand,
> And there his power was hidden.
> Before him went pestilence,
> And fever followed at his feet
>
> (3:3-5).

This description of God may have been taken from the earlier manifestations of the Lord: in delivering his people from Egypt, appearing upon Mount Sinai at the giving of the law, carrying them through the wilderness and settling them in the promised land.[6] On the other hand, comparing these words with the similar words of Moses in Deuteronomy 33:2, Keil notes a difference in tense in Habakkuk (not obvious in our translation) in which 'The LORD came' becomes in Habakkuk, 'He will come, or comes,' to indicate at the very outset that he is about to describe not a past, but a future revelation of the glory of the Lord. This Habakkuk sees in the form of a theophany, which is fulfilled before his mental eye.[7]

Habakkuk re-echoes the strong note struck by the prophet Nahum just a few years earlier, revealing God as the great Warrior.[8] Instead of using the designation 'LORD' (Jehovah, the name of God in covenant relationship with Israel), he uses the more general term 'God' *(Elohim)* which is used to designate God as the Lord and Governor of the whole world. He comes as the Holy One (1:12), who cannot tolerate sin and who will judge the world and destroy sinners (3:12-14). As Moses declared, following the destruction of the Egyptians, 'The LORD is a man of war; the LORD is his name' (Exod. 15:3).

Throughout the history of Israel the Lord exerted his mighty power in numerous miracles, overruling nature and nations (3:8-12). By these means he displayed his glory and saved his people. Habakkuk declares:

'You went forth for the salvation of your people, for salvation with your Anointed' (3:13). This is not so much a prophecy as a declaration about the past that is continually relevant. Nevertheless, what God has been doing in the past he will continue to do in the future. He has always been working in the world for the salvation of his people. He is always working to this end. He always will work for this purpose until the task is completed and 'the Son of Man' comes 'in the clouds with great power and glory' and gathers 'together his elect from the four winds, from the farthest part of earth to the farthest part of heaven' (Mark 13:26-27).

Who are God's people for whom he goes forth? In regard to creation, all people of the world are God's people. Under the Old Covenant, Israel was God's chosen people (Deut. 7:7-8), 'to whom pertain the adoption, the glory, the covenants, the giving of the law, the service of God, and the promises; of whom are the fathers and from whom, according to the flesh, Christ came, who is over all, the eternally blessed God' (Rom. 9:4-5). There never was a time, however, when *all* citizens of the nation of Israel were spiritual children of God: 'For they are not all Israel who are of Israel' (Rom. 9:6). Nevertheless the Lord always maintained a remnant, a spiritually quickened minority who loved him and were devoted to his worship and service. This expression, 'the salvation of your people', must refer, then, not to the nation of Israel as a whole, but to that 'remnant according to the election of grace' (Rom. 11:5).

This salvation of his people God accomplished (and continues to accomplish) by going forth with his Anointed (Hebrew — 'Messiah'). While the words of Habakkuk may signify men like Moses, Joshua and David, nevertheless the underlying truth has reference to the Son of God. 'God went forth with his Anointed, that is, with Jesus Christ, to save his people … and by this faith, by faith in this Messiah, the just shall live.'[9]

Application

1. Unbelief despite warnings

The judgement of God upon Judah, which was expressed in the invasion of the land by the Babylonians, is an illustration of an even more serious judgement from God coming upon the whole unbelieving world. Paul warns Jews in Antioch by quoting Habakkuk:

Behold, you despisers,
Marvel and perish;
For I work a work in your days,
A work which you will by no means believe,
Though one were to declare it to you

(Acts 13:41; cf. Hab. 1:5).

The quotation is applicable to all nations in all generations. Even though people are warned time and time again about the coming judgement of God, they stubbornly refuse to take notice. Many thousands have heard the gospel clearly and faithfully proclaimed and yet they refuse to repent and believe on the Lord Jesus Christ for salvation.

2. Living by faith

Scholars are divided as to the translation and therefore the interpretation of the words of Habakkuk: 'The just shall live by his faith' (2:4). Some give the sense: 'The one who is righteous shall live by his faith.' Others give the sense: 'The one who is righteous by faith shall live.' The first meaning appears to suit the context of Habakkuk (and that of Heb. 10:38), whereas the second is the evident meaning of the apostle Paul (Rom. 1:17; Gal. 3:11).

Through the prophet Habakkuk, the Lord declares the reason for his delay in delivering his people and punishing the wicked (2:2-4). Harsh difficulties in life make the distinction plain between 'the proud' (unrepentant sinners) and 'the just' (repentant sinners who are trusting in the grace of God). The just (righteous) 'shall live by his faith' (2:4). That person has confidence that the Lord's timing is the best timing. God knows *what* he is doing; God knows *when* he will do it. Let the believer rest in God's wisdom, power and grace. 'The Lord is not slack concerning his promise, as some count slackness, but is long-suffering towards us, not willing that any should perish but that all should come to repentance' (2 Peter 3:9).

Speaking of the great salvation 'ready to be revealed in the last time', the apostle Peter says, 'In this you greatly rejoice, though now for a little while, if need be, you have been grieved by various trials, that the genuineness of your faith, being much more precious than gold that perishes, though it is tested by fire, may be found to praise, honour, and glory at the revelation of Jesus Christ...' (1 Peter 1:6-7).

The second meaning of the words, 'The just shall live by his faith' (2:4), is found in the New Testament and is understood in the sense of 'The one who is righteous by faith shall live.' In other words, it is a declaration of the foundation of a right relationship with God. God is righteous; God demands righteousness; we live in the presence of God only by righteousness. This righteousness is provided by the Lord Jesus Christ (Jer. 23:6; 1 Cor. 1:30; 2 Cor. 5:21). It is the righteousness of God which is clearly revealed in the New Testament gospel and is ours only by faith (Rom. 1:17). 'But now the righteousness of God apart from the law is revealed, being witnessed by the Law and the Prophets, even the righteousness of God which is through faith in Jesus Christ to all and on all who believe' (Rom. 3:21-22).

No one is made righteous by obedience to the law of God because no one is able to keep the law of God in its entirety (Gal. 3:11). If any are righteous before God it is because they have received God's righteousness as a free gift through faith. This has always been the case, for Abraham 'believed in the LORD, and he accounted it to him for righteousness' (Gen. 15:6; cf. Rom. 4:2-5). While, as Calvin acknowledges, 'Habakkuk does not, it is true, explicitly deal with this question, and hence he makes no mention of free righteousness',[10] the New Testament nevertheless amplifies and clarifies the meaning intended by the Holy Spirit.

'The question is not what the Old Testament writers intended in such and such sayings, but what the Spirit which was in them did signify. The Prophets might often not know the full extent of their own prophecy, but certainly the Spirit, by which they spake, always did... And who dare say but that He may point out more fully under the New Testament what He intended in the Old, than ever could have entered into the heart of man? (1 Cor. 2:9-10). Surely the only wise God must be allowed to know the full sense of His own words.'[11]

There is, however, no real tension between the two interpretations, 'The one who is righteous by faith shall live' and 'The one who is righteous shall live by his faith'. As is often the case, the New Testament amplifies and clarifies the Old. We must first be 'righteous' before God, and that is only possible 'by faith', *and then* we 'shall live by faith' (2 Cor. 5:7).

It is evident that the phrase, 'The just shall live by his faith,' is applied with differing emphases according to the context: in Romans 1:17 the emphasis falls upon 'righteousness'; in Galatians 3:11 it falls upon 'faith'; while in Habakkuk 2:4 it falls upon 'live'. In Hebrews 10:38 the emphasis is that of Habakkuk: to continue to live firm in the faith. The passage that follows immediately afterwards in Hebrews 11 illustrates how God's people were saved *by faith alone* before the coming of the Messiah, even as God's people are saved *by faith alone* since the coming of the Messiah. Strictly speaking, of course, all who are saved are saved by grace through faith and even this faith is a gift from God (Eph. 2:8).

We stand firm and secure only when we rest on God by faith: 'Before a man can attain to a comfortable way of bearing trouble and waiting on God in hard times, he must first make sure of his personal reconciliation and righteousness before God, which will be only when by faith he lays hold on Christ's righteousness offered in the gospel. He must first be "just", and that "by faith", and then he "shall live by faith", in trouble…'[12]

3. Trust in difficult days

There are strong points of comparison between the book of Habakkuk and that of Job. Evil prospers and the righteous suffer. Habakkuk received the same basic message as Job that, 'In spite of all appearances to the contrary, and no matter how difficult conditions might become, he must continue to believe, continue to trust the promises of God and have confidence that the Lord of all the earth would do right.'[13] Years before Isaiah had expressed a similar thought:

> Who among you fears the LORD?
> Who obeys the voice of his Servant?
> Who walks in darkness
> And has no light?
> Let him trust in the name of the LORD
> And rely upon his God
>
>   (Isa. 50:10).

The most staggering illustration of a man clinging to God in the darkest hour is that of the Lord Jesus Christ. In the Garden of Gethsemane he prayed: 'O my Father, if it is possible, let this cup pass from me; nevertheless, not as I will, but as you will' (Matt. 26:39). Christ 'humbled himself and became obedient to … death, even the death of the cross' (Phil. 2:8). And on that cross at the height of his suffering he cried out, 'My God, my God, why have you forsaken me?' (Matt. 27:46).

Habakkuk concludes with some of the most moving words of faith and confidence. This is the hope of all believers: that when the day of trouble comes, when the harvest fails, when livestock die and the outlook in life is desperate, they will be able to say, 'Yet I will rejoice in the LORD, I will joy in the God of my salvation' (3:18).

Another suffering servant of God, the apostle Paul (cf. 2 Cor. 11:23-28), declared the same confidence in the Lord: 'Not that I speak in regard to need, for I have learned in whatever state I am, to be content: I know how to be abased, and I know how to abound. Everywhere and in all things I have learned both to be full and to be hungry, both to abound and to suffer need. I can do all things through Christ who strengthens me' (Phil. 4:11-13).

Conclusion

Why does the Lord allow his people to be persecuted? Why does the Father allow his children to suffer? Why does the Lord stand by while false religions sweep through one nation after another, debarring Christian preachers from freely proclaiming the glorious gospel? Why does the Lord permit impostors to deceive the people with a false Christianity?

The prophet Habakkuk faced the same kind of moral dilemmas. He could not harmonize his knowledge of the goodness and righteousness of God with the evil so prevalent in the world. While he was struggling in prayer, God gave the prophet 'a wonderful insight into biblical philosophy and history, and how these things are to be reconciled with His own holiness and greatness, and how everything will eventually be perfectly worked out'.[14] Habakkuk may not have understood God's ways, but he was confident in God's wisdom. God is consistent with himself even as he permits evil. The wicked may appear to prosper, but it is only for a little while. The judgement of God will fall upon them. Asaph faced the same dilemma as he witnessed the prosperity of the wicked:

> When I thought how to understand this,
> It was too painful for me —
> Until I went into the sanctuary of God;
> Then I understood their end

(Ps. 73:16-17).

Habakkuk began by questioning the Lord. He closed by praising the Lord. He praised God for his person, his power and his purposes. The Lord requires faith from his people. He does not give detailed explanations of his activity or his inactivity. The answer is consistently the same: God is good and God knows what he is doing.

Nowhere was the activity of God more baffling to human thought than in the death of the Lord Jesus Christ: scorned and abused by the Jewish leadership, crucified by Gentiles as a common criminal and deserted by his friends. The evidence would seem to suggest that God's purposes were frustrated. On the contrary, however, the purpose of God was not thwarted but accomplished. Isaiah had prophesied that 'It pleased the LORD to bruise him; he has put him to grief' (Isa. 53:10). While it is true that Jesus was 'taken by lawless hands ... crucified, and put to death', he was nevertheless 'delivered by the carefully planned intention and foreknowledge of God' (Acts 2:23). What appears to human eyes and reason to be evidence of failure is in reality the greatest success. What appears to be weakness turns out to be remarkable power (1 Cor. 1:23-25).

> 'For my thoughts are not your thoughts,
> Nor are your ways my ways,' says the LORD.
> 'For as the heavens are higher than the earth,
> So are my ways higher than your ways,
> And my thoughts than your thoughts'
>
> (Isa. 55:8-9).

God's ways are often baffling to his children, but he is under no obligation to explain himself to us. The Lord requires our devotion and our trust.

> God moves in a mysterious way
> His wonders to perform;
> He plants his footsteps in the sea,
> And rides upon the storm.
>
> Blind unbelief is sure to err,
> And scan his work in vain;
> God is his own interpreter,
> And he will make it plain
>
> (William Cowper, 1731-1800).

Whatever and whenever the children of God may suffer, they can be confident in knowing that God is fighting for them: 'If God is for us, who can be against us?' (Rom. 8:31). 'And shall God not avenge his own elect who cry out day and night to him, though he bears long with them? I tell you that he will avenge them speedily' (Luke 18:7-8).

Like Habakkuk all God's saints are to trust the Lord implicitly:

> Though the fig tree may not blossom,
> Nor fruit be on the vines;
> Though the labour of the olive may fail,
> And the fields yield no food;
> Though the flock be cut off from the fold,
> And there be no herd in the stalls—
> Yet I will rejoice in the LORD,
> I will joy in the God of my salvation

(3:17-18).

Zephaniah

('hidden by Jehovah')

Author: Zephaniah

Key thought: God's jealousy

Theme:
The searching judgements of God

'All the earth shall be devoured
With the fire of my jealousy.'
Zephaniah 3:8.

Summary

Zephaniah

At Sinai the Ten Commandments began:

> I am the LORD your God, who brought you out of the land of Egypt,
> out of the house of bondage.
> You shall have no other gods before me.
> You shall not make for yourself any carved image, or any likeness of
> anything that is in heaven above, or that is in the earth beneath,
> or that is in the water under the earth; you shall not bow down to
> them nor serve them. For I, the LORD your God, am a jealous
> God, visiting the iniquity of the fathers on the children to the third
> and fourth generations of those who hate me, but showing mercy
> to thousands, to those who love me and keep my commandments
> (Exod. 20:2-6).

The motivation behind these early commandments is given: 'For I, the LORD your God, am a jealous God.' Fundamental to all God's dealings with his people is his jealousy, but not the kind of jealousy so often demonstrated by human beings. Human jealousy often stems from insecurity, fear or resentment, and is expressed by suspicion of unfaithfulness. God needs no one to affirm his being or his worth. He is the only true God; he made all things; he is Lord of heaven and earth; he has the right to the entire devotion of all his subjects:

> I am the LORD, and there is no other;
> I form the light and create darkness,
> I make peace and create calamity;
> I, the LORD, do all these things...

> Woe to him who strives with his Maker! ...

And there is no other God besides me,
A just God and a Saviour;
There is none besides me.
Look to me, and be saved,
All you ends of the earth!
For I am God, and there is no other…

I have made, and I will bear;
Even I will carry, and will deliver you.
To whom will you liken me, and make me equal
And compare me, that we should be alike?

(Isa. 45:6-7,9,21-22; 46:4-5).

Zephaniah is the book of God's jealousy, God's demand for exclusive loyalty. It is a jealousy which is expressed in righteous judgement. Yet in the midst of judgement God expresses amazing love towards his chosen people and will go to great lengths to secure an exclusive place in their hearts.

Author

As Zephaniah is the only prophet to trace his ancestry back through so many generations there must be some significance in this. The conclusion seems therefore justified that Hizkiah (1:1, AV) is to be identified with Hezekiah,[1] the godly king of Judah (715–686 B.C.). Zephaniah is therefore the only Old Testament prophet of royal blood, a direct descendant of King Hezekiah, who was his great-great-grandfather. As such, he would have easy access to the royal court and therefore first-hand knowledge of the corruption of Judah's leaders in church and state.

Zephaniah means 'hidden or protected by Jehovah' and the prophet may have had his own name in mind when he wrote:

Seek the LORD, all you meek of the earth,
Who have upheld his justice.
Seek righteousness, seek humility.
It may be that you will be hidden
In the day of the LORD's anger

(2:3).

Historical setting

According to the opening words (1:1), Zephaniah exercised his ministry during the reign of godly King Josiah (640–609 B.C.) As the destruction of Nineveh (foretold in 2:13) occurred in 612 B.C., Zephaniah must have prophesied somewhere between 640 and 612 B.C. The imminent judgement of God which the prophet described occurred when Judah was invaded by the Babylonians (605 B.C.).

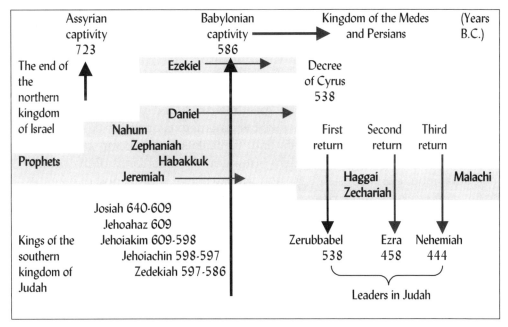

Judah and its prophets and kings before, during and after the exile

The northern kingdom of Israel (the ten tribes) had been invaded a century earlier and her inhabitants taken captive into the land of Assyria (723 B.C.). The small nation of Judah (the two tribes of Israel, Judah and Benjamin) remained with her capital at Jerusalem, but her days were numbered. Continuing rebellion against the Lord, with blatant idolatry and immorality, was to lead to her overthrow and subsequent captivity in the land of Babylon.

Born during the reign of evil Manasseh, Zephaniah would be all too aware of the corruption into which Judah had so easily and so often slipped. By the time his ministry commenced, a new king was on the

throne of Judah. It is generally thought that Zephaniah exercised his ministry in the early years of Josiah's reign before that godly king instigated a
religious reformation of Judah (2 Kings 23:2,8 — 627 B.C.). This would
place Zephaniah as a contemporary of Nahum and Jeremiah. It is most
likely that the two prophets Zephaniah and Jeremiah influenced King
Josiah in the religious reformation of the nation.

Josiah became king of Judah at the age of eight; at sixteen he turned to
God, and at twenty he began his first reformation of religion (628 B.C.). He
destroyed numerous idols, grinding them to dust, burned the bones of false
priests on their altars, and then demolished the altars themselves (2 Chr.
34:3-7). The discovery of the Book of the Law in the temple (2 Kings
22:8) had a profound effect upon the king and a second reformation was
undertaken.

The reign of a godly king (Josiah) and the ministries of worthy prophets
such as Zephaniah, Jeremiah and Habakkuk during those latter years of
the nation of Judah indicate the great mercy of God in giving the people
many warnings of their serious plight and numerous opportunities to return
to him. Zephaniah, Jeremiah and Habakkuk have been called 'the
eleventh-hour prophets to Judah'.[2] However, the repentance of the people
during the reign of Josiah was short-lived; within a short period of time the
nation was once more plunged into idolatry and immorality.

Outline

As with the books of Isaiah and Ezekiel, there is a similar threefold pattern
to the book of Zephaniah. Beginning with prophecies related to the immediate historical context of Judah, there follow prophecies of judgement
against foreign nations, concluding with prophecies of future restoration
and blessing for Israel.

The book makes solemn reading. It is filled with vivid expressions of
God's righteous anger:

> Neither their silver nor their gold
> Shall be able to deliver them
> In the day of the LORD's wrath;
> But the whole land shall be devoured
> By the fire of his jealousy
>
> (1:18).

My determination is to gather the nations
To my assembly of kingdoms,
To pour on them my indignation,
All my fierce anger;
All the earth shall be devoured
With the fire of my jealousy

(3:8).

Stern condemnations and severe threats pile one upon the other until the very last section, where the tone changes drastically to end in one of the most beautiful love songs found in the Old Testament.

Part I: The Day of the Lord is at hand (1:1 – 2:3)

The Israelites have once more failed in their covenant obligations. They have not remained true to the living God. His patience and long-suffering are exhausted. He expresses his great anger at the idolatry of Judah (1:2-7).

The expression, 'the day of the LORD', occurs seven times in this first section.[3] Zephaniah is probably aware of the earlier use of this theme by the prophet Amos (cf. Amos 5:18-20; 8:3-13).[4]

The first section ends with a call to repentance (2:1-3). God's mercy is wonderfully demonstrated as he reveals his severe judgement and then calls upon the people to turn to him and so escape his wrath.

Part II: Prophecies against the surrounding nations (2:4-15)

Although Zephaniah is a prophet to Judah, there is nevertheless a message for the heathen or pagan nations around. They are convicted by God of their sins and are without excuse. Non-Israelite nations must also answer to God. His fellow-prophets Jeremiah and Nahum proclaimed the same message:

But the LORD is the true God;
He is the living God and the everlasting King.
At his wrath the earth will tremble,
And the nations will not be able to abide his indignation

(Jer. 10:10).

God is jealous, and the LORD avenges;
The LORD avenges and is furious.
The LORD will take vengeance on his adversaries,
And he reserves wrath for his enemies;
The LORD is slow to anger and great in power,
And will not at all acquit the wicked

(Nahum 1:2-3).

The future of the nations is in the hands of the Lord, to dispose of as he sees fit. Zephaniah addresses first Gaza and the land of the Philistines (2:4-7); he pronounces judgement upon Moab and Ammon because of their hostility towards Israel (2:8-11); Ethiopia also comes under judgement (2:12); and the destruction of Nineveh is foretold in graphic detail (2:13-15). The prophecy was fulfilled when Nineveh was utterly destroyed approximately twenty years later, in 612 B.C., by the combined forces of the Medes and Babylonians.[5]

Part III: Judgement against the city of Jerusalem (3:1-8)

The Lord is particularly distressed about the spiritual and moral state of the capital city. The people of Jerusalem continue in their spiritual blindness and wickedness despite repeated warnings from the Lord through his prophets. Those who should have been leaders in righteousness are leaders in iniquity — princes, judges, prophets and priests (3:3-4).

Though the people of Judah have witnessed the fall of the northern kingdom of Israel they have not learned the lessons of history.

Part IV: Universal judgement: a righteous remnant preserved (3:9-13)

The prophet Zephaniah foretells a universal judgement at which only a small number of persons will be saved. There will be a 'remnant of Israel' who 'shall do no unrighteousness and speak no lies, nor shall a deceitful tongue be found in their mouth' (3:13).

Part V: The restoration and glory of Israel (3:14-20)

As the Lord is 'in the midst' for judgement (3:5), so he is also 'in the midst' for restoration (3:15,17). 'When the cup of wrath is drained, love is poured forth.'[6] Zephaniah rejoices in the prospect of the coming kingdom of God. He presents a remarkable picture of the Lord as one who with great tenderness and love will delight in his people:

> The LORD your God in your midst,
> The Mighty One, will save;
> He will rejoice over you with gladness,
> He will quiet you in his love,
> He will rejoice over you with singing
>
> (3:17).

God's people will be restored and they shall be famous throughout the earth (3:20).

Christ and his church

1. The Day of the Lord

In just three chapters there are twenty references to 'the day' of the Lord. Zephaniah's prophecy concerning the Day of the Lord, when he will visit the land with judgement (e.g. 1:14-16), found partial fulfilment in the invasions of Judah by Nebuchadnezzar and the Babylonian army, with the subsequent exile (605 B.C., 597 B.C. and 586 B.C.), but the full and complete fulfilment is yet in the future.

The New Testament writers refer to the Day of the Lord in two ways. On the one hand, the expression 'the Day of the Lord' is related to the first coming of Messiah, the Lord Jesus Christ (Acts 2:20, quoting Joel 2:31; cf. Mal. 4:5).

On the other hand, the apostle Peter uses it when he writes about the Second Coming of the Lord Jesus Christ: 'But the day of the Lord will come as a thief in the night, in which the heavens will pass away with a great noise, and the elements will melt with fervent heat; both the earth and the works that are in it will be burned up. Therefore, since all these things will be dissolved, what manner of persons ought you to be in holy conduct and godliness, looking for and hastening the coming of the day of God, because of which the heavens, being on fire, will be dissolved, and the elements will melt with fervent heat? Nevertheless we, according to his promise, look for new heavens and a new earth in which righteousness dwells' (2 Peter 3:10-13).

Paul also refers to the Day of the Lord as the return of Christ. Addressing the Thessalonians, he writes, 'For you yourselves know perfectly that the day of the Lord so comes as a thief in the night' (1 Thess. 5:2; cf. Matt. 24:43-44; 1 Cor. 5:5; 2 Cor. 1:14).

For Zephaniah the Day of the Lord is a complex interweaving of momentous events (3:8-13). It is not possible to determine dogmatically which predictions relate, firstly, to the invasion by Babylon and the subsequent exile; secondly, to the return of the captives under the leadership of Zerubbabel and Ezra; thirdly, to the coming of the Messiah in his mission as the Saviour; or, fourthly, to the return of the Messiah in glory and judgement. The same complexity is evident 500 years later in the teaching of the Lord Jesus. Speaking of momentous events in the future, he interweaves the invasion of Jerusalem by the Romans, international confrontations, worldwide gospel preaching and his return 'with power and great glory' (Matt. 24:1 – 25:46).

While so many of the prophecies relating to the Day of the Lord have now been fulfilled, there still remains the climactic Day of the Lord. Building up to that day is the fearful warning of the Lord Jesus when he asks, 'When the Son of Man comes, will he really find faith on the earth?' (Luke 18:8). The apostle Peter asks, 'What manner of persons ought you to be in holy conduct and godliness, looking for and hastening the coming of the day of God?' (2 Peter 3:11-12). The writer to the Hebrews urges Christians to wait 'eagerly' for him (Heb. 9:28). Paul sums up the importance of living faithful and obedient lives when he writes, 'For the grace of God that brings salvation has appeared to all men, teaching us that, denying ungodliness and worldly lusts, we should live soberly, righteously, and godly in the present age, looking for the blessed hope and glorious appearing of our great God and Saviour Jesus Christ…' (Titus 2:11-13).

2. The right clothing

Be silent in the presence of the Lord GOD;
For the day of the LORD is at hand,

> For the LORD has prepared a sacrifice;
> He has invited his guests.
> And it shall be,
> In the day of the LORD's sacrifice,
> That I will punish the princes and the king's children,
> And all such as are clothed with foreign apparel
>
> (1:7-8).

The sacrifice here is the nation of Judah; the invited guests are the Babylonians who come as priests to cut and slay the Israelites, and the birds and beasts will feed on their carcasses (cf. Ezek. 39:17-20).

The same kind of language is used in Revelation to describe the final judgement of God: 'Then I saw an angel standing in the sun; and he cried with a loud voice, saying to all the birds that fly in the midst of heaven, "Come and gather together for the supper of the great God, that you may eat the flesh of kings, the flesh of captains, the flesh of mighty men, the flesh of horses and of those who sit on them, and the flesh of all people, free and slave, both small and great"' (Rev. 19:17-18). This appears in the very same chapter as the marriage of the Lamb (Rev. 19:6-9).

The Lord Jesus may have had the words of Zephaniah 1:7-8 in mind when he spoke the parable of the marriage feast (Matt. 22:1-14). The king had *prepared* the celebration and *invited* his *guests*. One man was removed from the festivities because he did not have the appropriate 'wedding garment' (Matt. 22:11); in other words, he was 'clothed with foreign apparel' (1:8).

In Isaiah the appropriate clothing is referred to as 'the garments of salvation' and 'the robe of righteousness' that every true child of God wears:

> I will greatly rejoice in the LORD,
> My soul shall be joyful in my God;
> For he has clothed me with the garments of salvation,
> He has covered me with the robe of righteousness,
> As a bridegroom decks himself with ornaments,
> And as a bride adorns herself with her jewels
>
> (Isa. 61:10).

It is 'the best robe' in which the Father dresses his prodigal son (Luke 15:22). The 'foreign apparel' of Zephaniah 1:8 is a symbol of 'all our righteousnesses', which 'are like filthy rags' (Isa. 64:6) in the sight of a holy God and totally unsuited for his glorious presence. The Redeemer has commanded that the filthy garments be taken away from every child of God and has said, 'See, I have removed your iniquity from you, and I will clothe you with rich robes' (Zech. 3:4; cf. Rev. 19:7-9).

3. The end of shame

In that day you shall not be shamed for any of your deeds
In which you transgress against me;
For then I will take away from your midst
Those who rejoice in your pride,
And you shall no longer be haughty
In my holy mountain

(3:11).

What is said here cannot refer to those who were brought back from Babylon because there were hypocrites and unconverted among the returning exiles. The prophetic announcement, as Keil explains, 'refers to the time of perfection, which commenced with the coming of Christ, and will be completely realized at His return to judgement'.[7]

The Lord Jesus Christ 'was manifested to take away our sins, and in him there is no sin' (1 John 3:5). Here is complete salvation. The whole character and work of the incarnate Son of God has removed sin. The cross destroys both the guilt and the power of sin, for 'Righteousness is imputed and implanted in one act.'[8] The indwelling Holy Spirit brings his beautiful influence to bear upon the child of God, convicting 'of sin, and of righteousness, and of judgement' (John 16:8) and, at the same time, producing fruit that is honouring to God (Gal. 5:22-23).

Zephaniah declares the character of the preserved ones:

The remnant of Israel shall do no unrighteousness
And speak no lies,
Nor shall a deceitful tongue be found in their mouth...

(3:13).

The New Covenant reveals a wonderful parallel: 'And now, little children, abide in him, that when he appears, we may have confidence and not be ashamed before him at his coming. If you know that he is righteous, you know that everyone who practises righteousness is born of him' (1 John 2:28-29).

4. The Lord's remnant

I will leave in your midst
A meek and humble people,
And they shall trust in the name of the LORD.
The remnant of Israel shall do no unrighteousness
And speak no lies,
Nor shall a deceitful tongue be found in their mouth…

(3:12-13).

While the nation falls under the severe judgement of God, a small number, 'the remnant of Israel', are kept faithful by God's powerful grace. In every generation the Lord keeps for himself a 'remnant according to the election of grace' (Rom. 11:5). Even in the dark days of Elijah in the northern kingdom, when he thought himself alone the Lord showed him that he was much mistaken, for the Lord had kept 7,000 faithful souls in Israel (1 Kings 19:18). The preservation of the elect of God is a precious truth bringing great comfort to the people of God (1 Peter 1:5).

Application

1. The singing of the Lord

The Lord told Job that when he 'laid the foundations of the earth … the morning stars sang together, and all the sons of God shouted for joy' (Job 38:4,7), but there is no mention of the Lord himself singing.

When the church of Jesus Christ, which is the true Israel of God composed of believing Jews and believing Gentiles, is complete and glorified, God will sing:

The LORD your God in your midst,
The Mighty One, will save;
He will rejoice over you with gladness,
He will quiet you in his love,
He will rejoice over you with singing

(3:17).

'He will rejoice over you with gladness,' points to the inward delight in the heart of God, whereas 'He will rejoice over you with singing,' expresses the outward manifestation: '... as the bridegroom rejoices over the bride, so shall your God rejoice over you' (Isa. 62:5).

God deeply loves his people; which is the same as saying that the Lord Jesus Christ 'nourishes and cherishes' his church (Eph. 5:29).

2. The presence of the Lord

Jerusalem's princes, judges, prophets and priests have failed (3:3-4); consequently the Lord is 'in her midst' (3:5) to rectify a bad situation. When 'the Lord ... is in her midst' he takes the place of these leaders and fulfils each office in turn. The Lord comes, firstly, as Judge convicting of sin and bringing his justice to light (3:5-7; cf. John 16:8-11); secondly, as Prophet teaching the people to call upon his name with pure lips (3:9; cf. Joel 2:32; Acts 2:21; Rom. 10:13-17), humbling his people in his presence (3:12); thirdly, as King reigning in sovereign power and glory 'in your midst' (3:15); and, fourthly, as Priest, gathering his people, removing all obstacles and bringing them into the closest possible relationship with himself (3:17-20).[9]

The day will come when God will create 'a new heaven and a new earth' and a loud voice will declare: 'Behold, the tabernacle of God is with men, and he will dwell with them, and they shall be his people, and God himself will be with them and be their God. And God will wipe away every tear from their eyes; there shall be no more death, nor sorrow, nor crying; and there shall be no more pain, for the former things have passed away' (Rev. 21:3).

3. Right jealousy

As there is a jealousy in God that is holy and pure, so there is to be in believers a comparable jealousy. There are two kinds of jealousy: 'one that springs from our self-love which is evil and perverse, and another that we endure on behalf of God... There are many who are jealous on their own account and not on God's, but the only right and godly jealousy is that which looks to God's interest to see that He is not defrauded of the honour that is His due.'[10] When God's jealousy is understood as his demand for exclusive loyalty, his people share that jealousy in being passionately concerned for his honour and glory. The apostle Paul displays this spirit when he writes to the Christians at Corinth: 'I am jealous for you with godly jealousy. For I have betrothed you to one husband, that I may present you as a chaste virgin to Christ. But I fear, lest somehow, as the serpent deceived Eve by his craftiness, so your minds may be corrupted from the simplicity that is in Christ' (2 Cor. 11:2-3). He is passionately concerned that they retain their exclusive loyalty to Christ.

The people of God should be excited by strong feelings of concern for the name, honour and glory of the only true God, the Father of our Lord Jesus Christ — and our Father, by his grace!

Conclusion

Judgement and mercy, wrath and grace are the dominant themes of this book. Judgement is related primarily to the Day of the Lord, whereas grace is linked to a remnant and restoration. 'Wrath and mercy, severity and kindness cannot be separated in the character of God.'[11] 'Therefore consider the goodness and severity of God: on those who fell, severity; but towards you, goodness, if you continue in his goodness. Otherwise you also will be cut off' (Rom. 11:22).

The book of Zephaniah closes with six beautiful 'I wills' of what the Lord will do for his people:

'*I will gather* those who sorrow over the appointed assembly,
Who are among you,
To whom its reproach is a burden.
Behold, at that time
I will deal with all who afflict you;
I will save the lame,
And gather those who were driven out;
I will appoint them for praise and fame
In every land where they were put to shame.
At that time *I will bring* you *back*,
Even at the time I gather you;
For *I will give* you fame and praise
Among all the peoples of the earth,
When I return your captives before your eyes,'
Says the LORD

(3:18-20, emphasis added).

The ten tribes of the northern kingdom of Israel have long since been taken into captivity in Assyria. Soon the two tribes of the southern kingdom will suffer the same fate at the hands of the Babylonians. In the midst of declaring the judgement of God upon a wilful and rebellious nation, the Lord gives encouragement to the faithful that restoration will come about. The Lord will return them to their own land.

Beyond this, however, there is the glorious fine thread of the promise to Abraham (Gen. 12:3). Through the prophet Zephaniah there is the anticipation of a time to come when the nations will worship the Lord. Whereas there is judgement pronounced upon the whole earth, there is also predicted the conversion of the heathen nations to the living God:

> For then I will restore to the peoples a pure language,
> That they all may call on the name of the LORD,
> To serve him with one accord
>
> (3:9).

Through Israel, and especially through Israel's greatest Son, the nations will be gathered in. The promise of a new Israel composed of Jew and Gentile alike (Gal. 3:8-9,14,26-29) is already in the process of fulfilment.

Haggai

('my feast')

Author: Haggai

Key thought: 'Working for God'

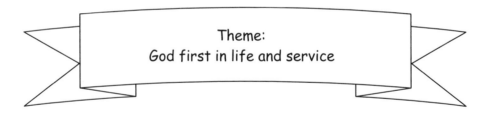

Theme:
God first in life and service

'Is it time for you yourselves to dwell
in your panelled houses, and this
temple to lie in ruins?'

Haggai 1:4

Summary

Haggai

The exile in Babylon was over. The Israelites had been encouraged to return to their homeland. But the early enthusiasm for rebuilding the temple in Jerusalem had waned. Setbacks and discouragements had hindered the work. After sixteen years the people had lost interest. The Lord called Haggai to the prophetic office to stimulate and challenge them to take up once more the task of rebuilding the temple.

Haggai, together with Zechariah and Malachi, faced a different situation from that which confronted the prophets who ministered before the Babylonian exile: 'Those earlier prophets confronted a people who tended to depend upon physical ceremonies and buildings... In contrast, the post-exilic prophets ministered to a discouraged and apathetic people who were tempted to believe that nothing they did made any difference from a religious standpoint. The destruction of Jerusalem had humbled a once-proud people and they were influenced by the Persian view of all religions as equal in value.'[1]

Author

Haggai was probably born in Babylon during the seventy-year exile.[2] The name 'Haggai' means 'my feast' and may have been given to him by his parents in anticipation of the return from exile. Alternatively, he may have been born at the time of one of the Jewish festivals. It is likely that Haggai journeyed to Judah with the first returning Jews under the leadership of Zerubbabel (1:1 — 538 B.C.). He was a colleague of the prophet Zechariah (Ezra 5:1; 6:14), beginning his ministry two months earlier than the latter (1:1; cf. Zech. 1:1). The recorded prophecies of Haggai were delivered within the space of just three months and twenty-four days, whereas those of Zechariah span three years.

Historical setting

The third and final invasion of Judah occurred in 586 B.C. The city of Jerusalem, with its temple and houses, was left in ruins by the invading forces of Nebuchadnezzar. The people of the southern kingdom of Judah were taken into exile in the land of Babylon. The Lord raised up prophets from among the exiles: Daniel served as a statesman in the royal court; Ezekiel ministered to the people. During the long years of captivity the godly yearned to return to Jerusalem (Ps. 137).

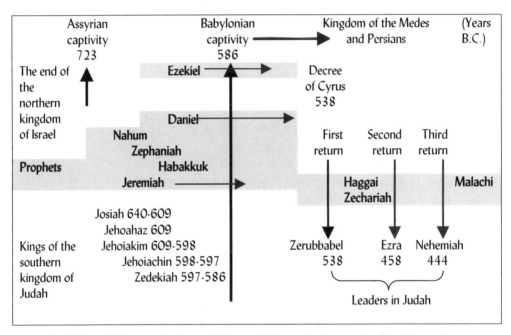

Judah and its prophets and kings before, during and after the exile

When Babylon eventually fell to the Medes and Persians, King Cyrus issued his decree encouraging the Jews to return to Judah to rebuild the Lord's temple at Jerusalem (538 B.C.; 2 Chr. 36:22-23; Ezra 1:2-4). The Babylonian exile was over. 50,000 Jews returned (Ezra 2:64-65; Neh. 7:66-67). Many more thousands of Jews chose to remain in Babylon. The prophet Jeremiah had counselled the exiles to 'Build houses and dwell in them; plant gardens and eat their fruit. Take wives and beget sons and daughters...' (Jer. 29:5-6) and it seems that many had settled down and prospered. After so many years Babylon had become 'home'; indeed, for the generations born there it was the only home they had known. When the opportunity came to return to Judah the Jews had to consider the lives they had built for themselves — the prosperity they enjoyed in business and commerce, the friendships that had been forged, the family networks which had developed and the poor state of the land of Judah, to which they were being encouraged to journey. It may be that most of those who made the long trek to Jerusalem were motivated by a concern for the honour and glory of God, or it may just have been the excitement of a new opportunity and a new beginning.

At first those who returned to Jerusalem were enthusiastic (Ps. 126), giving themselves to the rebuilding of the altar and to the laying of the foundation for the temple (Ezra 3:1-13). Within a short time, however, the neighbouring Samaritans proved a hindrance and hired 'counsellors against them to frustrate their purpose' (Ezra 4:5). The opposition proved effective and the reconstruction of the temple was hindered for a number of years. During this period the Jews became dispirited and lost interest in the project. By the time the Samaritan opposition had waned, the people had become absorbed in their own concerns, preoccupied with building and equipping their own homes. The temple still lay in ruins (1:4).

Disasters and afflictions struck the land: the harvests failed and there was a serious drought (1:6,9-11). The prophet Haggai was sent by God to interpret the calamities and to communicate the Lord's displeasure. Haggai and his colleague Zechariah were raised up by the Lord to challenge and to encourage the people to return to the building project (Ezra 5:1-2). Haggai is often called 'the prophet of the temple' and his prophetic ministry began 'in the second year of King Darius' (1:1 — 520 B.C.), King of Persia, eighteen years after the return from captivity. In just over three weeks the building work recommenced and the Lord sent new messages of encouragement and hope.

Outline

The style of this prophet is 'plain, simple, curt, business-like'.[3] Through Haggai, the Lord is challenging; he demands a hearing; he engages his hearers (1:4; 2:3,12-13). He uses repetition for emphasis: in just two chapters Haggai uses the expression, '… says the Lord,' nineteen times, 'the LORD of hosts,' fourteen times, and 'consider…' five times.

The book is composed of five distinct messages from God delivered on separate occasions.

Part I: First message (1ˢᵗ Day, 6ᵗʰ Month[4]): Rebuke (1:1-11)

Disheartened and dispirited, the people are not inclined to work on the rebuilding of the temple. They try to avoid their obligations and excuse themselves by claiming that it is just not the right time to build (1:2).

Their homes are fine, solid structures while the temple remains in ruins (1:4). Attention is drawn to the various calamities that have struck the land, such as the failed harvests and the prolonged drought. Haggai explains why these afflictions have come from the Lord: it is because they have neglected the rebuilding of the temple.

The people are encouraged to work for the Lord (1:8).

Part II: Second message (24ᵗʰ Day, 6ᵗʰ Month): Reassurance (1:12-14)

Just over three weeks after Haggai's first prophetic word, the people commence the reconstruction work on the temple, because they fear 'the presence of the LORD' (1:12). But it is not in judgement or punishment that the presence of the Lord is to be experienced; Haggai delivers a second message in which there is the reassurance of the *encouraging* presence of the Lord (1:13). Zerubbabel the governor, the civic leader, and Joshua the high priest, the religious leader, and 'all the remnant of the people' are stirred up in spirit by the Lord and put themselves to the task (1:14).

Like the tabernacle before it, the temple 'was not only the focus of the whole system of offerings and sacrifices, priests, and worship; it was also the symbol of Israel's spiritual identity and a visible reminder of the person, power, and presence of God'.[5]

Part III: Third message (21ˢᵗ Day, 7ᵗʰ Month): Comfort and hope (2:1-9)

There are evidently some older Jews among the returning remnant who had been born in Judah and who had actually seen the elaborate temple of Solomon (2:3) before it had been destroyed by Nebuchadnezzar, seventy years earlier. They are disheartened because they have not the necessary resources to build a similar fine temple. Had they not been led to expect the wealth of the nations to finance the rebuilding work? (cf. Isa. 60). Yet the building now being constructed seems more like a hut than a temple worthy of the Lord.

The leaders and the people are urged to work hard for the Lord: '"Yet now be strong, Zerubbabel," says the LORD, "and be strong, Joshua, son of Jehozadak, the high priest; and be strong, all you people of the land," says the LORD, " and work; for I am with you," says the LORD of hosts' (2:4).

The God of the covenant is with his people (2:5). The Lord reassures the people: the new temple may not be anything like the old one in terms of its size, structure and magnificence, but it will surpass it for glory. This simplicity is not, however, due to any lack of resources for, the Lord reminds them, 'The silver is mine, and the gold is mine' (2:8). The Lord gives a wonderful promise that he will send 'the Desire of All Nations' and he 'will fill this temple with glory', with the result that 'The glory of this latter temple shall be greater than the former' (2:7, 9).

Part IV: Fourth message (24th Day, 9th Month): Cleansing and blessing (2:10-19)

Two months after the last message, the prophet delivers another word from the Lord. By question and answer, Haggai explains that, just as a clean thing becomes contaminated by contact with the unclean, so 'The former attitude of the people towards the Lord and His house polluted their own labour and as a result the blessing of the Lord was withheld.'[6]

The situation is now changed. The impurity has been removed. Their obedience to the command of God and their return to work on the temple has resulted in the blessing of the Lord resting upon them. Their fields will be fruitful once more (2:18-19).

Part V: Fifth message (24th Day, 9th Month): Security (2:20-23)

The last message recorded by Haggai is received on the same day as the previous one. Governor Zerubbabel is assured of the Lord's blessing; the strength of the heathen will be broken; God will show mercy to his people.

Zerubbabel, a descendant of David, is God's chosen instrument, chosen as a twin-link in the chain of ancestry for the promised Messiah. By the sign of the 'signet' he is shown how much the Lord esteems, values and cares for him. The prophecies linked to David's line are to continue through Zerubbabel.

Christ and his church

1. The temple filled with glory

'For thus says the LORD of hosts: "Once more (it is a little while) I will shake heaven and earth, the sea and dry land; and I will shake all nations, and they shall come to the Desire of All Nations, and I will fill this temple with glory," says the LORD of hosts... "The glory of this latter temple shall be greater than the former," says the LORD of hosts. "And in this place I will give peace," says the LORD of hosts' (2:6-7,9).

The significance of the shaking of heaven and earth is explained by the writer to the Hebrews: '... whose voice then shook the earth; but now he has promised, saying, "Yet once more I shake not only the earth, but also heaven." Now this, "Yet once more," indicates the removal of those things that are being shaken, as of things that are made, that the things which cannot be shaken may remain. Therefore, since we are receiving a kingdom which cannot be shaken, let us have grace, by which we may serve God acceptably with reverence and godly fear. For our God is a consuming fire' (Heb. 12:26-29).

The Puritan theologian John Owen draws certain conclusions from these two passages in Haggai and Hebrews:

- That the events referred to by both authors are one and the same;
- That these things are spoken by the prophet expressly with respect to the first coming of Christ and the promotion of his gospel;
- That the apostle declares that believers are now actually receiving what was being promised, 'a kingdom which cannot be shaken' (v. 28) — in other words, a spiritual kingdom;
- That these words of Haggai 'are applicable to the first coming of Christ; they had a literal accomplishment in an eminent degree, in the announcement of His birth by an angel from heaven and

celebrated by a multitude of the heavenly hosts; the Holy Ghost descended on Him in the shape of a dove; and God gave express testimony unto Him from heaven, "This is My beloved Son"';
• 'This shaking of the earth and the heavens is descriptive of God's
dealings with His church, and the alterations He would make
therein.'[7]

This promise that '… they shall come to the Desire of All Nations, and I
will fill this temple with glory,' is Messianic (cf. Mal. 3:1). 'The Desire of All
Nations' is none other than the Messiah himself. 'It must be obvious to a
careful reader of this promise that the blessings which the Lord is here
promising are spiritual in nature.'[8] Over 500 years after Haggai, the incarnate Son of God, Jesus the Christ, visited that temple in Jerusalem on several occasions during his earthly life. He brought a greater glory to this second temple than the glory of the first one, for he is 'the brightness of
[God's] glory and the express image of his person' (Heb. 1:3). He is the
spiritual, eternal Temple (John 2:19-21), made without hands (Mark
14:58) and all who believe in him, come to him and, 'as living stones, are
being built up as a spiritual house, a holy priesthood, to offer up spiritual
sacrifices acceptable to God through Jesus Christ' (1 Peter 2:5). The temple
of Solomon and the rebuilt temple of Zerubbabel are symbols of Christ and
his church (1 Cor. 3:16-17; 6:19-20).[9]

The temple in Jerusalem is the place where God says, 'And in this place
I will give peace' (2:9). Jesus Christ is Shiloh, 'the Pacifier' or 'Peacemaker'
(Gen. 49:10), the 'Prince of Peace' (Isa. 9:6), 'for he himself is our peace'
(Eph. 2:14), 'having made peace through the blood of his cross' (Col.
1:20). In his death the Saviour unites believing Gentiles (nations) with believing Jews and forms one glorious spiritual building. All this was achieved
when the one who is the true Temple and who builds the true temple died
on a tree outside the walls of the city of Jerusalem.

The stone which the builders rejected
Has become the chief corner-stone.
This was the LORD's doing;
It is marvellous in our eyes.
This is the day which the LORD has made;
We will rejoice and be glad in it

(Ps. 118:22-24).[10]

2. The Messianic line

Zerubbabel was of the tribe of Judah, of the house of David. He never had a kingdom, nor ever wore a crown; nevertheless the Lord chose him and made him 'as a signet' (2:23). Thus 'Zerubbabel becomes the centre of the messianic line and is like a signet … sealing both branches together.'[11] Two lines of descent from King David unite at Zerubbabel and from him flow two lines which lead to Mary and Joseph, mother and step-father of the Lord Jesus (Matt. 1:12-13; Luke 3:27).[12]

Application

1. On His Majesty's service

Robert Lee describes Haggai as 'a model worker for God':[13]

- He spends no time talking about himself. He magnifies the Lord.
- He is the Lord's messenger. He is always saying, 'Thus says the LORD…'
- He not only rebukes, but encourages; he not only criticizes, but he commends.
- He stimulates the people by word and example.
- He not only preaches, but he is involved in the practical work (Ezra 5:1-2).

Working for the Lord should be the Christian's major concern: 'Therefore, my beloved brethren, be steadfast, immovable, always abounding in the work of the Lord, knowing that your labour is not in vain in the Lord' (1 Cor. 15:58).

In the days of Haggai, when the people concentrated upon their own concerns and neglected the Lord's work, their crops failed and they became increasingly poor (1:9-10). Conversely when the people committed themselves to the Lord's work they were promised sustenance and support (2:19). In a similar manner the Lord Jesus exhorts his followers not to be anxious about their food, drink or clothing, but rather to 'seek first the kingdom of God and his righteousness', with the promise that 'All these things shall be added' (Matt. 6:33).

2. Building the temple

The building of the temple in Jerusalem in 520 B.C. has a modern and spiritual counterpart today: the building of the church of Jesus Christ. The Son of God said, 'I will build my church, and the gates of Hades shall not prevail against it' (Matt. 16:18).

The Lord Jesus uses his people to build his church, for he said, 'All authority has been given to me in heaven and on earth. Go therefore and make disciples of all the nations, baptizing them in the name of the Father and of the Son and of the Holy Spirit, teaching them to observe all things that I have commanded you; and lo, I am with you always, even to the end of the age' (Matt. 28:18-20).

The task laid upon all Christians is to be engaged in the building of the true and spiritual church: by prayer (Eph. 6:18-20), by witness (1 Peter 3:15), by life (Phil. 2:14-16; Matt. 5:16), by labour (1 Cor. 15:58) and by financial support (Phil. 4:15-19).

'Haggai's message is full of stirring words to us today. If, as a church, we thought more of the Lord's work of saving souls than of our own comfort, there would be no lack of means to carry it forward.'[14]

Conclusion

Haggai was one of the few prophets who saw immediate and tangible results from his prophetic ministry. The people accepted his criticism and responded by putting their backs into the work of rebuilding the temple of the Lord. The temple was completed within four years (1:1; Ezra 6:15).

The church of Christ is continually in need of challenge in the area of priorities. Pressures are not easily balanced in relation to business and employment, parents and children, house and home, church and spiritual life. Failure to make a priority of worship and service for the Lord will inevitably bring problems. The Lord often withholds blessing where his worship and service have been neglected. To claim the extra stresses of modern living as an excuse for failure in worship or service is to show a lack of love towards the Lord.

'Do not be deceived, God is not mocked; for whatever a man sows, that he will also reap. For he who sows to his flesh will of the flesh reap corruption, but he who shows to the Spirit will of the Spirit reap everlasting life. And let us not grow weary while doing good, for in due season we shall reap if we do not lose heart' (Gal. 6:7-9).

Zechariah

('Jehovah remembers')

Author: Zechariah

Key thought: 'God loves his people'

Theme:
Encouragement to the disheartened

'Behold I will save my people…
They shall be my people
And I will be their God
In truth and righteousness.'
Zechariah 8:7-8

Summary

Zechariah

When the people of God become disheartened in their service for the Lord there are a number of approaches that may be used to stir and stimulate their enthusiasm. The approach taken by church leaders is most likely to be that of rebuke, censure and challenge. By contrast the Lord often reminds his people of how much he loves them, in order to warm their hearts and stir a new devotion within. A revival of the first love brings renewed endeavours in God's work. Zechariah is the Barnabas of the Old Testament — a true 'son of encouragement' (cf. Acts 4:36-37).

Zechariah revived the zeal of God's people by prophesying of the glory that was to come. His prophecies related to the first and the second coming of the Messiah. The adversities and hardships for the people of God are made bearable by the knowledge that there is a wonderful future ahead (cf. 1 Thess. 4:13-18; 1 Peter 1:3-7; 4:12-13; 2 Cor. 4:16-18; Rev. 21:1-4).

Author

Zechariah designates himself as 'the son of Berechiah, the son of Iddo the prophet' (1:1), whereas Ezra the historian calls him 'the son of Iddo' (Ezra 5:1; 6:14), Zechariah's father was Berechiah and his grandfather was Iddo. It was Jewish practice to call someone 'the son of' any of his male ancestors, not just his immediate father, and especially after a well-known ancestor. As Iddo the priest and prophet was well known in the Jewish community, Zechariah was known as 'the son of Iddo'. The combined names of the three men are prophetic of Zechariah's life: Berechiah means 'Jehovah blesses'; Iddo means 'the appointed time', and Zechariah means 'Jehovah remembers'.[1]

Zechariah was a priest as well as a prophet (Neh. 12:12,16). He was probably born in Babylon and, like Haggai, he would have made the long journey to Judah with the returning exiles under the leadership of Zerubbabel (538 B.C.). He was a colleague of Haggai (Ezra 5:1; 6:14) and probably the younger of the two (2:4). The recorded prophecies of Zechariah were delivered during a period of three years, whereas those of Haggai took just three months and twenty-four days.

Historical setting

As Zechariah commenced his prophetic ministry just two months after Haggai began to prophesy (1:1; cf. Hag. 1:1) the historical setting is the same for both prophets.[2] The year was 520 B.C.; 50,000 Jews had been back in Jerusalem for eighteen years; the foundations for the temple had been completed in the first two years, but the work had been interrupted by Samaritan interference and no work had been carried out on the temple since.

The Lord sent a message through the prophet Haggai, the people responded and three weeks after receiving that first message the work of rebuilding the temple began again (Hag. 1:1,12-15). Now, five weeks later, Zechariah joins Haggai to add his contribution to motivating the people to do the work of the Lord in the rebuilding of the temple (1:1). Zechariah ranks as one of the greatest prophets. He was a great poet and 'a fitting companion' of 'plain, practical Haggai'.[3]

Dates relating to Zechariah and Haggai

According to the day, month and year of the reign of King Darius of the Medes and Persians

Date			Content	Reference
Day	Month	Year		
1	6	2	The temple must be rebuilt	Hag. 1:1-2
24	6	2	Work on the temple recommences	Hag. 1:14-15
21	7	2	The promise of greater glory for this temple	Hag. 2:1,9
?	8	2	A call to return to God	Zech. 1:1,3
24	9	2	Cleansing and blessing for Israel	Hag. 2:10,17,19
24	9	2	Zerubbabel a chosen instrument of God	Hag. 2:20,23
24	11	2	Visions in the night	Zech. 1:7 – 6:8
4	9	4	A question about fasting	Zech. 7:1-7
3	12	6	The temple completed	Ezra 6:15

Outline

Part I: A call to return to God (1:1-6)

Zechariah introduces himself and then declares his first message. In the eighth month of the second year of the reign of King Darius (i.e. 520 B.C.), the Lord sends a word urging the people to return to him. They must not follow the behaviour of their sinful ancestors who disregarded the warnings of the prophets and consequently suffered under the judgement of God. The Lord lovingly pleads with Israel: 'Thus says the LORD of hosts: "Return to me," says the LORD of hosts, "and I will return to you," says the LORD of hosts' (Zech. 1:3).

Part II: Visions in the night (1:7 – 6:8)

Three months later, on the twenty-fourth day of the eleventh month, a second message is communicated to Zechariah. He receives eight visions in one night. In the first he sees the Angel of the LORD as a man upon a red horse. The Angel is co-ordinating the work of God's messengers and travelling throughout the world observing events on earth. All the earth is said to be 'resting quietly' (1:11), though Jerusalem and Judah are still suffering the effects of God's judgement. A time is coming, however, when the situation will be reversed and the nations will feel God's anger, but Jerusalem will know God's blessing and the temple will be rebuilt.

The four horns of the second vision represent the four empires in Daniel's vision: Babylon, Medo-Persia, Greece and Rome[4] (Dan. 7:1-8). In the third vision a man is measuring the walls of Jerusalem because its present size is not large enough to cope with the number of people whom the Lord will bring in to salvation. The high priest Joshua (at that time serving in Jerusalem), is pictured in the fourth vision. He stands before the Angel of the LORD. Satan stands by to accuse Joshua, but his accusations against the high priest are without effect. Joshua is confirmed in his office, with promises attached. The Lord commands the removal of Joshua's 'filthy garments', which symbolize his sin, and their replacement with 'rich robes' (3:4).

The golden lampstand and the two olive trees of the fifth vision symbolize the church (the people of God) and the source of their true power; the spiritual power of God's grace. In the sixth vision the prophet sees a flying scroll representing the judgements of God. The seventh vision pictures Israel's 'wickedness' as a woman being restrained in a basket with a lid of lead dropped on to the top (5:7). The night visions come to a close with a vision of four chariots, with red, black, white and dappled horses. These represent 'four spirits of heaven' (6:5) which go throughout the earth delivering the Lord's judgement.

Part III: The command to crown Joshua (6:9-15)

Messengers arrive from Babylon with gold and silver from the Jewish exiles still in that land, as their contribution to the rebuilding of the temple. Zechariah is instructed to use the gifts to make an elaborate crown and then engage in the symbolic act of crowning the high priest, Joshua. No man could occupy the position of priest and king according to the law of God, and the Lord goes on to explain that this act is a Messianic promise; Messiah will be king and priest:

> He shall bear the glory,
> And shall sit and rule on his throne;
> So he shall be a priest on his throne

(6:13).

Part IV: A question of observing additional fasts (7:1 - 8:23)

Two years later, on the fourth day of the ninth month, Jews living in the land of Babylon raise a question about the observance of fasts. The dating of this message is important since it indicates that the rebuilding of the temple had been underway for two years and was halfway to completion. The basic structure of the Lord's house would be in place by now and this would have been seen as indicating the return of the Lord's favour towards Israel. The observance of the extra fasts relating to the destruction of Jerusalem and the temple now seems inappropriate.

During the exile the Israelites were accustomed to observe a fast in the fourth, fifth, seventh and tenth months (8:19). In the fourth month, on the ninth day, they fasted to remember the conquest of Jerusalem by Nebu-chadnezzar in the eleventh year of Zedekiah (Jer. 39:2; 52:6-7). In the fifth month, on the tenth day, they fasted to remember the day Nebuchadnez-zar and the Babylonians destroyed Jerusalem and the temple (Jer. 52:12-13). In the tenth month, on the tenth day, a fast was observed to remember the beginning of the siege of Jerusalem by Nebuchadnezzar in the ninth year of Zedekiah (2 Kings 25:1; Jer. 39:1). In the seventh month, according to Jewish tradition they fasted on the third day on account of the murder of Gedaliah, the governor, and the Judeans who had been left in the land of Judah (2 Kings 25:25-26; Jer. 41:1-3). Now that the exile is over the exiles are questioning whether they should continue to observe the annual fasts[5] connected with the destruction of Jerusalem and its temple.

The answer from the Lord strongly indicates that the Lord delights in obedience rather than in fasting. Outward observances are meaningless without the engagement of the heart and mind. The failure of past gener-ations of Israelites is highlighted and the people are urged to avoid the same pitfalls.

If the people will respond and honour God in their behaviour, the Lord promises the restoration of Israel and his blessing upon the believing remnant.

Part V: The future of the world powers and of the kingdom of God (9:1 – 14:21)

The final part of the book contains two long prophecies (9:1 – 11:17 and 12:2 – 14:21). Both sections begin with the expression: 'The burden of the word of the LORD' (9:1; 12:1), which gives the 'character of a threatening prophecy or proclamation of judgement'.[6] The first 'burden' is 'against the land of Hadrach', while the second is 'against Israel', and throughout the six chapters the contrast and conflict between the heathen world and Israel are expressed.

The emphasis falls, in the first part, upon the destruction of the heathen world and Israel's being given strength to subdue all her enemies. The ulti-mate triumph of Israel will be accomplished through the coming of a humble king (9:9). The Lord will punish worthless shepherds and person-ally gather his chosen flock (10:3). The distinguishing features of good and bad shepherds are delineated (11:1-17).

The contents of the second burden emphasize the refining of Israel: the conflict with the heathen nations will be used by the Lord to sift out those who are genuinely the Lord's people. Interwoven is a promise of 'the Spirit of grace and supplication' bringing a true repentance (12:10-14), and the suffering of the Shepherd will result in the scattering of his sheep, but the Lord will ensure that a purified and totally committed minority will emerge (13:7-9).

Zion will be delivered and will triumph over the heathen world. When the Lord has completed his work of refinement he will be the King of the world and everything will then be devoted to his service. Even common utensils will be sanctified for the service of God (14:21). The distinction between sacred and secular will be abolished for ever.

Christ and his church

Zechariah contributes some of the most wonderful prophecies concerning the Lord Jesus Christ found anywhere in the Scriptures.

1. Messiah, *the* temple-builder

> Behold, the man whose name is the BRANCH!
> From his place he shall branch out,
> And he shall build the temple of the LORD;
> Yes, he shall build the temple of the LORD.
> He shall bear the glory,
> And shall sit and rule on his throne;
> So he shall be a priest on his throne,
> And the counsel of peace shall be between them both
>
> (6:12-13).

Since the promise is given to Zerubbabel that he himself will finish the re-building of the temple in Jerusalem (4:9), another temple must be intended here. God promises that the man spoken of as the Branch — that is the Messiah (cf. Isa. 4:2; Jer. 23:5-6) — will build, not a temple *to* the Lord, but rather *the* temple *of* the Lord.

Furthermore, the Messiah will himself be the glory of the new temple and he will rule in a dual capacity as king and priest. Such a double function, with the same person holding the two offices of king and priest, was impossible under the terms of the Old Covenant, since priests were to descend from Levi and kings from Judah. Consequently the Lord had prepared a priestly order *above that* of Aaron and Levi — the order of Melchizedek, the king/priest (Gen. 14:18-20; Heb. 7:1-10).[7] Messiah comes in this order of priesthood (Ps. 110:4). Christ rules the new temple, *the* temple *of* God, as King and Priest. He is King over his body the church (Eph. 1:22-23), ruling, controlling and guarding. He is Priest for his church, having presented the one supreme sacrifice for sin (Heb. 10:10) and ever living to make intercession for us (Heb. 7:24-25).

Zechariah prophesied that Messiah would personally build the temple of the Lord, the greater temple. That temple is currently under construction. It is the spiritual temple of which Christ is the foundation (1 Cor. 3:11), the cornerstone (Eph. 2:20), the centre and the heart (John 2:21). Believers are living stones who come to Christ to be 'built up as a spiritual house' (1 Peter 2:5) and with him and in him to form the true temple (1 Cor. 3:16; 6:19-20). The true Temple, the spiritual temple, is Christ and his church.

Connected with the arrival of God's servant the Branch (3:8) is the removal of guilt in one day (3:9) — a remarkable prediction of the work of Christ at Calvary!

2. Messiah, the humble Prince

Rejoice greatly, O daughter of Zion!
Shout, O daughter of Jerusalem!
Behold, your King is coming to you;
He is just and having salvation,
Lowly and riding on a donkey,
A colt, the foal of a donkey

(9:9).

The Jews always understood this passage to apply to the promised Messiah, until Christians used it as an argument in favour of Jesus Christ.[8] Messiah the King is described as just, possessing salvation, humble, outwardly poor (riding on a donkey), and as one whose kingdom is characterized by peace and is of universal extent (9:10). The Lord Jesus Christ deliberately enacted this prophecy by his triumphant entry into Jerusalem (Matt. 21:1-11).

3. Messiah, the Pierced One

Shortly after the Lord Jesus Christ died upon the cross, soldiers arrived with orders to break the legs of the three crucified men. The legs of the criminals on either side of the Lord were broken. The Saviour was delivered from this further barbarity because the soldiers were convinced that he was already dead. One soldier, however, made doubly sure by thrusting a spear into his side. Here was confirmation indeed concerning the actual death of Christ. This strange sequence of events served to fulfil prophecy once more. The apostle John sees the fulfilment of two Old Testament predictions (John 19:36-37). One concerned the Passover lamb: 'Not one of his bones shall be broken' (Exod. 12:46). The other referred to the piercing of Jehovah: 'And I will pour on the house of David and on the inhabitants of Jerusalem the Spirit of grace and supplication; then *they will look on me whom they have pierced*; they will mourn for him as one mourns for his only son, and grieve for him as one grieves for a first-born' (12:10, emphasis added).

'As God is here the speaker, this passage has always been a stumbling-block to the Jews, for how could God be pierced? The only fact that explains it is that which they have not yet admitted, that they have crucified and slain that prince of peace who was God manifest in the flesh. As soon as they admit this fact they will see the consistency of the passage, and will mourn the guilt of their fathers in crucifying the incarnate Son, and their own guilt in so long rejecting him.'[9]

Also predicted in this prophecy of Zechariah is a great spiritual awakening among the people of Israel (cf. Acts 2:41; 4:4; 6:7). In this mighty revival that will take place in the future there will be considerable penitence and considerable prayer.

4. Messiah, the Betrayed One

Did the chief priests and elders at the time of the crucifixion realize the parallels between Zechariah 11:12-13 and the sum of thirty pieces of silver paid to Judas and the subsequent purchasing of the potter's field? (Matt. 27:1-10).

> Then I said to them, 'If it is agreeable to you, give me my wages; and if not, refrain.' So they weighed out for my wages thirty pieces of silver. And the LORD said to me, 'Throw it to the potter' — that

princely price they set on me. So I took the thirty pieces of silver and threw them into the house of the LORD for the potter (11:12-13).

Then he threw down the pieces of silver in the temple and departed, and went and hanged himself. But the chief priests took the silver pieces and said, 'It is not lawful to put them into the treasury, because they are the price of blood.' And they took counsel and bought with them the potter's field, to bury strangers in (Matt. 27:5-7).

The parallels between the two passages are striking: firstly, the work of the Lord Jesus, as with that of Zechariah, was not valued; secondly, thirty pieces of silver was a trifling amount either for the shepherd's wages or the Saviour's betrayal (there is great irony in calling it 'that princely price'); thirdly, in both cases the silver was thrown down in the temple; and, fourthly, in both cases the thirty pieces of silver eventually arrived in the hands of a potter.[10]

5. Messiah, the stricken Shepherd

At the opening of Zechariah 13 the Lord had promised that a fountain would be opened by which the people of Israel might wash away their guilt and moral pollution (v. 1). The connection between this fountain for cleansing, the piercing of Jehovah (12:10) and the striking of Jehovah's shepherd and companion (13:7) only becomes evident in the suffering and death of the Lord Jesus Christ.

The night before our Lord's death, he walked with his disciples to the Mount of Olives and the Garden of Gethsemane. On the way the Lord predicted their weakness and failure, quoting Zechariah 13:7: 'All of you will be made to stumble because of me this night, for it is written: "I will strike the shepherd, and the sheep of the flock will be scattered." But after I have been raised, I will go before you to Galilee' (Matt. 26:31-32).

Thus the meaning of Zechariah 13:7-9 is made clear: First, Messiah will die for the sins of his people; secondly, the nature of his death will cause all his disciples to stumble ('probably referring to [their] "becoming untrue" to their Master');[11] and, thirdly, the salvation of the remnant will be through hardship and trial.

It is God the Father who strikes the Shepherd. 'There is in the whole compass of human knowledge, nothing more awfully sublime, than this seeming schism in the Godhead. It is as if sin was so dreadful an evil, that the assumption of its guilt by a sinless Mediator must for a time make a division even in the absolute unity of the Godhead itself. It is the most awful illustration of the repulsive and separating power of sin, that the history of the universe affords.'[12]

6. Messiah, the robe of righteousness

In Zechariah's fourth vision (3:1-5), Joshua the high priest is seen standing before the Angel of the LORD. Powerful symbolism is used which demonstrates that he has been rescued from hell ('a brand plucked from the fire' — v. 2); washed of all his sins ('Take away the filthy garments from him' — v. 4) and clothed in the righteousness of Christ ('See, I have removed your iniquity from you, and I will clothe you with rich robes — v. 4).[13] The foundation upon which this wonderful transaction takes place is further indicated when the Lord says, 'And I will remove the iniquity of that land in one day' (3:9; cf. Dan. 9:24).

Application

1. God's power to preserve his people

The Lord has a great love for his people: 'I am zealous for Jerusalem and for Zion with great zeal' (1:14). 'For thus says the LORD of hosts: "He sent me after glory, to the nations which plunder you; for he who touches you touches the apple of his eye"' (2:8). 'I am zealous for Zion with great zeal; with great fervour I am zealous for her' (8:2).

In his zeal and love for his people the Lord provides all that they need to fulfil his commands. This is demonstrated by the vision of the lampstand (4:2-3), which indicates both the responsibility of the church and the source of her power. Her mission is to be the light-bearer in a dark world (cf. Matt. 5:14-16). The lampstand is of solid gold, signifying purity, preciousness and indestructibility. The seven lamps and seven tubes indicate the varied ways in which the light is to shine. The two olive trees supply all the oil and represent the source of grace and strength to the church: the Holy Spirit of God. He constantly reassures his people: 'My grace is sufficient for you, for my strength is made perfect in weakness' (2 Cor. 12:9).

The vision conveys the message that the church will carry out her work in the world, not by human power but by the strength of God. As King Hezekiah had said regarding one of his enemies, 'With him is an arm of the flesh; but with us is the LORD our God, to help us and to fight our battles' (2 Chr. 32:8). The Angel of the LORD gives the interpretation of the vision of the lampstand:

This is the word of the LORD to Zerubbabel:
'Not by might nor by power, but by my Spirit,'
Says the LORD of hosts.
'Who are you, O great mountain?
Before Zerubbabel you shall become a plain!
And he shall bring forth the capstone
With shouts of "Grace, grace to it!" '

(4:6-7).

The power of God alone is sufficient to preserve the church. Each child of God is 'kept by the power of God through faith for salvation ready to be revealed in the last time' (1 Peter 1:5). Once God has begun a good work in the life of an individual, there is absolute certainty that he will 'complete it until the day of Jesus Christ' (Phil. 1:6). There is no power on earth or in hell that can thwart God's purposes in preserving every last one of his people. Hence we should not 'fear those who kill the body but cannot kill the soul. But rather fear him who is able to destroy both soul and body in hell' (Matt. 10:28).

Fear him, ye saints, and you will then
Have nothing else to fear;
Make you his service your delight,
Your wants shall be his care

(Nahum Tate / Nicholas Brady).

2. A great spiritual awakening

Amplifying the prophecies of Micah 4:2 and Isaiah 2:3, Zechariah predicts a great turning to God among the Gentiles (the nations):

Thus says the LORD of hosts:
'Peoples shall yet come,

Inhabitants of many cities;
The inhabitants of one city shall go to another, saying,
"Let us continue to go and pray before the LORD,
And seek the LORD of hosts.
I myself will go also."
Yes, many peoples and strong nations
Shall come to seek the LORD of hosts in Jerusalem,
And to pray before the LORD.'

    Thus says the LORD of hosts: 'In those days ten men from every language of the nations shall grasp the sleeve of a Jewish man, saying, "Let us go with you, for we have heard that God is with you"'
(8:20-23).

The nations are seized with a powerful desire to go to Jerusalem. They press towards it and want to be included in the community of Israel. The promise given to Abraham is being realized: through his Seed '… all the families of the earth shall be blessed' (Gen. 12:3; cf. Gal. 3:26-29; Rev. 7:9).

    Believing Jews joined by believing Gentiles form the true Israel through which Jehovah will make himself known as the God of the world's history and of prophecy — the believing Israel of the New Testament era.[14]

Conclusion

The task before the prophet Zechariah is to encourage the people in their God-given responsibilities of love and obedience. If they continue in sin they will be punished as in former days, but if they will humble themselves before the Lord they will have a glorious future. The heathen nations will be subdued, Jerusalem will prosper and great future spiritual blessings will be brought about through the Messiah.

    'Blessed be the God and Father of our Lord Jesus Christ, who has blessed us with every spiritual blessing in the heavenly places in Christ, just as he chose us in him before the foundation of the world, that we should be holy and without blame before him in love, having predestined us to adoption as sons by Jesus Christ to himself, according to the good pleasure of his will, to the praise of the glory of his grace, by which he has made us accepted in the Beloved' (Eph. 1:3-6).

Malachi

('my messenger')

Author: Malachi

Key thought: 'The Lord will come'

Theme:
Messages of love, rebuke and hope

'Behold, I send my messenger...
And the Lord, whom you seek
Will suddenly come to his temple,
Even the Messenger of the covenant...'
Malachi 3:1

Summary

Malachi

There is something peculiarly solemn about the closing book of the Old Testament. 'The stern vigour of its reproofs, the yearning tenderness of its appeals and the sublime sweep of its predictions combine to give it an intrinsic interest of the profoundest character.'[1] This interest is greatly enhanced by its position — standing as it does in the closing days of the Old Covenant revelation, yet looking to the future and the dawning of the New Covenant. The anticipated change is going to be dramatic.

Author

The name 'Malachi' means 'my messenger,' or 'my angel'. This has led some of the earlier commentators to conclude that God had communicated this prophecy through an angel. It is, however, evident, as Calvin asserts, that 'The Lord at that time did not send angels to reveal his oracles, but adopted the ordinary ministry of men.'[2] As the apostle Peter declared, 'Prophecy never came by the will of man, but holy *men* of God spoke as they were moved by the Holy Spirit' (2 Peter 1:21, emphasis added).

Some suppose Malachi may be another name for Ezra. The name 'Ezra Malachi', or 'Ezra the Messenger' would then be like 'John the Baptist', where the office, or title, had become, in time, a proper name. This is pure conjecture; the Bible gives no such information. 'Malachi is happy to remain anonymous so that people think, not about him, but about what God has to say.'[3]

Malachi is God's messenger fulfilling a priestly function. A priest is 'the messenger of the LORD of hosts' (2:7); Messiah is 'the Messenger of the covenant' (3:1); and the one coming immediately before Christ will be the 'messenger' of the Messenger (3:1).

Historical setting

No personal information about Malachi is given in the Scriptures and he himself provides neither ancestry, home location, nor even the designation of 'the prophet'. Unlike many of the writing prophets, he does not locate the time of his prophecies in the reign of a particular king (cf. Isa. 1:1; Zech. 1:1). There are nevertheless internal indications which enable an approximate date to be established:

- The temple had been rebuilt at Jerusalem and sacrifices were being offered (1:7-8,13-14; 3:8);
- The word translated 'governor'(1:8) is the Persian technical term *pehah*, probably indicating that a Persian governor was ruling in Jerusalem;
- The great similarity between the problems faced by Ezra and Nehemiah and those addressed by Malachi: such as, corrupt priests (1:6-2:9; Neh. 13:7-9), intermarriage with pagans (2:10-12; Ezra 9:1-2; Neh. 13:23-28) and the neglect of tithes and offerings (3:8-9; Neh. 13:10-11).

Nehemiah came to Jerusalem in 444 B.C., but it is unlikely that he was the governor mentioned in 1:8 since the Persian word is used. It is probable that Malachi's prophecies were delivered during Nehemiah's twelve-year absence in Susa with King Artaxerxes of Babylon (Neh. 13:6). That would place Malachi's prophecies between 432 and 420 B.C., about a century after Haggai and Zechariah began their ministries (520 B.C.). Malachi therefore probably stood in the same relation to Nehemiah as Haggai and Zechariah did to Zerubbabel, or Isaiah to Hezekiah, and Jeremiah to Josiah, in Israel's earlier history.

Before the Babylonian captivity (586 B.C.) the besetting sins of the Jews were idolatry and superstition. Afterwards, because of the influence of the Babylonian culture and mind-set, a change began in the thinking of the Jews which would lead ultimately to the rigid formalism of the Pharisees and the ridiculing scepticism of the Sadducees. The predominant outlook during the period of Malachi's prophecy was the Pharisaic 'spirit of proud and bigoted self-righteousness that claimed the favour of God with insolent haughtiness, at the very moment that this favour was forfeited by unbelief and neglect of duty'.[4]

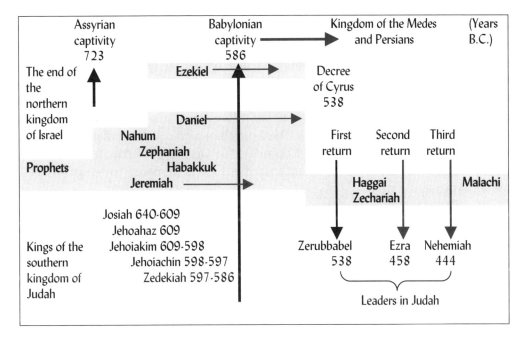

| Assyrian captivity 723 | Babylonian captivity 586 | Kingdom of the Medes and Persians | (Years B.C.) |

Judah and its prophets and kings before, during and after the exile

Outline

The book of Malachi is in the style of a dialogue between God and his people. Of the fifty-five verses in this book, forty-seven are spoken by God — the highest proportion of all the prophets.[5] Twelve times in the first three chapters 'you say' is contrasted with 'says the Lord'. God hears and remembers every word spoken by his people. Through Malachi the Lord answers their wrong thinking and challenges their sinful behaviour.

'Malachi … directed his message of judgement to a people plagued with corrupt priests, wicked practices, and a false sense of security in their privileged relationship with God. Using the question-and-answer method, Malachi probes deeply into their problems of hypocrisy, infidelity, mixed marriages, divorce, false worship, and arrogance.'[6]

Part I: A message of love (1:1-5)

A clear pattern is evident throughout the book: the Lord makes a state-ment; the people question it or deny it; and the Lord gives the answer.[7] The first instance of this (1:2-5) illustrates the common pattern. The Lord says, 'I have loved you,' to which the people respond with the question: 'In what way have you loved us?' (1:2). The Lord then replies by describing the de-struction of their enemies the Edomites, the offspring of Esau. It is an ad-ditional illustration of his patient love that God is prepared to reason with them.

Part II: A message of rebuke (1:6 - 2:17)

In spite of the numerous evidences of God's special love for his people, they have not responded by honouring and obeying him. The priests have neglected their responsibilities: the sacrifices they have brought to God are not fit even to set before an earthly governor (1:8); and they have failed to obey and to teach the law of God (2:5-9).

The behaviour of the Lord's people reflects badly upon the Lord him-self. He is being dishonoured by both priests and people; as in the days of Hosea it is 'like people, like priest' (Hosea 4:9). Following the bad example of their religious leaders, they have intermarried with their pagan neigh-bours (2:11) and have 'dealt treacherously' by divorcing their wives (2:14-16). They display a bad attitude towards each other (2:10). To all their faults and failings they add the greatest dishonour to the Lord by blasphemously claiming that 'Everyone who does evil is good in the sight of the LORD, and he delights in them' (2:17).

In spite of Israel's failure and neglect the Lord will vindicate his great name (1:11).

Part III: A message of hope (3:1 - 4:6)

The Lord gives the Israelites a message of hope, though it contains a sober warning. He will send the Messenger of the covenant, but his coming will prove devastating: 'But who can endure the day of his coming?' (3:2). The nation will be purified: witchcraft, adultery, dishonesty and oppression will be banished from the land (3:5).

If they will obey the terms of their covenant with God, then they will experience the singular blessing of the Lord.

The Lord accuses them of uttering more harsh words against him. They have claimed that there is no value in obeying the Lord (3:14) and they have honoured the wicked and blasphemous among them. There is, however, a righteous remnant to be found in Israel who encourage one another in the Lord. The Lord records their names in 'a book of remembrance' (3:16). When the Day of the Lord comes there will be a clear distinction drawn between the righteous and the unrighteous (4:1-4).

The people are again urged to keep the law of Moses and with patience to await the arrival of Elijah the prophet.

Christ and his church

1. The Messenger of the covenant

Covenants stand at the heart of the book of Malachi. Three covenants are specifically mentioned: the covenant of Levi (2:8), the covenant of the fathers (2:10) and the covenant of marriage (2:14). The special love which God displays towards Israel is intrinsically related to his covenant relationship with them (1:2-5). Furthermore, through Malachi the promised Messiah is called 'the Messenger of the covenant':

'Behold, I send my messenger,
And he will prepare the way before me.
And the Lord, whom you seek,
Will suddenly come to his temple,
Even the Messenger of the covenant,
In whom you delight.
Behold, he is coming,'
Says the LORD of hosts

(3:1).

The Messenger of the covenant is an apt name for the one who is also the Word of God (John 1:1). The Son of God is the ultimate communication from God (Heb. 1:1-2), since 'No one has seen God at any time.

The only begotten Son, who is in the bosom of the Father, he has declared him' (John 1:18; cf. John 14:9-10).

The 'covenant' here does not mean any specific outward transaction between God and the Israelites, but that deeper inner relationship 'which he has to the whole church, involving ... the great purpose and plan of redemption'.[8] The Lord Jesus Christ is also called 'the mediator of the new covenant' (Heb. 12:24; cf. Matt. 26:28; Jer. 31:31-34).

Four hundred years after Malachi prophesied, the Lord Jesus identified John the Baptist as the one who fulfilled the prophecy: 'Behold, I send my messenger, and he will prepare the way before me' (Matt. 11:10; Luke 7:27; cf. Mark 1:2-4). John declares his unique ministry as identifying and introducing Jesus of Nazareth as the Messiah, the Son of God, the King of Israel, the Lamb of God who takes away the sin of the world (John 1:29,34,36).

2. The coming of Elijah

> Behold, I will send you Elijah the prophet
> Before the coming of the great and dreadful day of the LORD
>
> (4:5).

Who is this Elijah? Is he the Tishbite (1 Kings 17:1), who is personally to reappear on earth? That is what the Jews and even some of the early Christian fathers thought. The question is resolved, however, by the Lord Jesus Christ himself when, referring to John the Baptist, he said, 'For all the prophets and the law prophesied until John. And if you are willing to receive it, he is Elijah who is to come' (Matt. 11:13-14). In a parallel passage Luke records the words confirming John the Baptist's representative character. Speaking about John, the Lord Jesus said, 'But what did you go out to see? A prophet? Yes, I say to you, and more than a prophet. This is he of whom it is written: "Behold, I send my messenger before your face, who will prepare your way before you"' (Luke 7:26-27).

Before the birth of John the Baptist, his father, the godly priest Zacharias, received a visit from the angel Gabriel, who applied the prophecy of Malachi (4:5-6) to the unborn child when he said, 'He will turn many of the children of Israel to the Lord their God. He will also go before him in the spirit and power of Elijah, "to turn the hearts of the fathers to the children," and the disobedient to the wisdom of the just, to make ready a people prepared for the Lord' (Luke 1:16-17). John the Baptist is the Elijah promised by the Lord through his servant Malachi.

While the two prophecies of the messenger of the Messenger (3:1) and the sending of Elijah the prophet (4:5) appear unrelated in the book of Malachi, in their fulfilment they are intrinsically united. John the Baptist is the man of God who unites both predictions in his person and office.

Application

1. The distinguishing love of God

> I have loved you…
> … Jacob I have loved;
> But Esau I have hated
>
> (1:2).

The apostle Paul quotes these words, along with others from the Old Testament, when explaining the electing love of God: 'For they are not all Israel who are of Israel, nor are they all children because they are the seed of Abraham; but, "In Isaac your seed shall be called" [Gen. 21:12]. That is, those who are the children of the flesh, these are not the children of God; but the children of the promise are counted as the seed. For this is the word of promise: "At this time I will come and Sarah shall have a son" [cf. Gen. 18:10,14]. And not only this, but when Rebecca also had conceived by one man, even by our father Isaac (for the children not yet being born, nor having done any good or evil, that the purpose of God according to election might stand, not of works but of him who calls), it was said to her, "The older shall serve the younger" [Gen. 25:23]. As it is written, "Jacob I have loved, but Esau I have hated" [Mal. 1:2-3]' (Rom. 9:6-13, references added).

Paul's logic is crystal clear: the whole human race is sinful by nature. The Lord would be entirely just to condemn every individual man, woman and child to everlasting punishment. We all deserve it: 'There is no one righteous, no, not one … for all have sinned and fall short of the glory of God' (Rom. 3:10,23). The Lord 'chooses and rejects as seems good to Him any of the sinful race of Adam, all of whom are justly objects of His displeasure, without regarding natural qualities which distinguish them from one another'[9] (cf. Eph. 1:3-5). 'For by grace you have been saved through faith, and that not of yourselves; it is the gift of God' (Eph. 2:8).

From the book of Malachi the Christian church may learn important lessons:

- They should remember how much God loves his chosen people (1:2; 3:17; cf. John 3:16; Rom. 5:8; 8:31-32; Eph. 1:3-7);
- Repentance is essential in maintaining a right relationship with the Lord (1:9; cf. Isa. 55:7; 2 Cor. 7:10);
- True faith in God is demonstrated by obedience to his Word (2:7-9; cf. John 14:15; 1 Cor. 7:10; James 2:18);
- The Lord's people should encourage one another (3:16) 'and so much the more as [they] see the Day approaching' (Heb. 10:25).

2. Stealing from God

Will a man rob God?
Yet you have robbed me!
But you say,
'In what way have we robbed you?'
In tithes and offerings

(3:8).

The people defrauded the Lord in tithes and offerings. The tithe, a tenth part of income devoted to the Lord's service, was based on Abraham's spontaneous gift to Melchizedek (Gen. 14:20), continued as part of Jacob's commitment (Gen. 28:22), established in Israel's law by Moses (Lev. 27:30-32; Deut. 14:22-26) and given for the support of the Levites (Num. 18:21-32).

Israel's repentance will be demonstrated by bringing 'all the tithes into the storehouse' (3:10) and the blessing of the Lord will fall upon them.

King Solomon recorded a spiritual proverb which expresses the same sentiment:

Honour the LORD with your possessions,
And with the first-fruits of all your increase;
So your barns will be filled with plenty,
And your vats will overflow with new wine

(Prov. 3:9-10).

The Old Testament contains 'spiritual laws of economics' which are diametrically opposed to the world's thinking:

> There is one who scatters, yet increases more;
> And there is one who withholds more than is right,
> But it leads to poverty.
> The generous soul will be made rich,
> And he who waters will also be watered himself
>
> (Prov. 11:24-25).

In the New Testament the words 'tithe' and 'tithing' appear only eight times (Matt. 23:23; Luke 11:42; 18:12; Heb. 7:5,6,8,9). All of these passages refer to the Old Testament practice, or the current Jewish interpretation. Under the New Covenant there is no express command to tithe, but Christians are commended for being generous in sharing their material possessions with the poor (Acts 2:44-45; 4:32-37) and instructed that gifts in support of the Lord's people and the Lord's work are to be given freely, cheerfully, generously and secretly (2 Cor. 9:6-8; Matt. 6:3-4). Rich Christians are 'to be rich in good works, ready to give, willing to share' (1 Tim. 6:18).

The Saviour is the Christian's ultimate example of giving (2 Cor. 8:9). All that we are and all that we possess have been entrusted to us by the Lord. We are called to be faithful stewards (1 Cor. 16:1-3; 2 Cor. 8:1 – 9:15). Love for the Lord demonstrated in generosity to the Lord's people and the Lord's work still results in blessing from the Lord (Gal. 6:6-10). When Abraham spontaneously gave a tithe he did so 430 years before the tithe was written into the Old Testament law at Sinai. The tithe remains a guideline, but for many Christians in the Western world it is a wholly inadequate amount.

3. The book of remembrance

The character of God and his relationship with his people is highlighted throughout the whole book of Malachi: God loves his people (1:2); God is Israel's Father and Master (1:6); God is without deceit and speaks openly and plainly (2:2): God is Israel's Father and Creator (2:10); God is the God of justice (2:17) and God does not change (3:6).[10] Everything about God's character and ways warrants the utmost respect, reverence, love and service. Those who delight in the Lord will also delight in speaking of him, especially to those who share such loving devotion:

> Then those who feared the LORD spoke to one another,
> And the LORD listened and heard them;
> So a book of remembrance was written before him
> For those who fear the LORD
> And who meditate on his name.
> 'They shall be mine,' says the LORD of hosts,
> 'On the day that I make them my jewels.
> And I will spare them
> As a man spares his own son who serves him'
>
> (3:16-17).

The Lord keeps a record of those in whom he delights and who delight in him. The coming of the Messiah will divide people into two groups — one for blessing, one for judgement. It will be a day 'burning like an oven' (4:1), or the day when 'The Sun of Righteousness shall arise with healing in his wings' (4:2). While the first advent of Christ brought judgement to some and healing to others (Matt. 8:16-17; 11:5), the Second Advent of Christ will bring in the final judgement and total healing (Rev. 21:4).

The apostle John describes a vision of the final judgement and the opening of the record books: 'Then I saw a great white throne and him who sat on it, from whose face the earth and the heaven fled away. And there was found no place for them. And I saw the dead, small and great, standing before God, and books were opened. And another book was opened, which is the book of life. And the dead were judged according to their works, by the things which were written in the books. The sea gave up the dead who were in it, and death and Hades delivered up the dead who were in them. And they were judged, each one according to his works. Then death and Hades were cast into the lake of fire. This is the second death. And anyone not found written in the book of life was cast into the lake of fire' (Rev. 20:11-15).

4. Preparing for the coming of Messiah

Malachi presents a vivid picture of the closing period of Old Testament history: reformation is needed in preparation for the coming of the Messiah. There is a parallel to be drawn between Israel's state and condition at this time and that of the church in our own day. Malachi closes with a forward look to the first coming of the Messiah. No one knew just when that day would come. The church of Jesus Christ today looks forward to the return, the Second Coming, of our Lord and Saviour Jesus Christ. God's people are to be those who are 'looking for the blessed hope and glorious appearing of our great God and Saviour Jesus Christ' (Titus 2:13). We are to be those 'who eagerly wait for him' (Heb. 9:28), which leads us to ask, 'What manner of persons ought [we] to be in holy conduct and godliness?' (2 Peter 3:11).

Conclusion

With the culmination of the book of Malachi the Old Testament preparation for the coming of the Messiah is complete.

Theophanies, types and prophecies have laid the foundation. The promise of a great champion, who would do battle royal with the enemy of God (Gen. 3:15) and rectify the appalling damage which resulted through the sins of unbelief and disobedience, has been elaborated.

Predictions have been made:

- The seed of Eve, the seed of Abraham, the seed of Judah, the seed of David — establishing the royal line;
- Son of God, God like God, possessing all the attributes of the eternal — revealing a unique personage;
- King, Priest, Prophet, Messiah, Mediator, Counsellor — forming a unique combination of offices;
- Peacemaker, kinsman-redeemer, sacrificial lamb, sin-bearer — indicating a remarkable responsibility and purpose.

The scene is set. The godly yearn; they watch; they wait and they pray. The 'just and devout' wait 'for the consolation of Israel' (Luke 2:25).

The Old Testament Scriptures are complete.

The prophet's voice is silent for the next four hundred years, until suddenly a man emerges in Judah crying out: 'Repent, for the kingdom of heaven is at hand!' (Matt. 3:2). John the Baptist breaks forth as 'the voice of one crying in the wilderness, "Prepare the way of the LORD"' (Isa. 40:3). He is the messenger of the Messenger of the covenant (Mal. 3:1). God has raised him up to reveal his Son to Israel (John 1:34,31). The fulness of the time has come. God sends 'forth his Son, born of a woman, born under the law ... that we might receive the adoption as sons' (Gal. 4:4-5). 'God, who at various times and in different ways' had spoken 'in time past to the fathers by the prophets', now communicates in a new and far more wonderful way, speaking 'to us by his Son' (Heb. 1:1-2).

The New Covenant is about to be established. The Old Covenant at Sinai is to be superseded by 'a better covenant' (Heb. 8:6), 'the everlasting covenant' (Heb. 13:20). The blood of this covenant is not like the old, 'the blood of bulls and goats' (Heb. 10:4), but 'the precious blood of Christ, as of a lamb without blemish and without spot' (1 Peter 1:19). The sins of God's people are to be removed for ever. Righteousness is to be imputed *and* imparted. The Spirit of God is to indwell every believer. The law of God is to be written on the heart. Believing Jew and believing Gentile are to unite into the new Israel of God, the true Israel of God, the spiritual Israel of God. Together the children of God of all nations unite in singing, 'Salvation belongs to our God who sits on the throne, and to the Lamb!' (Rev. 7:10).

The history of the Old Testament should thrill us; so too should its prophecies and teachings. The Old Testament should thrill us because it has one glorious and united purpose, one unifying subject: Christ and his church. The Bible should thrill us because it speaks of him (John 5:39) and what he has done for his people — at great personal cost, to bring us to God (1 Peter 3:18).

Amen! Blessing and glory and wisdom,
Thanksgiving and honour and power and might,
Be to our God for ever and ever.
Amen

(Rev. 7:12).

Placing the prophets (1)

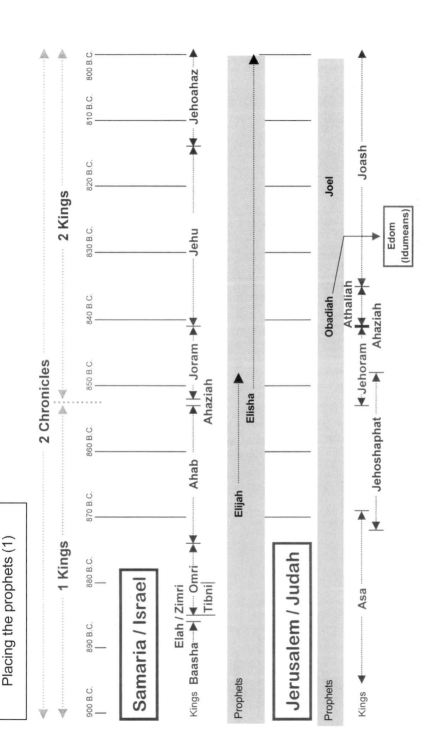

1 Kings · **2 Chronicles** · **2 Kings**

Samaria / Israel

900 B.C.	890 B.C.	880 B.C.	870 B.C.	860 B.C.	850 B.C.	840 B.C.	830 B.C.	820 B.C.	810 B.C.	800 B.C.

Kings: Baasha — Elah / Zimri — Omri |Tibni| — Ahab — Joram / Ahaziah — Jehu — Jehoahaz

Prophets: Elijah — Elisha

Jerusalem / Judah

Kings: Asa — Jehoshaphat — Jehoram / Ahaziah — Athaliah — Joash

Prophets: Obadiah — Joel

Edom (Idumeans)

How far the prophets extended into each reign is not known. Other, lesser-known prophets also ministered in the days before the Babylonian exile.

Dates of the kings of Israel and Judah are based on the work of Edwin R. Thiele, *A Chronology of Hebrew Kings* (Grand Rapids: Zondervan, 1977).

Placing the prophets (2)

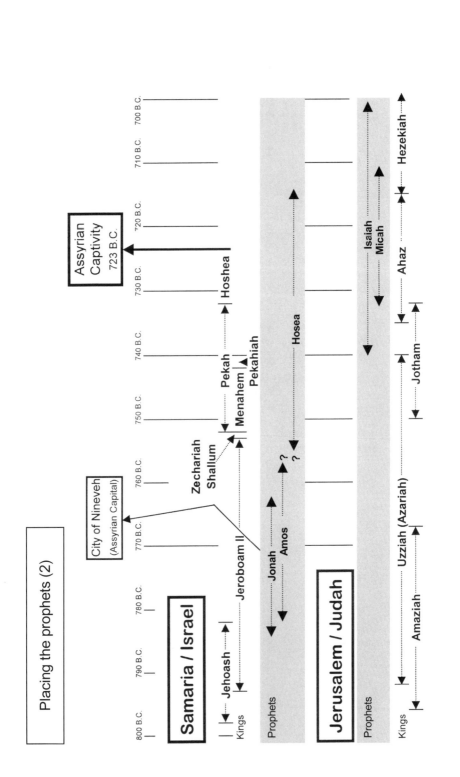

Placing the prophets (3)

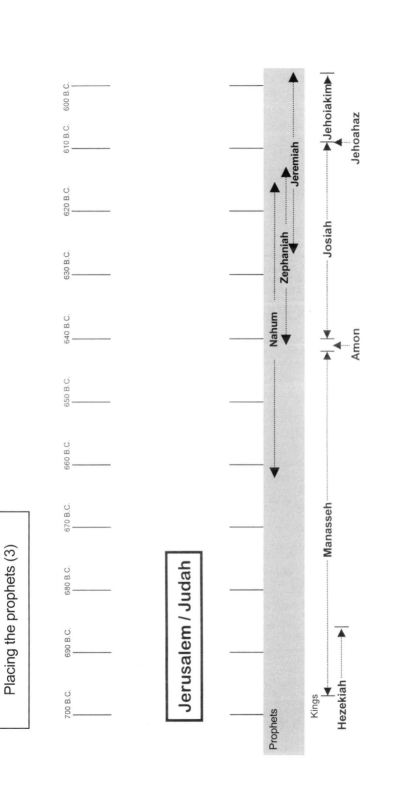

Jerusalem / Judah

| 700 B.C. | 690 B.C. | 680 B.C. | 670 B.C. | 660 B.C. | 650 B.C. | 640 B.C. | 630 B.C. | 620 B.C. | 610 B.C. | 600 B.C. |

Prophets

Nahum

Zephaniah

Jeremiah

Kings

Hezekiah

Manasseh

Amon

Josiah

Jehoahaz

Jehoiakim

Placing the prophets (4)

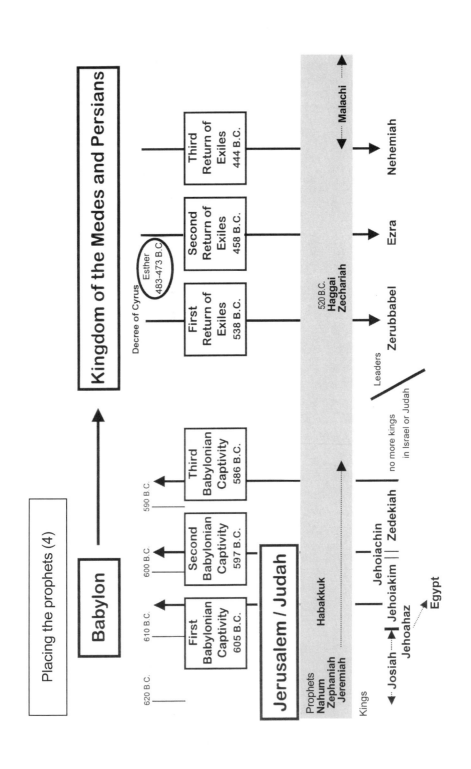

Kingdom of the Medes and Persians

Babylon

Jerusalem / Judah

First Babylonian Captivity 605 B.C.	Second Babylonian Captivity 597 B.C.	Third Babylonian Captivity 586 B.C.	

620 B.C. 610 B.C. 600 B.C. 590 B.C.

Decree of Cyrus

Esther 483–473 B.C.

First Return of Exiles 538 B.C.	Second Return of Exiles 458 B.C.	Third Return of Exiles 444 B.C.

Prophets
Nahum
Zephaniah
Jeremiah

Habakkuk

520 B.C.
Haggai
Zechariah

Malachi

Kings

Josiah
Jehoahaz
Jehoiakim
Jehoiachin
Zedekiah

no more kings
in Israel or Judah

Egypt

Leaders

Zerubbabel   Ezra   Nehemiah

The message of the writing prophets

Years B.C. (approximately)	Prophet	Nation(s) to whom prophecy addressed	Theme	Key thought
c. 840 or c. 580	Obadiah	Edom	Warning to the enemies of the people of God	As you have done, it shall be done to you
c. 820	Joel	Judah	The value and importance of repentance	The Day of the Lord
793-753*	Jonah	Nineveh	He is not the God of the Jews only	A gracious and merciful God
792-740*	Amos	Israel	National sin results in national punishment	Punishment
750-710*	Hosea	Israel	God's love for his wayward people	Return
740-700+	Isaiah	Judah	Salvation of the nation by the living God	The Holy One of Israel
732-715†	Micah	Judah / Israel	God hates sin and delights to pardon	The pardoning God
663-612*	Nahum	Nineveh	The destruction of God's enemies	Awful doom
640-612*	Zephaniah	Judah	The searching judgements of God	God's jealousy
627-586+	Jeremiah	Judah	Certainty of God's judgement; eternity of God's love	Early warnings
609-605*	Habakkuk	Judah	The mysteries of providence	Living by faith
605-522+	Daniel	Gentile nations	Jehovah is Lord of all	The universal sovereignty of God
592-570†	Ezekiel	Judah in exile	The severity and goodness of God	The glory of the Lord
c. 520	Haggai	Judah after exile	God first in life and service	Working for God
520-517	Zechariah	Judah after exile	Encouragement to the disheartened	God loves his people
538-458	Ezra	Judah after exile	The place and power of the Word of God	The Word of the Lord
445-433+	Nehemiah	Judah after exile	Building the kingdom of God	Prayer and hard work
432-420*	Malachi	Judah after exile	Messages of love, rebuke and hope	The Lord will come

* somewhere within this period   + and onwards   † at least this period

Notes

The inspiration of Scripture

1. Bruce Milne, *Know the Truth: a handbook of Christian belief* (Leicester: Inter-Varsity Press, 1982), p.39.
2. Brian H. Edwards, *Nothing but the Truth* (Welwyn: Evangelical Press, 1978), p.38.
3. R. C. H. Lenski, *Commentary on Colossians, Thessalonians, Timothy, Titus and Philemon* (Minnesota: Augsburg, 1964), p.845.
4. J. I. Packer, *'Fundamentalism' and the Word of God: some Evangelical principles* (Leicester: Inter-Varsity Press, 1958), pp.47,48.
5. Francis A. Schaeffer, *The Great Evangelical Disaster* (Westchester, Illinois: Crossway, 1984), p.57.
6. *The Works of Benjamin B. Warfield, Revelation and Inspiration* (Baker Book House Co., 1981 [first published 1927]), vol. 1, p.436.
7. C. Sydney Carter, *The Reformers and Holy Scripture: a historical investigation* (London: Thynne and Jarvis, 1928), p.17.
8. G. J. Collier, 'Notes on Inspiration' (*Gospel Tidings*, 9 [5] 1984), p.200.
9. Arthur W. Pink, *The Divine Inspiration of the Bible* (Grand Rapids, Michigan: Guardian Press, 1976), p.5.
10. E. J. Young, *Thy Word is Truth* (Edinburgh: Banner of Truth Trust, 1963), p.47.
11. A. M. Hodgkin, *Christ in all the Scriptures* (London: Pickering and Inglis, 1907), p.3.
12. Irving L. Jensen, *Jensen's Survey of the Old Testament: search and discover* (Chicago: Moody Press, 1978), p.21.
13. Edwards, *Nothing but the Truth,* p.50.
14. Albert Barnes, *Notes on the New Testament: explanatory and practical, Thessalonians, Timothy, Titus, and Philemon* (London: Blackie and Son), vol. 8, p.241.
15. Edwards, *Nothing but the Truth,* pp.112-13.

The central theme of Old Testament Scripture

1. E. A. Martens, *Plot and Purpose in the Old Testament* (Leicester: Inter-Varsity Press, 1981), p.12.
2. William J. Dumbrell, *Covenant and Creation: an Old Testament covenantal theology* (Exeter: Paternoster Press, 1984), pp.15-16.
3. Martens, *Plot and Purpose in the Old Testament*, p.33.
4. Walter C. Kaiser, *Toward an Old Testament Theology* (Grand Rapids, Michigan: Zondervan, 1978), p.11.
5. *Ibid.,* pp.12-13.
6. Thomas E. McComiskey, *The Covenants of Promise: a theology of the Old Testament covenants* (Nottingham: IVP, 1985), p.16.
7. *Ibid.,* p.10.

8. Martens, *Plot and Purpose in the Old Testament*, p.11.
9. *Ibid.*, p.15.
10. *Ibid.*, pp.16-17.
11. Ernest W. Hengstenberg, *Christology of the Old Testament: and a commentary on the Messianic predictions* (Grand Rapids, Michigan: Kregel Publications, 1970 [first published 1847]), p.24.
12. Martens, *Plot and Purpose in the Old Testament*, p.19.
13. Hengstenberg, *Christology of the Old Testament*, pp.1-2.
14. Andrew A. Bonar, *Christ and his Church in the Book of Psalms* (Grand Rapids, Michigan: Kregel, 1978 [first published 1861]), p.viii.
15. Franz Delitzsch, *Messianic Prophecies* (Edinburgh: T & T Clark, 1880), p.27.
16. Hengstenberg, *Christology of the Old Testament*, 1970, p.8.
17. James A. Borland, *Christ in the Old Testament: a comprehensive study of Old Testament appearances of Christ in human form* (Chicago: Moody Press, 1978), p.10.
18. *Ibid.*, p.4.
19. *Ibid.*, p.21.
20. Edmund P. Clowney, *The Unfolding Mystery: discovering Christ in the Old Testament* (Leicester: Inter-Varsity Press, 1988), p.14.
21. Andrew Jukes, *The Law of the Offerings* (Grand Rapids, Michigan: Kregel Publications, 1976 [first published 1854]), pp.14-15.
22. William Tyndale cited by Bonar, *A Commentary on Leviticus*, p.4.
23. Bishop Marsh cited by Patrick Fairbairn, *The Typology of Scripture: viewed in connection with the whole series of the divine dispensations* (Grand Rapids, Michigan: Baker, 1975 [first published 1900]), p.46.
24. John Calvin, *A Commentary on Genesis* (Edinburgh: Banner of Truth Trust, 1965 [first published 1554]), p.487.
25. Hengstenberg, *Christology of the Old Testament*, p.10.
26. Patrick Fairbairn, *Prophecy: viewed in respect to its distinctive nature, its special function, and proper interpretation* (Grand Rapids, Michigan: Baker, 1976 [1865]), p.178.
27. Geerhardus Vos, *Biblical Theology: Old and New Testaments* (Edinburgh: Banner of Truth Trust, 1975 [1948]), p.7.
28. Fairbairn, *The Typology of Scripture*, p.72.
29. Kaiser, *Toward an Old Testament Theology*, 1978, p.41.
30. Fairbairn, *The Typology of Scripture*, p.48.
31. William Hendriksen, *Survey of the Bible: a treasury of Bible Information* (Welwyn, Hertfordshire: Evangelical Press, 1976), p.298.
32. Jukes, *The Law of the Offerings*, p.18.

Genesis
1. H. C. Leupold, *Exposition of Genesis* (Grand Rapids, Michigan: Baker, 1942), vol. 1, p.9.
2. Vos, *Biblical Theology*, p.11.
3. 'cf.' means 'compare with'.
4. Homer C. Hoeksema, *'In the Beginning God...'* (Grand Rapids, Michigan: Reformed Free Publishing Association, 1966), p.45. Hoeksema enumerates the various alternative 'interpretations' of creation and demonstrates their weakness and inadequacy.

5. *Our World,* No. 18 (published by Creation Resources Trust, Somerset, England); and *Creation ex nihilo,* vol. 19, no. 2, pp.16-19 (published by Creation Science Foundation (UK), Swindon, Wiltshire).

6. For a detailed argument see Hengstenberg, *Christology of the Old Testament,* pp.24-5.

7. Fairbairn, *Prophecy,* p.181.

8. Hengstenberg, *Christology of the Old Testament,* p.26.

9. For an explanation of the name 'Shiloh' see page 72 (see also note 18 below).

10. Ernest W. Hengstenberg, *History of the Kingdom of God under the Old Testament* (Edinburgh: T & T Clark, 1877), vol. 1, p.2.

11. See pages 39-40. For a fuller treatment of theophanies as appearances of the Son of God, see Borland, *Christ in the Old Testament,* pp.34-49.

12. For an explanation of the meaning of the word 'type' see the chapter on the 'Central theme of Old Testament Scripture', pp.40-43.

13. Clowney, *The Unfolding Mystery,* p.64.

14. George Lawson, *Lectures on the History of Joseph* (London: Banner of Truth Trust, 1972 [first published 1807]), p.1. In this book Lawson does not develop the notion of Joseph as a type of the Lord Jesus Christ.

15. Robert Candlish, *Studies in Genesis* (Grand Rapids, Michigan: Kregel Publications, 1979 [first published 1868]), pp.608-16.

16. McComiskey, *The Covenants of Promise,* p.20.

17. Vos, *Biblical Theology,* p.43.

18. For the interpretation of 'Shiloh' see Leupold, *Exposition of Genesis,* vol. 2, pp.1178-85.

19. Arthur W. Pink, *Gleanings in Exodus* (Chicago: Moody Press, 1972), p.7.

20. Martens, *Plot and Purpose in the Old Testament,* pp.29-30.

21. Arthur W. Pink, *Gleanings in Genesis* (Chicago: Moody Press, 1922), p.168.

22. Leupold, *Exposition of Genesis,* p.479.

23. Vos, *Biblical Theology,* p.44.

24. Clowney, *The Unfolding Mystery,* p.73.

Exodus

1. The figure is calculated as 1,734,540 in James G. Murphy's *A Critical and Exegetical Commentary on the Book of Exodus* (Minneapolis, Minnesota: Klock and Klock Christian Publishers, 1979 [first published 1866]), p.131.

2. Robert Lee, *The Outlined Bible: an outline and analysis of every book in the Bible* (London: Pickering and Inglis), analysis no. 2.

3. *Ibid.*

4. Raymond Brown, *Let's Read the Old Testament* (London and Eastbourne: Victory Press, 1971), p.9.

5. F. B. Meyer, *Devotional Commentary on Exodus* (Grand Rapids, Michigan: Kregel Publications, 1978), p.219.

6. Thomas Watson, *The Ten Commandments* (London: Banner of Truth Trust, 1959 [first published 1692]), p.45.

7. Kiene gives the conversion of the old Hebrew cubit as 52.52cm or 20.7 inches (Paul F. Kiene, *The Tabernacle of God in the Wilderness of Sinai.* Grand Rapids, Michigan: Zondervan, 1977, p.30).

8. According to Hebrews 9:4 in the RAV, the altar of incense is located inside the Holy of Holies. The literal words of Hebrews 9:4 are 'having a golden censer' (see AV). The

censer from the altar was taken into the Holy of Holies once a year on the Day of Atonement (Lev. 16:12-13). The altar remained outside the Holy of Holies.

9. When the ark was eventually housed in the temple at Jerusalem it contained only the two slabs of stone upon which were written the Ten Commandments (1 Kings 8:9).

10. C. L. Maynard, cited by A. M. Hodgkin, *Christ in all the Scriptures* (London: Pickering and Inglis, 1907), p.21.

11. A type is a figure, episode, or symbolic factor resembling some future reality in such a way as to foreshadow or prefigure it (see pp.40-43).

12. For a detailed study of the furnishings and materials used in the tabernacle as representing the character and work of Christ, see Kiene, *The Tabernacle of God in the Wilderness*, pp.9-162.

13. Hendriksen, *Survey of the Bible*, pp.212-13.

14. The consecration of the high priest (29:1-37) and his sacred duties, together with their rich significance in relation to the Lord Jesus Christ, will be considered in detail in the next chapter on the book of Leviticus.

15. E.g. Kiene, *The Tabernacle of God in the Wilderness*, pp.162-73; Henry Law, *The Gospel in Exodus* (London: Banner of Truth Trust, 1967 [1855]), pp.134-9; Pink, *Gleanings in Exodus*, pp.259-72.

16. Law, *Gospel in Exodus*, p.134.

17. Pink, *Gleanings in Exodus*, p.7.

18. This is not a reference to Abraham, Isaac and Jacob — for whom circumcision was not a yoke but a promise — but the fathers since the time of Moses (Paton J. Gloag, *A Critical and Exegetical Commentary on the Acts of the Apostles*. Minneapolis, Minnesota: Klock and Klock Christian Publishers, 1979 [first published 1870], vol. 2, p.73).

19. Albert Barnes, *Notes, explanatory and practical, on the Acts of the Apostles* (London: Routledge and Sons, no date, p.238).

20. Gloag, *Acts of the Apostles*.

21. John Calvin, *The Acts of the Apostles 14-28* (Edinburgh: Saint Andrew Press, 1966 [first published 1554]), pp.37-8.

22. Watson, *The Ten Commandments*, p.6.

23. *Ibid.*, p.45.

24. It is not the purpose of this book to argue for one position in preference to another, merely to illustrate the diversity of opinion that exists among Bible-believing scholars and teachers.

25. R. C. H. Lenski, *The Interpretation of the Acts of the Apostles* (Minneapolis, Minnesota: Augsburg Publishing House, 1961), p.604.

26. *Ibid.*, pp.604-5.

27. Rudolf Stier, *The Words of the Apostles* (Minneapolis, Minnesota: Klock and Klock, 1981 [first published 1869]), p.239.

Leviticus

1. Pink, *Gleanings in Exodus*, p.7.

2. Samuel H. Kellogg, *The Book of Leviticus* (Minneapolis, Minnesota: Klock and Klock Christian Publishers, 1978 [first published 1899]), p.10.

3. Andrew A. Bonar, *A Commentary on Leviticus* (Edinburgh: Banner of Truth Trust, 1966 [first published 1846]), p.1.

4. Raymond B. Dillard and Tremper Longman III, *An Introduction to the Old Testament* (Leicester: Apollos IVP, 1995), pp.76-7.

5. Kellogg, *The Book of Leviticus*, p.156.

6. For a Christian GP's perspective on the benefits of the laws of Moses to the health of the nation, see S. I. McMillen, *None of These Diseases* (London: Marshall Morgan and Scott, 1966).

7. C. F. Keil & F. Delitzsch, *Biblical Commentary on the Old Testament, The Pentateuch* (Grand Rapids, Michigan: Eerdmans, no date), p.407.

8. Bonar, *A Commentary on Leviticus*, p.321.

9. There are about forty special references to Leviticus.

10. A type is a figure, episode, or symbolic factor resembling some future reality in such a way as to foreshadow or prefigure it (see pp.40-43).

Two books of particular help are:

(i) Bonar, *A Commentary on Leviticus*. C. H. Spurgeon recommended this book as: 'Very precious. Mr Andrew Bonar has a keen eye for a typical analogy, but he always keeps the rein upon his imagination, and is therefore safe to follow. He is a master in Israel.'

(ii) Jukes, *The Law of the Offerings*. This is also recommended by Spurgeon: 'A very condensed, instructive, refreshing book. It will open up new trains of thought to those unversed in the teaching of the types'(*Commenting on Commentaries*. Edinburgh: Banner of Truth Trust, 1969 [first published 1876], pp.60-61).

11. Edmund P. Clowney, 'Preaching Christ From All the Scriptures,' in Samuel T. Logan Jr. (ed.), *The Preacher and Preaching: reviving the art in the Twentieth Century* (Phillipsburg, New Jersey: Presbyterian and Reformed Publishing Company, 1986), p.175.

12. The self-sacrifice of Christ's holy, obedient life meets all the requirements of God's righteousness and justice. God is entirely satisfied. Believers are no longer children of wrath, but children of grace.

13. Hodgkin, *Christ in all the Scriptures*, p.24.

14. Law, *The Gospel in Exodus*, p.133.

15. William Arnot, *Studies in Acts: the church in the house*, Grand Rapids, Michigan: Kregel Publications, 1978 [first published 1883]), pp.38-9.

16. Law, *The Gospel in Exodus*, p.131.

17. Rudolf Stier, *The Words of the Lord Jesus* (Edinburgh: T & T Clark, 1985), vol. 5, p.278.

18. Robert Murray M'Cheyne, cited by Bonar, *A Commentary on Leviticus*, p.8.

19. Kellogg, *The Book of Leviticus*, p.4.

20. Cf. Lev. 26:12; Jer. 32:38; Ezek. 37:27; Isa. 52:11; Ezek. 20:34, 41; 2 Sam. 7:14.

21. Jukes, *The Law of the Offerings*, pp.33-4.

Numbers

1. E. J. Young maintains that Moses could have written these words (see Edward J. Young, *An Introduction to the Old Testament*. Grand Rapids, Michigan: Eerdmans, 1949, p.86).

2. Pink, *Gleanings in Exodus*, p.7.

3. Keil & Delitzsch, *The Pentateuch*, vol. 3, p.5.

4. This was not the first time that the Lord provided quails in the wilderness (Exod. 16:12-13; cf. Ps. 105:40).

5. G. Campbell Morgan, *Student Survey of the Bible* (Iowa Falls, Iowa: World Bible Publishers, 1993), pp.35-6.

6. For a detailed explanation of these types see Pink, *Gleanings in Exodus*, pp.136-40.

7. Hengstenberg, *Christology of the Old Testament*, p.34.

8. Keil & Delitzsch, *The Pentateuch*, vol. 3, p.194; cf. Delitzsch, *Messianic Prophecies*, pp.40-41.
9. Hengstenberg. *Christology of the Old Testament*, p.34.
10. Brown, *Let's Read the Old Testament*, pp.33-4.
11. Hodgkin, *Christ in all the Scriptures*, p.31.
12. Is there an intended connection between this man's illness as a result of his sin (John 5:5,14) and the thirty-eight years spent by the children of Israel wandering in the wilderness because of their sin? A number of Bible scholars believe there is such a link.
13. Campbell Morgan, *Student Survey of the Bible*, p.39.

Deuteronomy

1. Hendriksen, *Survey of the Bible*, pp.217-18.
2. *Ibid.*, p.210.
3. For a brief examination of critical theory against Mosaic authorship, see Dillard and Longman, *An Introduction to the Old Testament*, pp.93-7.
4. Lee, *The Outlined Bible*, analysis no.5.
5. R. C. H. Lenski at least concedes: 'We read about other periods of precisely forty days in the Scriptures, so that it seems as though some mysterious law underlies this number' (*The Interpretation of Matthew*. Minneapolis, Minnesota: Augsburg Publishing House, 1961 [first published 1943], p.141).
6. The obligation of a man to marry his deceased brother's wife who has no son in order to maintain the family name and inheritance.
7. The word 'covenant' appears twenty-one times in Deuteronomy (seven times in chapter 29).
8. Meredith G. Kline, cited by Jensen, *Jensen's Survey of the Old Testament*, p.131.
9. Clowney, 'Preaching Christ From All the Scriptures,' p.168.
10. Delitzsch, *Messianic Prophecies*, p.41.
11. John Bunyan, *The Pilgrim's Progress: from this world to that which is to come* (Edinburgh: Banner of Truth Trust, 1977 [first published 1676]), p.376. Application suggested by Brown, *Let's Read the Old Testament*, p.40.
12. Stier, *The Words of the Apostles*, p.90.
13. John Calvin, *A Harmony of the Gospels Matthew, Mark and Luke* (Edinburgh: St Andrew Press, 1972), vol. 3, pp.191-2.
14. William Hendriksen, *The Gospel of Luke* (Edinburgh: Banner of Truth Trust, 1979), p.1025.
15. Hodgkin, *Christ in all the Scriptures*, p.37.
16. Campbell Morgan, *Student Survey of the Bible*, pp.45-6.
17. Keil & Delitzsch, *The Pentateuch*, vol. 3, p.270.
18. Dillard and Longman, *An Introduction to the Old Testament*, p.102.

Joshua

1. Young, *An Introduction to the Old Testament*, p.163.
2. Lee, *The Outlined Bible*, analysis no.6.
3. Leupold, *Exposition of Genesis*, vol. 1, p.486.
4. Loyalty to the Lord is more important than loyalty to one's nation.
5. Arthur W. Pink, *Gleanings in Joshua* (Chicago: Moody Press, 1964), p.1324.
6. William G. Blaikie, *The Book of Joshua* (Minneapolis, Minnesota: Klock and Klock Christian Publishers, 1978 [first published 1908]), p.130.
7. Pink, *Gleanings in Joshua*, p.13.
8. Lee, *The Outlined Bible*, analysis no.6.
9. 'It was not customary to distinguish Israelites in this way, but only those who had come among them from other tribes, like "Heber the Kenite," "Jael, the wife of Heber

the Kenite" (Judges 4:11,17), Uriah the Hittite, Hushai the Archite, etc.' (Blaikie, *The Book of Joshua*, p.263).

10. O. Gerlach, cited by Carl F. Keil, *The Books of Joshua, Judges and Ruth* (Grand Rapids, Michigan: Eerdmans, 1950), p.95.

11. Pink, *Gleanings in Joshua*, p.388.

12. Jensen, *Jensen's Survey of the Old Testament*, p.137.

Judges

1. Andrew R. Fausset, *A Critical and Expository Commentary on the Book of Judges* (USA: James and Klock, 1977 [first published 1885]), p.4.

2. Lee, *The Outlined Bible*, analysis no. 7.

3. *Baba Bathra* 14b, cited by Young, *An Introduction to the Old Testament*, p.169.

4. The discrepancy between 340 years (1390 B.C. to 1050 B.C.) and 410 years (sum total of years related in the book of Judges) is explained in that the rule of the 'judges' overlapped. The Bible presents three different historic periods which must be reconciled with the inspired record in the book of Judges: 300 years (Judg. 11:26), 480 years (1 Kings 6:1) and 450 years (Acts 13:20). See Leon J. Wood, *Distressing Days of the Judges* (Grand Rapids, Michigan: Zondervan, 1975), pp.10-17; and Carl F. Keil, *The Books of Joshua, Judges and Ruth* (Grand Rapids, Michigan: Eerdmans, 1950), pp.277-92.

5. Young, *An Introduction to the Old Testament*, p.170.

6. Jensen, *Jensen's Survey of the Old Testament*, p.152.

7. Fausset, *Commentary on the Book of Judges*, p.1.

8. Wood, *Distressing Days of the Judges*, pp.6-7.

9. Bruce Wilkinson and Kenneth Boa, *Talk Thru the Old Testament* (Nashville, Tennessee: Nelson, 1983), p.62.

10. Jensen, *Jensen's Survey of the Old Testament*, p.158.

11. Dillard and Longman, *An Introduction to the Old Testament*, p.125.

12. Miriam was the first prophetess (Exod. 15:20). After Deborah there were others such as Huldah (2 Kings 22:14) and Anna (Luke 2:36).

13. Gordon J. Keddie, *Even in Darkness: Judges and Ruth simply explained* (Welwyn: Evangelical Press, 1985), p.49.

14. Descendants from Abraham's son Midian, born to Keturah (Gen. 25:2).

15. Jerubbaal is another name for Gideon (6:32).

16. Luke H. Wiseman, *Practical Truths from Judges* (Grand Rapids, Michigan: Kregel, 1985 [first published 1874]), p.230.

17. Ambros, cited by Keil, *The Books of Joshua, Judges and Ruth*, pp.417-18.

18. Keil, *The Books of Joshua, Judges and Ruth*, p.452.

19. *Ibid.*, p.407.

20. Fausset, *Commentary on the Book of Judges*, pp.224-5,255,262-3.

21. Keil, *Joshua, Judges, Ruth*, p.389.

22. Fausset, *Commentary on the Book of Judges*, p.204.

23. Keil, *Joshua, Judges, Ruth*, p.392.

24. Fausset, *Commentary on the Book of Judges*, p.205.

25. Wiseman favours the view that the young woman was put to death (see Wiseman, *Practical Truths from Judges*, pp.266-8).

26. Young, *An Introduction to the Old Testament*, p.175.

27. Wood, *Distressing Days of the Judges*, p.289.

28. Keddie, *Even in Darkness*, p.85.

29. Wiseman, *Practical Truths from Judges*, p.293.

30. Wiseman, *Practical Truths from Judges*, p.63.

Ruth

1. David Atkinson, *The Message of Ruth: the wings of refuge* (Leicester: Inter-Varsity Press, 1983), p.25.
2. Cited by Lee, *The Outlined Bible,* analysis no. 8.
3. The more usual practice is to calculate back from the birth of King David through Jesse and Obed, placing the marriage of Boaz and Ruth during the forty-year period of peace following Gideon's delivery of Israel (Carl Keil, Leon Wood, Gordon Keddie, Nelson). This results in too many years to be filled by the lives of Rahab and Boaz. A more accurate way of calculation is to work forward from Rahab, who was at least in her teens when Israel invaded Jericho, and is unlikely to have been more than fifty when she gave birth to Boaz. That would make the latest time for his birth to be thirty-five years after the invasion. If Boaz then fathered Obed as late as his eightieth year *the very latest period* into which the book of Ruth would fall is 105 years after possession of the land of Canaan — i.e. during the eighty years of rest following Ehud's delivery from the oppression of Moab.
4. The Moabites descended from Abraham's nephew Lot by his oldest daughter (Gen. 19:37; 11:27).
5. Naomi had prior legal claim to a kinsman-redeemer but gave this up in favour of Ruth.
6. Keddie, *Even in Darkness,* p.121.
7. Atkinson, *The Message of Ruth,* pp.113-14.
8. Jensen, *Jensen's Survey of the Old Testament,* p.166.
9. Atkinson, *The Message of Ruth,* p.59.
10. Lee, *The Outlined Bible*, analysis no. 8.
11. Hals, cited by Dillard and Longman, *An Introduction to the Old Testament,* p.133.
12. Dillard and Longman, *An Introduction to the Old Testament,* p.133.
13. Atkinson, *The Message of Ruth,* pp.27-8.
14. Leon Wood argues that these two marriages did not contravene God's law (Wood, *Distressing Days of the Judges*, pp.256-7).
15. Keil, *Joshua, Judges, Ruth,* p.483.

1 Samuel

1. Carl F. Keil & Franz Delitzsch, *Biblical Commentary on the Books of Samuel* (Grand Rapids, Michigan: Eerdmans, 1950), p.13.
2. Alfred Edersheim, *Israel Under Samuel, Saul, and David, to the Birth of Solomon* (London: The Religious Tract Society), p.2.
3. W. G. Blaikie, *The First Book of Samuel* (Minneapolis, Minnesota: Klock and Klock Christian Publishers, 1978 [first published 1887]), p.2.
4. Edersheim, *Israel Under Samuel, Saul, and David,* p.65.
5. Three explanations have been given for the 'appearance' of Samuel: (i) Samuel actually appeared to Saul; (ii) the medium at En Dor deceived Saul; and (iii) an evil spirit assumed the form of Samuel. For a discussion see Hengstenberg, *History of the Kingdom of God,* vol. 2, pp.104-6.
6. Edersheim, *Israel Under Samuel, Saul, and David,* p.12.
7. Wood, *Distressing Days of the Judges,* p.341.
8. Stier, *The Words of the Apostles,* p.191.
9. *Ibid.*
10. See chapter on Deuteronomy, 'The Great Prophet', pp.162-3.
11. The character of David's rule as a type of Christ's reign will become more obvious as we study 2 Samuel.
12. Blaikie, *The First Book of Samuel,* p.91.
13. J. E. Adams, 'The Pastor and his Family,' *Reformation Today*, 81, 1984, p.29.
14. F. W. Krummacher, *David — the King of Israel* (Grand Rapids, Michigan: Baker Book House, 1982 [first published 1868]), p.173.

Krummacher's writings are highly recommended for their faithfulness to Scripture, devotional emphasis and clear and easy style. Other titles (also published by Baker) include *Elijah the Tishbite, Elisha a Prophet for our Times, The Suffering Saviour* and *The Martyr Lamb.*

15. Edersheim, *Israel Under Samuel, Saul, and David,* p.36.

16. Brown, *Let's Read the Old Testament,* p.67.

2 Samuel

1. The Amalekite's account of events is untrue (see 1 Sam. 31:3-5), but David has no way of knowing this.

2. Arthur W. Pink, *The Life of David* (Grand Rapids, Michigan: Baker Book House, 1981), vol. 1 p.233.

3. Keil & Delitzsch, *The Books of Samuel,* p.292.

4. Charles Gulston, *David Shepherd and King: the life and heritage of David* (Grand Rapids, Michigan: Zondervan, 1980), p.98.

5. William G. Blaikie, *David, King of Israel: the divine plan and lessons of his life* (Minneapolis, Minnesota: Klock and Klock Christian Publishers, 1981 [first published 1861]), p.145.

6. David may have composed Psalm 63 at this time. While many commentators place Psalm 63 in the days when David hid from Saul in the wilderness of Judah, it is most unlikely that David would have called himself 'the king' at that time (v. 11). Spurgeon places it later, when David was fleeing from Absalom.

7. Keil and Delitzsch calculate twenty years to the victory at Ebenezer, forty years under Samuel and Saul, and about ten years under David (Keil & Delitzsch, *The Books of Samuel,* p.330).

8. Michal possessed an idol (1 Sam. 19:13; cf. Gen. 31:19) and evidently loved the courageous hero and majestic king. She had no sympathy with David's humility in taking the priestly ephod and behaving with such spiritual enthusiasm.

9. Gulston, *David Shepherd and King,* p.153 (emphasis his).

10. H. C. Leupold, *Exposition of the Psalms* (London: Evangelical Press, 1969), p.329.

11. Charles Haddon Spurgeon, *The Treasury of David* (McLean, Virginia: MacDonald Publishing Company), vol. 1, p.445.

12. Gulston, *David Shepherd and King,* p.170.

13. There are differences of opinion as to when these various clashes recorded in chapter 21 actually took place. Three of the wars are recorded in 1 Chronicles 20:4-8, being included in a general survey of David's war exploits. It is fair to assume, however, that at least the first battle is correctly located here since it records how David ceased from accompanying his men to war (21:15-17).

14. Blaikie, *David, King of Israel,* p.317.

15. The opening words of chapter 23 present something of a difficulty since David's life is not yet at an end; there is more to follow. Arthur Pink suggests a solution: '2 Samuel 23 refers to "the last words of David" not so much as those merely of a man, but rather as being a mouthpiece of God, thus forming a brief appendix to his Psalms' (See Pink, *The Life of David,* vol. 2, p.286).

16. Pink, *The Life of David,* vol. 2, p.309. Pink adds: '… nor do we profess to be able to solve it fully'!

17. Blaikie, *David, King of Israel,* p.300.

18. Alexander argues that on the basis of this revelation David wrote Psalms 2 and 110 concerning the eternal Son and Psalm 16:10 concerning the resurrection of Messiah (Charles D. Alexander, *The Heavenly Mystery of the Song of Songs.* Liverpool: Bible Exposition Fellowship, 1965 onwards, pp.12-15).

19. McComiskey, *The Covenants of Promise,* p.21.

20. *Ibid.,* p.26.

21. Fairbairn, *Prophecy,* p.179.

22. Delitzsch, *Messianic Prophecies,* p.51.

23. See section above, 'Part I: The Opening Years', pp.261-2.

1 Kings

1. Young, *An Introduction to the Old Testament,* p.189.

2. Hendriksen, *Survey of the Bible,* p.226.

3. The explanation for making one book into two is given in the introduction to the chapter on the book of 1 Samuel (p.238).

4. Keil & Delitzsch, *The Books of Samuel,* p.512.

5. Spurgeon, *The Treasury of David,* p.43.

6. Thompson Chain Reference Bible.

7. Graeme Goldsworthy, *Gospel and Kingdom: a Christian Interpretation of the Old Testament* (Carlisle: Paternoster, 1981), p.72.

8. Dates of the rulers of Judah and Israel are based upon the work of Edwin R. Thiele, *A Chronology of Hebrew Kings* (Grand Rapids, Michigan: Zondervan, 1977).

9. This prophecy against the altar was fulfilled three hundred years later (2 Kings 23:15-20).

10. Spelled Abijah in 2 Chr. 12:16, etc.

11. See the fuller account, including the first religious revival since the division of the kingdom, recorded in 2 Chr. 14:1 – 16:14.

12. See Arthur W. Pink, *The Life of Elijah* (Edinburgh: Banner of Truth Trust, 1956); and F. W. Krummacher, *Elijah the Tishbite* (Grand Rapids, Michigan: Baker, 1977).

13. The claim that Elijah was gripped by cowardly fear and running for his life is examined later in the section on application (see pp. 316-17).

14. Carl F. Keil, *Biblical Commentary on the Books of the Kings* (Grand Rapids, Michigan: Eerdmans, 1950), p.261.

15. See the fuller account, including the second religious revival since the division of the kingdom, in 2 Chr. 17:1 – 20:37.

16. Herbert M. Carson, *Hallelujah!: Christian worship* (Welwyn: Evangelical Press, 1980), p.36.

17. Cited by Charles Bridges, *A Commentary on Proverbs* (London: Banner of Truth Trust, 1968 [first published 1846]), p.300.

18. John Murray, *Principles of Conduct: Aspects of Biblical Ethics* (London: Tyndale Press,1957), p.46.

19. A clear allusion to the forbidden practice of yoking different kinds of animal together (Deut. 22:10).

20. John Calvin, *The Epistle of Paul the Apostle to the Hebrews and the First and Second Epistles of St Peter* (Edinburgh: St Andrew Press, 1963 [first published 1549], pp.74-5.

21. Keil, *The Books of the Kings,* p.166.

22. Hengstenberg, *History of the Kingdom of God,* vol. 2, p.134.

23. Alexander, *The Heavenly Mystery of the Song of Songs,* p.3.

24. Herbert Carson, *Depression in the Christian Family* (Darlington: Evangelical Press, 1994), pp.28-9.

25. Pink, *The Life of Elijah,* pp.196-7.

26. Charles D. Alexander, *Elijah: 'Crouching Coward' or Hero of the Faith?* (Liverpool: Bible Exposition Fellowship, no date), p.4.

27. The NIV has a footnote: 'Or Elijah saw'.

28. Keil, *The Books of the Kings,* p.253.
29. Campbell Morgan, *Student Survey of the Bible,* p.101.
30. Dillard and Longman, *An Introduction to the Old Testament,* p.165.

2 Kings

1. Dr Bullinger, cited by Robert Lee, *The Outlined Bible,* analysis no.12.
2. Dates of the rulers of Judah and Israel are based upon the work of Thiele, *A Chronology of Hebrew Kings.*
3. See Arthur W. Pink, *Gleanings from Elisha: his life and miracles* (Chicago: Moody Press, 1972); F. W. Krummacher, *Elisha: a prophet for our times* (Grand Rapids, Michigan: Baker, 1976); and F. W. Krummacher, *The Last Days of Elisha* (Grand Rapids, Michigan: Baker, 1981).
4. A. R. Buckland and A L. Williams (eds.), *Universal Bible Dictionary* (London: The Religious Tract Society, 1914), p.146.
5. 2 Chr. 22:6, etc.
6. Keil, *The Books of the Kings,* p.345.
7. Another devilish plot to try to destroy the covenant promises that the Lord made to David (2 Sam. 7:12-13,16).
8. It is most unlikely that Athaliah would have permitted her daughter to marry a godly high priest of Jehovah.
9. See the fuller account, including the third religious revival since the division of the kingdom, recorded in 2 Chr. 24:1-25.
10. The deliverer may have been either of the successors of Jehoahaz to the throne of Israel, Jehoash (13:25) or Jeroboam II (14:25); or it may have been Adad-Nirari III of Assyria, who blockaded Damascus about 803 B.C.
11. Keil maintains that this prophecy was given to King Jeroboam II by Jonah in person (C.F. Keil, *The Twelve Minor Prophets.* Grand Rapids, Michigan: Eerdmans, 1949, p.379).
12. Called Azariah in 14:21; 15:1-7, and Uzziah in 2 Chr. 26:1; Isa. 6:1, etc.
13. A reference to Uzziah's arrogance in burning incense in the temple in direct disobedience to the law of God (2 Chr. 26:16).
14. The prophets Isaiah and Micah specifically address this sinfulness (Isa. 2:5-9; 5:7-30; Micah 1:5; 2:1-2).
15. Yet another satanic plot to try to destroy the covenant promises the Lord made to David (2 Sam. 7:12-13,16).
16. This amazing prediction is a wonderful prophecy concerning Christ (Matt. 1:23). See the later chapter covering the book of Isaiah.
17. The precise relationship between the accounts in Kings and Chronicles is not easy to determine with the information available (Edward J. Young, *The Book of Isaiah.* Grand Rapids, Michigan: Eerdmans Publishing Company, 1965, vol.1, pp.267-8).
18. Some Bible scholars suggest Shalmaneser is to be identified with Shalman (Hosea 10:14) and Sargon (Isa. 20:1), while others suggest a co-regency for Shalmaneser and Sargon, and still others take Sargon to be the same as Sennacherib (18:13). There seems to be no way to form a conclusion based upon the evidence supplied in Scripture.
19. See the fuller account, including the fourth religious revival since the division of the kingdom, recorded in 2 Chr. 29:1 – 32:33.
20. In the New Testament the word 'hell' nine times translates the Greek word 'Gehenna' (e.g. Luke 12:5) which derives from 'the Valley of Hinnom', south of Jerusalem, where, in New Testament times, rubbish and dead animals from the city were burned.

21. See the fuller account, including the fifth religious revival since the division of the kingdom, recorded in 2 Chr. 34:1 – 35:27.

22. This may have been the original copy of the law of Moses (2 Chr. 34:14).

23. J. C. Ryle. *Expository Thoughts on the Gospels: St. Matthew* (Cambridge: James Clarke, 1973), pp.208-9.

24. Alexander, *Elijah: 'Crouching Coward' or Hero of the Faith?*, p.17.

25. Miracles are only associated with three sets of men: Moses and Joshua, Elijah and Elisha, Jesus and his apostles.

26. Pink, *Gleanings from Elisha,* p.47.

27. Ernest W. Hengstenberg, *Commentary on the Gospel of St John* (Minneapolis, Minnesota: Klock and Klock Christian Publishers, 1980 [first published 1865]), vol.1, p.230.

28. Young, *An Introduction to the Old Testament,* p.189.

29. Hengstenberg, *History of the Kingdom of God,* vol. 1, p.139.

1 Chronicles

1. Jensen, *Jensen's Survey of the Old Testament,* p.207.

2. *Ibid.*

3. According to the non-inspired historical record of 2 Maccabees 2:13-15, Nehemiah collected an extensive library which would have been available to Ezra for his research.

4. Wilkinson and Boa, *Talk Thru the Old Testament,* p.101.

5. *Ibid.*

6. Campbell Morgan, *Student Survey of the Bible,* p.123.

7. Included only to explain what led up to the purchase of the threshing-floor of Ornan the Jebusite for the erection of an altar to the Lord, and later to be used as the site for the temple.

8. William Hendriksen, *The Gospel of Matthew* (Edinburgh: Banner of Truth Trust, 1973), p.812.

9. See Stuart Olyott's highly readable and convincing books: *Jesus is Both God and Man — what the Bible teaches about the person of Christ* (Darlington: Evangelical Press, 2000); and *The Three are One: what the Bible teaches about the Trinity* (Welwyn: Evangelical Press, 1979).

10. Spurgeon, *The Treasury of David,* vol. 1, p.315.

11. *Ibid.*

12. Samuel Chadwick, *The Path of Prayer* (London: Hodder and Stoughton, 1931), p.16.

13. Oswald Sanders, *Spiritual Leadership* (Basingstoke: Marshal Morgan and Scott, 1967), p.78.

14. Andrew Stewart, *A Family Tree: 1 Chronicles simply explained* (Darlington: Evangelical Press, 1997), p.187.

15. Spurgeon, *The Treasury of David,* vol. 2, p.478.

16. Stewart, *A Family Tree,* p.11.

2 Chronicles

1. Jensen, *Jensen's Survey of the Old Testament,* p.212.

2. That is, the Pentateuch, the five books of Moses: Genesis to Deuteronomy.

3. The Talmud (a collection of ancient writings on Jewish civil and ceremonial law and tradition) deplores it as one of the most atrocious of Jewish crimes against God's servants (Lenski, *The Interpretation of St Matthew's Gospel,* p.919).

4. It was 250 years earlier that Jehoshaphat had instructed the Levites to go throughout Judah to teach from the Book of the Law of the Lord (17:9).
5. Wilkinson and Boa, *Talk Thru the Old Testament*, p.109.
6. The differences between the two lists may be explained in that Matthew presents the legal line through Joseph whereas Luke presents the natural line through Mary (See Hendriksen, *The Gospel of Luke*, pp.220-25).
7. Hengstenberg, *Commentary on the Gospel of St John*, vol. 1, p.146.
8. See under the heading 'Christ and his church' in the chapter on Genesis (p.66).
9. Charles Hodge, *Systematic Theology* (Grand Rapids, Michigan: Eerdmans, 1977), vol. 2, p.370.
10. The Epistle to the Hebrews teaches the spiritual significance of the Old Covenant temple and its spiritual fulfilment in Christ and his church. The temple furniture, ceremonies and sacrifices all point to the person and work of the Saviour — see the chapters on the books of Exodus and Leviticus under the heading of 'Christ and his church', pp.92-5,117-24.

Ezra

1. Hendriksen, *Survey of the Bible*, p.310.
2. See the books of these prophets.
3. This may have been a very small group. As well as soldiers sent to escort and protect him while in Judah, Nehemiah mentions 'my brethren and my servants' in a context which distinguishes them from those already resident in Judah (Neh. 5:10; cf. 4:10).
4. Brown, *Let's Read the Old Testament*, p.91.
5. C. F. Keil, *The Books of Ezra, Nehemiah, and Esther* (Grand Rapids, Michigan: Eerdmans, no date), pp.58-9.
6. That is, the remaining five years of the reign of Cyrus (4:5), seven and half years of Cambyses, seven months of Smerdis, and one year of Darius, until the second year of his reign (4:24).
7. Hodgkin, *Christ in all the Scriptures*, p.93.

Nehemiah

1. Hendriksen, *Survey of the Bible*, p.310.
2. See the books of these prophets.
3. It is beneficial to read the book of the prophet Malachi alongside that of Nehemiah.
4. Cf. Elijah (1 Kings 18:41-44), of whom James writes, 'The effective, fervent prayer of a righteous man avails much' (James 5:16-18).
5. See later section on 'Application', pp.404,405.

Esther

1. Lee, *The Outlined Bible*, analysis no.17.
2. Wilkinson and Boa, *Talk Thru the Old Testament*, p.133.
3. *Ibid.*, p.131.
4. Keil, *The Books of Ezra, Nehemiah, and Esther*, pp.308-9.
5. R. C. H. Lenski, *The Interpretation of the Epistles of St Peter, St John and St Jude* (Minneapolis, Minnesota: Augsburg, 1966), p.132.
6. William Still, *Eight Sermons on the Book of Esther* (Aberdeen, Didasko Press, 1973), p.22.
7. Thomas McCrie, *Lectures on the Book of Esther* (Lynchburg, VA: James Family Christian Publishing Co.), pp.306-7.
8. Dillard and Longman, *An Introduction to the Old Testament*, p.196.

Job

1. See introduction, pp.16-17.
2. Young, *An Introduction to the Old Testament,* pp.319-23.
3. Albert Barnes, *The Book of Job* (London: Blackie and Son), vol.1, p.x.
4. William Henry Green, *The Argument of the Book of Job Unfolded* (USA: James and Klock, 1977 [first published 1874]), pp.88-9.
5. Young, *An Introduction to the Old Testament,* p.324.
6. Barnes, *The Book of Job,* vol. 1, p.116.
7. Green, *The Argument of the Book of Job Unfolded,* pp.75-6.
8. Young, *An Introduction to the Old Testament,* p.326.
9. Barnes, *The Book of Job,* vol. 1, p.329.
10. Green, *The Argument of the Book of Job Unfolded,* pp.42-3.
11. Jensen, *Jensen's Survey of the Old Testament,* p.261.

Psalms

1. Quoted by Lee, *The Outlined Bible,* analysis no.19.
2. For a fuller discussion of the characteristics of Hebrew poetry see Young, *An Introduction to the Old Testament,* pp.291-6.
3. Leupold, *Exposition of the Psalms,* p.1.
4. Lee, *The Outlined Bible,* analysis no.19; see also Jensen, *Jensen's Survey of the Old Testament,* p.280.
5. Hendriksen, *Survey of the Bible,* p.282.
6. Augustine. 'Expositions on the Book of Psalms,' in Philip Schaff (ed.), *A Select Library of the Nicene and Post Nicene Fathers of the Christian Church* (Grand Rapids, Michigan: Eerdmans Publishing Company, 1974), vol. 8.
7. Leupold, *Exposition of the Psalms,* p.20.
8. *Ibid.,* pp.21-2.
9. Jensen, *Jensen's Survey of the Old Testament,* p.272.
10. Bonar, *Christ and his Church in the Book of Psalms,* p.ix.
11. Jensen, *Jensen's Survey of the Old Testament,* pp.275-6.
12. See Hengstenberg, *Christology of the Old Testament,* pp.91-2. It is not easy to explain the insertion of 'A body you have prepared for me' in place of 'My ears you have opened' (Heb. 10:5).
13. James G. Murphy, *A Critical and Exegetical Commentary on the Book of Psalms* (Minneapolis, Minnesota: James Family Publishing, 1977 [first published 1876]), p.29.
14. See chapter on the book of Leviticus, pp.117-19.
15. Krummacher, *David: the King of Israel,* p.509.
16. Albert Barnes, *Notes on the Old Testament: critical, illustrative and practical: Psalms* (London: Blackie and Son), vol. 2, p.212.
17. Fairbairn, *Prophecy,* pp.182-3.
18. Barnes, *The Book of Psalms,* vol. 1, p.xix.
19. For a sample of the subjects see the outline at the beginning of this chapter.
20. Bonar, *Christ and his Church in the Book of Psalms,* p.vi.
21. *Ibid.,* p.vii.
22. Spurgeon, *The Treasury of David,* vol. 3, p.454.

Proverbs

1. See introduction, pp.16-17.
2. Young, *An Introduction to the Old Testament,* p.311.

3. Hendriksen, *Survey of the Bible,* p.283.

4. About 800 are preserved in the final collection that forms the book of Proverbs.

5. Bridges, *A Commentary on Proverbs,* p.iv.

6. William Arnot, *Studies in Proverbs: laws from heaven for life on earth* (Grand Rapids, Michigan: Kregel Publications, 1978 [first published 1884]).

7. For a fuller discussion of the characteristics of Hebrew poetry see Young, *An Introduction to the Old Testament,* pp.291-6.

8. Olyott, *The Three are One,* p.65.

9. *Ibid.*

10. Jensen, *Jensen's Survey of the Old Testament,* p.291.

Ecclesiastes

1. Dillard and Longman, *An Introduction to the Old Testament,* p.247.

2. Derek Kidner, *The Message of Ecclesiastes: a time to mourn, and a time to dance* (Leicester: Inter-Varsity, 1976), p.13.

3. R. K. Harrison, *Introduction to the Old Testament* (Grand Rapids, Michigan: Eerdmans Publishing Co., 1969), p.1072.

4. Stuart Olyott, *A Life Worth Living and a Lord Worth Loving* (Welwyn: Evangelical Press, 1983), p.15.

5. Young, *An Introduction to the Old Testament,* p.348.

6. Wilkinson and Boa, *Talk Thru the Old Testament,* p.172.

7. The issue of Solomon's serious backsliding and restoration is discussed in the chapter on 1 Kings, pp.313-15.

8. Charles Bridges, *A Commentary on Ecclesiastes* (Edinburgh: Banner of Truth Trust, 1961 [first published 1860]), p.xvi.

9. H. C. Leupold, *Exposition of Ecclesiastes* (Welwyn: Evangelical Press, 1952), p.18.

10. Hendriksen, *Survey of the Bible,* p.302.

11. *Ibid.,* pp.302-3.

12. Olyott, *A Life Worth Living and a Lord Worth Loving;* Jensen, *Jensen's Survey of the Old Testament,* p.303.

13. Kidner, *The Message of Ecclesiastes,* p.12.

14. *Ibid.*

15. Bridges, *A Commentary on Ecclesiastes,* p.xi.

16. Olyott, *A Life Worth Living and a Lord Worth Loving,* p.15.

17. Lee, *The Outlined Bible,* analysis no. 21.

18. Leupold, *Exposition of Ecclesiastes,* p.43.

19. *Ibid.,* p.17.

20. Wilkinson and Boa, *Talk Thru the Old Testament,* p.172.

21. Hodgkin, *Christ in all the Scriptures,* p.123.

22. Dillard and Longman, *An Introduction to the Old Testament,* p.255.

23. Hodgkin, *Christ in all the Scriptures,* p.120.

The Song of Solomon

1. Jensen, *Jensen's Survey of the Old Testament,* p.306.

2. John Gill, *An Exposition of the Song of Solomon* (Grand Rapids, Michigan: Sovereign Grace Publishers, 1971 [first published 1854]), p.1.

3. Cited by Lee, *The Outlined Bible,* analysis no. 22.

4. Gill, *An Exposition of the Song of Solomon,* p.10.

5. Young, *An Introduction to the Old Testament,* p.332.

6. Olyott, *A Life Worth Living and a Lord Worth Loving,* p.74.

7. Lee, *The Outlined Bible,* analysis no. 22.

    A similar approach is taken in William Still's *Eleven Sermons on the Song of Solomon* (Aberdeen: Didasko Press, 1971).

8. Hendriksen, *Survey of the Bible,* p.297.

9. Adapted from H. A. Ironside, *Addresses on the Song of Solomon,* cited in *Jensen's Survey of the Old Testament,* p.308. Olyott, *A Life Worth Living and a Lord Worth Loving,* also follows this approach.

10. Young, *An Introduction to the Old Testament,* pp.333-7.

11. Rosenmüller, cited by George Burrowes, *A Commentary on the Song of Solomon* (London: Banner of Truth Trust, 1958 [first published 1853]), p.24.

12. Jensen, *Jensen's Survey of the Old Testament,* p.311.

13. Young, *An Introduction to the Old Testament,* p.336.

14. Olyott, *A Life Worth Living and a Lord Worth Loving,* p.74.

15. Lee, *The Outlined Bible,* analysis no. 22.

16. Henry Law, *The Song of Solomon: arranged for Sunday reading* (London: Hamilton, Adams and Co, 1879), pp.1-2.

17. Lee, *The Outlined Bible,* analysis no. 22.

18. Hendriksen, *Survey of the Bible,* p.298.

19. *Ibid.*; cf. William Hendriksen, *More than Conquerors: an interpretation of the book of Revelation* (London: Tyndale, 1940), pp.179-81.

20. Alexander, *The Heavenly Mystery of the Song of Songs,* p.21.

21. Cf. Ezek. 16:61 and Calvin's commentary on that verse; also Gill, *An Exposition of the Song of Solomon,* pp.27-8,201-2,19-21.

22. Alexander, *The Heavenly Mystery of the Song of Songs,* p.21.

23. *Ibid.,* p.1.

24. *Ibid.,* p.10.

25. *Ibid.,* pp.1-2.

26. Burrowes, *A Commentary on the Song of Solomon,* p.38.

27. Jay E. Adams, *The Christian Counsellor's Manual* (Phillipsburg, New Jersey: Presbyterian and Reformed, 1973), p.392.

28. Roger Ellsworth, *He is Altogether Lovely: Discovering Christ in the Song of Solomon* (Darlington: Evangelical Press, 1998), pp.175-6.

29. Burrowes, *A Commentary on the Song of Solomon,* p.16.

30. Olyott, *A Life Worth Living and a Lord Worth Loving,* p.79.

31. Cited by Burrowes, *A Commentary on the Song of Solomon,* p.26.

Isaiah

1. A brief outline of the arguments for and against a single authorship is provided in Dillard and Longman, *An Introduction to the Old Testament,* pp.268-75.

2. For full list see Young, *An Introduction to the Old Testament,* p.206.

3. Jensen, *Jensen's Survey of the Old Testament,* p.328.

4. Also called Azariah in 2 Kings 15:1.

5. Spelled 'Berodach-Baladan' in 2 Kings 20:12.

6. H. C. Leupold, *Exposition of Isaiah* (Welwyn: Evangelical Press, 1977), vol. 2, p.176.

7. *Ibid.,* vol. 1, p.397.

8. Edward J. Young, *The Book of Isaiah* (Grand Rapids, Michigan: Eerdmans, 1969), vol. 2, p.192.

9. Leupold, *Exposition of the Psalms,* p.494.

10. See the chapter on the book of Amos, the section on 'The remnant of Israel', pp.668-9.

11. Young, *The Book of Isaiah,* vol. 1, p.265.

12. John Calvin, *Commentary on the Book of the Prophet Isaiah* (Edinburgh: Constable, 1853), vol. 4, p.62.

13. Leupold, *Exposition of Isaiah,* vol. 2, p.167.

Jeremiah

1. Young, *An Introduction to the Old Testament,* p.234.

2. Thomas Nelson, *Complete Book of Bible Maps and Charts* (Nashville: Thomas Nelson Publishers, 1996), p.215.

3. The numbers indicate the order in which these men reigned over Judah.

4. Jeremiah's prophecies have been rearranged under the reign of the appropriate king.

5. Different names being used to refer to the same place is not uncommon. Depending on the context, a group travelling from York may be described as coming from the town itself, from Yorkshire, from England, from Great Britain, or from the United Kingdom.

6. The prophet Daniel cites this prophecy and pleads with the Lord to forgive Israel's sins and fulfil his promise to restore his people to their own land (Dan. 9:2,19).

7. Young, *An Introduction to the Old Testament,* p.233.

8. Hengstenberg, *Christology of the Old Testament,* p.632.

9. *Ibid.,* p.629.

10. *Ibid.,* p.634.

11. Adapted from *Nelson's Illustrated Bible Dictionary* (Nashville, Tennessee: Nelson, 1986).

12. Hodge, *Systematic Theology,* vol. 2, p.357.

13. John Owen, *Hebrews: the Epistle of Warning* (Grand Rapids, Michigan: Kregel, 1953 [abridged from eight volumes]), p.129.

14. William G. T. Shedd, *The Doctrine of Endless Punishment* (Minneapolis, Minnesota: Klock and Klock, 1980 [first published 1886]), pp.12-13.

Lamentations

1. Dillard and Longman, *An Introduction to the Old Testament,* p.304.

2. The letters of the Hebrew alphabet are shown in Psalm 119. This psalm is also presented in acrostic form.

3. Nelson, *Complete Book of Bible Maps and Charts,* p.220.

4. See explanation in the chapter on Jeremiah, pages 558-9.

5. Wilkinson and Boa, *Talk Thru the Old Testament,* p.207.

6. A woody plant with a bitter flavour.

7. Hodgkin, *Christ in all the Scriptures,* pp.172-3.

Ezekiel

1. Young, *An Introduction to the Old Testament,* p. 241.

2. Campbell Morgan, *Student Survey of the Bible,* p. 240.

3. The prophet Daniel is mentioned three times in the book of Ezekiel (14:14,20; 28:3). The prophet Jeremiah is mentioned in the prophecy of Daniel (Dan. 9:2).

4. The Babylonians are also known as Chaldeans (e.g., Jer. 32:5; Dan. 1:4).

5. Jensen, *Jensen's Survey of the Old Testament,* p.365.

6. Cf. Dan. 9:2; Zech. 1:12; 7:5; 2 Chr. 36:21; Ezra 1:1.

7. William Greenhill, *An Exposition of Ezekiel* (Edinburgh: Banner of Truth Trust, 1994 [first published 1645]), p.199.

8. Dillard and Longman, *An Introduction to the Old Testament,* p.324.

9. 29:1 (12th day of the 10th month in the 10th year); 29:17 (1st day of the 1st month of the 27th year); 30:20 (7th day of the first month of the 11th year); 31:1 (1st day of the 3rd month of the 11th year); 32:1 (1st day of the 12th month of the 12th year); 32:17 (15th day of ? month in the 12th year).

The reason for the departure from the strict chronological order of the second prophecy is explained in that the first two prophecies belong together. The second is a 'complement' of, or 'appendix' to, the first. See Patrick Fairbairn, *An Exposition of Ezekiel* (Minneapolis, Minnesota: Klock and Klock, 1979 [first published 1851]), p.326; Ernest W. Hengstenberg, *The Prophecies of the Prophet Ezekiel Elucidated* (Edinburgh: T. & T. Clark, 1874), p. 250.

10. Based on suggestions in the Thompson Chain Reference Bible.

11. Dillard and Longman, *An Introduction to the Old Testament,* p.322.

12. See the chapter on 2 Chronicles, section on 'Solomon's temple', pp.374-7.

13. Young, *An Introduction to the Old Testament,* p. 248.

14. Patrick Fairbairn, *An Exposition of Ezekiel,* p.492.

15. See the chapter on Jeremiah, section on 'The New Covenant', pp.559-62.

16. Delitzsch, *Messianic Prophecies,* p.82.

17. Ezekiel, Isaiah and Jeremiah together emphasize the Trinity: Jeremiah highlights the Father, Isaiah the Son and Ezekiel the Spirit.

18. Hengstenberg, *The Prophecies of … Ezekiel Elucidated,* p.321.

19. J. Oswald Sanders, *Spiritual Leadership* (Basingstoke, Marshall Morgan and Scott, 1967), p.39.

20. Hodgkin, *Christ in all the Scriptures,* p.175.

21. William Greenhill, *An Exposition of Ezekiel,* p.830.

Daniel

1. Young, *An Introduction to the Old Testament,* p.361.

2. Nelson, *Complete Book of Bible Maps and Charts,* p.234.

3. Edward J. Young, *A Commentary on Daniel* (London: Banner of Truth Trust, 1949), p.22.

4. Albert Barnes, *Notes on the Old Testament: critical, explanatory, and practical. The Book of the Prophet Daniel* (London: Blackie and Son, 1851), vol. 1. p.2.

5. John Calvin, *Calvin's Commentaries, vol. 5, Ezekiel and Daniel* (Grand Rapids, Michigan: Associated Publishers and Authors Inc. [first published 1554]), p.419.

6. A full explanation of the relationship between King Nabonidus (the official king) and King Belshazzar (co-regent) is given in Young, *A Commentary on Daniel,* pp.115-18.

7. Compare our Lord's use of parables (Matt. 13:13-16) and the visions recorded in the book of Revelation.

8. Young, *A Commentary on Daniel,* pp.373-4. This interpretation is favoured by Dillard and Longman, *An Introduction to the Old Testament,* p.350.

9. Dillard and Longman, *An Introduction to the Old Testament,* p.350.

10. Delitzsch, *Messianic Prophecies,* Edinburgh: T & T. Clark, 1880, p.91.

11. Calvin, *Commentaries: Ezekiel and Daniel,* p.601.

12. See the book of Esther (Esth. 1:1, etc.).

13. Calvin, *Commentaries: Ezekiel and Daniel,* p.620. E. J. Young sets out a number of alternative interpretations but all end with Xerxes identified as the fourth and far richer king (See Young, *A Commentary on Daniel,* pp.231-2).

14. Young, *A Commentary on Daniel,* p.94.

15. Barnes, *Notes on the Old Testament, Daniel,* vol. 1, p.221.

16. *Ibid.,* p.199.

17. Hengstenberg, *Christology of the Old Testament,* p.406.

18. Delitzsch, *Messianic Prophecies,* p.93.

19. Barnes, *Notes on the Old Testament, Daniel,* vol. 1, p.129.

20. Calvin, *Commentaries: Ezekiel and Daniel,* p.671.

Hosea

1. Young, *An Introduction to the Old Testament,* p.253.

2. Dillard and Longman, *An Introduction to the Old Testament,* 1995, p.357.

3. Jensen, *Jensen's Survey of the Old Testament,* p.412.

4. Keil argues for Hosea as a citizen of the ten tribes of the northern kingdom (see Keil, *The Twelve Minor Prophets,* vol. 1, pp.11-12).

5. Thompson Chain Reference Bible.

6. Young, *An Introduction to the Old Testament,* p.254.

7. See Hosea 1:1; cf. Isa. 1:1; Micah 1:1; Amos 1:1.

8. Lee, *The Outlined Bible,* analysis no. 28.

9. Keil, *The Twelve Minor Prophets,* vol. 1, pp.20-21.

10. John Calvin, *Commentaries on the Twelve Minor Prophets: vol. 1, Hosea* (Edinburgh: Banner of Truth Trust, 1986 [first published 1559]), p.55.

11. Keil, *The Twelve Minor Prophets,* vol. 1, p.61.

12. Hendriksen, *Survey of the Bible,* pp.235-6.

13. Calvin, *Hosea,* p.387.

14. John Murray, *The Epistle to the Romans* (London: Marshall, Morgan and Scott, 1967), part 2, p.38.

15. Calvin, *Hosea,* p.217.

16. Pusey, cited by Hodgkin, *Christ in all the Scriptures,* p.195.

Joel

1. Nelson, *Complete Book of Bible Maps and Charts,* p.246.

2. Young, *An Introduction to the Old Testament,* p.255.

3. John Calvin, *Commentaries on the Twelve Minor Prophets: vol. 2 Joel, Amos, Obadiah* (Edinburgh: Banner of Truth Trust, 1986 [first published 1559]), p.xv.

4. Campbell Morgan, *Student Survey of the Bible,* p.272.

5. Hendriksen, *Survey of the Bible,* p.277.

6. Calvin, *Joel, Amos, Obadiah,* p.53.

7. *Ibid.,* p.112.

8. Delitzsch, *Messianic Prophecies,* p.58.

9. Hengstenberg, *Christology of the Old Testament,* p.520.

10. Dillard and Longman, *An Introduction to the Old Testament,* p.370.

11. Hengstenberg, *Christology of the Old Testament,* p.525.

12. Cf. 1 Thess. 5:2-8. 'The Day of the Lord' is also called 'the day of our Lord Jesus Christ' (1 Cor. 1:8; 5:5).

Amos

1. Keil maintains that this prophecy was given by Jonah directly to King Jeroboam II (*see* Keil, *The Twelve Minor Prophets*, p.379).
2. Campbell Morgan, *Student Survey of the Bible*, p.283.
3. Young, *An Introduction to the Old Testament*, p.259.
4. Dillard and Longman, *An Introduction to the Old Testament*, p.380.
5. Ray Beeley, *Amos: introduction and commentary* (London: Banner of Truth Trust, 1969), pp.39-40.
6. Calvin, *Joel, Amos, Obadiah*, p.360.
7. Dillard and Longman, *An Introduction to the Old Testament*, p.384.
8. Stier, *The Words of the Apostles*, p.244.
9. Charles D. Alexander, *The Six Day War and the Future of Israel: an examination of the Jewish theory of prophecy* (Liverpool: Bible Exposition Fellowship, no date), p.19.
10. Hendriksen, *Survey of the Bible*, p.231.
11. Nelson, *Complete Book of Bible Maps and Charts*, p.249.
12. Campbell Morgan, *Student Survey of the Bible*, p.283.

Obadiah

1. Campbell Morgan, *Student Survey of the Bible*, p.291.
2. Edward Marbury, *Obadiah and Habakkuk* (Minneapolis, Minnesota: Klock and Klock, 1979 [first published 1649-1650]), p.1.
3. Dillard and Longman, *An Introduction to the Old Testament*, p.386.
4. Young, *An Introduction to the Old Testament*, p.260.
5. Delitzsch, *Messianic Prophecies*, p.57.
6. Marbury, *Obadiah and Habakkuk*, p.2.
7. Dillard and Longman, *An Introduction to the Old Testament*, p.387.
8. Hodgkin, *Christ in all the Scriptures*, p.201.
9. Lee, *The Outlined Bible*, analysis no. 31.
10. Clyde E. Harrington, 'Edom,' in *The Zondervan Pictorial Bible Dictionary*, p.234, cited by Jensen, *Jensen's Survey of the Old Testament*, p.423.
11. Calvin, *Joel, Amos, Obadiah*, p.449.
12. Lee, *The Outlined Bible*, analysis no. 31.
13. Campbell Morgan, *Student Survey of the Bible*, p.293.
14. Calvin, *Joel, Amos, Obadiah*, p.418.
15. Keil, *The Twelve Minor Prophets*, vol. 1, p.338.

Jonah

1. Gordon J. Keddie, *Preacher on the Run: the message of Jonah* (Welwyn: Evangelical Press, 1986), p.7.
2. There is also the question of the birthplace of the prophet Nahum. Capernaum, in Galilee, means 'village of Nahum'; even if it was not the prophet's birthplace its name at least suggests a strong connection with him.
3. Hodgkin, *Christ in all the Scriptures*, p.203.
4. Lee, *The Outlined Bible*, analysis no. 32.
5. Dillard and Longman, *An Introduction to the Old Testament*, p.395.
6. Hendriksen, *Survey of the Bible*, p.233.
7. John L. Mackay, *God's Just Demands: a commentary on Jonah, Micah and Nahum* (Fearn, Scotland: Christian Focus, 1993), p.34.
8. Harrison, *Introduction to the Old Testament*, p.908.

9. Frederic L. Godet, *Commentary on Luke* (Grand Rapids, Michigan: Kregel, 1981), p.327.

10. Keddie, *Preacher on the Run*, p.70.

11. The duration, 'three days and three nights' (1:17), is to be understood in terms of the Jewish reckoning that day and night are one unit and any part of that unit is thought of as the whole. This is important when reading of our Lord's death and resurrection, since he died on Friday afternoon and rose again on Sunday morning (Luke 23:50 – 24:8; cf. Matt. 12:40 — see Hendriksen, *The Gospel of Matthew*, p.534).

12. Keil, *The Twelve Minor Prophets*, vol. 1, p.383.

Micah

1. Keil and Delitzsch, *The Twelve Minor Prophets*, vol. 1, p.419.

2. Lee, *The Outlined Bible*, analysis no. 33.

3. See Micah 1:1; cf. 2 Kings 14:25-27; Amos 1:1; Hosea 1:1; Isa. 1:1.

4. Michael Bentley, *Balancing the Books: Micah and Nahum simply explained* (Darlington: Evangelical Press, 1994), p.50.

5. Compare also Micah 5:5 with Isa. 9:6.

6. Dillard and Longman, *An Introduction to the Old Testament*, p.402.

7. John Calvin, *Commentaries on the Twelve Minor Prophets: vol. 3. Jonah, Micah and Nahum* (Edinburgh: Banner of Truth Trust, 1986 [first published 1559]), p.342.

8. Mackay, *God's Just Demands in Jonah, Micah and Nahum*, p.105.

Nahum

1. Wilkinson and Boa, *Talk Thru the Old Testament*, p.267.

2. Dillard and Longman, *An Introduction to the Old Testament*, p.404.

3. Bentley, *Balancing the Books*, p.94.

4. Buckland and Williams, *The Universal Bible Dictionary*, p.339.

5. Wilkinson and Boa, *Talk Thru the Old Testament*, p.268.

6. Calvin, *Jonah, Micah and Nahum*, pp.436-7.

7. Lee, *The Outlined Bible*, analysis no. 34.

8. Dillard and Longman, *An Introduction to the Old Testament*, p.408.

9. Carson, *Hallelujah!*, p.34.

10. Buckland and Williams, *The Universal Bible Dictionary*, p.339.

11. Wilkinson and Boa, *Talk Thru the Old Testament*, p.268.

Habakkuk

1. D. Martyn Lloyd-Jones, *From Fear to Faith: studies in the book of Habakkuk — and the Problem of History* (London: Inter-Varsity Fellowship, 1953), p.10.

2. In 3:1 Shigionoth may indicate some musical notation.

3. The same Hebrew word occurs in 2 Kings 4:16, Eccles. 3:5 and S. of S. 2:6.

4. Lee, *The Outlined Bible*, analysis no. 35.

5. The prophet Jeremiah was ministering at about the same period in Judah's history.

6. George Hutcheson, *Exposition of the Minor Prophets: Obadiah, Jonah, Micah, Nahum, Habakkuk, Zephaniah* (Sovereign Grace Publishers, 1962), p.266.

7. Keil, *The Twelve Minor Prophets*, vol. 2, p.97.

8. See the chapter on the book of Nahum, pp.731-3.

9. Marbury, *Obadiah and Habakkuk*, p.674.

10. John Calvin, *The Epistles of Paul the Apostle to the Romans and to the Thessalonians* (Edinburgh: Saint Andrew Press, 1958), p.54.

11. Bell, cited by Robert Haldane, *An Exposition of Romans* (McLean, Virginia: MacDonald Publishing Co., 1958), p.54.
12. Hutcheson, *Exposition of the Minor Prophets*, pp.246-7.
13. Dillard and Longman, *An Introduction to the Old Testament*, p.413.
14. Lloyd-Jones, *From Fear to Faith*, p.13.

Zephaniah
1. As in the RAV and NIV.
2. Wilkinson and Boa, *Talk Thru the Old Testament*, p.279.
3. 1:7,8,14 (twice),18; 2:2,3.
4. Dillard and Longman, *An Introduction to the Old Testament*, p.419.
5. See the chapter on Nahum (especially pp.727-8) for fuller details about Nineveh, the capital city of Assyria.
6. Delitzsch, *Messianic Prophecies*, p.77.
7. Keil, *The Twelve Minor Prophets*, vol. 1, p.158.
8. George G. Findlay, *Fellowship in the Life Eternal: an exposition of the Epistles of St John* (Minneapolis, Minnesota: James and Klock), p.259.
9. Hodgkin, *Christ in all the Scriptures*, p.215.
10. John Calvin, *The Second Epistle of Paul the Apostle to the Corinthians* (Edinburgh: St Andrew Press, 1964), pp.139-40.
11. Wilkinson and Kenneth Boa, *Talk Thru the Old Testament*, p.279.

Haggai
1. *Nelson's Complete Book of Bible Maps and Charts*, p.276.
2. On the fragile basis of 2:3 some suppose Haggai to have been born in Judah and to have seen the temple as a child before being taken into exile. The prophet would then have been in his mid-to-late seventies when he delivered these messages from God.
3. Lee, *The Outlined Bible*, analysis no. 37.
4. The sixth month of the Jewish calendar falls roughly around August-September.
5. Wilkinson and Boa, *Talk Thru the Old Testament*, p.285.
6. Young, *An Introduction to the Old Testament*, p.277.
7. Owen, *Hebrews: the Epistle of Warning*, p.265.
8. Young, *An Introduction to the Old Testament*, p.277.
9. See chapter on 2 Chronicles, section on 'Solomon's temple', pp.374-7.
10. Psalm 118 was probably sung at the first Feast of Tabernacles celebrated in Jerusalem after the Babylonian exile, when the altar was first erected on the holy place (Ezra 3:4).
11. Wilkinson and Boa, *Talk Thru the Old Testament*, p.285.
12. Zerubbabel is found in both lists. For a comparison of the genealogies of Jesus given in Matthew and Luke see Hendriksen, *Survey of the Bible*, pp.135-7.
13. Lee, *The Outlined Bible*, analysis no. 37.
14. Hodgkin, *Christ in all the Scriptures*, p.217.

Zechariah
1. The name Zechariah is popular in the Old Testament, referring to over twenty-five different individuals.
2. See the section on 'Historical setting' in the chapter on Haggai, pp.772-3.
3. Lee, *The Outlined Bible*, analysis no. 38.
4. Young, *An Introduction to the Old Testament*, p.282.

5. These were not fasts instituted by God.

6. Keil, *The Twelve Minor Prophets,* vol. 1, p.383.

7. See the chapter on Genesis, p.66.

8. Thomas V. Moore, *A Commentary on Zechariah* (Edinburgh: Banner of Truth Trust, 1958), pp.145-6.

9. *Ibid.,* p.198.

10. For a number of possible explanations as to why Matthew quotes Zechariah 11:12-13 and yet credits the words to the prophet Jeremiah (Matt. 27:9-10), see Hendriksen, *The Gospel of Matthew,* pp.947-8.

11. Hendriksen, *The Gospel of Matthew,* p.913.

12. Moore, *A Commentary on Zechariah,* pp.211-12.

13. Compare the section in the chapter on the book of Zephaniah on 'The right clothing', pp.762-4.

14. Delitzsch, *Messianic Prophecies,* p.99.

Malachi

1. Thomas V. Moore, *A Commentary on Haggai and Malachi* (Edinburgh: Banner of Truth Trust, 1960 [first published 1876]), p.101.

2. John Calvin, *Commentaries on the Twelve Minor Prophets: vol. 5, Zechariah and Malachi* (Edinburgh: Banner of Truth Trust, 1986 [first published 1559]), p.459.

3. John Benton, *Losing Touch with the Living God* (Welwyn: Evangelical Press, 1985), p.11.

4. Moore, *A Commentary on Haggai and Malachi,* p.104.

5. Wilkinson and Boa, *Talk Thru the Old Testament,* p.297.

6. *Ibid.,* p.295.

7. Beginning at 1:2; 1:6; 1:7; 1:11; 2:13; 2:17; 3:6; 3:13.

8. Moore, *A Commentary on Haggai and Malachi,* p.149.

9. Haldane, *An Exposition of the Epistle to the Romans,* p.465.

10. Dillard and Longman, *An Introduction to the Old Testament,* pp.441-2.

Select bibliography

Alexander, Charles D. *Elijah: 'Crouching Coward' or Hero of the Faith?* (Liverpool: Bible Exposition Fellowship, no date)

The Heavenly Mystery of the Song of Songs (Liverpool: Bible Exposition Fellowship, 1965 onwards)

Alford, Henry. *The Book of Genesis and Part of the Book of Exodus: an explanatory commentary* (Minneapolis, Minnesota: Klock and Klock Christian Publishers, 1979; first published 1872)

Arnot, William. *Studies in Proverbs: laws from heaven for life on earth* (Grand Rapids, Michigan: Kregel Publications, 1978; first published 1884).

Atkinson, David. *The Message of Ruth: the wings of refuge* (Leicester: Inter-Varsity Press, 1983)

Barnes, Albert. *The Book of Job* (London: Blackie and Son)

Notes on the Old Testament: critical, explanatory, and practical. The Book of the Prophet Daniel (London: Blackie and Son, 1851)

Notes on the Old Testament: critical, illustrative and practical: Psalms (London: Blackie and Son)

Beeley, Ray. *Amos: introduction and commentary* (London: Banner of Truth Trust, 1969)

Bentley, Michael. *Balancing the Books: Micah and Nahum simply explained* (Darlington: Evangelical Press, 1994)

Benton, John. *Losing Touch with the Living God* (Welwyn: Evangelical Press, 1985)

Blaikie, William G. *The Book of Joshua* (Minneapolis, Minnesota: Klock and Klock Christian Publishers, 1978; first published 1908)

David, King of Israel: the divine plan and lessons of his life (Minneapolis, Minnesota: Klock and Klock Christian Publishers, 1981; first published 1861)

The First Book of Samuel (Minneapolis, Minnesota: Klock and Klock Christian Publishers, 1978; first published 1887)

Bonar, Andrew A. *Christ and his Church in the Book of Psalms* (Grand Rapids, Michigan: Kregel, 1978; first published 1861)

A Commentary on Leviticus (Edinburgh: Banner of Truth Trust, 1966; first published 1846)

Borland, James A. *Christ in the Old Testament: a comprehensive study of Old Testament appearances of Christ in human form* (Chicago: Moody, 1978)

Bridges, Charles. *A Commentary on Ecclesiastes* (Edinburgh: Banner of Truth Trust, 1961; first published 1860)

　　A Commentary on Proverbs (London: Banner of Truth Trust, 1968; first published 1846)

Brown, Raymond. *Let's Read the Old Testament* (London and Eastbourne: Victory Press, 1971)

Buckland A. R. and Williams A L. (eds.). *Universal Bible Dictionary* (London: The Religious Tract Society, 1914)

Burrowes, George. *A Commentary on the Song of Solomon* (London: Banner of Truth Trust, 1958; first published 1853)

Calvin, John. *Calvin's Commentaries, vol. 5, Ezekiel and Daniel* (Grand Rapids, Michigan: Associated Publishers and Authors Inc.; first published 1554)

　　Commentaries on the Twelve Minor Prophets (Edinburgh: Banner of Truth Trust, 1986; first published 1559), *vol. 1, Hosea; vol. 2, Joel, Amos, Obadiah; vol. 3, Jonah, Micah and Nahum; vol. 5, Zechariah and Malachi*

　　Commentary on the Book of the Prophet Isaiah (Edinburgh: Constable, 1853), vol. 4

　　A Commentary on Genesis (London: Banner of Truth Trust, 1965; first published 1554).

Candlish, Robert. *Studies in Genesis* (Grand Rapids, Michigan: Kregel Publications, 1979; first published 1868)

Carson, Herbert M. *Hallelujah!: Christian worship* (Welwyn: Evangelical Press, 1980)

Clowney, Edmund P. *The Unfolding Mystery: discovering Christ in the Old Testament* (Leicester: Inter-Varsity Press, 1988)

　　'Preaching Christ From All the Scriptures,' in Logan, Samuel T. Jr. (ed.). *The Preacher and Preaching: reviving the art in the Twentieth Century* (Phillipsburg, New Jersey: Presbyterian and Reformed Publishing Company, 1986)

Delitzsch, Franz. *Messianic Prophecies* (Edinburgh: T & T Clark, 1880)

Dillard, Raymond B. and Longman, Tremper III. *An Introduction to the Old Testament* (Leicester: Apollos IVP, 1995)

Edersheim, Alfred. *Israel Under Samuel, Saul, and David, to the Birth of Solomon* (London: The Religious Tract Society)

Ellsworth, Roger. *He is Altogether Lovely: Discovering Christ in the Song of Solomon* (Darlington: Evangelical Press, 1998)

Fairbairn, Patrick. *An Exposition of Ezekiel* (Minneapolis, Minnesota: Klock and Klock, 1979; first published 1851)

　　Prophecy: viewed in respect to its distinctive nature, its special function, and proper interpretation (Grand Rapids, Michigan: Baker, 1976; first published 1865)

　　The Typology of Scripture: viewed in connection with the whole series of the divine dispensations (Grand Rapids, Michigan: Baker, 1975; first published 1900)

Fausset, Andrew R. *A Critical and Expository Commentary on the Book of Judges* (USA: James and Klock, 1977; first published 1885)

Gill, John. *An Exposition of the Song of Solomon* (Grand Rapids, Michigan: Sovereign Grace Publishers, 1971; first published 1854)

Goldsworthy, Graeme. *Gospel and Kingdom: a Christian Interpretation of the Old Testament* (Carlisle: Paternoster, 1981)

Green, William Henry. *The Argument of the Book of Job Unfolded* (USA: James and Klock, 1977; first published 1874)

Greenhill, William. *An Exposition of Ezekiel* (Edinburgh: Banner of Truth Trust, 1994; first published 1645)

Gulston, Charles. *David Shepherd and King: the life and heritage of David* (Grand Rapids, Michigan: Zondervan, 1980)

Harrison, R. K. *Introduction to the Old Testament* (Grand Rapids, Michigan: Eerdmans Publishing Co., 1969)

Hendriksen, William. *Survey of the Bible: a treasury of Bible information* (Welwyn: Evangelical Press, 1976)

Hengstenberg, Ernest W. *Christology of the Old Testament and a Commentary on the Messianic Predictions* (Grand Rapids, Michigan: Kregel Publications, 1970; first published 1847)

   The Prophecies of the Prophet Ezekiel Elucidated (Edinburgh: T. & T. Clark, 1874)

   History of the Kingdom of God under the Old Testament, vol. 1 (Edinburgh: T & T Clark, 1877)

Hodge, Charles. *Systematic Theology* (Grand Rapids, Michigan: Eerdmans, 1977)

Hodgkin, A. M. *Christ in all the Scriptures* (London: Pickering and Inglis, 1907)

Hoeksema, Homer C. *In the Beginning God...* (Grand Rapids, Michigan: Reformed Free Publishing Association, 1966)

Hutcheson, George. *Exposition of the Minor Prophets: Obadiah, Jonah, Micah, Nahum, Habakkuk, Zephaniah* (Sovereign Grace Publishers, 1962)

Jensen, Irving L. *Jensen's Survey of the Old Testament: search and discover* (Chicago: Moody, 1978)

Jukes, Andrew. *The Law of the Offerings* (Grand Rapids, Michigan: Kregel Publications, 1976; first published 1854)

Keddie, Gordon J. *Even in Darkness: Judges and Ruth simply explained* (Welwyn: Evangelical Press, 1985)

   Preacher on the Run: the message of Jonah (Welwyn: Evangelical Press, 1986)

Keil, Carl F. *Biblical Commentary on the Books of the Kings* (Grand Rapids, Michigan: Eerdmans, 1950)

   The Books of Ezra, Nehemiah, and Esther (Grand Rapids, Michigan: Eerdmans, no date)

   The Books of Joshua, Judges and Ruth (Grand Rapids, Michigan: Eerdmans, 1950)

   The Twelve Minor Prophets (Grand Rapids, Michigan: Eerdmans, 1949)

Keil, Carl F. & Delitzsch, Franz. *Biblical Commentary on the Books of Samuel* (Grand Rapids, Michigan: Eerdmans, 1950)

   Biblical Commentary on the Old Testament, The Pentateuch, 3 vols. (Grand Rapids, Michigan: Eerdmans)

Kellogg, Samuel H. *The Book of Leviticus* (Minneapolis, Minnesota: Klock and Klock Christian Publishers, 1978; first published 1899)

Kidner, Derek. *The Message of Ecclesiastes: a time to mourn, and a time to dance* (Leicester: Inter-Varsity Press, 1976)

Kiene, Paul F. *The Tabernacle of God in the Wilderness of Sinai.* (Grand Rapids, Michigan: Zondervan, 1977)

Krummacher, F. W. *David — the King of Israel* (Grand Rapids, Michigan: Baker Book House, 1982; first published 1868)

   Elijah the Tishbite (Grand Rapids, Michigan: Baker, 1977)

   Elisha: a prophet for our times (Grand Rapids, Michigan: Baker, 1976)

   The Last Days of Elisha (Grand Rapids, Michigan: Baker, 1981)

Law, Henry. *The Gospel in Exodus* (London: Banner of Truth Trust, 1967; first published 1855)

Lawson, George. *Lectures on the History of Joseph* (London: Banner of Truth Trust, 1972; first published 1807)

Lee, Robert. *The Outlined Bible: an outline and analysis of every book in the Bible* (London: Pickering and Inglis)

Leupold, H. C. *Exposition of Genesis,* vols. 1 and 2 (Grand Rapids, Michigan: Baker, 1942)

   Exposition of Ecclesiastes (Welwyn: Evangelical Press, 1952)

   Exposition of Isaiah (Welwyn: Evangelical Press, 1977)

   Exposition of the Psalms (London: Evangelical Press, 1969)

Lloyd-Jones, D. Martyn. *From Fear to Faith: studies in the book of Habakkuk — and the Problem of History* (London: Inter-Varsity Fellowship, 1953)

Mackay, John L. *God's Just Demands: a commentary on Jonah, Micah and Nahum* (Fearn, Scotland: Christian Focus, 1993)

Marbury, Edward. *Obadiah and Habakkuk* (Minneapolis, Minnesota: Klock and Klock, 1979; first published 1649-1650)

Martens, E. A. *Plot and Purpose in the Old Testament* (Leicester: Inter-Varsity Press, 1981)

McComiskey, Thomas E. *The Covenants of Promise: a theology of the Old Testament covenants* (Nottingham: Inter-Varsity Press, 1985)

McCrie, Thomas. *Lectures on the Book of Esther* (Lynchburg, VA: James Family Christian Publishing Co.)

McMillen, S. I. *None of These Diseases* (London: Marshall Morgan and Scott, 1966)

Meyer, F. B. *Devotional Commentary on Exodus* (Grand Rapids, Michigan: Kregel Publications, 1978)

Moore, Thomas V. *A Commentary on Haggai and Malachi* (Edinburgh: Banner of Truth Trust, 1960; first published 1876)

A Commentary on Zechariah (Edinburgh: Banner of Truth Trust, 1958)

Morgan, G. Campbell. *Student Survey of the Bible* (Iowa Falls, Iowa: World Bible Publishers, 1993)

Murphy, James G. *A Critical and Exegetical Commentary on the Book of Exodus* (Minneapolis, Minnesota: Klock and Klock Christian Publishers; first published 1866)

A Critical and Exegetical Commentary on the Book of Psalms (Minneapolis, Minnesota: James Family Publishing, 1977; first published 1876)

Nelson, Thomas. *Complete Book of Bible Maps and Charts* (Nashville: Thomas Nelson Publishers, 1996)

Olyott, Stuart. *A Life Worth Living and a Lord Worth Loving* (Welwyn: Evangelical Press, 1983)

Pink, Arthur W. *Gleanings in Exodus* (Chicago: Moody Press, 1972)

Gleanings in Genesis (Chicago: Moody Press, 1922)

Gleanings in Joshua (Chicago: Moody Press, 1964)

Gleanings from Elisha: his life and miracles (Chicago: Moody Press, 1972)

The Life of David (Grand Rapids, Michigan: Baker Book House, 1981)

The Life of Elijah (Edinburgh: Banner of Truth Trust, 1956)

Spurgeon, Charles Haddon. *The Most Holy Place: Sermons on the Song of Solomon* (London: Passmore and Alabaster, 1896)

The Treasury of David (McLean, Virginia: MacDonald Publishing Company)

Stewart, Andrew. *A Family Tree: 1 Chronicles simply explained* (Darlington: Evangelical Press, 1997)

Stier, Rudolf. *The Words of the Apostles* (Minneapolis, Minnesota: Klock and Klock, 1981; first published 1869)

The Words of the Lord Jesus (Edinburgh: T & T Clark, 1985)

Thiele, Edwin R. *A Chronology of Hebrew Kings* (Grand Rapids, Michigan: Zondervan, 1977)

Vos, Geerhardus. *Biblical Theology: Old and New Testaments* Edinburgh: Banner of Truth Trust (1975; first published 1948)

Watson, Thomas. *The Ten Commandments* (London: Banner of Truth Trust, 1959; first published 1692)

Wilkinson, Bruce and Boa, Kenneth. *Talk Thru the Old Testament* (Nashville, Tennessee: Nelson, 1983)

Wiseman, Luke H. *Practical Truths from Judges* (Grand Rapids, Michigan: Kregel, 1985; first published 1874)

Wood, Leon J. *Distressing Days of the Judges* (Grand Rapids, Michigan: Zondervan, 1975)

Young, Edward J. *The Book of Isaiah* (Grand Rapids, Michigan: Eerdmans Publishing Company, vol. 1, 1965; vol. 2, 1969)

A Commentary on Daniel (London: Banner of Truth Trust, 1949)

An Introduction to the Old Testament (Grand Rapids, Michigan: Eerdmans, 1949)

Christ and his church:
topical index

Index of application topics

General index

Note: Where the name of a Bible character is the same as that of a book (e.g. Isaiah, Job, Esther), the entry below refers to the individual, not the book.

promised land (see also Canaan, land
of), 34, 61, 62, 69, 76, 102, 110,
132, 133, 134, 135, 136, 137, 138,
139, 140, 141, 144, 146, 148, 156,
158, 160, 161, 166, 169, 173, 175,
186, 187, 200, 305, 317, 380, 384,
387, 391, 572, 621, 743, 744
conquest of, 179-82, 187
division of, 181-4
entry into, 177-79, 187, 560, 626
promises,
amplification of to Moses, 33
blessing, 32-3, 46, 70-73, 84, 157
God's faithfulness to — see covenant, God's faithfulness to
reliance on God's, 284
seed of the woman — see Seed,
promise of the
to Abraham, 31-4, 37, 60-61, 69, 70,
133, 157, 164, 174-5, 183, 278-9,
383, 391, 462, 579, 685, 704,
707, 717, 768, 794
to David, 265, 277-9, 298-9, 301,
309, 314, 318, 343, 352, 366,
369, 374, 379, 534-5, 579, 825
proneness to wander — see backsliding
prophecies,
of Christ, 38, 43-6, 47, 58, 68-9, 71-2,
143-4, 162-6, 277-80, 351, 447,
452-62, 524, 528-39, 543, 557-62,
615-17, 633-6, 715-16, 825
of the church, 666-9, 716-17
of the remnant — see remnant, the
prophecy, 43-6, 76, 456, 650-51, 797,
807
fulfilment of, 734-5
Prophet, promise of the great (see also
Christ, as Prophet), 162-3, 239
identified with Messiah, 162, 163
prophetesses, 204, 821
prophets (see also entries for individual
prophets), 189, 191, 204, 241,
245-6, 304, 339-40, 522, 598
classification of, 16-17, 238, 424
historical setting of, 48, 809-12
Amos, 659-60
Daniel, 606-7
Ezekiel, 585-7
Habakkuk, 740-41
Haggai, 772-3, 784
Hosea, 627-9
Isaiah, 520-22
Jeremiah, 549-50

Joel, 644-6
Jonah, 694-5
Malachi, 798-9
Micah, 712-13
Nahum, 726-8
Obadiah, 676-8
Zechariah, 784
Zephaniah, 757-8
how to interpret, 668
inspiration and authority of, 28
message of, 813
schools of, 325-6
true and false, 159, 718-19
propitiation, 92, 119, 226, 561, 721
proverbs, 829
definition of, 467
New Testament references to, 476-7
purpose of, 471-2
on specific topics, 475-6
providence, 42, 140, 159, 168, 224,
228, 230, 232, 243, 253, 315, 343,
373, 398, 400, 414, 419, 432, 438,
463, 610, 634, 705, 743
punishment for sin (see also judgement,
God's judgement of sin), 42, 76, 137,
176, 196, 203, 252, 270, 272, 290,
291, 298, 315, 326, 344, 365, 378,
385, 430, 433, 568, 571, 573-4,
575, 578, 587, 588, 618, 630, 631,
632, 640, 643, 647, 654, 657, 661,
663, 671, 698, 704, 713, 715, 721,
730, 742, 794
everlasting, 565, 803
Purim, Feast of, 410, 412, 415
purposes, divine — see God, purposes

Rebekah (Rebecca), 62, 75, 679, 803
reconciliation, 90, 112, 118, 124, 276,
616, 748
Red Sea, crossing of, 85, 175, 178,
324, 705
redemption, 92, 95-6, 102, 108, 126,
133, 169, 226, 227, 232, 233, 376,
561, 633, 634, 636, 732
of land, 222, 223
the kinsman-redeemer, 222, 223,
226-7, 228, 807, 822
reformation in Judah, 367-72
Rehoboam, 299, 301-3, 322-3, 328,
366, 377, 469, 521
religion,
formality in, 539-40, 718, 719
true religion defined, 718